SUFISM AND THE 'MODERN' IN ISLAM

Sufism and the 'Modern' in Islam

Edited by
Martin van Bruinessen
and
Julia Day Howell

I.B. TAURIS

Revised paperback edition published in 2013 by I.B.Tauris & Co Ltd
6 Salem Road, London W2 4BU
175 Fifth Avenue, New York NY 10010
www.ibtauris.com

Copyright Editorial Selection © 2013, 2007 Martin van Bruinessen and Julia Day Howell
Copyright Individual Chapters © 2013, 2007 Rachida Chih, Celia Genn, Patrick Haenni, Julia Day Howell, Michael Laffan, Yoginder Sikand, Brian Silverstein, Benjamin Soares, Martin van Bruinessen, Matthijs van den Bos, Leonardo A. Villalón, Raphaël Voix, John O. Voll, Itzchak Weismann, Pnina Werbner
First published in hardback by I.B.Tauris & Co Ltd, 2007

The right of Martin van Bruinessen and Julia Day Howell to be identified as the editors of this work has been asserted by the editors in accordance with the Copyright, Designs and Patent Act 1988.

All rights reserved. Except for brief quotations in a review, this book, or any part thereof, may not be reproduced, stored in or introduced into a retrieval system, or transmitted, in any form or by any means, electronic, mechanical, photocopying, recording, or otherwise, without the prior written permission of the publisher.

ISBN: 978 1 78076 379 8

A full CIP record for this book is available from the British Library
A full CIP record for this book is available from the Library of Congress

Library of Congress catalog card: available

Camera-ready copy edited and supplied by the author

CONTENTS

Preface and Acknowledgements   vii

INTRODUCTION   1

1. Sufism and the 'Modern' in Islam   3
   Julia Day Howell and *Martin van Bruinessen*

PART I: MODALITIES OF SUFI ORGANIZATION AND PRACTICES IN MODERN SOCIETY   19

2. What is a Sufi Order? Revisiting the concept through a case study of the Khalwatiyya in contemporary Egypt   21
   Rachida Chih

3. Sufism and Modernity in Turkey: From the authenticity of experience to the practice of discipline   39
   Brian Silverstein

4. Elements of Neo-traditional Sufism in Iran   61
   Matthijs van den Bos

5. Saint and Sufi in Contemporary Mali   76
   Benjamin F. Soares

6. Saints, Politicians and Sufi Bureaucrats: Mysticism and politics in Indonesia's New Order   92
   Martin van Bruinessen

PART II: THE INTERRELATION OF SUFISM AND ISLAMIC REFORM   113

7. Sufi Fundamentalism between India and the Middle East   115
   Itzchak Weismann

8.	The Reformist Sufism of the Tablighi Jama'at: The Case of the Meos of Mewat, India *Yoginder Sikand*	129
9.	National Crisis and the Representation of Traditional Sufism in Indonesia: The periodicals *Salafy* and *Sufi* *Michael Laffan*	149
10.	Sufi Modernities in Contemporary Senegal: Religious dynamics between the local and the global *Leonardo A. Villalón*	172

PART III: BREAKING OUT OF THE MOULD: SUFISM IN NEW SETTINGS — 193

11.	Intimate Disciples in the Modern World: The creation of translocal amity among South Asian Sufis in Britain *Pnina Werbner*	195
12.	Modernity and Islamic Spirituality in Indonesia's New Sufi Networks *Julia Day Howell*	217
13.	God by All Means … Eclectic faith and Sufi resurgence among the Moroccan bourgeoisie *Patrick Haenni* and *Raphaël Voix*	241
14.	The Development of a Modern Western Sufism *Celia A. Genn*	257

CONCLUDING REFLECTIONS — 279

15.	Contemporary Sufism and Current Social Theory *John O. Voll*	281

Notes	299
Notes on Contributors	315
Note on Transliteration	321
References	323
Glossary	353
Index	361

PREFACE AND ACKNOWLEDGEMENTS

This book derives from the meeting of two initially separate but kindred projects carried out by the two editors. The projects were brought together by Azyumardi Azra, Rector of the State Institute of Islamic Studies (IAIN), currently the State Islamic University (UIN) Syarif Hidayatullah in Jakarta, and researchers at this institution's Centre for the Study of Islam and Society (PPIM), which acted as our institutional counterpart.

Martin van Bruinessen previously taught at an IAIN in Yogyakarta, where he was involved in historical and anthropological research on religious education and various Sufi orders in Kurdistan and Indonesia. That research was part of a larger Dutch–Indonesian research program on Muslim religious authority in Indonesia sponsored by the Royal Netherlands Academy of Sciences. Martin ran the project on Sufi orders and similar religious communities (*jama`at*) in modern urban environments. The project related to work on the transformation of similar forms of religious association worldwide, pursued at the International Institute for the Study of Islam in the Modern World (ISIM) based in Leiden, The Netherlands.

Julia Howell had earlier conducted research on Javanese syncretistic mysticism and New Religious Movements. She noticed the remarkable upsurge of interest in Sufism among Indonesia's urban middle classes in the 1990s while studying Javanese branches of an Indonesian Sufi order closely connected to Suharto-era political elites. While further investigating the new urban Sufism in Jakarta, she learned of the research on this topic already under way at the Department of Religion's Agency for Religious Research and Development under the direction of Djohan Effendi, and at PPIM in the State Islamic University. To facilitate scholarly exchange with these bodies, Julia and the PPIM (particularly Jamhari Makruf and Dadi Darmadi) organized a research planning seminar on 'Urban Sufism' on 8-9 September

2000, with support from the Australia Indonesia Institute. The seminar stimulated a number of research projects on the topic, including Julia's subsequent work on new urban Sufi networks in Jakarta.

Although the approaches taken by scholars associated with the Dutch and Australian cooperation programs differed, the considerable overlap in the phenomena we were studying provided ample reason for us to join forces. This was recognized by Azyumardi, who, as our colleague and facilitator of both the Dutch–Indonesian and Australian–Indonesian research cooperation activities, kindly assisted in forging links between these programs. He shared our interest and agreed with us that the resurgence of Sufism in various forms among the best educated and most modern segments of the middle class was an important and regrettably under-studied aspect of the encounter of Islam with modernity. Counter to popular understandings of Sufism as a fading vestige of the rural past, in Indonesia and apparently in some other regions of the world as well, Sufism has become part of 'modern' Islam. Yet journalistic as well as scholarly observers of Indonesian Islam have focused their attention almost single-mindedly on radical Islamist trends and inter-religious conflict. In terms of numbers of people involved, however, Sufi orders and Sufism-inspired currents in Islam are probably much more important, not only in Indonesia but throughout the Muslim world.

We were all thus convinced that the new developments in Indonesian Sufism had broader significance as part of little documented global trends, the strategic and theoretical significance of which had not yet fully registered on the sociology of Islam and on popular understandings of the contemporary diversity within Islam. Recent developments in Sufism challenge our understandings of how these expressions of the Islamic heritage may – or may not – be part of the lives of Muslims fully engaged with the modern world. But to properly assess this, we recognized that the Indonesian case and accounts of unexpectedly vigorous and even renascent Sufism elsewhere in the world needed to be canvassed systematically, taking a global, comparative perspective.

Encouraged by Azyumardi's and other Indonesian colleagues' interest and shared sense of the importance of the phenomenon, together with PPIM we convened an international conference entitled 'Sufism and the "Modern" in Islam', to explore this subject collaboratively. We invited to the conference colleagues currently engaged in relevant research in various parts of Asia, Africa and among Muslims in the West. The early versions of the chapters of this book were presented at the conference, held in the beautiful and quiet setting of Bogor, West Java, on 4-6 September 2003. We are grateful to the staff of PPIM (particularly Director Jamhari Makruf and his successor Fuad Jabali, Din Wahid and Ismatu Ropi) who did an excellent job on logistics and took care of most administrative requirements.

We thank the Ford Foundation, and especially its Representative in Jakarta at the time, Suzanne Siskel, for a substantial contribution to costs of both the conference and the editing of this book and its Indonesian translation and dissemination. Several academic institutions also contributed to conference expenses: the Griffith Asia Institute at Griffith University (Brisbane, Australia), the International Institute of Asian Studies (IIAS) and the International Institute for the Study of Islam in the Modern World (ISIM), both in the Netherlands, and the Melbourne Institute of Asian Languages and Societies (MIALS) at the University of Melbourne. Julia Howell gratefully acknowledges research grants from the Australian Research Council and Griffith University for her projects on Sufism in modern Indonesia, and Martin van Bruinessen acknowledges support from the Royal Netherlands Academy of Sciences (KNAW) for the program 'Dissemination of Religious Authority in Modern Indonesia', of which the Sufism project was part.

We thank all participants in the conference, both those who actually wrote chapters for this volume and those who enriched the discussions with their contributions. Two of the latter should be mentioned by name: Azyumardi Azra of the UIN, and Merle C. Ricklefs, then of Melbourne University, both of them senior scholars who have written extensively on many aspects of the history of Islam in Indonesia and its transnational connections. John O. Voll, who has been writing important studies of Sufism in changing societies since the late 1960s, presented at our request thoughtful reflections on the papers and suggested new theoretical approaches. He performs the same role in the final chapter of this volume.

Finally we wish to thank the publications team at Griffith University: Maureen Todhunter for her fastidious copy-editing and for her wise shepherding of the manuscript for this volume through the many stages of its preparation; and Robyn White, publications officer and formatter extraordinaire, for her expert assistance. We also acknowledge with appreciation the support of the Department of International Business and Asian Studies at Griffith University for the preparation of camera-ready copy.

INTRODUCTION

1

SUFISM AND THE 'MODERN' IN ISLAM

Julia Day Howell and *Martin van Bruinessen*

Islam and Modernity

Sufism, as a devotional and mystical current within the Islamic tradition, has been subject to the strains of modernization experienced across the Muslim world. Rapidly expanding urban populations, the diffusion of non-religious general education and the natural sciences, the erosion of family and village social hierarchies, the supplanting of royal with popular sovereignty, increased mobility and access to information – all have brought to Muslim communities stresses comparable to those experienced by Western societies in the course of their industrialization.

But in much of the Muslim world, where economic modernization has come relatively late and in the face of competition with non-Muslim societies that made their head-start partly at the expense of Muslim colonies, confrontation with modernity has been especially traumatic. The material prosperity of the Western early developers has been attractive to later-developing Muslim societies, but the social transformations associated with technological and economic change have not always been welcomed. Nor have the politics of post-colonial international relations between Western and Muslim-majority societies been reassuring, especially since the end of the Cold War and the post-September 11 'War on Terror'. The sense of heightened threat that many Muslims experienced at the end of the nineteenth century when colonial powers began introducing socially corrosive modern capitalism into their colonies has been reignited (Malik, 2004).

To the extent that religion has guided and become intertwined with local cultural practices of peasant communities and pre-modern states, Muslims (like Jews, Christians, Hindus and others) have had to question to what extent their religious traditions could, and should, accommodate modernity. If they should accommodate modernity, then in what areas and in what ways? Legal safeguards for religious pluralism, increments of democratic participation in government, and support for human rights and gender equality have to varying degrees accompanied the development of modern nation-states in the North Atlantic region.

In the twentieth century, Muslims in Muslim-majority societies that have adopted the nation-state model and Muslims in plural societies East and West have had to consider whether Islamic law (shari`a) as developed by the classical schools of religious law can be reconciled with Western discourses of democracy, pluralism and human rights. If not, might a re-examination of canonical texts (the record of Divine revelation in the Holy Qur'an and the example of the Prophet Mohammad and his companions recorded in the Hadiths) yield new interpretations of tradition, such as both Salafi and Modernist reformers have proposed? While Salafi readings of the Islamic canon have rejected the social forms of modernity (although, inconsistently, not its technology), Muslim Modernist reformists have deployed more fine-grained hermeneutical and historically contextual analysis of the Qur'an and Hadiths to permit the selective adaptation of modern democratic, pluralistic and egalitarian social institutions.

While Muslims have anxiously regarded Western societies and the modernity modelled by them in the early twentieth century, Westerners too have questioned the compatibility of Islam and modernity. After the dissolution of Cold War bipolar politics and the reorientation of Islamist movements from domestic to international, and especially Western, targets over the last two decades, substantial sections of Western publics have eyed the Muslim world with increasing concern. Influential scholars like political scientist Samuel Huntington (1997) and Middle East historian Bernard Lewis (2002) have reinforced popular scepticism about the capacity of the tradition, which was the scientific leader and a cultural benefactor of Europe in the Middle Ages, to support democracy in Muslim societies today. Such pessimism justifies their prognostication that Islam will define a crucial 'civilizational fault line' dividing the 'West' from 'the rest' in the twenty-first century.

There has, however, been substantial criticism of this position, pointing to the role of Western governments in suppressing democratic movements that have threatened these governments' autocratic allies in the Muslim world. Critics have also called attention to the more basic error of essentializing any religious tradition (whether Islamic, Christian or any other) by conflating particular contemporary ideological renderings of that tradition with what the canon 'really says'. As social realities, these universalistic religions are actually polyphonic heritages carried through diverse cultural practices, streams of scholarship and ideological movements. Islam, like the other major world religious traditions, includes currents that promote the positive engagement of its adherents in plural, egalitarian societies and their use of rational-critical approaches to knowledge in the physical and social sciences. Thus scholars like Charles Kurzman (1998) and Omid Safi (2003) have called attention to the development of a rich body of liberal and progressive Islamic thought in the latter part of the twentieth century and have worked to familiarize Western (and Muslim) publics with a broad range of contemporary Muslim intellectual discourse.

Sufism and Modernity

It is evident, then, that articulations of the Islamic heritage that strive for accommodation with modernity are being vigorously championed in the Muslim world. They are also increasingly appreciated in the West for their importance in Muslim societies. Nonetheless, Islam's Sufi traditions, which include metaphysics, ethical disciplines, devotional practices, music, poetry and mystical experience, are not so widely recognized as compatible with modern life, either within Muslim communities or by social scientists trying to understand the relationships between religion and modernization.

The social sciences for most of the twentieth century have been dominated by modernization theories (of both the left and right) according to which societies modernize by proliferating what Max Weber called 'rational' social forms. The rational-critical thought necessary to support the proper functioning of modern firms and other bureaucratic institutions, so the argument goes, would render religions less and less plausible and attractive. To the extent that religions survive in modern societies as meaning systems or 'sacred canopies' (Berger, 1967) legitimating polities, family systems and ethnic loyalties, they were assumed to be the more plausible the less prominently they featured 'magical' and ecstatic practices. Early versions of such evolutionary schemas of religious development justified colonial regimes in promoting Christian faith as a 'rational' improvement on the supposed 'superstitions' of colonized non-Christians.

Modernization theorists into the middle of the twentieth century built uncritically on late nineteenth century evolutionary schemas according to which an early stage of 'magic,' understood as a manipulative act in pursuit of self interest based on patently false beliefs, was superseded in more advanced societies by 'religion'. The truths of religion were construed as beyond factual confirmation or manipulation. Moreover, many social scientists unfamiliar with serious academic studies of the mystical traditions of self-transcendence in Buddhism, Hinduism, Islam and Christianity still erroneously use the terms 'magic' and 'mysticism' casually as synonyms for the most flagrantly implausible beliefs and practices of religions generally.

The re-emergence of ethnicity and religion into the political arenas of both non-Western and Western societies in the latter part of the twentieth century has forced the revision of the ill-fated 'secularization hypothesis' (cf. Casanova, 1994; Martin, 1978; Swatos and Christiano, 1999). That the equation of modernization with secularization is false is now widely appreciated in the social sciences, although what this implies about the supposed rationality of late-modern societies and the religious forms that flourish in them is matter of discussion.

Less widely understood (if broadly recognized on a superficial level), however, is the still growing popular appeal of ecstatic variants of Christianity born of the Pentecostal movement in the early twentieth century (cf. Martin, 2002). The same can be said of extra-ecclesial or non-denominational New Age 'spiritualities' that have emerged in Western societies and become popular in the last decades of the twentieth century (cf. Heelas and Woodhead, 2005; King, 1997). Although widely remarked upon, being politically innocuous they have drawn less scholarly attention.

The New Age spiritualities draw on a related phenomenon in the West: the mid- to late-twentieth century 'New Religious Movements'. These movements are denominationally structured and include new-to-the-West offshoots of 'old' Asian religions like Hinduism, Buddhism, Islam and Sikhism that carry mystical traditions. Rather more commonly than in their parent traditions as a whole, these movements feature practices of consciousness transformation and the possibility of experiencing the immanent presence of the Divine. Although Troeltsch (1931) presciently anticipated an upsurge of individualized mysticism ('Spiritualismus') among the educated classes in the West in the twentieth century, ecstatic religion generally was left to anthropologists studying traditional societies for much of that century (cf. Bourguignon, 1973; Lewis, 1971) and was even regarded as anti-modern. Nonetheless, the growing momentum of experiential religiosity in the New Religious Movements and the New Age in the 1960s and seventies has prompted Campbell (1978), Swatos (1983) and others to belatedly affirm Troeltsch's understanding that mysticism could well be integral to some religious accommodations to modernity.

Islam's Sufi tradition cannot be equated simply with mysticism. As amply evident in this volume, as elsewhere, Sufism includes many different practice regimes and their supporting social institutions, arts and scholarly justifications. Nonetheless, the common thread through all is the possibility of heightened awareness of the Divine. Moreover, many expressions of Sufism, particularly those embodied in the Sufi religious orders (*tariqa*) prevalent since the twelfth century, carry the hope that such a heightened awareness may open into a vivid sense of what Rudolph Otto (1970) called the numinous, the *mysterium tremendum et fascinans*. The Sufi orders connect Muslims seeking enrichment of their obligatory ritual regimes (the five daily prayers, fasting in the month of Ramadan, making the pilgrimage to Mecca when possible) with a spiritual director (the order's master or *shaykh, murshid, pir*) who is credited with great piety and an especially powerful sense of God's presence. The *shaykh*'s special gifts of intimacy with the Divine and his own tutelage under his master in a line of spiritual teaching (*silsila*) stretching back ultimately to the Prophet Muhammad, justify his role as guide in disciplines of ethical reflection, supererogatory prayers and fasting, and special extended litanies (*dhikr*) that call constantly to mind the names and qualities of God.

To the extent that Sufism does reference a radical shift in awareness through which God's presence is felt more intensely, Sufism has been connected justifiably with mysticism. In much of the social sciences and Western public discourse, however, this association suggests that Sufis are unsuited to the work of social and economic development as envisaged in twentieth century modernization theory scenarios.

Sufism has long been a target of Muslim reformers as well. As in other universalistic religions that have spread widely across the world through many cultures and forms of society, adaptations of Islam to local cultural practice have repeatedly been the object of reformist scrutiny. While traditionalist Muslims have allowed the elaboration of the obligatory prayers to the extent that the additions support the intent of the canonical ritual, Muslim Reformists of the twentieth century have condemned all 'innovations' (*bid`a*), including the Sufis' supplementary, supererogatory rituals. Reformists have regarded as particularly objectionable the Sufis' repetitive *dhikr* litanies, which can facilitate ecstatic experiences, especially in extended group performances where people may punctuate their utterances with emphatic bodily movements or accompany them with dance.

Muslim Reformists, and Muslims heavily engaged in the modern sector of their countries' economies, have also been critical of the roles assumed by the principals of the Sufi orders. Twentieth century reformist Muslims share not only the concerns of all Sunni Muslims that none of God's creation elevates itself to the level of a 'second to God' (thereby undermining the purity of Islam's monotheism). These reformists have also strenuously condemned initiations in which, as they understand it, a spiritual director requires a student to surrender his or her judgment. They also criticize the reputedly extreme deference required by masters of Sufi orders and the masters' supposed secretiveness and exclusivity. These features attributed to the *tariqa* have been deemed not only to violate basic religious doctrine but to be inappropriate to the personal autonomy proper to the modern subject, suggesting interaction between Western discourses of secular modernity and Muslim reformist discourse in the latter part of the twentieth century.

Throughout much of the twentieth century many Sufis themselves actually reinforced perceptions that their traditions were incompatible with modernity, presenting themselves as anti-modernist and anti-reformist. Nonetheless, the tradition has undergone much change over the past century, in no small part in response to reformist critics and even through the agency of sympathetic reformists. An appreciation of this, documented in many of the following chapters on contemporary Sufism, helps us to understand the otherwise perplexing, and wholly unexpected, efflorescence of Sufism in modern and modernizing settings across the Muslim world in the last decades of the twentieth century, along with the more general Islamic revival.

Islamic Revival, Fundamentalism and Sufism in the Latter Twentieth Century

The Islamic resurgence, whose onset may be traced to the 1967 Middle East war, received strong impetus from the Iranian revolution. The resurgence has not only brought a wide range of Islamist and neo-fundamentalist movements into the public sphere of the Muslim world but also appears to have occasioned a revival of Sufism and related devotional movements.[1] Contradicting the easy dichotomies of much popular writing on Islam, neither the Islamist nor the Sufi movements can be explained simply as traditionalist responses to modernity or to the secular modernism represented by the nationalist, socialist and populist elites of the preceding decades. Most scholars agree that Islamist ideology and Islamist movements are distinctly modern phenomena, and that to some extent even neo-fundamentalist movements are part of, and not just a reaction to, modernity. But until recently there has been little scholarly appreciation that this also applies to resurgent Sufism.

Questioning the Supposed Decline of the Sufi Orders

The resurgence of Sufism in modern environments calls into question a number of 0widely held assumptions about the impact of modernity on Islam and Muslim societies. Orientalists and social scientists working on Muslim societies through much of the twentieth century had long taken for granted that the Sufi orders were rapidly disappearing and only retained a foothold among the most backward, often rural, segments of the population. In a classic text of the mid-twentieth century, A.J. Arberry's *Sufism*, the author remarked that Sufi orders in many places were continuing to attract the 'ignorant masses, but no man of education would care to speak in their favour' (1950: 122). This perception became especially widespread due to the influential writings of Clifford Geertz and Ernest Gellner who examined the apparently inevitable shift from the 'classical styles' of Islam ('maraboutism', centred around rural miracle-working saints and mystics, and the scholarly replication of tradition centred around the urban-based *ulama*), to the dry 'scripturalism' of nineteenth and twentieth century urban reformists (Geertz, 1968; Gellner, 1981, 1992).

These studies continue to exert considerable influence among social scientists studying Muslim societies, in spite of serious flaws in the studies' argument. Geertz and Gellner declared Sufism moribund, but what they meant by Sufism was only its popular, rural, ecstatic and illiterate variant. They appeared unaware of the existence, all over the Muslim world, of learned urban Sufis, whose followings included members of the traditional elites (cf. Sirriyeh, 1999). The dichotomy of popular rural religiosity and sober urban-based scripturalism, to which both authors subscribe, is embarrassed by the observation that Geertz' archetypical marabout, Sheikh Lyusi, was also the author of learned books, and therefore also a representative of scripturalist Islam (Munson, 1993). Attributing Sufism to either 'popular' or 'learned', 'legalistic' versions of Islam is now recognized as untenable; many Sufis operate in both domains without appearing to perceive a contradiction.

Sufism's 'Survival' and Institutional Innovation

A more judicious argument concerning the apparent decline of Sufi orders was made by Michael Gilsenan (1967, 1973), who in the 1960s studied an Egyptian *urban* Sufi order. He reported some 60 orders in Egypt at the time of his field research, but he judged that relatively few people were actually involved in them, particularly in comparison to the pre-modern period when most men were reputedly members of orders. He attributed what he perceived to be declining membership to the loss of function of the Sufi orders in modernizing Egyptian society. The various social, economic and educational activities that the orders had supported in the past, Gilsenan argued, were by then better served by specialized modern institutions, such as trade unions, political associations and schools, already widespread in that urban environment. Nonetheless, that functionalist argument left open the possibility that certain orders might find new functions and grow rather than decline. In fact, the order he studied had expanded where others had declined. Gilsenan attributed this to a form of Weberian rationalization: the adoption of a formal structure and explicit written rules in the still vital Sufi order on which he focused. Although De Jong (1974) challenged Gilsenan's interpretation, attributing the order's continued vigour to state patronage, these explanations are not mutually exclusive. Both deserve further exploration in this case and others, as conditions that may enable a Sufi order, with its spiritual legacy and original institutional form rooted in pre-modern societies, to thrive in modernizing urban settings.

Hoffman (1995), however, took issue with the notion that Egyptian Sufism was in fact in decline. During her fieldwork in the 1980s, she found that the number of orders had actually increased, not just since the 1960s but throughout the century, and although the great bulk of those associated with Sufi orders were from the less privileged sectors of society, members of the new middle classes credentialed with modern, general educations where also patronizing Sufi orders. In fact certain orders like the Burhaniyya and the Muhammadiyya Shadhiliyya were successfully targeting such people with their modestly reformist presentations of a sober, clearly *shari`a*-based Sufism. And although it was clear to Hoffman that the Sufi orders no longer had the prominent social roles and political influence of times past, they were not socially marginal. Rather, they constituted an important but quietist arena in the lives of people who were otherwise active participants in the economic, social and political life of the country. Rachida Chih's contribution to this volume on the Khalwatiyya generally supports this interpretation, although certain branches clearly do play important social roles in particular local communities.

Elsewhere around the Mediterranean basin, scholars have found evidence of Sufi adaptations to modern environments. For example, Zarcone (1992), Yavuz (1999) and Silverstein (in this volume) have documented the remarkable resurfacing of the Naqshbandiyya in Turkey, where one branch of the order inspired the establishment of the first Islamist party and its various successors. Veritable business empires are now associated with the order as well. This case, along with a growing literature on Sufism in modern and modernizing environments elsewhere in the world, call even more seriously into question established views on the presumed incompatibility of Sufism with modernization. They also draw attention to Sufism's occasional connection with Islamism.

Sufism, Anti-colonial Militancy, and Pre-adaptation to Modern Nationhood

A number of entirely different arguments concerning the relationship of Sufism and modernity have been made in connection with the worldwide wave of Sufi-led *jihad* movements against colonial powers and/or indigenous elites of the late nineteenth and early twentieth century (e.g. Ansari, 1996, Voll, 1995). Evans-Pritchard (1949) earlier explained how the Sanusi order had provided an integrating structure to the fissiparous Bedouin tribes of Cyrenaica and was thereby able to play a role in Libyan nation building. This kind of explanation for the flourishing of Sufi orders in early-modern colonial contexts readily lent itself to application in other regions where segmentary lineages had structured social relations (e.g. Bruinessen, 1992). Sufi orders appeared in these cases to have adopted a new political role as predecessors and progenitors of modern nationalist movements.

Here and there in recent nationalist struggles, most notably in the Muslim-majority republics of the former Soviet Union, Sufi orders have continued to figure as bastions of ethnic distinctiveness and instruments of nationalist political mobilization, sometimes violently. In Chechnya, for example, the Sufi orders have been identified both with opposition to the Kremlin and as vehicles for pro-Russian rapprochement. The association of Sufi orders in such cases with 'traditional' culture belies the significance of the roles they have assumed in the ideally participatory politics of would-be modern nation-states.

The militancy of Sufi orders in late colonial and contemporary contexts contrasts sharply with common attribution to Sufis of peace loving, tolerant and inclusivist attitudes. To account for the apparently anomalous militancy of certain Sufi orders in the colonial period, a number of scholars (most prominently Fazlur Rahman) launched the concept of 'neo-Sufism'. This concept drew attention to a number of important changes in the nature of Sufism during the late eighteenth and early nineteenth centuries. 'Neo-Sufism' was claimed to distinguish itself by increased militancy, stronger orientation towards the *shari`a* (to which some orders had taken a rather casual approach), rejection of *bid`a*, and de-emphasis on, or rejection of, efforts to achieve ecstatic union with God in favour of imitation of the Prophet in daily life (cf. O'Fahey and Radtke, 1993; De Jong and Radtke, 1999).

A broader conceptualization of neo-Sufism de-emphasizes its occasional militancy and sees it more loosely as the reformism initiated within certain Sufi orders as a reaction against excesses among their own kind (e.g., Azra, 2004; Johansen, 1996; Weismann, 2000). A further extension of the term is found in late twentieth and twenty-first century renderings of Sufism by Muslim intelligentsias who use the term to designate a this-worldly ethical and devotional practice free of the Sufi orders (cf. Howell, 2001). These diverse conceptualizations of neo-Sufism highlight the participation of Sufis themselves in Islamic reform movements. They also contribute to the growing recognition among scholars, not simply of polar variants of Sufism, but of a spectrum of Sufi stances towards both orthopraxy and the wider political contexts within which Sufi groups have functioned, as argued and illustrated by Itzchak Weismann and Yoginder Sikand in their chapters in this volume.

Sufism, Globalization and the New Transnationalism

Sufi orders from their inception have been supralocal, with each master attracting students from near and far, and recognizing, at the same time, links with other masters authorized by the same predecessor and tracing the same chain of spiritual authority back to the Prophet. The major orders in pre-modern times already spread widely across the boundaries of traditional states through such informal bonds. Their networks of teachers and students spanned the orders' places of origin, the holy land, and the other regions of the Muslim world from which pilgrims and scholars came to the holy cities and to which they subsequently returned. This produced overlap with the networks of scholars specializing in other Islamic sciences (cf. Voll, 1980; Azra, 2004).

Modern communications and the emergence of significant Muslim diasporas throughout the world have introduced new modalities of global connectedness that can be conceptualized as varieties of transnationalism. The term signals the new strengthening of long-distance social ties made possible in the post-modern era by more regular, even instant, electronic communications. It also suggests the possible use of that pre-eminently modern form of association, formal organization, which is now pervasive in all sorts of voluntary groups. These technological and social innovations can be used to knit together previously loose networks of Sufis working overseas, international business travellers, migrant families and jet-setting *shaykh*s, into something more like a whole, transnational community.

The Mouride movement of Senegal, described earlier by Cruise O'Brien (1971, 1988) and Copans (2000) and further in this volume by Villalón, represents one special type of a travelling Sufi order in which membership in the order, trade and international migration are intimately connected. So also in the South Asian and Turkish immigrant communities of Western Europe and Australia one finds 'transplanted' Sufi networks that are extensions of networks in the home countries (Werbner, 2003 and in this volume). The rapid geographical expansion of the Fethullah Gülen branch of the Nurcu movement from Turkey to Central Asia, though not a Sufi order strictly speaking, represents a highly successful adaptation of a Sufism-inspired movement to the opening of the former socialist bloc (Yavuz and Esposito, 2003).

A rather different and more dynamic form of Sufi transnationalism is that of the Naqshbandi Haqqani order, in which the *murshid* and his chief khalifas are highly mobile and supervise communities of followers around the globe. Although there appear to be considerable differences in Sufi practice among the branches, close connections are sustained via a website maintained in the United States and other electronic communications as well as by the frequent visits of the chief spiritual directors (Atay, 1996; Damrel, 2006; Nielsen, Draper and Yemelianova, 2006).

Reconceptualizing Sufi Engagements with Modernity

Building on the growing recognition of the inadequacies of old models of 'Muslim society' that linked Sufism to dying pre-modern enclaves in modernizing states, this volume brings together new research on contemporary Sufism across the globe to reassess those old verities and propose new approaches to understanding the dynamic relationships emerging between Sufism, non-Sufi brands of Islam, and modernity. Each essay focuses on a particular region or movement, from Southeast Asia to West Africa, and from the Middle Eastern heartlands of Islam to the West. Most adopt a comparative perspective and attempt novel analytical approaches that account more adequately than previous studies for the ways the Sufi heritage of Islam is actually manifest in the contemporary social world. The authors focus particularly on the appeal of Sufism to urbanites and others at the forefront of modernizing social changes in Muslim communities across the globe. But they also look at the linkages Sufi networks form between urbanites and provincials, as well as between domestic groups and international movements and diasporas.

In the chapters in Part I, the emphasis is on shifts in Sufi practices, changing relations of authority and new patterns of association emerging in response to the broader social changes associated with modernity. In Chapter 2, focusing on Egypt, Rachida Chih questions a number of established views of what a Sufi order is, what membership in it entails, and how it is organized. She shows that one and the same order, the Khalwatiyya in this case, can assume quite different forms in different environments: devotional practices, patterns of association, and the nature of relations linking the disciples to the shaykh and to each other. These vary according to the locality, the personality of the shaykh and the needs of the community. The adaptability of the order, allowing it to invent new associational forms and social services and yet remain recognizable, appears to be a major factor in its survival and current resurgence.

An even more radical adaptability is shown by the Turkish Naqshbandi community studied by Brian Silverstein in Chapter 3. This study examines the Iskenderpasha congregation, whose members have played an important role in the political and economic life of the country during the past decades. Few of the practices and social forms commonly associated with a Sufi order are evident here, and Silverstein argues that this is not just because of the formal ban on Sufi orders but to a large extent is the outcome of internal developments that began well before the Kemalist period. Like the Egyptian Khalwatiyya, the Naqshbandiyya has a repertoire of devotional practices and spiritual techniques. According to Silverstein, some are emphasized and others de-emphasized according to need in particular situations. In this chapter he focuses on the disciplining practices, especially *sohbet*, which is particularly important in this congregation. He also shows how the order's emphasis on *hizmet*, understood as service to the community, is congruent with its functioning as a benevolent association that is formally registered as a foundation, *vakıf* (as are many NGOs in Turkey).

Under the Islamic revolutionary regime in Iran, Sufism and the Sufi orders have faced much suspicion and oppression. But, as Matthijs van den Bos makes clear in Chapter 4, Sufi orders there have found various ways of accommodating the new regime, as they had done previously under the modernizing Pahlavis. Currently, most Iranian Sufis appear to maintain a quietist attitude and van den Bos found little or no mutual sympathy between Sufis and the leading reformist thinkers and activists. Ali Shari`ati's militant sociology of Islam, that provided an intellectual impetus to the revolution in the late 1970s, has found a Sufi counterpoint in a spiritual sociology developed by the Sufi thinker Tanha'i, which is also analysed in this chapter.

In West Africa and Southeast Asia, at opposite reaches of the Muslim majority world, Sufi orders have long played prominent social roles and political leaders have commonly had Sufi shaykhs as their spiritual advisers. Perhaps it is in Senegal that social and political life has been most pervasively structured by adherence to Sufi orders and participation in their communal ritual activities. As Leonardo Villalón notes in his contribution in Part II, the orders act in independent Senegal as the civil society bases for democratic political mobilization and communication with the state. The Muridiyya, Tijaniyya and other orders there have also developed a unique form of local voluntary association, the *daaira*, which, like the *rawda* that Chih describes in Egyptian cities, provides mutual support for urban members.

In neighbouring Mali, as Benjamin Soares notes in Chapter 5, the number of people formally affiliated with a Sufi order is quite limited, but many have a relationship of some kind with one or more saintly persons (*'marabouts'*) believed to have supernatural gifts. Most of the latter have been associated with the Qadiriyya or Tijaniyya orders. Recently a new type of Sufi saint has gained public prominence: charismatic media stars whose styles play on modern urban youth culture and who appear to represent a break with the traditional types of *marabout*. Some of them are surprisingly heterodox, embracing a syncretism that combines Islam, Christianity and African religious elements and appears to be inspired by a pan-African nationalism.

In Indonesia too, some heterodox 'living saints' have emerged recently in otherwise orthodox Muslim environments. In Chapter 6, Martin van Bruinessen describes this phenomenon against the background of the expansion and increasing formalization (if not bureaucratization) of major Sufi orders during the Suharto era. This period saw a struggle between syncretistic and more puritan versions of Islam; 'orthodox' Sufi orders, caught in the middle, established their own political associations to defend their common interests and vie for government patronage or attempt to influence policies.

Sufism and Salafism have commonly been presented as inherently mutually opposed and thus incompatible manifestations of Islam. Salafi movements after all strive to purge Islam of beliefs and practices for which there is no precedent in the Qur'an or in the example of the Prophet and his immediate followers, whereas Sufism, certainly in its organized form, emerged several centuries after the golden age of the Prophet. Yet the relationship between Salafism and Sufism is a more complicated one, as the chapters in Part II illustrate. In Chapter 7, Itzchak Weismann discusses a network of Syrian and Indian ulama and thinkers who in different ways combined orthodox Sufism with a Salafi spirit and political activism. The scholar who played a key role in connecting Indian and Middle Eastern reformist circles, Abu al-Hasan `Ali Nadwi, had a Naqshbandi family background (as did the Syrian ulama studied here) but his first visit to the Middle East was as a representative of the Tablighi Jama`at, a reformist movement of Sufi inspiration.

Most of the founders and early leaders of the Tablighi Jama`at had family connections with Sufi orders and privately practised some Sufi devotions, but the movement firmly rejected Sufism as it existed in India, especially the veneration of saints. The Jama`at and its struggle against popular religious practices in India constitute the subject of Yoginder Sikand's contribution in Chapter 8. This chapter focuses on the region where the Jama`at first spread its message, among a peasant population that was nominally Muslim but whose pantheon was inhabited by Hindu deities and spirits besides Allah and Muslim saints. From humble beginnings, through its efforts to educate this marginal community and reform its religious practices, the Tablighi Jama`at has developed into the most truly transnational movement in Islam.

'Sufi' and 'Salafi' are juxtaposed literally in Chapter 9, in Michael Laffan's analysis of the two contemporary Indonesian journals bearing these names. Although he leaves no doubt that these represent currents between which there is no overlap and major points of disagreement exist between them, he finds that each rarely, if ever, engages explicitly with the other current. The journal *Salafy* polemicizes primarily with Salafis and Islamists; for the journal *Sufi*, it is as if Salafis do not exist.

In Senegal, reformist and Islamist discourses critical of Sufism have gained in prominence, even in some circles where adherence to a Sufi order is the norm. In Chapter 10, Leonardo Villalón explains how several leading Sufi personalities have adopted elements of these reformist discourses, without however giving up the 'maraboutic model' and affiliation with a *tariqa*. He portrays a number of such reformist or modernist Sufi movements, as well as another modern development, the Mouride brotherhood's leap onto the global stage through international migration. In just over two decades, this Senegalese order has become an impressive transnational movement, in which trade and Sufi practice are intimately linked.

This brings us to Part III, in which globalization, transnationalism and hybridity are central themes. In Chapter 11, Pnina Werbner discusses a number of 'British Pakistani' Sufi groups that range from fairly orthodox extensions of Pakistan-based Sufi networks to hybrid local formations that reflect a great variety of intellectual and spiritual influences. Werbner finds that the British Sufi orders provide forms of 'intimate sociality' among people who otherwise would not have known each other, or known each other well, disturbing simplistic understandings of the quality of personal relations in the public spheres of modern societies and cautioning against understanding modern societies (and religions in them) in terms of simple dichotomies between traditional and modern, community and association and the like.

In Indonesia's capital, Jakarta, Julia Howell reveals a lively interest in Sufism among the educated classes in her discussion in Chapter 12. This represents a rapprochement of Muslim 'modernizing elites' with Sufism. She explains how this reconciliation has been affected by Indonesian Muslim sophisticates who are conversant with global scholarship critical of narrowly rationalist constructions of modernity, such as those embodied in Islamic Modernism in Indonesia and in state-sponsored constructions of what constitutes proper 'religion' in the modern Indonesian state. She also describes how urbanites have formed new kinds of 'Sufi' networks linking not only established Sufi orders but a wide variety of spiritual service providers, from mosque-based adult education foundations to alternative health and spiritual psychology groups drawing on the global spiritual marketplace.

In Chapter 13, Patrick Haenni and Raphaël Voix note very similar developments among sections of the Moroccan westernized bourgeoisie who, after studies abroad and experiments with Asian religions and New Age movements, 'discovered' in the Budchichiyya order an attractive indigenous spiritual tradition. (The order is, incidentally, also expanding among Westerners with similar interests in oriental spiritualism.) Howell's chapter and this chapter respectively reveal how middle-class and elite urbanites in

Indonesia and Morocco are exercising unprecedented autonomy in their spiritual lives, in some cases even assimilating to Islam some of the practice regimes of other esoteric traditions via their understandings of Islam's Sufi heritage.

Celia Genn's discussion in Chapter 14 exemplifies another way in which Sufism, rather than being drawn more strictly within the bounds of legalistic Islam, has been opened out, in this case not to cultural borrowings from other traditions but to people from non-Muslim backgrounds who are not required to convert. Her subject, Hazrat Inayat Khan's International Sufi Movement, builds on the tradition of openness in South Indian Chishtiyya Sufi circles to Hindus and Sikhs. As a modern formal organization, the ISM and its offshoots have been able to regularize and coordinate the highly personalistic master-to-initiate spiritual teaching to which Inayat Khan was heir across several continents and many decades. Genn discloses how this formal organizational structure underpins a more robust form of transnationalism than the informal Sufi networks of old could sustain.

Sufism as a Category of Comparative Analysis in the Study of Contemporary Societies and Religion

The variety evident in the case studies of contemporary Sufism presented in this volume helps us to appreciate that Sufism, as practiced, has no necessary political stance or doctrinal colouration. Nor is it fixed immutably to local cultural traditions. The Sufi groups documented here range across the entire spectrum from the strictly *shari`a*-oriented to the latitudinarian, from Muslim puritan to perennialist. In the West where Sufi poetry, music and meditation now have an enormous appeal (Hermansen, 1998, 2000; Malik and Hinnells, 2006; Genn in this volume) and in some highly cosmopolitan Muslim communities elsewhere, it is impossible to make a strict separation between Sufi groups and New Age-type movements.

This raises the question of whether Sufism can be conceptualized as a coherent tradition with definitive core features present in all cases to which the term is appropriately applied. The authors in this volume explicitly or otherwise take local usages as a guide: what do the people who are actually involved mean by 'Sufism' or *tasawwuf*? This immediately brings into view the considerable diversity of ways in which Sufism has been socially constructed by Muslims over the last century. The very concept of *tasawwuf* has been intensely problematized and sometimes fundamentally reworked as Muslim proponents of Sufi heritages have tried to respond to the criticisms of reformists and secular modernists. In some cases (such as Naqshbandi practice in Turkey described here by Silverstein, the Tablighi Jama`at movement in India described by Sikand, or the Indonesian Muslim Modernist Hamka's reformulation of *tasawwuf* described by Howell), the social forms of the Sufi religious orders (the *tariqa*) have been drastically reworked or even renounced. Even the word *tasawwuf* has been excised from some purified and up-dated versions of Sufism (as in Weismann's account of certain Naqshbandi reformers in Syria), the better to re-seat Sufism within the Islam of the Qur'an and hadith. In contrast, some adaptations in the West (as we see in Inayat Khan's International Sufi Movement) have gone so far as to de-couple Sufism from Islamic law (traditionally recognized as the necessary grounding for Sufi spiritual work) and even from identification with Islam as a faith, making the mystical awareness of the One God accessible to non-Muslims.

Nonetheless, some authors (Chih, Silverstein, Werbner, for example) assert that there are paradigmatic concepts that shape both social relations and ritual practice across place and time wherever people draw on the Sufi heritage: the need for an intimate relationship of affection and trust between a spiritual guide (*shaykh, murshid, pir*, etc.) and a seeker (*murid, muhibb*, etc.), and the inevitable blossoming of bonds of solidarity among fellow seekers under the guidance of a particular master. These relations require, and typically find, a meeting place that provides a physical locus for the enactment of those relations (*zawiya, pesantren,* etc.), and the gifts and hospitality that support and literally feed those relations. Each author, however, shows through their distinctive case materials that there is considerable variation in the ways that such bonds are actually constructed, responding to local historical, cultural and political circumstances and making use of the distinctive personal and social assets of the guide. As Chih reveals, recognition of the actual flexibility of Sufi tutelary relations enables us to appreciate how Sufi institutions have been able to spread to so many places and endure over time (even in many modern contexts), and yet preserve a coherent Sufi tradition.

Models for Future Research

This leaves us to address the related question of what kinds of sociological approaches are appropriate to the enterprise of comparative sociological analysis of Sufism in contemporary social settings. The essays in this volume uniformly reject simplistic characterizations of Sufism that confine it inevitably to the dying rural spheres of 'Muslim society' as envisioned in Gellner's model, and they refute more general secularization models of the fate of religion in the process of modernization. They provide further proof of the inadequacy of simplistic contrasts between 'traditional' and 'modern' societies, showing how forms of social organization characteristic of pre-industrial societies can nonetheless function in modern settings and be reworked to meet newly emergent needs and sensibilities. We see that Sufism can take on both positive and defensive stances towards modernization, and even defensive postures may themselves promote certain kinds of social participation generally associated with modern individualism and universalism.

Several of the authors in this volume make use of classic conceptual tools used in the sociological study of modernizing societies, such as Max Weber's notions of institutional rationalization and bureaucratization and Ferdinand Tönnies' contrast between *Gemeinschaft* and *Gesellschaft*, community and association. However the articulations of such broad social processes in the lives of contemporary Muslims are critically examined, prompting reformulations that better account for how those processes actually operate today. In Chapter 15, John Voll's concluding essay in this volume highlights three newer bodies of social theory that are particularly likely to be useful for advancing Sufism research conceptually. He suggests insights that can be gained from using recent developments in social movement theory to understand Sufi elements in popular or mass culture and points to ways in which Robertson's (1995) concept of glocalization can model tensions playing out in contemporary *tariqa*. Finally, recollecting the overemphasis on materialist motivations in earlier modernization theory, he recommends that the current popularity of Sufism in its many forms can better be understood in light of the growing literature on post-materialist values in late- or post-modern societies.

PART I:

MODALITIES OF SUFI ORGANIZATION AND PRACTICES IN MODERN SOCIETY

2

WHAT IS A SUFI ORDER? REVISITING THE CONCEPT THROUGH A CASE STUDY OF THE KHALWATIYYA IN CONTEMPORARY EGYPT

Rachida Chih

In this chapter I present some reflections on the concept of the *tariqa* ('mystical path', pl. *turuq*) and on how a *tariqa* may be expressed socially within modern society. I take one local example, that of the Khalwatiyya order in contemporary Egypt, as my point of departure. I argue that the primary conception of the *tariqa* as an association with a hierarchical structure that exercises a degree of control over its adepts or followers, as reflected in the common translation as 'Sufi order' or 'brotherhood', is in need of revision. Such a conceptual framing has been the predominant model of the *tariqa* in studies since the 1950s, and predictions of its gradual but inevitable disappearance, made by various historians and anthropologists (Arberry, 1950; Geertz, 1968; Gilsenan, 1971; Trimingham, 1971; Gellner, 1981), were based on the perceived incompatibility of this type of association with modern society. The emergence of an educated urban middle class that embraced ideas of progress, individualism and democracy appeared to leave little space for the old-fashioned brotherhoods, which were believed to attract only marginalized segments of society with little education, low social status or ongoing rural connections.

A growing number of empirical studies have shown that the claims of such students of modernizing Muslim communities in the 1960s and 1970s concerning the decline of the *turuq* are no longer tenable.[1] It has become increasingly evident that the *turuq* not only have persisted but actually function meaningfully in modern societies, thereby refuting the view that Sufism, if not religion in general, is incompatible with modernity. However, the authors of these more recent empirical studies have also been confronted with the difficulty of developing more appropriate theoretical frameworks for explaining the nexus of relations between Sufism and modernity. A number of obstacles hinder the elaboration of new approaches in research. One of these has been a rigid and homogenous conceptualization of *tariqa* as a 'brotherhood'. Yet the social expression of the *tariqa* has, in the course of its passage through time and geographical space, from West and North Africa to India and Southeast Asia, been remarkably flexible. Its forms have been adapted to different social settings and cultural contexts, and no single rigid model of social organization can do justice to these forms. Although it may be true that the various *turuq* existing today share a common substrate of ideas and practices, they nonetheless present an immense diversity in forms of social organization.

Another problem is that scholars have often shown a clear preference for studying those *turuq* that have a distinct and clear organizational structure and, if possible, accessible archives (witness the studies by Gilsenan, 1973 and De Jong, 1978). The less tangible, more informally structured and perhaps less accessible *turuq* have received less scholarly attention. Finally, it should be noted that many studies have privileged those aspects of the 'path' that are more immediately perceptible, notably the patterns of formal organization to which it has given rise, at the expense of the spiritual aspects of the 'path' or the more fluid social patterns associated with it.

I therefore propose to explore another approach to the study of the *tariqa*, focussing on the types of spiritual affiliation between a master and his disciples, the forms of social relations between them, and those between companions of a same 'path' that these affiliations imply.[2] I show that, in the case of the contemporary Egyptian Khalwatiyya, the *tariqa* is based first on the person of the spiritual master (the shaykh), and more precisely on the idea of his role as heir of the Prophet and representative (*khalifa*) of God on earth on the esoteric level, and on the interpersonal relationships that the shaykh establishes with his disciples. In accordance with the social project he may have formed, the shaykh may have recourse to various social networks and intermediaries for expanding his *tariqa*. The malleable and elastic structure of the *tariqa* allows it to adapt to very different social environments. The longevity of the Sufi path – and implicitly its relevance in modernity – owes most to the fact that the *tariqa* is an individualized and humanized way of establishing a relationship with the Divine. This approach, I believe, enables us to better understand the religious culture of the Sufis and the spiritual and social implications of their practices in modern Egyptian society. What makes the case of the Khalwatiyya especially interesting is that this order has been expanding in urban environments while maintaining profound roots in the rural districts of Upper Egypt. It has been spread by learned shaykhs, often graduates of Al-Azhar, and it attracts disciples from all social circles.

The Khalwatiyya in Egypt: One path, various branches

In spite of the Turco–Persian origins of the Khalwatiyya, Egypt is now its most important centre in the entire Muslim world. For the past two centuries the Khalwatiyya has been spreading from Cairo to the Delta and all along the Nile valley. In the 1980s the Khalwatiyya was the largest of the officially recognized paths according to the Supreme Council of Sufi Orders (the official body that monitors the activities of the *turuq* in Egypt). At that time it had 19 distinct branches or sub-orders. The second and third largest *turuq* were the Ahmadiyya and the Shadhiliyya, with 18 branches each (Luizard, 1990). Although one has to be cautious with all statistics concerning the *turuq* (if only because the Council does not take account of the *turuq* lacking official validation), this placement indicates that the Khalwatiyya is by no means a marginal phenomenon in Egypt's spiritual and religious field. The Khalwatiyya owes its position to the ties that were established with the religious elite educated at al-Azhar in the eighteenth century. Those ties were crucial to its subsequent diffusion across the whole country.

The Khalwatiyya first arrived in Egypt in the late fifteenth century but initially remained restricted to Turkish and Persian circles in Cairo (Chih, 1998). It became an Egyptian order properly speaking with the initiation into the *tariqa* of the Egyptian shaykh of al-Azhar, Muhammad b. Salim al-Hifni (d. 1767), at the hands of the Syrian-born Mustafa Kamal al-Bakri (d. 1749). Al-Hifni's biography, written during the master's lifetime by one of his closest disciples, gives a clear description of the beginnings of the Khalwatiyya in Egypt (cf. Chih, 2000b). It presents the shaykh as a man of action, engaged in the revitalization and propagation of the Sufi path on the ground. Nonetheless al-Hifni left very few writings behind, devoting himself entirely to teaching and above all to the training of numerous disciples whom he then dispatched all over the country to spread the *tariqa*.

With al-Hifni, we also witness the beginning of the close association of the Khalwatiyya and the al-Azhar elite. From his time as shaykh, affiliation with the Khalwatiyya became a major factor, if not a necessary condition, for entering the higher echelons of al-Azhar hierarchy. This quasi-corporate identity of the Khalwatiyya in its connections with al-Azhar has continued until the present day.

The degree of attention given to proselytization has varied over the years, depending on the personality of the shaykh. Al-Hifni, as said, was very active in this respect. He allowed the rapid expansion to result in the emergence and functioning of quasi-independent branches of the *tariqa*, between which he was the only intermediary.

Al-Hifni's successor, Ahmad al-Dardir (d. 1786), also devoted much energy to the propagation of the *tariqa*. He hailed from Upper Egypt, and his activities ensured that this region would become the major seedbed of the order in Egypt. Al-Dardir was one of relatively few men with a provincial background who succeeded in making a brilliant career at al-Azhar. Trained in

Maliki jurisprudence (*fiqh*) in his native town of Bani `Adi, he came to occupy important positions at al-Azhar, including that of shaykh of the *riwaq* or dormitory for students from Upper Egypt, administrator of their pious foundations (*awqaf*), and Maliki *mufti*. These functions made him the most important person at al-Azhar for any student originating from the Nile valley, and the vast network of Upper Egyptians at al-Azhar served him well in his efforts to spread the *tariqa*. Most of the branches of the Khalwatiyya in Upper Egypt today go back to the shaykh al-Dardir.

The expansion of the *tariqa* continued during the following century, and Delanoue's study of intellectual life in nineteenth century Egypt shows that persons affiliated with the Khalwatiyya dominated the religious field (Delanoue, 1982). Until recently it was widely assumed that in the late nineteenth century a turning point was reached and that the order suffered a gradual but unstoppable decline in the twentieth century as a result of, on the one hand, modernization and secularization and, on the other, the rise of Salafism and Wahhabism (cf. Trimingham, 1971: Ch. IX).

My field research in Upper Egypt, however, has led to a different conclusion. The Khalwatiyya continued its expansion there due to the activities of three Sufis, discussed below, who played influential roles in the course of the second half of the nineteenth and into the first half of the twentieth century. They are the founders of various new branches of the Khalwatiyya that are presently very active in the region, both as spiritual movements and as welfare associations. Frederick De Jong earlier made an inventory of the various Khalwatiyya branches active further north, in Middle Egypt (De Jong, 1978). One has the impression that these various branches together form a fine grid overlying the entire Nile valley. This raises the question about what sort of relations exist between these various branches.

The three Sufis on whom my research has focused were all Khalwatis, but they represent quite different types of spiritual masters (Chih, 2000a). The first, Ahmad Sharqawi (d. 1899), who was active in Jirja in the province of Suhaj, surrounded himself with an elite group of scholars based in both Cairo and Upper Egypt. However, he did not aim through his teaching to found an institutionalized *tariqa* and the chain of transmission (*silsila*) to which he belonged became extinct with the death of his sole spiritual heir (*khalifa*). His influence continues, however, because he wrote several books on Sufism and doctrine, most of which were published and remain in print. These works give the reader some insight into the mystical path and its future as understood by a learned Sufi in the late nineteenth century. The other two Sufis, `Abd al-Jawad al-Dumi and Ahmad al-Tayyib al-Hasani, have not left writings behind (or no works of importance, at any rate), but they devoted themselves throughout their lives for the spiritual training of disciples and the propagation of the Sufi path.

Al-Dumi (d. 1943), who hailed from Tahta in the province of Suhaj, studied at al-Azhar, and after completing his studies established himself as the imam of a mosque in Sabtiyya, a ward of Cairo with a large community of migrants from Upper Egypt. He soon found himself at the centre of a large group of Azhar students who were Upper Egyptians like himself. Being Malikis, the Upper Egyptians studied at al-Azhar under shaykhs of the Maliki school of law, and they lived together in the same *riwaq* (dormitory) at al-Azhar or around the same mosque. Like al-Hifni, al-Dumi used this regional network to spread his *tariqa*. Many of his closest disciples made their careers in mosques or as teachers, inspectors or directors of the various new Azhar-affiliated institutes that were being established in the provinces. Thanks to their mobility and their strategic location in the system of religious education, these disciples were in a position to recruit numerous further disciples both among the future ulama and among the `amma (the common folk) in Cairo as well as in the provinces.

Ahmad al-Tayyib al-Hasani (d. 1955) represents a third category of shaykh. According to oral tradition, al-Hasani established himself, after his studies at al-Azhar, in a village near Luxor, where he married the daughter of a man locally considered as a saint. Al-Hasani then became a peripatetic teacher of the basic precepts of Islam and of the Sufi path, moving from village to village on horseback. His reputation as a learned and holy man spread like an oil slick and a steady stream of disciples, mostly belonging to the peasantry, came to visit him. The shaykh built a special structure called the *saha* (literally, 'court') to receive all these visitors. After his death, his son, and later his grandson continued his religious and social activities: a new sacred lineage was born.

These three Sufis have a number of traits in common with other masters of the Khalwatiyya. They were educated at al-Azhar and their ideal, reflecting their educations and expressed in their writings as well as their disciplining activities, was to lead people towards God through Qur'anic instruction. They refrained from extravagant claims concerning sainthood (*walaya*), divine grace (*baraka*) and supernatural powers (*karamat*). Even though much of their teaching in fact revolved around sainthood, they preferred discussing this indirectly through references to the Qur'an and Sunna. To some extent, perhaps, this was to protect themselves against criticism from circles that were hostile to Sufism and saint worship, but it was just as much from conviction and training. The learned Khalwati shaykhs, with all their variety, distinguish themselves quite clearly by their sobriety from the shaykhs of more popular (folk-oriented) *turuq* such as the Ahmadiyya and Burhamiyya. The latter orders, often originating from the Delta, are characterized by a conception of sainthood that openly gives rise to veneration of the master as the bearer of the *baraka* of the founding saint.

The three Khalwati shaykhs, in spite of having gone through the same process of initiation and disciplining, had quite different approaches to their roles as teachers, leading to different modes of mobilization of disciples and different patterns of interaction with society. One chose to transmit his message to a small circle of educated followers, a *khassa* (elite), whereas the other two wished to reach out to the masses, the `*amma* – al-Dumi at the national level and al-Hasani at the local level. The teaching of these three resulted in not two but three new branches of the Khalwatiyya. Each distinguishes itself from other branches by adding the name of the founder of the branch to that of the mother *tariqa*. The teaching of Shaykh Ahmad al-Tayyib al-Hasani thus gave rise to the emergence of the Khalwatiyya Hasaniyya and that of Shaykh `Abd al-Jawad al-Dumi to two distinct new branches, the Khalwatiyya Dumiyya and the Khalwatiyya Dumiyya Ramliyya. The *silsila* of Shaykh Sharqawi, as noted above, is extinct so there is no branch named after him.

We speak of branches here, implying that they issued from the same trunk, but properly speaking these bifurcations do not constitute new paths. They share the same spiritual heritage and it is only in social appearance that they differ from, and are independent of, one another. A single *tariqa* may thus exist in a variety of social forms one beside the other, which makes it different from the monastic orders of Christian Europe. Most, if not all, *turuq* have at most times shown this tendency towards segmentation and the emergence of autonomous subdivisions. The Egyptian Khalwatiyya is, from the point of view of social organization, not a single, unitary, hierarchical organization with a pyramidal structure. It has constantly divided itself into new segments and this is precisely what has helped it to propagate and extend itself all over the country, into various geographical and social environments. The Khalwatiyya is not a network either; its branches have no connections with one another and in each of them the pivot of the path is the shaykh. Each of the branches however can be considered as a network in the sense that it consists of all individuals who interact with the shaykh and with each other.

Affiliation with the *Tariqa*

Just as the common translations of *tariqa* as 'order' or 'brotherhood' may carry unwarranted connotations, the terms 'adept' or 'member' do not adequately represent the forms of spiritual affiliation or initiatory attachment to a *tariqa*. In the Egyptian Khalwatiyya, one does not become a member or adept of a *tariqa* but one attaches oneself to a master, who transmits the teachings that he has himself received from another master, following an initiatory chain of transmission (*silsila*) that goes back to the Prophet. Each branch has its own *silsila*, and the only ritual detail that distinguishes the branches from each other is the prayer invoking the spirits of the masters of the path (*al-tawassul bi-rijal al-tariqa*) at the end of the *dhikr* session. This minor difference is quite significant, however, as the following incident illustrates. At the end of the *dhikr* session held by a group of disciples of the Khalwatiyya Dumiyya in a town in the province of Qina, a disciple from a distant town asked the person who acted as the leader in the absence of the master whether he would be allowed to attend the weekly meetings held by the Khalwatiyya Dumiyya Ramliyya in his hometown. The latter refused, saying, 'Those people (i.e. the Khalwatiyya Dumiyya Ramliyya) belong to one *mashrab* (initiatory tradition going back to the Prophet) and we to another; they have their own *madad* (invocation of assistance, protection) or *tawassul* (prayer for intercession by the masters of the path) and we another'.

In the Khalwatiyya, there are also different degrees of attachment to a master. One can be the *murid* (disciple, pl. *muridin*) of a shaykh or simply his *muhibb* (devotee, pl. *muhibbin*). At the moment of affiliation, a *murid*, a person who commits himself to the mystical path, concludes a pact (`ahd) with his shaykh and submits himself to the master by an oath of allegiance (*bay`a*). The term `ahd can also mean 'contract', and the term *bay`a* carries the connotation of an agreement between buyer and seller, as Denis Gril has explained (Gril, 1996: 92). The *murid* thus submits himself to the shaykh and through him to the Prophet and to God. The shaykh commits himself in exchange to guiding the disciple on the path but also to protecting, supporting and helping him. As we see below, for the disciple the shaykh is a *wali* ('friend of God', saint), meaning a person protected by God, as well as a protector, a patron and a client.

For the vast majority of the *muridin*, affiliation with the *tariqa* remains restricted to their reciting its litanies and prayers (*wird*, pl. *awrad*), participating in the congregational *dhikr* sessions, and regularly visiting the shaykh. Only those who share the life of the shaykh for many years may be further initiated into the spiritual secrets of the path and may become the master's *khalifa*. The latter are very few: Shaykh Sharqawi had only one *khalifa*, Shaykh al-Dumi three; and Shaykh al-Tayyib transmitted the path to a single person, his own son. These *khalifa* had a lifelong and intimate attachment to the shaykh. The *suhba* (companionship) of Shaykh Muhammad al-Tahir with his master `Abd al-Jawwad al-Dumi lasted for more than 20 years. As Shaykh Muhammad al-Tahir testified himself, this long friendship was of great influence in the formation of his own religious, spiritual and moral personality. He explained during an interview with me, 'I was constantly together with my shaykh, whether in Cairo or when travelling; I was with him during the *dhikr* sessions and in the classes and interviews that he gave. Through this *suhba*, the shaykh transmitted his knowledge in Qur'anic exegesis and Sufism'. After the shaykh's death, Muhammad al-Tahir renewed the pact of allegiance (`ahd) with the Shaykh al-Ramli, whom he was to succeed as the shaykh of the Khalwatiyya Dumiyya Ramliyya.

Unlike the *muridin* (the disciples), the *muhibbin* (the devotees) are not connected to the shaykh though an initiatory link but through a link of *mahabba*, love. The *muhibbin* have not passed through an initiation to the formulas of the *wird* because, in their own words, they do not feel capable of making the personal effort that the path demands, or they are simply not ready to make the effort. (This does not mean, however, that they might not join in reciting the *wird* during collective rituals.) The affiliation to a *tariqa* is perceived as a very serious act that implies a change in behaviour, for the pact with the shaykh is considered to be a pact concluded with God. The new disciple is expected to lead henceforth a life in accordance with all that God has commanded and to refrain from all He has forbidden. One person strongly attached to a Khalwati shaykh in Karnak near Luxor claims he refuses formal affiliation out of fear he might stray from the straight path and thereby betray the commitment made in the `ahd*.* A trader in the well-known Cairo market, the Khan al-Khalili, declared himself to be a *muhibb* of Shaykh al-Tayyib, whom he met on the occasion of a *mawlid* of Husayn, the grandson of the Prophet, which was held in his neighbourhood. Before this encounter, he never prayed or fasted; it was the shaykh, he explained to me in interview, who had set him on the right path. He had prayed regularly and fasted during Ramadan over the subsequent three years, but he still did not feel up to taking initiation. For such disciples, the shaykh represents a model of perfection that they are incapable of ever attaining themselves. The efforts demanded from a practising *murid* are also beyond them; the constraints of modern life make it even harder to reach such a degree of proximity to God. The *muhibbin* expect, however, that their weakness will be forgiven because of their attachment to and love of the *awliya* (pl. of *wali*).

Neither *muhibbin* nor *muridin* see their attachment as being first and foremost to a *tariqa*. The terms they use to describe themselves and their relationship with the shaykh are quite significant: they do not speak of themselves as Khalwati but as the children (*abna, awlad*) of the shaykh, or as his companions (*ashab*). This practice is not unique for the Khalwatiyya either. At the saints' day celebrations (*mawlid*) that are at the core of popular religiosity, various *turuq* erect their own tents with flags and banners, and the writing on the banner typically identifies the groups as the children or companions of such and such a shaykh, from this or that village, adding only at the end the name of the *tariqa*. When one asks Sufis what distinguishes them from those who are not Sufis, one receives answers such as 'love of the shaykh' (*mahabba li-l-shaykh*), 'attachment to the shaykh' (*mulazamat al-shaykh*), or 'putting oneself at the shaykh's service' (*khidmat al-shaykh*). This relationship is what the classical Sufi manuals call *suhba*, 'companionship', and it is modelled on the reciprocal affective relationship between the Prophet and his companions. In referring to spiritual fatherhood, to the proximity characterizing the relationship of master and disciple, and to intercession and guidance, as well as in invoking rules of proper behaviour and respect towards the master, people are ultimately referring to the example of the Prophet.[3]

An influential model of Muslim society contrasts the Islam of the saints with the scripturalist Islam of the ulama (the jurists). Sufi Islam is cast as hierarchical and the Islam of the ulama as more egalitarian (Gellner, 1969, 1981). The type of authority exercised by a saint allegedly demands unquestioning allegiance and submission, which would explain why it is supposed to be incompatible with modernity and particularly with the primacy of the individual in modern societies. Such a model ignores the reciprocal dimension present in the *bay`a* (as explained above) and the agency inherent in the choice of the pious followers. Religious authority in Islam has in fact always been fluid and fluctuating and has frequently been questioned (Gaborieau and Zeghal, 2004). In the domain of sainthood, it has usually been the *vox populi* that has prevailed (Goldziher 1880).

But what are the criteria for recognizing the authority of a shaykh, and what is the basis of his legitimacy in the eyes of the community? A study of the connections between Sufism and sainthood would exceed the limits of the present chapter, but one might state briefly that the authority of a shaykh amounts to the application of the various modalities of *walaya* and/or *wilaya*, concepts translated as 'sainthood'. Important recent studies on the subject have noted that in the Qur'an the term *walaya* refers to proximity but also to command (Chodkiewicz, 1986; Cornell, 1998). For the Sufis, this *walaya* is the result of access to an esoteric and inspired knowledge of God: the shaykh is an *`arif bi-llah*, one who has knowledge derived from God. This knowledge confers on him a form of spiritual authority that may eventually be converted into social authority. Esoterically, the shaykh may be invested with functions similar to those of the *khalifa*, God's representative an earth. He is an heir to the Prophet, whose behaviour he emulates. His proximity to God allows him to intercede on behalf of those who place themselves under his protection and come to their support. This is what Egyptians refer to by the term frequently uttered in the presence of a living saint or to call upon the spirit of a deceased saint: *madad*, 'assistance, protection'. A shaykh's disciples offer him allegiance in exchange for his *madad*. It is in recognition of this reciprocity that the social ties between the disciples and their shaykh and between companions on the path take their shape. There is, however, a wide variety of social arrangements in which this reciprocal relationship between master and disciples can be expressed. Within each branch of the *tariqa*, the forms of affiliation with the shaykh and the ties between disciples vary according to social environment and personality of the master. The following section illustrates this variety by comparing the functioning of Khalwatiyya branches in a rural and an urban setting.

The Social Setting: Shaykh al-Tayyib and his *saha*

In his village near Luxor, Shaykh Muhammad Muhammad Ahmad al-Tayyib is a popular and influential personality. From his *saha* (court), he oversees various matters concerning the village and its surroundings. He belongs to the social class of local notables, but he is much more than that; he is a shaykh, like his father before him and like his grandfather, the first to spread the *tariqa* Khalwatiyya in the village. Certain anthropologists have analyzed the hereditary transmission of the *baraka* (blessing) as amounting to the routinization of charisma, as theorized by Max Weber. The authority of the shaykh is, in this view, explained in terms of his management of symbolic capital, which he may turn into material capital, to be redistributed among his faithful followers. There is some confirmation for this view in the fact that Shaykh Muhammad M. Ahmad al-Tayyib's *saha*, which was originally constructed to respond to the needs of the *tariqa*, now responds to the needs of the entire village community. It is here that the shaykh feeds the people, arbitrates in conflicts, receives government officials, and listens to the complaints of the inhabitants.

However, as explained above, the shaykh is a *wali*, who needs to be engaged as a party to a *bay`a* in order to fulfil the role expected of him. His designation as a shaykh by a master or not is irrelevant as long as he has not also been designated as such by his community, which shows its recognition by renewing the pact of allegiance, thus transferring loyalty from the deceased master to the new shaykh. The three shaykhs of the al-Tayyib family have acquired this public recognition due to qualities that were, in the eyes of their followers, different in each case but that made them all nonetheless true holders of *walaya*. Family background, relations with the state and the support of local networks played crucial parts in the present shaykh Muhammad M. Ahmad al-Tayyib's rise to religious authority; but for his followers these are the external signs of his election by God.

Shaykh Muhammad al-Tayyib (d. 1988) received from his father, Shaykh Ahmad al-Tayyib, a proper written *ijaza* (authorization), which made him both genealogically and spiritually his *khalifa*. Everybody in the region remembers this strong personality, who was so different from his father. The latter was, in the memory of the old people of the village, a warm and genial personality, close to the people, accepting their hospitality and happily sharing their meals on his never-ending tours through the district to spread the Word. The son, shaykh Muhammad, was a very different type of Sufi. His presence would inspire awe and fear, even when he would be sitting, in the way of all spiritual masters, in the circle of his disciples. His behaviour and his physical appearance reinforced this impression. He never spent the night away from his *saha*, always returning home from his visits on the same day, and he refused the food and gifts that were offered to him.

Only one person, his daughter Kulthum, was allowed to prepare his single, sober daily meal, consisting mostly of vegetables and some meat cooked without salt or spices. He drank no tea, coffee, or any other drink, apart from a glass of aniseed tea in the evening. Towards the end of his life he reduced his intake of food to a few spoonfuls of milk. His skin became so delicate that he had to cover his hand with a shawl so that his numerous visitors could touch him. He spent long periods of retreat in a cell that was connected with the mosque of the *saha* by a small door and which he left only to perform his prayers. His physical appearance added to the fascination: he was entirely dressed in white, from his shoes to the scarf that covered his head. Following the example of the Prophet, he used perfume and he wound his turban so that a loose tail would hang down on his neck. People say that he inspired a mixture of respect and fear (*hayba, rahba*) so that they would lower their eyes in his presence. 'When I found myself in the presence of the shaykh', one disciple remembered to me, 'I was overcome by a feeling of fear, as if I had unwittingly done something wrong'.

Anthropologists and sociologists have analyzed sainthood in terms of the ways in which the shaykh constructs his charisma through his self-representation (e.g., Gilsenan, 1973; Elboudrari, 1985; Touati, 1989). Even where succession to the position of shaykh generally follows the line of family descent, being the son or other descendant of the founding master is not sufficient either for selection by the shaykh or for the chosen descendant's acceptance by others as a legitimate successor. The successor also has to be acknowledged by the people as one who has inherited his predecessor's knowledge and spiritual stature. Austerity, self-denial and humility are recognized as external signs of sainthood; these traits may help the successor to gain recognition of his status as the new shaykh. To his faithful followers, Shaykh Muhammad al-Tayyib was a saintly person of great majesty who had devoted his life, which was marked by extreme self-denial, entirely to God. He inspired a reverential fear in his followers but at the same time a profound love. His body was, as some say, 'pure and luminous as those of the saints' for he was himself one of the Friends of God.

The present shaykh, Muhammad Muhammad Ahmad al-Tayyib al-Hasani, is Shaykh Muhammad's eldest son. One could hardly imagine a greater difference from his father, who was likewise very different from the grandfather. The grandson has a round face and does not hide his corpulence, showing that he appreciates a good meal. He dresses according to the local custom. He is a friendly and genial man who loves a good joke, especially at the expense of others, and he enjoys pulling your leg in public. He is, finally, a man of action, *`amal*, rather than a man of knowledge, *`ilm*. He has, it is true, studied at al-Azhar, but not up to a high level – unlike his brother Ahmad, who holds a doctorate in Islamic philosophy from that institution's Faculty of Theology (*usul al-din*). However, in spite of this mild and good-natured appearance he inspires fear and respect like his father, for he is a man of power who reigns in his *saha* with an iron fist.

It has to be said that the times have changed: administering the *saha* he inherited from his father has become a heavy task. There are many *saha* in Upper Egypt, both small ones that are closed and reserved for a narrow circle of disciples, and large ones that are open to all visitors. All depends on the social and economic as well as the therapeutic roles played by the shaykh concerned. The present *saha* probably resembles only in a few respects the *saha* that the grandfather had built to house his family and receive his disciples. The family has expanded but even more so has the number of disciples, which increased as the population of the village and the wider region increased and as the shaykh came to play a more important role in society. The original structure of sun-baked clay bricks has been replaced by one of concrete and cement. Since the 1970s, the *saha* has had its own mosque, and in the 1990s it also received a minaret. Rooms have had to be added to provide lodging for visitors coming from afar, and a large kitchen was built to prepare dozens, or even hundreds, of meals served after the weekly *dhikr* sessions following the Friday prayer and at the larger celebrations of the religious holidays. The *saha* is always open; any passer-by can enter it to pray, meditate and pass the night if he wishes, or simply to take a rest, seated on a bench in the courtyard, in the shadow of the trees, in the calm and quiet atmosphere of this holy place. A servant will offer the visitor tea, and even a meal.

Besides the weekly distribution of food after the *dhikr*, more substantial food distributions take place in the *khidma* organized by the shaykh on the occasion of major religious festivals.[4] He organizes such *khidma* at the time of the two great annual *mawalid* of Cairo, the festivals in honour of the Prophet's grandchildren sayyida Zaynab and sayyid al-Husayn, and during the *mawlid* of the al-Tayyib shaykhs in Upper Egypt. The organization of these festivities obviously requires considerable financial resources. The shaykh also provides sustenance to the needy. Whereas the state has been failing as a provider of social security and of redistribution, the shaykh has stepped in and assumed these functions. This helps to explain why the *saha* has been so successful.

It proved impossible to measure the economic flows that make the *saha* the centre of redistribution. Like every Sufi establishment, the *saha* no doubt owes much to alms and to private gifts. Whatever may have been the forms of material accumulation and enrichment of the al-Tayyib family, in the eyes of their followers the present shaykh is a rich man because he is pious; this manna is the fruit of his *baraka*, the sign of God's beneficence towards him. The shaykh's *walaya* is revealed, made visible, through these daily actions of his for the well-being of his community. Generosity is one aspect of sainthood: the shaykh gives to the faithful without keeping anything for himself. He is said to 'serve the people [for free]' (*yakhdam al-nas*), i.e. to serve them for the love of God. The *wali* is at the same time also a man of power, and this quality is also recognized in Shaykh al-Tayyib, who acts as the mediator and arbiter of conflicts in his village.

The *saha* of Shaykh al-Tayyib receives a continuous stream of visitors, some of them people from the village or its surroundings, others from nearby towns or more distant cities such as Aswan, and including not only Muslims but also Christians; not only adult men but also women and youths. Some come to request his intercession with local authorities, others to ask his advice, moral support or material assistance. Women come to seek his protection against a violent husband or father; young people seek his blessing before undertaking a voyage, investing money or contracting a marriage. But it is especially to seek his help in arbitration that people come to see the shaykh. His father and grandfather already functioned as arbiters and mediators in the feuds that for a long time caused much bloodshed in the region. The feuds have not disappeared, but the present shaykh is especially active in resolving conflicts between spouses, brothers, cousins and neighbours – conflicts that are often about land or questions of inheritance. In arbitration he presides over a council consisting of the important personalities of the village, named the *majlis al-`arab*. His intercession is made more effective due to his connections with the local authorities.

The shaykh is also a political notable, even though he would not describe himself as such. He holds local power as a result of his political connections with the government, due to which he can intervene effectively on behalf of the community. He is a member of the ruling party, the NDP (National Democratic Party). Government officials often have recourse to him for taking care of problems in the village, and he regularly obliges them, assisted by his council of local notables. His authority and the prestige of his family increased even further when his learned brother, the said doctor Ahmad, was appointed as the *mufti* of the Republic by the Egyptian President himself and later was promoted to the position of president of al-Azhar university. For his followers, these relations of the shaykh with the holders of political power are not at all in contradiction with his status as a saint. They are perceived as recognition of his authority and as a form of allegiance of the powerful of this world to his spiritual leadership. They are seen as proof that the invisible power of the saint is superior to worldly power.

Once the followers have recognized the presence of *walaya* in the shaykh, they establish a relationship of allegiance with him that sociologically takes the form of a patron-client relationship. The shaykh protects the interests of the village and in exchange the people show him their recognition and allegiance. This is not very different from the way sainthood functioned in early Christendom. Students of the history and anthropology of Sufism may learn much from the methodological advances made by historians of sainthood in Christianity, among which especially Peter Brown's work on Late Antiquity (1982) has become a major reference. The relations of patronage that we have noted in the Egyptian case, where the shaykh takes care of the needs of the community, are inherent in the very concept of *walaya*: proximity to God implies patronage. As Michel Chodkiewicz has noted, the Sufi concept of *walaya* corresponds with the Roman term *amicitia*, which likewise, as Brown has shown, denotes simultaneously friendship, protection and power: 'The saint was the *patronus*, the protector with whom it was desirable to enter into a client relationship' (Brown, 1982: 15).

The people of the village experience their relationship with the shaykh as one of exchange and mutual benefits, which they exploit themselves. The shaykh is arbiter and intermediary at the same time: he intercedes with God, through the intermediary of the Prophet, on behalf of individuals and he intercedes with the state on behalf of the community. He represents in this sense the ideal patron as defined by Peter Brown:

> He is a man who would use his power to smooth over the thorny issues of village life. He would provide – and help distribute – the all-important water supply of the village. He would arrange the cancelling of debts. He could settle disputes among the villagers on the spot, and so save them the long trek to the local town to conduct their litigations. (Brown, 1982: 117)

The *walaya* of a saint, here in Upper Egypt, has a clear territorial dimension, which reminds us of the dual meaning of the pair of homonyms *walaya* and *wilaya* – the former primarily referring to proximity to God, the latter to territory and authority. Against this background it is understandable that the ties to Shaykh al-Tayyib were complemented by ties of family, regional, or ethnic identity. The affiliations with the shaykh have a collective aspect and are often (though not always) hereditary.

This contrasts with the state of affairs in the two other branches of the Khalwatiyya discussed below. These have established themselves primarily in the urban environment, thanks to networks of institutions of religious studies and later of mosques. They are not localized *turuq* linked to a specific territory (whether a village, an urban neighbourhood or a town). From Cairo they have spread everywhere in the cities of Upper Egypt, where they have built some new kinds of social settings for their gatherings. Because the shaykh resides in Cairo, the primary social ties in these Upper Egyptian branches are those between brothers on the path rather than between master and disciple. Adherence to the *tariqa* is a matter of personal choice rather than heredity.

Another Social Setting: The *rawda*

Shaykh `Abd al-Jawad al-Dumi preferred the spiritual transmission from master to disciple over that by inheritance. During his lifetime he issued *ijaza*s (certificates of permission to provide guidance) to three of his disciples, who became his *khalifa* after his death. When a shaykh opts for transmitting his path to more than one disciple, he cannot logically choose a single successor among them. As a result, schisms are almost inevitable; these make up much of the vitality of a *tariqa*.

After the death of Shaykh al-Dumi, the majority of his followers elected his eldest disciple and *khalifa*, Shaykh al-Ramli, as the new spiritual master of the *tariqa*. Shaykh Sulayman, who also had an *ijaza* from Shaykh al-Dumi defected from the *tariqa*, accompanied by another group of followers. They considered that Shaykh al-Ramli was not sufficiently learned to become their new shaykh. Shaykh Ramli was but a modest employee of the railways, whereas Shaykh Sulayman had a diploma from al-Azhar. The group around Shaykh Sulayman grew into a new branch, which took the name of Khalwatiyya Dumiyya, and the group led by Shaykh al-Ramli took the name of Khalwatiyya Dumiyya Ramliyya.

These two branches are completely independent of one another at present. Even when they celebrate the *mawlid* of their common master, `Abd al-Jawad al-Dumi, they do so separately. Shaykh al-Ramli lies buried beside his master al-Dumi in the graveyard of Imam Shafi`i, south of the City of the Dead in Cairo (the Qarafa). But when Shaykh Sulayman died in 1959, his followers built a luxurious mausoleum for him in the graveyard of al-Basatin, further north. In spite of this evident break, however, both shaykhs and their *khalifa* in turn have followed Shaykh al-Dumi's ways of organizing their *tariqa* and functioning in society.

The various activities of these two branches take place in a number of different settings: in private apartments, often in mosques, and especially in the *rawda*, an institution specific to these branches. The *rawda* (literally 'garden') is in fact a rather large building, usually consisting of a simple hall for gatherings but in some cases a building of several floors with a social and cultural centre attached. The first *rawda* was established by Shaykh al-Dumi as a meeting and gathering place for his disciples in Cairo but especially for those who came to visit him from Upper Egypt. Then the members of the Khalwatiyya Dumiyya, whose shaykh resides in Cairo, built a *rawda* in the capital (the one of al-Basatin) and established other *rawda* in most big cities of Upper Egypt. As for the *rawda* of the Khalwatiyya Dumiyya Ramliyya, they are all located in Upper Egypt where its successive shaykhs have lived. A biography of shaykh al-Dumi records a disciple's memories of the founding of the *rawda*:

> The shaykh held *dhikr* sessions on all Sunday and Thursday evenings, following the class and the evening prayer (`isha). Some people came from very far away to take part in the *dhikr*, and when they had no relatives in Cairo, they were lodged in the *rawda* that their shaykh put at their disposal. (Tahir and Mahmud, 1961: 179)

Unlike the *saha* in the Upper Egyptian context, the *rawda* is not open to the general public; it is reserved for the disciples. It is here that disciples who are passing through can spend the night, as does the master himself during his visits. Only rarely will a disciple stay in a *rawda* permanently, although such cases do occur. One such long-time resident whom I encountered was Ibrahim, a student at al-Azhar. Ibrahim came from a village in the district of al-Maragha and he was initiated into the Khalwatiyya Dumiyya by Husayn Mu`awad, the present shaykh of the *tariqa*. Upon arrival in Cairo, he first found a place to stay in the *rawda* of al-Basatin, in the Qarafa, and later moved on to that of Giza. He stayed in both places free of charge.

In the course of the 1970s, the number of such *rawda*s in Cairo and the cities of the Nile valley increased rapidly, due to the propagation of a network of associations for carrying out the religious and social activities of both branches of the *tariqa*. These associations collected voluntary contributions (*tabarru`at*) for the construction of social and educational centres run by the *tariqa*. These complexes usually comprised a mosque and sometimes a Qur'an school, but also a clinic and sometimes even a hospital. The *rawda*s are often attached to these complexes.

The *rawda* is an essentially urban institution. The size and splendour of the *rawda* depend of course on the importance of the *tariqa* in the town. Most *rawda* are of modest size. The *rawda* in the town of Suhaj may serve as an example of an average one. It consists basically of a single large room, with lots of carpets and cushions on the floor and portraits of the shaykhs of the *tariqa* as the only ornaments on the wall. On one side, there is a bedroom, a tiny kitchen and a bathroom. One of the largest *rawda* is that in the town of Jirja – a five-story building on the Corniche, built in the 1980s. On each floor there are rooms with two or three beds, intended for disciples who are passing through. A better-appointed bedroom, with attached bathroom and toilet, is reserved for the shaykh's use during his stays in the town. This *rawda* also has a prayer hall and a modest library. The construction of such a *rawda* may take many years and demand considerable funds. Rooms and facilities may be added when funds become available. Another exceptional *rawda*, with a more specialized function, is the one that was established in the garden around the mausoleum of Shaykh Sulayman to provide lodgings to disciples and followers who come from afar to visit the shaykh's grave or to take part in his *mawlid*, which is celebrated every year on the first Friday of the month Muharram. For the rest of the year, the *rawda* serves as a holiday retreat for the shaykh and his family; it is located at a quiet and airy site in the foothills of the Muqattam cliffs. This *rawda* has several floors. On the ground floor are the kitchens and on the first floor are two salons, the smaller of which is reserved for women and also holds the shaykh's personal library. The upper floors have rooms for guests, and on top there is a terrace.

The *rawda* was from the beginning conceived as the place for the brothers of the path to experience companionship among themselves, companionship (*suhba*) being one of the pillars of the path according to all classical Sufi manuals. This is where they meet after the collective *dhikr* session. Seated in a circle and sipping tea, sometimes served with sweets, they discuss or follow lessons. These *rawda* are run by the oldest and closest disciples of the master, all of them Azharis and usually retired men, who have both enough free time and sufficient religious knowledge to organize the *majlis* (the *dhikr* session), to lead the prayer, and sometimes to initiate new disciples. It is these meetings in the *rawda* that keep the ties between brothers on the path intact. Associating in the *rawda* also contributes an internal cohesion to the group that compensates for the absence of the shaykh most of the time. The emphasis in the *rawda* is on companionship and brotherhood. In this context, *suhba* refers not only to the attachment to the shaykh but also to the sense of unity among companions at the *rawda* as brothers on the path (cf. Gril, 1986: 43). The disciples feel united by their common loyalty and love for the shaykh and by extension for the Prophet and all saints This common sentiment exemplifies the convivial and fraternal nature of Sufism.

The *rawda* have other important social functions: they provide a meeting point for non-resident urban followers and help to integrate new urban migrants into the urban environment. The recent massive migration from the countryside to the cities and the emergence of proletarian urban classes have influenced the ways in which the *turuq* are integrated into society. The *turuq* traditionally depended strongly on kinship, tribal relations, and local and regional ties for recruitment and cohesion. All of these traditional forms of social organization have been profoundly affected by the rural exodus, although they have not entirely disappeared. The Khalwatiyya Dumiyya and the Khalwatiyya Dumiyya Ramliyya reproduce in Cairo and the cities of the Nile valley local and regional solidarities that are still very strong. The *rawda* make it possible to maintain ties of solidarity among the disciples who are rural migrants to the urban environment. In Cairo, new migrants, who are often quite young, find a new family with their shaykh and with their brothers on the Path.

Conclusions

The debates on Sufism and modern society in Egypt have been and remain dominated by Michael Gilsenan's study of an urban branch of the Shadhiliyya and Fred de Jong's study on the institutionalization of the *turuq* by the state. Gilsenan attributed the survival of the *turuq* in modern urban society to a Weberian rationalization of its forms of organization and its practices. De Jong attributed the changing organization of the *turuq* in Egypt primarily to the role of the state.[5] Official support and a certain degree of modern organization no doubt played a part in the development and the religious and social integration of the *turuq* into modern Egyptian society, but these have not been decisive or dominant factors. It is true that the connections between the holders of political power and the Sufi shaykhs have a long history and are well established in Egypt. At least since Ottoman times, the state has made efforts to intervene in the functioning of the *turuq*. Towards the end of the nineteenth century, the government established a Sufi council, which had the task of overseeing and administering the social world of mysticism (De Jong, 1978). In the 1980s, some 70 *turuq* were registered by this council, but at least as many if not more had to do without its stamp of recognition.

The branches of the Khalwatiyya examined in this chapter have always refused official registration. Their shaykhs are not public personalities like the shaykhs studied by previous researchers.[6] They do not take part in the conferences and public discussions of religious questions that are organized by the state, nor are they present at the official openings of religious ceremonies, and they do not have seats on the Sufi council. Like many Azharis, they have experienced as traumatic events both the reforms of al-Azhar carried out under Nasser in the 1960s, and the transformation of its ulama into civil servants. Many men of religion (and this includes many Sufis) feel in their hearts a strong wish to free themselves from control by the state (cf. Zeghal, 1996).

The shaykhs of the Khalwatiyya did not need the state to have their authority recognized; it exists outside the state. Their authority has to do with exoteric knowledge, acquired at al-Azhar, and with a spiritual transmission that makes them guides in this world and in the hereafter. It is true that from the moment a *tariqa* takes form as a social body it cannot completely escape interference by the state. However, it is not as easy for the state to reform the *turuq* as it was to reform al-Azhar; neither their ideology nor their social or institutional form is susceptible to such intervention. The common approach therefore has been to establish patron–client networks with the shaykhs. Sufi shaykhs have themselves also engaged in a reciprocal strategy of seeking patronage from bureaucrats and politicians. The social microcosm studied here illustrates a situation that is prevalent in the entire country: the state exerts administrative power, but moral authority is exercised by informal leaders who are accepted by the government but not directly controlled by it.

It is not possible to fully separate analysis of the *tariqa* as a spiritual path and as a pattern of social relationships. The *turuq* represent only one aspect and only one vector of a religious culture that has been forged in Islam in the course of the centuries. This culture revolves around sainthood. The saints follow models that have been transmitted to them in the course of their initiation and education, and all emphasize some particular attribute or quality of the Prophet.[7] Each shaykh or saint represents a spiritual profile. The profile of the Khalwati shaykh is that of a Sufi attached to the principles of the Sunna, who is engaged in a form of social activism adapted to his environment. For his disciples he is himself a model to emulate, and if the shaykh's example is too difficult to imitate, the disciple may at least seek daily contact and proximity to him. Communication with the shaykh, the love felt for him, and the services willingly rendered to him are also forms of spiritual realization. This personal relation transforms the disciple, and the transformation affects his relations with his companions on the path, with his family, and with his entire universe.

Acknowledgement

I thank Malika Zeghal for her incisive and illuminating comments on an earlier version of this article.

3

SUFISM AND MODERNITY IN TURKEY: FROM THE AUTHENTICITY OF EXPERIENCE TO THE PRACTICE OF DISCIPLINE

Brian Silverstein

> To a considerable extent ... the characteristic quality of the Turks in the modern Muslim world seems to rest on the uniqueness of their immediate past. (The prime matter here is continuity: the unbroken sequence from their medieval grandeur, including a persisting independence – and therefore active responsibility.)[1]
> Wilfred Cantwell Smith

> *Asrımız tarikat asrı değildir.* (Ours is not the age of the Sufi orders.)[2]
> Said Nursî

In the Ottoman Empire until 1923 and briefly in the Republic of Turkey, Sufi orders were of major importance to social, political and economic life. Many `ulama actively cultivated their devotion in one (or more) of the numerous idioms of Sufism available in the Empire.[3] However, in 1925 the Republican administration proscribed the orders and closed their lodges. It has since been technically a punishable offence to be involved in a Sufi order – as shaykh (a title not recognized by the Turkish state) or as devotee – although a number of orders have continued to function in a somewhat 'public secret' fashion.

What becomes of Sufism as an Islamic tradition of practice in such an environment?[4] What is the status of such traditions of Sufi Islamic discourse and practice in Turkey as the country is increasingly self-conscious of its Ottoman heritage, and yet has seen dramatic social, economic and political transformation during the last two centuries, culminating in serious bids for entry into the European Union? While participation in a Sufi order is not a mass phenomenon in contemporary Turkey, Sufism in the country is, as Crapanzano has said of a brotherhood in Morocco, 'peripheral but by no means unrelated to the mainstream' (Crapanzano, 1973: 7). Moreover, the characteristically modern ways of defining and organizing space, time, experience and bodies as objects of calculation situate contemporary practice in the context of the history of profound and intimate articulation with modern techniques of governance since the eighteenth century. These ways of defining and organizing suggest that the structure and form of continuity in practice, which is central to the functioning of Islamic traditions, has unfolded not in a relation of alterity to the geography of these specifically modern techniques, but coextensively with it.

Power and Islamic Traditions on the Margin of Europe

In a now seminal article, Asad (1986) argued that social scientists (and anthropologists in particular) should define Islam – like Muslims themselves do – as a discursive tradition. The timing of the appearance of the piece, in the mid-1980s, seems to have ensured that the vast majority of its readership took the emphasis in this definition to be on the discursive. However, and as subsequent publications have made clear, Asad himself would have us put the emphasis on the notion of tradition; Islam is a tradition, among others. Asad operates in this article with the formulation of tradition elaborated by Alasdair MacIntyre in his work in moral philosophy, and specifically in his controversial 1984 work, *After Virtue*.

A tradition, on Asad's adaptation of MacIntyre, is an ongoing set of discussions (a 'discourse') and practices that are closely interlinked and have been so continuously and over time. One of the most important practices is discussion and debate about correct practice. To belong to a tradition involves sincere commitment to the value and normatively binding character of past precedent and to the validity of the discussions and debates received from the past. Normative judgment is an important part of any tradition; there are better ways to do things, and therefore there are ways that are less good. Here we need to keep in mind that these discussions about correct practice are always evolving, and the judgments reached are constantly changing. Stasis is not a characteristic of tradition.[5] Indeed, Asad notes that one must wait for the appearance of the modern bureaucratic nation-state in order to arrive at an unprecedented homogenization of discourse and practice in society. However, to say that traditions are always changing does not amount to saying they are 'constructions', 'inventions', or do not exist.[6] Living traditions change through engagement with the received, ongoing sets of discussions; doing otherwise is by definition abandonment of the tradition.

Elsewhere (Silverstein, 2003) I have proposed a modest corrective to recent work in this vein with respect to what I argue is an unduly narrow, localized (postcolonial Arab Middle East-centred) definition of which specific discourses and practices Islamic traditions consist of today (and what their

relationship is to modernity). In this chapter, I build on that conception of
Islam as a discursive tradition. Work in this vein among Muslim communities
often under-elaborates the nature of continuity in practice and discourse,
which is considered to be crucial to the functioning and definition of
traditions. Muslims see that it is important to legitimize their practice through
reference to the tradition, to past precedent. A relation of continuity with the
past is thus desirable, while a form of censure and reproach is to judge a view
or practice to be without basis in the traditions. In the legitimacy of a given
practice or discourse aspiring to 'Islamic' status, the politics of continuity is
central.[7]

The notion of continuity becomes problematic in many parts of the
Muslim world because of the perceived ruptures of European imperialism and
colonialism. How does one, as a Muslim, consider the character of discourses
and practices in recent centuries and the judgments arrived at in those
contexts, vis-à-vis those of previous periods? Even though certain areas of
the Muslim world were not formally colonized (e.g. Turkey and Iran), the
entire world was, and continues to be, convulsed by the ascendance of
European, 'Western', non-Muslim power. Hence I argue that the question is
one of defining modes of power and their relationship to Islamic traditions.
In this chapter I examine the specific articulation of Sufi institutions with
Republican social and institutional forms to illustrate the shared historicity of
Islamic traditions and characteristically modern modalities of power and
subject formation.[8] I draw from my research with a Gümüşhanevi branch of
the Khalidi sub-order of the Naqshbandi Sufi order.[9]

In attending to the relationship between Islamic traditions and specifically
modern techniques and practices in the context of Turkey, we need to keep in
mind that the Turkish present is not post-colonial in any direct sense. This is
not to celebrate 'successful resistance'. Rather, the point is to recall that in the
Ottoman and Turkish case, a radical rupture does not characterize the specific
contexts and imperatives of power in which Islamic traditions continually
evolved while characteristically modern forms and techniques were
incorporated (in spite of the rhetoric of the Revolution beginning in 1923
with the proclamation of the Republic by Mustafa Kemal).[10] The Ottomans
were like several other powers in the political geography of Europe (e.g.
Russia and Austro-Hungary) that were close to the margin of the emergence
of industrial capitalism, and sought to incorporate techniques of modern
governance as a way of prosecuting more effective warfare by rationalizing
and bureaucratizing the identification and exploitation of resources
(Silverstein, 2003). This history of the incremental reform of institutions,
according to the Ottoman authorities' own criteria, has bequeathed a situation
in which modernity has been experienced not as a conspiracy of outsiders but
as an integral part of the status of the Turkish present.

Utterance and Companionship as Sufi Practice: *Sohbet*

Sohbet (Arabic *suhba*) is a devotional practice of particular prominence in the Naqshbandi order, as it is among Mevlevis. It consists of 'keeping the company of the shaykh and of one's fellow disciples in accordance with precise behavioural norms' (Algar, 1992: 213), with the 'disciple's firm conviction in the exclusive effectiveness of his shaykh's *suhba*' (Algar, 1992: 215). I translate *sohbet* as companionship-in-conversation, and will describe its form and function below.[11] During my fieldwork in the late 1990s with the Gümüşhanevi branch of the Khalidi Naqshbandi order,[12] members would gather after `asr prayers on Sunday afternoons in the main area of a mosque in the Fatih neighbourhood of Istanbul to attend a *sohbet*, similar in outward form to a lesson. This was led by an authorized stand-in (*vekil*) for the shaykh, Esad Coşan Hoca Efendi (commonly known as Esad Hoca), who was abroad – mainly in Australia – from 1997 until his sudden passing in a car accident there in 2001.[13]

The *sohbet*s were structured around the reading and discussion of two or three *hadith* (accounts of exemplary sayings and deeds of the Prophet). The *hadith* were first read aloud by the *vekil* in Arabic, translated, and then interpreted, giving examples from daily occurrences and historical anecdotes.[14] The exercise generally lasts about an hour and a half, with very little coming and going, no talking on the part of listeners, and almost no note taking. At the end of the *sohbet*, supplicatory prayers (*du`a*) were said, asking God to accept the efforts of the *sohbet* and the prayers of its participants. This became seamlessly an abbreviated version of the *khatm-i Khwajagan*, an invocation of the memory of earlier pious personalities, with special emphasis on figures in the Naqshbandi order's chain of initiation (*silsila*). It was followed by a *zikir* (*dhikr*), invocations and remembrance of the Divine names and attributes.[15]

Those participating in the sohbets in Fatih were members of the Gümüşhanevi branch of the Naqshbandi order of Sufis. Members comprise a community known as a *cemaat*[16] (Arabic *jama`a*), as members of the Order refer to their community, in preference to *tarikat*, Sufi Order. During the *sohbet*, there were ritual recitations of cycles of prayers and invocations of the memory of Sufi luminaries considered to be predecessors in the Naqshbandi order. Yet there was nothing ostensibly 'mystical' about the content of the discussions that took place, occupying roughly 95 per cent of the time of the *sohbet*. I had attended *sohbet*s and socialized with *cemaat* members for several months when I realized that almost no one had ever discussed the classic themes of Sufism emphasized in Western literature on the topic, such as 'intimate experience of God' and 'self-effacement (in the Reality of God)'. Not only were these techniques not discussed during *sohbet*, they were not discussed among the many followers outside of *sohbet*s. It became quite obvious that the members of the *cemaat* simply were not particularly concerned with these themes on a daily basis.

They were, however, clearly very concerned with what was a constant topic of lessons and informal discussion: the good (*iyilik*) and morality (*ahlak*), and how one can become predisposed to ethical practice and avoidance of sin. For the practitioners who I came to know, Sufism is essentially an ethical discipline (the term they used was *terbiye*, Arabic *tarbiya*), a self-reflexive effort to constitute moral dispositions (*hal-tavır*) in oneself through repetition according to precedents considered to be binding and authoritative.[17] These practitioners' concerns with ethical practice and the formation of their dispositions suggest that in analyzing the practices of this order, our focus should not be on something called 'mystical experience', but rather on disciplinary practice, which Asad (1993: 130) defines as 'programs for forming or reforming moral dispositions (organizing the physical and verbal practices that constitute the virtuous ... self)'. Hence an interpretation of the nature of Sufi practice in contemporary Turkey (and likely in other contexts as well) requires an analytic shift away from the infinite calculus of 'real Sufi' *experience* (or its absence) and toward the relationship between traditions of discourse and practice and the kinds of ethical selves associated with them.

The term *sohbet* is used in modern, every day Turkish to mean 'conversation'. But in classical sources it has a more nuanced meaning of companionship, including shades of fellowship and discipleship (Trimingham, 1998: 311). There is a sense among Sufis that companionship is linked intimately to conversation, and conversely that conversation engenders companionship. The term '*sohbet*' itself derives from the same Arabic root as the word '*sahaba*', companions, and the terms participate in the same semantic extension. *Sohbet* is what, by definition, companions do. The figure of the companion in Islam is modelled on the Companions of the Prophet, those who were closest to the Prophet during his lifetime, sought out and frequently kept his company, and strove to assimilate his teachings. The Companions' significance can hardly be overstated, since it was they who transmitted the *hadith* and the Quran before these were written down and compiled, ensuring a critical structural role for companionship and face-to-face speech in Islamic disciplines.

Those with whom I worked in the Gümüşhanevi branch of the Naqshbandi order emphasized that it was in emulation of the *sunna* (exemplary precedents) of the Prophet that they practiced *sohbet* (as well as *dhikr*). Indeed, this principle of the authoritativeness of the source was often cited as the most important reason why members of the order continued to associate with that order, rather than with one of the other groups in Turkey oriented toward the observant and pious (e.g. the Nurcu movement). 'This group's teachings have a clear and known source (*belli bir kaynağı var*)', I was told repeatedly, referring to the fact that the shaykh of the order was himself trained by a previous shaykh, and so on, back – as nearly all Sufi orders consider – to the Prophet Muhammad himself.[18] Important here is the role of precedent in the formulation of right practice, and sustained, explicit reflection on the relationship between the status of sources and correct practice.[19] Among Naqshbandis specifically, *sohbet* has been emphasized since at least the time of 'Ubaydullah Ahrar (d. 1490) and Ahmad Sirhindi (d. 1625). It was also emphasized by Mevlana Khalid ('al-Baghdadi' d. 1827) who was the major shaykh in the chain of initiation of the Khalidi sub-order of the Naqshbandis, from which the Gümüşhanevi is a branch.[20]

There is thus a strong sense of belonging to a tradition, and Naqshbandis in Turkey today often refer to themselves and like-minded (not necessarily Sufi) Muslims as '*ehl-i sünnet*', or 'Those of the Tradition'. Through *sohbet*, Naqshbandis have structured their main group activities besides canonical worship around the discussion of *hadith*, in a form that self-consciously conforms to what they construe as the privileged mode of knowledge transmission between the Prophet and his companions. Naqshbandis therefore embody what they see to be the quintessential mode of Islamic religiosity, namely the formation of a moral disposition to practice through companionship and discourse modelled on the *sunna* of the Prophet. The emphasis is on face-to-face presence of both the seeker and the one who is considered ethically mature because these relationships are considered most likely to lead to certain sentiments – the technical term here being 'love' (*sevgi*, *muhabbet*; Arabic *muhabba*)[21] – and hence dispositions to ethical practice.

These Naqshbandi practices of virtue are intimately tied to practices of self-formation that are embedded in networks of companionship and contexts of disciplined utterance. The metaphysic of influence is embedded in an ethic of companionship that is understood to be central to the functioning of the constitution of morally structured dispositions to do the Good. It has been embodied in what I propose to call disciplines of presence. The most important of these disciplines for those in this branch of the Naqshbandi order is *sohbet*.[22] The embodiment of voices in gendered bodies is a condition for the functioning of these disciplines, as is repeated interaction with specifically structured environments, through which such habits and dispositions are embedded.[23] The structural transformations of the social environment are thus of major importance to how these practices function over time.[24]

The central concern of the Naqshbandi Sufis with whom I worked was thus not the so-called mystical union with God (and annihilation of the self). Their concern was with the disciplining of the base self (*nefs*), in order to form a proper disposition to do the Good (*iyilik*) as commanded by God. A member of the order in Sivas told me:

> It's kind of like in the circus – the animals there. One gives them little food, breaking them in and training (*eğitmek*) them, not giving them the things they want. Maybe one animal wants to go out today; nope, we're not going to. To the extent that the reins are in our hands, we'll take the horse where we want to go. But without a horse, one can't go anywhere,

one definitely must have a horse. So, Sufism does this. It disciplines the *nefs*, and this thing called *nefs* is actually us ourselves (*biziz*). Me. You know, we say, 'I don't want any' (*canım istemiyor*). That me – self – is the *nefs*. 'I' don't want to go out. 'I' am bored. That term 'I', this is the *nefs*. 'The self inside (*içimizdeki ben*)', they say. So, the point is to discipline (*terbiye etmek*) this. Because (otherwise) one goes where it wants to go, one acts as it wants us to act. The reins, the bridle of the horse, must be in our hands. This is the goal. And we have no choice but to make use of this (*nefs*). The goal is NOT to kill or destroy the *nefs*. To kill the *nefs* is not the thing to do (*iş değil*). But to discipline it, THAT's it (*iş*).

Several senior Naqshbandis explained to me their understanding that people are influenced most in their behaviour by other people. For the proper formation of character, then, one should try to always be with 'good people', defined as those who seek the approval of God, and only God, and are not led astray by such things as popular fashion, prestige or power. The Quranic verse, 'O ye who believe! Fear Allah and be with those who are true in word and deed (*al-sadiqin*)' (Quran 9: 119) was frequently cited in this context. Sufis claim that everyone needs a shaykh, whether they know it or not, and behind this claim is recognition of the need for upright, 'mature' guides to train and discipline the self. It is important to be with someone who is aware of his responsibilities toward his disciples, to instil in them the proper *adab* (moral etiquette). The physical space where these practices have traditionally been undertaken in Muslim communities in Anatolia and the Balkans is the *tekke*, or Sufi lodge.

Legacies of the Late Empire: The structure of a contemporary absence

The lodge (*tekke*, *dergâh*, or, less commonly, *zaviye* in the Turkish speaking context) has been the centre of associative life of Sufis throughout the history of most of the orders. Here travelling Sufis would be accommodated, students housed, a shaykh often lived with his family, and a kitchen functioned.[25] During the last century of the Ottoman Empire from 1820 to 1920 it is estimated that there were between 1,000 and 2,000 *tekke*s in the core provinces of Anatolia and Rumelia (the Balkans) (Kreiser, 1992: 49). Estimates put the number of *tekke*s in the capital of Istanbul alone at around 300 by the late nineteenth century.[26] The upkeep of most was provided by a foundation (*vakıf*), from which modest stipends to some residents and provisions such as food for the kitchen were ensured. State policies concerning such foundations were therefore of extreme importance to the life of the *tekke*s and orders. When the state sought to inaugurate a new policy toward the Sufi orders – as the Republican administration did in 1925 when it proscribed the orders and closed their lodges – this involved new procedures in the administration of *vakıf*s.

The Republic of Turkey was proclaimed by Nationalists in 1923 from the ruins of the Ottoman Empire, after ten years of almost continuous warfare in the Balkan Wars through World War I and the War of Independence. It is striking that between 1920 and 1925, the Nationalist movement's leader, Mustafa Kemal and those around him in the movement, did not take hostile actions against the orders. Indeed, the Constitution of 1924 included in its Article 75, 'No one may be persecuted on account of the religion, *madhhab* (school of *shari`a* jurisprudence), *tarikat* or school of philosophy to which he or she belongs. Provided they are not contrary to public order and decorum (*asayiş ve umumî muaşeret*), all types of religious ceremonies (*ayin*) are permitted' (cited in M. Kara, 2002: 101).

Law number 429 was promulgated on 3 March of the same year, abolishing the Ministry of the Shari`a and Evkaf, and establishing the Ministry of Religious Affairs. The former ministry had existed only since 1920 when it was created as an alternative to the *Meşihat*, the office of the Shaykh al-Islam in Istanbul that had collaborated with the Western powers against the Nationalists. Article 5 of this law stipulates that, 'All appointments and dismissals of imams, *khatib*s [preachers], *va`iz* [preachers], shaykhs, *muezzin*s [reciters of the call to worship], caretakers and various personnel to and from all mosques and *tekke*s shall be undertaken by the Ministry of Religious Affairs'. Shaykhs, *tekke*s and *zaviye*s were thus officially recognized and placed under the control of the new Ministry, itself a part of the streamlined and more tightly structured administration in Ankara. Imams of mosques and shaykhs of the orders were made State bureaucrats, as they were in the later Empire. This incorporated form of social and legal life of the orders in the new Republic was, however, short-lived.

The turning point was the Shaykh Said rebellion in the (predominantly Kurdish) Southeast of the new Republic, beginning around 13 February 1925. It is clear that Mustafa Kemal and his close associates were badly shaken by these events, and used them as an occasion to deal swiftly and decisively with numerous individuals and movements suspected of being less than enthusiastic in their support for the ongoing reforms. The legal grounds for doing so were prepared by amending the High Treason Law of 1920 (previously amended in 1923) to include on 26 February 1925 the 'use of religion for political purposes' and on 4 March 1925, the establishment of Independence Tribunals. The amendment enabled sentencing of Shaykh Said and dozens of others to death, and the tribunals continued through 1926 (Zürcher, 1994; M. Kara, 2002).

In July 1925, a commission of inquiry sent from Ankara to Istanbul to ascertain the situation of the *tekke*s there reported that the majority were close to ruin (*harap durumunda*) (Jäschke, 1972: 36).[27] In September the Cabinet of Ministers prepared a bill to close the *tekke*s and this bill was subsequently debated in the Parliament. On 30 November, passage of law number 677 formally abolished the orders and closed the *tekke*s (whose numbers seemed to have declined to around 250).²⁸ The *tekke*s with mosques attached or that were also used as mosques would continue to be used solely as mosques; those not used as mosques would be used as schools, and those unable to be so used would be sold, with the proceeds going to the education budget. Titles such as *hoca, shaykh, baba* and *dede,* given to leaders of religious communities, were banned, as was wearing turban and robes for all but official (i.e. state) functionaries (e.g. imams and *müftü*s) while conducting their duties.²⁹

It is striking to see in the minutes of the parliamentary debates over proscription of the orders that almost no one came to the defence of the orders and *tekke*s. This was true among the numerous MPs with *medrese* (advanced Islamic) education and even among those with Sufi backgrounds, such as Shaykh Esad Erbilî (former chairman of the Assembly of Shaykhs), Shaykh Safvet (editor of the important Second Constitutional period journal *Tasavvuf* and author of the bill to abolish the Caliphate) and Chelebi Efendi (former *postnişin* [lodge head] of the Konya Mevlevihane) (M. Kara, 2002). The incremental steps leading to the proscription had seemed to the vast majority of prominent people involved to be reasonable, if unfortunate. To many, then and today, proscription of the orders was merely 'locking the doors of the *tekke*s which were in any case already closed'.³⁰ The subtleties of this point may be difficult to appreciate for those unfamiliar with the transitional period from the late Ottoman to Republican environments. Only very recently have scholars interested in something other than Kemalist or Islamist apologetics paid serious attention to this period.³¹

The main point to understand here is the near collapse of the residual prestige of the Sufi orders and Sufism in general, in the wake of the collapse of the Empire. This prestige was already in tatters by the Ottoman second constitutional period, beginning in 1908. Indeed, the vast majority of those who considered themselves to be working and living in contribution to Islamic traditions from within, generally accepted that Sufism was an important part of the rich Islamic heritage but it had for all practical purposes ceased to function and was unlikely ever to again. The issue was brought to a head by the dramatic dimensions of the political, military and economic problems facing Ottoman Muslims, and the broader issue of the scope and function of Islam in Ottoman society in general. At a time when Muslims themselves were interrogating the very nature of Islam and Islamic institutions and practices in an attempt to reinvigorate these practices, many came to consider Sufism a luxury that Ottoman Muslims in the heartland of the Empire could not afford (İ. Kara, 1997). The Empire needed schools to provide training in modern disciplines and Islamic sciences; the Sufi lodges, almost without exception, needed major repairs. Resources were extremely limited. Which do you choose? All of the available evidence suggests that even among Sufis themselves the answer was obvious.³² Abdülaziz Bekkine Efendi (1895-1952), trained in late Ottoman *medrese*s and *tekke*s and shaykh of the order studied here from 1949 to 1952, said in response to a question about the *tekke*s' closure, 'My son, those *tekke*s deserved to be closed. Among them the ones that were maintaining [*muhafaza etmek*] Islam had dramatically diminished. And so Allah closed them' (İ. Kara, 1991: 20). Today one continues to find ambivalence on the part of participants in this order on the issue of the *tekke*s, and it is clear that their ability to re-establish *tekke*s is not a high priority for them.

The Space of Sufism in Contemporary Turkey

Today there are no functioning *tekke*s as such in Turkey, although their traditional functions do not go entirely unfulfilled. The Gümüşhanevi branch under discussion here is well known for its activities among personnel and students at universities. A number of branch members informed me that this orientation continues the scholarly identity of Ahmed Ziyaüddin Gümüşhanevi (d. 1893), the internationally renowned scholar of Islam who developed this branch in the Khalidiyya lineage of the Naqshbandi order. It seems likely that growth of interest in this branch of the order among university professors and students dates to the period of Abdülaziz Bekkine Efendi. According to *mürid*s (initiated members loyal to the shaykh) who participated, in warm weather Aziz Efendi used to hold *sohbet*s after *juma`* (Friday) prayers on a raised platform, shaded under trees behind the Ümmü Gülsüm mosque in Zeyrek, where he was the imam; in colder months the *sohbet*s would take place in his wooden two-storied house behind the mosque (Ersöz, 1992). There were usually many students and academics in attendance (including Nureddin Topçu), especially from Istanbul University, which is relatively close to Zeyrek. Several accounts by participants in these *sohbet*s attest to their power and subtlety, including that of the Egyptian Turkologist and Cairo University professor Ahmad Sa`id Sulayman (d. 1991), who spent some 20 months in Istanbul in the early 1950s: 'I was deeply impressed by the shaykh [Abdülaziz] Efendi's *sohbet*s. In Egypt I am someone who has been a member of the Bayyumi *tarikat* long enough to attain khalifa status, but I must admit that among those groups in the old wooden house I just melted away [*eridim*]' (İ. Kara, 2004: 18).[33] In 1952 Mehmed Zâhid Kotku (d. 1980) took up leadership of the *cemaat*, continuing and increasing its popularity among student circles. Upon Kotku's passing, leadership of the community passed to his son-in-law Esad Coşan. Coşan's appointment was not without controversy since Kotku had himself been trained by the last generation of Ottoman shaykhs and several long-time Kotku *mürid*s found it difficult to place themselves in the hands of someone of Coşan's generation. Coşan was nonetheless well respected for his knowledge of Islam and Sufism as a professor at Ankara University's Theology Faculty, and he began to attract younger generations of disciples.

At the time I conducted my research in the late 1990s, it was clear that the *cemaat* had continued to draw members primarily from among academic circles under Coşan. This was reflected in the claim by most of the people with whom I spoke in Istanbul and Anatolian cities that they had encountered the group during their studies at various universities. Finding suitable accommodation is one of the major concerns of incoming university students in Turkey (as elsewhere) and with liberalization of Turkey's legal and economic structures, in the 1980s there was expansion of the private dormitory sector where private interests run dormitories for profit or as a non-profit activity. The *cemaat*'s *vakıf* ran two non-profit dormitories in Istanbul, one in the heart of the old city and one just beyond the Byzantine walls. Each had around 30 student residents, the one beyond the walls all male, the other with about a 3:1 male to female ratio, men and women on separate floors. Each dorm had about ten residents who were on scholarships that covered the students' room costs. Not all student residents were members of the *cemaat*, however, since membership was not a condition of residence in any formal sense. More important to fitting in at the dorm was residents' general observance of Islam in their daily lives, e.g. discipline in prayers and care in one's social relations and lifestyle.

A typical day for those residing in one of the *cemaat*'s dormitories would begin pre-dawn when the lights were turned on in the sleeping rooms, while the resident 'on duty' that week said in a soft tone, 'Friends, let's do our morning prayers, *inshallah*'. After making their way out of the room, down the hall and past the Atatürk memorial (with flag and bust), residents would head downstairs, then past the laundry room, past a ping-pong table and into the washrooms. These were immaculately clean and well-appointed like the rest of the facilities, with a row of doored lavatories on the right, eight sinks on the left, and facing them, a trough with eight spigots at waist height for ablutions.

Canonical worship was then performed upstairs in the room for socializing, where low divans rimmed the room. The senior student on duty who usually acted as imam would swing around on his haunches to face the congregation, and lead a brief *khafî* (silent) *dhikr* (remembrance of God) and *du`a* (supplication). He then would ask, 'Who will start?'. Then began the recitation of *Evrad-ı Şerif* (sing. Arabic *wird*), which a quorum of at least around ten tries to do every morning after *fajr* (dawn) prayers. The recitation takes about 40 minutes and is entirely in Arabic, with the 'Abi' or elder brother (relatively more knowledgeable, senior resident disciple) on duty, asking different people to take turns. Those who presented themselves more prominently, with a visible desire to recite, do so without the text of the prayers before them. However some took recourse to a neighbour's copy to refresh their memory if they strayed or couldn't remember and someone else did not correct them out loud first. This daily recitation of *Evrad* was also an occasion for members to memorize these prayers, the accomplishment of which is understood to be a sign of a *mürid*'s spiritual progress. He is thus able to perform the recitations himself and for others, and can teach it to others.

The recitation was closed by another short *khafi dhikr* of 33 '*Subhanallah*', 33 '*Alhamdulullah*', and 33 '*Allahu akbar*', to which 33 '*Istaghfurullah wa alaytu l-alayh*' are often added.

A member of the Gümüşhanevi branch in Sivas said of his time in a *vakıf*-run apartment:

> At first, there isn't really a 'Sufi' atmosphere. After all, you can't really explain Sufism directly anyway. And since it's something based on request, they didn't really direct us to Sufism at first. It was more just about Islam. The first steps are not about Sufism.

Indeed, this attitude on the part of the *cemaat* regarding its own Islamic identity and how it relates to others who are observant (but not initiated members of the order) indicates well the Naqshbandi mode of Sufism. Those with whom I worked in conducting my research emphasized continually that their practices were nothing more and nothing less than Islam itself. A typical comment to me explained:

> This is true Islam. Being able to live as our Prophet lived, this is Sufism. Now, obviously it isn't possible to really live like him. But we can try – try to do like him, try to do like the Companions (*sahaba*). It's about not retreating into one's own shell, but being together with people, talking with them. You know, Ibrahim Abi, 'enjoin the lawful and prevent the forbidden'.

Coşan continued and intensified the *cemaat*'s engagement with daily life and with the modern technologies that Kotku had encouraged through his *sohbet*s and publications. In his publications, Kotku exhorted Muslims to seek the best possible education for themselves and their children (boys and girls), including knowledge of Islam as well as of 'secular' disciplines such as economics, laboratory sciences, management and medicine. These emphases can be seen in the *cemaat*'s publishing and media projects, most prominently the monthly magazines *Islam* from 1983 and *Kadın ve Aile* (Woman and the Family) from 1985, in addition to publications by the Seha publishing house.[34] From 1994, the emphases could also be heard on the *cemaat*'s radio station and for a brief interim on a television station that was short-lived in the late 1990s.

On Friday evenings, residents of the dormitories and *vakıf* apartments would gather and listen to Esad Hoca's *sohbet*s broadcast by satellite from Australia. The text of his *sohbet*s was published in *Islam* from 1990, and the radio *sohbet*s reinforced what many commentators have called a transition from a face-to-face sociality based on presence to a mediated sociality. The influence of this mediation on Naqshbandi practice concerns the centrality of *sohbet* to the devotions as we have considered above, and it has been a major part of the structural transformation of this Sufi order as a *tarikat*, *vakıf* and *cemaat*.

New Forms of Tasavvuf through *Vakıf* and *Cemaat*

During my time with the Gümüşhanevi branch of the Naqshbandi order, I observed a number of developments that underscore the importance of *vakıf* and *cemaat* in contemporary Sufi life in Turkey. One that was particularly striking concerned this branch's response to the crisis in Kosovo that involved upheaval and tragedy for fellow Muslims not far from Turkey. The response provided a palpable demonstration of Sufi life directly through the *vakıf*. In June 1999, comings and goings at the office of the *vakıf* informally associated with this Gümüşhanevi branch (located in the old *külliye* facilities facing the mosque where *sohbet*s are held) came to increasingly involve people with dossiers and forms and a distinctly urgent tone to their affairs. Dreadful events had been unfolding in Kosovo for months, but now a slaughter by Serb security forces and irregulars was well under way. In Istanbul, almost everyone who is not a migrant from Anatolia knows someone who has relatives from the Balkans (from where the narrative of migration to Turkey is inevitably one of escaping from persecution). People in Istanbul were painfully aware of the news then coming from the Balkans.[35]

The *vakıf*'s dealings with government bureaus, especially the Directorate of Foundations, were again uneasy after a period of eased tensions under the *Refah*–True Path coalition until 1997. But what was now going on at the *vakıf* office was a response to the tragedy unfolding a few hundred miles away in Kosovo, about which we had come to hear more and more direct and indirect reference in Friday sermons. Donations – mainly of tents, clothes, blankets, boots and bottled water – and logistical arrangements were being coordinated through *vakıf* across the country. These donations were organized into convoys with the Turkish Red Crescent Society that had permission from Bulgarian authorities to transit the shipments through. Because these were Red Crescent convoys, to be received by Red Crescent and Red Cross officials upon arrival, there was no question of anything other than humanitarian aid being sent through these channels.[36]

During this time, one would encounter a few Kosovar refugees at the *vakıf* office and some of them spoke Turkish. The eyes of these young men bore the distinct, unmistakable look of gratitude for every moment of being alive. These men were quiet, polite and entirely overwhelmed by uncertainty, having placed themselves utterly in the hands of people who they wanted to trust. Their presence at the *vakıf* office is significant, as is the fact that it was the *vakıf* that coordinated the collection and transport of donations. The significance of an activity 'as Sufism' does not derive from the topics of conversation or the specific actions performed, but rather from their link to broader traditions of Islamic discursive practice. In this case, the Kosovar visitors who the *vakıf* assisted were not Naqshbandis, but the response of those in the *vakıf*, taking Muslims from danger and caring for their welfare is seen as action that one should take as a Muslim.

The Turkish government Directorate of Foundations had issued directives banning private initiative in organizing transport to Kosovo. A number of reasons were given, foremost among them that by coordinating the efforts, the Red Crescent would know what had already been collected and what was still needed. Periodic announcements were made to this effect in the media. There was, however, speculation about other reasons why the Red Crescent wanted to monopolize the transport and logistics of this aid. Those at our local *vakıf* office grumbled that this was typical behaviour – that the state and Red Crescent wanted to keep people who 'think differently' as distant from the process as possible, while taking credit for the effort. As for the state itself, and others less sympathetic to perceived Islamist initiatives, the main explanation was that lack of coordination and rationalization of procedure signifies incompetence on the part of governmental authorities anywhere, and tends to lead to inefficiency and ineffectiveness. In such a grave crisis as was then at hand, they claimed, it would be an outrageous scandal to allow such incompetence.

Another concern I heard voiced by politicians was that without centralized coordination it would be difficult to know who was doing what. They claimed that this would lead not only to the problem of some needs being oversupplied and others unmet, but also to diplomatic problems with countries receiving the aid, and/or those through which the aid would transit. Sometimes the initiatives of private individuals are taken to have official Turkish government approval, while reports go out in international media to the effect that 'the Turks' are supporting this or that controversial group, a scenario that seems to have played out in the early days of the deteriorating situation in Kosovo.

That the government was ready so quickly with this response also points up the central function of *vakıf* institutions in Turkey today as a form of incorporation. Particularly among groups such as a Sufi order, which cannot exist legally as such, incorporation as a foundation enables them to have some institutional form of existence in Turkish society. Government policy toward foundations is therefore extremely important to the tone of civil associational life in Turkey, as it was in Ottoman days.[37]

The chairman of the foundation informally affiliated with the Gümüşhanevi branch graduated from university in 1993 with a degree in administration, making him barely 30 years of age in 1999 when the Kosovo developments I describe above unfolded. Speaking of Sufism in Turkey, the young director said to me, 'You know, most of Sufi life (*tasavvuf hayatı*) in Turkey these days is *vakıf* activities. But most of the *vakıf*s get politicized, break up and disappear, as I'm sure you've noticed'. He was referring to the precarious nature of functioning as a foundation, i.e. a body recognized by the government, especially for religious activists. This *vakıf*, he observed, is trying to 'not be political', but rather to carry out '*hizmet*' (Arabic *khidhma*, service to the community). Some commentators have described this as emblematic of a '*vakıf*-ication' of the Sufi orders in Turkey.[38]

Along with *vakıf* activities, the main mode of sociality of Sufis in Turkey is as a community, a *cemaat*. No formal, public functions take place in Turkey as Sufi events, since these are, by definition, illegal. Nonetheless, Sufis come together, lessons are taught, ethical disciplines are inculcated, and even larger events are held. What matters is the status of the event. Here a judicious equivocation is the norm. For example, a public lecture or symposium on a particular Sufi luminary may be organized, with many of the organizers belonging to a particular Sufi order. The aim of the conference is for those attending to broaden their appreciation and knowledge of the figure and his contribution to Islamic traditions. Is this a 'Sufi' event?

Alongside the noted '*vakıf*-ication' of the Sufi orders in Turkey, some commentators (and even practitioners) believe that one also ought to speak of a '*cemaat*-ification' of the orders, in the sense that the dynamics of their social life correspond to those informally characteristic of *cemaat*s in general. This relates to one aspect of Sufism in Turkey that may be specific to the Turkish context, namely that the proscription of the orders – and their status and social standing on the eve of that proscription – have impacted on organizational dimensions in subtle as well as more obvious ways. In particular, the notion of stages and ranks (*makam, derece*) along the path to spiritual maturity certainly appears to operate, but it is much less a topic of discussion and daily concern than it was likely to have been in the past. Another way to put this is to say that the orders in Turkey have moved in the direction of 'association' and somewhat away from 'organization' on the continuum outlined by Gilsenan (1973). It is difficult for them to show outward signs of organizational function and status in the prohibitive environment that is contemporary Turkey.

Another aspect of changes in Sufi culture over the last 80 years is arguably equally important, even if under-appreciated. It is that much of the criticism of Sufism and Sufi orders, from the later Ottoman period to the present, has centred on 'superstitions' and 'charlatans', and especially on those who were felt to manipulate the ignorant for personal gain. In the late Ottoman context of collapse of an entire political, economic and social order, radical interrogation of the underpinnings of that order were to be expected, and indeed proliferated.[39] In this context, the severest condemnation of superstition and obscurantism was a major feature of the discourse of reform. This reform discourse was considered to be the only hope for the *umma* – the moral and political community of Muslims – (particularly since in the later Ottoman environment this term came to be identified with the 'nation') to defend itself against (infidel) aggression, such as had just brought on the collapse of the empire.[40]

The notion that alongside knowledge of the canonical sources and practice of canonical worship there are yet 'other sources' of Islamic authority continues to be controversial among observant Muslims, in Turkey and elsewhere. The effects of decades of discrediting and casting doubt on Sufism have been considerable in Turkey, and many Sufis whom I worked with in the Gümüşhanevi branch of the Naqshbandi order were very concerned that there be no straying from the path of *sunna*, the exemplary precedents of the Prophet. These Sufis remained in that particular branch because they had not detected any such straying.

One point of practice that occasioned some controversy was *rabıta*, the link or 'bond' between the shaykh and disciple. The mechanics of this technique of spiritual realization have been outlined elsewhere (Meier, 1994, Abu-Manneh, 1990). Problematic for some who encountered the *cemaat* and subsequently disassociated themselves from it was the practice of concentrating one's attention and affection so enthusiastically on the shaykh that it became confounded with one's devotions, which should naturally be reserved for God alone. Those with whom I worked took care to emphasize that the various techniques of *rabıta*, which they all practiced, were less 'formal' and less structured than worship, and needed to be done very 'carefully'. One *cemaat* member in Sivas, originally from Siirt in the Kurdish southeast, told me that *rabıta* was nearly cause for his departure from the *cemaat*; it was only upon careful reflection and consultation over the course of his theology studies at the university that he found *rabıta* 'acceptable' and continued to participate in the *cemaat*. The environment of generalized hostility toward the orders in Republican Turkey, and especially a heightened contempt for 'charlatanism' among the more observant and pious may have led to the diminished profile of *rabıta* in favour of *sohbet*. If so, it is not the first time the practice has been secondary to *sohbet*. In both Sirhindi's *Maktubat* and Kashifi's *Rashahat* (*`Ayn al-Hayat*), the emphasis is on *sohbet* over *rabıta* (Abu-Manneh, 1990: 286).

The History of the Present

Sufi orders remain illegal today. Nevertheless, prosecution of the relevant laws has varied over the decades, with a general relaxation noted just before the 1950 general elections (the first truly competitive ones), in which the Democrat Party (DP) emerged victorious over the Republican People's Party (CHP) (Sitembölükbaşı, 1995). By the late 1960s, a relatively small but increasingly active group of outwardly pious and politically oriented people emerged within what was generally called the political Right.

Mehmet Zahid Kotku encouraged his *mürid*s as loyal initiated members to be active in worldly affairs, specifically in capacities that would enable Turkey and the Muslim world to stand up to the cultural, political and economic domination by the 'West'. Echoing ideas expressed since the late Ottoman period, Kotku considered Western domination to be based on the West's clever development and use of technology, albeit in a way that is out of balance with ethical considerations concerning family life, the environment and so forth. Kotku made it clear that not only was there no problem with Muslims industrializing their societies based on the latest technology, it was positively incumbent upon them to do this (Gürdoğan, 1991). This was the context in which the continually growing numbers of attendees at Mehmed Zahid Efendi's sohbets during the 1960s began to take their places in increasingly influential institutions such as the State Planning Organization (SPO) (*Devlet Planlama Teşkilatı*), created in the wake of the 1960 coup to coordinate industrialization through investment and allocation of subsidized inputs and foreign exchange. The SPO quickly became an extremely powerful mechanism for political bargaining over scarce resources (Keyder, 1987: 148).

The idea of freeing Turkey from the logic of the Western market also led to Kotku's suggestion to establish the Gümüş Motor Company (the name invoking the memory of the nineteenth century Naqshbandi scholar Ziyaüddin Gümüşhanevi), with Necmettin Erbakan, who was later to become prime minister, as its director. However, the company did not last long. Having lost the investment in the motor company, many in the *cemaat* concluded that there was a direct connection between being able to create an alternative market and moral economy, and the political-economic environment in which transactions take place. In other words, they would need to participate in institutionalized politics.

The two political parties that attracted those who felt this need were the *Milli Selamet Partisi* (MSP, the National Salvation Party) and later the *Refah Partisi* (RP, the Welfare Party). It is significant that almost all of the major figures in the MSP–RP incubus came out of the Iskender Pasha community, which was once famous as a centre for the Naqshbandi order. Pre-eminent among these political figures are Necmettin Erbakan (prime minister 1996-97) and current Prime Minister Recep Tayyip Erdoğan (from 2003), who participated in Mehmed Hoca's *sohbet*s in the 1970s. As Yavuz wrote in his recent study:

> (T)he Naqshbandi Sufi order served as the matrix for the emergence in the 1970s of the four leading contemporary Turkish Islamic political and social movements: the neo-Nakşibendi (sic) Sufi order of *Süleymancı* and other orders [including the Iskender Pasha group discussed in the present article]; the new Islamist intellectuals; the Nurcu movement of Bediüzzaman Said Nursî, with its offshoot led by the charismatic Fethullah Gülen; and the *Milli Gençlik Hareketi* of Necmettin Erbakan. (Yavuz, 2003: 11)

After the closure of the short-lived National Order Party (Milli Nizam Partisi or MNP) in 1971, some of its personnel formed the MSP in 1972, with Necmeddin Erbakan as its chairman. The new party fared well in the 1973 elections and entered the ruling coalition. However during the mid- to late-1970s, the political landscape in Turkey was utterly radicalized into 'Right' and 'Left', with youth groups and gangs sympathetic to, or directly organized by, each side viciously and murderously attacking and counter-attacking each other publicly. A number of those on the Right who considered themselves to be politically conservative (*muhafazakâr*) emphasized the political language of Islam and Islam as the bastion of true Turkish culture and values.

A coup in 1980 brought an immediate end to the street-level violence. Nonetheless, the military administration and the then elected government under general-cum-president Kenan Evren began to emphasize what came to be called the 'Turkish–Islamic synthesis' (*Türk–İslam sentezi*) as a formulation for national identity. This was an attempt to preserve nationalist sentiments while drawing on the heritage of Islam as culture and general ethic, a move that appeared to be the height of irony to many secular, liberal Turks. The aim was to remove any remaining wind from the sails of the Left and to appropriate the discourse of Islam for the mainstream, while re-exerting state control over Islamic institutions. These efforts were largely successful by all accounts.

In this context, both participation and scholarly interest in Sufism have risen (Kafadar, 1992), even though the statutes banning orders have not been changed since the early years of the Republic. Books are published on the orders in general and on this or that particular order. Many publications are quite hostile to the orders, to be sure, but many are not. Magazines publish dossiers; scholarly journals publish articles. The continuing existence of the orders is, in short, an open secret; just how open depends almost literally on the month, if not the week.

Welfare (*Refah*) Party candidates won many of the country's major municipal elections in 1994 (including Istanbul and Ankara). In the national elections of 1995, *Refah* emerged as the leading party, with the most seats in the national assembly and a major role in the ruling coalition, including the Prime Ministry. It is difficult to exaggerate the suddenness with which Islam seemed to become the main issue in politics and culture,[41] and the key issue for social science research in Turkey, only to be dropped unceremoniously a year or two later. Questions about the continued existence of Sufi orders and Sufi practices were revived and attempts were made to make sense of the rise of *Refah* in terms of these orders. Even within the orders themselves, members engaged in discussions about whether or not the orders should clarify their political views among themselves.

Within the Iskender Pasha community, discussions began in the early 1990s about whether leader Esad Hoca should become involved in party politics, either in an established party or as founder of a new one. He did not in the end enter party politics and the *cemaat*'s relationship to *Refah* during the years of *Refah*'s rise and time in power was often strained. It appears that several points of disagreement centred on what could be called a struggle for authority and prestige. As a key player in the MSP–RP formation, Necmeddin Erbakan was reported to have made critical remarks suggesting that he himself had and should have more authority among Muslims than Esad Hoca. The disagreement spilled into the open by 1990, when Esad Hoca, under his well-known pseudonym Halil Necatioğlu, published an article in *Islam* entitled, 'The Indisputable Value and Superiority of the Islamic Scholar (*Alim*)' (Necatioğlu, 1990). The article was directed specifically at Erbakan and the *Refah* cadres, as the implicit ending of the tide was 'over the politician'. However it needs to be noted here that members of the order were not monolithic in their politics so that the order could not speak with one political voice. A significant number of members of the order supported the Motherland Party (*Anavatan Partisi*, ANAP), which is the party of former President Turgut Özal (1989-93). Özal had only thinly veiled his sympathy for Naqshbandi Sufism, and his mother is buried in the Süleymaniye cemetery near Mehmed Zahid Kotku and Ahmed Ziyaüddin Gümüşhanevî (Çakır, 1990: 17-76).

In February 1997, the military officers on the National Security Council essentially presented an ultimatum of measures that the *Refah*–True Path coalition government would have to undertake to reverse what the Council saw as explicit 'Islamicizing tendencies' in the bureaucracy and even in the armed forces. The coalition unravelled by the middle of June. The event is remembered as '*28 Şubat*' (28 February), which came to be used as a euphemism among many conservative Muslims for the beginning of a 'crackdown' led by the military against 'political Islam'. Commentators generally agree that the ultimatum represented a statement by the generals of the measures necessary to prevent them from carrying out a *coup d'etat*.[42] Following *28 Şubat*, the military continuously made it known in meetings with politicians and in published statements that it considered one of the gravest threats to the country's security to be 'those who wish to exploit religion for political purposes'. The armed forces directed considerable energy toward combating such people. Elected officials, such as the extremely popular mayor of Istanbul (now Prime Minister) Tayyip Erdoğan, were tried and spent time in jail. Journalists and writers were harassed and arrested. And most importantly for this discussion, associational life for the outwardly pious was more restrictive. An incipient trend to stage conferences and symposia on Islamic and/or Ottoman topics (often with the participation of municipalities) waned.

In 1994, Erdoğan was elected mayor of Istanbul, proving to be extremely popular and effective. He was clearly a rising star in the *Refah* Party. In 2001, after months of thinly veiled tensions within the now *Fazilet* Party over the inability of members critical of Erbakan to rise in seniority, several *Fazilet* members including Erdoğan and the charismatic Abdullah Gül founded the Justice and Development (*Adalet ve Kalkınma*, AK) Party, largely comprised of intellectuals and technocrats. Again, several of the founding members of the

AK Party had experience with the Iskender Pasha community, and the exceptionally high training and competence of the cadres, their own adherence to Islamic norms in their personal lives, and their attempt to fashion a politically liberal Muslim society can be seen as a legacy of their Iskender Pasha experience.

The elections of 2002, 2007 and 2011 gave the AK Party overwhelming majorities in the assembly and enabled it to form single-party governments. With respect to foundations and the incorporation of civil groups as associations, the AK Party favoured liberalizing regulation, which was conveniently in line with the views of its center-right supporters and with EU entry protocols. This and similar convergences between this liberalization (sometimes given the shorthand 'neoliberal reform') and the discourse of the moderate religious right (as it is known in Turkey) made the Kemalist establishment – not to mention the military – nervous. While initially appearing committed to an overall program of liberalization, in more recent years the controversial Ergenekon and KCK cases, as well as other pressure on critics of the AK Party in the media and various institutions have led to questions emerging about the AK Party's commitment to freedom and equality before the law.

Conclusions: Islamic disciplines and modern forms of power

The experiences of Sufis in the Republic of Turkey have been deeply conditioned by the legacies left to the Republic by the late Ottoman Empke (Silverstein, 2003). Proscription of the orders was one of a series of events begun a century earlier (which is not to say that this proscription was somehow inevitable). Thus the characteristically modern modes of power that Foucault (1991) identified as governmentality – redoubled rationalizing of administration and normalizing the objects of governance – and the particular kinds of knowledge and subjectivities associated with them, had profoundly rearticulated the nature of discourse and practice among Sufis by the last third of the nineteenth century. This was well before there was any question of a Republic (Silverstein, 2009).

The study of Sufi practice and discourse in Turkey – like the study of Islamic institutions in Turkey more generally – illustrates how characteristically modern social forms and techniques are now among the conditions of possibility for a great many movements that are concerned to extend Islamic traditions of practice and piety. Perhaps the most important instance of this is in the ways that such movements depend for their coherence and compelling-ness on their ability to refer to micro-levels of bodily comportment and practice. These were never publicly discussed as such before they were rendered 'visible' and 'calculable' by two primary sources. One is the modern state-sponsored development programs in which domestic family life has been 'variously defined, manipulated, and generally subjected to the regulation of health, educational and welfare programs' (Ong, 1995: 161). The other is such quintessentially modern cultural productions as the (psychological) novel and film.

These have been major features of Turkish state governance with a profound impact on the minutiae of daily life in Turkey (Navaro-Yashin, 2002). Hence, instances of renewed and intensified interest in such virtues as modesty and bashfulness in women, or the visceral qualities of experience in ethically disciplined bodies, are all linked inextricably and intimately to the techniques of micro-level visibility, calculability and objectification. These are central to the exercise of what Foucault called bio-power, 'what brought life and its mechanisms into the realm of explicit calculations and made knowledge-power an agent of transformation of human life' (1980: 143). Observant Muslim selves in Turkey are traversed and organized by these modern regimes of knowledge and power.

Some of the effects on Sufi practice of the liberalization of associative life in Turkey in line with EU norms are arguably discernable. The issue of Sufism and the political in Turkey is less defined by the influence of the orders on party politics than by the relationship between ethical solidarity of the type cultivated by Sufi orders and the place of moral discourse in liberal political culture, which, whatever the shortcomings of Turkish implementation according to its norms, *has* been taken as the norm of Turkish politics. The privatization of Islam into a religion is essentially a *fait accompli* in Turkey. It results superficially from the Republican reforms but more substantially from centuries of Ottoman institutional reform and incremental shifts in the authority and prestige of Islamic regimes of knowledge and power vis-à-vis other ones (Silverstein, 2003).

The AK Party initially included and addressed itself to a wide spectrum of people of the sort who had brought other center-right, not specifically Islamist parties to power in past elections, in addition to many others who supported an easing of state regulation of economic and social arenas. The AKP also took a pro-EU entry stance, in contrast to previous Islamist parties. While many of the reforms the party has undertaken were initiated by previous governments, their single-party administration has made it more efficient in passing legislation and passing reforms. For anyone who spent time with the Iskender Pasha community in the years before the formation of the AK Party, the fact that it continued Turkey's post-1980s liberalization came as little surprise, nor did the fact that many of the party cadres can be seen as Muslims attempting to live in continuity with their history while rejecting neither their religious heritage nor a great deal of the inheritance of the Republic.

Acknowledgement

I am grateful to Hamid Algar, Martin van Bruinessen and Julia Howell for comments on versions of this chapter, as well to Michael Meeker and colleagues at the İslâm Araştırmaları Merkezi in Istanbul, Recep Şentürk and Semih Ceyhan especially, for their helpful suggestions along the way. Ersin Nazif Gürdoğan, Mahmud Erol Kılıç and İsmail Kara were generous with their time and knowledge on several occasions. My invitation to participate in the seminar in Bogor, Indonesia was a welcome opportunity to present my work to a critical and knowledgeable audience, and it is a pleasure to thank the conveners and participants. My continuing thanks to the members of the *cemaat* who received me with such warmth and generosity. Several audience members at the American University of Beirut also provided thoughtful comments on some of the material here; thanks to Karla Mallette, Brian Catlos and Mia Fuller for the invitation. I conducted the research on which this chapter is based with funding from a Fulbright Grant and with Dissertation Write-Up and Postdoctoral Research Grants from the Institute of Turkish Studies, Washington DC. I gratefully acknowledge this financial support. Naturally, I alone am responsible for the views presented here.

4

ELEMENTS OF NEO-TRADITIONAL SUFISM IN IRAN

Matthijs van den Bos

Iran and Persian culture have been the cradle of great Sufi orders, both Sunni and Shi`i. Of the Sunni orders, the Qadiriyya and Naqshbandiyya have been the most important in Iran. These orders are mainly associated with the Sunni parts of Kurdistan (the present provinces of West Azerbaijan and Kurdistan) and fall outside the scope of this chapter. Among the Shi`i orders, the Dhahabiyya and three subdivisions of the Ni`matullahiyya – the Safi`alishahi, Sultan`alishahi (also known as Gunabadi), and Dhu'l-Riyasatayn (or Munawwar`alishahi) orders – predominate. Much less is known about the contemporary existence of a third major Shi`i order, the Khaksar; comprehensive research is lacking.[1] Occasionally one comes across references to other, smaller Shi`i orders such as the Kawthar`alishahi branch of the Ni`matullahiyya and the Maktab Tariqat Uwaysi Shahmaqsudi.

Ni`matullahi and Dhahabi houses of worship are to be found in all major cities of Iran, and beyond. The Dhahabiyya used to be concentrated in Shiraz, but their supreme master now resides in Southampton, Great Britain. There are also Dhahabi centres in North America. The Dhu'l-Riyasatayn branch of the Ni`matullahi order is similarly organized transnationally. The supreme master resides in Britain, but the order is particularly widespread in North America. Safi`alishahi Sufis, on the other hand, are strongly Tehran-centred. By far the most important Ni`matullahi branch is that of the Sultan`alishahis, which has for many decades eclipsed the other two branches in numbers of adherents (cf. Lewisohn, 1999: 48) and in social impact. The order is based in Tehran and Khurasan and also has a global network of devotees. This chapter focuses mainly on the Safi`alishahi and Sultan`alishahi orders, which have retained Iran as their geographical and spiritual home. Occasionally discussion will refer to the other orders.

The development of institutional Sufism in Iran since the Islamic Revolution of 1978-79 remained until recently largely unknown to the outside world. Even the Sufi orders' existence under the second Pahlavi Shah (1941-79) was, on the whole, *terra incognita* until the appearance of the first volume of Richard Gramlich's groundbreaking study in the 1960s (Gramlich, 1965). Only from the early 1990s have several authors begun to fill the gap (e.g., Lewisohn, 1998, 1999; van den Bos, 2002a, 2002b; Nasr, 1991; Algar, 1993). These accounts generally point to the decline in number and importance of Sufi orders since 1979. I have frequently encountered the same assessment of their circumstances among Sufis in Iran. Nevertheless, Sufism has lived on in revolutionary and post-revolutionary Iran.

In this chapter I briefly sketch the major known developments in Iranian Shi`i Sufism in the twentieth century and their linkages to socio-political and religious regimes. I compare these developments to social facts of Shi`i Sufism in contemporary Iran up to the end of Mohammad Khatami's presidency in August 2005, drawing upon earlier publications of my field research in Iran between 1996 and 2002. I argue that the quietism characteristic of the orders in Iran in this era under reformist Khatami does not represent a retreat into socially disengaged Sufi traditionalism, but a rather more complex and self-conscious engagement with the modern context of the nation-state.[2]

Trajectories of Sufi Modernity in the Iranian Nation-state

Sufism in Iran is often thought to have shrunk into insignificance with the collapse of the Qajar polity (1785-1925).[3] However, the biographies of several modern mystics suggest otherwise. These accounts point to a new, activist Sufism in the twentieth century, with numerical strength and social importance in the emerging nation-state (e.g., van den Bos, 2002a).

The Constitutional Revolution (1905-11) had a protagonist in the master of the Dhu'l-Riyasatayn-Ni`matullahi order, Hajj `Ali Dhu'l-Riyasatayn (also known by his dervish name of Wafa`alishah, d. 1918). In the words of his biographer, the present Dhu'l-Riyasatayn master Javad Nurbakhsh, Wafa`alishah was 'the first man among the clergy of the province of Fars to self-sacrificingly devote himself to [...] the Constitution' (Nurbakhsh, 1980: 114). He and his followers are reported to have dressed in military garb (Chardahi, 1973: 530). The lodge of his successor, Sadiq`alishah, was, according to the same source, 'a sanctuary for the politically oppressed'. During the Constitutional Period his house 'served as a hide-out for distinguished opposition figures' (Nurbakhsh, 1980: 115). Political involvement by Sufis was not restricted to the Dhu'l-Riyasatayn order. In the chaotic aftermath of the Constitutional Revolution, the master of the Sultan`alishahi order, Nur`alishah II (d. 1918), is alleged to have spread all over Persia a pamphlet, in which he pledged to remove discord from the nation, on condition that the nation accept him as its (spiritual) head (Miller, 1923: 353-4).

In the Reza Khan (later Reza Shah) era (1921-41), the engagement of Sufis with the shaping of the modern nation-state became even more pronounced. Hajji Dadash (d. 1948), a master of the Safi`alishahi order, published the journal *Majalla-yi ukhuwwat*, which was decisively this-worldly and discussed such issues as women's rights and the economy, often treating patriotic themes. The more powerful leader from 1924, Binish`alishah (d. 1932), served as Minister of the Interior in one of Reza Shah's nationalist and modernizing cabinets (Azimi, 1998: 461). He headed the Consultative Committee (*hay'at-i mushawara*) in the order's Brotherhood Society (*Anjuman-i ukhuwwat*) as first among equals, departing from the practice of his predecessors who were traditional autocratic masters.

The *Anjuman* had been founded by the charismatic Zahir al-Dawla (d. 1924), who had assumed leadership of the Safi`alishahi order soon after the founder's death in 1899. It was a formal association, with registration cards, formalized procedures for the admission and expulsion of 'members' and a central administration of membership. Its Consultative Committee was an administrative body that assumed authority over the authority of the Safi`alishahi order's 'elected' shaykhs. These instances of bureaucratization and centralization in the Brotherhood Society mark the high tide of Sufi modernity in Iran, and both phenomena resemble developments within the state realm. Unlike the Turkish cases that Brian Silverstein has examined in this volume (Chapter 3), however, where bureaucratization and centralization of the orders commenced from the early nineteenth century under pressure from the state, these processes were not directly state-imposed in the Iranian case of the Safi`alishahi *Anjuman*.

At the leadership level, the Safi`alishahi order lost its reformist zeal under the second Pahlavi ruler (1941-79). Leaders such as Farajullah Aqawli (d. 1974) distinguished themselves not by reform-mindedness but by their devotion to the Shah. But all the same, the nation-state remained an important frame of reference in late twentieth-century Sufism. This orientation became apparent in, among other things, royal patronage and intimate regime relations. `Abdullah Intizam (d. 1983), the last Safi`alishahi leader, was a personal friend of the Shah. The Shah's brother, `Ali-Riza, extended royal patronage to Sufis and was initiated into the Safi`alishahi order, and the Shah and the Empress Farah had Sufis in their entourage as religious teachers and advisors (Chahardahi, 1982: 60; Gramlich, 1965: 50). Subordinate Sufis in the order resisted these connections in a 'war of words' that was waged in pamphlets and national magazines.[4]

As for the Sultan`alishahi order, its grand master Hajj Sultanhusayn Tabanda (Riza`alishah, d. 1992) had maintained relations with people in high places for decades. But on the occasion of an international human rights conference in Tehran in 1968, he wrote a pamphlet that on the one hand lashed out against the secular Universal Declaration of Human Rights and on the other contained sharp religious and political criticism of the government (Tabanda, 1975). This tract implicitly targeted the royal regime itself.

Another object of criticism exercised by Sufis in this period concerned the various forms of mystical syncretism that became increasingly prominent in the late Pahlavi era.[5] One such trend was the so-called 'New Sufism' launched in 1942 by the scholar and author Husayn Kazimzada Iranshahr on the basis of his notion of an 'esoteric mysticism', `irfan-i batini* (Ghaffari, 1964: 247; Chahardahi, 1982: 377). This was to accomplish a union of science, technology and religion (Ghahari, 2001: 67-8). In the circle around Seyyed Hossein Nasr, in post-war Iran, Sufism blended with perennialist philosophy, while the Uwaysi Sufis Muhammad and Sadiq `Anqa (d. 1980) sought to marry Sufism and the natural sciences (Baldick, 1993: 28; Chahardahi, 1982: 436-7). In 1963, the Kawthar`alishahi-Ni`matullahi master Mas`ud Humayoni established, under the name of *Anjuman-i Adyar*, an Iranian branch of the international Theosophical Society in Tehran (Homayouni, 1991: 231).

Under the Islamic Republic from 1979, Ni`matullahi Sufis sought to accommodate with the new regime. In the Sultan`alishahi order, this accommodation involved public expressions of sorrow for deceased revolutionary clerics, such as the ayatullahs Taliqani and Mutahhari, and of sympathy with their struggles against the (Pahlavi) 'regime of oppressors'. The order also gave financial support to victims of the war with Iraq. The supreme master's medical trips abroad were scrupulously announced in national newspapers to pre-empt any misinterpretation that might construe his departure abroad as a flight from Iran. The announcements documented the master asking for Khomeini's permission and wishing for the success of the 'brothers in faith' in the 'continuance of the movement on the way of the true Islamic revolution' (Humayuni, 1992: 222).

These expressions of religious nationalism on the part of the master indicated that the Sultan`alishahi order continued to position itself in the framework of the modern nation state. Riza`alishah made the national wartime agony into a patriotic topic for a New Year's address in March 1989, in which he emphatically pleaded with God to remove the terrible plight from his country. Years earlier, in May 1982, he had stated in public with regard to the Iran–Iraq war that 'the *fuqara* (the 'poor', i.e. devotees) of the order are proud that several from their ranks have become martyrs' (van den Bos, 2002b: 158-9).

A public and apparently indisputable record of good relations between the Sultan`alishahis and Imam Khomeini was beneficial to accommodation as well.[6] This came to the fore in 1979, for instance, when Riza`alishah met with the Imam and the latter explained to him the aims of the revolution (Mahbub`alishah, 1994: 81). One Sultan`alishahi Sufi emphasizes a shared spiritual ancestry, observing that both Khomeini and a Sultan`alishahi shaykh named `Izzat`ali were disciples of ayatullah Mirza Muhammad `Ali Shah-

Abadi (d. 1950). By means of this master–disciple (*murshid–murid*) relation, he traces one of Khomeini's intellectual pedigrees back to the Kubrawiyya order. The chain in question runs through Khomeini's 'perfect mystic' (`arif-i kamil*), i.e., Shah-Abadi, and the latter's own teacher, Aqa Sayyid Muhammad Bid-Abadi, who commanded an authorization (*ijaza*) of both the Nurbakhshiyya and the Dhahabiyya branches of the Kubrawiyya *tariqa*.[7]

At the same time, Sufism also was perceived as a form of religiosity uncorrupted by affiliation with the regime. Affiliates of the orders often read into their masters' words esoteric subtexts that subverted exoteric facades. For instance, some Sufis claimed that Riza`alishah's treatise on human rights, mentioned above, was only a juristic statement that disguised the master's true Sufi essence. But while the orders were to some extent counter-hegemonic on the symbolic level, they and their leaders did not represent dynamic forces in the emergence, development and growth of Iran's civil society that began around 1995.

In the Islamic Republic

In spite of the above-mentioned efforts to show that Sufism and the spirit of the Revolution were compatible, Sufism's reputation had to some extent been tarnished as anti-revolutionary by the time of the revolution (cf. Fischer, 1980: 143). Members of the *ancien régime*'s elite were associated with or had prided themselves on their Sufism, and mystical Shi`ism was played off against revolutionary Islam (e.g., Nasr, 1979: 11). If only for these reasons, Sufi masters and their disciples have often kept a low profile since the revolution.

One noticeable device employed to avoid undue attention was the labelling of mystical spirituality. In the Sultan`alishahi order, which is in all outward respects a Sufi order, with lodges (*husayniyya*s), a spiritual genealogy (*silsila*) and an ethos of veneration towards the supreme master or 'Pole' (*qutb*), the master denied that one entered the realm of 'Sufism' (*tasawwuf*) through him. Instead, he argued that he and his disciples engaged in `irfan*, the learned variety of mysticism or gnosis. This is a largely respectable phenomenon within Iranian Shi`ism, in which Imam Khomeini and several others among the revolutionary clergy were also known to have been trained. This identification with `irfan* strongly dissociated the Sultan`alishahis from the popular Sufism of wandering dervishes (*darwishi wa qalandari*), of which the Khaksar dervishes were the prototypical example, and which is widely associated with anti-social behaviour, drug abuse and blasphemy.

Naturally, such finer taxonomic distinctions were considered mere sophistry by that stratum of the Shi`i clergy who felt simply that any claim to mystical insight, especially one originating from within an 'order' (*tariqa*), was a dangerous heresy alien to Islam. This viewpoint was abundantly evident in my interviews with clergy. It did not take long for an ayatullah whom I interviewed in Qum in 1997 (a man as convivial as he was sour) to rule

Sufism as a whole 'outside Islam'. Similarly, grand ayatullah (*ayatullah al-`uzma*) Nasir Makarim-Shirazi held Sufism generally to consist of illegitimate aberrations.[8] In so far as the Sufis' post-revolutionary prudence did not result directly from state pressure or violence, they obviously observed it to thwart such traditional ulama's rejections of Sufism, which could be dangerously amplified in the context of the new puritan regime.

Fortunately for the Sufis, under the new regime there were still (as indeed there always had been) among the jurists some scholars who held more benign views of their mystical fellow Muslims. `Abd al-Karim Musawi-Ardabili, for instance, another grand ayatullah, put forward several reservations about and objections to Sufism to clarify my understanding, but also added, subtly, that jurists who were knowledgeable of the issues involved were less inclined to flay the Sufis.[9]

Other rejections of Sufism that have been voiced by traditional jurists are similar to those of modernists, expressed most forcefully by the nationalist historian Ahmad Kasrawi (d. 1946) in his *Sufigari* (Kasrawi, 1963; Ridgeon, 2006). Modernists, too, criticized Sufism for its alleged otherworldliness, idleness, and anti-social character. Sufis were said not to marry or provide for posterity, and to use drugs instead of working. At the level of common rumour mongering, suspicions even circulated that Sufis might cook and eat children in Satanic rituals. With much hilarity, the middle-aged, informal leader in Safi`alishah's lodge who I interviewed in 1997 supplied such an anecdote, which revealed the prevailing anti-Sufism of his youth.

Most importantly, exclusivist political readings of Shi`ism have been institutionalized in the new state structures. Therefore, Sufis have had to downplay associations between Sufism and alternative spiritual authority as embodied in the figure of the *shaykh*, *pir*, or *qutb*. Concepts of *wilayat* (or *walayat*), roughly translating as 'guidance', 'sainthood', 'friendship with God', or 'spiritual power', are central to both Islamic Republican ideology and Sufi notions of spiritual authority, and the relations between the two readings are complex (cf. van den Bos, 2002c).

There have been divergent articulations of Sufi authority in the Islamic Republic. Some have held that Sufi and jurist authority are completely unrelated qualities; others would stress their competitive relationship. A third view, current in Sultan`alishahiyya circles, has it that spiritual authority during the Larger Occultation – the period since the disappearance of the Twelfth Imam in 941 – is divided into a realm of the jurists and a complementary realm of the Gnostics (i.e., a sphere including the Sultan`alishahi Sufis). This view can be traced to at least 1906-07, when it was expressed in a Sultan`alishahi publication (van den Bos, 2002c: 362-3). Other expressions of Sufi authority in harmony with the Islamic Republic's state/jurist authority include photographs of the Iranian leadership beside portraits of masters of the orders, on the walls of Sufi houses of worship.

Precisely how regime change has altered opportunities for the expression of Sufism in the Islamic Republic remains difficult to pin down, but it is vividly suggested in private narrations of repression. These contain chilling images such as 'beards [that] were set on fire' (interview, 5 December 1996). Other violence that may explain the public silence of the Sufis includes an arson attack on the Amir Sulaymani house of worship of the Sultan`alishahi order in Tehran in 1979, in which the building was completely destroyed. The circumstances of the attack remain unresolved (van den Bos, 2002b: 154-6). The mausoleum of Sultan`alishahi master Salih`alishah (d. 1966) in Tehran was also destroyed in the early 1990s on the orders of the authorities, allegedly to 'make more space for public worship' (Lewisohn, 1998: 452).

Silence was also upheld in the face of a post-revolutionary genre of heresiological literature containing vitriolic denunciations of the orders and their teachers.[10] In addition to launching the traditional religious and modernist charges against Sufism, this literature frames the orders as reactionary and subversive of the Islamic Republic. These books, essays and pamphlets drag the names of Sufi masters through the mire, alluding to illegitimate sources of huge wealth and to relations with representatives of the *ancien régime*, including the feared and hated secret service, Savak (e.g., Salih`alishah, 1996: 215-16). It remains unclear whether state involvement in this anti-Sufism campaign was limited to the publication permits issued by the Ministry of Islamic Guidance (*irshad*), or extended to the Ministry of Intelligence (*ittila`at*) and affiliated state and semi-state agents as well.

During my fieldwork in 1996, an Iranian informant reflected on how Sufis in Iran had moved back into the social configuration in which Sufism had started: with Sufis practicing as individuals and in small groups without any formal organization (i.e., without religious 'orders'). He suggested that worldly forms (i.e., the Sufi orders) had polluted an ideal Sufism that was without formal organization. In his view it was only natural that Sufism should have come full circle to its original self – masters and disciples assembling in a setting of intimate personal contact. (My informant did not seem to attribute this development to the regime.)

Under the Islamic Republic, several orders have suffered closure or occupation of their lodges (Hasuri, 1997: 8). According to an affiliate of the Dhu'l-Riyasatayn order in Tehran, 25 of their lodges were closed down after the revolution. The central Tehrani Safi`alishahi lodge was occupied for about one year early in the revolution. One revolutionary committee after the other took over the premises, but they apparently allowed Sufi visits to continue. Through these events, a new leadership emerged that managed to secure official registration for the lodge (van den Bos, 2002b: 160-8).

Since the revolution, some of the orders have crumbled or have regrouped abroad.[11] For example, the Safi`alishahi order, some of whose leaders had been associated with the Pahlavi court, only nominally retains a religious centre at the founder's grave in central Tehran, having disintegrated into much smaller assemblies and alliances in Iran. But in the Netherlands, a previously local Safi`alishahi master from Isfahan has proclaimed himself to be the overall Safi`alishahi master (styling himself Safi`alishah II, to which I have not encountered objections in Iran). He commands a mixed, émigré-Iranian and Dutch audience. People of both cultural backgrounds join together in *dhikr* sessions, which because of linguistic and other barriers carry with them very diverse religious understandings. Similarly, spiritual masters of transnational orders such as the Dhahabiyya, the Dhu'l-Riyasatayn-Ni`matullahiyya (both UK based), and the Maktab Tariqat Uwaysi Shahmaqsudi (US and UK based) at present guide their Iranian disciples from foreign quarters. The International Association of Sufism developed from another American Uwaysi lineage centring on Sayyida Dr Nahid Angha [`Anqa], the daughter of the forty-first master of the order, Shah Maqsud Sadiq `Anqa. The Association is very much in the avant-garde of transnational Sufism, hardly resembling traditional orders or spirituality at all. Instead, it represents itself as an 'educational organization' and a United Nations-affiliated NGO that carries out a United Nations Human Rights project.

While Sufis in Iran have kept a low profile in contrary circumstances, institutional Sufism never vanished from Iranian society after 1978/9. In 1991, the authoritative analyst of Islamic mysticism, Seyyed Hossein Nasr, wrote in a passage on 'Sufism and Islamic spirituality in contemporary Persia' that 'the Qadiriyya and Naqshbandiyya have continued to be strong' (Nasr, 1991: 218). Although the Dhahabiyya's administration of the Shah Chiragh shrine in Shiraz was discontinued (Algar, 1993: 580), the order's supreme master reported in January 1997 that no Dhahabi lodges had been confiscated and no Dhahabi Sufis persecuted (Lewisohn, 1999: 48). As for the Dhu'l-Riyasatayn-Ni`matullahiyya, leading authorities of the order stated in 1998 that some 60 of its lodges were still in operation (Lewisohn, 1998: 461).

In spite of, and perhaps partly as a response to, the dominant Islamism, some lodges reportedly flourished (Hasuri, 1977: 8). I may add in confirmation that the places of congregation of the various orders that I visited between 1996 and 2002 were always filled to the brim when meetings took place. The facts on the ground in post-revolutionary Iran, in other words, do not indicate that Iranian Sufism suffered repression to the point of extinction or that it was forced to return, full circle, to an atomized, socially disembodied existence. Rather, Sufis have made particular, post-revolutionary accommodations.

The Riddle of Sufi Quietism in Khatami's Iran
After Muhammad Khatami's assumption of the presidency of Iran in August 1997, one would have expected a gradual return of the Sufi orders to the public sphere. There seemed to be a widening space for the public assertion of Sufi identity, and it seemed possible for Sufis to abandon their earlier

repertoire of silence and accommodation. An indication of the improved circumstances for Sufism was the return to Iran from exile abroad of a Kurdish Sufi, the Qadiriyya shaykh Hasan Hashimi, with permission from the government (Bianchi, 2000). Similarly, a youthful admirer of Sufism nicknamed 'Sultan of the Dervishes' was registered as a candidate for the June 2001 presidential elections (AFP despatch, 3 May 2001). And with fear rapidly diminishing at that time, the Sufi orders' continuing silence could not be attributed to state intimidation alone.

Moreover, there was an area of overlap between Sufi mystic religiosity and the religious ideology associated with Khatami's political reform program. Even before the reform movement proper, authors such as H. Hamid had written about the reformist potential of 'social mysticism', *'irfan-i ijtima'i* (cf. Alinejad, 1999: 489-93). In Abdolkarim Soroush's thought, newly articulated religious ideas of relativism and pluralism blended with an older mystical perspectivism even though he strongly disapproved of organized Sufism (Matin-Asgari, 1997: 100-2). The compatibility with the 'new religious thought' associated with the reform movement seemed to make for a new and safer public space for Sufi religiosity.

Moreover, one could predict the revival of a Sufi presence in public life in the Khatami reform era from revisiting the history of early twentieth-century Sufi activism. Leading early twentieth-century Sufis had been political activists, strongly oriented to the here-and-now. Under the second Pahlavi shah (1941-79), Sufism became an important social vehicle as elite Iranians joined its ranks and linkages emerged between royalty and (Sufi) mysticism. There was nothing intrinsic to Iranian Sufism, therefore, which would impede its worldly engagement once the socio-political circumstances became more favourable after 1997.

But Iranian Sufism remains insular and aloof from new social forms in the emerging civil society. Sufi masters have not made themselves visible as authority figures in Iranian society, and no coalition has emerged between Sufi leaders and the new reformist religious intellectuals. In this respect, the social universe of Iranian Sufism contrasts with the British–Pakistani cases described by Pnina Werbner in this volume (Chapter 11), which appear to represent an expanding religious social world. The British–Pakistani networks in question exhibit boundary-transcending and integrative traits that signal their participation in what may perhaps be called an ethno-religious civil society.

Manifestations of Shi`i Sufism in Contemporary Iran

State strictures on Sufism have loosened under Khatami, and beyond that Sufism has attained a new societal legitimacy in Iran (Khosrokhavar and Roy, 1999: 180). One indication of the new legitimacy is the uninhibited display of books on Sufism and other mystical subjects in urban shop-windows. Before 1997, the public presence of Sufi symbols remained limited largely to dervish dolls and Sufi paraphernalia (such as begging bowls, *kashkul*) in souvenir shops.

In 2002, the authorities still prohibited an international congress of the Sultan`alishahi Ni`matullahiyya in Mahan (Iran House, 2002). But in the same year, the Fajr Music and Theatre festival in Tehran enabled Sufi music masters from different regions of Iran to become known internationally and perform abroad (Sauerwein, 2002). In 2003, the Culture House of the Islamic Republic of Iran in New Delhi organized a seminar on 'Islamic mysticism and Sufism' (Iran House, 2003). Another, paradoxical indication of the new openness consists of the complaints by Dhu'l-Riyasatayn Ni`matullahi dervishes and lodges throughout Iran that had experienced harassment and aggression. The parliamentary commission investigating these complaints exculpated the Sufis in 2003 (Afarinish, 2003). A Sultan`alishahi Ni`matullahi source told me that his order has faced similar cases of harassment.[12] But except for the commission and the publicity surrounding such cases, Sufism remains virtually absent from the public sphere.

In spite of the improved conditions, one cannot rule out prudence or fear as partial explanations of the quietism that prevails among Sufis in Iran. In the midst of Iran's current ideological wars, Sufis presumably would make themselves vulnerable to political machinations and easily become scapegoats when speaking out in public for or against a given politico-religious cause. During my fieldwork in 2001, informants referred to these factors in response to my questions concerning the Sufis' current conditions. But beyond these external factors there are other inhibitions that are at least as important in explaining the virtual absence of Sufism from the public sphere.

The conviction among many Sufis that state Islam is not the real Islam does not help to relax the mutual reservations that Sufis and religious reformists have about each other. This became evident in my interviews in September 2001 with the reformists Muhammad Mujtahid-Shabistari and Muhsin Kadivar. When our conversation touched upon Sufism, they indicated their disapproval of it with their raised eyebrows and emphatic silences. Although Abdolkarim Soroush's work is pervaded by laudatory references to Sufism, and more specifically to Rumi, at the same time Soroush is strongly critical of Sufism's worldly manifestations.[13] For their part, some Sufis may have a jaundiced view of Soroush. A shaykh told me that Soroush had visited him and had won his respect for his formal grasp of an essential Sufi text, Rumi's *Mathnawi*. But the shaykh was also scornful of what he perceived as Soroush's inability to really comprehend the deeper meaning of even a single verse; Soroush's reading remained, the shaykh suggested, an exoteric one.[14]

In the face of contradictions between regime jurist and Sufi religiosity, there were Sufi sympathies for reformist thought at a political level, but these were not enough to forge a coalition of Sufis and reformists. Between the Sufis' spiritual hours and their ordinary daily lives there seems to exist, certainly from an outsider's perspective, an almost impenetrable mental boundary, even though they conceive of Sufism as an overarching Way, encompassing all of life. There are other areas of potential tension as well. Whereas Sufis expressed sympathy for democracy as opposed to state Islam, they also insisted that democracy and Sufism belong to different realms. Sufis were unwilling to have spiritual authority subject to questioning, to the sort of intrusive inquiry that is central to democracy. From this it would seem that the current manifestations of Shi`i Sufism in Iran are fully open to modernist critiques of Sufism as anachronistic and otherworldly.

On Sufism and the 'Social'

In a different respect, however, post-1997, Khatami-era Sufism does contrast with Sufism earlier in the Islamic Republic. The ideological make-up of the Sufi orders now takes shape in the context of what Olivier Roy calls post-Islamism, in which 'the fields of the political and the religious become autonomous but stand in a relation of conflict vis-à-vis each other. Religion frees itself from the state, even if this be itself the Islamic state (Iran)' (Roy, 2001: 53). The present autonomy of Sufi religiosity vis-à-vis the state contrasts with the celebration of regime martyrs and with the religious nationalism professed by the Sultan`alishahi order during the war with Iraq.[15] Presently there appear to be no equivalents for those gestures. The elders of the orders do not play public roles in post-Khatami Iran, and Sufi attitudes towards the state are generally distant. In this regard, the Shi`i orders exemplify the larger process of emancipation in Iran wherein Shi`i religiosity attains significantly greater autonomy vis-à-vis its clerical overlords.[16]

In addition, greater autonomy becomes visible in that the orders elude what remains of the Islamist state (while previously, their 'uncorrupted religiosity' represented only tacit protest against it). The Sultan`alishahi master Nur`alishah Tabanda (Majdhub`alishah) was well aware of a new presence of youth and women in his order, and he felt uninhibited in discussing the issue openly with me.[17] The master frankly explained his view that these changes in membership related to the developments in Iranian society associated with the *duwwum-i khurdad*, the day of Khatami's election as president in May 1997. He also stressed, however, that this was a social (and therefore ephemeral) matter, as opposed to religious matters. Clearly the master did not wish to elaborate on this issue.

Indeed, life had been quite different for Nur`alishah Tabanda before he became supreme master (*qutb*) of the Sultan`alishahi order (after the death of his nephew Mahbub`alishah on 16 January 1997). Before the Islamic revolution, he had been a judge in the Supreme Court and he had translated Frantz Fanon's *Sociologie d'une révolution* and other writings into Persian (Madani, 1997: 162), which suggests an ideological proximity to `Ali Shari`ati (see below). He was affiliated with the oppositional Freedom Movement (Nahzat-i Azadi),[18] and was known for his activism during the revolution

(Madani, 1997: 162), although he downplayed these activities when I interviewed him on 7 May 1997. After the revolution, he again assumed high offices, including membership of the Board of Trustees and Directors of the Hajj Organization (Tanha'i, 2000: 600).

After becoming Sultan`alishahi *qutb*, Majdhub`alishah published a collection of papers on social and other issues of worldly import that stemmed from his pre-*qutb* years. The foreword to these 'jurisprudential essays' (*maqalat-i fiqhi*) explicates the writings are not 'mystical' (`*irfani*) but 'social' (*ijtima`i*). They comment, for instance, on the national Islamic identity of Iran, on Malthus, and on the significance of the family. They exhibit lay conceptualizations of society, which is to say that they clearly do not proceed from mystical conceptualizations of society.

Apparently, the first modern Sultan`alishahi effort to do precisely that, i.e. articulate mystical conceptualizations of society, is presented in some of the works of Dr. Husayn Abu'l-Hasan Tanha'i, a well-known affiliate of the Sultan`alishahi order, who studied sociology in the United States (Tanha'i, 1999, 2000).[19] Tanha'i apparently did not hold a position of authority in the order at the time his writings were published and they ought not be taken as straightforward representations of Sultan`alishahi doctrine. Nevertheless, a former supreme master, Riza`alishah, requested Tanha'i to write a sociology of religion in 1989-90 and the two supreme masters succeeding Riza`alishah also endorsed this venture (Tanha'i, 1999: 19). There is thus reason to believe that whether or not this project was sanctioned by the Sultan`alishahi order, at least it does not deviate from Sultan`alishahi doctrine.

Tanha'i's sociology of Islam is actually Islamic sociology. It seeks to debunk Western social science to make room for an Islamic alternative. The Islamic sociology project is reminiscent of an older Iranian nativism in that it relates uneasily to Western intellectual sources that actually lie at the root of its own writings. Chief ideological forebears of the Islamic revolution such as Jalal Al-i Ahmad and `Ali Shari`ati were thoroughly acquainted with secular and leftist European intellectualism, which marked their formulations of an authentic, besieged Iranian self. And through the West, paradoxically, they had also rediscovered Shi`ism (Boroujerdi, 1996).

In another respect, however, Tanha'i's project reverses Shari`ati's Sociology of Islam. Having translated Frantz Fanon's *Damnés de la terre* into Persian and, reportedly, corresponded with Fanon (Dabashi, 1993: 110), Shari`ati founded his Shi`i ideology upon secular categories. Among his neologisms were 'independent judgement/interpretation' (*ijtihad*) as a means to transform reactionary 'Safavid' Shi`ism, corrupted by state power, into revolutionary 'Alid Shi`ism' (cf. Rahnema, 2000: 306). Marx's concept shone through the idea of man's alienation without divine unity/monotheism (*tawhid*), and it is probably fair to argue, as Daryush Shayegan has done, that in the final analysis Shari`ati 'explain[ed] everything in Marxist terms of infrastructure and superstructure' (Shayegan, 1992: 55). In the end, Shari`ati reads Islam sociologically; Tanha'i, on the other hand, reinterprets sociology Islamically. Indicative of this difference is the fact that Tanha'i conspicuously ignores Shari`ati's work, even though it is such an obviously relevant *oeuvre*.

Tanhai'i's sociology sets out to define the ideal structure of a healthy society from a Qur'anic viewpoint (2000: 32). To that end, it identifies historical deviations since the earliest days of Islam. Among these deviations were all-too-human creations, such as the Umayyad state, often mistaken for truly Islamic institutions, and the emergence of regional and sectarian divisions within Islam.

In summary, Tanha'i's works articulate negative social–historical correlates of Shi`i theology, describing the drama of non-Alid developments after the demise of the prophet. Islamic deviations, he argues, would not have occurred had mainstream Islamic history taken a Shi`i course. In subsequently building up the ideal Islamic social, his Islamic sociology explores Shi`i themes that without exception refer back to one source. This is the concept of *walayat*, Shi`i guidance, friendship with God, or alternatively, in this case, the Imamate.

The Place and Shapes of *Walayat*

For Tanha'i, *walayat* represents a panacea for all the ills and deviations afflicting Muslim societies (2000: 31). His explications of the authentic message of Islam do not involve a substantial political sociology, but they do elaborate on relations between *walayat* and authority in the Sufi tradition and the Qur'an. The Qur'anic meaning of *walayat* concerned the appointed, as opposed to chosen, 'friend' (*wali*) or 'executor' (*wasi*) on earth who is the people's 'leader' (*rahbar*) and 'guide' (*rahnama*) (2000: 67).

The author divides the concept into several varieties, among which two are basic. 'Complete' (*kulliyya*) *walayat* remains the prerogative of the Imams, while the 'partial' (*juz'iyya*), derivative variety branched off into *wilayat-i faqih* ('Rule of the Jurist', the central concept of Khomeini's political theory), and 'mystical/gnostic' (`*irfani*) *walayat*, commonly glossed as 'sainthood' (cf. 2000: 126-7, 216). Tanha'i's Islamic sociology postulates a corresponding functional division of spiritual authority between jurists and Sufis during the 'larger occultation' (*ghaybat-i kubra*) of the twelfth Imam. This formulation in fact reiterates similar views expressed by Sultan`alishahi masters under the Islamic Republic and before. It is, however, certainly not the established or standard view, and some other contemporary views of Sufi *walayat* fail to see any relation to jurist authority or non-Sufi conceptions of *walayat/wilayat* whatsoever.[20]

The author also mentions the two partial branches of *walayat* in connection with the concept of 'absolute' (*mutlaqa*) *walayat/wilayat*, which more commonly refers to Khomeini's widened, post-1988 notion of the jurists' political authority. The relevant passage ends with the tacit comment that *wilayat-i mutlaqa* had never meant 'absolute dictatorship' in any historical record, or according to Islam's logical requirements (Tanha'i, 2000: 216). Furthermore, the sociology opposes *walayat* to monarchy (as well as absolute dictatorship) and associates it with the implementation of social justice (Tanha'i, 2000: 216). In one statement, the concept is brought to bear on pluralism and democracy (Tanha'i, 2000: 216).

Yet, the Islamic sociology does not relate *walayat* to a more explicitly defined ideal socio-political order. In this respect, it bears no relation with the current debates in Iran and the rather more mundane terms in which these are expressed. There is neither reference to nor engagement with, for instance, the writings of Soroush that connect mysticism and reformism. The interpretive principle is not developed into the kind of hermeneutics that allows Muhammad Mujtahid-Shabistari to develop a radically different, democratic reading of Shi`ism (Mujtahid-Shabistari, 2000). Nor do these writings resemble those of Muhsin Kadivar, who re-examined the main theories of *wilayat* and thereby discredited the Rule of the Jurist (Kadivar, 1999, 2001). In a comment on my reading of his books, the author stressed that (Sufi) *wilayat* has nothing at all to do with *sulta* (political rule).[21] In sum, Tanha'i's Islamic sociology stands in contrast to Iran's 'new religious thinking' (*naw-andisha-yi dini*) in that it does not have a clear-cut worldly orientation, except for being a 'sociology' – which is a marker of post-Khatami progressive discourse. Viewed in the context of Sufi ideology emerging from the current Sufi literature, however, Tanha'i's sociological framing of *walayat* clearly renders his project unique.

Conclusion

The other-worldly quietism that outwardly characterizes Shi`i Sufism in Khatami's Iran came as a relative novelty after prior twentieth-century developments. Sufism in the Reza Shah era was marked by ideological and organizational renewal with a distinct societal focus. Varieties of religious syncretism developed under Mohammad Reza Shah Pahlavi. Royal patronage reached certain quarters of Sufism, while politicized Sufi opposition emerged against the regime and against elite spirituality.

Even under the Islamic Republic, instances of Sufi regime religiosity indicated that the nation state remained a major frame of reference for the Sufi orders. This focus on the nation state was especially conspicuous in the religious statements of Sultan`alishahi authorities with respect to Iranians' martyrdom in the Iran–Iraq war.

In addition, certain intellectual expressions after the 1997 reformist turn in the Islamic Republic contradict the apparent other-worldly quietism of Iranian Shi`i Sufism. Tanha'i's Islamic sociology and constructions of 'the social' are not immediately relevant to the here-and-now, but they do not represent a disengaged mystic traditionalism either.

The Islamic social, emanating from within and unintelligible without the grid of Shi`i jurisprudence and theology, is pre-sociological in the sense that it lacks Durkheim's prerequisite of autonomy.[22] The surrogate social is also elusive in its theological abstraction, compared to the objects defined by new religious thinkers: the sociological implications of their work are often manifest. But in reading *walayat* into the social order of things, the Sufi studies represent an unparalleled effort, within the sphere of modern Shi`i Sufism in Iran, to come to terms with this-worldly social science and society.

Acknowledgement

Fieldwork and other research for this paper were funded by the International Institute for the Study of Islam in the Modern World (ISIM) in Leiden.

5

SAINT AND SUFI IN CONTEMPORARY MALI

Benjamin F. Soares

Beginning in the late 1990s, a group of young Muslim religious figures, who call themselves Sufis, started to attract considerable attention, particularly in urban Mali. The most prominent are based in Bamako, Mali's capital and largest city. There is much agreement among Malians that these contemporary Sufis are new kinds of Sufis. Indeed, they are markedly different from both other Sufis in Mali and their historical predecessors from the colonial and pre-colonial past, all of whom have been closely associated with one of the main Sufi orders found in this country.

In this chapter I consider some of these Sufis – 'new Sufis' for convenience here – who have become influential religious figures with many followers and clients in Mali. The recent and ongoing processes of liberalization in Mali – political, economic and social – have profoundly influenced the practice of religion and Islam in particular. Over the past few years, new forms of associational life, increased transnational and global interconnections, and the use of new media technologies have had a major impact on Mali's religious economy, which has become more diverse and complex. The new Sufis offer a significant opportunity to reflect upon some of the changing modalities of religious expression in a place like Mali, which has undergone rapid processes of liberalization over the past 15 years.

Islam as an Object of Study

Many observers of Islam and of Muslims in West Africa have long assumed that the Sufi orders were the most important institutional form for the practice of Islam in much of Muslim West Africa (e.g., Hiskett, 1984). The attention to Sufi orders during the colonial period was of course directly related to both British and French colonial administrators' overtly political objectives of attempting to thwart any challenges or threats to colonial authority that might possibly come under the banner of Islam (Seesemann, 2002). Given that the organized Sufi orders in West Africa were and remain to one degree or another corporate groups with identifiable leaders, they were obvious areas of interest and study from the nineteenth century through the colonial period in the twentieth century. In the late colonial period from around the 1940s, colonial observers shifted their attention to include the latest perceived challenge to colonial rule, those reformist and modernist Muslims who sometimes articulated critiques of the Sufi orders, their leaders, doctrines and practices. In the postcolonial period, with a few notable exceptions, observers of Islam in West Africa have continued to work within this same problematic by focussing on Sufism and Sufi orders and, to a lesser extent, on reformist Muslims. Thus, there have been various studies of those Sufi orders that historically have been the most important in West Africa, particularly the Qadiriyya, the Tijaniyya, and their various branches, as well as anti-Sufi groups and movements within various countries in West Africa or more generally across the region.[1]

Such a problematic, which might even be called a preoccupation with Sufi orders and their opposites, Muslim reformist critics, is perhaps best exemplified in the case of Senegal. Here there has been sustained scholarly production about the Sufi orders and especially the Mourides – a branch of the Qadiriyya – that has proceeded almost uninterrupted since early in the colonial period. Given the role Sufi orders and their leaders have played in national politics in Senegal, it is not at all surprising that political scientists have been in the forefront in analysing them (e.g. Cruise O'Brien, 1971, 1975; Villalón, 1995). Just when one thought that enough had been said about the over-studied Mourides, the scholarly production about them seems to have taken on a new life now that scholars have decided to pay attention to Senegalese migrants in Europe, North America and beyond.[2] However, the attention of scholars on Sufi orders in West Africa and especially in Senegal has only helped to reinforce the view that somehow the practice of Islam in Africa is equivalent to that of the existing organized Sufi orders. As Villalón suggests in this volume, Senegal represents a rather exceptional case for the importance of the Sufi orders even in West Africa. If one looks elsewhere in West Africa, for example Mali, Niger and Côte d'Ivoire, it is readily apparent that Sufi orders have never had the importance they may have in Senegal, not to mention other places in the Muslim world.

My objective in this chapter is not to downplay the importance of Sufism or Sufis in West Africa. To the contrary, it would be difficult to understand the history and contemporary practice of Islam in West Africa without comprehending the centrality of Sufism. But Sufism and its influence cannot, and should not, be reduced to its presumed institutional forms such as the handful of Sufi orders whose history we already know something about. While there have been very good studies of individual Sufis and the Sufi orders they have founded, led and propagated in West Africa, there has been insufficient attention to how Sufi organization and practice may have actually changed over time. In fact, attention to the existing organized Sufi orders might obscure from our view other possibly newer ways of being Muslim in West Africa and therefore some of the important transformations in the practice of Islam, of which the new kinds of Sufis in Mali are a perfect illustration.

The History of Islam

Here I cannot enter into the intricacies of the history of Islam in West Africa. Rather, I present the following brief historical sketch as background information for understanding contemporary religious practice and the new Sufis in particular. It is quite clear that Islam has been present and practiced in West Africa for more than a millennium. In some places, including urban centres such as Jenne and Timbuktu to cite two of the best-known Islamic centres in West Africa, Muslims were a clear majority and dominated the affairs of state for centuries. In many other places in West Africa, Muslims often lived as a minority among non-Muslims. Wherever they lived, Muslims regularly interacted with various groups of non-Muslims through trade, marriage alliance, political alliance, warfare and so forth.

Not until the twentieth century did Islam become the religion of the majority of people living in what is present-day Mali. The unprecedented spread of Islam during French colonial rule was as much a surprise to colonial administrators as it was to many Muslims. Unlike many other places in West Africa, there were very few converts to Christianity in Mali despite the long presence of Christian missionaries in the region. Today, less than 2 per cent of Malians consider themselves Christians, and most of these Christians are Catholics.

Various individuals and groups who were not Muslims at the onset of colonial rule embraced Islam during colonial rule. In becoming Muslim, many people gave up a range of ritual objects and practices that sometimes involved blood sacrifice and were deemed to be un-Islamic – 'fetishes' and 'fetishism', 'animism', or 'paganism' in the colonial lexicon. At the same time they usually also adopted a set of standardized ritual norms – regular prayer and fasting during the month of Ramadan – that indexed them as Muslims. In many cases, being Muslim also included affiliation to a Sufi order – the Qadiriyya or the Tijaniyya, through one of their various branches. If before the twentieth century, affiliation to Sufi orders was a private affair limited exclusively to Muslim scholarly elites, during colonial rule affiliation to Sufi orders became much more widespread among many ordinary Muslims, both men and women. But formal membership in a Sufi order never became as prevalent in Mali as it did in neighbouring Senegal. This may be why the organized Sufi orders have never been key factors in Mali's national political culture, as they have in Senegal and, at some points in time, in northern Nigeria.

Some scholars, who have conducted research outside Senegal in contemporary West Africa, have noted that many Muslims emphasize the importance of Sufi orders, all the while lacking any affiliation to a Sufi order (e.g., Launay, 1992; Soares, 2005). Indeed, most Malian Muslims today have no formal affiliation whatsoever to a Sufi order. Even so, certain practices closely tied to Sufism, Sufi orders and their leaders, including the veneration of certain persons with reputations as saints and the use of the Islamic esoteric sciences (*'marabouts'* and *'maraboutage'* in the French colonial lexicon), remain central to what it means to be Muslim for many Malian Muslims. Indeed, the most palpable influence of Sufism on Malian society has come by way of elaborate discourses about esoteric knowledge, 'secrets', and miracles associated with various past and present Muslim religious figures, who usually have had some association with a Sufi order.

Despite the somewhat limited role of the organized Sufi orders in postcolonial Mali, various individuals with reputations as Muslim saints who are associated with the Qadiriyya and the Tijaniyya have been key religious figures in the society. In fact, until very recently, the career of nearly every Muslim with a saintly reputation seemed to be contingent upon a close link with a branch of one of these Sufi orders. Like their Senegalese counterparts, Muslim saints in Mali have been almost without exception members of lineages of hereditary Muslim specialists, who have distinguished themselves through charismatic abilities or qualities. As I have argued elsewhere (Soares, 2004b, 2005), certain Muslim religious leaders in Mali have personalized religious authority. These saintly superstars attract followers from all sectors of society, but in their relations with some of their followers, particularly members of the political and economic elite, in recent years they have become more privatized religious figures. In exchange for often sumptuous gifts, elite followers have relatively unfettered access to the saints, their blessings, and religious services such as personalized prayers and amulet-confection. These saintly superstars live in small provincial towns or other regional urban centres known as important Islamic religious centres. In fact, none of the heads of the existing Sufis orders are based in Bamako.[3]

While the saintly superstars living outside Bamako are among the most prominent religious figures in Mali, there are many more religious figures in the broader religious economy. Bamako is the most populous city in Mali, with a population estimated at over one million. It is also the country's most important centre of economic activity, politics, education, cultural activities and international assistance, since Mali, on the French model, remains a highly centralized state. Perhaps not surprisingly, the city has become a centre for Islamic religious activities. Mali's reformist and modernist Muslims have their highest profile in Bamako and here they have built many schools, mosques and modern Islamic educational institutions. But Bamako has also become the country's most important urban centre of what can be called fee-for-service religion. Throughout the country, one finds a broad range of

Muslim religious specialists who draw on Sufism and the Islamic esoteric sciences and make a living, or supplement their income, through the use of special prayers, blessings, spiritual retreat and exercises, instruction or guidance in alms-giving and various forms of divination. Many of these religious figures frequently spend time in Bamako or have moved there.

In the postcolonial period, every Malian regime – democratically elected or not – has sought to associate itself in one way or another with Islam and Islamic religious practice. The Malian state's association with Islam was most pronounced in the 1980s under the regime of President Moussa Traoré, who identified himself and his regime with various high-profile Muslim religious leaders, including certain leaders of Sufi orders with saintly reputations (Soares, 2004b, 2005). By the time of the coup that replaced Traoré's authoritarian regime in 1991, Islam had come to play a dominant role in the public sphere in Mali. Various modernizing critics, including prominent Sufi leaders and Muslim reformists, openly and regularly castigated people for engaging in all sorts of allegedly un-Islamic activities (read 'fetishism'). This contributed to a climate in which allegedly un-Islamic 'traditions' were relegated to private or at least semi-public venues.

After 1991, political reforms eventually led to multi-party elections. More vigorous implementation of economic reforms and economic liberalization in line with IMF/World Bank policy prescriptions accompanied this political liberalization and the so-called transition to democracy. Significant changes in the religious economy have also come in the wake of such political and economic liberalization.[4] Given the state's commitment to freedom of association and expression, there has been a proliferation of newspapers and private radio stations, many of which feature a range of regular Islamic religious programming. Many members of a highly educated Muslim elite, which has grown in numbers, have also founded dozens of new Islamic or Muslim associations and organizations. These include associations for Muslim youth, women and reformist Muslims, for Muslim preachers and other associations that promote development. While some of the associations advocate ethical improvement and/or Islamist agendas, many have complex transnational connections for funding, personnel and support.

Along with the liberalization that permitted the formation of new Islamic associations and new media outlets, one now finds a wide range of new Muslim public figures, almost all of whom are men. They include the writers of books, pamphlets and newspaper articles about Islam, preachers whose sermons are aired on radio and television and circulate on audiocassette, video and DVD, those involved in Muslim educational institutions, and activists and leaders of the many Islamic associations that have been founded since the early 1990s. However, with the exception of one popular preacher, Chérif Ousmane Haïdara who is a veritable media star (see Soares, 2004a, 2005), most of these new Muslim public figures have little widespread popular legitimacy or even constituencies. It is nevertheless important to consider the phenomenon of new Sufis, who have become significant and influential actors in a religious economy that has become more complex, competitive and diverse. I focus here on two of the most prominent of these new religious personalities in urban Mali.

Marketing Sufism

Cheick Soufi Bilal (hereafter Bilal) is a young self-described Sufi and shaykh, as his name indicates, who is also a prolific writer of short pamphlets and primers about Sufism and ritual practice. From the late 1990s, Bilal has developed a reputation for piety, miracles and the large gatherings for the *mawlid*, the celebration of the birthday of the Prophet Muhammad, which he organizes and hosts. One of his major claims to authority is that he has reached the highest stage of Sufism and is a *murshid* or '*grand guide spirituel*' (as he translates it into French). Bilal does indeed have many followers and deputies, that is, *muqaddam*s and *khalifa*s, and he has opened several *zawiya*s or Sufi centres in different neighbourhoods in the capital and in certain villages. Like many Sufis in this region, he does not mention or discuss any of his own teachers or those who may have initiated him into Sufism or a particular Sufi order. Rather, he makes reference to his many visits to the tombs of saints in Mali and elsewhere in North and West Africa.

Unlike many Muslims with saintly reputations here, he does not make a specific claim to be a descendant of the Prophet Muhammad. His genealogical claims do, however, figure in his claims to authority. Interestingly, Bilal traces his ancestry through his father to Muhammad Taqiyyu Allah, a famous twentieth-century Sufi and member of the Qadiriyya from near Néma in present-day Mauritania, who is known for his many miracles and followers during the colonial period.[5] Many, perhaps even most, Malians are today unfamiliar with Muhammad Taqiyyu Allah's illustrious history, and this may help to explain why Bilal's ancestry through his mother is more frequently invoked. Bilal's mother comes originally from Timbuktu. This city is closely connected with Islam in the social imaginary, not least because 333 Muslim saints are said to be buried there. In Bilal's books, the paid advertising, newspaper articles,[6] and his website,[7] there is repeated reference to the 'saintly' character of Timbuktu and his association with the city through his mother.

Bilal's name in itself is rather interesting, given that this was the name of the Abyssinian slave who was the Prophet Muhammad's companion and the first *muezzin*, the person who calls people to prayer. Muslims throughout the world have great respect for this figure in Muslim history.[8] Although the name, Bilal, frequently indexes someone as being of hereditary slave status in this part of West Africa, it would be tendentious to claim that such a marginal identity was of importance to Bilal or his followers.

In the late 1990s, Bilal moved to Bamako from the country's second largest city, Ségou, which is also closely linked with Islam in the social imaginary. He lives in a fairly modest home in a neighbourhood not far from the densely populated city centre where he receives many visitors. On the main road outside his home, there is a large sign with arrows, which indicate the location of his house. This is not merely a roadside sign, but rather a small billboard, a form of advertising that has become increasingly popular in Mali. The star and crescent motif features prominently on the billboard, at the top of which is the saying written in Arabic script, 'God is one'. Bilal's name transliterated into French, his standing as a 'great spiritual master' [*grand maître spirituel*], and his two mobile telephone numbers follow on the billboard.

For someone aspiring to a career as a Muslim religious specialist, Bilal has a rather unconventional appearance, and this has generated much discussion in Mali. He is rather youthful in appearance, and those around him often emphasize how young he is to be both a shaykh and a Sufi leader of such high stature. When seen in public or photographed, he always wears the West African *boubou*, a long robe that is considered normal West African Muslim attire and which he sometimes covers with a long, brightly coloured cape on ceremonial occasions. He usually wears a turban or fez on his head, or occasionally the long, white head-covering that indicates the wearer has performed the *hajj*. All of this is rather unremarkable. But immediately striking in his appearance are his dreadlocks, which many Malians refer to as 'rasta hair'. He wears his dreadlocks shoulder-length, hanging loosely from the base of his turban or fully exposed.

Such a 'rasta' hairstyle certainly adds to Bilal's appearance of youthfulness, and I have heard many Malians comment upon it. This is because such hairstyles – and long hair for men more generally – were among the signs that historically indexed people in the broader region as non-Muslims. Indeed, many Malians still associate such signs with non-Muslims, who usually abandoned these when they adopted Islam. However, in the 1980s and 1990s, through the media of reggae music, videos, and the widely circulating images of such much-loved reggae stars as Bob Marley and the Ivoirien Alpha Blondy, many youths appropriated certain Rastafarian elements of style and integrated these elements into youth culture (Savishinsky, 1994). These elements became influential and popular among many young men, especially, although not exclusively, in urban areas in Mali. In some cases, people also adopted some of these elements of style through the Muslim Baye Fall, a subgroup of the Mourides with certain pan-Africanist ideas, who are present in small numbers in Mali.

In the 1990s, Ségou gained a reputation as a city where young men, including some of those involved in Islamic education (especially those enrolled in private Islamic educational institutions, not 'modern'-style madrasas) adopted dreadlocks. Some of these young men said they let their hair grow long and matted as Sufis did in the past when they spent long periods alone in the countryside, engaging in prayer and fasting. Although some Malians refer to these young men as 'the Ségou rastas', their links to

Rastafarianism (or the Muslim Baye Fall for that matter) were in most cases rather tenuous. Some urban youth emulating or borrowing from Rastafarianism also took up the practice of smoking cannabis, but this was not an element of Rastafarianism that most young Muslim students in Islamic education adopted in places like Ségou. In any case, Bilal was just one of a rather large group of young Muslim students who began to wear their hair in the 'rasta' style, indexing their affinities with contemporary urban youth culture and possible aspirations as Sufis. Such a style also pointed to a clear generational shift in acceptable appearance and attire for Muslim youth and men.

Bilal is set apart from some of his contemporaries by the series of pamphlets he has written and published at his own expense, dealing with Sufism, ritual practice, and most recently, the celebration of the Prophet Muhammad's birth. Since his first pamphlet on the Qadiriyya appeared in late 1999, he has published five other books.[9] His various pamphlets provide rather elaborate discussions and instructions about Sufism, esoteric doctrines, the special litanies of prayers, and supererogatory prayers for which Sufis and Sufi orders are well known. It is likely that the popular and widely available books of the Senegalese author, Cheikh Ahmad Tall, on 'secrets' (see, e.g., Tall, 1995) provided a model for some of Bilal's pamphlets in both their content and style.[10] All of the information Bilal provides in his pamphlets is ostensibly to enable Muslims to move closer to God, which is said to have potential benefits in this world and in the next. One theme in some of the pamphlets is the danger that 'animism', 'paganism' and 'polytheism' pose to Muslims. The author suggests that the prayers detailed in his publications when properly recited should be able to help Muslims avoid such evils. In this respect, the subjects covered in Bilal's pamphlets are not at all unusual and in fact follow in a long tradition of such books that West African Muslims have written.[11]

It is, however, rather significant that Bilal has published separate pamphlets about different Sufi orders and even seems to suggest in these publications that he has affiliations to multiple Sufi orders. This must be understood in the context of the history of the practice of Islam in this part of West Africa. Before the twentieth century and into the first decades of colonial rule it was quite commonplace for members of the Muslim scholarly elite to have affiliations to multiple Sufi orders, but this practice changed in the twentieth century. By the 1930s or so, exclusive affiliation to a Sufi order effectively became the norm for most Muslims. A main impetus for this shift came with the spectacular spread of the Tijaniyya with its doctrine of the exclusiveness of affiliation. Those who wished to join the Tijaniyya were expected to renounce any earlier affiliations, which in this part of West Africa were usually to the Qadiriyya. However, certain members of the Qadiriyya in West Africa did not adhere to the doctrine of exclusivity of affiliation and continued to initiate people into both the Qadiriyya and the Tijaniyya. One example is

Muhammad Taqiyyu Allah and other members of the Fadiliyya, the branch of the Qadiriyya to which he was affiliated. Another is Chérif Fanta Mady (d. 1955), one of the most prominent Muslim religious leaders in late colonial French West Africa, who lived in Kankan, Guinea, but also had followers in Mali. Nevertheless, these people with multiple affiliations and the propensity to initiate people into different Sufi orders were part of a small and aging minority of Muslim religious leaders in Mali.

With the appearance of Bilal's pamphlet on the Qadiriyya (Bilal n.d. 1), many, if not most, Malians would probably have assumed him to be a member of this Sufi order, who would be neither interested in, nor able to promote, any other Sufi affiliation. The pamphlet presents a history of the Qadiriyya and the special litanies of this Sufi order in some detail. It lists some of the most prominent West African Qadiris from the twentieth century and identifies them as Muslim saints, beginning with Chérif Fanta Mady. However, Bilal's purported ancestor, Muhammad Taqiyyu Allah, is conspicuously absent from this list. Towards the end of the pamphlet, Bilal instructs members of the Qadiriyya and their 'brothers' from the Tijaniyya not to be divided against each other since 'we all aspire ... to a *tariqa* of peace, unity, and devotion' (Bilal n.d. 1: 31). This is rather important given that historically there has been considerable rivalry and sometimes antagonism and outright conflict between members of the two Sufi orders, beginning in the nineteenth century. However, calls for unity between Qadiris and Tijanis are not completely lacking. In recent years, some prominent leaders of Sufi orders in Mali have made public appeals for such unity, which seems to have been in part a response to Muslim reformist criticisms of Sufi orders.

Bilal published a similar pamphlet on the Tijaniyya (Bilal n.d. 3) a few years after his pamphlet on the Qadiriyya appeared. The Tijaniyya pamphlet does not state explicitly, but does leave readers with the impression, that the author has also been initiated into the Tijaniyya. In fact, he refers to his fond memories of having recited the litanies of the Tijaniyya at the mosque of Ahmad al-Tijani, the founder of the Tijaniyya, in Fez, Morocco. After a discussion of Sufism and the claim that the Prophet Muhammad was a Sufi, Bilal makes the controversial claim that access to heaven is guaranteed to members of the Tijaniyya. In this pamphlet, too, he calls for unity, specifically among Tijanis, and emphasizes that the differences between the main branches of the Tijaniyya in Mali are unimportant. He includes a discussion of Mali's most famous twentieth-century Tijani leader, Shaykh Hamallah, who was the leader of a branch of the Tijaniyya – the Hamawiyya – and was deported to France in the 1940s. Here Bilal remains in keeping with popular discourse about Hamallah, referring to Hamallah's absence but not mentioning his death in exile.

More controversially, Bilal claims that members of the Tijaniyya are not forbidden to frequent other non-Tijani religious leaders. This claim seems to explicitly contravene Tijani doctrine, if not practice, as scholars have noted (see Abun-Nasr, 1965). Bilal concludes this pamphlet with a list of important families in Mali who are associated with the Tijaniyya, but he does not name any prominent living Tijanis in the country. He does, however, list a number of prominent Tijanis living outside of Mali. One is Hassan Cissé from Kaolack in Senegal, a leading figure in the branch of the Tijaniyya, which Ibrahima Niasse propagated in large parts of West Africa. This is perhaps to be expected since Bilal's hometown, Ségou, is one of the few places in Mali where Ibrahima Niasse attracted a substantial number of followers.

When one looks closely at what Bilal has written about Sufism, his ideas seem to be a veritable *bricolage* of ideas and techniques from different Sufi orders, especially from the Qadiriyya and the Tijaniyya. The contents of his pamphlets aside, what is unusual is the new kind of religious marketing developing around Bilal. The publications, advertising, media coverage, billboards, and website all help to market Bilal, promoting his reputation and career. Before publication of his pamphlets, paid advertising has appeared in *Kabako*, one of Mali's newspapers that started in the 1990s. *Kabako* means literally 'astonishing things' in Bambara (Mali's most important *lingua franca* and also the name of the country's largest ethnic group), and it is one of Mali's most sensationalist newspapers. It provides regular coverage of scandal, fraud, rumour and astonishing things more generally. In fact, '*kabako*' is the usual Bambara translation for the Arabic '*karamat*' or miracles associated with Muslim saints, and the newspaper takes a particular interest in the miraculous. On several occasions, *Kabako* has published write-ups about Bilal's latest pamphlets, either shortly before or after the pamphlets have appeared (Anon., 2000; Anon., 2003; Bouaré, 2003).

Advertising about Bilal's publications also regularly appears on some of Bamako's and Ségou's private radio stations, sometimes in conjunction with recorded songs in praise of Bilal. Although Bilal has financed the publication of his pamphlets, they have been not only commercially viable, but even profitable. The author himself apparently set the list price for the pamphlets. As many Malians note, Bilal's pamphlets are considerably more expensive than other pamphlets on similar topics and of similar length, quality of paper, binding, and so forth. Bilal's pamphlets are available for sale in all the main Islamic bookshops in Bamako and in other urban centres such as Ségou where they are prominently on display. Malian bookshop owners and employees confirm brisk sales of the pamphlets.

It is striking how all of the pamphlets are very much focused on Bilal as an individual religious figure whose claims to superior, secret, esoteric knowledge are proclaimed. This is certainly in keeping with ordinary Sufi practice in Mali, but the way in which the publications serve as marketing tools for Bilal is truly a new phenomenon in this country. Every one of the pamphlets features a photograph of Bilal on the cover, and photographs inside present him in telling poses alone or surrounded by his followers. In some of the photographs he is offering blessings to individuals or groups who sometimes have their heads bowed toward him, as in one photograph with the caption 'the Shaykh with his students' (Bilal n.d. 4: 47). Use of Muslim religious leaders' images on video dates from the 1980s and use of their images in photographs, on lapel buttons, and printed on fabric goes back much further (see Soares, 2004a). Yet Bilal seems to be the first Malian Muslim religious figure to use his own image on publications for promotional purposes, as Cheikh Ahmad Tall began to do in Senegal in the mid-1990s.

Apart from his first pamphlet, which was published before mobile telephones were widely available in Mali, all of the other pamphlets list his mobile telephone numbers. The latest pamphlets also list his email address and website address, where one can find a short biography of Bilal, photographs of him and some of his followers, and the ubiquitous mobile telephone numbers. As far as I am aware, Bilal is Mali's only Muslim religious leader with his own website. Whatever other purposes it serves, this contact information is one part of the greater marketing activities of this religious entrepreneur and his version of Sufism.

It is not easy to make sociological generalizations about Bilal's followers since they range from agriculturalists, merchants and petty traders to dropouts from public schools and Islamic education, university students and graduates, clerical workers in offices, and civil servants. However, the overwhelming majority of followers and deputies seems to be members of the young, urban poor. Indeed, they tend to be social marginals, including the recently urbanized, who are trying to eke out an existence under very difficult conditions in this era of neo-liberal reforms, declining real wages and living standards, and cutbacks in public services and education. Bilal's religious marketing is directed not just toward these people, but also to the general public – potential followers and clients – who might want to contact this new Sufi for his services in trying to attain wealth, good health, and success in these times of economic uncertainty.

Religious Synthesis

The second of the new Sufis I consider here is Adama Yalcouyé, who most people know as Sufi Adama. He too is relatively young, born in 1960. Adama's father is Dogon, from the ethnic group that French anthropology made famous partly by holding up as quintessential 'traditional' Africans practicing 'traditional' African religion. Adama's father comes from a Dogon village near Bandiagara where Muslims and non-Muslims have lived in proximity for many decades. Adama's mother is Bambara. She comes from a small village in the Bélédougou, a region with a reputation for being one of the most 'animist' in Mali.

As a child, Adama grew up in a large village in the Bélédougou where a number of people, including some of his father's affines, are Catholics. Adama did not attend state schools where instruction is in French, and he apparently had no Qur'anic or Christian education. Some of his brothers engaged in Islamic education, including one who continued with advanced studies in Mali. Adama instead sought initiation into some of the non-Islamic men's secret societies that are still important in various places in Mali.[12] As a young adult, Adama gained a reputation as a hardworking and formidable agriculturalist. He worked as an agricultural labourer in various places in Mali and in Côte d'Ivoire, where he lived for several years. Eventually, Adama moved to the outskirts of Bamako where he built a house on the edge of the river that bisects the city. The place he selected for his home is known in the social imaginary for its powerful and dangerous spirits, which is why it remained largely uninhabited until Adama moved there with members of his large extended family and some of his followers. They have no immediate neighbours, but many people go to this area at all times of day and night to propitiate the spirits that are said to inhabit the landscape.

Although Adama calls himself a Sufi, he is not a member of any Sufi order and states this quite openly. Unlike Cheick Soufi Bilal, Adama seems almost completely uninterested in the different Sufi orders present in Mali. But he does take an avid interest in Mali's various living and deceased Muslim saints. In fact, Adama and many others say that he is in this world to complete the mission of Sékou Salah Siby (circa 1888-1982), a Dogon with a widespread reputation as a Muslim saint. Sékou Salah Siby is one of the people largely credited with spreading Islam among non-Muslim Dogon during the colonial period.[13] One of Mali's quality newspapers has even reported the widely discussed rumour that Sékou Salah Siby had predicted that Adama would come into this world (Anon., 2002). As a prominent member of the Qadiriyya, Sékou Salah Siby had ties with all the important branches of the Sufi order in the broader region. In fact, Muhammad Taqiyyu Allah initiated Sékou Salah Siby into the Qadiriyya. Sékou Salah Siby had a reputation as a Sufi who performed many miracles, not least of which was the massive Islamization of the non-Muslim Dogon and some of their neighbours, and the destruction of un-Islamic ritual objects (read 'fetishes'). However, the Qadiriyya was always central to Sékou Salah Siby's career, and it remains of paramount importance to his descendants and associates who seem to have adhered to the doctrine of exclusiveness of affiliation.

While like Sékou Salah Siby, Adama presents himself as a Muslim and a Sufi, unlike Sékou Salah Siby, Adama seems not particularly concerned to have non-Muslims embrace Islam. What Adama means by Sufi relates to the special mission he and many of his followers say God has communicated to him. When I have asked Adama and some of his associates about his being a Sufi, they have replied that it relates to his stature and mission. Some have insisted that Adama is much higher in stature than a Muslim saint. On several occasions I have heard some of his followers even refer to him as a prophet, using the word '*nabi*' from the Arabic. When some of Adama's followers discuss Adama, their discourse echoes elements of black nationalism and is reminiscent of both Rastafarianism and the Muslim Baye Fall. One of

Adama's closest followers and companions told me the Arabs have their prophet (presumably Muhammad) and so do the whites (presumably Jesus Christ). To his followers, Adama is the prophet for black people. I have been unable to ascertain how widely such views are shared or even understood, but most Malian Muslims find this completely heterodox, given that most Muslims maintain that the Prophet Muhammad was the last and final prophet.

Adama's so-called mission centres around a few basic elements, which he states in some of his public pronouncements and more privately to some of his followers. First, he emphasizes a strict moral code of conduct, inveighing against stealing, dishonesty and illicit sexual relations. In this way Adama's discourse is similar to that of some earlier new religious movements among non-Muslims elsewhere in Africa (see Jules-Rosette, 1979 and Hackett, 1986). It also resembles the moralizing discourse of some Malian Muslim preachers who talk frequently about moral decline and the general state of permissiveness in the present era (see Soares, 2006). Second, Adama urges people to unite. While Bilal calls for the unity of all Muslims and members of different Sufi orders and their branches, Adama calls for the unity of all people – Muslims, Christians and other non-Muslims. Here he seems to advocate a rather innovative religious synthesis. To the best of my knowledge, in his call for unity Adama goes much further than other Muslims involved in religious movements elsewhere in Africa.

Adama sports dreadlocks like some of the other new Sufis such as Bilal, although Adama's dreadlocks are very long and matted and appear to have taken several years to grow. Many Malians see that this places Adama in the same generation as some of his contemporaries like Bilal, who have adopted some of the trappings of urban youth culture. Like many members of Sufi orders in Mali, Adama also wears prayer beads around his neck. Unlike most Sufis, Adama attaches a large silver Christian cross to his prayer beads, although the cross is inscribed with the Prophet Muhammad's name in Arabic. On public occasions, Adama's younger brothers often wear large white mitres, the liturgical headdress worn by high-ranking Catholic clergy. The mitres have inscriptions in Arabic about God, the Prophet Muhammad and the *shahada* (the Muslim profession of faith). Some of Adama's followers carry small portable Christian crosses painted red, yellow and green, the colours of the Malian flag and also associated with Rastafarianism and pan-Africanism. These colourful Christian crosses also have the *shahada* painted on them.

Adama is not simply trying to synthesize Islam and Christianity, as the use of the Christian cross and the Catholic headdress might suggest. In fact, unlike many Malian Muslims who warn of the dangers of paganism, animism, and polytheism, Adama actively incorporates various allegedly un-Islamic symbols and elements into his own ritual objects and public persona. He usually wears what Malians recognize as Muslim garb, but regularly carries a long wooden staff with equally recognizable Dogon 'pagan' iconography. Most notably, the *kanaga*, the most well-known Dogon mask, a symbol the Malian government has used to promote the country's culture and heritage, appears in miniature form in silver on the tip of his wooden staff. This Dogon 'pagan' symbol is superimposed with the Christian cross and Islamic inscriptions in Arabic. Adama carries such a staff with him whenever he travels or goes on visits into town. He has told me that such Dogon iconography is very important to him and his identity as a person. However, it is less clear how important this iconography is to his very diverse followers, who come from all sectors of society and from various ethnic and linguistic groups in the country.

As well as using such 'pagan' signs, Adama has openly made overtures towards non-Muslims and non-Muslim ritual specialists in particular, including 'traditional' healers, diviners, and sorcerers who promise their clients good health, progeny, wealth and success. Adama is associated publicly with one of the most prominent of these Bamako-based non-Muslim ritual specialists, Daouda Yattara a.k.a. Satan, who has drawn much media attention over the past few years.[14] In fact, Adama and Daouda are friends, and regularly spend time together at each other's homes in Bamako. On one occasion, I saw them at Daouda's house and the two of them posed together for a photograph with an un-Islamic ritual object,[15] precisely the kind that many Muslim religious leaders in Mali have encouraged or forced people to abandon.

At midday on Fridays, hundreds of people, mostly women, travel to Adama's home to pray with him in the mosque he has built near the spirits' abode. Many who come have heard about Adama's reputation for miracles. They hope to receive Adama's blessings and frequently bring him gifts of money. Some attending might record the songs of praise of the Prophet Muhammad that Adama's followers sing and make the recordings available for airing on local radio programmes. Before and after the canonical Friday midday prayers, vendors work the crowds selling photographs of Adama including some of him posing with famous guests like Daouda Yattara, or buttons with Adama's name and photograph, sometimes side-by-side with Sékou Salah Siby's photograph.

On other days in the week, there is a steady stream of visitors who come as individuals or in groups. I have met among them students, school teachers, employees of various government ministries, people working in development assistance, market vendors, and unemployed youth. Once I saw an entire amateur football team who had come as a group to receive Adama's blessings before one of their matches. Sometimes there are also very high-profile visitors to Adama's home. On one Friday the former Malian President Moussa Traoré (1968-91), who was released from prison in 2002, went to meet Adama and the two posed together for photographs. One evening at

Adama's, I encountered a famous Malian pop star, ostensibly looking for blessings on the eve of her latest European tour.

In the years since President Traoré lost power, the subsequent governments in Mali have been relatively more secular in orientation. Some of Mali's non-Muslims (who are not Christians) have noted that this has allowed them the space to engage in their 'religious' practices more freely and openly than in the past. In fact, non-Muslim religious specialists like Daouda Yattara have an increasingly high profile in the public sphere and engage in their own forms of religious marketing, using print and audiovisual media to considerable effect. Some of these non-Muslim religious specialists welcome recent Malian government policies to promote Mali's cultural heritage and 'traditions', which include certain traditions that most Muslims condemn as un-Islamic. In early 2001, the government sponsored a major gathering of 'traditional' non-Muslim hunters and even erected a statue in honour of the hunters' 'pagan' deities in central Bamako. Many Malian Muslims and reformist Muslims in particular have been very critical of the government's new public association with the un-Islamic. But such open association with the un-Islamic seems to have helped make what Adama is promoting less unthinkable than in the recent past.

Certain forms of religious synthesis are known of in this region prior to colonial rule (see Soares, 1999) and during colonial rule, particularly in rural areas (e.g., Cardaire, 1954; Royer, 1999; Mann, 2003). Yet the urban-based synthesis that Adama seems to be advocating is a new phenomenon. Indeed, many Malians claim that they have never seen someone try to synthesize different religious traditions with any measure of success in urban Mali. As many remark, before the period of liberalization Mali's Muslim religious leaders could restrain religious entrepreneurs like Adama whose practices they found unacceptable.

Over the past few years, Adama and his activities have generated enormous public attention and discussion. It is not at all surprising that Adama and his followers with their crosses, Catholic headdresses, and pagan symbols have drawn criticism in Mali. I have heard both Malian Muslims and Christians say that they are perplexed or uneasy by his provocative use of symbols from different religions and his apparent attempt to mix Islam with Christianity. Some of these people claim they are offended and repulsed when they learn of the possible addition of African 'traditions' and Adama's close association with the self-styled Satan. Many claim that Adama and those around him are wrong in mixing Islam with Christianity, 'animism' and talk of prophecy. While some Muslims have told me it is the duty of Adama's fellow Muslims to show him the error of his ways, others say wistfully that this can only end badly. There have been no reports of violence against Adama and his followers, but conflicts between Muslims and non-Muslims over such matters have a long history in this region of West Africa.

Conclusion

In this chapter I have suggested that the present age of economic and political liberalization has led to an opening of the religious market in Mali and facilitated shifts in the country's religious economy. The newly liberalized environment has enabled the activities of new kinds of religious entrepreneurs and new kinds of Sufis in particular. The new Sufis who I have considered here help to illustrate some of the changing ways of being Muslim in Mali. In making claims to religious authority, both of the two new Sufis seem to be acting as individuals and not as part of the established Sufi orders that have been important in Mali. The Muslim women and youth of Mali have been significant in this development, sometimes as the key actors and constituents in making the careers of these new Sufis. Moreover, the print and audiovisual media have been important in helping to spread the reputations, messages, and fame of the new Sufis.

Neither of these youthful Sufis makes political pronouncements or intervenes in politics. However, the activities of both have come under increased scrutiny, not least because of the ways they depart from their predecessors. If certain Malian Muslims assert that Bilal is just another person involved in Mali's burgeoning fee-for-service religious market, his many followers, clients, and the public reading his books suggest he cannot be dismissed so easily. Adama, who so clearly and unambiguously acts contrary to received ideas about religion of most Malian Muslims and even of Christians, has attracted even more followers than Bilal. What kinds of challenges Adama might encounter from his many critics is an open question, but these challenges would seem to be almost inevitable in the context of a more liberalized religious economy in Mali.

Acknowledgement

I am grateful to Rosalind Hackett, Julia Howell, Rüdiger Seesemann, and Martin van Bruinessen for comments on earlier drafts. As always, I am most indebted to my Malian friends and informants, who have helped with this material and analysis of it.

6

SAINTS, POLITICIANS AND SUFI BUREAUCRATS: MYSTICISM AND POLITICS IN INDONESIA'S NEW ORDER

Martin van Bruinessen

Indonesia's New Order, roughly coinciding with the years of Suharto's rule, 1966-98, can be seen in retrospect as a period in which orthodox Islam gradually replaced syncretistic religiosity. The architects of the New Order made concerted efforts to weaken the political muscle of Islam (and they were largely successful in doing so) but at the same time endorsed the dissemination of Muslim personal piety. The period witnessed considerable change in the sociological landscape of Indonesian Islam, the most visible aspect of which was perhaps the emergence of a relatively affluent, self-consciously Muslim, urban middle class. The eclectic fascination with the spirit world and with techniques of harnessing it in the pursuit of supernatural power, which hitherto had been part of the habitus of the elite, gradually faded into the background. *Shari`a*-oriented Sufism experienced a noticeable upsurge in popularity, at first among the rural population where Sufi shaykhs became influential and politically powerful figures, then later also among various urban classes. The informal structure of Sufi orders, based on loyalty between teacher and disciple, came to be supplemented by more formal associations led by committees elected by and answerable to national congresses. The process of gradual rationalization and bureaucratization of Sufism was not without its conflicts between the charismatic saint and the bureaucrat.

New Order Modernization and Religious Change

Sociological research of the 1950s pointed out the existence of two distinct patterns of belief and ritual among the nominally Muslim population of Java. These became widely referred to as *santri* and *abangan*, the terms chosen by an American research team to describe these patterns. (Jay, 1957; Geertz, 1960). The *santri* were the more or less *shari`a*-obeying stricter Muslims, who prayed regularly, fasted during Ramadan, and hoped to save enough money to perform the *hajj* at least once in their lives; the *abangan* held syncretistic beliefs and carried out various other rituals, many in the form of a *slametan* – an offering to the spirits and communal meal. Although Geertz rightly observed that one and the same person might act as *santri* on some occasions and as *abangan* on others, most later authors used these terms as referring to distinct social categories, roughly the constituencies of the Muslim political parties, Masyumi and NU (Nahdlatul Ulama, 'Awakening of the Scholars') on the one hand, and the Communist and Nationalist Parties on the other. By this rough indicator, less than half of Indonesia's Muslims were actually *santri* at the time of the first general elections in 1955.

Many *abangan* beliefs and rituals were associated with the life world of the peasantry, the hazards of the agricultural cycle, and local or ancestral spirits. There were also urban and elite varieties of this syncretistic culture (for which Geertz used the term *priyayi*). The term *santri* in the strict sense referred to students of the *pesantren* – Islamic boarding schools – and most of these *santri* had rural backgrounds. Their religious training consisted mostly of the study of Arabic *fiqh* books and inculcating respect for *ulama* of the past. As well as canonical obligations, common *santri* religious practices included grave visiting (*ziyara*) and recitation of sacred texts to ward off danger or call for supernatural support.

Urban pious Muslims tended to be influenced by modernist or reformist thought and to reject many of the traditional practices of the rural *santri* and the *abangan*. The most important reformist association, Muhammadiyah, established in 1912, had always been urban in character, and its activities focussed on education and social welfare. It established numerous modern schools, modelled on mission schools rather than on pesantren or madrasa, and engaged in charitable work besides *da`wa* (spreading the message of Islam). Much of the teaching and preaching in which Muhammadiyah engaged was concerned with purifying the faith and combating syncretistic practices, including traditional *santri* devotional practices. The NU had been established in 1926 as an association for defending traditional *santri* practices and the interests of traditional scholars against the reformist onslaught. After Indonesia gained Independence in 1945, the NU became a political party and Muhammadiyah became a major component of the other major Muslim political party, Masyumi. Political struggles and rivalries at the centre often exacerbated religious contradictions and tensions at the local level. There were heated debates between reformists and traditional *santri*, and between *santri* and *abangan*. Some of the *abangan* movements adopted a stridently anti-Islamic tone, and the balance of power in the 1950s gave little reason to predict that *santri* Islam was to prevail so soon.[1]

The physical elimination of the Communist Party and its rural followers in 1965-66 and the enforced depoliticization of society under the New Order dramatically reduced the intensity of religious debates and conflicts. Many rural *abangan*, to avoid being taken for communists, asserted their formal adherence to one of the officially recognized religions (i.e., Islam, Christianity, Hinduism or Buddhism), even though they did not at once give up their old beliefs and dispositions. Suharto and several of his closest collaborators adhered to elite varieties of the *abangan* worldview and were themselves extremely suspicious of political Islam.[2]

During the New Order's first decades, *santri* Muslims remained seriously underrepresented in the military, administrative, political, business and cultural elite. But a gradual Islamicization from below set in, in spite of the regime's distrust of Muslim political aspirations. Increasing numbers of students of *santri* family background took up places in the various institutions and moved upward into positions previously held by the older 'secular' elites. Intensive *da`wa* activities were successful in spreading more orthodox Islamic ideas and practices to previously *abangan* circles. Increased geographical mobility marginalized local cults and village-based rituals and strengthened the shift from *abangan* to *santri* orientation. The 'Islamic turn' in Suharto's policies around 1990, when he allied himself with the new Muslim middle class and made a number of important symbolic pro-Islamic gestures, confirmed the religious changes in society at large that had empowered many previously marginalized actors of *santri* background. Sufi orders have played a major role in the shift from *abangan* to *santri* type religious orientations. The following sections trace the development of Sufi orders and their role in this process of further Islamicizing Indonesian society.

Sufi Teachers, Sufi Devotions and Sufi Orders

Sufi orders as actual associations of devotees are a relatively recent phenomenon in Indonesia.[3] In the earliest extant texts, which date from the late sixteenth century, we find (diluted) influences of the metaphysical Sufism of Ibn Arabi and al-Jili as well as Ghazali's Sufi ethics, but no references to specific orders. The great Indonesian Sufi authors flourished in the seventeenth and eighteenth centuries. They had been initiated into one or more Sufi orders (*tarekat*; Ar. *tariqa*) during long sojourns in Arabia and they taught the doctrines and exercises of these orders to selected students, but these do not appear to have been organized into orders strictly speaking. Sufi ideas, notably those of the world as an emanation from God and of the parallelism of microcosm (the human body) and macrocosm, were easily assimilated to pre-existing systems of classification and magical control of the world. Sufi exercises – recitations, breathing techniques, methods of meditation and contemplation – were added to an already vast repertoire of techniques for acquiring spiritual power, martial prowess and invulnerability. In various later '*abangan*' mystical movements, including some overtly anti-Muslim ones, we may recognize traces of Sufi ideas. Especially the Shattariyya, which always adapted easily to local cultural traditions, made an impact on Indonesian indigenous mystical and magical movements. However ideas and techniques introduced by other orders too have been adopted into syncretistic formations.[4]

In the final decades of the nineteenth century and the first half of the twentieth, a period about which we have relatively rich information, there were all over the Indies local teachers of spiritual doctrines and techniques for acquiring supernatural powers and knowledge, surrounded by groups of disciples and followers. Only a minority of them – often the relatively well-to-do, who could afford to make the pilgrimage to Mecca – were affiliated with one of the great international Sufi orders. Most had compiled their own eclectic mixture of spiritual techniques and metaphysical speculation from a variety of sources including visions and inspirations induced by fasting and other forms of self-mortification, meditation and wakes in spirit-haunted forests or caves, on mountain tops or holy graves. Some claimed royal or noble descent or had a degree of formal Islamic learning, qualities that propped up their charisma. Others were of peasant background and catered primarily to the needs of peasant followings, as healers, magicians and shamans. In terms of religious orientation, they covered the entire range from strict *santri* to teachings without any noticeable Islamic influence. They all drew selectively on a common stock of mystical ideas and techniques that was increasingly enriched by Sufi influences but in which Indic and indigenous elements remained strongly present. A frequently recurring element in the teachings was the messianic expectation of a just ruler, the Ratu Adil. In many cases, the teacher was simply an individual and his teachings vanished with his decline or death. Other teachers handed down teachings that survived them; often these were local adaptations of an existing Sufi order or they constituted a new, local variety of Sufi order.[5]

The affiliation of a teacher with one of the large international orders was generally conducive to a broader geographical orientation: most of these teachers had travelled widely and were at the centre of a network of *khalifa* (deputies) and *khalifa* of *khalifa* that could stretch over a wide region. These networks also had greater stability over time than those of most local teachers, because of a degree of institutionalization and more or less agreed succession rules. The networks' larger size and (where they existed) continuing contacts with centres of learning abroad also made for greater stability of doctrine and praxis, preventing lapses into heterodoxy.

This period also saw the rapid expansion of the number of pesantren, the Javanese variety of the madrasa.[6] Besides the basic doctrines and rituals of Islam, two types of subjects were taught in these schools: *kitab*, i.e. written texts, mostly *fiqh*, and *kanuragan*, the magical skills used in martial arts.[7] The education of a pesantren teacher or *kiai* usually took him from pesantren to pesantren to study the specific *kitab* or other subjects for which each was renowned. Ideally he completed his education with a few years study in Mecca before starting to teach, and thus would have acquired a broader mental horizon than most villagers living around the pesantren. Like the Sufi teachers of the large orders, such *kiai* had networks of contacts in many different parts of the country and comprising members of different social classes. (Virtually all Sufi shaykhs in this period were also *kiai* and headed some sort of pesantren; the Sufi orders expanded only the range of their social networks and the extent of their influence.) It is not surprising that we find many of these shaykhs and *kiai* in contact with, or even actively involved in, the first Indonesian nationalist activities and later as active members of social and political associations, where their *tarekat* following was considered as an asset.

Sufi Orders and Modern Civic Associations
A Sufi order is, in a sense, a voluntary association that members join for purposes related to a conception of the common good. The degree to which the followers of a shaykh actually perceive themselves as a community and act as such varies, as does the degree to which they admit common objectives beyond the performance of ritual. Among those who regularly take part in collective rituals, affiliation with the order generates social trust and often a degree of mutual support. For this reason, some observers would see Sufi orders as the seeds of civil society and of an incipient public sphere. The essentially charismatic and authoritarian character of leadership in the orders makes them different from modern civic associations with elected and representative leadership, but the twentieth century brought about various forms of accommodation between these two types of organization. Sufi orders have been incorporated in various ways in formal associations that were established and run in accordance with Dutch (and later Indonesian) law on associations.

Indonesia's first modern nationalist organization with a mass following, Sarekat Islam or SI ('Islamic Association', established in 1912), was a surprising phenomenon that appeared to break rapidly through established social patterns. The enthusiasm it aroused and the pace of its growth were truly amazing. It successfully brought together indigenous Indonesians of all walks of life: from members of the traditional aristocracy to peasants, from graduates of Dutch schools and pesantren to illiterates, *abangan* as well as *santri*, Javanese as well as other ethnic groups. Established by western-educated urban intellectuals and traders as a movement for emancipation of the indigenous population, it drew, to its leaders' surprise, a large rural following that perceived a fulfilment of millenarian expectations in the new movement. The SI leader Tjokroaminoto was, to his embarrassment, hailed as the expected just ruler, Ratu Adil; huge masses flocked to the meetings where he spoke to receive the blessing emanating from his presence. Other SI leaders were similarly welcomed as heralds of the millennium, and all over the country there were rumours of impending revolutionary change.[8]

The SI leaders rejected the mass enthusiasm as irrational and made efforts to contain it by imposing strict discipline and the trappings of modern formal organization. The central committee established regional branches all over the country; annual congresses were convened at which the official representatives of these branches discussed matters of common concern and decided on policy. Within a few years, the SI had branches in almost every district town, each with its local committee and by-laws registered by the colonial administration. The growth was spectacular, and largely spontaneous. The largest categories of members were traders and lower-level civil servants, but almost 10 per cent of the branch committee members were religious teachers and officials.[9] In several branches, a Sufi shaykh dominated the local committee and the following of the *tarekat* and the membership of the Sarekat appeared to overlap considerably. There were repeated conflicts between the SI central committee and these local branches: clashes between different types of leadership and authority. In other places, there was fierce competition between the Sarekat Islam and a Sufi order that represented rival elite families, each with their networks of patronage. In at least one region, tensions between relatively 'orthodox' Muslims and adherents of local syncretistic cults caused the latter to respond to the Sarekat Islam by organizing a competing association that they called Sarekat Abang ('Red Association').[10] This was one of the first instances where syncretists rallied together and organized a common defence against the perceived threat of orthodox Islam. Many more instances followed.

Organized Syncretism: *Kebatinan* Movements and Local *Tarekat*

The twentieth century saw the emergence of numerous syncretistic mystical movements. In earlier times, the following of a spiritual teacher would dissipate after his death. Other teachers might emerge who passed on (part of) his teaching, recombined with other teachings, and some of the old master's disciples might move on to one of these successors. Only in the Sufi orders was there continuity in organization. In the early twentieth century, however, organized movements emerged around some of the more influential syncretistic mystics, and these survived the original teacher as self-perpetuating associations with more or less formalized doctrines and rituals. Most of these movements – known as *kebatinan* ('esotericism') movements – were directly or indirectly influenced by Sufi doctrines and methods, and most presented themselves as spiritual alternatives to excessively *shari`a*-oriented, exoteric versions of Islam; the movement studied by Howell (1976) constitutes a particularly clear example. Another significant influence on at least some of these *kebatinan* movements was from Freemasonry and the Theosophical Movement, the first European associations that admitted highly educated indigenous (and Chinese) Indonesians as equal members.

Some *kebatinan* movements had an aristocratic following and espoused sophisticated metaphysical doctrines and meditation methods; others catered primarily to peasant audiences and taught a variety of cosmological classification systems and methods for communicating with or controlling the spirit world. Meditation was not so much intended to lead to illumination but was a means to acquire spiritual power (*kasektèn*), the quest for which was central to both aristocratic and peasant movements.

Freemasonry and Theosophy may have provided a model of organization for some of the 'aristocratic' movements, and Sufi orders a model for other movements. Yet the experience of nationalist politics in colonial times and political party struggles after independence also had an impact on the structure of the movements. Several adopted a formal structure much like other formal associations, with a class of administrators assisting and managing the spiritual teachers. *Kebatinan* was not necessarily an other-worldly mysticism; the spiritual powers that were sought could be put to very this-worldly uses, and some *kebatinan* movements were involved in radical politics. One of the more respectable movements of the New Order period, Sumarah, provided young fighters in the independence struggle with magical prowess and invulnerability (Stange, 1980). In the years of political polarization, the 1950s and early 1960s, many *kebatinan* movements directly opposed the Muslim parties and were allied with the left. One of the most openly anti-Islamic *kebatinan* movements of that period, Permai, was led by a leftist labour organizer who structured it much like a political party.[11] During the New Order, some of the *kebatinan* movements, especially the non-elite kind, aroused the suspicions of the Suharto regime because of their earlier association with *abangan* and left-wing politics.

Besides the kebatinan movements, there were also various new mystical movements that defined themselves as Muslim and Sufi but were regarded as heterodox by established Sufi orders and even more so by Muslim reformists. Such local *tarekat* straddled the boundary between *santri* and *abangan*, drawing followers from both. The two best known of these local *tarekat*, the Wahidiyya and the Siddiqiyya, were founded by East Javanese *kiai* and at their centre are pesantren in which some bookish knowledge is also taught (Abdurrahman, 1978; Effendi, 1990b). Both *kiai* had reputations as successful healers, which was probably the chief factor increasing their following. The devotions of these *tarekat* were not different from the devotions of the established, 'orthodox' Sufi orders. (In the case of the Wahidiyya, for instance, the chief devotion consists of the congregation reciting a long prayer composed by – or, as the followers believe, revealed to – the founder, in the course of which all participants burst out crying.) The absence of an authenticated spiritual genealogy and the founders' leniency towards their followers' poor conformity with the *shari`a* drew to these movements the stigma of heterodoxy. Both orders allegedly had many *abangan* adherents, and in the days of mass killings of communists, many more *abangan* were said to have flocked to these teachers and sent their children to these pesantren. Although these orders appear to have played a role in the gradual further Islamicization of the countryside, they were often treated with suspicion by orthodox Muslims for their rumoured harbouring of former 'communists'.[12]

Tarekat into Political Party: Perti and PPTI

Sufi teachers became actively involved in the two major traditionalist Muslim associations that emerged in the second quarter of the twentieth century, the aforementioned Nahdlatul Ulama in East Java (1926) and Persatuan Tarbiyah Islamiyah or Perti ('Union for Islamic Education') in West Sumatra (1930). (Both became political parties after Indonesia's independence and gradually expanded over all of Indonesia but were to remain dominated by the Javanese and Minangkabau ethnic groups respectively.) For most of the ulama who founded the NU, Sufi devotional practices were an integral part of their religiosity but few of them appear to have been actual *tarekat* teachers. The Sufi orders became more prominent within the NU after Indonesia's independence, when electoral politics strengthened the position of ulama who could mobilize many votes. In the case of Perti, Naqshbandi shaykhs were prominent from the very beginning – which is not surprising, for the order had a very strong presence in West Sumatra. The association consisted of two major factions, one basically a network of Naqshbandi teachers. The expansion of Perti into other parts of Sumatra went hand in hand with expansion of the Naqshbandiyya, for the *khalifa* of this network also became Perti activists. Ethnic and family networks provided a solid core for both the *tarekat* and the party.[13]

A conflict between the senior Naqshbandi teachers in West Sumatra and an ambitious colleague, Haji Jalaluddin, gave rise to the emergence of a rival party to Perti. Haji Jalaluddin was a Dutch-trained schoolteacher without formal Islamic education, but he wrote some popular books that gave a very clear didactic exposition of Naqshbandi spiritual techniques. The most prominent Naqshbandi teacher in Perti accused Jalaluddin of misrepresenting certain teachings and introducing unacceptable innovations, and ordered him to withdraw and correct these books. Jalaluddin refused to comply and instead established his own association, which after national independence he called Partai Politik Tarekat Islam or PPTI.[14] Haji Jalaluddin, politically astute and a gifted pamphlettist and organizer, succeeded in drawing many of the Minangkabau Naqshbandi shaykhs to his organization. When the PPTI fared well in the 1955 elections – in some Sumatran districts it won as much as 10 per cent of the vote – Haji Jalaluddin became a man of influence in Jakarta. Perceived to be close to President Sukarno, he persuaded influential shaykhs of various *tarekat* throughout the country to lend their names to the PPTI by formally joining its 'Council of Spiritual Guides' (*Dewan Mursyidin*). In Sukarno's experiment with corporatist representation to replace the party system (Reeve, 1985), Jalaluddin managed to insert his PPTI into the Golkar ('functional group') structure as the sole body representing the 'functional group' of *tarekat* followers. Throughout the New Order period, when Golkar functioned as the government party, the PPTI was to remain the only association of *tarekat* that enjoyed government recognition and the facilities that came with it.

The PPTI exemplified the problems inherent in incorporating Sufi orders into formal organizations and the incompatibility between charisma and bureaucratic rules. Like the NU and several other associations, it had a dual leadership: the *Dewan Mursyidin* consisted of senior *tarekat* shaykhs and formally constituted the highest authority, but the executive committee actually ran the organization and took most decisions. Until 1975, Haji Jalaluddin was both president of the *Dewan Mursyidin* and chairman of the executive, and it was obvious that the other shaykhs had little effective influence. Many of the organization's active members believed that matters of organization and spiritual authority should be separated more strictly than they were, and that year the PPTI congress re-elected the nonagenarian Jalaluddin as the president of the *Dewan Mursyidin* but chose one of his collaborators, Sutan Amiruddin, as the new chairman. Jalaluddin had not attended the congress due to poor health and was furious at what he perceived as rebellion. He expelled Amiruddin and his allies from the organization and ordered loyalists to organize another congress. Jalaluddin died before this congress was over, and two of his most loyal followers were chosen to head the *Dewan Mursyidin* and the executive.

Henceforth there were two rival PPTIs, led by Amiruddin and Djumingan Afiat, respectively. Neither managed to keep the support of all the senior shaykhs who had given their names to the *Dewan Mursyidin* of Jalaluddin's days, but Djumingan's PPTI had the considerable benefit of official recognition by Golkar, making it attractive to local teachers in search of government patronage. The ranks of its members were strengthened by civil servants. Lacking major charismatic shaykhs, however, it gradually turned into an organization of Sufi bureaucrats, a formal association that had no purpose other than its own continued existence.[15]

Nahdlatul Ulama, the 'Orthodox' Orders, and Golkar

As remarked above, Sufi teachers had been members of Indonesia's largest traditionalist association, Nahdlatul Ulama, since its inception, but they had not been among its foremost leaders. In fact, the organization's highest religious authority, Hasjim Asj'ari, had banned *tarekat* activities from his own pesantren, at Tebuireng near Jombang, which concentrated exclusively on textual studies. (Later, in the 1970s and 1980s, we find several of the teachers at Tebuireng involved in *tarekat*, but they did their *tarekat* teaching elsewhere.) Four large pesantren in Jombang district, where most of the other prominent *kiai* had studied, constituted for a long time the most prestigious centre of the NU. Only one of them, at Rejoso, was a '*pesantren tarekat*', where the leading *kiai* was also a teacher of the Qadiriyya wa-Naqshbandiyya. It is perhaps significant that after Hasjim Asj'ari's death, supreme leadership of the NU passed in succession to the *kiai* of two other Jombang pesantren but none of the Rejoso *kiai* was ever considered for this position. *Kiai tarekat* enjoyed a lower prestige in NU circles than the scriptural specialists, *kiai kitab*, but they usually had a much larger following among the peasantry and after national independence they were often patronized by military and civilian officials.

Many of the older pesantren were, according to oral tradition, originally *pesantren tarekat* until a reformist *kiai* turned them into centres of *fiqh* and other textual studies. The term 'pesantren tarekat' did not necessarily indicate the presence of one of the great Sufi orders but denoted more generally that the *kiai* specialized in *kanuragan* and other forms of magic. In some, the *kanuragan* practices disappeared completely; in others they persisted alongside *kitab* studies, to resurface very prominently in times of crisis such as the independence struggle, the mass killings of 1965-66 and, most recently, the final months of Abdurrahman Wahid's presidency in 2001.[16] Sufi orders occasionally caused some controversy and debate in NU when the orthodoxy of a specific *tarekat*'s teachings was questioned, as happened in the case of the Tijaniyya in the late 1920s and early 1930s (van Bruinessen, 1999: 720-22), but the organization managed to contain such conflicts and maintain tolerance of a wide range of Sufi beliefs and practices. Nevertheless, some of the local orders that emerged in the second half of the twentieth century, such as the Wahidiyya and Siddiqiyya and some Javanese Shattariyya branches, were not accepted in NU because their devotions were invented by their founders and so could not claim a genealogy going back to the Prophet.

From the 1970s or perhaps a little earlier, Sufi orders assumed a more prominent presence in the NU. A number of Sufi teachers, who had been meeting since the late 1950s to discuss matters of common interest, established an association of 'orthodox' orders, the Jam'iyyah Ahlith Thoriqah Mu'tabaroh (*jam`iyyat ahl al-tariqa al-mu`tabara*). Their use of the term *mu`tabar*, 'respectable', indicates their desire to distinguish their 'orthodox' Sufism from the mysticism of both the *kebatinan* movements and the local *tarekat*, which had been the targets of increasing criticism from reformist and conservative traditionalist Muslim circles.[17] The *kebatinan* movements had been striving for recognition on a par with religion and were perceived to have strong political support under Sukarno and in the early Suharto years (see Howell's chapter in this volume), and some *kebatinan* movements (especially the most *abangan* ones) and local *tarekat* were stigmatized because of their alleged association with communism.[18] The founders of the Jam'iyyah apparently sought to be *mu`tabar* in the eyes of *shari`a*-oriented Muslims as well as those of government authorities.[19]

The driving force behind the Jam'iyyah was Kiai Musta'in Romly, who in 1960 succeeded his father as the *kiai* of Rejoso and shaykh of the Qadiriyya wa-Naqshbandiyya. He inherited a vast network of local branches of the order, covering a large part of East Java.[20] He cultivated excellent relations with the local government (and with the Chinese business community), which helped him to attract even more followers; by the late 1970s the number of his disciples in the various branches of the *tarekat* all over East Java reportedly reached 150,000. This made him a person to be reckoned with even by the central government. In 1975, Kiai Musta'in organized the first large congress of the Jam'iyyah, bringing together *tarekat* teachers from all over Java.[21] The congress was opened by President Suharto and many other high officials were present, an indication of the importance then attached to the Sufi orders. In his own opening speech, Kiai Musta'in stressed the role Sufism had to play in the New Order's development effort, for material development had to be balanced by spiritual growth. He spoke of a widespread misunderstanding that *tarekat* are just an attribute of traditional or rural societies, claiming that in truth the *tarekat* is of much more universal value and helps in personality building by strengthening one's morality and belief in God. As he put it, *tarekat* teachings should be directed not just to certain social classes but to all, and especially to those groups most directly involved in the development effort, who need a strong moral grounding.

Kiai Musta'in thus presented the Jam'iyyah as a vehicle through which, on the one hand, the government could reach out to the peasant masses and involve them in Development (*pembangunan*, the catchword summing up New Order policies) and through which, on the other hand, the Sufi teachers could take part in the modernizing project and recruit bureaucrats, technicians and professionals as disciples. And, for whatever personal or pragmatic reasons, increasing numbers of officials did seek out Kiai Musta'in and other Sufi shaykhs as spiritual advisers. Mutually profitable relations of patronage developed.

However Kiai Musta'in went further in accommodating the government than his colleagues in NU found acceptable. In 1971 the NU had contested the first elections in the New Order as the only significant opposition to the government's Golkar and was at the receiving end of heavy-handed disciplining efforts and pressure on NU members to vote for Golkar. In 1974 it was forced to merge with other Muslim parties into the United Development Party (PPP), one of the two remaining non-government parties (the other, PDI, was a conglomerate of nationalist and Christian parties). But towards the following elections in 1977, while the leading *kiai* of NU issued fatwas declaring it a religious obligation to vote for PPP, Kiai Musta'in actively campaigned on behalf of Golkar. His reasons for this apparent disloyalty towards the NU were very transparent: it was public knowledge that he had received lavish government patronage since the late 1960s, including the grant of a large tract of land on which he built a private university. His pesantren and the university prospered as showcases of Development, whereas most other pesantren suffered permanent financial shortages and faced bureaucratic obstruction. Moreover, he probably genuinely believed that Development was beneficial and that he could make an impact on the direction it would take.[22]

The NU *kiai* decided to punish Musta'in for his treason and to persuade his disciples to leave him. The initiative for this spectacular action came from *kiai* and politicians at Tebuireng (there was definitely an element of interpesantren rivalry as well) but it received broad support. One of the Tebuireng teachers, Adlan Aly, who had been a disciple of Musta'in's father and was a member of the Jam'iyyah's ulama council, was put forward as the spiritual guide who would not sell out to the government and deserved to take Kiai Musta'in's place. The leading Central Javanese shaykh of the Qadiriyya wa-Naqshbandiyya, Kiai Muslich of Mranggen, who was the most prominent shaykh in the Jam'iyyah's ulama council, was persuaded to appoint Kiai Adlan Aly as his *khalifa* with full authority for East Java. One by one, Kiai Musta'in's local deputies were canvassed and persuaded to transfer their allegiance to Kiai Adlan. The vast majority deserted and if not to Kiai Adlan, they turned to Kiai Usman al-Ishaqi in Surabaya, who was Musta'in's father's chief *khalifa*. Musta'in lost control of most of his *tarekat* network, thereby decreasing his usefulness to the government.[23]

At the subsequent NU congress in 1979, a new *tarekat* association was inaugurated that was more explicitly affiliated with the Nahdlatul Ulama, the Jam'iyyah Ahlith Thoriqah al-Mu`tabaroh *al-Nahdliyyah* (JATMN). Many of its board members had been on the board of Musta'in's Jam'iyyah and were seconded by some prominent and well-connected NU politicians, including the long-time NU chairman who was past master of patronage politics and political intrigue, Idham Chalid. Well before the 1982 general elections, the *tarekat* networks had been harnessed to grabbing a large percentage of the rural vote for PPP. Musta'in meanwhile continued as the chairman of his own Jam'iyyah (which came to be named JATMI, the final I standing for 'Indonesia') as if nothing serious had changed. He replaced the board members who deserted him with a few men who were personally loyal to him and in 1982 again campaigned for Golkar. After Musta'in's death in 1984, JATMI continued its activities – Rejoso alone could still boast 20,000 disciples, and there were many more in other parts of East Java – but it lacked a charismatic leader. Musta'in's widow, who was its major strategist, made efforts to have JATMI recognized as an official component of Golkar, which might have strengthened JATMI. But Golkar already had its official *tarekat* representation in PPTI, and JATMI never gained the same degree of endorsement from the government.

The conflicts around the Jam'iyyah point to the increasing political significance of the Sufi orders, with elections held at five-year intervals from 1977. Electoral politics raised the importance of anyone who could deliver a significant number of votes, and *tarekat kiai* controlled the largest and most obedient followings. It was not accidental that the *kiai* who worked hardest to organize JATMN and to weaken Musta'in's authority were among the most politically astute *kiai* in NU. Kiai Adlan Aly was a simple, quiet man with a reputation for self-effacing piety, but his two colleagues at Tebuireng who did much of the organizing and propaganda work, *kiai*s Syansuri Badawi and Makky Makshum, were primarily *fiqh* teachers with strong political instincts and a firm loyalty to PPP. The *tarekat kiai* who became most active in the association in the following years, representing several other large orders, notably the Tijaniyya and Naqshbandiyya Khalidiyya, also tended to be staunch PPP supporters (and were courted by the PPP political leadership).

Tarekat and the Ongoing Islamicization of Indonesian Society
At the 1984 NU congress, it was decided that NU would no longer participate directly in politics and henceforth would be only a social and religious association. It would not endorse any particular party (in other words, it broke with PPP) and left its members free to join the party of their choice (in order words, to seek patronage from Golkar).[24] The *kiai* who offered the fiercest opposition to these decisions were those who had fought Kiai Musta'in; the JATMN remained the only NU-affiliated association that maintained a close connection with PPP. The 1984 congress elected Abdurrahman Wahid as the new NU chairman, a position he would hold for the next 15 years. Defeated at this congress, the previous chairman, Idham Chalid, thereafter used his position in JATMN as the basis from which to maintain both an influence in NU affairs at the top and a link to the grassroots of the organization.

During the following decade and a half, Sufi orders were increasingly prominent both within NU and in the Indonesian public sphere in general. Rural *tarekat* networks expanded and several *tarekat kiai* became well-known personalities nationwide due to the large numbers of their rural followers and their contacts with members of the elite. Several *kiai* who had until then taught only *fiqh* and other bookish subjects, sought an *ijaza* (formal permission) to teach a *tarekat* to strengthen links with their rural constituencies. Most of the leading *kiai* in JATMN were not only initiated into a Sufi order but also taught Islamic law and firmly opposed antinomian Sufism.

Not only the 'orthodox' but also various local *tarekat* contributed to the general drift from syncretistic to orthodox, *shari`a*-oriented Islam. Orders like the Siddiqiyya and the Wahidiyya (but also the Shattariyya and to some extent the Tijaniyya) attracted mostly *abangan* followers but in the course of one generation considerably changed the religious predispositions of their constituencies, contributing to what some Indonesians have called the '*santrinisasi*' of the *abangan*. Golkar was widely considered in the 1970s as representing *abangan* and *kebatinan* interests – this was one reason contributing to the anger in NU over Kiai Musta'in's desertion to Golkar. Two decades later, however, Golkar appeared to have been changed from within, with its leadership shifted from secular and *abangan*-oriented men and women to an all-*santri* team. The Sufi teachers who had joined Golkar in its early days were not the only or even the most influential actors behind this development, but they did play a role. And as a result of the accommodation between Sufi orders and Golkar, some Sufi teachers came to replace *kebatinan* gurus as the favourite spiritual counsellors of the New Order elite.

One teacher whose impact exemplifies, perhaps better than anyone else's, the changes in New Order Indonesia is the West Javanese *kiai* and *tarekat* shaykh Abah Anom, another master of the Qadiriyya wa-Naqshbandiyya and ultimately the most successful one. His pesantren at Suryalaya in Tasikmalaya, which is located close to the heartland of the Darul Islam rebellion, was always a fortress of loyalty to the central government and was entrusted by the military with the task of re-educating captured Darul Islam activists. In the early years of the New Order, he was also asked to give religious instruction to suspected ex-communists (Soebardi, 1978: 229). Abah Anom was the most prominent member of the *Dewan Mursyidin* of Haji Jalaluddin's PPTI (see above), but it appears he did not play an active role in that association. As a government loyalist, he supported Golkar but unlike Musta'in Romly never campaigned for it. Rival *kiai* in the same region rumoured that he was a *kebatinan* teacher, but there was never a concerted action against him as there was against Kiai Musta'in. In fact, although he was not a member of NU, Abah Anom gained an enormous following among NU members, especially outside Java.

The pesantren of Suryalaya was originally a *pesantren tarekat*, where Sufism and allegedly *kanuragan* were taught, but Abah Anom, who had a thorough training in the Islamic sciences, turned it into a centre of bookish learning as well, where general subjects were taught alongside the strictly Islamic ones. In expanding the *tarekat* network, he connected with the numerous local communities in West Java where an old cult of Shaykh `Abd al-Qadir Jaylani was still alive, with periodical recitations of a magically powerful text relating the great saint's miracles (Millie, 2006). Although affiliation with Suryalaya did not entirely replace or transform the old cult, it helped to integrate these communities into a wider social world and offered an alternative, less 'magical' ritual reading of a similar hagiography.

In the early 1980s, Abah Anom gained nationwide renown for his allegedly successful treatment of drug addiction and various diseases through intensive application of the methods of the *tarekat*. The patients were kept in isolation from the rest of the world, slept and ate little, and spent their days in prayer and *dhikr*. In spite of occasional negative publicity, many members of the elite sent their children to be disciplined at Suryalaya or in one of the dependencies that sprang up all over the country. The Ministry of Social Affairs rewarded Abah Anom for his contribution to solving this problem with a medal of merit and a handsome grant of money; many parents, impressed by the results obtained, became his followers and advocates.

It appears to have been this healing practice that helped Abah Anom to reach out beyond his growing rural constituency to a considerable modern urban following. Even so, the attention he attracted in Jakarta was not a matter of accident. As one knowledgeable observer writes, Suryalaya deliberately sent a number of lobbyists to the centres of political power (Effendi, 1990a: 97). Abah Anom was probably more successful than other *tarekat* teachers in attracting high military and civilian officials and university graduates (including a few well-known university professors) as his disciples and in building up significant urban followings. Yet on a more modest scale, many other Sufi teachers also found new urban constituencies.[25] Abah Anom exemplified wider changes in Indonesian society in another respect too: he became increasingly intimate with President Suharto, who appears to have greatly appreciated his spiritual powers. It is believed that in the first decades of the New Order, Suharto had only *kebatinan* teachers as his spiritual advisers (McDonald, 1980) but in later years he drew closer to orthodox Islam, and Abah Anom is said to have become the most favoured counsellor. It is difficult to assess trends in such private matters with any certainty, yet Sufism appears to have replaced *kebatinan* to quite some degree as a source of legitimization and spiritual succour.

The Emergence of Living Saints

The trend towards increasing orthodoxy, apparently sealed by the 'Islamic turn' in Suharto's policies, received a contrasting note in the New Order's final decade with the sudden appearance of a number of quaint charismatic personalities. Their erratic and often antinomian behaviour persuaded the public that they were friends of God (*wali*) – holy men whose spiritual attainment placed them above the religious obligations incumbent on ordinary mortals. A surprising aspect of these *wali* of the 1990s is that they did not emerge in the *abangan* circles where heterodox or non-Muslim holy men known as *wali* were not uncommon,[26] but in the centre of traditionalist orthodoxy, the Nahdlatul Ulama. These *wali* with pesantren backgrounds were seen as living saints, and they owed much of their public prominence to NU chairman Abdurrahman Wahid who patronized them. Gus Mik (Kiai Hamim Djazuli) and Mbah Lim (Kiai Muslim Rifa'i Imampura) displayed behaviour that would have been seen as outrageous in others but because of their perceived status as *wali* it only increased their charisma and attracted followers. Wahid surrounded himself with many other 'weird' people and built up a considerable reputation as a *wali* himself.

Javanese conceptions of sainthood are modelled on legends about the *wali sanga*, the 'nine saints' believed to have Islamicized the island and whose shrines, mostly on the north coast, are important places of pilgrimage. It is believed that the preaching of the *wali sanga* involved the adaptation of Islamic ideals to local cultural styles, and the shrine complexes and rituals surrounding the pilgrimage still reflect a cultural synthesis of elements drawn from various civilizations along the coasts of the Arabian Sea to the South China Sea. Most of the prominent families of *kiai* claim descent from one or other of these *wali sanga*, although they may not endorse the cultural syncretism associated with their cult. Some of the *wali* have a reputation for piety and orthodox learning, others for spiritual knowledge not transmitted through books. Both the pesantren tradition and various *kebatinan* movements trace their ancestry to the *wali sanga*, emphasizing different aspects of their legendary biographies.

The most Javanese of these *wali* was Sunan Kalijaga, a prince, vagrant mystic and reformed robber, who acquired his profound knowledge of Islam through silent meditation rather than textual study. He is credited with adapting Javanese cultural forms such as the *wayang* puppet theatre and *gamelan* music to spread Islamic teachings and with reinforcing the old Javanese techniques for acquiring supernatural powers with secret Islamic knowledge.[27] The most controversial of the *wali* was Shaykh Siti Jenar, who echoed al-Hallaj's famous words and proclaimed his essential identity with God. He was sentenced to death and executed by the other *wali* – because of his heterodoxy according to some, but for divulging an esoteric truth to the uninitiated according to others. Siti Jenar has appealed more to the popular imagination than any other *wali*, and some later mystics appear to have deliberately modelled themselves after him.[28] The ulama have usually fiercely opposed the 'teachings of Siti Jenar', which they have seen as legitimizing all sorts of antinomian behaviour; if there is no difference between worshipper and Worshipped, the rationale behind the *shari`a* obligations is undermined. But the fact of Shaykh Siti Jenar's recognition as a *wali* remains, despite the threat to the religious and political establishment that the teachings attributed to him represented.

Kiai Hamid of Pasuruan

Among the holy men of contemporary Indonesia we find several types of *wali* – from *kebatinan* gurus whose teachings show no ostensible relationship with Islam, to pious *shari`a*-abiding scholars, and a range of Muslim seers and healers in between. The most famous of the orthodox *wali* is Kiai Hamid of Pasuruan in East Java (d. 1982), who was known during his life as the greatest *wali* of NU and whose reputation overshadowed that of all others during the first decades after his death (Ahmad, 2001). Kiai Hamid hailed from a family of ulama. As did many *santri* in his youth he studied *kanuragan* and absorbed himself in the recitation of litanies (*wird, hizb*). Nevertheless his reputation as a *wali* was more to do with his self-effacing modesty and avoidance of all outward display, his quiet counsels of Sufi morality in the mould of Ghazali's *Ihya* and Ibn Ata'illah's *Hikam*, and the alleged effectiveness of his prayers for divine intervention. He seemed to have foreknowledge of events; unannounced visitors found that he was expecting them and heard him answer their questions even before they had posed their questions. Stories of his healing diseases or redressing disaster through an effective prayer were numerous, as were claims that he appeared to people in need, across large distances and through closed doors. He avoided spectacular miracles but people noticed that when he walked in the rain, his clothes seemed not to become wet – a well-known indication of sainthood. He urged those who asked his advice on Sufi practice never to stray from the *shari`a* under any circumstances. At least, that is what a recent biography of him (Ahmad, 2001) insists; the praise of Kiai Hamid appears to be a thinly veiled polemic against the less orthodox *wali* who gained prominence in the final decade of the New Order.

Gus Mik (Kiai Hamim Djazuli)

Gus Mik emerged suddenly in the public awareness as a *wali* of the more eccentric (*nyeleneh*) kind, his spiritual powers implied but never spelled out explicitly. Journalists were fascinated by his partiality to Guinness beer and his frequent though allegedly chaste visits to bars and night clubs in Surabaya, where he was feted by admiring queens of the night. In the pesantren world he was known as the son of a well-known and learned *kiai* in Kediri (the term 'Gus' is a title given to the sons of established *kiai*s), and his eccentricities were forgiven because of his pedigree. As a *santri* he had often defected from his classes and run away, sleeping on graves and in forests, engaging in ascetic exercises and the recitation of magically powerful formulas, and letting his hair grow long, all as signs of his quest for a deeper truth than that found in scripture. As an adult, he never behaved or dressed as other *kiai*, wearing jeans and a simple black shirt instead of white robes and a turban, but his prestige came to surpass that of more orthodox teachers.

His knowledge of scripture may have been spotty, but some very senior *kiai* (including the NU's highest religious authority, Kiai Achmad Siddiq) became his disciples in the discipline of reciting one particular litany, the *dhikr al-ghafilin*, which was believed to have powerful effects. He developed a new ritual for concentrating spiritual power, consisting of mass meetings for the collective recital of the entire Qur'an, *Sama'an Qur'an manteb*. In these all-night performances, a number of *hafiz* (people knowing the Qur'an by heart) would take turns chanting the holy book from the first chapter to the last. These *Sama'an* drew enormous crowds, mostly peasants but also officials who wished to take part in the blessing generated by the recital. After his sudden death in 1993, it was found out that he had been preparing for a lasting concentration of sacred energy. He was buried in a plot of land that he had carefully chosen and designated as the resting place of 40 *hafiz* and 40 'heirs of the saints': a permanent *Sama'an* of the spirit world, as it were, and likely to change the spiritual geography of Java and become a major centre of pilgrimage.[29]

Many Muslim men consume alcoholic beverages, chat with women in the entertainment business, and skip prayers from time to time. The average *santri* would be considered deficient in piety for doing so, or a hypocrite if he tried to keep up appearances. In a man of Gus Mik's stature, however, these were considered signs that he had reached a level where the everyday *shari`a* prescriptions no longer counted. The more the press reported on his ventures into Surabaya's night life, the stronger his reputation as a *wali* (of the Siti Jenar kind) grew, and the more people in high places requested his services in the pursuit of political goals. Gus Mik was believed to have attained such a spiritual stature that he could sway the balance of powers in the spirit world – he was said to have regular meetings with the spirits of the *wali* who guard Java – and thereby influence events in this world. Some people close to him attributed his sudden death to his too deep involvement in the struggle for Suharto's succession.[30]

Mbah Lim

Another *kiai* whose reputation as a *wali* ('the greatest *wali* of Java', according to some) peaked around this time is the diminutive, modest Mbah Lim of Klaten in Central Java. The first thing that strikes most people when they meet Mbah Lim is a speech defect, attributed to his early encounter with death. At the age of 20 he appeared to have died; his body was washed and prepared for burial. Just in time, people recognized a sign of life – he urinated – and cancelled the funeral. He was revived but his speech has been impaired ever since. People close to him have learned to understand his speech and translate his words for visitors. Even after translation, however, much of what he says remains obscure – like messages from another world.

Mbah Lim's grandfather had been the chief imam of the Surakarta court, and he was educated at a pesantren with court connections, which no doubt helped his reputation. In 1959 he settled in an *abangan* village in Klaten district. For many years, he remembers, he was the only person in the village who performed the Muslim prayers. The villagers sympathized with the Communist Party and mocked religion; Mbah Lim remembers a *wayang* performance on the death of God that gave them much pleasure. He built a simple mosque in the village, and at the time of mass killings of communists, with numerous victims in Klaten, he protected the people of his village from the killing squads, saying 'Who will pray in my mosque if you kill them?'. Little by little, he changed the religious life of the village, teaching the village children to practice Islam the *santri* way and indirectly influencing their parents too. It is said that he met much angry opposition from the spirit world as local spirits and heathen jinn fought back fiercely, occasionally taking possession of villagers' bodies and manifesting themselves in trees, rocks and disembodied voices. Mbah Lim's exploits as a fearless warrior of the spirit world who successfully expelled evil spirits and negative forces were recounted in ever wider circles. People from near and far flocked to his village to see him and ask for his blessing or advice. By 1990 these included members of the highest military and bureaucratic circles.

Mbah Lim's counsel was not always entirely comprehensible and it could be blunt. During consultations he would ask for paper and start writing at great pace, in large script, what appeared to be a formal statement or an instruction, affixing the exact time and date and completing it with a stamp and signature. Many people felt that such statements were inspired messages, with Mbah Lim acting, as it were, as the secretary of higher powers. The letters were treated with great respect and, even when not acted upon, taken home as amulets. I first heard of Mbah Lim when in one of these statements, given to a high-placed person, he called upon Suharto to step down and hand the reins of power to General Try Sutrisno and Abdurrahman Wahid, both of whom were *santri* who distrusted Suharto's recent alliance with reformist Islam. Unlike earlier messages purportedly from the spirit world to the same effect, this one had no negative consequences for the messenger; Mbah Lim appeared immune to repercussions.

Mbah Lim had not been active earlier in the NU, and his knowledge of scriptural Islam was quite basic, but from 1990 he appeared at all major NU congresses and conventions. Abdurrahman Wahid, who showed him much respect, appeared to consider him as his personal talisman, whose very presence influenced the outcome of internal power struggles in Abdurrahman's favour. I often wondered how much the public careers of people like Gus Mik and Mbah Lim owed to the stories that Abdurrahman Wahid circulated about them among the Jakarta elite. He did believe in their special gifts and powers, but he was also very much aware of the utility of other people's beliefs in such individuals' extraordinary qualities. Mbah Lim publicly proclaiming that the NU and the country needed Abdurrahman Wahid could only strengthen support for the latter, among the common members of NU and even among sections of the elite. The perception of support from the unseen world might well increase support in the visible world as well. Abdurrahman continued to surround himself with a strange assortment of mystics and seers, and increasingly indulged in grave visitations. His interest in the spirit world increased in proportion to his stature as a national political actor.[31]

Not everyone in the NU was happy with the emergence of these *wali* and their popularity among the NU's constituency. Several *kiai* told me that such men were little evident in the organization before Abdurrahman Wahid's leadership; some were sceptical about the status of these *wali*, or even scornful. One senior *kiai*, Mustofa Bisri (popularly known as Gus Mus), told me that in his youth he was a close friend of Gus Mik and had often joined the latter in his spiritual experiments, until his father, the formidable Kiai Bisri Mustofa, ordered him to stop. 'If you go on like this you'll end up as a *wali*', his father had warned him, 'Cut your hair, settle down, study books, and become a decent *kiai*'. Gus Mus obeyed his father and became a man of great moral prestige within the NU and beyond, an original poet as well as a scholar, and deeply committed to the interests of his organization. He seemed to imply it was a pity that Gus Mik had not been similarly disciplined by his own father, and that the heterodox *wali* were a threat to the NU's culture of sober learning. He later joined efforts to counter the belief in these heterodox saints.[32]

Although few people were more influential in national life during the 1990s than Abdurrahman Wahid, and although he probably played a part in launching the careers of some of the famous *wali*, the sudden visibility and apparent prestige of these charismatic personalities during the same period cannot be attributed simply to Abdurrahman's fascination with the unseen world, or his clever appeal to other people's superstitions (as some sceptics would have it). The same phenomenon could be observed beyond NU circles during those years. The West Javanese Qadiriyya wa-Naqshbandiyya master Abah Anom, whose following increased dramatically during the 1990s, may have represented the style of the sober and *shari`a*-oriented *wali*, but the equally influential Naqshbandiyya teacher from Sumatra, Kadirun Yahya, was a more flamboyant type of saint, believed to have power over nature and even over life and death, due to his having reached the stage of union with God.[33] Shaykh Kadirun, too, was patronized by people in high places, who were convinced they owed major successes in their careers to him.

The single most important factor in the emergence of these living saints of dubious orthodoxy was probably the struggle between different interest groups in preparation for the succession of Suharto. Abdurrahman Wahid's prominence, in the press and in public life in general, was another aspect of the same struggle. That some of the saints were heterodox miracle-workers was perhaps less significant than the fact that they emerged in the bona fide *santri* environments of the NU and the Naqshbandi order, and not in *abangan* or *kebatinan* movements. Their emergence, I venture to suggest, is consistent with the overall trend towards Islamic orthodoxy rather than contradicting it.

Conclusion

Urbanization, globalization, economic growth and the education revolution have not led to the marginalization of Sufism in Indonesia but rather to increased social and political prominence. The local horizons within which *abangan* beliefs and practices flourished have broadened, strengthening the appeal of *santri* Islam with its universal claims and transnational connections. Sufi orders and other mystical movements have felt pressure towards rationalization and adopted more formal modes of organization, in some cases giving rise to proper political parties or associations. Electoral politics had the effect of turning some Sufi teachers, because of their loyal and obedient following, into significant vote-getters and political entrepreneurs. The potential political weight of Sufi orders, with their large following, gave the government (at local and national levels) a strong incentive to control or co-opt them and attracted politically minded men as organizers and bureaucrats of Sufi associations. The cases discussed in this chapter indicate that contemporary Sufism in Indonesia has not been exclusively or even primarily an other-worldly affair but deeply involved in practical politics.

Indonesian politics, on the other hand, has been profoundly intertwined with mysticism as the major political actors have reached for charismatic mystical teachers – not only for legitimization, but also to sway elections, to provide spiritual counsel and, perhaps especially, as sources of supernatural power to bolster their own. New Order policies privileged formal associations of Sufis and gave a wide berth to the organizers, the Sufi bureaucrats. Individual political actors, however, needed charismatic Sufis for the various reasons set out above. The really successful Sufis, such as Haji Jalaluddin, Musta'in Romly and Abah Anom, were both charismatics and administrators. Where the two roles did not coincide, conflicts between the two types of leaders were almost inevitable, to the detriment of both parties. The overall trend towards greater Islamic orthodoxy and remarkable strengthening of scripturalist Islam has not led to a declining significance of charismatic mystics with a reputation for miracle-working. The most remarkable recent living saints emerged not from the margins but from the heart of orthodox Islam.

PART II:

THE INTERRELATION OF SUFISM AND ISLAMIC REFORM

7

SUFI FUNDAMENTALISM BETWEEN INDIA AND THE MIDDLE EAST*

Itzchak Weismann

Introduction

Contemporary Muslim perceptions of Sufism, and following them much of the scholarly literature, are dominated by the radical Islamist viewpoint. According to this perspective, Sufis are the most prominent example of deviation from the pure religion of the forefathers (*al-salaf*) and therefore are largely to be blamed for the so-called decline of Islam. Yet such a view ignores the major role that Sufism played in religious revival and reform efforts in latter-day Islam, as well as in the struggle against European colonialism (Levtzion and Voll, 1987; Sirriyeh, 1999). It also overlooks the fact that despite their criticism of popular mystical practices, leaders of the early fundamentalist trends of the second half of the nineteenth century, prominent among them the Ahl-i Hadith in India and the Salafiyya in the Arab world, remained committed to Sufi revivalist ideas and did not reject Sufism as such (Weismann, 2001: Ch. 8). When Salafi concepts were embodied in the following century in socio-religious movements such as the Muslim Brothers in Egypt and the Jama`at-i Islami in the Indian subcontinent, these still drew on the modes of organization of the Sufi *tariqa*s (Mitchell, 1969: 2-7, 214-16; Nasr, 1994: 11-13).

Without doubt, in the course of the twentieth century, Sufism and 'traditional' Islam in general, were subjected to an increasingly ferocious attack and their hold on both elites and the masses declined. In this attack, the fundamentalist critique combined with other 'modern' forces. Most important among these was Western-inspired rationalist philosophy with its typical contempt for mysticism, and the authoritarian State bent on suppressing civil society associations such as the brotherhoods. The

---

* In memory of Prof. Nehemia Levtzion.

prominence of radical Islamism in today's media and in the public discourse does not, however, mean that it has remained the sole alternative in the Muslim arena.

On the contrary, rather than a dichotomous presentation of radical as against conservative Islam, it would be more accurate to chart a spectrum of currents encompassing a wide-ranging middle strand between these two poles. Here belong the contemporary heirs of the various reformist trends of the past: revivalist Sufi shaykhs who have managed to adapt the spiritual path to the modern environment, fundamentalist ideologues who continue to respect Sufism as the moral–spiritual aspect of Islam, and Islamist movements that preserve Sufi populist and hierarchical conceptions within their structures. Scholars have tended to treat the Islamist middle strand principally as a moderate discourse facing the radicals' totalitarian and violent inclinations (e.g. Moussalli, 1999). Yet our analysis shows that in terms of its religious composition, a major element in this middle strand is what may be referred to as Sufi fundamentalism.

South Asia has served as a focal point in the dissemination of Sufi, Sufi-related, and anti-Sufi reformist ideas in both the pre-modern revivalist phase and the modern era of fundamentalist and radical transformations. Unlike other major Muslim concentrations, that of the subcontinent was always a relatively small minority living in the midst of vast Hindu populations. From the orthodox viewpoint, this state of affairs was the cause of a perpetual threat, motivating constant reformist thinking. Particularly in contrast to their Ottoman counterparts, even in the heyday of Muslim rule in India in the sixteenth and seventeenth centuries, the political culture of the Mughals was based on religious coexistence and the incorporation of local non-Muslim elites. These policies were epitomized in Emperor Akbar's (1556-1605) syncretistic 'divine faith', a court religion centred on his quasi-divine person (Ahmad, 1964; Nizami, 1989).

The last of the major Mughal emperors, the shari`a-minded Aurangzeb (1657-1707), tried to reverse this trend and partially excluded the Hindus (Hodgson, 1975: Ch. 3). Consequently, while the decline of other major Sunni Muslim governments during the eighteenth century normally meant decentralization, the decline of the Mughals resulted in total disintegration into mostly non-Muslim regional states. These were reunified in the following century by the British colonial power (Alam, 1986; Bayly, 1988). Since independence and partition in 1947, the Muslim communities in India have more than ever felt threatened by an increasingly hostile Hindu majority (van der Veer, 1994; Hansen, 1999: Ch. 6). Thus, as political decay was faster and deeper in South Asia than in other parts of the Muslim world during the past several centuries, it was here that ideas of religious revival and reform were first conceived. When other Muslim countries followed suit, their men of religion could draw on the already available reformist ideas of their Indian counterparts.

The principal agent in transmitting reformist ideas from South Asia to the Ottoman Empire and its Arab provinces in the pre-modern era was the Mujaddidi branch of the Naqshbandiyya.[1] The Mujaddidiyya was founded toward the end of Akbar's reign and partly in opposition to his religious policies, by Ahmad Sirhindi (1564-1624), 'the renewer of the second millennium'.[2] The Mujaddidiyya laid emphasis on the duty of spiritual masters to guide rulers on the path of the shari`a. Yet this markedly political orientation was more evident in the Ottoman realm than in India itself, where the adverse political situation turned the Mujaddidiyya increasingly quietist.

This activist streak reached the Ottoman Empire and its court at the turn of the eighteenth century, through the work of Murad al-Bukhari, founder of the notable Muradi family of Damascus (Babir, 1983). It came to fruition at the beginning of the nineteenth century when the Khalidi offshoot backed the Sultans' efforts to set the Empire on the course of reform (Abu-Manneh, 2001). Later in the century, the initiative moved to India's first 'fundamentalists', the Ahl-i Hadith (Metcalf, 1982: 268-96). The leaders of this trend also claimed roots in the Naqshbandi revivalist tradition (Saeedullah, 1973: 150-7). Under Western influence, they developed a new rationalist concept of *ijtihad*, which was instrumental in the formation of the modern Salafiyya in Iraq and Syria (Weismann, 2003b). In the mid-twentieth century, the chief ideologue of the Indo-Pakistani Jama`at-i Islami, Abu'l-A`la Mawdudi, influenced radical vanguards in the Arab world. Mawdudi was no longer committed to Sufism, and his paired concepts of *hakimiyya* (sovereignty) and *`ubudiyya* (worship) were the cornerstone of Sayyid Qutb's Islamist manifesto, *Ma`alim fi al-tariq* (Kepel, 1985: 47-52).

In this chapter I trace another, little noticed but no less important, recent line of transmission of reformist religious concepts from India to the Middle East. This line belongs to the moderate Sufi fundamentalist strand and is closely connected with the Naqshbandi revivalist tradition. At its core lies the idea of doing away with the conventional Sufi terminology and modes of organization as a means to preserve the spiritual essence of Sufism in the face of the 'modern' in general and the radical Islamist critique in particular. This concept, which may be described as 'Sufism without *tasawwuf*', became part of the Islamic discourse in Syria in the early 1980s in the context of the Islamist uprising against the Ba`th regime of Hafiz al-Asad. It had its origins several decades earlier in South Asia within the Lucknow-based organization of Nadwat al-`Ulama.

The chapter begins with analysis of the background and specific use of this concept among three of its major proponents who formed the contours of the middle Islamist strand in Syria. These are, on the one hand, Ahmad Kuftaru, the government-backed Grand Mufti and Naqshbandi shaykh, and on the other hand, `Abd al-Fattah Abu Ghudda and Sa`id Hawwa, the Naqshbandi-related leaders of the Muslim Brothers opposition, the former a hadith scholar and the latter a religious activist and ideologue. I then examine the background of Abu al-Hasan `Ali Nadwi, the Indian leader who formulated the concept in the 1950s, and the ways through which this concept reached his fellows in Syria. Through these examples, I wish to illustrate that not only have Sufi and Sufi-related ideas continued to flow in the twentieth century from south Asia to the Middle East along with the radical–fundamentalist ones, but also that movements embodying such ideas are bent on playing a moderating role in the contemporary Islamist scene.

'Sufism without *Tasawwuf*'

The idea of doing away with Sufi terms, including even those of *tasawwuf* and *tariqa*, is explicitly mentioned in a book that appeared in Syria in 1990 under the title *al-Tarbiya al-ruhiyya bayna al-sufiyin wa-l-salafiyin* (Spiritual Education between Sufis and Salafis) (al-Shaykhani, 1990). The work represented the teachings of the then Grand Mufti of Syria, Ahmad Kuftaru (1915-2004), who for 40 years was the foremost religious leader in the country.[3] Kuftaru was also the head of today's most widespread Naqshbandi–Khalidi branch in Syria, generally referred to as the Kuftariyya (De Jong, 1990; Böttcher, 1998: 164-93).

Of Kurdish extraction, Kuftaru's Sufi affiliation goes back through his father[4] to `Isa al-Kurdi (1831-1912), who was an important figure in the regeneration of the Khalidiyya in Damascus at the turn of the twentieth century. `Isa was faithful to the Ottoman Sultan, but became alarmed at the growing Western influence on the urban elite of his time. Therefore he turned his attention to the lower strata of the city and to the countryside (Weismann, 2003a). Kuftaru himself assumed public activity after Syrian independence in 1946 as a founding member of the professional association of Damascene men of religion, Rabitat al-`Ulama, which was dominated by `Isa's foremost deputies and other like-minded Sufi `ulama (al-Hafiz and Abaza, 1986: 725-6). Concomitantly, he began a career in the *ifta* administration and became involved in politics.

In line with the Naqshbandi–Mujaddidi precept of seeking influence with the rulers, Kuftaru was ready to collaborate with the Ba`th despite its minority character and secular ideology. This led to his nomination to the Syrian muftiship in 1964, a year after the establishment of the new regime. His alliance with the Ba`th was tightened in 1971 following Hafiz al-Asad's takeover, when Kuftaru was named Member of Parliament and his humble mosque was made headquarters of a government-sponsored religious trust. Within this foundation, he inaugurated in 1982, at the height of the Hama uprising, a college for Islamic propagation (*da`wa*) (Böttcher, 1998: 154-223; Stenberg, 1999; Geoffroy, 1997).

As reflected in *al-Tarbiya al-ruhiyya*, and on numerous other occasions, Ahmad Kuftaru readily concurred with the Salafis' censures against deviating Sufis, who he understood primarily to be proponents of the Ibn `Arabi school. Kuftaru also accepted his adversaries' call to return to the pristine ways of the forefathers, as well as their denunciation of legal school partisanship and advocacy of *ijtihad* as a means to progress. He likewise stressed the need to interpret Islam in a reasonable and activist manner and to fight religious innovation and superstition. On the other hand, Kuftaru reproached the Salafis for their literal interpretation of the scriptures and insisted that the spiritual aspect of Islam was essential for overcoming the temptations of the modern age. It was to allay the Salafis' misapprehensions that he suggested introducing a spiritual kind of education in which controversial Sufi terms will give way to those derived from the Qur'anic vocabulary.[5] Kuftaru accordingly defined his educational method as purifying the soul (*tazkiyat al-nafs*) and making it constantly aware of God's presence (*ihsan*). Its principal means were recollection of God's name (*dhikr*), along with a moral kind of asceticism and the specifically Naqshbandi practice of binding the heart to the master (*rabita*). Kuftaru expressed his hope that this method would bring about reconciliation between the orthodox Sufis and the Salafis as against the radical Islamists, on the one hand, and deviating Sufis and conservative `ulama generally, on the other (Shaykhani, 1990: 287-97).

Reviving the *Rabbaniyya*

Shaykh Ahmad Kuftaru's elaboration of the middle-strand concept of 'spiritual education' should be seen within the wider context of the conflict between the Ba`th regime that he served and the Islamist opposition. More specifically, it was a reaction to a series of Sufi-oriented books published in the preceding years that expounded this same concept. The author of this series was Sa`id Hawwa (Weismann, 1993; Hawwa, 1987) the foremost ideologue of the Muslim Brothers in Hafiz al-Asad's Syria. A son of a poor family from Hama, Hawwa (1935-89), too, adhered to the Naqshbandi-Khalidi brotherhood. He inherited this combination of Sufi affiliation and membership in the Muslim Brothers from his teacher, Muhammad al-Hamid (1910-69). The latter, in his turn, was a disciple of Abu al-Nasr Khalaf (1875-1949), an extremely popular Khalidi master who, not unlike `Isa al-Kurdi in Damascus, spread the path in the towns and villages of northern Syria during the French Mandate. Hamid helped in founding the Muslim Brothers' branch in Hama after independence and subsequently became its spiritual guide.[6]

Following Hamid's advice, Hawwa joined the Muslim Brothers in 1953 and ascended to a position of leadership in the movement in the wake of the rise to power of the Ba`th, when the old leaders were forced to flee the country. Subsequently he was charged with the task of reformulating the Brothers' doctrine in the face of the new circumstances. Compelled to flee Syria too, Hawwa was allowed to return after the establishment of the Asad regime. He was imprisoned in 1973 and on his release five years later left the country for good. He was thus prevented from exercising his moderating effect on the radicals, who led the Islamic movement of Syria to a bloody confrontation with the regime.[7]

The first book in Sa`id Hawwa's Sufi series is titled *Tarbiyatuna al-ruhiyya* (Our Spiritual Education) and it was published in 1979 when the Islamist uprising was gaining momentum. This book was complemented by a short epistle called *Ihya al-rabbaniyya* (Reviving [the way of] the Godly Men), which appeared in 1984 after the Syrian security forces had brutally suppressed the uprising.[8] Hawwa's stated aim in *Tarbiyatuna al-ruhiyya* was to familiarize the Islamist activists with the revivalist Sufi tradition and thus provide them with spiritual 'depth'. He points out in his introduction that he originally wanted to title the book 'The *tasawwuf* of the contemporary Islamic movement' or merely 'The spiritual life of God's army', but for various reasons that were undoubtedly connected with the prevalent revulsion at Sufism, he chose the existing title.

Hawwa was convinced that a clear view of Sufism was essential to protect the Islamist movement from being attracted by either the radicals, who threatened to drag it into a hopeless struggle with the Ba`th, or by their rivals who, like Ahmad Kuftaru, were ready to collaborate with the un-Islamic regime. As against these two poles, Hawwa set out to expound the foundations of a middle-strand Salafi Sufism. This was to be a 'book for the people' and not merely for the elite (Hawwa, 1981: 6-8). Following his scheme to deemphasize the Sufi vocabulary, the spiritual education he proposed consisted of a combination of `*ilm* (religious knowledge) based on *ijtihad*, and *tazkiyat al-nafs* leading to *ihsan* (Hawwa, 1981: 277, 313). Such education, Hawwa believed, would also guarantee the political goals of the Islamist movement in the modern age, the age in which apostasy (*ridda*) threatens to return (Hawwa n.d.: 5-11): the establishment of an Islamic government in each Muslim country and the restoration of the overall unity of the *umma* under the Caliphate (Hawwa n.d.: 120-1, 147-9).

The disastrous outcome of the radical-led Islamist uprising in 1982 drove Sa`id Hawwa to further elaborate the idea of 'Sufism without *tasawwuf*' into an alternative, more prudent, course of action. At the core of his scheme, as delineated in *Ihya al-rabbaniyya*, lay the reorganization of the Islamist movement 'from below'. Hawwa suggested forming study and *dhikr* groups in every neighbourhood and village, which would exemplify the path of the *salaf* and engage in propagating and instructing Islam among the people. Such a loose grassroots organization appears to be a continuation of the populist strategies of Abu al-Nasr Khalaf, the great Naqshbandi master of northern Syria during the Mandate era. Beyond the traditional Sufi framework, however, Hawwa, in the footsteps of his master Muhammad al-Hamid, emphasized in his treatise that the *rabbaniyyun*, the leaders and members of these groups, must be steeped not only in the religious sciences and Sufi practices, but also in modern culture. As such, their principal tasks are to serve as the common denominator of all religious forces striving to defend Islam in the face of the modern onslaught and, more particularly, to provide the Islamist movement with balanced spiritual as well as practical guidance in its struggle against un-Islamic autocratic regimes such as the Ba`th (cf. Hawwa, 1984; Weissman, 1997).

In the Name of the Tradition

Neither the concepts of *tazkiyat al-nafs* and *ihsan* nor of *rabbaniyya* figure prominently in the work of `Abd al-Fattah Abu Ghudda, the leader of the northern branch of the Syrian Muslim Brothers who had lived in Saudi exile since 1966.[9] His entire scholarly oeuvre, however, testifies that he too adhered to the principle of 'Sufism without *tasawwuf*'. Born into a well-to-do merchant family from Aleppo, Abu Ghudda (1917-97) also had roots in the Naqshbandi–Khalidi tradition. His first teacher was `Isa al-Bayanuni (1873-1943), the local deputy of Abu al-Nasr Khalaf, whom he describes as 'a lover of the Prophet and follower of the righteous, pious and pure way with abstinence, godliness and devotion', but without mentioning his Sufi affiliation (Al Rashid, 1999: 150).[10] While completing his studies at al-Azhar in the second half of the 1940s, Abu Ghudda became attached to Muhammad Zahid al-Kawthari (1878-1952), the conservative ex-deputy of the last Ottoman Shaykh al-Islam, who also belonged to the Khalidiyya (Algar, 1990: 43).

On the other hand, Abu Ghudda is credited with the foundation of the first Islamic youth association in Aleppo in 1935, when he was a mere 18 years old (Batatu, 1982: 14). He had come under the influence of Hasan al-Banna while in Egypt, and upon returning to his native city in 1951, he assumed teaching and preaching positions and came to be regarded as the figurehead of the Muslim Brothers' local branch. In this respect he was similar to Muhammad al-Hamid in Hama.

In 1962, Abu Ghudda was elected as a Member of Parliament on the Muslim Brothers' ticket, and as a founding member of the Saudi-sponsored Muslim World League on behalf of the Syrian `ulama.[11] Imprisoned for 11 months following the rise of the Ba`th, Abu Ghudda left for Saudi Arabia, where he dedicated himself to teaching, research and political activity. In these capacities, he also travelled extensively among the Muslim countries. In the escalating conflict with the Ba`th, Abu Ghudda emerged as the leader of the moderate faction of the Muslim Brothers, which by the mid-1980s was seeking to come to terms with the regime (Hinnebusch, 1990: 282-6). In 1995, the aging scholar was allowed to return to Syria, where he spent the last year of his life.[12]

Of `Abd al-Fattah Abu Ghudda's 70-odd books, the great majority are scholarly editions of works on hadith and to a lesser extent on jurisprudence.[13] Only one is a classical Sufi work, Muhasibi's *Risalat al-mustarshidin* (The Epistle for the Seekers of Spiritual Guidance). In this case too, Abu Ghudda refrained from mentioning that the author was indeed a Sufi. He defines Muhasibi as one of the forefathers (*salaf*) and characterizes him as an ascetic, a scholar and a religious propagator who left precious works concerning the purification of man's deeds and the mending of his soul.[14] The books that Abu Ghudda composed himself are likewise mostly concerned with moral–spiritual education, a subject in which he specialized for two years after completing his studies at al-Azhar (Al Rashid, 1999: 125).

Most important among these compilations is *Safahat min sabr al-`ulama `ala shada'id al-`ilm wa-l-tahsil* (Anecdotes on the Steadfastness of the Religious Scholars in the Face of the Hardships of Science and Learning), which was modelled on Ibn Jawzi's critical summary of Abu Nu`aym al-Isfahani's Sufi hagiographical work, *Hilyat al-awliya* (The Ornament of the Saints) (Abu Ghudda, 1992). Here Abu Ghudda aimed at the contemporary educated youth, who under the influence of Western culture belittled the Islamic heritage. He assembled in the book a wealth of reports on the hardships endured by students and men of religion throughout the ages, to obtain and record it. Abu Ghudda explicitly avoided, however, dealing with the afflictions that the `ulama suffered at the hands of the rulers, and his primary concern was with Sufi-tinged themes such as hunger and thirst, little sleep and much travel, poverty and chastity. He believed it is the example of such godly men, most of them, he claimed, of a humble artisan and peasant background, who could bring about a moral regeneration among the Muslim youth and evoke in them a spirit of sacrifice for the cause of Islam (Abu Ghudda, 1992: 7-21, 32).

The South Asian Connection

The respective schemes of 'spiritual education' of Ahmad Kuftaru, `Abd al-Fattah Abu Ghudda, and Sa`id Hawwa seem to widely diverge from each other. They differ in their point of departure – the Sufi brotherhood, the scholarly endeavour, and Muslim Brothers' activism – as well as in their political direction – cooperation with the Ba`th regime, acquiescence in it, or resistance. Yet the three schemes converge, largely on the basis of their common reformist Naqshbandi background, in the program of combining a moderate Salafi ideology with an orthodoxy-bound spiritual quest. The three may thus be regarded as different responses within the broader Islamist middle strand to the 'modern' in general, and to the Syrian reality of a non-Sunni secular government in particular.

A similar situation was encountered more than a century earlier by the Muslim minority of India, which lost the last vestiges of its political dominance on the subcontinent with the suppression of the Great Revolt and the disappearance of the Mughals in 1857-58. Under British colonial rule, Indian Muslim leaders founded a variety of socio-religious movements. These movements promoted different projects of reform while sharing a basic understanding that to preserve Muslim culture, and their own status, they must pay more attention to the religious education of the common people (Ahmad, 1967; Hardy, 1972; Lelyveld, 1978; Metcalf, 1982). Nadwat al-`Ulama stood out among these reformist associations in the special importance it attached to interaction with the Arab world. The Nadwa's prominent leader in the second half of the twentieth century, Abu al-Hasan `Ali al-Nadwi, conceived and disseminated the idea of doing away with Sufi terminology, as well as the concepts of *ridda and rabbaniyya*, in response to the situation of the Muslim minority in the independent secular Indian state.

Nadwat al-`Ulama (the Council of Religious Scholars) was founded in 1891 in Kanpur, Uttar Pradesh, by a group of religious-minded government officials, local notables and `ulama.[15] A leading figure among the founders was the Naqshbandi–Mujaddidi shaykh Muhammad `Ali Mongiri (1846-1927), who became its first administrator. Working in alliance with the colonial power, but alarmed at Christian missionary activity and the resurgence of Hinduism, the fundamental aim of the new association was to produce modern `ulama capable of standing up to these challenges. More specifically, the Nadwa leaders proposed to reform the old educational system and to promote unity among the religious scholars of various opinions. Posing between the earlier-established modernist trend of Aligarh and the tradition-bound Deoband, the Council's activity resulted, as in their cases, in the establishment of a new *madrasa*, whose cornerstone was laid in Lucknow in 1898.

Other important objectives were the creation of *dar al-ifta* (office for religious counselling) and the propagation of Islam abroad. For a while, the Nadwa came under the spell of Shibli Nu`mani (1857-1914), a former teacher at Aligarh University with mild modernist views.[16] Following his death, the more conservative elite of the surrounding small towns (*qasba*s) gained the upper hand with the nomination of `Abd al-Hayy al-Hasani (1869-1923), a close associate of Mongiri, as director of the school. His descendants, the Nadwis, turned the position into an actual family patrimony and brought the course of study in Nadwat al-`Ulama closer to the traditional syllabus of higher education in Muslim India.

The Nadwis are a notable `ulama family claiming descent from the Prophet (*sadat*), which settled in India after the establishment of the Delhi Sultanate in the thirteenth century (Bredi, 1999). Their principal Sufi affiliation goes back via Sayyid Ahmad Barelwi (Shahid), the famous nineteenth-century *jihad* leader,[17] to Adam Banuri, a prominent deputy of Ahmad Sirhindi and the first to spread the Mujaddidi teachings in the Hijaz.[18] Pursuing this tradition, `Abd al-Hayy became a disciple of Fadl al-Rahman Ganj Muradabadi (d. 1894), an influential Naqshbandi master with whom many of the founders of Nadwat al-`Ulama were associated (Hartung, 2003; Mukarram, 1992: 145-50). This Sufi connection was continued by his sons: `Abd al-`Ali (b. 1893), who was elected life-chairman of the Nadwa in 1931, and Abu al-Hasan `Ali (b. 1914), who succeeded him in 1961 and kept office until his own death in 1999.

According to his testimony, Abu al-Hasan became acquainted with Ahmad Sirhindi's *Maktubat* (collection of letters) when he was 17 years old, at the instigation of his brother (Nadwi, 1994: 1-2).[19] As Hartung shows, the

Naqshbandi affiliation remained always close to his heart. Nadwi's first Naqshbandi master came from the Northwest province in today's Pakistan, but then he became a disciple of `Abd al-Qadir Ra'ipuri (d. 1962) closer at home. This shaykh had close ties with the Tablighi Jama`at, a grassroots organization founded in the mid-1920 with the aim of propagating Islam among the Indian Muslim masses.[20] Nadwi remained a Naqshbandi–Mujaddidi master for the rest of his life, combining it with an enduring interest in the study of hadith (al-Nadwi, 1998). However, he carried out the major part of his activities through the Sufi-related organizations with which he was associated: Nadwat al-`Ulama and the Tablighi Jama`at (Hartung, 2003: 250-63, 322-9). Through these organizations, Nadwi and his ideas became known to his Syrian colleagues: Ahmad Kuftaru, `Abd al-Fattah Abu Ghudda, and Sa`id Hawwa.

As a graduate of Nadwat al-`Ulama, Abu al-Hasan al-Nadwi had not only mastered the Arabic language but was also well acquainted with the history and current situation of the Arab world. Nadwi's first visit to the Middle East was the *hajj* he performed in 1947, which was aimed at buttressing the propagation efforts of the Tablighi Jama`at (Mukarram, 1992: 269). His second pilgrimage, which he undertook three years later, was extended into a comprehensive one-year *da`wa* journey in the region, during which he established contacts with many leading Arab Islamic figures.[21] In Egypt, one of his major targets, Nadwi was much impressed by the political and intellectual activities of the Muslim Brothers movement, which seemed to him a complement to the quietist populism of the Tablighi (al-Nadwi, 1975: 26-33, 86-9, 99-103).

However, the oft-repeated claim that it was Nadwi who transmitted the radical ideas of Abu'l-A`la Mawdudi to Sayyid Qutb[22] must be seriously qualified. He certainly joined the Jama`at-i Islami upon its foundation in 1941 and helped translate some of Mawdudi's basic writings. Moreover, in his influential 1944 book, *Madha khasira al-`alam bi-inkhitat al-Muslimin* (What the World Lost with the Decline of the Muslims), he followed Mawdudi by referring to the Arabs' departure from Islam as a modern *jahiliyya* (the era of ignorance that preceded the rise of Islam) (Zaman, 2002: 162-3). Nevertheless, by 1950 the two had already long parted ways (Hartung, 2003: 297-305). Undergoing what Mukarram describes as a transformation from a governance- to Guidance-oriented framework, Nadwi felt much closer to Muhammad al-Ghazali and al-Bahi al-Khuli. These Muslim Brothers' leaders had Sufi inclinations and perpetuated the original, more moderate ideas of the organization's founder, Hasan al-Banna (al-Nadwi, 1975: 59, 64-6, 100-3).[23]

Abu al-Hasan `Ali al-Nadwi was uneasy about the moral and social malaise that he observed in Egypt and felt much more at home in the still traditional religious atmosphere of Syria. His principal associate during his first visit to the country was Ahmad Kuftaru, his Naqshbandi colleague. Nadwi became acquainted with Kuftaru a few months earlier during the *hajj*, and it was with

Kuftaru that Nadwi spent the major part of his time in Damascus. Attending the young shaykh's popular lesson in the Umayyad Mosque, Nadwi admired his method of interpreting the scriptures in light of current issues and everyday experiences, as well as his ability to express himself in simple language intelligible to the common people (al-Nadwi, 1975: 224-5). Subsequently, he listened with interest to Kuftaru's scheme of bringing religion back to personal life and to society by forging connections with the politicians in power, and through them giving an Islamic direction to public education and the mass media (al-Nadwi, 1975: 236-7).

Apart from Ahmad Kuftaru, Abu al-Hasan `Ali al-Nadwi was naturally also eager to get to know the Syrian Muslim Brothers, as well as Salafi `ulama and reformist Sufi shaykhs who backed them. His first encounter with their leader, Mustafa al-Siba'i, took place in the parliament, where the representatives of the Brothers were engaged in an ongoing struggle over Syria's Islamic character (al-Nadwi, 1975: 227-9). Nadwi later toured the country, partly in the company of Siba'i, visiting major Muslim Brothers centres and meeting, among others, `Abd al-Fattah Abu Ghudda in Aleppo and apparently Muhammad al-Hamid in Hama (al-Nadwi, 1975: 282-94).[24]

Nadwi returned to Syria in 1956, this time at the invitation of Siba'i, who meanwhile had been nominated dean of the newly founded Shari`a Faculty of the Syrian University in Damascus. He exploited his half-year stay, during which he delivered a series of lectures on the great Islamic reformers of the past, to tighten his relations with the Syrian men of religion. When in 1960 the Muslim Brothers established their organ, *Hadarat al-Islam*, Nadwi was entreated to send contributions. These dealt mainly with the impact of Islam on India (Hartung, 2003: 418-21; al-Nadwi, 1964: 8-15). In 1973 Nadwi paid yet another visit to Syria, which was by then under the Ba`th regime, as part of a delegation of the Muslim World League. He took the opportunity to meet with Kuftaru again, noting that most of his friends, namely those attached to the Muslim Brothers, were no longer there. The visit was abruptly interrupted when the delegation was inexplicably expelled from the country (al-Nadwi, 1974).

Ahmad Kuftaru's suggestion to do away with the Sufi terminology is taken from an article by Nadwi that appeared in the ninth issue of *Hadarat al-Islam* (The Civilization of Islam) under the title, 'Vacuum that must be filled' (al-Nadwi, 1961: 25-33). Nadwi opens his article with the postulate that concepts often misrepresent the things they denote and thus give birth to distorted entities that in their turn arouse scepticism and factionalism. He claims that such is the case with the term *tasawwuf*, which has no root in the Qur'an and the Sunna or in the sayings of the first generations, and around which fierce battles have been fought throughout Islamic history. Nadwi maintains that if the Muslims were to free themselves from this innovative concept and return to the sources, they would fall back on the Qur'anic terms of *tazkiyat al-nafs* and *ihsan*, the two spiritual pillars upon which the righteous society and just government of the forefathers were founded. The science that explores the 'inner' aspects of the shari`a may accordingly be called *fiqh al-batin*.

Nadwi admits that Sufism played a part in the degeneration of the *umma* in the later generations, as heretics, philosophers and monks were allowed to act under its banner. Yet in every generation there have emerged people of God, *rabbaniyyun*, who renewed and propagated Islam through their call upon rulers and common people alike to adopt the path of *tazkiya* and *ihsan*. Nadwi concludes that the specific Sufi way may have become obsolete in view of the modern materialist condition, yet the social and moral vacuum thus created can be filled by neither science nor political independence, but only through the perpetuation of the spiritual work of *rabbaniyyun*.

`Abd al-Fattah Abu Ghudda's debt to Abu al-Hasan al-Nadwi may have been less direct than Kuftaru's, but it was nonetheless substantial. Abu Ghudda's academic work was inaugurated in the wake of a three-month visit to India and Pakistan in 1962, during which he was received in Nadwat al-`Ulama by no other than Abu al-Hasan, who was recently nominated director of the school. He also met the leaders of the Tablighi Jama`at and numerous other respected men of religion (Al Rashid, 1999: 155-7, 216).

The first scientific editions that Abu Ghudda then published were three works by `Abd al-Hayy al-Lakhnawi, followed by Muhasibi's epistle (Al Rashid, 1999: 180-1). `Abd al-Hayy was a conservative Indian scholar, who Abu Ghudda had first heard about from his erstwhile Turkish teacher, Kawthari. It was Nadwi, however, who supplied him with a copy of the first manuscript (al Hindi, 1963). In his introduction to another of Lakhnawi's epistles on Sufism, which he edited a quarter of a century later, Abu Ghudda takes the middle stand of extolling the silent and loud forms of *dhikr* as cures for body and spirit, while recommending avoidance of dubious actions in their performance (al Hindi, 1988: 7, 13).

Abu Ghudda visited India several more times in the following decades and maintained close relations with Nadwi (Al Rashid, 1999: 34). Among the numerous praises he received for his major work, *Safahat min sabr al-`ulama*, he chose to adorn the second edition with that from the Indian scholar, as one of 'three dear words of distinguished, venerable, great teachers who hold a special place in my soul and have great love in my heart'. Nadwi had praised Abu Ghudda as 'the godly (*rabbani*) educationalist scholar who recalls `ulama al-salaf` in his great determination, his lofty vision, and his mastery and precision in all sciences' (Abu Ghudda, 1992: 10, 12).

Sa`id Hawwa was a generation younger than Abu al-Hasan `Ali al-Nadwi and connected with him in a way that was less personal than Kuftaru or Abu Ghudda had done. He may have heard of Nadwi from his teacher, Muhammad al-Hamid, and may have also attended his lectures in the Shari`a Faculty in 1956, which he himself joined as a student that same year (Hawwa, 1987: 44). Hawwa must have read Nadwi's contributions to *Hadarat al-Islam*, as he occasionally cites him in his books. The notion of contemporary

Muslim apostasy that Hawwa adopted was probably from another article of Nadwi first published in 1959 in the journal *al-Muslimun* in Geneva, and later as a separate epistle in several prints under the title '*Ridda ... la Abu Bakr laha*'. In this article, Nadwi argued that owing to the political and cultural invasion of Europe, the Muslim elites were almost imperceptibly inflicted with *ridda*, and that their empowerment after independence made their apostasy the most dangerous since the original *ridda* of Abu Bakr's times. He prescribed a way to fight the atheistic trend not through war or revolution, but through a modern reformulation of the Islamic culture and a dedicated organization for its propagation (*da`wa*) (al-Nadwi, 1980).

Moreover, in many of the ideas that Sa`id Hawwa developed after 1979, and especially that of *ihya al-Rabbaniyya*, he was inspired by Nadwi's book *Rabbaniyya la rahbaniyya*, a second edition of which appeared in Beirut in 1978.[25] The first chapter of this book is a reprint of the above mentioned article 'Vacuum that must be filled', and in the following chapters, Nadwi clarifies that the term *rabbaniyyun* refers primarily to the great Sufi masters and Sufi-inclined scholars. Among these he counts not only classical figures such as `Abd al-Qadir al-Jilani and Jalal al-Din al-Rumi (al-Nadwi, 1986: 26-35; 55-73), but also Ahmad ibn Taymiyya, who Nadwi claims was just as adamant in approving the exigency of the spiritual–moral path (al-Nadwi, 1986: 74-94). Nadwi also mentions more recent Sufi masters and Sufi-inclined leaders who undertook the jihad against the European onslaught, for example, `Abd al-Qadir al-Jaza'iri, the Sanusis, and Hasan al-Banna (al-Nadwi, 1986: 119-27). The most prominent place in Nadwi's book is reserved for those Naqshbandi–Mujaddidi shaykhs, the followers of *imam-i rabbani* Ahmad Sirhindi, who were instrumental in the formation of Nadwat al-`Ulama and the Tablighi Jama`at: Fadl al-Rahman Ganj Muradabadi, `Ali Mongiri, and `Abd al-Qadir Ra'ipuri (al-Nadwi, 1986: 36-54, 95-112, 132-41).

Nadwi depicts the present as the age of passions and temptations, and in line with the goals of the Tablighi Jama`at, the principal task that he assigns to the *rabbaniyya* is to propagate the Qur'anic message among the people and urge them to purify their souls. Still, as the examples of the movements of Sayyid Ahmad Shahid in India and of Hasan al-Banna in the Middle East demonstrate, in times of crisis such as the modern one, spiritual training must not be confined to personal devotion but must also include love of the *shahada* (self sacrifice) and jihad (al-Nadwi, 1986: 113-31, 142-58).

Conclusion

Ahmad Kuftaru, `Abd al-Fattah Abu Ghudda, and Sa`id Hawwa represent different ways within the broader Islamist middle strand of coping with the political and religious challenges of modern Syria. Kuftaru has kept to the traditional Sufi framework while allying with the State. Abu Ghudda and Hawwa transcended this framework while joining the opposition movement of the Muslim Brothers, the former being primarily a religious scholar (*`alim*), the latter an Islamist ideologue and activist. All three were influenced by the ideas of the eminent Indian scholar and propagandist Abu al-Hasan `Ali al-Nadwi, who like them came from a Naqshbandi–Mujaddidi background and lived under a non-Islamic government. Each of the three further elaborated Nadwi's ideas into a scheme of 'spiritual education' in accordance with his own point of view and needs.

For Kuftaru, the notion of doing away with the Sufi terminology serves as a means to lure the moderate Islamists to make peace with the government. Abu Ghudda implemented the same idea in order to focus on what he regarded as the most urgent task of preserving the Islamic heritage in a secularized age. Finally, Hawwa relied on the complementary concept of *rabbaniyya* to propose a grassroots organization that would allow the opposition to continue its work under a hostile and vigilant regime. Their different solutions notwithstanding, these three Syrian men of religion thus ultimately shared with their Indian colleague the ideal of combining a Sufi type of spirituality with a fundamentalist ideology as the basis for a moderate alternative to both backward Sufis and vociferous radical Islamists.

Acknowledgement

The research for this paper was supported by the Israel Science Foundation, to which I express my gratitude. I also wish to thank Dr Jan-Peter Hartung of Erfurt University for his comments on an earlier draft of this paper.

8

THE REFORMIST SUFISM OF THE TABLIGHI JAMA`AT: THE CASE OF THE MEOS OF MEWAT, INDIA

Yoginder Sikand

The twentieth century witnessed the emergence of a number of movements for religious revival, revitalization and reform among Muslims all over the world. One of these, probably the largest Islamic movement in the world today, is the Tablighi Jama`at (TJ).[1] Although it has its roots in the South Asian Muslim environment, with which it is still closely identified, the TJ is now said to be active in almost every country with a significant Sunni Muslim presence (Faruqi, 1992: 43). Its founder, the charismatic `alim, Maulana Muhammad Ilyas (1885-1944), believed that Muslims had strayed far from the teachings of Islam.[2] Hence, he felt the urgent need for Muslims to go back to the basic principles of their faith, and to observe strictly the commandments of Islam in their own personal lives and in their dealings with others. This alone, he believed, would win for Muslims the pleasure of God, who would then be moved to grant them 'success' (*falah*) in this world and in the life after death.

Although not identified as a specifically Sufi movement as such, the TJ emerged from the reformist Sufi project represented by the renowned Dar ul-`Ulum *madrasa* located in Deoband, a town not far from Delhi. It first took root in the mid-1920s in the area of Mewat, south of Delhi, among a community of Muslim peasants known as the Meos. The Meos continue to be closely involved in the work of the TJ, although their involvement has declined somewhat in recent years as the movement has assumed global proportions. Yet, as TJ ideologues and activists see it, Mewat is said to be the most successful experimental ground of the movement.

This chapter examines the reformist Sufi project of the TJ as it has come to be expressed among the Meos of Mewat. It begins with a brief description of the Meos and the early twentieth century Meo popular religion. It then discusses the intervention of the TJ in Mewat, looking at what this has meant for popular Sufism in the region. It goes on to examine the new form of Islam – reformist, *shari`a*-centred Sufism – that the TJ has sought to introduce in the region, examining ways in which the Meos have sought to incorporate the TJ's project in their daily lives. It also considers the implications of this new conceptualization of Islam, and particularly what it has meant for how religious authority is imagined, understood and articulated. Finally, the chapter examines how, in the face of urbanization, education and the intervention of the modern state, Meo attitudes towards the TJ are gradually undergoing a transformation.

The TJ and the Reformist Sufi Tradition

The TJ has its origins, as mentioned above, in the reformist Sufi project represented by the Dar ul-`Ulum *madrasa* at Deoband. Established in 1867, the Deoband *madrasa* set in motion a powerful movement to reform popular tradition, exhorting Muslims to closely follow the Prophetic model and to abandon what it condemned as 'un-Islamic' customs (Metcalf, 2002). This entailed a fierce attack on beliefs, customs and practices that were seen to have no sanction in the *shari`a* and the practice of the Prophet, and which were consequently declared as *bid`at* or wrongful 'innovations'. It also entailed the definition of what constituted 'orthodox' Islam. As the Deobandis saw it, 'true' Islam lay not simply and entirely in the classical scripturalist sources, including the Qur'an and the canonical collections of Hadith or Prophetic traditions, but also in the writings of the Hanafi `ulama. As strict *muqallids*, the Deobandis insisted on rigid *taqlid* of the *ijma`* of the Hanafi `ulama, and even went to the extent of condemning inter-*mazhab* eclecticism. They were fiercely opposed to western culture, represented by the British colonial regime, which they saw as threatening the integrity of Islam and the Muslims' commitment to their faith. They roundly condemned Muslim modernists who advocated reforms in the historical *shari`a* in the name of *ijtihad*. Yet they did not oppose modern technology or forms of organization as such, and in fact willingly embraced modern methods of communication, such as the printing press, to spread their doctrines to a wider audience.

While insisting on the need for Muslims to closely abide by the *shari`a* and internalize its norms, the `ulama of Deoband also sought to cultivate a rich inner life. Leading Deobandi `ulama also acted as Sufi *shaykh*s, serving as spiritual preceptors for many of their students, and initiating them into various Sufi orders. Metcalf (2002) deals extensively with the reformed Sufism of the Deobandis, and so this does not need to be repeated here. To summarize, the Deobandis were particularly concerned to reconcile the *tariqa* with *shari`a*, the inner mystical journey with the externalist path of the law.

This entailed new definitions of what constituted 'orthodox', and hence acceptable, Sufism in the Indian context.

The founder of the TJ, Maulana Ilyas, was himself a student of several of the leading `ulama of Deoband, including a number of its foundering fathers. He was born in 1885 in the town of Kandhla, in the district of Muzaffarnagar in the erstwhile United Provinces, not far from Delhi. His family claimed Arab origins, and was known for having produced numerous leading Islamic scholars. In 1897, at the age of 12, Ilyas travelled to the town of Gangoh, not far from Kandhla, then a major centre for reformist Islamic learning. After spending nine years there in the service of the renowned Deobandi `alim, Maulana Rashid Ahmad Gangohi (1829-1905), he went on to Deoband. There he studied Hadith from Maulana Mahmud ul-Hasan (known to his followers as Shaikh ul-Hind or 'The Teacher of India'), to whom it is claimed that he gave an oath (*bay`at*) of *jihad* against the British. While at Deoband he also came into contact with other leading Deobandi `ulama, including Maulana Ashraf Ali Thanwi, arguably the greatest reformist Sufi of his times, and Maulana Shah Abdur Rahim Raipuri. Later, Ilyas would refer to them as his 'very body and soul' (Sikand, 2002: 127). Ilyas' years at Gangoh and then at Deoband instilled in him a deep reverence for the Deobandi `ulama and their mission, inspiring him to later launch his own powerful movement of Islamic scripturalist reform in the early 1920s. Ilyas would later insist that the TJ aimed at spreading the reformist doctrines of the Deobandis, albeit using different means of popular preaching.

Ilyas' Reformist Sufi Program

The Tablighi Message

Ilyas wrote almost nothing about his own project of reformed, *shari`a*-centred Sufism, stressing that 'practical work' (*`amali kam*) for the sake of Islam was more important than merely writing about it. Here he followed the path of the early Sufi masters, who insisted that Sufism was, above all, a practical, rather than simply an intellectual, discipline. Nevertheless some of Ilyas' disciples collected his letters (*maktubat*) and utterances (*malfuzat*), which they published after his death (Numani, 1991; Bakhsh, 1995). These are important traditional genres of Sufi writings and provide us with valuable insights into Ilyas' own understanding of his work.

Ilyas' *malfuzat* and *maktubat* reveal a man passionately concerned with the fate of the Muslim community — both its worldly conditions and what he saw as its digression from the Prophetic model. The community's fortunes, Ilyas was convinced, depended critically on strict observance of the *shari`a*. As he saw it, the Muslims' plight owed simply to their having strayed from the path of God's law and having 'adopted' the ways of the 'disbelievers' (Sikand, 2002: 64-71). Hence, he regarded the need to reform popular tradition as particularly urgent. In this view, of course, he was not alone. Early twentieth century Indian Muslim reformists of all hues, including the Deobandis as well as Islamists and Muslim modernists, railed against popular customary practices, exhorting Muslims to 'return' to the path of the 'authentic' Islamic tradition. Although the ways that they envisaged Islamic 'orthodoxy' and 'authenticity' varied considerably, and were often mutually opposed, the reformists were united in their opposition to custom, which they roundly castigated as 'un-Islamic'.

Yet, whatever their concern for 'orthodoxy', the entire effort seems to have been deeply influenced by an overriding concern on the part of Muslim reformers to draw rigid boundaries between Muslims and others (mainly 'Hindus') as part of a wider project of constructing an 'imagined community' of Muslims. This must be seen in the context of Muslim marginalization following the collapse of Mughal political authority, and the growing challenge of Hindu 'nationalism' that threatened to absorb the Indian Muslims into the Hindu fold. In Ilyas' particular case, it appears that the growing success of the Arya Samaj, a neo-Hindu revivalist group, in bringing into the Hindu fold large numbers of what were seen as 'nominal' Muslims (generally referred to as *nau musalman* or 'new Muslims') goaded him on to realize the importance of inculcating a deep sense of unity among Muslims of all classes based on a common commitment to the *shari`a*. Only in this way, he believed, could Muslims stave off the Arya challenge and preserve their faith and identity intact, as I discuss below.

In other words, the growing stress that late nineteenth and early twentieth century Indian Muslim reformists placed on *shari`a*-centred Islam and their attacks on popular custom must be seen as intimately related to the particular political context of colonial north India, one characterized by growing and increasingly fierce rivalry between Hindu and Muslim elites. Here it is important to note the concern of Muslim elites with the *shari`a* as a symbolic marker of identity, uniting Muslims while at the same time distinguishing them clearly from Hindus. This concern had much to do with the fact – which the reformists lamented – that the Muslims of India (like the Hindus) did not actually constitute a single community. Sharp divisions of language, locality, ethnicity, sectarian affiliation and even caste divided the Muslims of the country, and in no sense of the term could they be considered a single homogenous, monolithic group. The attack on local customary practices, and their replacement by commitment to the universal, normative standard of *shari`a*-centred scripturalist Islam, thus served as a powerful symbolic resource in the process of constructing a pan-Indian Muslim community transcending internal divisions.

At the same time, by attacking customary practices that were condemned as borrowings from 'infidel' Hindus, the reformers helped undermine traditions of popular religiosity and religious culture that brought Hindus and Muslims together in a shared cultural universe. Stressing the distinctions between Muslims and their Hindu neighbours, based on a firm commitment to *shari`a*-centred Islam, reformists exhorted Muslims to remain deeply conscious of their separate communal identity, for only then could Muslims effectively meet the perceived threat of being absorbed into the Hindu fold by organized Hindu revivalist groups. This had its counterpart on the Hindu side as well, as Hindu reformers strongly condemned the visiting of Sufi shrines by Hindus and the widespread observance of what were seen as 'Muslim' practices. In turn, these attacks on popular religious traditions bolstered the process of constructing sharply defined boundaries between Muslims and Hindus.

Ilyas' own reformist Sufi project grew out of these powerful concerns for identity and normative Islam of the Muslim reformers of his time. As Ilyas saw it, the decline of Muslim political authority in India, and what he referred to as Muslim 'degeneracy' (Ilyas, 1989), owed entirely to Muslims having strayed from the path of strict observance of scripturalist Islam. By abandoning that path, and 'adopting' what he saw as un-Islamic customs that he traced to their Shi'a and Hindu neighbours, Muslims had courted God's wrath. Also branded as 'un-Islamic', and occupying a central place in what Ilyas saw as 'un-Islamic' customary tradition, was the entire domain of popular Sufism. This included practices related to worship at the shrines of saints, such as prostration before their graves, musical sessions and unrestricted mixing of the sexes.

Equally condemnable was a range of beliefs and associated practices relating to the authority of the Sufis, whether living or dead. The notion that the buried Sufis were still alive and could intercede with God to grant one's requests was fiercely condemned as 'un-Islamic' and as akin to *shirk*, the sin of associating partners with the one God. It was also said to be a reprehensible innovation (*bid`at-i siyah*) that had no legitimacy in Islam. Likewise, the notion that one could attain unity with God, which the *wujudi* Sufis stressed, was branded as heresy. As Ilyas saw it, the *shari`a* was to be taken as setting down the parameters of normative Islam. Practices associated with popular Sufism that were regarded as exceeding those boundaries were to be regarded as 'un-Islamic', and hence to be abandoned.

In other words, Ilyas did not condemn Sufism outright, as did, for instance, the followers of the Ahl-i Hadith, a group of reformists who emerged in the late nineteenth century, who identified themselves with the Wahhabis of Arabia. Ilyas' *shari`a*-centred Sufism insisted on the unity of the *shari`a* and the *tariqa*. Ilyas, like many of his Deobandi masters, functioned as both an `alim as well as a Sufi, and in the latter capacity as a guide to his followers on the spiritual path. His *maktubat* and *malfuzat* are replete with Sufistic terms, such as *lutf* (joy), *sukun-i qalb* (peace of heart), *nur-i basirat* (the light of insight), *ma`rifat* (gnosis) and so forth (Metcalf, 2003: 145). Yet these are to be understood as states that are experienced not in mystical flights of fancy and self-absorption, but in the course of missionary work, abiding faithfully by the *shari`a* and exhorting others to do the same. Several of the practices that Ilyas enjoined upon his followers are clearly associated with Sufism. The 'six points' (*chhe batein*) that he laid down for his followers, which now serve to encapsulate the Tablighi program, have remarkably Sufi associations.

The first of these was the *kalima shahada*, the Islamic creed of confession of the faith (*la ilaha illa llah muhammadan rasul allah*). Muslims were first to memorize the *kalima shahada* and learn to pronounce it properly. Then, they were to internalize it, seeking to realize its essence – that God alone is the Master of all, which means that His will alone, as expressed through His Prophet, alone should be obeyed. The second point was *namaz* (Arabic: *salah*), or ritual worship. Muslims were to learn the rules of *namaz* and regularly perform it. This was to accompany the cultivation of the appropriate inner attitude, for it was not enough simply to go through the worship as a mere physical exercise. The third point was `*ilm-o zikr*` (knowledge and remembrance). Muslims were to seek to acquire knowledge of the faith, particularly of the *shari`a*, and also to engage in various *zikr* practices, many of these being clearly Sufi in substance and form.

Fourth was *ikram-i muslim*, or 'respect for [all] Muslims'. The ideal Muslim was one who loved and respected all fellow believers, overlooked their follies and ignored their bad qualities, focusing instead on the good that they might possess. Fifth was *tashih-i niyyat* ('purification of intention'). All actions, whether worldly or religious, were to be motivated by pure intention, that is, by the desire to win God's favour, to do His will, and to earn merit (*sawab*) in the hereafter. This meant that one's actions were to be untainted by any worldly motives. Finally, was *tafrigh-i waqt* ('spending time'). A true Muslim was one who actively worked for the cause of the faith, taking time off from his worldly responsibilities to travel to engage in *tabligh* or missionary work, both in search of religious knowledge and to impart that knowledge to others. Ideally, a Muslim was to spend three *chilla*s[3] a year doing *tabligh* work. Overall, the *chhe batein* reflect an activist, *shari`a*-centric Sufism that, while borrowing heavily from the Sufi heritage, seeks to root itself within the boundaries of normative or scripturalist Islam.[4]

Popular versus Shari`a-*centred Sufism*

Ilyas' reformed Sufism, as expressed in the form of the TJ, had crucial implications for the constitution of religious authority. By attacking popular custom, the TJ directly challenged the authority of the custodians of the Sufi shrines (*sajjada-nishin*), who were seen as having a vested interest in preserving popular custom for their own claims to authority rested on these. Since a true Muslim was sought to be defined as one who carefully followed the *shari`a* in his own life, the claims of the *sajjada-nishin* to authority on the basis of their special links with the buried saints, generally as relatives or descendants, were effectively challenged. As Kelly Pemberton perceptibly notes, by making access to fundamental texts and teachings of scripturalist Islam available to all

Muslims, the TJ, like the Deobandis, 'sought to undercut the intercessionary role of the Sufi *shaykh*' (Pemberton, 2002: 72).

This did not, however, mean doing away with the position of the *shaykh* altogether, but recasting his role from that of an intermediary between God and man, to that of a teacher of the *shari`a*. In other words, the TJ put forward a new basis of religious authority. Authority to speak for and to represent Islam was, Ilyas suggested, to be earned through personal effort – by strict compliance with the *shari`a*, rather than simply gained through inheritance from one's ancestors. Ilyas suggested that every Muslim, no matter what their status in life, could be considered a true *wali* or friend of God, provided they followed the *shari`a* faithfully. One did not require the 'right' family connections for that, contrary to what many *sajjada-nishin* claimed.

As Ilyas saw it, one's faithful observance of the *shari`a* alone qualified one to be considered a *wali*. He therefore effectively dismissed as ultimately of little worth the claims to authority of the *sajjada-nishin*, based on the reports of the miracles (*karamat*) performed by the saints whose shrines they tended. He stressed that punctilious observance of the *shari`a*, and not *karamat*, was the only way to rise in God's eyes. Even 'despicable' non-Muslims were said to be capable of performing miracles, and so that could not constitute a basis for authority. One's claims to religious authority, Ilyas suggested, also had nothing to do with mediating between God and man, as in the case of popular Sufi cults, for this was considered as 'un-Islamic'. Rather, he seems to have believed, one earned religious authority by strictly following the *shari`a* and dedicating one's whole life for the sake of the propagation of Islam. In other words, the role of the Sufi *shaykh* was now no longer that of an intermediary, but that of a guide. Alongside this, the ways in which the Sufi path was understood also underwent a crucial transformation. The *shari`a*, rooted in this-worldly practices, took over from the mystical quest of abandoning the world or absorbing oneself in God. There could thus be no contradiction between the *shari`a* and the *tariqa*.

In other words, attempts were made to transfer the locus of authority in the TJ from the deceased Sufi or the *sajjada-nishin* to the charismatic community, the roving *jama`at* or preaching party of Tablighi missionaries. The Sufi discipline was to be cultivated within the *jama`at*, rather than in a Sufi hospice (*khanqah*) associated with a particular Sufi order *(silsila)*. God was believed to grant His blessings and even sometimes to arrange for suitable *karamat*, in the context of working in the *jama`at*. In a sense, then, the TJ represents a significant democratization of religious authority, at least in comparison to the closely controlled and steeply hierarchical cults of the Sufis centred on the shrines.

All Muslims were exhorted to gain knowledge of Islam, and access to the resources of scripturalist Islam was no longer to be regarded as a closely guarded monopoly of the `ulama or high-ranking Sufis. All Muslims could, indeed should, be actively involved in the 'work' for the faith. *Tabligh* was no longer to be regarded as the duty of the `ulama and Sufis alone. Earlier, the *tabligh* was considered a *farẓ-i kifaya*, a duty fulfilled if even a section of the community, in this case the `ulama and the Sufis, performed it. Now *tabligh* was to be considered as *farẓ-i `ayn*, a responsibility binding on every single member of the community, no matter how humble his or her origins. One's stature in God's eyes was said to be dependent not on family origins, wealth or power, and not even on Islamic knowledge, but simply on one's dedication to Islam and to the work of *tabligh*, expressed in the form of faithfully following the dictates of the *shari`a* in one's own life. Naturally, such a stance worked to undermine the influence of the *sajjada-nishin* and of many `ulama, even as it sought to impose the vision of one section of the `ulama – those `ulama associated with the TJ – as hegemonic.

The Meo Popular Tradition: From *bid`at* to *shari`a*

Ilyas' reformist project was first launched in a culturally distinct region south of Delhi called Mewat, comprising large parts of the Alwar and Bharatpur districts of the present-day Indian state of Rajasthan and the Gurgaon and Faridabad districts of Haryana state. Mewat is the land of the Meos, a Muslim community who are for the most part peasants, and who today number some one million. The Meos were regarded, and in some sense continue to be seen, as *nau*-Muslims, although their first contact with Islam goes back several centuries. The Meos claim to be of 'high' caste Hindu Rajput origin, but although some of them may well be of Rajput stock, the vast majority of Meos appear to be descendants of 'low' caste and tribal converts, who now claim a 'high' caste origin for themselves.

Mewat's first encounters with Islam date to the twelfth century, when the Meos living in the vicinity of the imperial capital of the Sultanate of Delhi often came into conflict with the Turkish Sultans. Drought and famine sometimes forced hordes of Meos to attack and loot Delhi, which then brought violent reprisals upon them. On several occasions, the Meos were forced to convert to Islam as a punishment and as a means to combat Meo lawlessness. Yet, although the Sultans were apparently rather ineffective in converting the Meos to Islam, numerous Sufis who settled in the region seem to have been more successful. Today, scores of Sufi shrines dot the Mewati countryside, testifying to the many centuries of Sufi presence in the area. The vast majority of the inhabitants of Mewat came to identify with Islam, at least nominally, under the influence of these Sufis. Yet, Meo forms of Islam continued to be deeply rooted in popular traditions, leading observers to comment that the Meos were Muslim in name only. Thus, writing in the last quarter of the nineteenth century, Major Powlett, the British settlement officer of the Alwar state, observed:

> The Meos are now all Musalmans in name, but their village deities are the same as those of the Hindus, and they keep several Hindu fasts ... Meos, in their customs, are half Hindu. The Meo places of worship are similar to those of their Hindu neighbours ... As regards their own religion [Islam] the Meos are very ignorant. Few know the *kalima*, and fewer still the regular prayers, the seasons of which they entirely neglect. (Powlett 1878: 38)

According to another source, in Mewat:

> Reading of the Qur'an was less popular than reading the Hindu epics Ramayana and Mahabharata. Hindu shrines far outnumbered mosques in Mewat. Few Meos prayed in the Muslim manner, but most of them performed the *puja* – worship at the shrines of the Hindu gods and goddesses. (P.C. Aggarwal, quoted in Sikand, 2002: 113)

As an almost entirely peasant community, the Meos had few religious specialists of their own. Instead, they sought the help of Hindu *pandit*s as well as Muslim *faqir*s, custodians of the Sufi shrines, for various ritual purposes. Meo religion was, above all, practical – rooted in specific life-cycle events and geared to the propitiation of deities. These included Allah, and a host of spirits and hidden saints for favours or to ward off misfortune. As for the way the Meos identified themselves, the notion of 'Muslim' as clearly excluding and being set apart from or against 'Hindu' was quite unknown.

From the late nineteenth century onward, and gaining particular momentum from the 1920s, a complex set of developments set in motion a process of radical redefinition of Meo self-perceptions, including religious identity.[5] These developments included the introduction and spread of reified notions of religion and community identity popularized by colonial administrators, particularly census officers, as well as Muslim and Hindu elites; growing competition between Hindu and Muslim elites, leading to Hindu–Muslim conflict in large parts of northern India; a series of Meo peasant revolts in the context of the Great Depression of the 1930s that the Hindu rulers of the Bharatpur and Alwar states saw as 'Islamic' movements and accordingly sought to brutally crush; the role of external Muslim organizations and leaders in assisting the Meos in their revolt and articulating their grievances to a wider audience; and, finally, the role of Ilyas and his movement in the area from the mid-1920s, seeking to save the Meos from the threat of being absorbed into the Hindu fold at the hands of the Hindu revivalist Arya Samaj.

All of these developments appear to have fostered an increasing stress on the Islamic aspect of Meo identity. The TJ had a crucial role to play in this process. Its call for the Meos to identify with and observe the rules of the *shari`a* struck a receptive chord among many Meos, who now sought to distinguish themselves clearly from their Hindu neighbours. Yet, as I have shown in my study of the TJ in Mewat, the TJ really took off in a major way among the Meos only in the aftermath of the Partition of India in 1947, after the bloody rioting in Mewat in which tens of thousands of Meos were killed. Faced with the fierce hostility of their Hindu neighbours, most Meos found in the TJ a source of strength, and its calls to eschew 'Hindu' customs and beliefs were now certainly more acceptable than before (Sikand, 2002: 147-56).

To understand the success of the TJ in Mewat, it is useful here to examine how the TJ's followers sought to root the movement among the Meos, and in particular how they related it to the Meo popular religious tradition. As we have seen, the Meo tradition had for centuries resisted pressure to conform to normative understandings of Islam. Ilyas therefore insisted on a gradual process of Islamization, following in the footsteps of his Sufi forebears. The Meos were not to be forced to accept and follow the entire edifice of the *shari`a* all at once. Rather, Ilyas stressed, they must be first encouraged to follow the *chhe batein*, based on a firm cultivation of their faith (*iman*) in Islam. Once their faith was sufficiently fortified, he argued, they would themselves work to create a 'truly' Islamic society, replacing their 'un-Islamic' practices and institutions with those in line with the *shari`a*.

Hence, TJ missionaries were asked in their preaching work simply to focus on the great divine rewards (*faza'il*) that the Meos would receive if they followed the *shari`a*, with promises of immense blessings (*sawab*) assured for those who 'revived' even the most minor *sunnat* or practice of the Prophet. In matters other than ritual worship, the missionaries were to clearly avoid the *masa'il*, the detailed aspects of Islamic jurisprudence and law that in many respects conflicted with Meo customary practice. This approach was particularly important given the deep-rootedness of the Meo tradition. It reflected Ilyas' astute awareness that even though this tradition flagrantly violated the *shari`a* in many crucial respects, attempting to combat this tradition directly would inevitably result in stern Meo opposition to the TJ movement. Put differently, Ilyas insisted that in their missionary work, TJ activists avoid all reference to what he called *ikhtilafi* matters that might promote dissent and conflict. Instead, he stressed, they must focus only on *ittifaqi* issues, such as the need for piety and prayer, on which there could be no dispute or opposition (Sikand, 2002: 83-9).

With Ilyas' pragmatic missionary strategy, the TJ was able to establish a firm foothold in Mewat by the end of the 1940s. This process responded to the Meos' quest for a more unambiguously 'Muslim' identity built in opposition to what they had come to see as the menacing Hindu 'other'. The bloody events of 1947, when several thousand Meos were slaughtered by Hindu mobs, provided further boost.

We can thus appreciate that with the growing spread of Hindu militancy in large parts of India today, including in Mewat, association with the TJ and its program of *shari`a*-centred Islamic reformism has much to do with Muslim insecurities and fear that their lives, faith and identity are under grave threat. Formal affiliation or identification with the TJ has become, in a sense, an integral part of Meo identity. However this does not mean that the TJ has made much headway in bringing the Meos to lead their personal and collective lives in accordance with the *shari`a*. Several pre-Islamic customs and institutions of the Meos remain deeply rooted, and the commitment of many Meos to TJ-style reformism is nominal. The TJ's own style of missionary activism appears largely responsible, since it leads most Meos to only a very partial acceptance of the movement's total message.

As noted above, TJ workers are strictly forbidden from raising 'controversial' (*ikhtilafi*) matters and must restrict themselves to the *ittifaqi masa'il* matters on which all Muslim groups agree. In the Meo case, stressing the *faza'il* and the *ittifaqi*, as opposed to the *masa'il* and the *ikhtilafi*, has enabled the TJ to gain accommodation in Mewati society without major controversy. But the deep-rooted 'un-Islamic' traditions and institutions of the Meos that TJ activists see as 'un-Islamic' are not directly challenged or opposed. These include the traditional Meo prohibition of cross-cousin marriage (the preferred form of marriage for many other Muslim groups in South Asia), the custom of dowry paid to the groom by the bride's family, the practice of women working in the fields in the presence of unfamiliar men, and the almost complete denial of inheritance rights to women, all of which have no sanction in the *shari`a*.

The TJ and Modernity

The TJ's response to the manifold challenges that modernity poses is a complex one, fraught with tensions and ambiguities. On the one hand, in line with the general Deobandi position on the matter, the TJ enjoins strict *taqlid* or imitation of past precedent in matters of *fiqh* or Islamic jurisprudence. On the other hand, the TJ explicitly condemns *ijtihad* or creative reasoning and development of *fiqh* in accordance with changing conditions. The TJ sees *ijtihad* as a threat, since while claiming to reform the *shari`a* (which followers believe were revealed by God), it regards unrestrained *ijtihad* as diluting Muslims' faith and undermining the *shari`a*.

The TJ regards such changes as dangerous *bida'at* or 'innovations' that are to be fiercely condemned, for every such 'innovation' is said to lead to hell-fire. In other words, in several crucial respects the TJ appears to be vehemently hostile to the changes that modernity brings in its wake, including changing value systems and laws. Notwithstanding, Meo identification with the TJ today also has much to do with distinctly modern concerns. Thus, the TJ's opposition to the cults centred on the Sufi shrines ties in with contemporary Meo aspirations for equality and self-respect. As a Meo respondent, an active TJ worker, put it:

> In the past, we served the *faqir*s of the shrines, for they insisted that they were of pure Muslim descent and that we were Hindu converts. They claimed that they had special access to the Sufis whose shrines they looked after, and through those saints, to God. We would serve them to pass on our requests to God through the saints. In return we had to pay them regular sums of money and a share in their harvest. Despite that, they treated us as lowborn, almost like their own servants, and looked upon us as uncivilized and uncouth.

In contrast, the TJ is seen as considerably more 'democratic', challenging the notion of the privileged access of the Sufis and the *faqir*s to religious knowledge and authority. As the Meo respondent quoted above continued:

> In the work of the *jama`at*s there is no high and low. All of us are equal, being fellow Muslims. It does not matter in Allah's eyes how much money you have, how much land you own, how many degrees you have earned or even how many books you have read on Islam. Without faith and willingness to work for the sake of Islam, all such things are useless. Here, in our movement, even the poorest Muslim feels he is the equal of a rich landlord and can even exercise the right to gently admonish him when he does something wrong.

The *shari`a*-centred form of Islam that the TJ represents is also seen as relieving the Meos of a heavy economic burden, which has come to be associated with popular Sufism. The TJ makes no financial demands on its followers, other than exhorting them to spend on going out themselves to conduct *tabligh* work. Generally, this is not very expensive, as activists sleep in mosques and cook their own food or are entertained by local Muslims. This is often presented as in sharp contrast to pre-Tablighi Meo popular religion centred on the Sufi shrines. Thus, a Meo respondent explained:

> In the past, each time we went to a shrine, which was very often because we always wanted something from the saints who are buried there, we were expected to pay something to the *faqir*s and the other *sajjada-nishin*s. Sometimes we would give them wheat or vegetables or maybe a chicken, and at other times cash. If you didn't pay you sometimes were made to feel that you were not welcome. Some *faqir*s would even quarrel with us, demanding to be paid more. And then, we had an extra burden of expenses each time we organized a festival, and there were so many, as we celebrated both Hindu and Muslim festivals. There are so many *dargah*s (Sufi shrines) in Mewat, and each shrine has its own large annual festival. So, sometimes poor Meo families landed deep in debt to meet the expenses involved in these festivals and the payments to the shrine custodians. But there's nothing of this sort at all in the Tablighi Jama`at.

> In fact, it seems that Allah has sent the *jama`at* to rescue us from our economic plight.

Association with the TJ today also represents new and distinctly modern ways of imagining Muslim communal identity. In the years after the Partition, Mewat gradually opened up to the wider world and the developments taking place within it. This led to an increasing crisis of Meo parochial religious identity tied to local cults of the saints and various folk heroes and deities, and a consequent further shift to a 'world religion' as represented by the *shari`a*-centred Islam of the TJ. The Meo popular tradition was clearly inadequate in confronting the new challenges that modernity posed for the Meos, for which the tools provided by the reified Islam of the TJ seemed far more effective and useful. Before the Partition, literacy was almost non-existent among the community. Post-Partition, the state established a number of schools in the region, which led to the gradual emergence of a class of literate Meos. This, and improved means for communications with the outside world, meant that Meos could now seek to establish closer links with the wider Indian Muslim community. These links were often facilitated through the Tablighi network, for by this time the TJ had gradually expanded from its confines in Mewat to become an India-wide movement with a significant presence in several other countries as well.

Influenced by the TJ, growing numbers of Meo students took admission in *madrasa*s or Islamic schools in other parts of India, thus facilitating a crucial process of geographical as well as upward social mobility for many Meos. Going on missionary tours to other parts of India and increasingly abroad has led many Meos not simply to new understandings of Muslim identity, and a growing commitment to global Muslim unity and to Islam. It has also brought distinct worldly benefits for several Meos. As one Meo respondent explained:

> In theory Tablighi activists are meant to travel simply to increase their knowledge of Islam and to impart that knowledge to others. Indeed, that is what many of them actually do. However, travelling to other places on *tabligh* work naturally opens up the minds of many of the activists. They see new places, new things, and meet new sorts of people, and come to know how other people live. They come to know of the whole world outside Mewat, about new developments in the rest of the world, which can really open their minds. Some of them might even strike business deals with people they might meet on their journeys or establish business contacts or get new business ideas, although the Tablighi elders actually strictly forbid this.

In matters of education, gender relations and inter-community relations – three areas of particular concern to Muslims living as a minority in India today – the TJ advocates what some observers may see as a rigid conformism and a stern refusal to recognize the need for change or reform. Thus, for instance, Ilyas himself is said to have condemned as a 'Satanic institution' the first modern school in Mewat, set up in 1923 at the town of Nun (Sikand, 2002: 121), warning the Meos to stay away from it and to send their children to Islamic *madrasa*s instead. Even today, many TJ leaders insist (quoting a Meo `alim) that 'the only form of education that is valuable in God's eyes is knowledge of the *shari`a*, which alone can win success for Muslims in this world and in the hereafter'. In Mewat's leading *madrasa*, the Madrasa Morin ul-Islam at Nun, founded in the early 1940s by Maulana Ilyas himself, no 'worldly' subjects are taught, and students are forbidden from reading newspapers for fear that they might be attracted by the snares of the world (Sikand, 2002: 164). Some Meo *maulvi*s associated with the TJ are said to go so far as to declare that learning English and Hindi are *haram*, strictly forbidden in Islam (Sikand, 2002: 165).

The TJ also exhibits a distinctly anti-modernist impulse in matters of gender relations. It represents an extremely patriarchal understanding of Islam, one in which women are clearly subordinate to men.[6] Many Meo TJ leaders and activists continue to condemn modern education for girls, seeing that it threatens to tempt girls away from commitment to Islam and opens the doors to all manner of *fitna*: worldly – including sexual – temptation, strife and insubordination. Female Meo literacy rates remain among the lowest in India, estimated at no more than 5 per cent, and this owes much to the distinct lack of enthusiasm by TJ activists in Mewat for girls' education.

In matters of inter-community relations too, the TJ's position might seem to militate against modern sensibilities. It refuses to recognize the truth claims of other faiths, insisting that Islam, as the TJ understands it, is the only way to win God's favour and enter paradise. All other religions are regarded as either human creations or representing distorted versions of divine religions that have become corrupted over time. Other religions are therefore false and their followers, consequently, doomed to hell. TJ activists are constantly reminded that non-Muslims, no matter how pious and noble they might be, are all veritable 'enemies of God'. Nevertheless, TJ activists are expected to behave with courtesy and kindness towards non-Muslims, although strictly within the limits set by the *shari`a*. This derives from the hope that non-Muslims might be thereby suitably impressed by Islam and even consider accepting it.

A common refrain heard in TJ circles is that the movement is concerned 'only about the heavens and the brave below, and never about the world in-between'. This is often employed as an argument to convince others that the TJ has no political or worldly motives. Yet precisely because of what is seen as the TJ's distinct lack of concern for the worldly affairs of Muslims, today a small but growing number of Meo youth increasingly voice their protest against what they see as the TJ's rigid understanding of Islam. These youths have been influenced by 'modernist' as well as Islamist understandings of

Islam, and, ironically, helped by the TJ in their first exposure to Islamic structuralism. They regard what they see as the TJ's indifference to the this-worldly concerns of the community as wholly 'un-Islamic'. In their view, the TJ's obsessive concern with the ritual minutiae of the *shari`a*, and its silence on the social, economic and political affairs of the community, have only contributed to the further backwardness of their community.

Comparisons are often drawn between the Meos and their Hindu Jat neighbours. For the most part, the Jats are associated with the Hindu revivalist movement Arya Samaj, which took off in the region at almost the same time as the TJ. The Jats, like the Meos, were traditionally a peasant community. In recent years, the Jats have made impressive strides in education and economic development, and today they are a powerful political force. Their development owes partly to the work of the Arya Samaj, which set up a number of schools, hospitals, orphanages and training centres in Jat territory. Contrasts drawn between the TJ and the Arya Samaj often lament that the TJ has done little for the Meos; as a Meo informant puts it, the TJ is almost 'completely blind' to the real-world concerns of the Meos. This approach is said to be profoundly 'un-Islamic', for in Islam, it is claimed, there is no distinction between religion (*din*) and worldly affairs (*dunya*). As some Meos see it, the TJ appears to make such a distinction to the point of insisting that the two realms are mutually opposed to each other. They therefore claim that the TJ is propagating an 'un-Islamic Sufism' (*ghayr islami tasawwuf*) or 'monasticism' (*rahbaniyyat*) that has no legitimacy in Islam itself. A Meo student opined:

> The division that Tablighi activists make between *din* and *dunya* is itself un-Islamic, for in Islam the world is part of the *din*. They see the *din* as lying simply in prayers and fasting and going on *tabligh* tours, the rest being *dunya*, and these two are perceived as fundamentally opposed to each other. That is why they do not pay any attention to the worldly concerns of the Meos, dismissing them as *dunyavi*, and hence of little worth. In fact, I have often heard Tablighi *maulvi*s in Mewat lament in their lectures the little economic progress that we have experienced, saying that when we were poor and nearly starving we were very pious Muslims, but that today some of us are a little more comfortably off but we have forgotten God. This attitude of the *maulvi*s is something that many educated Meos resent today. Undoubtedly, this has caused a growing disillusionment with the movement on their part.

There are various interpretations of the TJ's perceived indifference to the worldly concerns of the Meos. Some explain it as a consequence of an 'un-Islamic' Sufism that encourages flight from this world, while for others it is the product of a distinctly this-worldly concern of TJ leaders and `ulama to enhance their own authority and their access to, and control over, the Meo's community resources. Thus, it is often alleged that while TJ leaders preach the virtues of poverty and exhort Muslims to remain content with the bare minimum of worldly goods – only enough to survive – many of these leaders run what one Meo respondent claims are 'large religious rackets of their own'. These rackets are said to operate through the institutions that the leaders manage, which are financed by donations from the Meo community, from Muslims elsewhere in India, and some even from abroad. The TJ leaders are also often accused of preaching against modern education, which their critics claim to be a fundamental Islamic duty. The critics explain this move as inspired by the TJ leaders' fear that educated Meos might challenge their own claims to leadership of the Meo community.

Yet, despite its apparent lack of concern with the this-worldly affairs of its followers, the TJ has been able to accommodate some of the challenges that modernity is bringing about in Mewat today. Indeed, some of the values that the TJ sees as central to Islam bear a striking resemblance to the Protestant ethic that Weber ties in with the spirit of modernity in his classic work on the evolution of capitalism (Weber, 1930). In a manner similar to the Protestant case, in some respects the TJ might be said to effectively be promoting an inadvertent modernization, albeit with a suitable 'Islamic' gloss. As the TJ sees it, the individual believer is armed with an instrumentality in realizing the Islamic mission in this world. The fortunes of Islam are thus seen to be determined not by the presence of a Muslim ruler, as in the past, but by the active and conscious involvement of every Muslim individual, all of whom are charged with a new sense of agency and mission to change the world by working to implement God's will on earth.

Some of the values that the movement stresses, such as punctuality, the value of time, cleanliness, the equality of all believers and concern for others, derive from certain strands of Sufism. These values have powerful echoes in modernity and tie in with what the TJ sees as its 'civilizing' mission, rescuing Muslims from both 'superstition' and 'corrupt' and wasteful practices. The TJ's attack on the mediational cults of popular Sufism, and in the case of the Meos, on the widespread belief in spirits, ghosts and local deities, represents a distinct, albeit limited, rationalization of the world that modernity also seeks to promote. The TJ's stress on Islamic scripturalism and the universal Muslim *umma* works to undermine locally rooted identities. In Mewat and in much of the rest of India, these identities are predicated on caste and sect, major hurdles with which modernity has to contend.

Travelling on *tabligh* work outside one's own locality to other villages and towns and even to other countries promotes a new sense of shared Muslim identity that transcends the local. It thereby promotes what could be called a 'transportable Islam' that is at home all over the world, since TJ missionaries carefully seek to make TJ practices and methods uniform and standardized wherever they are active. This represents a standardization of Islam rooted in Islamic scripturalism, bringing together Muslims from different regions in a shared universe of discourse and with a common commitment to the Tablighi project. It also serves to undermine local forms of Islam that are seen to divide the universal *umma*. In these senses, then, the movement represents a novel form of Islamic modernity.

Two factors in particular facilitate the TJ's ability to come to terms with some of the most pressing challenges that modernity poses in its wake. One is the movement's lack of a centralized organizational structure and the other is the nature of its missionary strategy, seeking to steer clear of *ikhtilafi* issues and focusing on the *faza'il* instead of the *masa'il*. Since the TJ issues no official statements and has no official publications of its own, at the local level TJ activists are somewhat free to interpret the TJ message in their own ways, albeit within certain broad limits. Thus, while some TJ activists today lament many Meos' growing enthusiasm to send their children to modern schools, the movement as such does not explicitly condemn this.

Indeed, some TJ leaders actually welcome this development, although they insist on the primacy of Islamic education, and argue that Meo children studying at modern schools must also receive traditional Islamic knowledge so that their faith in Islam is not diluted or compromised by studying in general schools that often betray a distinct Hindu bias. Today some TJ activists may go so far as to insist that Muslim children acquire modern education, for only then can Muslims establish their supremacy over other communities. In a similar vein, they argue that if pious Muslims armed with knowledge of the world excel in various fields of worldly activity, the non-Muslims with whom they come into contact may be suitably impressed and even consider embracing Islam. Thus, modern education is grudgingly accepted by some TJ activists, and warmly embraced by others. Both camps regard this as a means to promote what they see are the interests of Islam, and not simply as an end in itself.

In political matters too, the TJ displays a remarkable flexibility despite its apparent rigidity. Here it follows in the general Deobandi tradition. The elders of the Deoband *madrasa*, while rigid in matters of religion, were flexible pragmatists in matters of politics. They stood for strict conformity to the *shari`a*, as they understood it, condemning Muslim 'modernists' as veritable apostates, and seeing all religions other than Islam as pathways to hell. Yet most of them were also enthusiastic supporters of the Hindu-dominated Indian National Congress and its project of a united India. Numerous Deobandis were in the forefront of the Indian independence movement, and were among the bitterest critics of the Muslim League and its demand for a separate Muslim state of Pakistan. The rector of the Deoband *madrasa*, Maulana Hussain Ahmad Madni, went so far as to insist that nationality (*qawmiyyat*) was determined not by religion but by common land of birth. The Hindus and Muslims of India, he insisted, arguing against the claims of the Muslim League, were members of one national community.[7] On the other hand, a minority among the Deobandis, led by Maulana Ashraf Ali Thanwi, lent its support to the Pakistan demand, insisting that the Muslims and the Hindus were indeed two separate nations. Ilyas was influenced by both groups among the Deobandis, with several of his teachers and mentors from either group. Yet even at the height of the Pakistan movement in the mid-1940s, Ilyas steered clear from overt political involvement, preferring to focus on strengthening and reinforcing Muslims' commitment to Islam. This, he believed, was the only way in which Muslims could regain God's favour and establish their political supremacy over others in the future, as the people charged with spreading God's chosen faith.

In Mewat today, the TJ's silence on political affairs enables its followers to make pragmatic political decisions. They can thus accommodate themselves to a non-Islamic and non-Muslim state, implicitly accepting the principle of secularism and the personalization of religion. The Meos are left free to decide which political parties to vote for and with which groups to enter into alliances. Thus, most Meos vote for political parties that are largely controlled by non-Muslims and have no commitment to an Islamic state, which is what Ilyas himself believed to be a central component of an ideal Islamic society.

The TJ justifies this accommodation to practical politics and acceptance of secularism as a necessary step in the path of ultimately establishing an Islamic state in the distant future. TJ leaders and activists believe that Muslims are today living in a state similar to that of the Prophet at Mecca (*makki daur*). This was a period when Muslims were learning their faith in the face of active persecution by their enemies, and when the Prophet lacked political power. The culmination of the Prophet's life was the establishment of an Islamic state at Medina, ruled according to the *shari`a*. Muslim societies should thus aspire to establish the Medinan period (*madni daur*) as the ultimate state. However, to reach that goal, they must first eschew all concern with politics. They must focus, as the Muslims in the Meccan period are said to have done, simply on cultivating their faith in and knowledge of Islam, for only then will they win God's pleasure. Political power represented by the Medinan phase of the Prophet's life is not something for which one should struggle actively. Rather, it is a gift that God gives to Muslims if they strictly abide by the commandments of the faith.

Contemporary Muslims the world over, who are seen as still in the Meccan phase after 'straying' from the path of Islam, must therefore concern themselves with strengthening their faith. In effect, the establishment of an Islamic state – the ushering in of the Medinan phase – is postponed into the indefinite future. As the TJ sees it, the cultivation of faith which is the defining feature of the Meccan phase is a long drawn-out process virtually without end, given the constant presence of worldly temptations and distractions. The followers of the movement in Mewat and elsewhere are thus able to conduct their politics on pragmatic, as opposed to ideological, lines and to come to terms with the absence of non-Muslim rule and the presence of a secular polity. Here the TJ stands in marked contrast to Islamist movements that see their primary and immediate goal as the establishment of an Islamic state, ruled in accordance with the laws of the *shari`a*.

Conclusion

As this general survey of the TJ in Mewat suggests, the emergence and development of the TJ in Mewat is a distinctly modern, although not quite modernist, phenomenon. The launching of the TJ movement by Maulana Ilyas in the 1920s in Mewat was prompted largely by distinctly modern developments. These were primarily the obtrusive presence of the British colonial state and the competition between Hindu and Muslim elites for numbers, leading to new understandings of community identities and confessional boundaries. The TJ was not opposed to Sufism as such, and following in the general Deobandi tradition in which it is rooted, the TJ sought to redefine Sufism by bitterly critiquing what it saw as 'un-Islamic' influences and insisting on the need to conform to the commandments of the *shari`a*. In turn, this *shari`a*-centred scripturalist form of Sufism helped further galvanize the process of redefining Muslim identity, seeking to clearly demarcate Muslims from their Hindu neighbours, in part to meet the grave threat of Hindu missionaries working among *nau*-Muslim groups.

The TJ's reformed Sufism has had important consequences for religious authority and how this authority comes to be imagined and articulated. It therefore ties in with distinctly modern concerns. In challenging the claims of the custodians of the Sufi shrines as intermediaries, in insisting on the need for every Muslim to be armed with a knowledge of the faith, and in stressing the duty of all believers to carry out the work of *tabligh*, the TJ promotes a de-centring of authority, or what can be called the priesthood of all believers. Consequently, the role of the Sufi *shaykh* comes to be imagined differently. From a spiritual guide who leads his disciple on the mystical path or *tariqa*, he is transformed into a teacher who instructs his followers on the path of the *shari`a*. The ideal Sufi is no longer one who escapes the world into mystical, transcendental states. Rather, he is one who actively works in this world for the realization of God's will on earth. The charisma of the medieval Sufi *shaykh* and the *silsila* or Sufi brotherhood is now sought for endowment upon the charismatic community of Tablighi activists as a whole, although within the community those with more knowledge or experience of *tabligh* work are accorded a special status and respect.

The TJ's message of scripturalist reform, which it sees as a civilizing mission, promotes certain values that bear a distinct resemblance to those associated with the project of contemporary modernity. Further, while not uncritically embracing all that modern life brings in its trail, its conscious refusal to address *ikhtilafi masa'il* enables its followers to make pragmatic adjustments to the challenges and prospects of living under a non-Muslim state, including accepting, in practical terms, the principle of secularism. Given the loose organizational structure of the movement, its activists are able to adjust within broad limits to what might otherwise be seen as 'un-Islamic' institutions. Here they are free from the rigid controls of a central authority, which makes the TJ unlike most Islamist movements. These circumstances help to promote a distinctly Tablighi approach to modernity. While not fully approving of all or even most of what dominant contemporary forms of modernity entail, this approach is nevertheless willing to accept some aspects of them, suitably reinterpreted. The TJ then makes these an integral part of what it sees as its own divine mission, as the movement charged with spreading God's chosen faith.

9

NATIONAL CRISIS AND THE REPRESENTATION OF TRADITIONAL SUFISM IN INDONESIA: THE PERIODICALS *SALAFY* AND *SUFI*

Michael Laffan

The struggle between Sufis and anti-Sufis as rival claimants to a discourse of Islamic authenticity has a long and varied history. The story of that contest in Indonesia shares many features with the struggle in other contexts (De Jong and Radtke, 1999; Sirriyeh, 1999). Just as the boundaries of the future state were being finalized by Dutch colonialism at the turn of the twentieth century, this contestation became particularly intense, as it was coupled with debates about national identity and progress. With the rise of vernacular newspapers and competing discourses of modernity – whether Westernized or the Islamic variant formulated by the Cairo-based reformers Muhammad `Abduh (1849-1905) and Rashid Rida (1865-1935) – the exponents of the Sufi orders were often consigned to the rural periphery of a new imagination that was urbanizing and nationalized.

Certainly the ideas of `Abduh and Rida concerning the need to return to an understanding of Islam based only on Qur'an and *sunna*, set in harmony with all forms of modern technological progress, seemed to hold sway in the emergent Indonesian public sphere over the first half of the century. This was especially marked in the ranks of the urban-based Muhammadiyah movement which, following its inception in 1912, spread its network of schools and hospitals across the country. The debate between Muslim modernists and their rural opponents was further radicalized in the 1920s with the ascent in Arabia of the Saudi dynasty that many modernists supported due to their shared distaste for the alleged excesses of the Sufi shaykhs. Equally it has become common for enemies of the modernists to brand them as puritanical Wahhabis under the spell of the most famous critic of Sufi heresy in the eighteenth century, Muhammad bin `Abd al-Wahhab (1703-87), even if Wahhabis and modernists alike renounce the term in favour of the ascription as 'Unitarians' (*muwahhidun*) or, increasingly, the true Salafis, that is: the followers of the pious forebears of Islam (*al-salaf al-salih*).

The single most influential movement founded to defend 'traditionalist' Islam in Indonesia is the Nahdlatul Ulama (NU), founded in 1926. As such, NU defends the form of Islamic teaching and practice that recognizes the authority of the four *madhhab*s (the orthodox schools of law), the charismatic authority of the shaykhs, the importance of visiting holy graves, and the validity of Sufi ethics and ritual. Ever since the early years of the independent Republic of Indonesia, the sympathizers of NU have competed with their rivals from the modernist end of the Islamic spectrum for access to power and position with the government of the day. At times, some groups have sought support from abroad. The doctrinaire Indonesian Council for Islamic Propagation (DDII), for example, has to a degree served as the Indonesian arm of the Saudi-sponsored Muslim World League, founded in 1962, even if the latter league was often seen as a source of funding more than of dogma (van Bruinessen, 2002).

The last three decades of the twentieth century, and especially the 1990s, saw a greater distancing of the Saudi-oriented Salafis from the modernists and a reappearance of Sufis in state discourses, and not just in Indonesia. Skovgaard-Petersen (1997) has argued that the twentieth century has seen a Salafizing trend in Egypt's premier *fatwa*-issuing body, the Dar al-Ifta. However it seems remarkable that the Mufti of the Egyptian Republic in 2006, Dr `Ali Gum`a, is a prominent member of the Shadhiliyya order, while his predecessor, Ahmad al-Tayyib, was a member of the Khalwatiyya. In Indonesia, too, there has been a rapprochement between leading modernists and traditionalist thinkers, many of whom emphasize the shared heritage of a distinctly Southeast Asian Islam.

Meanwhile the earlier debates about orthodoxy and Sufism in the public sphere have been obscured by arguments about the interactions between Islam and the state. There has been a certain degree of engagement between these mass-organizations – with members of both serving on the *fatwa*-issuing panels of the Majelis Ulama Indonesia – and their respective leaderships speaking out on common concerns like the US invasion of Iraq. Yet such cooperation usually recognizes, rather than resolves, differences between them. NU-sponsored lessons on classical *fiqh* and the rituals of the *tariqa*s still contrast with the organized classrooms of Muhammadiyah's universities.

Certainly contestation about Sufism is ongoing in Indonesia. However its contemporary expressions have been little documented because they fall beyond either the Muhammadiyah–NU fault line or the pale of discussions of modernity. Moreover, as I now suggest, they are not necessarily foregrounded in the radical Salafist discourse that is so often in the headlines, whether in connection with *jihad* in the Moluccas or the reported plots of Jamaah Islamiyah.

This chapter is thus an attempt to trace the echoes of an old but still ongoing debate through a reading of two recent periodicals that claim to represent opposite ends of the spectrum of Islamic opinion in Indonesia. I argue that the positions taken in these journals – appropriately entitled *Salafy* and *Sufi* – show the sharply divergent visions of Sufism still held by some elements of Indonesian society. Still, the fact that each perceives the other as a force to be opposed is not always immediately discernable, especially as they often share an elementary vocabulary of faith and practice and openly agree that a proper understanding and practice of Islam (as each understands it) is essential to the salvation of the nation from its perceived ills. To explore their differences, one must look closely at their differing modes of explicating these basic elements of practice, which in turn shows what form of religiosity each actually sanctions or condemns.

Furthermore today's Sufis and Salafis share in something else, viz. the very means of communicating with their partisans in the Umma. Indeed it is significant in itself that Sufis and their sympathizers have launched their own magazine(s) to put forward their point of view, taking fuller advantage of the modern media than they have in the past.

The *Salafi* Path: Saving Indonesia with Shari`a

In July 2002, I was struck by the numerous banners draped from bridges crossing Jakarta's arterial toll-ways. At this time a motion was before Indonesia's upper house urging that it affirm – at least in name – support for Islam as the fundamental basis for the state by reinstating the long-erased Jakarta Charter.[1] Many of the banners supported the parties advocating the motion, among them the local branch of the transnational movement for a global caliphate, Hizbut Tahrir. But one pennant in particular seemed to sum up the principle concern of the various Islamist factions; it read *Selamatkan Indonesia dengan Syariah*, 'Save Indonesia with *shari`a*'. Certainly Indonesia was then a crisis zone. With the fall of Suharto in 1998 after the onset of the Asian economic crisis, the archipelago was peppered with violent conflicts over rights to land and property, widespread confusion about the impact of regional autonomy (initiated in January 2001), and the mass dislocation of populations in the Eastern half of the archipelago along religious and ethnic lines.

The first journal I wish to examine, *Salafy* (1995-2000), born before this atmosphere of crisis, developed in what history will adjudge to have been the twilight years of Suharto's New Order (1966-98). In the early and mid-1990s the regime, which had come to power in the aftermath of the communist putsch of 30 September 1965, was actively courting Islam. Suharto himself – previously noted for his opposition to political Islam and his trust in Javanese spiritualism – had performed the pilgrimage to Mecca in 1991 and was supporting the development of a Salafi-inclined association for self-proclaimed 'Muslim intellectuals' under the leadership of his deputy B.J. Habibie. A sense of crisis may not then have been palpable for most Indonesians, but the advocates of *Salafy* were united in a sense that their nation needed saving from itself, and especially from the deviant versions of Islam that seemed to permeate the nation. Had they been allowed, they would have condemned Suharto's state-backed Islamization as insincere. For them, and like the makers of the Islamist banners fluttering over Jakarta's toll-ways, *shari`a* was the only solution. But unlike many of the parties that would press for the revival of the Jakarta Charter, they rejected participation in the democratic process, regarding the extant form of representational politics as being intrinsically contrary to Islam.

Salafy, which first appeared in December 1995, was subtitled 'the effort to emulate the steps of the generation of the Pious Forebears' (*upaya miniti jejak generasi salafus shalih*), meaning the generation of those Muslims who formed the first community of Islam under the leadership of Muhammad. *Salafy* was an offering of the *pesantren* Ihya'us Sunnah. This institution, located in Degolan, some 16 kilometres north of Yogyakarta, was one of the first of a number of openly Wahhabi institutions founded in the mid-1990s.[2] Its leader, Ja'far Umar Thalib (b. 1961), had modelled the curriculum on that of his teacher in Yemen, Muqbil ibn Hadi al-Wadi`i, with whom he had studied after participating in the Afghan conflict, an experience that he often emphasized along with his heritage as the descendant of a Hadrami migrant to Southeast Asia.

Thalib and his lieutenant Muhammad Umar as-Sewed determined the content of *Salafy*, which could not be any closer to the semi-official *da`wa*-oriented doctrine propagated by Muqbil ibn Hadi, and his mentors in Saudi Arabia, the late Nasir al-Din al-Albani (1909-99), and `Abd al-`Aziz `Abd Allah bin Baz (1912-99). In this respect, then, they were the Central Javanese representatives of a specific Saudi-sponsored Salafi movement in Indonesia. Thalib and his followers would later be propelled to national prominence due to their involvement in the fratricide in the Moluccas in 2000-02, for which they sought *fatwa*s from their `*ulama*-masters in Arabia as justification, claiming that it represented a defensive *jihad* (Hasan, 2005).

Their initial foray into publishing in late 1995 was a modest affair. According to the first editorial (Thalib and as-Sewed 1995), *Salafy* aimed to disseminate understanding of the steps of the Pious Forebears in terms of doctrine (`*aqida*), moral behaviour (*akhlaq*) and *shari`a*. This was to raise various issues to combat those who falsely claimed to represent the Salaf and orthodoxy under the slogan of being 'people of the practice of the Prophet and consensus' (*ahl al-sunna wa-l-jama`a*; a name usually claimed by NU) when in fact they were a 'people of heresy' (*ahl al-bid`a*) who spread their teachings alongside the 'secularists' (*orang sekuler*).

Much of the content of *Salafy* was taken directly from the writings of the Salafi `ulama* of the Hijaz. For example, a feature article by al-Albani on 'authenticity' (*asala*) outlined the necessity for true Muslims to identify themselves as Salafis in order to transcend *madhhab*-centric particularisms and to distinguish themselves from the many factions of misled groupings of the times (al-Albani, 1995).[3] Here al-Albani mentioned all manner of Islamic sects, past and present, including Rafidi Shi`a, `Ibadis, Qadiyanis and various 'other groups', leading me to wonder how highly the Sufis actually ranked on the ever lengthening list of the lost. This was made clear, however, in his conclusion. Here, in his critique of partisan fanaticism (*ta`assub*) and of believers unable to transcend a basic social identification as Muslims, al-Albani makes mention of those unable to detach themselves from membership of sects, *madhhab*s, and mystical orders – even if 'all such ascriptions are not in accordance with the *shari`a* and are unsound'.

The call of al-Albani for the widespread adoption of the Salafi *manhaj* (program) is followed by articles by Thalib on deviant groups (Thalib, 1995a) and on the history and correct understanding of orthodoxy (Thalib, 1995b). Here he makes use of a dictionary of classical Arabic and *hadith* to discuss the key terms of *sunna* (tradition), *jama`a* (community), *bid`a* (innovation), *khalaf* (successor) and *salaf* (generation). As-Sewed then interposes an article on the history of *shirk* (the ascription of divine power to deities other than Allah) in the Arabian peninsula (As-Sewed, 1995), before Thalib gives his outline view of 'Salafi propagation at the crossroads' and announces the goals of the Salafis. These goals are (1) to return mankind to its position as a servant of God and to affirm His oneness as Lord and Divinity through His names (*asma*) and 'qualities' (*sifat*); (2) to purify hearts, tongues and acts of all *shirk*; and (3) to save all humanity from Hell and to bring them to God's mercy (Thalib, 1995c).

Broadly speaking there is little in the stated goals of *Salafy* that most *shari`a*-oriented Sufis would contest, apart from their being grouped with the lost by the self-appointed partisans of orthodoxy. Indeed at many levels even the mystics share the terminologies adopted by the *Salafy* authors for discussion in their journal. Various issues contain discussions of such words as *dhikr* (recollection of God), *tawassul* (mediation with the Divine), *baraka* (Divine blessing), *tawba* (repentance), *wara`* (piety), *zuhd* (ascetic withdrawal or renunciation), *sabr* (patience) and *tawakkul* (absolute trust in God). However, the similarity ends here. The Salafi authors usually commence their articles with a rigid literalism, often proceeding from a dictionary definition or one found in a work of exegesis, before moving through a hierarchy of authoritative usage, from Qur'an and *hadith*, followed by the Pious Forebears, the Successors, and lastly the jurists.

One of the first terms to be addressed in *Salafy*, and one that sets the pattern for future issues, is that of *dhikr* (al-Salafi, 1995: 74). Here `Abd al-Mu`ti al-Salafi provides an excerpt from a passage on 'the excellence of recollection' by Imam Nawawi (1233-77), who in turn cited *hadith* from Muslim bin al-Hajjaj (d. 875) on the four most-favoured formulae; *subhan Allah* (praise God!), *al-hamdu lillah* (praise be to God), *la ilaha illa Allah* (there is no god other than God), *Allahu akbar* (God is great). No mention is made, however, of any communal uttering of these phrases to the accompaniment of physical movements or music, as is often done in the context of a Sufi gathering. As such, there is no obvious critique of Sufism. Instead it is ignored or relegated to the margins by foregrounding one understanding of practice to the exclusion of all others. A similar method, literal and *hadith*-based, is employed in later articles dealing with *akhlaq* (morals) and *zuhd* (renunciation).[4]

The first developed statement of distaste for the Sufis, and indeed for the undifferentiated grouping of Sufis as representatives of the *tariqa*s, actually comes in the fifth issue (Dhu 'l-hijja 1416/1996). Here the cover, under the heading 'answering the problematics of the *umma*', portrays a modern Indonesian book on Sufism bedecked with a set of prayer-beads and sitting amidst money, flowers and signet rings. The implication is obvious: the community is plagued by its recognition of the teachers who often wear these rings and carry the beads, and who sanction the offerings of flowers and money at the tombs of the departed (or who covet the money for themselves).

The substantive article that is related to the none-too-subtle cover is in the form of a book review written by Junaidi. This review is of the very book displayed, being an examination and presentation of the thought and poetry of a famous Sumatran mystic of the sixteenth century (Hadi, 1995).[5] This book was written by the well-known litterateur, poet and now lecturer at Jakarta's Universitas Paramadina, Abdul Hadi W.M., and it was published in 1995 by the innovative Islamic press, Mizan.[6] Certainly, *Salafy*'s juxtaposition of the work with the paraphernalia of corruption is problematic, as Abdul Hadi's book is by no means a manual of the dark arts. Rather it is a scholarly treatment of manuscript versions of Hamzah Fansuri's poetry.

Regardless of this, the *Salafy* reviewer is less interested in examining Abdul Hadi's book than attacking the misguided travellers on the mystic path in general, and identifying them all, along with the contents of the book, as manifestations of the purportedly heretical doctrine of the *wujudiyya* that allows for the possibility of human recognition of the Divine.[7] Indeed the bulk of the review is in fact a restating of the purported views of Ibn Taymiyya (and Bayruni Abu Rayyan) that Sufism was a twisted form of the Greek concept of 'wisdom' (*sophia*, glossed in *Salafy* as *sophos*) that could only serve to confuse, or worse that it is some bastardized and outmoded incorporation of Indic pantheism.

The attitude of the *ulama* of the Ahl al-sunna wa-l-jama`a towards *tasawwuf* since the first time it appeared as a teaching/faith (*ajaran/aqidah*) and until today is the same. They have come to the same conclusion that *tasawwuf* – as a teaching or way of thought – is an innovation because it is attributed to Islam, whereas the ideas of its thought actually deviate from Islam itself. (Junaidi, 1996: 68)

Various charges follow, including that Sufis believe Hell is a garden-paradise and that even unbelievers will benefit from God's mercy and grace. These are capped off by the reviewer's own surprise and concern:

Regardless of the intention of the publisher in releasing this book, [its] appearance ... is extremely ironic amidst the rising call to return to the true understanding of Islam based on the Qur'an and *hadith*. If we are not careful, this book, with its many footnotes, will be a loose cobble [that could trip up] the propagation of [correct] Islam. (Junaidi, 1996: 69)

By and large, however, the critique against Sufism found in *Salafy* is not so direct. Issue number 7 (*Safar* 1417/1996), for example, condemns the celebration of the Prophet's birthday as favoured by the Sufis, while issue number 12 (Rajab 1417/1996) critiques the common Sufi practice of building structures over tombs and making a journey (*rihla*) with the aim of visiting a tomb (*ziyara*). The latter article (al-Kaf, 1996), which frequently cites al-Albani, repeats the *hadith* that one should not set out on a journey except to visit three mosques: the Meccan Haram, that of the Prophet in Medina, and the al-Aqsa Mosque in Jerusalem. This implies that the various *ziyara*s of the Sufis are invalid.

On other occasions, the opportunity to ridicule certain practices is missed, or put in a tangential way. In issue number 15, Ahmad Hamdani discusses whether a Muslim could ever see the face of God without suffering destruction, and focuses on the promise that God will be seen only after death (Hamdani, 1997a). The argument is that given Muhammad was not able to see God when he was alive, and as nobody can claim to be greater than the Prophet, the claim of any other mortal to be able to see Him is ludicrous. It appears that here some potential is missed, as the opportunity seemed available to criticize the claims of certain ecstatic Sufis who are said to be *majdhub*, that is, they experience a sense of 'attraction' (*jadhba*) to God.[8] Such questions had animated Kelantanese society on the northeast coast of the Malay Peninsula at the turn of the twentieth century. In 1905, the Raja of Kelantan had requested a *fatwa* on the matter from the eminent Patani scholar and resident of Mecca, Ahmad bin Muhammad Zayn al-Fatani (1856-1906).[9] In his request, the Raja mentioned that some of the ecstatic Sufis of the Ahmadiyya order claimed to have seen God in various unlikely places. The *shari`a*-oriented scholar (*and* Sufi) al-Fatani replied that such was not possible, and supplied the standard answer that such visions could only be inspired by malignant *jinn* who could affect the visions of weak students or those whose teacher or knowledge of the *shari`a* was deficient (al-Fatani, 1957; cf. Kraus, 1999).

Perhaps, though, the editors of *Salafy* felt that such purported excesses as the *majdhub* no longer trouble Southeast Asian Islam. Instead, a far more direct critique of the Sufis is found in the discussion of a *hadith* regarding the status of being a '*wali*' (a saint or friend of God) (Al-Medani, 1997). At the same time, the article on this *hadith* carries a description of a believer enraptured with love for God. The tradition itself runs as follows:

> The Prophet (p.b.u.h.) said: God has said: I shall declare war upon whosoever makes an enemy of my *wali*. No servant of mine shall approach me other than through doing what I love most of the things I have made obligatory for him, and a servant shall be constantly approaching Me (*yataqarrub ilayya*) by doing what goes beyond the incumbent so that I shall love him. When I love him, I shall be the auditor of what he hears, the witness of what he sees, the hand with which he strikes and the leg with which he walks. And if he asks aid of Me, then I shall give it, and should he ask My protection, I shall protect him. (as quoted by Al-Medani [1997: 40])

The article gives the various sources for this *hadith*, noting their transmitters and assessing their chains of transmission, before pronouncing a final assessment that it had been elevated to the level of being sound (*sahih*) by the ultimate authority of the Salafis, Nasir al-Din al-Albani. Further affirmation of its reliability is proven with references to Muhammad al-Shawkani of Yemen,[10] a certain al-Tuqi, and `Abd al-Fadl bin `Ata, before a definition of *wali*-ness (*ke-wali-an/walaya*) is given from Ibn Mansur's dictionary (*Lisan al-`arab*) and various works of exegesis. In short, for the editors of *Salafy*, *walaya* entails (divinely sanctioned) 'power', and like the various exegetes they consulted, they hold that it can only be achieved through *iman* (faith) and *taqwa* (piety).

The main point the author makes in the article is that 'the door of *wali*-hood is still open' (*pintu kewalian tetap terus terbuka*) to any believer who practices the *sunna*. Further, there is an especially exalted rank of *wali*, and it is at this point that reference is made to the pseudo-*wali*s, with the statement that 'the noble *wali*s are the Prophets and Messengers, which makes the errors of the extremist Sufis very clear' (p. 42). No others may hope to claim immunity from error (as is alleged by some Sufis), and once the believer is vouchsafed the love of God through his or her sincere practice of the *sunna*, then the words of the *hadith* will be realized.

> Thus, whoever really approaches God (*bertaqarrub kepada Allah*) with actions that are *wajib* (obligatory) or *sunna*, God will bring him close to

Him and raise the status of His servant from *iman* (faith) to *ihsan* (spiritual perfection). Thus the servant shall worship God as if in constant dread of seeing Him. His heart is filled with knowledge of God, love, awe, fear and the like as if he is just about to see God. Once his heart is filled with the awe of God, then he will forget all beyond God. No trace remains of his self or lower passions, or of his will, save that which is willed by his Lord. At that moment the servant cannot speak other than by pronouncing *dhikr* to Him, he cannot move save by His decree. This is the understanding of the *hadith* in question. (Al-Medani, 1997: 44)

It is interesting here to note a concern with a hierarchical differentiation between *iman* and *ihsan* as levels of spirituality, much as is found in Sufi understandings of the levels of Islamic practice.[11] But this comes with a caveat:

Whoever understands [this *hadith*] in any way other than this is directed towards heterodoxy (*ilhad/pengingkaran*), that is *hululiyya* and *ittihadiyya* ([the belief that] Allah shall join and merge with the body of the servant). God and His prophet disassociate themselves from this matter. (Al-Medani, 1997: 44)

Despite this caveat, however, the passage on *taqarrub* is still redolent of the deep spirituality of the Sufis. And one should certainly not deny that the Salafis, too, value emotive forms of spiritual devotion and sincere love of God. Seen in this light, their aspirations may align but their methods differ. Moreover, as their earlier reference to 'extremist' Sufis suggests, the Salafis abhor the excessive philosophizing of the *hululiyya* or *ittihadiyya*. The person who truly loves God and who has advanced to the stage of *ihsan* may have his or her actions guided by the Divine, but he or she is absolutely passive in this, and at no point does the created *become* the Creator.

This becomes clearer after another page when the article turns its sights on the Sufis once more, noting that the great jurist Ibn Hajar al-`Asqalani (1372-1449) made mention of the many ignorant Sufis who believed that their movements were guarded by God and that they were protected from error:

This *hadith* is not to be understood as it is by those of the *wahdat al-wujud* and *ittihadiyya* ... who ultimately declare infidel things like 'I am God', or 'God is I', like al-Hallaj. We take refuge in God from *shirk*. Hey, all you who equivocate! Concentrate yourselves on the oneness of God. Amen. (Al-Medani, 1997: 45)

Despite the apparent overlap in depiction of experience of oneness, the key difference between the Salafis and their Sufi opponents lies in relation to the question of the unity of being (*wahdat al-wujud*); a doctrine that not all Sufis embrace but that all Salafis nonetheless ascribe to them. There is also a sharp difference on authority, specifically on how knowledge of divinity is to be mediated, and how God's favours are to be distributed. This is made all the clearer in issue number 21, when the rubric of 'doctrine' is devoted to the question of *tawassul* (Hamdani, 1997b). Here the author sharply condemns those who believe that God will bestow His miracles (*karamat*) upon people who ask for them via a third party or, worse, that they will gain blessings through proximity to allegedly blessed people or objects:

> Even more astray are the group of people who allow *tawassul* to God via some part of His creation which is not properly deserving of honour, such as the graves of *wali*s, the buildings erected over those tombs, and the stones and trees in vicinity of something noble. (Hamdani, 1997b: 42)

'What, then, is *tawassul*?', ask the editors before commencing, once more, with a linguistic treatment of the term followed by *hadith*. Final say is given to al-Albani, who concludes that the only proper form of *tawassul* is the carrying out of good deeds. In all cases, the act and the benefit are entirely individual, and he pointedly rejects the practice of applying to deceased saints and the pious for aid in a time of crisis.[12] He asserts that only proper *tawassul* is to beseech God for aid by enacting the *shari`a*, calling directly in His name – or with any one of His names – by use of prayers deemed sound and used in the correct context, and, lastly, by good acts. This last form – *tawassul* through good acts – is illustrated with a long *hadith* about three believers trapped in a cave by a stone, which is moved by God only when they recount their most pious actions (Hamdani, 1997b). The remainder of the article is a series of refutations, some in the form of *fatwa*s, affirming that no boon can be granted by any of the dead, nor can they intercede on the behalf of a believer, even in times of peril.

A similar approach is manifested in a subsequent feature on *tabaruk*, i.e. seeking the blessings of God, where the actions of the misguided who seek such at the tombs of saints and the pious are cast as trying to destroy Islam from within (Nur and Al-Makasari, 1997). The surest proper way to carry out *tabaruk* is with *dhikr*, or by visiting the mosque, but not for the sake of the place itself:

> Carrying out *tabaruk* with the mosque does not entail covering it or its walls in a shroud. This is because *tabaruk* is the act of worship which must be in accordance with the practice of the Prophet (p.b.u.h.). Seeking *tabaruk* through mosques consists of remaining there for a time, awaiting the five prayers, praying together on Friday, attending *dhikr* sessions there, and other approved practices. Any practice not approved

by the *shari`a* will not bring *baraka*, and moreover shall constitute *bid`a*. (Nur and Al-Makasari, 1997: 37)

Here readers are reminded that only the three holiest mosques are valid destinations for Muslim travellers. It is then explained that *baraka* can be gained through 'time' – for example at such auspicious times as the month of Ramadan, Laylat al-Qadr, Fridays, and ten days before the month of Dhu 'l-hijja – before the briefest of paragraphs concludes with the mention that *baraka* might also be obtained from certain foods as mentioned by the Prophet, such as olive oil, honey, water from the well of Zamzam, and dates (Nur and Al-Makasari, 1997: 39).

Perhaps the sturdiest, though still ambiguous, assault on the Sufis comes in issue number 24 (Mu`thi, 1998). Here, under the rubric of 'the traps of Satan', the people of the mystical orders are accused of believing that once they have obtained gnosis (*ma`rifa*) they are no longer subject to the *shari`a*, or may follow a *shari`a* of their own. I say that the article is ambiguous because there seems to be some room left for the proper, '*shari`a*-oriented' Sufis in the justificatory text quoted in *Salafy*, the *Mukhtasar minhaj al-qasidin* of Ibn Qudama al-Maqdisi (1147-1223):

[On] The followers of the Sufi orders

First are those who appear to be Sufis from their clothing, their speech and their situation, despite the fact that they have never trained themselves to distance themselves from faulty qualities or base acts. Indeed they have fallen into forbidden things that incur God's wrath.

Second are those who claim to possess knowledge [of God], who claim to have witnessed God, are close to God, and to occupy elevated positions in God's eyes. As a matter of fact, in God's eyes they are deemed to be hypocrites who commit great evil. This is caused by their not possessing knowledge (about *shari`a*), they cannot inculcate moral values (which are truly Islamic), and have never guarded their hearts from following base passions.

Third are those who deviate from the *shari`a* and reject it, making *halal* the same as *haram*, whilst among them there are those who say: 'Actually God has no need of my actions, so I shall not trouble myself'. Others say: 'There is no measure (*nilai*) for the external acts of one's limbs, the measure is only of one's heart, hence we fulfil carnal desires only with the limbs of the body, whereas our hearts are turned towards God'. They believe that they have advanced to a more exalted position than the common people and thus feel that they need not educate themselves with external things whilst their heart is close to God.

Fourth are those who have no care for the *shari`a* and who busy themselves seeking direct knowledge of God, so that when the door of *ma`rifa* is opened to them (in truth by Satan), they feel proud and pour all their attention into thinking about this science of *ma`rifa*. (al-Maqdisi, in Anon., 1998: 15)

Regardless of the assumed existence of real Sufis (as opposed to pseudo-Sufis), and the fact that these categorizations of al-Maqdisi could just as easily be found in the works of their *shari`a*-oriented masters (the last passage, for example, is redolent of al-Fatani's *fatwa* about the *majdhub*), the intent of the editors is made more than clear:

In our current day we often witness people talking about religion without knowledge of the *shari`a* which God has brought down through His divine inspiration. They consist of various groups, both commoners and Muslim intellectuals. They are bold indeed to talk about religion without knowledge, and make their statements some sort of work motto. Thus we meet many Muslims who only have the religion of Mr X or Mr Y without the support of the *shari`a* which God brought down. And when we produce the *shari`a* evidence proving their erroneous thought and action, they will respond by saying: 'Kiai X said this, or Ustadh Y said so', without wanting to return to the Qur'an and *sunna* before the understanding of the Companions as the best generation. This attitude is one of Satan's most dangerous traps. It is developing because the community has been truly overwhelmed by the Sufi orders, which teach blind fanaticism to the Kiais, right or wrong. (Anon., 1998: 17)

This, then, is the final point of critique of Sufism as an undifferentiated array of antinomian and pantheistic heresies: the place of the Kiai as unquestioned master. Indeed it is made all the clearer in what seems to be the last word on Sufism found in *Salafy*, which comes, just like the first word, in the form of a book review. In issue number 25, Abu Fairuz (1998) sets out to comment on the 1998 translation of a work by one of al-Albani's students, `Ali Hasan `Ali `Abd al-Hamid, entitled *al-Bay`a bayna al-sunna wa al-bid`a* (The Pledge of Allegiance: Between Sunna and Bid`a). Fairuz's own review is badged as 'Bay`a: a strategy to catch people', and he provides thereby a positive view of the work as a useful warning to the community.

Abu Fairuz notes that the matter of the pledge to the master (*bay`a*) is of concern at many levels in Indonesian society, whether in any of the '45 or more' orders (glossed here as *aliran* in order to denigrate them as a form of Javanist piety) found in the homeland, or indeed among the various *da`wa* organizations that have taken on the structural forms of the Muslim Brothers.

Mention here of the 45 orders is a pointed reference to the NU-affiliated organization for the *tarekat*, the Jam'iyyah Ahlith Thoriqah Mu`tabaroh (JATM, 'the Association of People of the Reputable Path'), which recognizes 45 orders as being legitimate (see below), while the attack on the once-allied Muslim Brothers is phrased in terms of an accusation that its founder, Hasan al-Banna (1906-49), had modelled its system of allegiance on that of a (nonexistent) *tariqa*, the Hashafiyya.

Abu Fairuz further claims that the matter of *bay`a* had split the many factions of the old Negara Islam Indonesia (or Darul Islam) movement, and had permeated the nationwide branches of the LDII (Lembaga Dakwah Islam Indonesia). According to Shaykh `Ali, the various movements required a program (*manhaj*) and not a system of blind obedience to the dictates of a leader. The only true *bay`a* could be to the Imam, or Caliph of the entire Muslim community, but there was clearly no such person at the present time.

Yet even with the rejection of the principle of *bay`a* in favour of a *manhaj*, and in order that the student follows the true *sunna* that rejects blind allegiance, both author and reviewer alike are at pains to urge Muslims not to read many of the books mentioned in the (very modern) footnotes. It is to be taken on equally blind trust, then, that the various works of Muslim Brothers – like Sayyid Qutb, Hasan al-Banna or the more recent critic of Saudi policy, Muhammad bin Surur Zayn al-`Abidin – constitute a dangerous deviation to tempt believers from the true Salafi *manhaj*. The books of the Sufis, meanwhile, gain no mention at all.

One should still remember that the explicit statements found in the articles discussed above are uncommon in *Salafy*'s pages, especially once the war in the Moluccas took centre stage. Apart from the odd shot across the bows of the pseudo-*wali*s and their post-mortem devotees, the general tenor of the discourse in *Salafy* was that there were bigger fish to fry in the global war on *bid`a* than the degenerate masters of (past) Sufi deviation. Prior to issue number 28 (no month, 1419/1998), far more space is devoted to decrying the errors of the Muslim Brotherhood – and especially the followers of Muhammad Surur – than the errors of Sufis. Other prime targets include westernized intellectuals, and those who allegedly seek to destroy Islam from within, such as the teachers of the State Institutes for Islamic Studies (IAIN).

With the fall of Suharto and the ensuing chaos, the focus of *Salafy* became even more parochial, leading in time to the bloody intervention in the Moluccas that consigned Sufis and Sufism to an even smaller corner in the Salafi discourse of *jihad* against the Judeo-Christian plot to destroy Islam. In a sense, *Salafy* was rather like the older scripturalist journal *al-Lisaan* of the Persis-leader Ahmad Hassan in Bandung, which, despite the anti-Sufism of its editors, more usually turned its ideological assaults against whatever seemed to be the greater threat of the day. In the late 1930s, for example, the overriding concern was with the Ahmadiyya movement, which had been initially welcomed by the reformist movement on Java in the 1920s (Ichwan,

2001). Comparison might also be made with the Singaporean journal *al-Imam* in 1908, which joined in the debate about the place of Sufism in Malay society only after it had dealt, in far longer articles, with the need for Islamic education, political emancipation and modernization.

One might ask, then, what value there is in examining the content of another anti-Sufi journal that seems to be the latest in an ongoing stream of international disputation between the Wahhabiyya and the Sufi orders. I suggest that there is value in reading these in light of the fact that there is now a very major (and modern) change in the context of the debate. Unlike the first part of the twentieth century, Sufis now have their established voice in the public sphere of mass organizations and the press, just like the Salafis. Bearing in mind the above criticism of the Sufis by the Salafi movement, it is worthwhile identifying what kind of image is projected by urban elites connected to the traditional orders. I will show that while the Sufis have their modern voice, they are, like the Salafis, actually more interested in criticizing fellow travellers on their own side of the modernist/traditionalist divide than those who should be their diametric opponents.

Revived Sufism Defined in Jakarta:
A modern corporate voice for the *tarekat*[13]

From April 2000, at a small office in the suburbs of Jakarta, Luqman Hakiem (b. 1962) first oversaw a small staff to produce a monthly magazine on Sufism of 50 to 60 pages, called *Sufi*. Despite his relative youth, Luqman already gave instruction to members of the Shadhiliyya order, although it is unclear as to whether he was a *murshid* in his own right given that he does not have his own *pesantren*.[14] Luqman himself would not make any claims as to his own ranking in the mystical order of things, but suffice it to say he evinced the manner of someone very knowledgeable in his subject area. His manner is relaxed, and from our very first meeting he was an engaging discussant on the subject of the history of Sufism in Indonesia and its role in national life today.

As Luqman painted it, Sufism had long been a spirit pervading the activities of the Indonesian people. He recalled that Islam is popularly believed to have been brought to the principal island of Java by the famous *wali songo*, nine saints said to have Islamized the island by using methods consonant with its cultural values and aesthetics. Sunan Kalijaga, for example, is said to have invented the shadow-play for the very purpose. Luqman outlined how the *wali songo* had in turn sent their students as envoys to the people, establishing *pesantren* throughout the countryside at which instruction in the practices of the mystical orders was also given.

According to Luqman, some *pesantren* were refuges for ascetics, while others were exclusive domains for an elite under royal patronage. However, reformist currents within some Sufi orders in the eighteenth and nineteenth centuries, followed by open rivalry with the modernists in the early part of the twentieth century, began to impact on traditionalist Sufis of the *pesantren*, leading some to come together in the framework of the mass organization NU. Finally, the *pesantren* underwent a profound intellectualization in the 1980s when that organization was under the leadership of the charismatic *kiai* (and quixotic future president) Abdurrahman Wahid.

It is worth noting that Luqman is allied to Wahid's faction within NU. And that his journal did not appear from thin air; it required the kind of support that the organization could provide when Wahid was president. Yet such was not mentioned in our interviews, as Luqman explained how the idea for *Sufi* had been formed while writing a column for the Java-based tabloid *Posmo* – a contraction from 'Post-Modern' – aimed at anyone interested in 'Metaphysics and alternative medicine'. With its pages full of stories of magic, mysteries and the paranormal, *Posmo* would be anathema to the Salafis. One issue, for example, related the account of a pilgrim who claimed to have observed the great saint `Abd al-Qadir al-Jilani flying around the Ka`ba (Mufid, 2002).

Midst such a sea of distraction sat Luqman Hakiem's column '*konsultasi sufi*', in which he attempted to provide simply worded answers to people's problems. According to Luqman, this column generated significant interest, attracting 20 to 30 questions by email each week. He also averred that all these questioners emphasized they wanted Sufi, rather than juridical (*fiqhi*) answers. The comparison merits noting as over the course of the twentieth century various Muslim organizations, including Muhammadiyah and NU, have developed mechanisms to produce such juridical solutions for contemporary problems of the nation which are disseminated in their various journals and, increasingly, on their websites. The opening up of the public space for Islamic propagation since the early 1990s has also seen a surge in the number of books interpreting Islam for the average reader, including among them numerous texts on *fiqh* for modern times. Luqman was cynical about the general quality of these materials. And, much as he disdained the very idea of '*shari`a* banking' or '*shari`a* business', he used the analogy of drinking coffee to illustrate that while a legal scholar could tell you whether coffee was licit or otherwise, the Sufi knew the correct way to drink it by virtue of the proper knowledge of moral behaviour (*akhlaq*).

Luqman was also critical of the division that had emerged in Indonesian Islam over the course of the twentieth century between the modernists and traditionalists. To his mind, the former have become obsessively rationalist and doctrinaire, while the latter are now undergoing a spiritual crisis that commenced some two decades ago. Even worse, the financial crisis of 1998 deepened the overall malaise. He therefore asserted that people were (and are) in desperate need of a spiritual solution to their problem, a solution that is nonetheless practical or, more specifically, a 'liberal' Sufism.

Luqman's reference here to liberal Sufism seems to be an attempt to link the traditionalist Sufism of NU to the public 'neo-modernism' of Nurcholish Majid and Ulil Abshar Abdalla. Abdalla in particular has attracted widespread attention and controversy with his Liberal Islam Network (*Jaringan Islam*

Liberal), and at various public forums, both in Indonesia and abroad, he has enunciated a line that the Qur'an also needs to be understood as a product of its historical context.

Sufi itself first appeared in April 2000 and appeared regularly for the following 22 months before a hiatus of several months. Such a short initial print run is by no means unusual in the history of the Islamic press in Indonesia, or in Southeast Asia for that matter, where publishers are subject to the vicissitudes of paper prices, tastes and patronage. The theme of *Sufi*'s first issue announced the dawning of the third millennium, regardless of the Islamic date being Muharram 1421. According to *Sufi*'s first issue, in the aftermath of the parties that celebrated the end of the last millennium, with its 'exoticism, hedonism and dehumanism', people were faced with the new challenge of globalization.

> The fact is that as the global village becomes ever smaller, the solutions offered to mankind are no simpler, but rather are ever more complex, ever more barren and, finally, ever more removed from the oasis of this illusory life. The hell of the world becomes as a prison for the soul. The world of Sufism offers an escape from this prison through the heaven of the heart and inner peace of the soul. ... It is no exaggeration to say that the editorial team [of *Sufi*] wants to make this Sufi world more actual, bearing in mind that this Sufi world is growing at such a rapid rate today. (Hakiem, 2000a: 1)

The editors then affirm an intention to give practical advice to those seeking the mystical path by presenting general themes within the rubric of *tasawwuf*, and that they would consult with the leading Sufis of the nation. Several readers' letters give an idea of what would come. One claims that he found the standard books on Sufism far too dry and humourless and that they contain too little background on the lives of the great masters. Another urged that the web pages of the journal be updated with an English version 'to help those interested from abroad'.[15]

Clearly the journal had high ambitions, which might be taken as a sign of some interest in gaining a place in the global imagination, much as NU is now concerned with increasing its international profile with the mooted founding of a study centre in Cairo.[16] Still, one has to start somewhere, and after Luqman Hakiem's own introduction entitled 'Escape from the barren oasis' (Hakiem, 2000b), the leading feature consisted of an interview with former NU chairman Sahal Mahfudz. Here he reiterates that modern life is a strain, but that religious communities everywhere, and the Muslim *umma* in particular, know that the values of the past cannot simply be abandoned. Yet true Islam has seemingly been relinquished, and what has emerged in its place is an urban Sufism, whether practiced by cohorts of tie-wearing executives at five-star hotels or obscured by the gloss of performing artists.[17] Luqman then summarizes the contributions of Sahal Mahfudz, Said Aqil Siradj and Abdul Hadi, noting that the first would point out that modernity need not be in conflict with Sufism, Aqil would emphasize the inseparable nature of *tasawwuf* and *shari`a*, and the last would discuss the current tendency to run off to the clinics of quacks and paranormals instead of taking advantage of serious programs like those offered by the reputable institutions such as Universitas Paramadina. Finally, Luqman noted how their investigations had revealed 'the tragedy of Western society', which was suffused by fear and in danger of imminent breakdown. These circumstances highlighted the real need for a reconnection with God in this new millennium – and not just in Indonesia.

The very first question put to Sahal Mahfudz concerned how to face the 'tragedy' of modern life, which he answered with the straightforward imperative to look at Sufism in terms of three mutually reinforcing dimensions: *`aqida*, *shari`a* and *akhlaq*. That is, Sufism is a part of orthodoxy. Certainly this is the standard view of NU, which often claims the exclusive rights to the mantle of representing the Ahl al-sunna wa-l-jama`a in Indonesia. However we might also recall here that this same claim was made by the anti-Sufi editors of *Salafy*, who also emphasized the importance of *`aqida*, *shari`a* and *akhlaq*. Of these three dimensions of Sunni Islam in the conception of Sahal Mahfudz and NU, Sufism is but a facet of *akhlaq* to be studied only after all the other dimensions had been mastered. When Luqman put the question as to whether *tasawwuf* is a religious obligation, Mahfudz replied that it is, 'in order to make one's belief and practice of *shari`a* complete' (Hakiem, 2000c: 6).

Such themes are by no means new in Sufi thought, but this all served as an introduction to the main question on the matter of 'modernity':

L.H.   Modernity has caused a spiritual crisis. Can *tasawwuf* provide a solution?

S.M.   I see modernity as the crest of materialism that leads ultimately to secularism. A contradiction has emerged between modernity and Sufism, yet the fact is that we cannot avoid modernity in our lives. Because of this, perhaps there needs to be a fusion of the functions of Sufism and modernity. Sufism must become a guide to modernity itself.

L.H.   But if modernity ends in secularism, are not the values of Sufism quite separate from this?

S.M.   As a matter of fact it cannot be so. When talking of modernity we cannot separate it from rationality, efficiency, democracy, the acknowledgement of plurality and human rights. None of this conflicts with Sufism. If we can say that humanity (*manusia*) consists of a soul (*jiwa*) and body (*raga*) then one's material needs must also be answered, and in this Sufism has a role to play.

	Namely people's material needs can be directed by its ethics or morals.
L.H.	Where, then, is the meeting of Sufism with its spiritual morality, and modernity with its materialism?
S.M.	Modernity can still connect with Sufism. We know in Sufism that this world is a means (*sarana*) and not an end (*tujuan*), it is not a goal (*ghaya*) but just the means (*wasila*). One can reject wealth, but do not regard such a rejection as the final goal. As a means it can enrich and remind one of fraternal matters. For such reasons Sufism might become a way out for modern people. Let Sufis not be too exclusive or separate themselves from modernity. As modernity itself cannot be avoided and stands as an inevitability, there must be an effort to return to understanding the world as a tool and not a goal. (Hakiem, 2000c: 6-7)

The discussion continues in this vein for a little longer, with Luqman asking if current exclusivist practices by some Sufis constituted deviation or misuse, to which Sahal Mahfudz says that they are more in the nature of a distraction and he reiterates the need to grapple with the modern world. The main point should be that people should hold to their values and be motivated by their `aqida. And if they could not enact the *shari`a* in their daily lives, then any attempt to carry out *tasawwuf* can only fail.

Discussions then switched to the umbrella organization for the orders in Indonesia, the Jam'iyyah Ahlith Thoriqah Mu'tabaroh (JATM) now headed by the prominent Habib Luthfi of Pekalongan. On this grouping, Sahal urged that they not be regarded as an organization that managed Sufism, but rather as a forum to represent their interests. And finally, when asked for his opinion on criticisms that the JATM was 'unable to develop intellectually or artistically', Sahal Mahfudz responded:

> We do not say that Sufism progresses or declines, whatever the estimations of writings [on the subject] may be. In the field of Sufi writing, for example, one might ask what the *tarekat* people could say on the matter. Has there not already been much written by way of explanation in all sorts of books on Sufism? What is the use then of making new ones? I think that the real achievement of the Sufis has been to strengthen the morality of the community, this has been their greatest result. ... Who else is there that still holds up high moral values? We might well ask what has been the role of the *pesantren* in the life of the nation, what are the books that have been written [there] and how many university graduates have they produced, in which case the answer is: none. To write a book or produce a graduate is easy. Yet to make people good is truly difficult. That is what we want to see as the role of the Sufis today. (Hakiem, 2000c: 10)

While for Sahal Mahfudz modernity, however defined, is inescapable, he is well aware of the standard (and unsatisfactory) present responses to that modernity as may be noted in his reference to books and university graduates. Of course there have been some notable successes, and the next interview in *Sufi* was with Abdul Hadi from the Universitas Paramadina (Hakiem, 2000d). Abdul Hadi, whose book on Hamzah Fansuri had been so loudly denounced in *Salafy*, stresses that Sufis needed to bring themselves from isolation and into public life. His colleague at Paramadina, Rifa'i Hasan, then describes its new study program on 'Positive Sufism' that does not separate itself from daily life – although he disavowed the ideas that Sufism could, or should, become a mass movement (see Hakiem, 2000e). Here Rifa'i Hasan makes a comparison with the various mystical movements in the West, which he alleges have degenerated into schemes for the accumulation of wealth or which have even led to mass suicides. When asked if these could occur in Indonesia he expresses doubt, and points out that most popular practices are centred around simple or erroneous beliefs in magic and ritual – whether in drinking specially blessed water or visiting holy graves like those of the *wali songo*. He suggests that the JATM has a (national) role to play in distinguishing correct Sufism from such practices, but urges that this does not become one more way of pigeon-holing people, given that Sufism is about universality, not formalization.

The Sufis of the *pesantren*s may well feel that they have at times been pigeon-holed by their rivals from the modernist camp, which includes Ahmad Rifa'i and Abdul Hadi who came to Sufism by an academic rather than traditional road. Such a feeling of having been misunderstood is evinced in an article by NU's Said Aqil, entitled 'The Reconstruction of Sufism' (Aqil, 2000). According to Aqil, too many people have a distorted view of the true essence of Sufism as merely consisting of such ritual behaviour as the repetition of pious phrases. This, he said, was because of the propaganda of the modernists (also glossed in English as: 'Islamic movement') who Aqil argues aim to create a community that exhibits only the formal symbols of Islam in which every aspect of life has to be labelled as 'Islamic' in order to be deemed in step with modernization. But what, Aqil asks rhetorically, has this movement actually given Indonesians in the last 100 years? How has it contributed to the advancement of the *umma*? According to Aqil, it would be far better if people steep themselves again in the accumulated knowledge and spiritual values of Sufism, which are applicable to any place given that, to use the language of al-Junayd, 'Sufis are like colourless water'. That is, they take on the hue of their surrounds and yet suffuse it.

Aqil also attempted to counter the modernist presentation of Sufism as intellectual stagnation by presenting it as dynamic, using the example of the various different stages that the Sufi must transcend on the path to gnosis, such as penitence (*tawba*), piety (*wara'*), renunciation (*zuhd*), patience (*sabr*) and absolute trust in God (*tawakkul*). *Salafy* used these same terms, but in very different senses given that they are all conditions to be enjoined rather than a hierarchical schema of progress in quest of knowledge of, and, most anathemized, unity with, God.

Despite his arguments against the modernist labelling of Sufism as a cause of stagnation, Aqil seems in general agreement with the modernists (and their Salafi cousins) that stagnation itself is a present reality. Yet unlike the modernist discourse that ascribes an immediate decline in Muslim fortune and learning after the period of the Rightly Guided Caliphs (632-661), and a concomitant insistence on a return to Qur'an and *sunna* alone in order to reclaim the purity of the past, Aqil proposes return to a later past that also preserves the achievements made in the Golden Age of the Ayyubids (661-750) and Abbasids (720-1258).

> Ultimately in order to reconstruct Sufism, and especially in Indonesia, what is clearly needed are precise and accurate works of reference. The ultimate references must be compiled from the primary sources in the field of *tasawwuf* written by the Sufis of the second and third centuries of Islam, which were constantly examined in each successive period. After this, in the Middle Ages they were augmented by the compilations of the `ulama, at which time the Muslim World began several centuries of intellectual stagnation. (Aqil, 2000: 20)

While *Sufi* is not the source book visualized by Aqil, it is clearly an attempt to engage with modern people by providing them with accessible information about past greats and pointers to the primary sources. It also nudges them in the direction of the 'reputable orders' that carry on the traditions of that scholarship and practice.

When I asked a son of the then *kiai* of the famous Buntet *pesantren*, near Cirebon in West Java, whether he was familiar with the journal *Sufi* and Luqman Hakiem in particular, he replied that he certainly was, and that his father, Ki Fuad Hasyim, was a subscriber. He then remarked that it was a very useful journal for people in general given that it gave them the chance to familiarize themselves with the great mystics of the past, whose pictures adorn many walls of the *pesantren*. From July 2000, there were indeed features in *Sufi* on great shaykhs, naturally beginning with al-Ghazali (issue number 3), then moving to al-Jilani (issue number 4), Rumi (issue number 5), and 'the great tragedy of al-Hallaj' who had famously declared his union with God (issue number 7). Nevertheless this emphasis from the classic past soon changed to include local heirs to the *tarekat* tradition, such as Ahmad Khatib Sambas (d. 1876), the Borneo-born founder of the Qadiriyya wa-Naqshbandiyya order (issue number 10), or Ismail Minangkabau (issue number 13), who spread the Khalidiyya variant of the Naqshbandiyya in Singapore and the Riau archipelago in the 1850s and 1860s.

It was soon apparent that *Sufi* was providing information about the many orders deemed by the Jam'iyyah Ahlith Thoriqoh Mu'tabaroh as valid, such as the Shadhiliyya, Shattariyya, Sanusiyya, Naqshbandiyya, Qadiriyya and Tijaniyya, while demonstrating the weakness of New Age cults. Furthermore, it pointed out that the Sufi path required proper supervision and that one needed a *murshid*. The dangers of not having such a spiritual director are laid out in Luqman's article on 'the various deceptions on the Sufi path' (issue number 13) (Luqman, 2001). Luqman also gave this the subtitle *ghurur* (i.e. delusion), the same term used by Ibn Qudama al-Maqdisi in his passage describing the errors of the Sufis, which was quoted in *Salafy*.

Throughout *Sufi*, too, there were also regular articles by NU *kiai*s and the modern intellectuals aligned broadly with them, such as Nurcholish Madjid, Komaruddin Hidayat, and Jalaluddin Rakhmat, most of whom had been singled out in *Salafy* as the local representatives of an enervating impulse from within the *umma*. There are also references to the scholarly contributions of Martin van Bruinessen on the *pesantren* tradition,[18] reflecting an awareness of western scholarship that is widely available in translation. The very presence of such books in the bookshops of Jakarta also reflects an engagement with Western scholarship by Indonesian scholars. (The back cover of *Sufi* often featured advertisements for the Indonesian translation of the *Oxford Encyclopedia of Islam*.) The various State Institutes for Islamic Studies – particularly those of Jakarta and Yogyakarta – have many members of staff who have completed advanced studies in North America or Europe, which are places *Salafy* informs its readers are hostile territory (*dar al-harb*) to be avoided.

While *Sufi* regularly praised the *pesantren*s for their role in keeping the *tarekat* vibrant in Indonesia, and cited the works of Western scholars, the visit to Indonesia of a leading international shaykh, Muhammad Nazim `Adil al-Haqqani of Cyprus, and his deputy and brother-in-law Muhammad Hisham al-Kabbani, was also well covered. Issue number 13 features an Indonesian translation of a final speech given in English by Nazim `Adil at the Suryalaya *pesantren* led by the aged shaykh of the Qadiriyya wa-Naqshbandiyya order, Abah Anom. Here he gave a critique of the `ulama and leaders of the community for their blindness to the light of true religion.

> Many `ulama give candles to the people, but not light! Both candle and light can only be handed on through a *tarekat*. There are 41 *tarekat* at the moment, 40 connected to Ali and one which draws light from Our Lord Abu Bakr Siddiq, being the Naqshbandiyya *tarekat*. The `ulama and the intellectuals can hand out candles as big as coconut trees, but what meaning have they without light? What is needed now is the light that shall set aflame the candles of knowledge. Many `ulama only look outside in quest of knowledge. They know much ... but what is the benefit of knowledge without divine illumination? The saints abide in

hidden places and people may only know their knowledge from the books they wrote. In the past many `ulama established *madrasas*, but at the moment when the students finish, all they are given is an *ijaza*. The teachers say: 'We have given you knowledge from intellectual (`aqli) and transmitted (*naqli*) sources'. But these are only candles. And what is the meaning of a candle without light? (al-Haqqani, 2001: 50-1)

Shaykh Nazim's tour, which was repeated the following year, can only have helped affirm the impression that the Haqqaniyya branch of the Naqshbandiyya will continue with its winning formula as one order among the 41 judged to be valid by virtue of reputable pedigree. Still, the Haqqaniyya does not focus its attention only on the traditional vessels of the *pesantren*, and there are apparently numerous branches of the order throughout Southeast Asia. In discussions with the host of another Naqshbandi gathering in Jakarta, it was claimed that Kabbani's regional deputy hoped to link the various chapters in Southeast Asia. The host also spoke at some length about the historical friction in Southeast Asia between 'modernists' and members of the *tarekat*.[19] He himself was the son of such a modernist from Pariaman in West Sumatra, a region famous for the depth of antagonism between the two rival claimants to the mantle of orthodoxy. This competition is often dated back to the Padri wars of the early nineteenth century, inspired in part by the first Wahhabi interregnum in the Hijaz. Certainly the members of the various *tarekat* remain very much 'disreputable' in the eyes of the current authorities in Saudi Arabia, and the host explained that both Shaykh Nazim and his kinsmen were still denied access to the Holy Places.

Regardless of whether the Holy Places are officially off-limits to some prominent international heads of Sufi orders, the Sufis are ever more visible in Indonesia, and in the aftermath of the Bali Bombing of October 2002 and the winding up of groups like Laskar Jihad, which had been mobilized by Ja'far Umar Thalib and his partisans, they would seem to have before them the chance to make further gains in a still worried national community.

Conclusions

In the ongoing dispute over rights to claim superior understanding of the Islamic tradition, Sufis and anti-Sufis alike utilize modern print media to advance their message. As for the two journals examined here, it is the Sufis who are the more explicit in rising to any suggestion – explicit or implicit – that their practices are not based on a sound understanding of *shari`a* or that they have little to offer Indonesians in the form of practical solutions to their national problems. Certainly they pin the blame for what they see as a misconception of Sufism on the modernist movement, whose partisans many Sufis still see as fellow travellers with the new Salafi movements. Nonetheless, the younger generation from within NU, as represented by people like Luqman Hakiem, is willing to work closely with the new streams of thought emerging from among the modernist camp in the form of such contextualists as the late Nurcholish Madjid and Ulil Abshar Abdalla.

On first inspection it seems that the Salafis are far less concerned with the Sufis than with expunging any form of deviation within their own ranks. And on another level, the *Sufi* and *Salafy* authors share the same basic convictions about Islam as a solution to the nation's ills. They also share much in the way of terminology. But beyond this, a close reading of *Salafy* shows that its authors (and readers) remain deeply opposed to Sufi understandings of proper practice and theology, and they are most certainly vociferous critics of the neo-modernists of Paramadina embraced by journals like *Sufi*.

As long as there are various conflicts labelled as part of the War on Terror, the Salafis are far more likely to be concerned with these than with their traditional, and traditionalist, opponents. Meanwhile we should bear in mind that Indonesia's Sufis are not a monolithic group welded together only by their shared distaste for the Wahhabiyya and its local allies. Nevertheless, any decline in the strength of their Salafi enemies – as with the ongoing schism within the Salafi groupings between Sururis and anti-Sururis, or the winding up of both Thalib's Laskar Jihad and the Ihya as-Sunnah *madrasa* in the aftermath of the first Bali Bombing – can only loosen the bonds between the Sufis. Even before this latest crisis of authority, Aqil Siradj had his own mouthpiece for the dissemination of information about Sufism. When I asked him about the differences between it and *Sufi*, he responded that there were none, and left it at that.[20] Perhaps the existence of his own journal, *Jurnal Khas Tasawuf*, simply reflects his own control of funds and access to different networks of patrimony within NU after the decline of Abdurrahman Wahid, who seems to have been the unmentioned Grey Eminence behind *Sufi*. Certainly the journals show remarkably similar content, and both share a concern for the atmosphere of crisis in Indonesia, with one issue featuring a full page appeal calling on Indonesians to save Indonesia, not with *shari`a*, but with *santun*, 'polite respect' (see *Jurnal Khas Tasawuf*, 1(6)). Given *Salafy*'s problematizing of the notion of pluralism, this call will not be universally heeded, but given the statistically small numbers of their form of Salafism in the nation of Indonesia, there is still hope for the future.

Acknowledgement

I wish to thank Julia Day Howell, Martin van Bruinessen, Michael Feener and Tom van den Berge for their advice and encouragement, and the Royal Netherlands Academy of Arts and Sciences for its support – especially via its program, SPIN (Scientific Program Indonesia–Netherlands).

10

SUFI MODERNITIES IN CONTEMPORARY SENEGAL: RELIGIOUS DYNAMICS BETWEEN THE LOCAL AND THE GLOBAL

Leonardo A. Villalón

Introduction

Senegal has long seemed an anomaly from the perspective of much of the scholarly literature on Africa or on the Muslim world. This black African Muslim society on the Atlantic edge of the *Dar al-Islam* has seemed exceptional to academic analysts in terms of both religion and politics. If, as the editors of this volume point out in their introduction, the scholarly literature on Islam has ill-prepared us to understand current developments across the Muslim world, the political science literature is, if anything, even less well-equipped to handle Senegal. This includes the broad inability to understand religion, and especially Islam, as compatible with 'modernity' in any form, and perhaps to see it as especially incompatible with political modernity in the form of democracy.

Yet against the expectations raised by this literature, Senegal is both a democracy and an oasis of stability in a troubled zone. If its colonial background, sharp poverty, ethno-linguistic heterogeneity, and African culture would all seem to militate against democracy in the country, many might expect Senegal's overwhelmingly Muslim and deeply religious society to ensure democracy's virtual impossibility.[1] But this seeming anomaly, I have argued elsewhere, is not just coincidental; the specific forms of religious organization in Senegal have not only made democracy possible in the country, but have been a major element contributing to that democratic system. Senegal's vibrant and religiously based 'civil society' has facilitated a popular engagement with the state that is in many ways unique in the region.

The Senegalese democratic polity has been built on religious foundations (Villalón, 1995).

From the perspective of this book, in religious terms Senegal also presents a highly interesting case given the long and sustained overwhelming dominance of the Sufi orders (*turuq*). In contrast to many of the other cases discussed in this volume, we cannot speak of any 'revival' or 'renewal' of Sufism in the country because in fact it has never been in decline. Allegiance to one of the major Sufi orders and its leadership has never seriously been called into question as the public and dominant mode of religious devotion for the great majority – some 90 per cent – of the Senegalese population.

It bears emphasizing, perhaps, that this situation is unique even in the West African context. To be sure, Senegal shares many characteristics with its neighbours, but nowhere else has the model of religious organization that I describe below been institutionalized to a comparable degree. It is instructive to contrast this discussion of Senegal with Benjamin Soares' discussion (Chapter 5 in this volume) of neighbouring Mali. While the saints he examines share spiritual genealogies with their Senegalese cousins, and their followings are built on comparable social foundations, their organizations lack the degree of institutionalization and routinization that we find in Senegal. Senegal's very uniqueness, however, makes it not only an interesting case, but one that is potentially instructive of the broader range of possibilities in Sufi encounters with 'the modern'.

This chapter explores this exceptional case and its contemporary adaptations to both local and global elements of modernity. In the section that follows, I first provide a description of the distinctive forms and nature of the established Sufi model in Senegal. The next section turns to the current internal debates within Senegal about the Sufi bases of that system in terms of its relations to forms of 'Muslim modernity'. This section focuses in particular on the challenges to Sufism from the modern sectors, and of the adaptations and responses of Sufis within the discussion of what it means to be Muslim in the local context. The final section turns to the adaptations of the Sufi model as a form of social organization in a globalized context, examining how forms of Sufi organization have adapted and facilitated the creation of a transnational movement fully at home in a global modernity.

The Senegalese Sufi Model

Given the broad range of phenomena to which the term is applied, it bears specifying that the Senegalese model of religious belonging is classically 'Sufi' in two crucial definitional senses. First, there is an absolutely central role for an 'exemplar', a teacher-guide or *shaykh* – most commonly referred to in Francophone West Africa as a 'marabout' – to whom disciples owe allegiance and submission.[2] Second, this allegiance implies not only vertical relations of deference but also horizontal ones of solidarity in terms of a high degree of social organization among the community of disciples. To be a Sufi in

Senegal, therefore, involves both having a maraboutic guide and sharing a conscious identity as part of a 'brotherhood' or 'order' (*tarixa* in Wolof), an identity held in common with fellow disciples.

Both of these elements draw on deep Sufi traditions, and this model has a long history in northwest Africa, on both sides of the Sahara. Given the local specificities of history and politics, however, in Senegal the model has also taken on distinctive national forms. Religious organization in Senegal today has been heavily shaped and influenced by the state context, beginning with the French colonial administration. In the first few decades following the French conquest in the last quarter of the nineteenth century, colonial authorities presided over a significant spread of Islam as it became the religion of the vast majority. This period also planted the seeds of the local institutional forms of the Sufi orders (see Triaud, 2000; Robinson, 2000).

Two major orders dominate religious organization in Senegal today: the dynamic Mourides (or Muridiyya)[3] and the demographically predominant Tijaniyya. The Qadiriyya, of which the Mourides is an offshoot, has a long history in the region, but in Senegal today it is a distant third in terms of the number of disciples or the influence of its *shaykh*s. The Layène, with origins as a mahdist movement in the colonial period, constitutes a fourth order, and one of some importance primarily due to its geographic proximity to the capital city of Dakar on the Cap Vert peninsula. While the Tijaniyya is of Maghrebian origin, founded in Fez in the eighteenth century and widespread throughout the region, the Mourides constitutes an indigenous Senegalese order, born in the Wolof heartland in the peanut-growing region of Baol.[4]

Regardless of their origins, the orders in Senegal today are centred both geographically and spiritually in specific locales, in the households or *zawiya*s of Senegalese holy lineages. The Mourides maintain a centralized allegiance to the city of Touba, established by the founder Shaykh Amadou Bamba, and which today includes the residences of his sons and other descendants. Touba is also the site of the massive central mosque and pilgrimage centre of the order, built around the founder's tomb. While widespread and more numerous, the disciples of the Tijaniyya divide their allegiances among several maraboutic lineages, of which two are most important: the Sy family of the city of Tivaouane, and the Niasse family from Kaolack. In each case these centres were established by an original charismatic figure or exemplar, who gathered disciples around him in the context of colonial upheaval.

Shaykh Amadou Bamba Mbacké, E.H. Malik Sy, and Shaykh Abdoulaye Niasse were all born around 1850 and lived into the 1920s. The coincidence of their life-spans and the fact that their movements all took form at the turn of the century suggest that the political context of conquest and collapse of the pre-colonial states was an instigating element in these movements' formation. The initial French reaction to these movements was one of fear, as demonstrated by the various deportations of Amadou Bamba and the initially tense relations with the others. Eventually, however, these teachers of Sufi paths found what David Robinson has called 'paths of accommodation' with the French colonial system (Robinson, 2000). The relations varied among men and over time, but the organizations founded by these saintly figures flourished and expanded in the late colonial period, and fully dominated Senegalese society by the time of independence in 1960.

Today, all of the major maraboutic figures in Senegal are the direct descendants of these charismatic lineage founders, and the saintly families maintain their central positions in terms of religious organization in the country. At the death of each founder, the eldest surviving son was appointed as the *khalifa* (deputy and successor) of his father, although among the Niasse family lineage, a younger son, Shaykh Ibrahima 'Baye' Niasse, was to surpass his elder brother's influence. Following crises of succession at the death of the first caliphs, a system was established for lateral inheritance across the founder's sons, before the passage to the next generation. While the aged Mouride caliph today, Shaykh Saliou Mbacké, is the last surviving son of Amadou Bamba, among the Tijani lineages the transition to the third generation has occurred.[5] The *zawiya*s have maintained their importance and there is still broad allegiance to the family lineages, but given the sheer number of descendants among highly polygamous families, each is marked by increasingly significant rivalries for influence among the grandsons and great-grandsons of the founders. There is thus today a multiplicity of claimants to maraboutic authority in Senegal, and disciples of any given family will most often identify one specific descendant as his or her own *shaykh*.

The core institutional organization for these allegiances is the *daaira*, the specific Senegalese contribution to the Sufi model (Villalón, 1995: 150-62).[6] The first *daaira*s were founded in the urban colonial setting as local associations of Tijani disciples of a common marabout, but the model was eventually adopted by all of the orders. Analogous to other urban voluntary associations in Africa, *daaira*s provide both social solidarity and tangible benefits to their followers in the form of mutual aid and support. In addition, they play a central role in linking disciples to their common shaykh, often organizing communal visits or the collection of funds for the marabout. Today *daaira* membership is the standard mode of participating in all of the Sufi orders in Senegal, and across all sectors of society, comprising the most significant institution of Senegalese Sufism. In neighbourhoods of all classes, factories and other workplaces, government offices, and university faculties, numerous *daaira*s to different marabouts are found.

From their informal origins with direct links to the marabout, the *daaira*s have often been more formally institutionalized over the post-colonial period. At the local level this is reflected in the proliferation of officers paralleling those of other formal organizations, and invariably bearing French titles: *président, secrétaire administratif, responsable cellule feminine*, and such. In addition, *daaira*s in different locales with allegiance to the same marabout are at times organized into formal federations, paralleling the hierarchical organizational structure of the Senegalese state with divisions into regions, departments, and local collectivities. Similar federations have been formed internationally in the Senegalese diaspora, and as with the national federations these organizations have expanded the meaning of the term by also labelling themselves *daaira*s.

A major activity of all *daaira*s is the organization of ritual ceremonies and the facilitation of attendance at the major events sponsored by the holy lineages. In addition to the main annual pilgrimages to the *zawiyas*, namely the *grand màggal* for the Mourides and the *gàmmu* for the Tijans, there has been a proliferation of such events organized by different branches of maraboutic lineages and, as we shall note below, this model continues to expand in the country. The purposes and impact of these ceremonies is varied, but one can identify two main audiences (Villalón, 1994). Internally, the ritual ceremonies serve to reinforce the ties of solidarity among disciples as well as the links to the maraboutic guides; they are the principle locus for the public celebration of allegiances. Externally, the ceremonies are central to defining and negotiating relations between the orders and the state. State officials are almost invariably present as invited guests, where they are presented both with visible evidence of the dynamism of these religious organizations and often with specific requests or suggestions by the religious leaders whose powers are being celebrated.

Given both the mass participation in this system across Senegalese society and the Sufi orders' high degree of organization and activity, the political potential of the Sufi orders was evident from early in the colonial period. The eventual pattern of collaboration and 'accommodation' that the French established with the saintly founders of the major lineages was inherited and adapted by the heirs to each lineage. With the expansion of party politics in the colony after the Second World War, the (Catholic) poet-turned-politician Léopold Sédar Senghor was to build the political machine that was to serve as the basis of his 20-year presidency on close relations with the caliphs of the major *zawiya*s. Senghor's hand-picked successor, Abdou Diouf, was in turn to inherit and maintain these ties. These involved the exchange of mutual benefits between the religious and the state elites. While the state provided sponsorship for various maraboutic initiatives and a tacit recognition of maraboutic pre-eminence in certain social domains, the marabouts in turn issued injunctions (*ndigal* in Wolof) calling for cooperation with state ventures and – most importantly – directing their followers in electoral contests. The merits of this system have been the subject of varying analyses (e.g., Behrman, 1970; Copans, 1980; Coulon, 1981), but it is clear that the reciprocal exchange of favours was a key element of the stability and quasi-democratic nature of the system ruled over by the *Parti Socialiste* for the first three decades or so of independence. In contrast to Turkey in the period before 1925, for example, the Sufi orders in Senegal have represented a strong form of social organization that has remained uncaptured by the state, yet also capable of engagement and interaction with it.

If these relations have been central, they have also evolved over the post-colonial period with political changes, and especially with the increasing pressures towards further and more substantial democratization of Senegalese politics. As elsewhere in Africa, by the late 1980s economic decline and political stagnation had produced widespread public anger and dissatisfaction in Senegal. Massive protests thus broke out in urban areas when Abdou Diouf was again declared the winner of the 1988 presidential elections, initiating a crisis of the regime that was in many ways to continue for over a decade. In this context of growing popular dissatisfaction with the political elite, the religious leaders similarly adjusted their stance. While the Mouride caliph had issued a strong electoral *ndigal* in favour of Abdou Diouf's re-election in the campaign of 1988, this was to be the last such pronouncement by any of the caliphs. The relations between political and religious authorities in Senegal were to further evolve over the course of the 1990s as generational tensions within maraboutic families and the deepening crisis of legitimacy of what appeared to be a politically blocked system eroded the foundations of these relations (Villalón and Kane, 1998).

This political stasis was broken dramatically with the historic elections of 2000, when the victory of the long-time opposition candidate Abdoulaye Wade over incumbent president Abdou Diouf ended the long monopoly of power of the *Parti Socialiste*. The uncertain and fluid period leading to the elections provided opportunities for various young marabouts to gamble at aligning themselves politically with different candidates. But, having gradually distanced themselves from the ruling party and direct involvement in the electoral process over the course of the previous decade, the major marabouts remained neutral throughout the campaign. As a result, and even though the caliphs had been most often seen as the political base of the *Parti Socialiste*, the position of the orders was by no means eroded because of Wade's election.

It was, in fact, quite to the contrary. On the very night of his election, the new president's first action was to leave the capital for the Mouride caliph's compound in Touba, where he was photographed kneeling to receive a blessing from the aged marabout, before spending the night there. Although the act provoked a major outcry among intellectuals and much consternation among Tijans and other Muslims, Wade was to repeat the gesture following legislative elections a year later, this time bringing along the newly elected members of his government. A committed Mouride himself, Wade is unapologetic about the act, insisting that it was not a political one but only a gesture of humility; having been charged with the destiny of the nation, he argues, it was only natural for him to seek blessings and guidance from his own spiritual guide.[7] The tensions between the new president and the other caliphs, as well as those between Mourides and Tijans as a result of this highly public gesture, were the subject of much debate in Senegal (see, e.g., *Nouvel Horizon*, 299, 324). But the preference for the Mourides that it seemed to indicate has in fact not materialized in terms of governmental policy.

The changes and tensions of the period between 1988 and Wade's election certainly introduced new elements into the religious dynamics of Senegal, and the positions of the Sufi orders and especially of the numerous and younger claimants to the saintly heritage of the founders is in flux and evolving. Nevertheless, it is important to note that the core understanding of the mutuality of relations between the religious and the political elite in the country remains intact. What one journalist described as the 'profound respect for republican institutions' of the long-time Tijan caliph Abdoul Aziz Sy (*Nouvel Horizon*, 277) continues to characterize the majority of major religious figures. And while the religious elite draws benefits and support from the state, the state in turn, in Cheikh Guèye's felicitous phrase, 'cleanses itself of the sin of secularity' by its association with the religious elite.[8] The highly organized and dynamic religious system in Senegal, therefore, has not only proven itself compatible, but has in fact been closely intertwined, with the development of that hallmark of political modernity: a functioning electoral democracy.

Shifting Muslim Modernity: Sufi responses to reformist critiques
Much as there have been subtle shifts in the politics of relations between the orders and the state over the past few decades, the dynamics of the Sufi model in terms of individual conceptions of what it means to be a 'modern' Muslim have also been evolving in Senegal. In part this has been linked to broader debates across the Muslim world in the wake of the Iranian revolution, but in part it has also been shaped by local issues. Throughout much of Africa – and indeed across other parts of the Muslim world – this has frequently taken the form of a debate about the continued validity of Sufism in the face of severe criticisms by 'reformist' and anti-Sufi Muslims. The choice has at times been presented as one between practicing 'African Islam' and following 'Islam in Africa' (Rosander and Westerlund, 1997). In such places as northern Nigeria, and across large sectors of the urban population and especially those involved in the modern economic sectors, the debate has had the effect of casting Sufism as 'folk' religion, the peasant and uneducated form of religious practice.

In this context, the first and crucially important observation that must be made in the Senegalese context is that, despite some evolution, the 'classic' Sufi model is still largely and overwhelmingly dominant in the country. Even in the urban and 'modern' sectors of Senegalese society, an identity as a Sufi disciple is seen by the vast majority not as an anachronism but rather as itself a normal element of being a Muslim, clearly integrated into the fabric of everyday Senegalese life across generations and social strata. The evidence of this continued vitality is myriad and publicly visible. On any street in urban areas, the signs of all sorts of commercial activities are most often identified by Sufi affiliation. Within university faculties, banners, public meetings and pamphlets attest to the dynamism of Sufi student associations. On the walls of government ministries, one finds posted announcements of upcoming *daaira* meetings for ministry employees. On the airwaves (and in Dakar nightclubs), popular songs by Senegalese pop stars are dedicated to singing the praises of marabouts (McLaughlin, 1997, 2000). Children's school notebooks with photographs of local wrestling heroes on the cover, list '*guide spirituel*' along with weight, age and other vital data on these athletic stars.

Indeed, there are many indications that the system is expanding and being strengthened as the more peripheral areas of the country are being integrated into the core. In the Fuuta Toro region, for example, along the Senegalese river valley on the long border with Mauritania, the primarily Haalpulaar (Fulani) populations of the region are overwhelmingly nominally Tijans, and most owe some allegiance to the descendants of the nineteenth century jihadist El Hadj Umar Taal, a hero of local resistance to French colonialism in the Sahel. But the Senegalese Sufi model has never enjoyed any significant degree of institutionalization in the region. Nor has the status of being a disciple of a given family or marabout been particularly central to individual identity or social relations. Yet in the past decade or so, the region has experienced a flourishing of associations and activities replicating the core model; *daaira*s are being formed and local marabouts are increasingly organizing annual ritual ceremonies and pilgrimages to their religious centres. Strikingly, this phenomenon is linked directly to the influence of the huge émigré community from the region. In many villages and towns along the river valley, economic difficulties mean that the majority of men spend a significant portion of their adult years away, in Paris or New York or other centres of Senegalese diaspora communities. Coming into contact with other Senegalese in these settings, this émigré community has been largely responsible for sponsoring the adoption of the Sufi model in their home region, often subsidizing it financially. Most importantly, this is seen as part of the émigré contribution to the 'development' of the region; *daaira*s and ritual Sufi ceremonies become a mark of 'modernization' in these settings.[9]

Yet despite this dynamism, it is also true that the model has been challenged in recent years by 'reformist' or 'Islamist' critics of the maraboutic system. Such critiques have relatively long roots in Senegal. Already in the 1950s in the late colonial context there were urban Muslim intellectuals who issued explicit and modernist attacks on the Sufi religious elite (Gomez-Perez, 1991). While their public pronouncements and publications brought them some attention, for our purposes here the most notable aspect of these movements was their lack of any significant popular appeal and their miniscule demographic importance. Indeed, the various movements founded by such individuals were gradually obliged to temper their critiques, and in fact moved frequently to reconcile their public stances with the realities of the overwhelming predominance of the Sufi maraboutic model. Thus such associations as the Union Culturelle Musulmane (UCM), which in the years after independence espoused a strongly reformist ideology under the leadership of the well-known Cheikh Touré, was gradually brought under the control of marabouts from the major lineages, and devoted itself primarily to promoting hagiographic events about Senegalese Sufi figures.

At the same time, over the course of the 1980s and 1990s, and linked to the increasing frustration about the political system and the socio-political models on which the post-colonial state had been built, reformist groups maintained their presence among a limited urban population. As in other places in the Muslim world, the main locus of the reformist movement has been within the universities, where groups such as the reformist *Jamatou Ibadou Rahmane* or the *Mouvement Al-Falah pour la Culture Islamique Salafiyya*, found an echo. Over the course of the 1980s, these groups grew in importance, eventually winning the symbolic victory of building a mosque on the Dakar campus (Bathily et al., 1995; Loimeier, 1996). The unprecedented adoption of a form of veiling by young university women was the most visible manifestation of the dynamism of these movements in the 1990s. While the practice was virtually unheard of in the early 1990s, with the endorsement of these groups it came to include perhaps some five to 10 per cent of university women within the space of a few years.[10] A formal organization, the *Mouvement des Étudiants et Élèves Jamaatou Ibadou Rahmane* (MEEJIR), was founded in 2002 and established chapters at the two universities. Given their location and their youthful and educated membership, these movements cannot be dismissed, but it must also be noted that they have a very limited popular appeal outside the class of young intellectuals.

However their influence has been felt in other, less direct ways. Gradually, since the late 1980s, religious figures from within the Sufi tradition have borrowed from and aligned themselves with elements of reformism, while maintaining the core of the maraboutic model. This evolution has been driven at least in part by a response to critiques of the classic maraboutic model, but it has also been motivated by generational tensions and succession struggles within maraboutic families themselves, and by the opportunities provided by the political context.[11] For many Senegalese youth and university students in particular, and even though most remain closely attached to their Sufi affiliations, the critical stances of the reformist groups have at times struck a sympathetic cord. Remaining rooted in the Sufi tradition, such people have also been willing to thus undertake a critical examination, and at times a consequent reinterpretation, of that tradition. As Bakary Sambe (2003) has pointed out, this dynamic has in many ways led to a blurring of the Sufism/reformist dichotomy.

In this respect, a particularly important case is that of the *Dahiratoul Moustarchidina wal Moustarchidaty*. The Moustarchidine are led by Moustapha Sy, a young Tijan marabout from the Sy family (he is a great-grandson of the founder, E.H. Malik). As the name suggests, the movement was built on the *daaira* model, but consciously portrayed itself as an effort to be more 'rationalized' and modern, and in this effort it borrowed themes and rhetoric from the reformist movements. Moustapha Sy builds his own image on multiple sources. Young, cosmopolitan, at ease in three languages and cultures (Wolof, French and Arabic), he portrayed himself as a spokesman for the crucial and disaffected social category of urban youth. The movement itself was built over the 1980s to emerge as a strong and hierarchical organization, with a national structure paralleling the administrative divisions of the state, constituting the most significant elaboration and institutionalization of the *daaira* model to date.

By the late 1980s, Moustapha Sy had also situated the movement as a potential political force, initially positioning himself as an arbiter between an increasingly unpopular regime and urban youth. As the political tensions mounted and the 1993 presidential elections approached, however, the young marabout changed his strategy. In the midst of the electoral campaign he made a dramatic public attack on incumbent president Abdou Diouf, linking it in part to a critique of the older maraboutic alliance with the secular state. With this act, followed by involvement in violent protests in the year following Abdou Diouf's re-election, the Moustarchidine emerged as what could be called the first serious contestatory political movement built on a religious basis in Senegal. In some Western media and elsewhere, this was described as the arrival of 'fundamentalism' in Senegal – 'shades of Algeria' as one journalist entitled his account (da Costa, 1994).

Its subsequent history demonstrated that this was hardly the case, but the movement was significant in that it signalled a major departure from the established relations between maraboutic authorities and the political elite, and especially in that it positioned itself ambiguously 'between sufism, reformism, and Islamism' (Kane and Villalón, 1995). While this movement was clearly driven in part by generational issues and questions of succession to leadership within the family, at the broader social level its dynamism must also be explained by the appeal to its young urban disciples of a more 'modernized' version of the classic Sufi model, one willing to make at least some of the critiques that had been developed by the reformists. Moustapha Sy nevertheless simultaneously rooted his claim to leadership of the movement directly in the hereditary charisma of his family.

Within the Mouride order, a somewhat different movement paralleled this development, similarly reflecting an evolution of the Sufi model in the context of reformist critiques. The Hizbut Tarqiyyah was founded in 1975 as a *daaira* of Mouride students at the University of Dakar (Guèye, 2002: 239-49; Sene, 2003). Under the dynamic leadership of its founder, Atou Diagne, the movement grew quickly in importance, securing the patronage of the caliph himself. By the mid-1980s, the Hizbut Tarqiyyah had established itself as central to the organization of the *grand màggal*, the annual pilgrimage to Touba. In ideological terms the movement displayed a simultaneous strong attachment to the Sufi model and a strict devotion to the figure of the founder/exemplar, Amadou Bamba, along with a commitment to the need to 'modernize' the forms of allegiance and social organization of the movement. Thus, for example, the group organized an exhibit in Touba on the life and work of Amadou Bamba every year on the occasion of the *grand màggal*, intended to 'demonstrate the specificity of the *daaira* in relation to the rest of the order'. At the same time, the exhibit was 'addressed to intellectuals to whom it wanted to demonstrate that Mouride culture could be expressed in a modern framework', investing heavily in the new technologies of communication and information (Guèye, 2002: 243).

The Hizbut Tarqiyyah expanded and grew throughout the 1980s and into the 1990s, establishing local *daaira*s in schools throughout the country. The group distinguished itself by its discipline and organization, including a hierarchical system of administrative posts within each local cell. It encouraged its young members to pursue their studies in the state French-language schools, yet also worked hard to resist their cultural assimilation to the francophone intellectual class, insisting on distinctive dress and rejection of much of 'Western' entertainment, sports and culture. By its very success, the growth of the movement produced tensions within the order and the maraboutic family itself, culminating in a major conflict in 1997. Taking his message of 'modernizing' the order a step further, Atou Diagne eventually dared to question the deeply enshrined notion of hereditary leadership by the Mbacké family. In the ensuing outcry and showdown, the movement was forced to retract, quickly losing much of its dynamism and strength as it lost followers around the country. While the position of the Hizbut Tarqiyyah has thus been significantly eroded, its place has nonetheless been taken by a number of splinter groups and offshoots, which maintain a very comparable ideology. At the universities and in high schools, and consequently in other modern sectors and increasingly in the émigré community, Mouride *daaira*s share a strong devotion to the founding saint of the order, along with an insistence on the 'orthodoxy' of his message and its compatibility with modernity in all its forms.

The impact of the reformist movements on the Sufi model in Senegal has been felt not only in the new organizations founded by the younger heirs to the maraboutic families, but also at the level of individual behaviour and of Muslim identity – of what is expected of a young and modern Muslim, Sufi or otherwise. Striking symbolic indications of this phenomenon were visible at a series of public presentations by representatives of Muslim students associations at the Université Gaston Berger in St. Louis in June 2003. The representatives of the *daaira* of Tijan student disciples of the Sy family, for example, included a young man who began his presentation with a long invocation in Arabic, very much in the style of reformist associations. Most surprisingly, the young woman representing the group was dressed in the veiled style of the *Ibadou Rahmane* students. Such veiling emerged as a new phenomenon in the 1990s, serving as the distinctive female marking of the anti-Sufi movement. Yet both of these young representatives of the Tijaniyya

Sufi order demonstrated their strong attachment to their Sufi fundamentals, insisting explicitly on the importance of having a marabout guide. Borrowing directly from the symbolic repertoire and the discourses of the reformist movements on campus, however, such young disciples are willing to engage in a re-examination of the Sufi tradition, and to suggest the reinterpretation of elements of that tradition.

In the international political context following the events of 11 September 2001 in the United States, and especially following the US invasion of Iraq in March 2003, such reinterpretations have also taken on a more explicitly political tone. Thus in a June 2003 lecture on 'Sufism and the State' at the West African Research Center (WARC) in Dakar, Sidi Lamine Niasse, editor and founder of the important media group *Wal Fadjri*, made a distinction between what he labelled the three faces of Sufism, illustrating his points with key historical figures of Senegalese Islam.

Sufism, he began, has often been marked by an attitude of dialogue and engagement with political authorities. He noted that the founder of the Tijani maraboutic lineage at Tivaouane, E.H. Malik Sy, might exemplify this stance in Senegal. Additionally, Sufi relations with political authority have at other times been marked by a position of respectful withdrawal – *hijra* in Arabic – maintaining a distance between the secular and the sacred. This was the position of the founder of the Mouride order, Cheikh Amadou Bamba, in his eventual cohabitation with colonial authorities, and the order has maintained such relations with the state since then. To be sure, Niasse suggested, these two figures, and their respective attitudes, have historically dominated the relations between Sufi Muslims and the state in Senegal. But, he insisted, it is important to remember that a third aspect of Sufism may at times be relevant: the attitude typified in Senegal by E.H. Umar Taal, the nineteenth century jihadist leader who resisted the French conquest. This attitude of militant resistance, he suggested, is the appropriate Sufi disposition when confronted with political aggression, and every indication is that such is the nature of the times in which we are living.

Niasse is himself related to the important Tijani family, but he began his career as an Islamist sympathizer of the Iranian revolution, and this attitude echoes his well-known public persona. What is striking, however, is his willingness to directly evoke the Sufi tradition to suggest a political stance of armed resistance to the West, a position that today is most directly rooted in Islamist movements.

This trend of staking out positions explicitly stated as being within the Sufi tradition, but also engaging in a rethinking of what that tradition entails, is clearly manifest in Senegal today. In a variety of domains one finds an intellectual search for models and examples within Sufism that might usefully be appropriated to modern situations and contexts. This dynamic certainly has the potential for significant transformations in religious practice and identity, not as a rejection of Sufism, but rather as a reformulation of the meaning of maintaining allegiance to these traditions that in many ways have defined Senegalese identities. The dynamic also has potential political consequences. Thus a major public intellectual in Senegal, Professor Penda Mbow, worries that 'reformist' or 'Islamist' groups are now 'using' and manipulating the Sufi orders to get what they want – rather than attacking them as in the past – and especially that these groups are using the third-generation young marabouts whose own rivalries push them to stake out distinctive positions for themselves.[12] The seeming rise in public visibility of the long-marginalized anti-Sufi groups in Senegal is thus producing a sincere soul-searching in the country, reflected at times in the press. The weekly magazine, *Nouvel Horizon*, for example, has devoted extensive cover stories to such sensationalist questions as 'Are our Islamists Dangerous?' (296) and 'Are Muslims Bin Laden?' (351).

The same intellectual cited above poses the issue as the central question for Senegalese society today: 'How to be Muslims, but to keep our traditions and identities as Africans?'. The implicit premise of the question suggests a renewed salience of an older issue: while the 'traditional' Sufi model to which the vast majority of Senegalese have adhered has presented little tension with the 'Africanness' of disciples, in the new contemporary contexts it appears – at least to such intellectuals – to pose the issue of their 'Muslimness'. Becoming a more modern 'Muslim' seems to be at some tension with remaining 'African', in a way that classic Sufism did not. While the maraboutic model remains strongly central in Senegal, in recent years a variety of efforts have been made to reconcile it with new strains of modernity, resulting in an internal process of debate and self-examination that will certainly lead to reformulations of the Sufi tradition.

Being Sufi in the Modern World: Situating the local in the global

In many ways, Senegal is increasingly an émigré society and economy. There is a large and growing Senegalese diaspora abroad – in various African countries, Europe, the United States, and elsewhere – forming distinct enclaves that most frequently maintain close ties with their home societies.[13] There are a number of distinct Senegalese émigré communities, and these can be based on a variety of common ties: religious, regional, or ethnic. For example, Linda Beck (2003) identifies in New York one ethno-linguistic and two religious communities: the Haalpulaar, the Mourides and the Niassène Tijan. Given the dominance of the Sufi orders as a mode of social organization in Senegal, however, in all cases the Senegalese émigré phenomenon is inevitably to some extent shaped by the Sufi system and, in turn, affects it. Indeed, religious ties are frequently at the organizational heart of the émigré experience.

The phenomenon of religious transnationalism is especially true for Mourides, although it is important to note that this is by no means linked specifically to that order, nor is it completely new. The Niasse family branch of the Tijaniyya, for example, from the time of its charismatic leader Ibrahima 'Baye' Niasse, has maintained an extensive network of ties throughout West Africa as well as in the Middle East, and increasingly in Europe and the United States (O. Kane, 1997). Today representatives of the family have a mosque in the Bronx, which includes in its community not only Senegalese but also a number of American disciples. In Dakar, *Cheikhna* Marième Niasse, daughter of Baye Niasse and granddaughter of the founder, maintains a *zawiya* with activities that include a network of schools under the name of Dar al-Qur'an al-Karim, frequented by students from across West Africa, including Moorish children from Mauritania, as well as the occasional American child. Wolof, Arabic, Hausa, English, French and Hassaniya are regularly spoken in her household, and her website documents this international, cosmopolitan, and multilingual community with text and photographs of her travels throughout the Arab world, West Africa and Europe (http://www.daralquran alkarim.org/).

Nevertheless, the most notable Senegalese religious diaspora today, and certainly the most studied, is that of the Mourides. Indeed, the element of migration has become closely associated with the identity of the order itself, producing what Mamadou Diouf (2000) has called a 'vernacular cosmopolitanism'. The Mouride order has always been closely linked to its economic base, and its origins, as Diouf notes, are rooted in an 'economic project'. From the order's historic base in the production of peanuts for the colonial economy, Mouride disciples shifted gradually into trading networks, moving geographically from the heartland in the region of Baol to the markets of Dakar in the post-World War II epoch. From there Mouride traders gradually expanded to various West African cities and beyond. By the 1970s, significant Mouride communities were based in Marseille and other European cities, and in the 1980s the United States, and especially New York, became the destination of choice.

Importantly, however, the geographic centre of Mouridism has always stayed central to the emigrant experience. The city of Touba, and the great mosque containing the founder's tomb in particular, have remained not only the spiritual anchor of émigré communities, but the economic capital and the political reference point as well. This orientation has maintained the historical status of Touba as retreat, from the colonial authorities and indeed from the Senegalese state itself. Touba has always been first and foremost Mouride ground, controlled by the leadership of the order and guided by its principles. Increasingly, it has also become the geographic centre of a network of religious associations with a global reach.[14]

The extension from Touba to the rest of the world has been accomplished by building heavily – indeed almost completely – on the Mouride Sufi model. Mouride *daairas* organize and sponsor the movement of disciples, and once established abroad they replicate and sustain the model, sponsoring the visits of Mouride marabouts to these new sites, and channelling the remittances of distant disciples to the holy city. The resulting cosmopolitanism has been strongly embraced by the order. In the heart of the hot and dusty Senegalese Sahel, the sprawling town of Touba has thus become a bustling city charged with signs of the international connections of its inhabitants. Scattered visitors from around the world are greeted at the mosque (reputedly the largest in sub-Saharan Africa) by self-appointed tour guides who in multiple languages will explain the universality of the founding shaykh's message, and hence the openness of the order to all people. In any household in Touba, one finds various young men who speak perfect Spanish, English, Italian and other languages, and who will recount their long stays abroad.

The significant increase in the number of Senegalese in the United States over the past two decades has included people from a variety of religious and ethnic communities. The Mouride community, however, is clearly the most organized and visible, and 'little Touba' has dominated a large part of Harlem. This New York community includes many émigrés involved in economic activities on the edges of the formal economy, legal or not – including street vendors of cheap Asian goods, taxi drivers, and hair braiders among women. Increasingly, however, it also includes a white-collar Senegalese diaspora: university professors, bankers, computer scientists and others (Babou, 2002b; Beck, 2003)

The first Mouride *daaira* was founded in New York in the mid-1980s, and by 2001, Cheikh Babou estimates, there were some 30 Mouride *daaira*s functioning in the city (2002b: 163). As the community expanded, the mid-1980s also saw the creation of a major umbrella association know as MICA, the 'Murid Islamic Community in America', duly registered officially as a 501 c3 non-profit organization. MICA maintains an elaborate website (http://www.micasite.org), publishes material on Mouridism and on its own activities in the United States, and organizes religious events and the celebration of the *grand màggal*. In 1988, with MICA influence, the City of New York declared 28 July 'Cheikh Amadou Bamba Mbacké day' (Villalón, 1995: 69) and the annual celebration since then includes a parade through Harlem that draws thousands. The events surrounding the celebration also regularly included a visit by Shaykh Mourtada Mbacké, the younger brother of the Mouride caliph in Touba, until his death in 2004.[15] This annual visit has now become in itself a major event linking New York disciples to the saintly family, and celebrated on both sides of the Atlantic. In 2002, for example, MICA produced a special glossy publication to mark the event, entitled 'Education: A Key Function in Muridism' and billed as 'A message from Shaykh Mourtada Mbacké, ibn Khadimou Rassoul' (MICA, 2002). In Dakar, the popular magazine *Frasques* devoted a large special edition full of photographs to the Shaykh's visit, under the title 'Un Jour de Bamba à New York'.[16]

In an interesting further twist of the transnational context, the fascination of Western intellectuals with the Mouride phenomenon has in many ways become part of the phenomenon itself, contributing directly to the 'cosmopolitanism' of this black African Sufi vernacular. In 2003, for example, the distinguished Fowler Museum of Cultural History at the University of California at Los Angeles organized an extensive and spectacular exhibit focused on the Mourides, under the title, 'A Saint in the City: Sufi Arts of Urban Senegal'. The beautiful and weighty catalogue that accompanied the exhibit must in many ways be seen to be at least as much a celebration as an analysis of the order (Roberts and Roberts, 2003). The exhibit drew not only the expected visitors to a university museum, but large numbers of Mouride disciples from around the country, as well as a visit by a Mouride *shaykh*, celebrated with lots of fanfare.[17] Covered in the Senegalese press – the daily *Le Quotidien* (12 March 2003) ran a headline, 'Serigne Touba à Los Angeles' – the exhibit was interpreted by many in Senegal as another indication of the international success of Amadou Bamba's ('Serigne Touba's') message.

In this global diaspora, the far-flung disciples of the order stay connected very directly, moving people and resources back and forth from the centre in Touba. In Senegal local *daaira*s pool their resources to send representatives abroad, that they might in turn return resources home. This global reach has come to be seen as an integral part of the strength and dynamism of the order, and it very clearly receives the implicit blessing of its leadership. When the old caliph, Serigne Saliou, receives crowds in Touba, among the disciples pressing around him to seek his blessings and help are many with their passports in hand, hoping that his spiritual intercession might facilitate that most desired of things in Touba: a visa to Europe or America. As the caliph mutters prayers and sprinkles his holy spit, he does his part to send off young Mourides on the international adventures that have become central to the order's strength and identity.

In the past few years, the most significant symbol of the tangible benefits of this cosmopolitanism is the huge new hospital that has been built in Touba, financed completely by an extensive international association of Mourides abroad, which identifies itself as the '*daaira* des émigrés' under the name Dahiratoul Matlabul Fawzayni (Guèye, 2002: 249-58). Founded by a Mouride émigré who had worked across a number of African and European countries, as well as in the United States, before settling in Spain, the movement was created for the specific purpose of fundraising among émigré *daaira*s to support projects in Touba. Beginning with the symbolically powerful project of a major modern hospital in Touba, where there was no comparable facility, the group is now moving into other projects focussed on the development of the city. As an umbrella organization linking local *daaira*s across the world, the Matlabul Fawzayni builds on, but differs significantly from, the classic *daaira* model. With an estimated 60,000 members, united not in allegiance to a specific shaykh or marabout but rather to the Sufi order as a whole, it reflects the innovative adaptation of the model to the new world of an international Senegalese diaspora.

The intentionally remote small Sufi *zawiya* of a rural Sahelian village in the early twentieth century has been transformed by the cosmopolitanism of its Sufi adepts to a sprawling and bustling dusty city of perpetual construction sites, and its dynamism is celebrated in the museums and conferences of American and European universities. Both are integral parts of the reality of the Mouride disciple today. In a day spent in the compound of the caliph at Touba, periodically being moved in incremental steps before being finally ushered into the presence of the holy man, I meet a group of men also waiting for an audience. These Mouride disciples sitting on a mat in the sandy courtyard are also bankers, and officials of the Senegalese Ministry of Finance. They have advanced degrees from the West, and are fluent in French and English. One of them knows the Western scholarly literature on Senegalese Sufism. Another returned the previous week from Washington, where he has been spending much time as part of a Senegalese delegation negotiating with the World Bank. In the presence of the caliph, they sit humbly and request his blessings before leaving.

How is this world lived and understood – and how is it theorized – by Mouride disciples today? Given the deep-rootedness of the Mouride Sufi experience in a specific holy site, in a history and a cultural specificity, how is this highly localized identity lived globally? In this regard, the statement of a young student in Sociology at the Université Gaston Berger in St. Louis is worth quoting at length. Speaking as a representative of the university's Mouride Students' *daaira*, and in response to a question about the *daaira*'s socializing mission among Mouride students, the young man reflected a widely shared understanding of what it means to be Mouride in the modern world.

> At this moment of globalization, when a single way of thinking is attempting to eliminate cultural specificities, Mouridism, or the Muridiyya, adopts a logic of a strategic return to its bases. But this is not a return to a position of isolation, but rather only a pulling back so as to better jump. That is, this is a way of rooting ourselves, followed by an opening up.
>
> You must understand one thing: Mouridism was born in a context of colonialism. It is thus a dissident way of thinking, intended to express a culture in opposition to the culture that the colonizer attempted to impose. There is thus a need for methods and rigorous mechanisms of socialization in order to maintain this success: a particular language, a particular way of dressing, a way of seeing. That is why when you see a Mouride walking, you know automatically, by his dress, that this person is a Mouride. Thus you have the model of dressing such as the Baye Lahatte, wearing the *maxtume*, a sort of mobile library which contains the *khassaides* of Amadou Bamba[18] .... If you go to China, the traditional dress is the Mao collar; it carries an ideology. If you go to India it is the

sari; when you go to Italy you have a particular Italian way of dressing – one dresses as a playboy. When you go to the United States it is Levi jeans, and the jacket …. Thus in the encounter of giving and taking [*au rendez-vous du donner et du recevoir*], this is what Mouridism brings ….

In a world and in a context where the policies of structural adjustment have emptied villages of their populations, the *daaira* came as a way of reinterpreting or recreating the traditional *daara* [Qur'anic school]. It is thus an ideology, a philosophy which is moving and which always adapts to the context. And this ideology is based on faith and on work, because as the Shaykh used to say: 'Work as if you were never to die; and pray to God as if you were to die tomorrow'. Today Mouridism attempts to marry globalization and the new methods of communication, information and technology in general. We have in our *daaira*, for example, a committee charged with popularizing the values of the shaykh, using such techniques.

In short, I can say that the Mouride is someone who aspires to go to God, but in going to God he also wants – given his largesse and generosity – to take others with him. It is thus an open ideology and not a closed one. And you can see this in Europe, in the US where there is a 'little Senegal' – there are many Mourides there. And in Italy. They are there. They are also open; they are polite. And it is the socialization that they received here that predisposes them to this type of adaptation.

At a moment when people speak of fundamentalism and of terrorism, Mouridism comes as an antidote, given the fact that it integrates all of man's dimensions.

The striking element of this discourse is its integrated view of a complex and multiple lived reality. Where the outside observer might see contradiction and dichotomy, a disjuncture between the 'modern' and the 'traditional', this cosmopolitan Mouride perspective posits the rooting in the local as the very means of managing the global. As Sophie Bava suggests, 'The current preoccupation of the émigrés is to connect the Mouride religious project to their mobile way of living the religion' (Bava, 2002: 593). The elaboration of a shared Mouride ideological understanding such as that eloquently articulated by this young student-intellectual serves to render the migrant experience both cohesive and manageable.

Concluding Comments

There may be little need at this point to insist on the remarkably dynamic nature of the Senegalese Sufi model. Religious institutions as well as religious ideology in Senegal have continually demonstrated their capacity to be highly adaptive to a changing world. In dialogue with others, and in the give and take of contact with various models of religious belonging and identities, the Sufi orders participate in the elaboration of new forms of modernity. In the past few decades they have been influenced both domestically and internationally by the intense discussion of what it means to be a Muslim, both at home in the historical context and more broadly in a globalized world. The future of Senegalese Sufism is thus being shaped at the intersection of these two contested domains of discussion.

To be a Muslim in Senegal was long synonymous with being a Sufi. As Cruise O'Brien phrased it more than 20 years ago, 'Sufism is the Senegalese mode of Islamic devotion' (1983: 122). More concretely within the Senegalese worldview, to be Muslim was to follow the rituals of a given *tarixa*, to join with fellow disciples in the shared community of a *daaira*, and most significantly to identify a spiritual guide whom you could claim as your own. This affiliation long provided disciples with an identity in a social order, and a place within the broader political and economic context of both the colonial and the independent state. To be sure, some few Muslims occasionally rejected such an identity on religious grounds, embracing as more authentic the models of religious devotion espoused elsewhere, and especially on the Arabian peninsula. Perhaps slightly more numerous were the French-trained intellectuals whose secular orientation led them to reject the maraboutic tradition as incompatible with development and modern political systems. Yet not only were these groups small and relatively marginal to broader Senegalese society, but they tended historically to mute their criticisms in the search for a popular audience.

Nevertheless, and given the deep implication of the marabouts in Senegalese economics and politics, increasing difficulties in these areas over the first two decades of independence fed growing questions about the appropriate scope of their influence, though only rarely about their religious legitimacy. The formulation of these domestic questions was accelerated significantly in a context of rapid transnationalization of religious movements, and especially in the context of the profound questioning within the Muslim world of what it means to be Muslim, both in terms of how one lives one's life and in terms of relations with the rest of the world. Between an attachment to deeply rooted and rich local Muslim traditions, and the perceived need for adaptation to rapidly changing contexts and responding to alternative models of religious life, the future of Senegalese religious 'modernity' (like that of elsewhere) is in flux.

The uncertain directions of change raise fears in some. Thus Senegalese francophone intellectuals long ambiguous about the backwards and even 'feudal' nature of the maraboutic worldview are now willing to embrace it as more authentically 'African' than the Arabized versions of reformist Islam being espoused by some religious intellectuals. In religious circles the tendency is for discussion and dialogue in a sincere effort to find common ground in a context of perceived outside challenges to Islam. In the mix one notes both a willingness to reinterpret elements of the Sufi tradition and a new openness to rapprochement and mutual borrowing between Sufis and

Islamists. Thus Sambe's (2003) suggestion that the classic distinction between Sufis and reformists or Islamists only imperfectly reflects today's complex realities of new identities and positions seems increasingly accurate. Yet every indication is that far from disappearing, these dynamics are feeding an evolution of Senegalese Sufi traditions as they both integrate and contribute to newly emerging modernities.

In the current globalized context the model is transformed, but also strengthened, as it is being reinvented in various ways. To be a Mouride disciple in New York, Rome or Madrid today now involves a new sense of this Mouride identity in relation both to the host society and to other émigré communities – including other Africans and other Muslims. There is thus an evolving template in any given locale for how – as a Mouride – one is to live in both religious and practical terms: where prayers are said and rituals performed; what you eat, where you sleep, how 'papers' are secured and traded, and how relations with police forces and other authorities are navigated. As individuals and groups move back and forth to Touba and other Mouride communities, this also involves redefinitions of local identities. The sense of self and understanding of his life chances of any young Mouride man in Senegal today are defined not just in terms of relations to the holy city or to the religious hierarchy, but in terms of a position within a globalized religious network: connections with *daaira*s, for example, that might get you to New York or Milan, and teach you to function and survive once you are there.

There are, to be sure, uncertainties about the ultimate direction of the changes under way, and there are real questions as to whether this will at some point undermine core elements of the model. But it also seems clear that for the moment, the Senegalese Sufi orders are very much capable of articulating forms of modernity in all of its dimensions: in the business networks of the international economy; in the political modernity of a democratic polity; and indeed, in the religious modernity of an Islam that is situated in the specific locale of a saintly tradition, but lived globally.

PART III:

BREAKING OUT OF THE MOULD: SUFISM IN NEW SETTINGS

11

INTIMATE DISCIPLES IN THE MODERN WORLD: THE CREATION OF TRANSLOCAL AMITY AMONG SOUTH ASIAN SUFIS IN BRITAIN

Pnina Werbner

Intimate Relations in the Modern World

Modernity is usually conceived of as constituted by a radical shift from *Gemeinschaft* to *Gesellschaft*: from community to association, *conscience collective* to individualism, status to contract, feudalism to capitalism, particularism to universalism. The point about such dichotomous contrasts is that they highlight the possibility in modern society of forging relations *between prior strangers,* and point to the emergence of forms of sociality beyond the reach of the state or any patriarchal or political authority. No longer tied from birth to grave to closed communities, lineages or feudal lords, modern individuals, so the argument goes, are free to move, and to choose their associative ties in a society protected and governed by equality before the law.

By the same token, the move from community to association is assumed to imply an attenuation in communal relations of close, personal, face-to-face intimacy, and a breakdown of the shared world of traditionally legitimated values. Instead, modern democratic societies have been characterized by the growth of civil society: an efflorescence of voluntary associations, clubs, religious organizations, trade unions, new social movements and market-oriented interests groups mediating between the state and individuals. Although many of these associations promote and debate moral issues, they do not necessarily foster a world of social intimacy. Such intimacy is regarded as the preserve of the familial, 'private' domain or of dyadic friendships beyond the public sphere.

This type of strict opposition between modernity and pre-modernity has been challenged, however. Hetherington, for example, following Schmalenbach (1977), suggests that some forms of modern human sociation 'cannot be neatly fitted into any of the old dichotomies: rational/irrational, pre-modern/modern or *Gemeinschaft/ Gesellschaft*' (1994: 1). There are, he argues, elective forms of modern association which nevertheless promote 'affectual solidarity' (1994: 2). Similarly, preconceptions regarding the traditional closure of pre-modern feudal and tribal societies have been challenged by theorizations of pilgrimage and regional cults that define these movements as social formations posed against and beyond the territorial community, fostering relations of amity or 'communitas' among communities of strangers who cross over territorial boundaries and meet at central places or sacred shrines, a feature I analyze below.

Much of the discussion of traditional Sufi cults and orders in Pakistan has tended, however, against such theories, to assume that local Sufi orders are perpetuated through inherited traditional village and familial ties (see, e.g., Lewis, 1984: 12).[1] So too, discussions of Pakistani labour migration to Britain have tended to stress the continued embeddedness of migrants in pre-migration village, family and *biradari* (caste cum kinship) ties.[2] Whether as migrants or Sufi followers, the assumption is thus that Pakistani settlers remain locked in traditional, pre-modern forms of sociality. A break from these implies either a modernist quest for individual spirituality, as in the Sufi groups described by Howell in this volume (Chapter 12), or a move to modernist, reformist and often politically activist Islamic groups. This chapter suggests, contrary to these assumptions, that Sufism in Britain has created the potential for a myriad of local and translocal elective relations of intimacy between prior strangers. It thus opens up new worlds of association and trust within the modern nation-state, which are governed neither by the state nor by prior village or kin relations.

Intimacy is always gendered. As the cases analyzed below show, some Sufi groups open up spaces for legitimate intimacy between the sexes, in shared sociality, camaraderie and cooperation, and for female leadership. In the most reformist groups, by contrast, there is strict separation between men and women grounded in ethical assumptions about sinful contact, although intimacy with the (male) shaykh is for women a felt experience even in these groups.

Localism and Transnationalism in Modern Sufism

South Asian Sufi activities in Britain, as on the subcontinent, vary widely in size, form and content.[3] They encompass all the major Sufi orders active on the subcontinent (Qadiriyya, Chishtiyya, Suhrawardiyya, Naqshbandiyya) and many smaller fraternities focused on more localized Pakistani saints, alive or dead. In Manchester, Sufi orders range from a very strict Naqshbandi Mujaddidi order to more traditional Sufi orders at one end of the spectrum and, at the other extreme, somewhat eclectic and idiosyncratic Sufi fraternities. Despite this variability, all the different Sufi circles meeting in the city have developed translocal relations and mutual visiting throughout Britain, extending into Pakistan. Seen as voluntary organizations, Sufi groups have created new national and international networks that bridge towns and cities and link members of different kinship, regional and caste groups in relations of amity and quasi-kinship. At the same time, the majority of followers remain Pakistani, despite the fact that groups perceive themselves as inclusive and open to non-Muslims and non-Pakistanis. In practice, however, cultural strangers rarely integrate into the Urdu and South Asian dominated cultural milieu in which Pakistani Sufism in Britain is practised.

Recognizing the variability of Sufi groups and practices in any single locality and, at the same time, the continuities across localities, is critical to comprehending Sufism as a global movement. It refutes the counter-globalization approach that argues that Islam is always locally unique since it is embedded in distinctive ways in different cultural systems. According to this view, Sufi groups resemble each other in particular localities while differing radically between localities, from Morocco to Indonesia, as Clifford Geertz (1968) famously proposed. Against Geertz I have argued elsewhere (P. Werbner, 1995, 2003) that Sufism as a discursive formation encapsulates an integrated set of assumptions about saintly world renunciation, spiritual authority and closeness to God, which travels globally and is widely shared across the Islamic world. At the same time, there are surface variations between groups in any particular locality.

This is not to deny, however, the concrete rootedness of Sufi cults in local contexts, or indeed the positive ways in which Sufi disciples embrace modernity (see P. Werbner, 1996a, 2003). It is to argue, nevertheless, that the deep structural logic of Sufism contains a determinative symbolic force that shapes the cultural environments where new saints settle. This is so even when – as in the four cases discussed here – Sufi cosmology and practice are inscribed through high-powered modern technologies, glossed in quasi-modern medical and political vocabularies, or fostered through relations of cooperation with the secular British, local state.

If Sufi cults are translocal, the variability of Sufi shaykh–disciple relations that they foster even in a single locality exposes the limitations of historical theories that posit the linear development of Sufism, from *khanqah* to Sufi order to *ta'ifa*,[4] or from directing-shaykh to mediating-shaykh, as proposed by Buehler in a version of modernization theory (Buehler, 1998: 191 and *passim*). This theory of historical phases – from the living, directing-shaykh to the mediating, dead shaykh or peripatetic, media-cum-mediating-shaykh – poses a false historicity: it fails to recognize the cyclical features of Sufi orders and regional cults, which are characterized by periodic waxing and waning, rise and fall, growth and decline (Trimingham, 1971; R. Werbner, 1977). At any historical period, only rare individuals rise to be new living saints and directing-shaykhs of real distinction. The cults they found seldom retain the same charismatic aura of the original founders under their successors.

Buehler's argument fails also to recognize that saints are perceived and experienced differently by different disciples, who make different demands on a living shaykh. Some followers approach a saint in the hope of obtaining intimacy with God via the saint; others regard him or her as the subject of love who mediates their mundane life desires with God. The very same saint can thus be both mediating and directing, depending on the situation, or on a disciple's expectations. In this sense it is the disciples who define and determine the nature of the connection between saint and follower, as much as the saint him or herself does. In practical terms, the result of these fluctuations in time and variations in perception gives rise to an apparently diverse range of Sufi circles, yet followers continue to recognize an affinity to one another and to share some basic assumptions.

Islam in Britain

Like the Sufi *tariqa*, the wide variety of different religious streams, denominations and movements evident in South Asia has been transposed into Britain, along with the migration of Muslims from the sub-continent. Manchester, a large industrial Northern British city with around 23,000 Pakistani settlers, is part of a much larger conurbation with a population of some 100,000 Asian Muslim immigrant settlers. The city is home to many Muslim independent associations and branches of national Muslim organizations. Major modernist groups such as Tablighi Jama`at, Jama`at-i Islami or the Deobandis compete with new Islamic movements such as the al-Muhajiroun (now banned) or Hizb ut-Tahrir, imported from the Middle East, which are attractive to some young South Asian Muslims. Most of these different groups have their own mosques. So far, however, the vast majority of Punjabi Pakistanis in Manchester, and in Britain more generally, have tended to identify themselves with the Barelvi movement. They emphasize love of the Prophet and his continued active existence, and many come from families that are, or were, affiliated to a particular saint in Pakistan.

Despite this acceptance of saints and cults, most UK Punjabi Pakistanis are not active followers of a particular saint or *pir* locally. They see themselves as the people of the Prophet's *sunna* in general, are happy to host and attend the lectures of visiting *pir*s or Barelvi `ulama, and to seek protective amulets or healing from local and subcontinental Pakistani *pir*s. They participate in processions on `id milad al-nabi (the Prophet's birthday) and sometimes attend a local commemorative `urs festival (the annual gathering to commemorate the mystical union of a saint with God at the moment of his death), but without being initiated to a particular saint, a step taken only by a few. Nevertheless, the performance of *zikr*, the remembrance of God's name, is very popular. In the early days of immigration, I was told, the practice of *zikr* was unknown and, in the rare instances when *zikr* circles were held, they were condemned by orthodox `ulama. Today some Barelvi mosques are reputed to have very large *zikr* circles, and although in Manchester *zikr* is still performed by a select few rather than the majority, there are many *zikr* circles in the city.

A major further feature of Islam in Britain is that on the whole it remains nationally and ethnically divided. There are Pakistani, Bangladeshi and Arab mosques, as well as Turkish and Shi`a mosques, and the language of sermons and even supplicatory prayers in the Pakistani mosques, whatever their tendency, is Urdu rather than Arabic. At the same time, children are taught to read the Qur'an in Arabic, and few youngsters can read and write in Urdu unless studying it in school as an examination subject. Mosque attendance among the younger generation is also a matter of choice and by no means universal, even though most youngsters remain pious and stress their Islamic identity, which they feel to be beleaguered both locally and globally.

In this context, the Sufi groups I studied, with one important exception, were relatively small and intimate. The main source of recruitment in all of them remained the older generation of migrants, but membership was augmented by recent younger immigrants from Pakistan, mostly in-marrying spouses, and by young Pakistanis, born or brought up in Britain, who were mostly well educated, with the exception of one traditional order that had a young, working class following.

Universalism and Particularism in Sufi Regional Cults

Despite their small size, Sufi groups in the city were enmeshed in translocal, transregional and transnational networks. They resembled other regional cults in having a sacred centre with branches linked to it in different localities in both Britain and Pakistan, and sometimes elsewhere. Typically also, they combined a universalistic orientation to a high God with a particularistic orientation to a specific sacred site or holy person. This mix of what are often regarded as opposed modern and traditional religious orientations is a key feature of regional cults. The same orientational conjuncture was also evident in the way modern, educated disciples sought logical, scientific knowledge through their shaykhs' esoteric speculations.

Second, rather than marking contiguous, bounded territories, Sufi groups co-exist side by side in a single locality, while expanding across ethnic and territorial boundaries, to create their own sacred topographies and flows of goods and people. Like in other regional cults, these sacred topographies cut across, rather than being congruent with, the political boundaries and subdivisions of nations, ethnic groups, or provinces (see R. Werbner, 1977: XI). There is no correspondence, in other words, between political territory and Sufi order. Nor can Sufi centres or saints be studied in isolation from the wider regional and transnational cult generated around the sacred centre, or the political contexts in which the cult operates.

Sufi cults remain in many ways autonomous organizations, outside any political order. It cannot be said, for example, that Sufi ritual and belief are mere reflections of political divisions or economic interests.[5] Yet they continue to accommodate to this order. Indeed, historically, certain Sufi groups have played prominent political or economic roles. By the same token, however, Sufi cults are often perceived or perceive themselves to be in tension with the postcolonial and capitalist economies of modern-day Pakistan or post-imperial Britain (P. Werbner, 2003). This is despite the fact that they thrive on the spaces opened up by modernity for independent organization and mobilization.

Regional cult analysis aims to disclose such hidden structural interdependencies and disjunctures between different domains of action (social, political, ritual, economic, and so forth).[6] As Villalón documents in this volume (Chapter 10), Sufi regional cults are both linked to centres of political power and in tension with them. Various historical studies have highlighted the pragmatic tendencies of Sufism that have enabled Sufi saints in South Asia to accommodate to changing political regimes and circumstances, over many centuries of imperial and postcolonial rule.[7] The relationship between the political centre and the sacred centre is a historically contingent one, and in this sense, as in others, regional cults are historically evolving social formations. This is evident in the cases presented below.

Victor Turner's argument that pilgrimage centres foster *communitas*, an alternative egalitarian ethical order uncircumscribed by territorially defined relations of power and authority, has been challenged by scholars who recognize a more complex *conjuncture* of politics and amity coexisting in a single cult (Eade and Sallnow, 1991; R. Werbner, 1977: XII *passim*). Hence, for example, Sufi regional cults are not simply inclusive. They foster a specific local membership, and yet the sacred centre and the major festivals around it are open to all. Relations between initiates are said to be (generic) relations of love and amity, stripped of any prior status, idealized as beyond conflict or division. Yet the organization of major regional cults is based around the ingathering of elective groups from particular, defined political and administrative communities – villages, towns, city neighbourhoods – and relationships between disciples in these larger cults can be marred by interpersonal rivalries and jealousies. The intimate Sufi groups described here were, however, free of such rivalries that typify larger orders.

Intimacy and Social Networks across Gendered Divisions

Whereas some of the larger Sufi fraternities were enmeshed in local mosque politics in Manchester (P. Werbner, 2002), most Sufi groups were too small to be regarded as significant political actors. They did, however, in other respects, resemble regional cults: they were inclusive, boundary-crossing, centrally focused social formations. A key feature was their shared sense of intimacy generated not only with the Sufi saint or guide, but among the followers, with each other. One of the groups, affiliated to the Azimiyya order with its centre in Karachi, was led by a woman saint, Baji Saeeda.[8] The

Azimiyya order was founded in 1960 and Baji Saeeda regarded herself as the third master and head of the order in the UK and Europe. The founder of the order was Mohammed Azim Barkhia, known as Qalandar Baba Auliya. He died in 1979 and was succeeded by Khawaja Shams-ud-Din Azeemi, an author of many books on Sufism, who is still alive and lives in Karachi. It was he who appointed Saeeda as head of the order in Europe, with the right to initiate followers, both male and female. I was told that the order has 70 *muraqaba* halls (visualizing, meditation or contemplation halls) throughout Pakistan, 12 in England, one each in Norway, the Netherlands, Sweden, Canada and Moscow, and six or seven in the United States.

The South Manchester Azimiyya group had its *muraqaba* hall above the supermarket of a keen female follower, a relatively educated woman from Lahore who was the right-hand woman of Baji Saeeda. She and Baji Saeeda also ran workshops on diet and complementary medicine in community centres and at Salford University. The group met twice a week, on Wednesday and Sunday evenings, for repetitive prayers, *zikr* and meditation. On Sunday these were followed by a *langar* (meal cooked voluntarily and distributed freely, provided in South Asia at Sufi lodges), prepared by members of the group and by Baji Saeeda herself. Every week there were visitors from elsewhere: from Huddersfield and Bradford in Yorkshire, from Nelson in Lancashire, from Birmingham and Glasgow. The *chapatti* (flat bread) for the *langar*, for example, was baked by a keen follower from Bradford. Although the group composition changed from one meeting to the next, there was a core of regulars, and even the visitors from other towns were intimately known since many of them had been to Manchester before, or had been visited in their cities by delegations from Manchester.

Seen in class terms, the attendants were a mixed group, from an educated, left-wing Gujarati woman town councillor to older people of village background, young men recently arrived from Pakistan as marriage spouses, computer experts and businessmen. The group was also a mixed gender group and the sexes mingled easily and did not form separate circles. Relations across both sex and generation were casual and friendly. Baji Saeeda herself was forthright, friendly, confident and genuine, but never distant. She radiated kindness in a motherly sort of way.

There was a good deal of gossip and joking during meetings. Most people had been coming for a long time and they clearly enjoyed the gatherings. The group was as much a social club as a religious association.

Yet the themes and events were typically Sufi: the stress on experience as well as formal knowledge, on *zikr, du`a* (supplicatory prayer), *langar, `urs* and religious inclusiveness. A good deal of time was spent discussing Sufi concepts and ideas. However to my Naqshbandi-trained ears, the Sufi speculations appeared rather confused, being a hybrid of lay scientific notions of healthy eating, nature, astrology, and homeopathy with standard Sufi and Islamic terms regarding the Day of Judgement, the journey of the soul, the

Platonic worlds of Sufi realities and so forth. So too, rituals deviated from the traditional standard. For example, Baji Saeeda gave the sermon but did not herself perform the *du`a* after the *zikr*, a peculiarity I observed in no other group. Similarly, the *`urs* was more like a public meeting than a ritual event.

Meditation meetings were not very large: during winter, when it is bitterly cold, the number of participants varied from 15 to 25, including visitors from other cities. Baji Saeeda visited other congregations throughout Britain regularly, usually on Saturday evenings.

Talking to one of the keen followers, a pleasant woman in her mid-forties, I asked if it was not strange to have a woman *pir*? She responded that everyone is an *insan*, a human being; there are no differences between men and women, young and old. 'I come here every week; it's like my family. It gives me a real boost for the rest of the week. I never pay attention to whether they are men or women'. She used to take anti-depressants but they did not help and had bad side-effects so she stopped.

On the night of the 27th of Ramadan, the *tarawih* prayers started at 10 in the evening rather than the usual time of 7.30pm. Baji Saeeda sat on a raised podium, reclining on brocade cushions. The *tarawih* were scheduled to go on all night. Like the regular meditations, the prayers took place in the dark, with the lights turned out.

On this occasion delegations were present from other cities: Bradford, Birmingham, Accrington, Nelson. Altogether there were about 35 people gathered in the hall. Most of the men and women were in their thirties and most looked as though they had grown up in Pakistan. One woman was a college Urdu teacher in Bradford. Talking among the *murid* was animated, and they participated in preparing and serving the midnight feast.

One evening we celebrated the recovery of a woman from Bradford who had suffered from a badly dislocated jaw, a condition that doctors were unable to cure. Baji Saeeda had blown *dam* (a spell consisting of a Qur'anic verse) on her, I was told, and totally cured her. She sat beside Baji Saeeda on the raised cushions, alongside her husband and three sons. This was an event of friendship and communal support, which was also an occasion to eat a commensal meal and hear a lecture on Sufism.

Magic Squares and the Quest for Cosmic Knowledge

Like the Azimiyya group in Manchester, Shaykh Abidi's group of devoted followers is an extremely intimate one. Indeed, several core followers are siblings of a single family, a sister and three brothers and their spouses. Shaykh Abidi is a well-known Sufi faith healer who, until his retirement, travelled widely in the Middle East and England. His miraculous healing was, in the past, regularly reported in the press, both in Britain and in Morocco, Tunisia and Egypt. He says that he has in his possession a gift given to him by one of the Gulf shaykhs whose wife he treated successfully. Sufism, he says, is his hobby.

Shaykh Abidi is addressed by his devoted followers as Sufi Sahib or simply Shahji. He used to live in Manchester where, in addition to his healing activities he was also a businessman, before returning to his home in Karachi. He moves back and forth between his homes in Manchester and Karachi. A Shiite with broadly tolerant views on matters of gender, music and religious difference, during his prolonged return visits to Manchester he holds a communal meal at his home every evening, starting at 8pm and going on sometimes until well after midnight. Followers sit on the floor in the company of the shaykh, and as in the Azimiyya group, the meal is laid on a giant plastic tablecloth spread over the carpet. Before the meal there is a prayer and sometimes a *zikr* session. Followers are educated people, many of them successful firm managers, business people or professionals, both men and women. One follower is a (Sunni) psychiatrist in a local government hospital. They all speak fluent English but the conversation usually flows in Urdu and Punjabi, as in Baji Saeeda's group.

Shaykh Abidi dresses dramatically, Middle East style, in kaftans and turbans of varying colours, or a red Arab *kafiya*, over a pure white tunic. He is a true eccentric who refuses to fit into any mould. During most evenings he (and the group) continue to watch television out of the corner of their eyes while they discuss his latest mystical projects. He took up playing the sitar some years ago, and among his followers are a couple of Sikhs. His enthusiasms and obsessions infect the whole group. He has cured people of all nationalities, and various religious faiths including Hindus and Mancunian Jews.

Distinctively, Shaykh Abidi has been working on a series of projects that all involve numerological or alphabetical computations of the Qur'an and other sacred texts. He uses a very powerful computer and laser printer, helped by some of his more technologically minded followers. He also writes prophetic books that comment on and predict world events. His quest for esoteric knowledge is thus all-embracing.

The regular group that meets daily is usually quite small, about ten people. Now and then, visitors come from elsewhere – London, Slough (near London), Peterborough, Southampton, Leeds and Blackpool. Shahji used to have a house in the Slough area of London and he still has a large following there. The evenings pass in relaxed talk, joking and gossip or in discussions of the latest numerical project. Very often the group videos itself and later watches videos of past gatherings. Members of the group are also involved in translating some of their guide's prophetic books.

One of his most devout followers told me, 'You know, Shahji tells those of us who can't keep in tune to say *zikr* quietly because it has to be said in harmony, all together. But at the Dar-ul-Uloom [the rival Sufi group's mosque in Manchester affiliated to Zindapir's order, which has a large following] the *zikr* sounds just horrible – a cacophony of voices'. The harmony of group sociality and the harmony of the sound produced in *zikr* are thus intimately linked in the eyes and experience of followers.

At the airport on the day of Shahji's departure for Karachi there are delegations from as far afield as London. He is showered with expensive gifts, including a diamond ring and a wide-screen television set.

Abidi claimed that his knowledge was passed down to him from his father and forefathers. This includes his knowledge of *hikmat*, Greek or Unani medicine. His genealogy, *shajara nasb*, stretches all the way back to Ali, he said, the original Caliph and companion of the Prophet. He was born in United Provinces, India, and arrived as a refugee to Karachi in 1948 when he was a child. The experience of Partition left him deeply unhappy. He sought a real *pir*, a person whom he had heard lived near Muree. Finally, after some searching, he reached a mud hut where there was an old man with a long beard. He began to visit him daily. There was an elderly postman there who wrote down all the *pir*'s words. He told Shahji that when he started as a young postman, the *faqir* was exactly the same age as now. One day Shahji tried to count the large number of stray dogs around the hut. He counted a particular number but the *faqir* said, 'You have forgotten that dog over there'. And these dogs all have families (in other words, the *pir* had extramundane knowledge and a superhuman psyche). The *pir* had come from the direction of Gilgit and was also a descendant of Ali. After the *pir* died, without even knowing where his grave was located, Shahji found the grave immediately, just where the wagon stopped, even though it was located in the wilderness and there were no signs leading to it.

This *murshid* visits Shaji in visions. Once, Shahji told me, he started a new *wazifa* (a Sufi repetitive set prayer or liturgy) in England, a very powerful *wazifa*, and he had a vision of drowning. He was in a small boat, being tossed up and down by giant waves, and he could not swim. Then his murshid came along, the water reaching only up to his knees, and carried him safely to the shore. After that he promised not to read the *wazifa* in England, and wait until he got back to Pakistan. What is the name of his *silsila*? Is it Naqshbandi or Chishti? He dismissed this with a wave of his hand. It is just Abidi.

Among followers in England, Sufism represents a form of esoteric knowledge of a hidden reality that may be mastered as objective fact. Some also stress meditation, *zikr*, dreams and visions as leading to such knowledge. Abidi, for example, spends a good deal of time interpreting the visions seen or experienced by disciples during the performance of *zikr*. These are aired and discussed in public for all to hear during the nightly sessions at the shaykh's home.

But the hallmark of Abidi's current project is the numerical and lexical manipulations of the Qur'an, using letter values as equivalent to numerical values, *alif* being 1, *ba* 2, *ya* 10, *mim* 40, and so forth, much like the numerical system used by Jewish kabbalists. Indeed, Shahji reads any kabbalist literature he can lay his hands on in English.

Abidi was described to me by his followers as the most knowledgeable person alive, and the last living Sufi in the world. On my first visit to him I was shown a giant, intricate chart of numbers hanging on the wall. The saint explained to me that the table represented the sum of the seven most important suras of the Qur'an in numerical form. It consisted of 25 x 25 large squares (total 625), each of which was divided into 4 x 4 small squares (16). The total number of small squares is thus 10,000 (100 x 100). Each number in the chart is different. Despite this, each row and column of four small squares adds up to exactly the same number, and so too do all the larger squares. Each row and each column of 100 small squares also adds up to the same number. One can then multiply the sum of one row or one column by 100, or of a row of 4 by 625, to get the total numerical value of the seven suras. Abidi proved all this to me, drawing out of his pocket a largish pocket calculator. The chart is called a '*naqsh*'. The very same table had also been copied by Shahji in Arabic numericals in his meticulously neat handwriting on to a silk cloth. This silk cloth, followers told me, is totally unique. If I placed it on my head, they said, I would have visions, and I would also receive blessings and solutions to all my problems.

The chart, as it turned out, was only the most modest of all Abidi's projects. During his stay in Manchester in 1999-2000, he was working on a much more ambitious *naqsh*, this time of the whole Qur'an as well as the Torah. This *naqsh* consisted of a million squares (1,000 x 1,000 small squares or 250 x 250 large squares = 62,500). The same principles applied to the larger chart as to its smaller equivalent, but this time all the work had to be done using a powerful computer. He already knew the numerical value of the whole Qur'an and Torah (which had both been computed by others). To produce the chart, his computer printed out strips of tiny numbers, using a PC Excel program. The strips were then stuck together on an enormous sheet to be taken to the printer.

To his young and highly educated followers, mostly born or educated in England, the magic charts reveal a miraculous knowledge which is divinely inspired. This knowledge enabled their shaykh to unlock a hidden, deeper reality through highly scientific numerical computations. The charts proved the holiness and perfection of the Qur'an, one that their shaykh was able to demonstrate scientifically through his amazing mathematical genius. The chart revealed that a book which might seem on the surface arbitrary and complicated is, in reality, divinely constructed as a perfect order.

Hence, the awe-inspiring numerical perfection of Shahji's magic squares reveals for followers the mysteries of divine universal perfection. This esoteric practice of numerical and alphabetical combinatorial manipulation, known in the Islamic world as *jafr* and more common among the Shi`a, is thought to contain 'the Universal intellect' (Fahd, 1999a) so that, in the words of one anonymous author, 'to understand the mystery of numbers is to penetrate that of the Divine intelligence' (Fahd, 1999b). It is based on the belief that, as

Schimmel tells us, 'letters are a veil of otherness that the mystic must penetrate' (1975: 411).

In February 2000, several months after I first met him, Shahji announced that the million square chart, referred to as the 'ark', was now complete. The reference to the ark was to the Ark of the Covenant housing the Ten Commandments that followed the Children of Israel through the desert, but Shahji sometimes conflated it with Noah's ark (an unintended and unconscious English pun). He continued to perfect the chart. One day, for example, towards the end of the project, he realized that there were mistakes in two of the sheets, and it had taken his nephew 24 hours to locate them. The 1,000 x 1,000 squares of numbers, a million different numbers, each number different and unique, which added up together to the same number in all the columns and rows, was being printed out first on a high-powered laser printer. The numbers were tiny, almost microscopic, and were printed on 100 sheets of 100 x 100 squares, each about the size of an A3 sheet, before being taken to the printer to be produced as a single whole.

Two weeks later the ark arrived back from the printer and was unfolded for us to behold. A large, laminated scroll, some three by three meters in size, it was opened by one of the disciples on the living-room floor, with everyone present gazing at it in awe. The thousands of tiny numbers and squares merged at a distance into intricate patterns, almost like a Persian carpet. The chart was framed in dark gold and bore the title, 'The Eleven Commandments' (a reference to the original Ten Commandments plus the Qur'an). For the onlookers it was replete with mystery and power. Shahji explained to me that it was based around sacred numbers such as 19, 10, 11 and 2.

He showed me a recently published American book in English that reported on how, through the use of modern technology, the Torah was discovered to be based on a complex code which, once cracked, could be used to generate all kinds of prophecies (such as the assassination of Yitzhak Rabin, the then Israeli prime minister). This discovery linked into one of Shahji's other major projects.

Hence, in addition to his numerical projects, Shahji had also written out a 'book' which was said to replicate the *Jafr Jama`a*, an esoteric book supposedly authored by Ali and subsequently lost without a trace. A description of how this book had been constructed was discovered by Shahji in an Egyptian text in Arabic, and formed the basis for his own project of reconstruction. Arabic has 28 sounds, he explained. The *Jafr Jama`a* was divided into 28 chapters, each with 28 pages. The whole book consisted of four-letter word combinations that were never repeated, much like in the *naqsh*.

In February 2000, as the ark was being completed, Shahji's version of the *Jafr Jama`a* was flown over to Manchester from Karachi on a Pakistan Airlines flight and unveiled in front of the assembled disciples. Written on a scroll, the book was treated with great veneration, covered with two cloths and raised above the floor on a table. The outer cloth, a heavy brocade, was removed first, followed by the green and gold inner cloth in which the scrolls were wrapped. I was told that the opening of the inner cloth was a moment to make a wish. An aura of sanctity and awe prevailed among the assembled congregation as the book was slowly unwrapped. Everyone stood around silently, the women with their heads covered.

Interpreting the *Jafr Jama`a* (also sometimes referred to as the ark) is the responsibility of an expert with divine inspiration since this book is said to contain all the knowledge in existence – past, present and future. For this reason the book is regarded as immensely powerful and is opened with such great reverence. Nevertheless, followers were still concerned with the meaning of the book. In the absence of a key to unlock the mostly meaningless alphabetical combinations, the book remained for them a frustrating mystery that even Shahji's genius could not fathom.

Hybrid Knowledge Systems

Although his imagination is undoubtedly more original and powerful than Shaykh Abidi's, the Azimiyya, too, engaged in speculations that mixed lay science with Sufi cosmology, like Shaykh Abidi's speculative flights. One example may suffice to give a taste of the hybrid juxtapositions of Azimiyya thought.

The high point of the Azimiyya *muraqaba* meetings was the lecture or sermon delivered by Baji Saeeda in which she explained the inner truths of Sufism and Islam. Her lectures were always followed by a group discussion in which she encouraged all the disciples to participate. She spoke forcefully and inspirationally, without notes, and her talks were recorded by some disciples, with her closest companion taking detailed notes which she subsequently retold with her own gloss to more lay audiences.

For the Azimiyya, a theory of colours and attributes as sources of spiritual energy was constantly linked to modern-day phenomena. Baji Saeeda's right-hand woman explained:

> We have 11,500 colours, each a different force, working within ourselves. The Qur'an says, 'We take Allah's colours', we are living on *nur*, light. There are ten lives of the soul. God said '*kun*' (be), and all the creative forces, attributes of God, were gathered together, that is the *ruh* (eternal soul). 11,500 attributes of God created us. Without *ruh* nothing can exist; without it nothing can manifest itself. A mountain could not exist without *ruh*; it has its own way of existence. He said the mountains and trees exist for me. They have a *shu'ur* – an intelligence, consciousness, though not like ours. There are reptiles, fruit – everything that exists contains *ruh*, energy, which can be perceived with an infra-red camera which outlines fields of energy. That is not the *ruh* but a reflection of it, evidence that something exists. It is a creative

force. If we are made of 11,500 attributes of God, a fish may have only 20 attributes.

> So too, she explained on another occasion, all the holy places have enormous energy that can be seen by infra-red light, and Mecca shows the most energy, more than any other place on earth when this technology is used. Colours are reflections of specific attributes. Each attribute has a job to do. Attributes send messages that are called hormones in the human body. The messages to the hormones are from the attributes.

The speaker drew several lines on a flip chart around the contours of the body that she said were the body's 'aura'. She also drew lines between `alam-i arwah* (the world of the souls) and the mind, which she explained was different from the brain. The *ruh* descends into the body with God's light (*nur*). The *ruh* creates communication and the mind receives the communication. The pineal gland in the brain responds to moods, positive or negative. It can cause illness. Bad thoughts prevent the receptiveness to Allah's light. They make the body opaque. This was an extremely scientific explanation.

Intimacy with the Shaykh

The intimacy of *zikr* circles is commented on by all disciples, and I discuss it further below. Those groups that hold regular `urs*, such as Zindapir's regional cult in Britain, gather together followers from all over Britain for one or two days (P. Werbner, 2003, 1996b). But one of the key groups in Manchester, a Naqshbandi Mujaddidi group headed by Shaykh Farooqui, a reformist saint who is in many ways close to the Deobandis and even to the Taliban, has no `urs*. Instead, the group holds an annual cricket tournament in the summer. Disciples, I was told, come from London, Bristol, Longsight (in Manchester), Croydon and many other places. The two young *murid* who told me about the cricket match said that it 'increased brotherhood'.

The mutual love between all Muslims, over and above the love of the shaykh, was very much stressed by these two young disciples. One of them told me:

> We come here just to do *zikr*, for the sake of *Allah subhanahu wa ta`ala*. It's love, when I go to my cousin, his shaykh is from Syria – Jordan – and he's a convert, a great shaykh and scholar. When I go and see him I feel extreme love, genuinely I love all Muslims, because when I go down, in town, and I meet someone and have a conversation and even if I don't know him, just because he's a Muslim I feel extreme love straight away, and we start talking as though we'd known each other for years and years and we sit together and start praying. You know, like if

we go to a mosque, like the Islamic Academy and some people come, we feel love. It's not just love for the shaykh. It's love for all Muslims as well.

Ultimately, however, it is intimacy with the shaykh that draws most of these *murid* into the *zikr* or contemplation circles.

Shaykh Farooqui, the Naqshbandi Mujaddidi Sufi, dresses like a classical saint, with a white gown and turban, and sits in traditional style in a room in his *khanqah* (study centre, which includes a mosque), reclining on brocade cushions, surrounded by pictures of holy sites and learned tomes in Urdu and Arabic, with the Qur'an placed on a small lectern in front of him. The shaykh has been extremely successful in fostering the cult-like features of his group. All members are enjoined to wear distinctive white turbans at all times, even in public. Men are expected to grow beards (for young men, an embarrassing deviation from the British norm), and women are required to wear the *hijab*. Women are expected to veil even in front of the shaykh and to expose only their faces, feet and hands. The rhetoric of the order is replete with references to hell and damnation. The group is renowned in Manchester for casting away and destroying all its members' television sets. Shaykh Farooqui stresses the gaze as a source of Satanic temptation and lust, and his vision of the world is, in general, guided by the sense he conveys to followers that they are surrounded by sinfulness. This is very much in contrast with the Azimiyya and Abidi groups that are enjoined to 'think positively'.

Shaykh Farooqui teaches his disciples the silent *zikr*, although this is a recent innovation of the cult. He has been particularly successful in attracting young, British-born, Pakistani students and some young converts, although most of his disciples are still first-generation migrant-settlers along with some of their children. Described by one young disciple as 'the most traditional of all saints', he nevertheless uses the Internet to publicize his group and his teachings, and has a relatively sophisticated Internet site, updated with his weekly sermon by young followers in London. In the past, he travelled throughout Britain. Now, due to ill health, he remains in the Manchester region where he has acquired and renovated his own *khanqah*.

Shaykh Farooqui is something of an autodidact, according to the prevailing local view of those who knew him in his previous, secular incarnation. For a long time he seemed to be just another market trader coming from an urban, middle-class background in Pakistan who, by his own account, enjoyed playing harmonium and tabla, presumably at middle-class musical gatherings. He is still a poet who writes *na`t*, praise poems to the Prophet. He claims a spiritual genealogy from Ali Murtaza whose shrine (*mazar*) is in Multan. The full spiritual genealogy of his order is published on the Internet and in the glossy monthly magazine his group produces. He delivers his sermons in Urdu with simultaneous English translation for disciples who are converts, and it is the English version that is published. His own spoken English is excellent.

The *khanqah*, a relatively new building that used to be a warehouse and has been converted into a mosque, with the shaykh's room on the upper floor, has no place for women. Women disciples can see him only on Friday afternoons, when he meets supplicants one at a time. His *zikr* circles, held in the evenings, are thus all-male events. I heard from a congregant that after September 11, he asked the congregation during the *jum`a* (Friday) prayers to raise their hands in support of the Taliban, revealing, perhaps, his radical Deobandi tendencies. Hearing about this clarified what seemed at the time an odd conversation I had with two of his young followers. The discussion began quite innocently when I asked them at the very end of an interview on how they became Sufis if they thought it was important to have democracy. One of them said he was not bothered either way. I was surprised, and commented that without democracy, a ruler opposed to Islam could arise in Britain.

'If you can't practice your religion', he responded, 'you should leave the country'. 'Would you just leave Britain?' I asked, puzzled. 'But don't you feel yourself to be a citizen of this country?'. He replied that he did not believe a Muslim should serve in the police force in Britain, although both he and his friend stressed the need to obey the laws of the land.

Farooqui rejects the title of *pir*, associated in South Asia with charlatanism, but he does disburse amulets and blow *dam* as most *pir*s do, and in his appearance and manners, he resembles the classical pose and repose of a South Asian Sufi living *pir*. Yet he clearly inspires a sense of integrity, selflessness and love in his young disciples. One of them, a university student studying ophthalmology, described to me during an interview his first meeting with the shaykh.

Ahsan: In a second, I can't explain it, it's like one day, you get an attachment, personally I just fell in love straight away, I just went there, I just fell in love with everyone there. Everyone was so, you felt so humble and it felt so nice and everything, you know, you felt this was Islam, you know, and it was so beautiful, it was so beautiful, everyone in white, this is so beautiful. At the time, shaving, one had to stand up, out of love and respect, it's like you have to stand up, but I found myself standing up, even though at the time I had no connection with the shaykh. Just feeling love and affection for someone. You know when someone is a fine person, you know that, when you have love and affection for him, when someone is a pious person, you know that. Then they went and brought the shaykh, and they came back and shook my hand and we went together (he and Noman, his fellow student), we went to see him, you know, and ask him questions. It was so different, we went to see the shaykh one-to-one and I was sitting there, he was totally different to how I thought it would be, just like me and the shaykh and that's what it was, no-one else was there, it was so beautiful, it was unbelievable. I can remember when I took *bay`at*, I just started shaking, and it was just like, you know, I couldn't believe it, you know, nervous and everything, you know, I was shaking because I just couldn't believe it, you know, I'd taken *bay`at*. Then I met Noman afterwards and I said, I took *bay`at*, and he said: so did I. O-o-o-o-okay.

Pnina: You didn't know about each other?
Ahsan: No, we didn't think ...
Noman: We had no intention of taking *bay`at*.
Ahsan: We just went there and when I spoke to him I thought to myself, there is no way I can leave here, you know, this is the truth, this is the *haqq*, you know, this is the ... I can't stay away, this is like unbelievable, it's like he knew what to say to me even before I asked him a question ...

Ahsan and Noman described the shaykh as being 'like a magnet' to which one feels religiously attracted. Yet, they claimed, the shaykh was 'so humble', so 'down to earth'. Sufism, they told me, is about 'perfecting yourself', just like wearing the turban, which is not obligatory in Islam.

Pnina: You seem to like the fact that it's strict? That seems to be part of his attraction. It's a challenge?
Noman: In Sufism, this is like that. You keep extra things out of love, everything is out of love, you keep a turban out of love, you wear this out of love, everything's out of love.

The sense of intimacy with the shaykh is a deep experience:

Noman: He [the shaykh] says: Don't come to this *masjid*, the reason you come to me is for *zikr*, for God, that's it, 'cause that's why you're there for'. He says, 'Just come to me for *zikr*', he makes you more aware of God, that's it. I'm not here to make a grand speech and then go home, that's not the aim of Sufism, *tasawwuf*, that's it, you never see anything (around you), every speech is for you. You think every speech is for you, I think, Oh my God, that Khan Sahib is talking to me, one to one, that's what it's like, every time. Even when I listen to cassettes, on tapes, it's like the same thing.

The connection is also deeply experienced during *zikr*:

Noman: You concentrate on God. It's like, when the lights are on, you keep looking around, but in the dark, it's brilliant, I mean, for me, my shaykh, when we do *zikr* in the dark, sometimes people could stand, like, he can spend 25 minutes just doing silent *zikr*, sitting in the dark there, I wouldn't even realize, you know, you're concentrating yourself, you don't care about anything else …

In other groups too, being in the presence of the shaykh is experienced as deeply moving. Baji Saeeda claimed visionary insight into events and an ability to see God since childhood. She was a writer who contributed regularly on her visionary insights to *The Roohani Digest,* the monthly magazine in Urdu produced by the Azimiyya order, and she had published several pamphlets as well as a volume of her essays. Her insight and powers of healing were aligned to her ability to give sensible and kindly advice. At every gathering, some disciples spent time in a corner talking with her quietly on their own about their problems and afflictions. Sometimes she would lay hands on a child or on an older person. But beyond that, those present felt that they absorbed some of her spirituality just by being in her presence. One woman told me:

> If you come repeatedly, you gain in spirituality from her and it really strengthens you in your daily life. It gives you power. And then you can also come to her after the *langar* with your problems and she solves them. She knows the answer. And you learn from her.

Another disciple told me he had spent the whole day with the head of the order, Babaji, in Karachi, so he felt that he had a special relationship with him. Baji Saeeda's close helper told me of travelling with Baji Saeeda on her second trip to Mecca. Her most exciting moment, she said, was when she was in the Haram Sharif in Mecca, standing on a praying mat with Baji Saeeda on one side and Baba Sahib (from Karachi) on the other. That was an incredibly moving moment. She just could not believe it. To think she was there in close proximity with both of them!

I asked one of Shaykh Abidi's young British Pakistani followers, a journalist married to a solicitor, why he spent evening after evening with the Shaykh. He explained that this was because Shahji could show him the way to reach closer to God. This disciple's sister cooks the evening meal almost every night, apart from occasions when everyone contributes a dish. She told me, 'I am the chosen one'. She said that people can't approach close to the shaykh because he is surrounded by a protective shield of *muwakkil*, which she translated into English as angels, guardian angels. She said her family had always been very close to him and this was a great blessing. She regarded it as something of a miracle that she could cook for so many people every night; that there must be *muwakkil* helping her.

Despite the awe in which Abidi is clearly held, when people greet him, they come close to him and kiss his shoulder. He is easygoing and welcoming, with a bright smile constantly lighting his face. He is regarded, and presents himself, as a seer of the future, both personal and political. He can issue warnings of dangers to come. His most recent book, *Divine Prophecy Divine*, was translated into English (Al-Abidi, 2002). Apart from being a healer with great powers, he is also believed to bring blessing and fertility.

Yet like Farooqui, Abidi's followers too deny that he is a *pir* or that they are his *murid*s. The negative connotations of the term *pir*, associated with superstition, manipulation and scurrilous exploitation, make it unacceptable to those who believe they are seeking, above all, true knowledge on the path to God.

Traditional Sufi Orders and the Mediational-Direction Opposition
In contrast to these more eclectic or extremely orthodox Sufi groups, the majority of Sufi groups in Britain conform to a more conventional and pragmatic familiar pattern of Sufi orders. There are three such traditional groups in South Manchester, all of them reformist. One is led by a senior Qadiri khalifa whose *pir* lives in London and whose order extends to various localities in Britain. Another is a Naqshbandi *sajjada-nishin* of Muhammad Qasim of Mohra Sharif who claims to be a *pir* in his own right and has a small following nationwide, composed to some extent of disciples of Mohra Sharif who live in Britain. The third is the Manchester branch of a major saint, Zindapir, whose lodge is located in the North West Frontier of Pakistan, and which is centred in Britain on the Dar-ul-Uloom in Birmingham. This is where Zindapir's senior khalifa, Sufi Abdullah, regarded as a *pir* in his own right, reigns supreme. Sufi Abdullah has created by far the largest and most successful of the Sufi orders in Britain, well connected politically to the local authority in Birmingham, and his order has recruited a large number of young British Pakistanis. Many of them are children of *murid*s. Some had attended Qur'an classes at his mosque or were students at the school for *hafiz* which his organization runs.

These khalifa and their shaykhs embrace the title of *pir* without hesitation, along with the range of customs associated with saintly veneration in South Asia, albeit in their reformist version. They articulate familiar Sufi cosmologies in the reformist tradition, practise a loud, melodious form of *zikr* and perceive the saint to be a powerful conduit of grace (*fayz*) and blessing (*barkat*). They hold monthly *gyarvi sharif* meetings in which food is prepared and served to commemorate Abdul Qadir Jilani. They march in public processions on the occasions of the `urs and `id milad al-nabi, distribute amulets and engage in other forms of healing. In these groups, it is the saint who always says the *du`a*, since it is he who is believed to intercede for followers on the Day of Judgement. Saintly predecessors are believed to be alive from the grave and to intercede with God for the sake of the living. At the same time, members of these groups lead ordinary, relatively secular, day-to-day lives. They certainly do not destroy their television sets or grow beards for the sake of the *pir*.

These groups could be interpreted in many ways as representatives of classic mediational Sufism. Indeed, *pir*s such as Sufi Abdullah are ridiculed and denigrated by the young, educated followers of Shaykh Abidi, for example, who regard them as power seekers lacking any true mystical inspiration or knowledge. In fact, however, in all the traditional Sufi orders there is a strong emphasis on Sufi practices of self-purification through *zikr*, and *zikr* sessions are highly organized and quite lengthy events. Moreover, at least some disciples desire intimacy in the company of the shaykh.

There is also, however, an ethical and social dimension to Sufism as practised in these traditional groups. This was made evident in my conversation with two young, relatively educated, British-born Pakistani women, both followers of the *pir* in Birmingham. The fathers of both young women were social workers by profession, were close *murid* of Zindapir in Pakistan and loyal followers of Sufi Abdullah.

I asked one of them, Ansa, what she got from being a *murid*? She told me that for her, Sufism is a refuge from the materialistic world. It creates a community of spirit and mutual help. It gives a purpose in life that is transcendent, above material interests. Ansa was very knowledgeable about the basic principles of Sufism and the Sufi path. She stressed that to advance on the path one must change oneself. It is not enough to repeat a *wazifa* given by the shaykh, in this case, by Sufi Abdullah. She said she participates regularly in *zikr* and *gyarvi* because these events give her a sense of community. I asked her if she had experienced any mystical visions. Her response implied that this was not a major concern of hers. But she and her friend both said that they liked performing *zikr* very much. It gives them, they said, a sense of going beyond themselves (sort-of like transcendental meditation, one of them explained). Ansa said that during *zikr*, one is supposed to focus on the image of the saint and remove all other thoughts from one's mind. Apparently, they found this to be a liberating experience. Ansa's friend said that Sufi Abdullah's *du`a* after the *milad* procession makes her proud to be a Muslim, perhaps because he asks for blessings for everyone in such detail.

At the same time they stressed that Zindapir, who had died the previous year, was not dead. Ansa said that he had died during his lifetime by denying himself all material things – he ate very little and hardly ever slept; he dedicated himself to God. Because of this he remains alive after his death. Zindapir was a very distant figure for the two young women and they wanted to hear as much as possible about him from me, since I had actually met him and spent time in his company.

They felt that Sufi Abdullah gave them enormous support. He was always there, as for Ansa's mother when she had serious medical problems. He was always ready with advice. Both girls' grandfathers had died while their families were in Britain and Sufi Abdullah had given their families enormous support. The shaykh is for them a protective figure, a rock in times of need, they said.

All these different cases, seen together, show that for young people in Britain of Pakistani origin, Sufism is grasped in social and ethical terms, while at the same time it is perceived to lead to an experience of transcendence and to a deeper, more real, form of knowledge. In all the groups, being a disciple leads to a broader exposure to like-minded Pakistanis living in different towns and cities in Britain, and to new kinds of links with Pakistan and Islam.

Conclusion

The varied cases I have drawn upon here highlight the complex conjunctures of tradition and modernity, universalism and particularism, community and voluntary association, scientific and esoteric knowledge, that typify Sufi practice in contemporary Britain.

The comparison discloses that despite the apparent variety and heterogeneity of Sufi groups that co-exist in a single British city, these groups bear, at a deeper level, many similarities. It is significant, I think, that all the groups analyzed here foster national networks that connect Pakistani settlers from different places in new social configurations, which are both voluntary and intellectually exploratory. In all the groups, the shaykh is not merely a mediatory figure but a source of inspiration. In addition, he is the locus of national and international organizational relations.

Not all the groups are equally politicized, or politicized in the same way. I found the Azimiyya and Abidi group to be openly and explicitly tolerant but to have little contact with the state or its representatives. They did, however, have contacts with local MPs and a range of English institutions such as the University. By contrast, Sufi Abdullah works closely with the local government in Birmingham, whose representatives are always invited to the *`urs* and a meal following the procession on *`id milad al-nabi*. In meetings with local councillors, bureaucrats and the police, members of the group stress the peaceful nature of Islam. The mosque in Birmingham hosts school visits and delegations coming to the city on a regular basis, and cooperates with the local authority on various work and educational projects. At the same time, the cult is secretive and contains elements antagonistic to non-Muslims (see P. Werbner, 2003). This antagonism seemed even more evident in the Naqshbandi Mujaddidi group, yet there was no evidence of any attempt by this group to reach the local state.

Similarities are most striking in the relations between disciples and the shaykh. Can we say, perhaps, that Pakistanis in Britain are returning to a *khanqah* style of Sufism? This, I think, would be to gloss over the complex mix of mediation and direct intimacy that marks all the groups, even where their leaders refuse the title of *pir*. Even if some groups are larger and more organized than others, shaykhs and *khalifa* – at present all are still living shaykhs – do have direct contact with young disciples. When Sufi Abdullah, for example, travels with his young disciples to Ghamkol Sharif, the cult centre in Pakistan, he spends all his time in their company, eating and sleeping with them. He rarely instructs them on the intricacies of Sufi cosmology. Nevertheless, they feel they benefit directly from his divine grace (*fayz*). At the same time, Zindapir, the living saint who died in 1999, is regarded by followers as alive from the grave.

It is perhaps a mistake to focus exclusively on relations between saint and disciple. Above all, intimacy is a quality of social relations between disciples themselves. Seen in a broader sociological perspective, Sufi cults in Britain, like other forms of religious organization, create links between Pakistani communities which go beyond prior kinship or village relations. Such cross-cutting ties across British cities, extending into Pakistan, create a consciousness of a broader community that is at once actively chosen by individuals, and at the same time reinforces their sense of identity as Muslims.

Acknowledgement

I conducted the research on which this chapter is based in 1999-2000 with a grant from the Leverhulme Trust. I wish to thank the Trust for its generous support. An earlier version appeared as Werbner, Pnina, 2004. Sufi Cults, Intimate Relations, and National Pakistani Networking in Britain. In *Muslims in Europe: From the Margins to the Centre*, edited by Jamal Malik, pp. 227-46. Munster: LIT.

12

MODERNITY AND ISLAMIC SPIRITUALITY IN INDONESIA'S NEW SUFI NETWORKS

Julia Day Howell

Throughout much of the twentieth century, Indonesian Sufi traditions were subject to a dual marginalization. This came from within the local Muslim community by Muslim Modernists and, from the outside looking in, by social scientists using the Indonesian case to test theories about how religions fare in the process of modernization. At the turn into the twentieth century, Muslim Modernists in the Dutch East Indies, inspired by reformers in the Islamic heartlands of the Near East, undertook a new kind of revitalization of their religion (Azra, 2004; Noer, 1973). Not only did they seek to expunge local accretions to the pure faith of the Prophet Muhammad, as so many reformers had done in the past, but they sought to reopen Islam's canonical texts, the Qur'an and Hadith, to new interpretations (*ijtihad*) unprecedented in scope. Their goal was to free the faith of archaisms and release its potential for spiritual leadership in the modern world.

Although some of the early Modernist reformers in the Near East had retained some appreciation for the Sufi tradition, in the Indies the Sufi orders came in for particularly scathing criticism from Modernists. They were accused of tolerating (or even, through their ignorance, actually encouraging) lax attitudes towards local spirit beliefs (*shirk*) and customs (*adat*) that contradicted Islamic law (*shari`a*). They were also suspected of promoting adulation of the principals of their orders (their *syekh*, Ar. *shaykh*) as virtually 'seconds to God', thereby violating the monotheism at the core of the faith.[1] The founding in 1912 of an organizationally modern (i.e., formally constituted and bureaucratic) Muslim Modernist voluntary organization, the Muhammadiyah, and its vigorous growth among urban Muslims throughout the late colonial period and into the Republican period, greatly facilitated the spread of such suspicions about the Sufi orders (*tarekat*, Ar. *tariqa*) and their teachings in the Indonesian islands.

Similarly, later in the twentieth century, some of the most influential scholarly observers of Muslim societies saw Sufism as marginal to Islam's future, whether in Indonesia or elsewhere. Arberry (1950), Geertz (1960b, 1968) and Gellner (1981, 1992), working in academic environments strongly influenced by post-Enlightenment Protestantism and various forms of modernization theory, all read Sufism as a remnant of traditional village and tribal life. In their view, Sufism was doomed to fade as modernizing social changes increasingly facilitated the displacement of emotive Sufi rituals and mystical practices by the sober scripturalism of city-based legal scholars and exegetes (*ulama*).

As noted in the Introduction to this volume, such characterizations of Muslim societies in terms of over-extended contrasts between city and countryside, scholars and ecstatics, have now been widely criticized, and in the cases of both Gellner and Geertz, attributed in part to a too-ready sympathy with their Muslim Modernist informants (cf. Hodgson, 1974; Woodward, 1989). Nonetheless, it is probably true that by the 1950s in Indonesia strict Muslim urbanites subscribed to Modernists' criticisms of the Sufi orders and of 'Sufi' devotional practices. They especially disapproved of extended and intensely repetitious forms of *dzikir* (Ar. *dhikr*, recitations of the names of God or of short phrases from the Qur'an) that can facilitate dramatic spiritual experiences. Certainly the characterization of Sufism as 'the Islam that isn't Islam' (*Islam yang bukan Islam*) was current from this time.

For 'lay' urbanites of Modernist leanings the unattractive features of the *tarekat* were not simply their supposed doctrinal infringements. Modernist urbanites were particularly concerned about the orders' reputation for having an objectionable social ethos: a rigid hierarchy and demand for uncritical obedience to the *syekh*, pressures on initiates to disengage from everyday social life, and a secretiveness and exclusiveness. With such stereotypes circulating in the 1950s and 1960s, and after half a century of politically propelled polarization of so-called 'strict' (*santri*) and casually observant Muslims, those more lax Muslims still interested in intimate spiritual experience or occult aid for the most part looked outside Islam, gravitating instead toward Sufi-derived,[2] but clearly heterodox, mystical groups (*golongan kebatinan*) and syncretic 'new religions' (*agama baru*) (Howell, 1982: 530-4; Stange, 1986).

From the 1970s, however, this situation began to change rapidly, despite some persistence of earlier stereotypes. The intellectual *avant-garde* spearheaded the rapprochement of Modernist-leaning Muslim urbanities with things 'Sufi'. Thus, in 1970 poet and scholar Abdul Hadi inaugurated a genre of 'Sufi' poetry, turning away from the socialist realism of the sixties (Aveling, 2001). Also around that time, the distinguished Islamicist and Muslim Modernist Hamka moved into television broadcasting and began reaching a much broader audience with the theme of one of his popular books *Tasauf Moderen* (*Modern Tasawwuf,* [1939] 1990). He encouraged modern Muslims to appreciate that the essence of 'tasawwuf' (which for him was personal ethical cultivation and philosophical reflection) was positive and could be learned by the general reading public without recourse to long periods of training in a Sufi order. This, he urged, would enable busy urbanites, fully engaged with work and family, to cultivate ethical discernment and enjoy spiritually enriching devotions that would enliven the otherwise flat Modernist regimen of minimalist ritual and compliance with religious law.

Indeed as the broader Islamic revival took shape in the later 1970s and 1980s, books on 'tasawwuf' and 'Sufisme' (the latter term just recently popularized through more widely accessible European publications) became best sellers. University student groups played an important role in promoting the urban 'Sufi' revival, featuring discussions of Sufism in their campus meetings and boosting Sufi book sales.

Then in the mid-1980s the mass media began to report that members of the urban middle class were joining a 'rush to the *tarekat*',[3] evidencing a remarkable softening of attitudes by some sophisticated urbanites to the once anathematized Sufi orders. Over the 1990s the popularity of the *tarekat* continued to draw comment, as the nation enjoyed impressive economic growth prior to the Asian financial collapse of 1997. However, even after that, and some say especially from 1998, in the troubled period of struggles to democratize that followed autocratic President Suharto's resignation, the *tarekat* have continued to attract well educated urbanites. Further, since the 1990s the range of activities involving 'tasawwuf' or 'Sufisme' has broadened considerably.

The surprising recent popularity of 'Sufi' spirituality in Indonesia, especially among the well-educated and religiously committed Muslim middle and upper classes, challenges us to understand how 'modern' Muslims could overcome, at least in part, the prejudices of earlier generations. This in turn requires us to understand how the negative stereotypes of Sufism became so entrenched in earlier decades of the twentieth century, given that Islam in Indonesia before the twentieth century was predominantly Sufi in tone and was supported by internationally well-regarded spiritual leadership and scholarship.

This inquiry, I argue, requires an appreciation of the evolving national legal and administrative environments in which religions have been regulated in Indonesia and of how discourses of modernity of various provenances (religious and secular, domestic and international) have interacted and become incorporated into Indonesians' perceptions of what constitutes proper 'religion' for 'modern' people. It also requires an understanding of how social changes from the mid-1970s that created a religiously committed new Muslim middle class have generated new demands in Indonesia's religious market.

Thus I argue that the legal and administrative structures that defined 'proper' religiosity for Indonesian citizens of the Republic in Suharto's New

Order Indonesia (1968-98) came to embody what I will call 'high modern' constructions of modernity. According to such constructions, religion suitable for people in a modern nation had to be scripturalist (i.e., focused on the observance of specific legal and moral codes and on prescribed worship), 'rational', congregational and exclusive. Such a construction was gradually articulated in law and state administrative practice in Indonesia under the influence of Modernist Muslims, mainline Christian churches and secular elites imbued with mid-century social science modernization theories. Not coincidentally, it devalued the experiential religiosity and eclecticism associated with Sufism. Not only were such emotive and 'inward' forms of spirituality castigated by scripturalists as violations of Islamic orthodoxy, but modernizing elites in general hoped to move the nation beyond such 'irrational' and outmoded 'superstitions'.

However, social changes associated with the New Order's highly successful economic development programs (rapidly increasing levels of secular education, entry of middle-class Muslims into upper-echelon jobs in the modern sector of Indonesia's economy, and increasingly cosmopolitan life experiences in the middle and upper classes) have generated new demands in Indonesia's religious marketplace for renovated elements of Islam's Sufi heritage. Those modernizing social changes have also stimulated much creativity to meet the new demands in the Muslim religious marketplace, prompting cosmopolitan Muslims to rework 'high modern' constructions of religiosity in general and Islamic spirituality in particular in what may be called 'late-', 'advanced-' or 'ultra-modern' terms (cf. Lambert, 1999; Voye, 1999). Thus, I argue, sections of the intelligentsia and other Muslim cosmopolitans are attaching a new, positive valence to autonomy in religious learning. They are also newly attributing positive value to certain types of eclecticism (although not syncretism) and experiential religiosity. Practices held over from the traditional past like *dzikir* and meditation that were once seen as embarrassingly superstitious, now appear to many Indonesian Muslim cosmopolitans as attractive, even 'scientifically' validated, ways to enhance a modern lifestyle. Contemporary constructions of Sufism, projected through the print and new electronic media, novel Muslim educational institutions and progressive Sufi orders, have facilitated this broadening of Indonesian conceptions of religion (*agama*).

Discourses of High Modernity and National Regulation of Religions in the Early Decades of the Republic

While Modernist Muslim critiques of the Sufi orders played the leading role in tarnishing the orthodox credentials of Sufi traditions among urbanities in the late colonial period, other factors came into play at the founding of independent Indonesia in 1945 and in the life of the young Republic. Controversies surrounding the relationship of Islam to the state lead to a compromise in which not Islam but 'belief in One Supreme God' (*keTuhanan*

Yang Maha Esa) became one of the founding principles of the state. That compromise generated more than three decades of public debate and government-civil society negotiation over what should constitute a proper religion (*agama*) in Indonesia.

In this unsettled period, non-Muslim and non-Christian ethnic groups that after Independence became targets for state-authorized mission activity, together with a plethora of Sufi-derived but independent and syncretic mystical groups (*golongan kebatinan*), some of which were patently heterodox Sufi orders, contested the terms of national religious legitimacy. In doing so, successful groups were obliged to undertake structural and doctrinal rationalization (in the Weberian sense) that helped them approximate the features of the established Muslim and Christian religions. This process of reformation was shaped by a modernist ethos, prevalent in both mainstream religious and secular nationalist circles. In this view, proper religions, that is, religions appropriate for a modern state, should focus through sober congregational worship on a transcendent deity. The capitulation of minority religious groups to such expectations in this early period of societal modernization contributed to the evolution of a normative standard for religion that went beyond the vague formulation of the nation's religious character in the first constitution.[4]

At the time of the first constitutional convention in 1945, nine out of ten Indonesians were Muslims and Islam had been an important bond joining the more than 300 ethnic groups in their anti-colonial struggle. Nevertheless, the nation was not founded as an Islamic state. Non-Muslim ethnic and religious minorities were able to win the support of Muslims wary of creating an Islamic state for an alternative basis of national identity: a set of five religiously neutral principles of Indonesian nationhood (the *Panca Sila*), including the non-denominational affirmation of 'belief in One Supreme God' mentioned above. This principle, incorporated with the other four in the Preamble to the 1945 Constitution, in effect made religious commitment a basic requirement of good citizenship. The body of the Constitution also obliged the state to support and protect citizens in their practice of religion (*agama*) (cf. Boland, 1971: 25-33) but it did not specify what qualified as religion. This was left to administrative regulation by the Department of Religion and the long term process of legislative clarification (including the possibility, which so far has not eventuated, that supporters of an Islamic state might win the numbers in Parliament to establish Islam as the state religion).

For more than a decade, in the absence of legislation clarifying what was to constitute 'religion', it was the administrative structure and procedures of the Department of Religion that in effect defined religion. Founded as an instrument to carry out the constitutional obligation of the state to support the religious life of citizens, but also as a mechanism for compensating disappointed proponents of an Islamic state, the Department of Religion has from its inception committed the bulk of its resources to Islam. Nonetheless, at its very beginnings in 1945, it was established with small directorates for Protestantism and Catholicism, thereby manifesting the earliest formal expression of constitutional religious pluralism (Boland, 1971; Steenbrink, 1972). In the absence of a definition in law, the Indonesian religions appropriate for good citizens were to be understood as the fraternal Abrahamic religions then present in substantial numerical and institutional strength in Indonesia.

However, the Department's need to develop procedures for dealing with other religious currents across the nation in the early days of the free Republic (from 1950) prompted it to articulate a working definition of religion. Not surprisingly, that definition was derived from Islamic understandings of 'Peoples of the Book', namely that a religion should have a prophet, a holy book and places of regular worship. The Department of Religion used that standard to identify and evaluate the numerous other religious currents extant or newly emerging across the country. Members of ethnic groups like the Balinese feared that their traditions, once branded 'animist', would be targeted for missionary work.

The rapidly multiplying independent mystical groups were treated differently. They were put under review and placed administratively under the Justice Department for surveillance. These mystical groups mostly had historical roots in the Sufi orders and used Sufi practices, concepts and names, but claimed a new revelation and wove elements of other religious traditions into their teachings. However, many of these groups contested the Department of Religion's determinations, and in so doing brought out into the open additional layers of meaning in the original Departmental definition of 'religion'. Thus the independent mystical groups (*golongan kebatinan*) formed an organization in 1956, the *Badan Kongres Kebatinan Seluruh Indonesia* (BKKI), to represent their interests to the public and win government support on the grounds that they, like Islam and the Christian churches, promoted the constitutionally enjoined *keTuhanan* (Subagya, 1976). The BKKI also pressed the claims of those mystical groups that purported to be religions in their own right.

Numerous *golongan kebatinan* actually operated as religions anyway, regardless of the Department's determinations, using names like *Agama Adam Makrifat* (Adamic Realization Religion), *Agama Jiwa Asli Republik Indonesia* (The Original Spirit of the Republic of Indonesia Religion), *Agama Islam Sejati* (Genuine Islam Religion) and *Agama Jawa Budo* (Javanese 'Buddhist' Religion) (cf. Subagyo, 1976). Yet throughout the 1950s and 1960s they persistently failed to win recognition as proper 'religions'. This was despite the fact that such groups technically fulfilled the Department of Religion's criteria for 'religion'. They had founders who received revelations (i.e., a 'prophet' of sorts), and in many cases recorded those revelations as the basis of the teachings of the group (producing something like a 'holy book') and had regular meetings in a building dedicated to the practice of communing with the Divine (i.e., a regular weekly or monthly 'place of worship').

Clearly those mystical groups that claimed to have a new revelation offended both Christian and Muslim beliefs that a definitive revelation had been given many centuries ago by their own religions' founders. The mystical groups thus stimulated opposition from mainstream religious interests reluctant to extend religious legitimacy any further, regardless of any apparent fit of the claimants' organizational profile with the Department of Religion's criteria for a religion. But even the more modest of the *golongan kebatinan*, which taught practices to facilitate experience of God's immanence in order to enhance Christian or Muslim faith in a transcendent God, were treated as highly suspect. At a time when even long-established, orthodox[5] Sufi orders were on the defensive against Modernist Muslims seeking to discredit the irrational ecstasies and claims to supernatural powers of the *syekh*, the syncretistic *kebatinan* mystics who no longer accepted the discipline of Islamic law were not to be encouraged with government privileges (cf. Rasjidi, 1967).

President Sukarno responded to these sentiments against the *kebatinan* groups in 1965 when he made the first legally binding government decision (Pen. Pres. 1, 1965) to recognize religions other than Islam and Christianity. Naming Islam, Protestantism, Catholicism, Hinduism, Buddhism and Confucianism as religions deserving the full support of the state, the decision also explicitly urged the *kebatinan* groups to 'return to their sources' (*kembali ke induk masing masing*) in the legitimized religions. Mystical groups persisting in calling themselves 'religions' were shut down; others charged with sullying the good name of religion were prosecuted. This was not simple capitulation to mainstream Muslim and Christian scripturalists, however. Not only did the Decision legitimize religions other than Islam, Protestantism and Catholicism, but its rejection of legitimacy for the mystical groups made plain and gave the force of law to ideals that secular modernizers such as Sukarno shared with Muslim Modernists and post-Enlightenment Protestants. Specifically, the Decision made manifest the objective that the religions of Indonesians should promote the country's advancement as a modern nation. Indeed Sukarno himself explicitly championed Enlightenment values in religion, urging his compatriots in August 1965, just a month after the promulgation of his Decision on religion and a month before the attempted coup that would lead to his political demise, 'Religion is not only concerned with feelings, but also with reason, reason, understanding, *ratio, ratio* and once again *ratio*!' (Boland, 1971: 131).[6]

That there was an evolution in normative standards set for religions over the early decades of the Republic, and that these were not in any simple sense just 'Islamic' or even 'Abrahamic', is further evident in the ways members of the Balinese and Chinese ethnic groups (together with some sympathetic Javanese) represented their cultural heritages in order to eventually win recognition for Hinduism, Buddhism and Confucianism as proper Indonesian religions (*agama*).

All three of the recently recognized Indonesian 'religions' (Hinduism, Buddhism and Confucianism) had their origins in minority cultural nationalist movements of the late colonial period. The scripturalist tone ultimately evident in the religions they produced, and the focus of those reconstructed religions on a transcendent deity emerged through processes of Weberian rationalization (selection, differentiation and systematization) evident in the cultural nationalist movements as they matured (Howell, 1978, 1982). These processes of community adaptation to rapid, modernizing social changes began in the late colonial period and continued in the Republican period. They have been as important as political pressures from the dominant religions in shaping the evolution of the minority traditions towards scripturalism and congregational organization.

Hinduism and Buddhism, which in Western New Religious Movements over the last half century have been embraced as ways of exploring meditation and experiential religiosity, in Indonesia actually evolved, by the time of their official recognition, along scripturalist lines. Also, both official Hinduism and Buddhism have been obliged to foreground a transcendent deity (at least in publications subsidised by the Department of Religion and in state-school-based religious education programs). At the same time, they have theologically reconstructed popular folk rituals that used to address a multifarious spirit world and down-played meditation practices aimed at experiencing an immanent Otherness.

Both 'Hinduism', adopted by Balinese reformists as the most appropriate identifier for their religious traditions, and 'Buddhism', formulated by Chinese Indonesians, sophisticated Javanese from Theosophy circles and a few Balinese, required a good deal of theological creativity to be reconciled with the constitutional requirement for 'belief in God' (*keTuhanan Yang Maha Esa*). Since the Indonesian original suggests by most interpretations a single divinity ('One Supreme God' or '*the* One Supreme God'), the Balinese had been obliged to select, from obscure texts, doctrines and images of the Absolute that could be popularized as the Supreme Deity among the polytheistic laity. The Hindu Bali Council facilitated a consensus around the transcendent and previously little supplicated Sang Hyang Widi (Sekretariat PHDP, 1970). Similarly, Buddhist organizations, heavily influenced in the 1950s by infusions of Theravada Buddhism and strict non-theism, nonetheless capitulated to national standards and nominated a figure from ancient Javanese Vajrayana texts, the Adi Buddha, as the Buddhist Supreme Being. Sunday worship was established to support congregational worship.[7]

These constructions could be construed as at best monistic; Indonesian reformers did not try to represent either Hinduism or Buddhism as strictly monotheistic on the model of the original established religions, Islam and Christianity. Thus the inclusion of Hinduism and Buddhism in the

Department of Religion and their later full legal recognition effectively broadened the range of permissible beliefs. But that extended scope still represented a compromise around a distinctively post-Enlightenment ideal: worship was to be regularized around that transcendent being, and the divine was to be approached via sober weekly collective worship, codified doctrines and official texts. Moreover those doctrines were to represent an exclusive commitment on the part of a clearly defined and bounded membership.

Confucianism, recognized as a religion in Sukarno's August 1965 Presidential Decision, soon lost that status after the alleged Communist coup attempt of September 1965 due to the too close association of Confucianism with the Chinese, and hence with Communism. It was not until after the resignation of Suharto, who rose to power by suppressing the coup attempt, that Confucianism regained its former legitimacy. By then it had been more fully reformulated, not just as a religion (*Agama Khonghucu*), but, in effect, as monotheistic, scripturalist and congregational (cf. Suryadinata, 1998).

These crisply formulated and neatly administered religions of the modern Republic were meant to stand in sharp contrast to traditional folk religious heritages, with their loose collections of untidy 'superstitions', irrational trances, and shifting, opportunistic patronage. They also stood in partial contrast to the independent mystical groups, the *golongan kepercayaan*. These had also assumed many of the trappings of rationalized religion, with their formal organizations and, in many cases, codified beliefs, but they bore obvious signs of recent syncretism and actually promoted experiential realization of immanent divinity. Some of them also maintained a specific ethnic or national referent.

The *golongan kepercayaan* represented by the BKKI umbrella body during the Old Order (1950s to the mid-1960s), differed among themselves not only in their aspirations toward the status of 'religion', but in the extent to which they fostered a universalistic as opposed to a local identity, and, related to that, the extent to which their leadership worked to synthesize cultural elements of different provenances into a coherent theology. The degree of universalism or cultural particularism of many groups was readily apparent in their names. Some clearly promoted local ethnic identities and heritages, for example, Kejawen Asli Hindu-Budo-Islam (Original Hindu-Buddhist-Islamic Javanism), *Agama Suci Jember* (the *Pure Religion of Jember* [a place in East Java]), and *Jawa Budo Budi Sejati* (the True Buddhist-Javanese Character [Movement]). Another type linked their practice regimes to a national identity and the 'national character' (*kepribadian nasional*) (a concept much in vogue at the time), as, for example, *Aliran Jiwa Indonesia* (The Spirit of Indonesia Movement) and *Pancasila Majapahit* (referencing both contemporary Indonesia's *Panca Sila* principles and the glory of the ancient, pre-Muslim kingdom of Majapahit). Some apparently non-parochial groups nonetheless asserted a particularly local or national appropriation of a universal religion, as in *Kejiwaan Islam Sejati* (True Islamic Spirituality), *Dharma Allah* (The

Teachings of God), and *Islam Murni* (Pure Islam), suggesting 'improvements' on the normative, international version of the religion that would have been offensive to the mainstream. Yet others proclaimed the universalism of their message, freed from both ethnic and national references (e.g., *Ngelmu Sejati* [True Knowledge] and *Perjalanan* [The Way]).

It was this latter type – those disengaged from an ethnic or national identity and focus – that developed the strongest national presence under the Old Order and adapted best to the New Order (Stange, 1986; Mulder, 1998). The largest of them (*Pangestu, Sumarah*, SUBUD [*Susila Budhi Dharma*] and *Sapta Dharma*), moreover, were not only universalist but monotheistic. They all survived the post-coup-attempt purges of the later 1960s, whereas many other groups quickly disbanded or were shut down. These latter groups were particularly the presumptuous 'improvers' on Islam – those with more floridly syncretic names linking Christianity and Islam in exotic pastiches like *Agama Islamisa* (The Jesus-Islam Religion), the frankly occultist, like *Klenik Islam* (Islamic Hermeticism), and those suspected of covering for 'atheistic communists'. All the surviving groups either never had, or came to disavow, claims to being a 'religion'. The highly visible *Sapta Dharma*, for example, changed its pre-1965 name '*Agama Sapta Dharma*' (the Sapta Dharma Religion) to '*Kerokhanian Sapta Dharma*' ('Sapta Dharma Spirituality').

The remaining mystical groups of the early 1970s were thus sufficiently adapted to the prevailing requirements for religion to win, at last, in 1973, an equivocal and separate but equal status beside the official religions. Having come on side with the new Suharto regime in the previous election, the independent mystical groups were accorded the status of 'faiths' (*kepercayaan*) nominally equivalent to the legitimate religions (*agama*) but administered within the Department of Education and Culture.[8] As such they enjoyed a very modest amount of enhanced protection and promotion, but were subjected to further pressures for rationalization and denomination-like exclusivity, while never quite overcoming lingering community suspicions.

Among the *kebatinan* groups that survived into the New Order, only SUBUD has become a major, fully international movement. Even so, it has a rather low profile domestically. Sumarah for many years was popular with foreign spiritual seekers in the Javanese cities of Solo and Yogyakarta and has a modest overseas presence through retreats offered in Germany, Italy and Australia by some of those ex-patriot seekers. Domestically, it suffered declining prominence, along with other independent mystical groups, as the Islamic revival gained momentum during the 1980s and as Suharto shifted his public support away from *kebatinan* and towards orthodox Islam in the 1990s. The most theologically sophisticated of the universalist mystical groups (indeed of all the mystical groups), Pangestu, curiously did not internationalize organizationally, although it was popular among the founder's[9] aristocratic friends who studied in Holland, and until recently maintained a large membership among upper echelon civil servants in

Indonesia. Sapta Dharma has remained a wholly domestic movement, but was rumoured to have the highest level connections with the Suharto regime.

The many other independent mystical groups or 'faiths' seem to have enjoyed little benefit from their registration as at least nominally confessional, congregational groups under the guidelines of the Department of Education and Culture during the New Order. Although under law an Indonesian citizen may profess a 'faith' instead of a 'religion', in practice people have been obliged to record one of the five unequivocally recognized religions on their identity cards. They are then under pressure to have the ceremonies of that religion for all their life cycle events, for taking oaths of office, and the like. This continually signals the marginal status of the 'faiths'. And as the economic development programs of the 1970s began to yield their benefits and the deregulation of the economy in the mid-1980s brought into the country more and more international influences, the *kebatinan* groups began to appear to the increasingly cosmopolitan middle and upper classes as not only suspiciously syncretic, and possibly occultist, but unappealingly parochial.

In sum, then, at the transition from the Sukarno period to Suharto's New Order, the normative standard for religion embodied in legislation and public administration of the modernizing state had come to embody the Enlightenment ideals of highly rationalized social forms and scripturalist religious expression. This normative standard struck a balance between the broad public affirmation of religiosity as a core feature of the national identity and the versions of modernization theory then current among secular elites, according to which religions were not really compatible with modernity and, in their 'traditional' forms, were suspected of being 'obstacles to progress' (cf. Soedjatmoko, 1965; Geertz, 1960a).

The New Muslim Middle Class and Changing Religious Markets: The impact of late-modern development and globalization

Remarkably, Suharto's New Order program of accelerated economic development eventually unsettled high modern notions of what religions ought to be among the growing numbers of urbanites whose cultural horizons rapidly broadened through cosmopolitan life experiences and exposure to increasingly globalized communication networks. Making 'development' (*pembangunan*) a primary goal of his government, Suharto put the economy in the hands of American-trained 'technocrats' and opened up the country to unprecedented levels of foreign investment and exchange. These development strategies stimulated rapid economic recovery and growth, and with that, an accelerating shift from rural to urban residence (Hill, 2000: 11-29; Hugo, 1997). Jobs proliferated in the increasingly sophisticated modern sector of the urban economy (Dick, 1985; Robison, 1996; Tanter and Young, 1990). Not only did more people experience employment and work places structured by instrumental rationality and rational-critical thinking, but work environments and middle-class residential neighbourhoods in major cities became more ethnically mixed (Robison, 1996). The growth of the major cities and upper-echelon white collar employment thus drew increasing numbers of people out of the largely ethnically homogenous rural regions and affected a version of cultural 'deterritorialization' such as Roy (2004) identifies as a major driver of religious change in Muslim minority communities in the West in the last 30 years and in the cosmopolitan sectors of other Muslim majority countries.

The culturally transformative residential and social mobility experienced by many Indonesians under the New Order was fuelled by the government's education policies. These enabled people from less privileged rural and urban backgrounds to obtain the kind of general education in the sciences and humanities that enabled them to take advantage of new job opportunities alongside the offspring of the old educated elite. Increased government support for education resulted in literacy rates for young adults rising from 40 per cent in 1970 to 90 per cent in 1990 and senior high school completions rising from 4 per cent in 1970 to 30 per cent in 1990 (Hefner, 2003: 4). By that time nearly all primary school-aged children were enrolled in school (Oey-Gardiner, 1997: 11; Hugo, 1997: 96) and participation in both secondary and tertiary education had expanded substantially. Tertiary course enrolments diversified from the late 1980s to respond to the expansion of the private sector of the economy over the government sector and to meet the rising demand for highly trained labour in both technical and managerial fields (Oey-Gardiner, 1997: 158-61; Robison, 1996).

Significantly, the expanding new middle class of white-collar workers in large businesses, bureaucracies and the professions included not just people who came through the secular government school system (generally people of less strict Muslim backgrounds), but also people coming through the Islamic school system. The New Order education extension programs included funding for Islamic religious schools (*pesantren*) to enable them to introduce subjects from the general school curriculum alongside classic Islamic studies. The government also provided increased funding for high schools associated with the *pesantren* and the tertiary education institutes (IAIN) attended primarily by *pesantren*-educated students. These educational opportunities for the first time enabled substantial numbers of 'strict' Muslims (*santri*), including those whose families had a strong scripturalist orientation, to find well-remunerated jobs in the modern service sector (Hefner, 2003; Jabali and Jamhari, 2002). Muslims in Indonesia's new middle class during the later New Order thus included not only people from less observant peasant and bureaucratic strata families (what Geertz [1960b] called *abangan* and *priyayi* families) but also people from *santri* backgrounds in the old merchant class and rural *pesantren*-oriented communities.

Increased access to secular education and the heightened pace of economic development in an international environment of post-industrial technological change thus stimulated the spread of cosmopolitan life-ways and attitudes among the expanded Indonesian middle and upper classes, particularly from the 1980s and 1990s. But this was also a time when many Indonesian Muslims, like Muslims elsewhere in the world, discovered a new interest in exploring their natal religion and deepening their personal piety. The Islamic *esprit* created by the Iranian Islamic Revolution of 1979 and other international events inspired many non- or loosely-observant Muslims to rediscover their faith. Descendents of the old bureaucratic stratum whose families had previously de-emphasized Muslim piety were in any case becoming better educated in their religion than their parents as a result of strict New Order requirements for students, even in secular schools, to have a least one hour of formal education in their religion each week at every level of education. The popular rehabilitation of visible Islamic piety (through, e.g., the use of Islamic greetings, women wearing the veil, and the inclusion of Friday religious observances in the regimes of major companies) was reinforced by President Suharto's own shift in public religiosity in the 1990s when he down-played his long known sympathies for *kebatinan* mysticism and began featuring in the press his performance of the *hajj* and his family's home tutoring in Qur'anic studies.

Middle-class and elite Muslims of the 1980s and 1990s were able to pursue their interests in deepening their faith through an unprecedented array of Islamic education resources. These included not only books, magazines, pamphlets and newspaper columns, but greatly increased television programming on Islam and, from the late 1990s, internet sites. As in the Arab world where rising rates of literacy and general education supported a proliferation in print and electronic media materials on Islam (Eickelman, 1992; Eickelman and Anderson, 1999), so also in Indonesia the new media gave voice to new types of religious authorities: not just *pesantren*-trained *ulama*, but university academics, journalists, self-taught preachers and so forth. These Muslim public intellectuals and mass-media preachers displayed a wide range of textual interpretations and religious styles (Hefner, 1997; Riddell, 2001: 287ff). So popular have some of the new media preachers become that they are veritable celebrities. In the 1990s, the 'million-follower preacher' (*dai sejuta umat*) Zainuddin MZ, for example, built a following through preaching at mass outdoor rallies and on television and then moved into party politics on behalf of the consolidated Muslim Party PPP. He has since launched his own political party drawing on that popularity and made a bid for the Presidency in 2004. Since the turn of the century, a younger cohort of TV preachers such as Abdullah Gymnastiar ('Aa Gym') and M. Arifin Ilham have drawn thousands of well-heeled urbanites to observances broadcast from the major mosques. Other top-rating TV personalities like Jefry Al Bukhori and Yusuf Mansur mix talk-show or soap-opera style entertainment with messages conveying Muslim values or provide more conventional didactic messages as edifying fillers between, or commentaries on, other television programming.

Other innovations by and for the new Muslim middle class – Islamic think tanks and commercial adult Islamic education institutes – offer structured religious education to Muslims accustomed to university-style courses and eager to see high standards of historical research and critical analysis applied to their religious studies. This type of institution was pioneered in Jakarta in 1986 by the Paramadina Foundation under the direction of prominent intellectual Nurcholish Madjid. While such modern-style educational foundations have differed in outlook, Paramadina under Nurcholish's leadership promoted a socially progressive approach to the reading of Islam's canonical texts. Through Paramadina publications, lectures and courses, Nurcholish and a group of like-minded Muslim intellectuals associated with the *pembaruan* ('renewal') or 'Neo-Modernist' movement showed how fuller understandings of the historical context of revelation could reveal universal ethical meanings beneath conventionally understood literal interpretations. This they hoped would free Muslims from culturally limited understandings of Islam that have tied Muslims to outmoded social forms. Their 'contextual' or 'substantial' methods thus formed the basis for a new wave of liberal readings on the compatibility of Islam with democracy, human rights, religious pluralism and scientific inquiry (cf. Barton, 1991, 1995; Hefner, 2000; Kull, 2005). From the 1990s, Nurcholish also gave increased attention to how modern Muslims can cultivate their personal spiritual lives, much along the lines advocated by Hamka, whose writings on *tasawwuf* he admired (Kull, 2005: 149-61).

Teaching in the short courses offered through the foundation's *Pusat Studi Islam Paramadina* (Paramadina Centre for the Study of Islam) modelled the approach advocated by Nurcholish and his colleagues. Not only did lecturers introduce students to their 'findings' on the meanings of texts, but they marshalled the hermeneutical and empirically grounded historical analyses through which these more rigorously contextualized interpretations were derived. Because different lecturers took somewhat different approaches and a discussion period was provided at the end of lectures, the courses stimulated students to form their own opinions in matters of religion, just as in other areas of their lives. Keen students continued their discussions after class and attended special lectures and the seminars with multiple speakers held by Paramadina at their own venue or at a major hotel.

Towards the end of the 1990s, a number of other modern-style adult education institutions had been established using the Paramadina model, that is, a formally constituted institute or foundation offering university-style short courses with a defined syllabus and lecturers drawn from the State Islamic Institute or another major university. Thus not only Paramadina but other institutes like Tazkiya Sejati, ICNIS (Intensive Course and Networking for Islamic Sciences), IIMaN (Indonesian Islamic Media Network), and the educational wings of some of the major mosques like At-Tin, Al-Azhar and Istiqlal, began meeting the demand for rational-critical approaches to religious knowledge and further stimulated it through their programming. The emphasis in such programs is on 'book learning', which in settings like the university-based student *tarbiyah* movement (cf. Damanik, 2002; Kraince, 2000) has promoted simplistic, literal readings of canonical sources and scripturalist styles of religiosity. Nevertheless the text-oriented scholarship examined in courses offered by institutes like Paramadina has tended rather to encourage personal autonomy in religious matters.

Certainly the emphasis on open exploration of the Islamic tradition in such institutes has varied from one program to another and even from one lecturer to another. But the availability in institutes like Paramadina, ICNIS and IIMaN of a variety of scholarly lecturers, each with their own approach, in a single institution and even in a single program, has encouraged many patrons to form a personal view where interpretations of Qur'anic texts or legal prescriptions differ. This type of religious learning environment also encourages students to pursue an independent line of questioning or search for more satisfying guidance. In other words, this kind of advanced 'book learning' need not, and in fact did not, wholly underwrite the Muslim scripturalist agenda. Nor did it unequivocally reinforce high modern conceptions of rationality according to which experiential religiosity and taking inspiration from other religions was seen as woolly headed indulgence in magic and heretical syncretism.

Far from dissociating themselves from Sufism, the new commercial adult Islamic education institutions like Paramadina, Tazkiya Sejati, ICNIS and IIMaN actually included *tasawwuf* studies in their course offerings. At Paramadina, *tasawwuf* courses were among the most popular offerings, even though students had to take prerequisite introductory courses in the fundamentals of Islam before they were eligible for that course. Many students repeated the *tasawwuf* course several times.[10]

By displaying the sophisticated theological and ethical scholarship of the Sufi tradition, the new commercial adult Islamic education institutions helped counter some of the negative stereotyping of Sufism as little more than the superstitious practices of country *syekh*. They also stimulated many 'alumni' to search further, beyond their *tasawwuf* courses, for ways to develop a personal practice with some kind of experiential or inner-depth dimension. The intellectual autonomy fostered by their university-style courses (as well as by the wider Indonesian religious market with its diverse array of Islamic products and providers) could as easily be exercised in seeking out Sufism as in looking for scripturalist learning. And with public interest in things 'Sufi' increasingly reinforced by exposure of the new Muslim middle class and elites to the global spiritual marketplace through cable TV, the internet, women's magazine features, visiting New Age gurus and imported growth movement programs, many highly committed 'modern' Muslims have sought out yet more opportunities to learn about the deeper 'spiritual'[11] dimensions of their own faith through various forms of Sufism.

New Urban Sufi Networks and the Late-modern Religiosity of Cosmopolitan Muslims

It might be supposed that contemporary Muslim sophisticates interested in 'Sufi' spirituality would avoid the *tarekat,* given the negative image that has burdened the Sufi orders in Muslim Modernist circles. Indeed, many Muslim Modernists and other scripturalists are 'still allergic' (as it is popularly put) to the *tarekat.* Yet news stories that have run since the mid-1980s and the small number of scholarly studies of particular Sufi orders that have well-educated, middle-class and elite participants (Howell, 2001; Syafi'i, 1996; Sila, 2000; Thoyibi, 1996) show that this is not universally the case.

My interviews conducted in Jakarta between 2001 and 2005 with patrons of *tasawwuf* courses at Paramadina and Tazkiya Sejati who have also moved on to explore other 'Sufi' activities help to explain this. These interviews, and observations of the organizations and activities that past short-course patrons have moved on to, show complementarities between the novel, commercial institutions through which formal studies in Sufism are available and the *tarekat.* The *tarekat* and commercial adult Islamic education institutions are part of a larger network of social resources being created to meet the new demand from cosmopolitan Muslims for ways to learn about and use Islamic devotional and mystical practices to cultivate a richer inner life, what we might call 'depth spirituality'. Significantly, in this, as it were, new urban Sufi network, 'traditional' institutions like the *tarekat* show distinctive adaptations to the modern urban environment; conversely, modern-style, highly specialized and narrowly contractually based formal organizations like the commercial adult education institutions also act as bases for recruitment to *pengajian* (religion study classes) and other traditional-style tutelary clienteles. At the same time, the modern, commercial Islamic education institutions act as platforms from which lecturers can launch careers as celebrity preachers, moving into television and other mass media. Moreover, students who have taken the university-style courses have developed an appreciation for their organizational templates and have thereafter launched their own 'spin-off' organizations and courses.

The shape of this new urban Sufi network can be glimpsed by looking more closely at the way the commercial adult Islamic education foundations cater for interest in Sufism. Paramadina Foundation, which pioneered the field of up-market short course provision to make its Neo-Modernist scholarship more widely available to the public, has offered studies in *tasawwuf* as part of a broader suite of courses on Islam. Students are required to do three other courses on the basics of the faith, conducted once a week over a period of several months, before undertaking the introduction to *tasawwuf.* Other occasional lectures and advanced courses on *tasawwuf* have been offered from time to time. The occasional lectures were originally held at the Foundation's headquarters in the up-market Jakarta neighbourhood of Pondok Indah. Then, after the unprecedented launch of Paramadina's *Klub*

Kajian Agama (Religion Study Club) in a five-star city hotel, lectures and discussions of *tasawwuf* were also held in that somewhat incongruous setting. Nonetheless, the combination of a social venue that urban sophisticates enjoyed patronising on a Friday evening and the format of several short lectures by guest speakers and Paramadina's figure-head, Nurcholish Madjid, followed by an extended discussion, proved popular, especially when the topic treated religion and politics or *tasawwuf*. Imitations of the hotel-based religion-study workshop flourished. The Foundation eventually established a university of its own, Universitas Paramadina,[12] which from time to time also offered weekend courses in *tasawwuf* to non-degree students.

IIMaN, sponsored by founders of the Islamic book publishers MIZAN, attempted to extend liberal, university-style Islamic education, including *tasawwuf* studies, to the public via the internet. After limited success on the web, IIMaN shifted the business to face-to-face courses offered from commercial premises. ICNIS was founded by lecturers from Jakarta's State Islamic University (most notably Nasaruddin Umar) who also lectured at Paramadina. ICNIS, too, made creative use of the internet but primarily operated courses out of rooms attached to the UIN mosque, offering basic courses on Islamic studies and *tasawwuf* studies. ICNIS also provided a forum for alumni of Paramadina interested in some of the international growth movement and New Age ideas beginning to circulate in the late 1990s (like Parent Effectiveness Training, Quantum Learning, Emotional Intelligence and Spiritual IQ, Reiki and the *Celestine Prophecy*) to explore their relevance to Islamic life and spirituality.[13] Some programming on growth movement and New Age topics was later introduced into the Paramadina occasional lecture series.[14]

Tazkiya Sejati Foundation, in contrast, was founded specifically to introduce *tasawwuf* to urban sophisticates through the short-course format. Its courses were offered on a commercial basis, but with generous subsidies from the Foundation's founder and patron, Sri Adyanti Rachmadi ('Ibu Yanti'), daughter of former Vice President Sudharmono and wife of Indonesia's McDonald's franchise millionaire. Ibu Yanti, a former Paramadina student, was inspired to establish the organization after enjoying lectures by Jalaluddin Rakhmat on *tasawwuf* at Paramadina and seeing the benefit his lectures on *tasawwuf* gave to her private women's study circle.

While all of these organizations have provided at least some introductory studies of *tasawwuf*, and Tazkiya Sejati actually devoted the bulk of its curriculum to it, the short-course providers have not attempted to offer the full range of supports for spiritual development that the Sufi orders have provided. In the *tarekat*, teaching is conducted through long-term, diffuse relationships between the *syekh* or one of his deputies and the students. While these spiritual directors may supervise group study of Sufi texts in their roles as *pesantren* teachers, as masters of the *tarekat* based at those *pesantren* they give initiates personal guidance in their efforts to follow individualized spiritual regimens aimed at ethical refinement and mystical experience. This generally consists of assigning particular regimes of *dzikir* recitation and supererogatory prayers, counselling initiates on their experiences with these practices, and offering general guidance in life conduct with a special emphasis on the shaping of character that will support heightened spiritual awareness through the exercise of repentance (*tobat*), piety (*warak*), patience (*sabar*), trust in God (*tawakal*) and other virtues.

The *tarekat* also offer opportunities for collective enjoyment of the emotional richness of the extended recitations of God's name (*dzikir*) and chanted prayers for the Prophet and his family (*shalawat*, Ar. *salawat*). These are attractive to many initiates, regardless of their dedication to a difficult path of mystical realization. The collective rituals also form the occasion for socializing and forming intimate friendships among fellow initiates, which have personal and spiritual value in their own right for participants, as shown by Chih (Chapter 2) for new urban migrants who use the *rawdas* established by the Khalwatiyya Dumiyya orders in Upper Egypt and by Werbner (Chapter 11) for the orders patronized by South Asian migrants in the United Kingdom.

In contrast, the modern, commercial adult education institutions, which are based on time-limited, contractual relationships, cannot offer open-ended, highly personalized spiritual direction or much in the way of devotional satisfaction and social enjoyment of collective ritual. This raises an issue for students of these institutions who wish to go beyond theory to practice. Where can they go for help?

Most Muslims learn some ways of performing *dzikir*. Short *dzikir* recitations are commonly appended to the obligatory prayers (*sholat*, Ar. *salat*) in 'traditionalist' (loosely speaking, Nadhlatul Ulama-oriented) circles. It is just the longer forms of *dzikir* (that through their repetitive structure may facilitate mystical ecstasies) for which the special guidance of a Sufi *syekh* is sought and which form the distinctive ritual elaboration of Sufi-style devotions. Theoretically, then, anyone can do *dzikir* meditation alone simply by multiplying the repetitions of commonly used phrases from the Qur'an. Also, the ethical values in which initiates are schooled are familiar topics of sermons, pamphlets and popular books. However, it is commonly held that the benefits of *dzikir* recitation are amplified in a setting of communal worship. Conventional wisdom also holds that those intent on a path of serious spiritual development need initiation and ongoing guidance from a *syekh*, in both their meditational practice and personal comportment, which should support that practice and through which its fruits will be expressed. The commercial adult Islamic education institutions, whose brief does not include such services, nonetheless have offered students some pathways to devotional practice and even the means of connecting with providers of conventional Sufi tutelage.

While Paramadina and the other commercial short-course providers have kept strictly to the academic lecture format, Tazkiya Sejati, consistent with its more thoroughgoing focus on *tasawwuf,* actually began and ended its classes with brief sung prayers that set a devotional and reflective tone. Tazkiya also published a book of Sufi prayers, *Mafatihul Jinan* (*Keys to Heaven*), compiled by its principal lecturer, Jalaluddin Rakhmat. Tazkiya students were encouraged to use such prayers in support of their personal practice of purifying the heart.

Both Paramadina and Tazkiya Sejati, however, linked their students in various ways to actual *tarekat* where they could, if interested, receive a broader range of supports for a Sufi practice. Paramadina did this in the 1990s by occasionally organizing bus trips to Pesantren Suryalaya in rural West Java, which is the centre of the Tarekat Qadiriyya wa-Naqshbandiyya (TQN) headed by KH Sahibul Wafa Tajul 'Arifin (or Abah Anom). One of Paramadina's regular lecturers, Asep Usman Ismail, who also lectures at Jakarta's State Islamic University and whose father was a preacher for TQN Suryalaya in the Pelabuhan Ratu region, organized the first visits so students doing the basic *tasawwuf* course could see first hand the life of one of the more open and progressive *tarekat.* Formerly, Paramadina also arranged weekend retreats in pleasant surroundings outside Jakarta with authorized spiritual directors from TQN Suryalaya, but these were discontinued to avoid suggestion of promoting a *tarekat.* Tazkiya Sejati, on the other hand, positively encouraged the students in its courses to join a *tarekat* to benefit from the support and spiritual direction the *tarekat* can offer. Its members became affiliated with several *tarekat,* including the Qadiriyya wa-Naqshbandiyya, Rida'iyya, Shattariyya and Tijaniyya.

Regardless of whether or not the commercial short-course providers actually arranged exposure to the *tarekat,* students could connect with the tarekat through those lecturers who were themselves authorized *tarekat* spiritual directors (*wakil talqin*). Some of these, like Asep Usman Ismail, are career academics (mostly at the State Islamic University). Others, like Zainal Abidin, head of a *pesantren* in Sukabumi, are *ulama* who teach the classical Islamic sciences to rural school children but have the intellectual stature and social flexibility to mix well with urban sophisticates and adapt to the university lecture format.

Short-course lecturers who represent a *tarekat* can also connect students with a local city branch of their *tarekat.* In the city branches of *tarekat* like TQN Suryalaya, it becomes readily apparent that the purportedly extreme hierarchical relationships and otherworldliness of the archetypal rural *tarekat* do not hold. The spiritual directors who live in the cities and make a living from the urban economy interact with their initiates on much the same terms that they would with anyone else. And branch meetings held locally in the homes of friends or at a neighbourhood mosque enable city initiates to carry on with their regular jobs and family life. Moreover, the *tarekat* have adopted formal organization structures to handle the administrative work associated with organizing branch meetings and contributions to the central activities of the organization. This gives considerable scope for people other than spiritual leaders to exercise a degree of influence. Meetings of these organizing committees use the same democratic forms of association that would be practiced in any voluntary organization. Ordinary members also assert their own preferences over the conduct of the regular prayer meetings by attending the branch meetings where their preferred prayer leader or preacher will be present, regardless of the distance. While this has generated tensions, little social pressure can be exerted to restrain the exercise of choice in such circumstances.

By no means all short-course lecturers, however, are exponents of *tarekat* or are even sympathetic with them. In any case, there are other ways in which lecturers at the commercial adult Islamic education institutes can facilitate either further text-based study of *tasawwuf* or opportunities to try out some kind of Sufi devotions or discipline. One way is through conventional informal tutelary relationships formed on a personal interest basis. Thus students of a popular lecturer wishing to keep studying with that teacher on a private basis will attend one of his ongoing informal *pengajian* classes or charitably sponsor that lecturer to give classes on a regular basis. The emphases in these informal and smaller charitable *pengajian* vary considerably, but include text-based *tasawwuf* studies (as e.g., the lessons from Jalaluddin Rakhmat that Ibu Yanti sponsored for her women's circle, and the private classes taught by Asep Usman Ismail with the support of one of his former students). They also include healing clinics (such as offered by Islamic law lecturer Zen al Hadi), personal counselling and charismatic assistance (e.g., that offered by Paramadina lecturer Agus Abubakar) and even practicums in the use of *dzikir* and *wirid*[15] to build the inner strength necessary to face personal trials or physical threats (such as formerly offered by Nasaruddin Umar at the State Islamic University mosque).

Lecturing at the commercial adult Islamic education institutes also gives teaching staff, many of whom are drawn from the universities, the opportunity to develop a somewhat more popular style and make contacts that become the basis for a second career as a public speaker and preacher. Major corporations hire popular lecturers through Paramadina, as well as directly at their universities, to give talks at executive development workshops that may draw on, for example, Sufi modes of ethical reflection. Corporations also commission popular lecturers who have a Sufi practice to conduct *dzikir* prayers and give a sermon in conjunction with the Friday services at their office blocks. Such lecturers may also offer commercial workshops on Islamic spirituality that introduce Sufi practices, or guide *hajj* and *umroh* (holy land tours outside the *hajj* season) tours that give them opportunities to colour their commentaries with Sufi insights. These latter activities, as well as television and radio teaching engagements, have become the basis of full-time careers for some short-course lecturers like Wafiudin, who comes from a business and IT background rather than from a university position and who acts as a spiritual director for the Tarekat Naqshbandi Haqqani.

The creativity that cosmopolitan Muslim intellectuals have exhibited in taking sophisticated Islamic studies, including *tasawwuf,* out of the *pesantrens* and universities and into the public arena has been matched by the initiative of many former short-course students in pursuing their religious interests after exhausting the courses. Not only have they followed their lecturers into private *pengajian,* workshops, *tarekats* and religious tour programs, but some have set up their own groups on the Paramadina format. These 'spin-off' groups, like the parent organization, bring in academics and other religious authorities to lecture to groups too far away from the main short-course providers in Jakarta to comfortably travel there on a regular basis. However their programs are not exact copies. A Bogor group modelled on Paramadina by past students, for example, follows Paramadina in offering a broad curriculum of Islamic studies but also teaches use of the Tazkiya Sejati prayers and organizes expeditions to attend a broad range of 'spiritual' activities like Sufi music events. The founder, Ibu Deti, has also written her own prayers, with which she opens the group's programs and other social gatherings.

Past students interested through their Paramadina, Tazkiya Sejati and other short-course studies in *tasawwuf* have also moved off on their own to explore the possibilities for spiritual and personal enrichment offered by the international growth movement and New Age organizations unconnected to Islam. Some of the most popular are Parent Effectiveness Training, Asia Work, Reiki, and the Brahma Kumari's Raja Yoga. Lectures, discussions and workshops held at Paramadina and ICNIS on such programs have helped introduced them to Muslims. Some Muslims are prepared to see their techniques for personal and spiritual development as essentially 'Sufi', in the sense that they may enhance self-reflection and purification or deepen meditative awareness. Articles in women's magazines also psychologize spiritual practices like Reiki and Raja Yoga, presenting them as methods of stress reduction that have health benefits and can be used as aids to confidence and concentration in business and study. In that way any competing religious representations of the spiritual forces energizing those techniques can be set aside and the practices adopted without perceived offence to an Islamic faith. The religiosity of such cosmopolitan Muslims can thus be eclectic (in the sense of drawing on practices other than those in prescribed orthodox Islamic ritual) without being syncretic.

Conclusions

The enthusiasm that numbers of well-educated Indonesian Muslims have shown in recent years for Sufism, once beyond the outer limits of Modernist Muslim conceptions of orthodoxy, reveals a little noticed current of change in understandings of what it is to be a good Muslim and what constitutes 'modern' Islam for those Indonesians highly committed to their faith. Whereas the rationalist agenda of earlier generations of Muslim Modernists in Indonesia required expunging Sufi devotional and ecstatic traditions from the faith and basing it solely on scripturalist practice, the Neo-Modernist and other new-wave adult education institutions responding to the needs of the expanding Muslim middle classes have actually provided courses in Islam's Sufi heritage. Moreover, the new adult Islamic education institutions have in various ways, directly and indirectly, helped their students locate other institutions that support them to further develop personal Sufi practices of ethical reflection, ritual devotion and meditation (*dzikir*).

These other institutions include the traditional Sufi orders whose headquarters had been for the most part removed from urban areas in the late colonial period and which came to be associated in Modernist circles with retrograde village religiosity. The *tarekat* and commercial adult Islamic education institutions founded since the 1980s offer services that are in some respects complementary with the newer university-style education institutions. The university-style short courses are attractive to urbanites who appreciate rational-critical and historical approaches to religious studies. Cosmopolitan Muslims appreciate them for their relatively non-hierarchical and casual commercial setting. Nonetheless some still value the *tarekat* for the opportunities they provide for long-term spiritual guidance and for regular group devotional and meditation practice.

Past students of the commercial adult Islamic educations institutes also use contacts made in those places to pursue their interests in Sufism elsewhere in a variety of other settings. These include personal tutelary relationships with lecturers who specialize in *tasawwuf* or have a Sufi practice; the lecturers' informal religion study groups (*pengajian*); formally constituted study clubs and institutes set up by alumni of the original short-course institutes; workshops and pilgrimage tours run by Sufi-oriented celebrity lecturers and preachers; and an array of growth movement and New Age activities whose 'spirituality' is selectively assimilated to Sufism.

These institutions together constitute nodes in what might be called new urban Sufi networks. Some of the most significant connectors in these networks are the lecturers from the university-style adult Islamic education institutes and their students. Both have exhibited considerable initiative in adapting religious education and guidance to the emerging markets created by the 'greening' and expansion of the Indonesian middle class. Students, in particular, have exercised qualities of critical judgment and autonomy in seeking out forms of Sufism (both traditional and avant-garde) that have had negative associations in the past but which they reinterpret as compatible with Islamic orthodoxy and rework to meet their needs.

Interestingly, the international growth movement and New Age spiritual fringe have proven highly attractive to many Muslim cosmopolitans over the last two decades, but only when their techniques and concepts have been religiously de-contextualized and psychologized or medicalized. They have then been read as 'spirituality' (*spiritualitas*) and, via 'Sufism', assimilated to Islam. In the growth movement and New Age the attractive world of international products and ideas meets the world of natal religious identity and pride in one's own tradition. This has happened even while the independent mystical (*kebatinan*) groups have waned in popularity. The *kebatinan* groups also teach depth spiritualities and personal development regimes, but they retain distinct, generally parochial identities, their own revelations and pre-packaged doctrines that set them apart as quasi-denominations at a time when identification with Islam as a global religion and authentic Islamic piety have become far more important to Indonesian Muslims. Those *kebatinan* groups that have remained modestly vigorous down-play religious imagery that would otherwise advertise their recent syntheses of world and local religious traditions. Nonetheless, while more Muslim urbanites are now prepared to include Sufism within the borders of authentic Islam, *kebatinan,* marooned within the 'faith' groups under the administration of the Department of Education and Culture, has been effectively excluded.

In taking up academic studies of Sufism at the new-style adult education institutes and then finding ways to practice it, Indonesia's cosmopolitan, largely Modernist-oriented Muslims are not only endorsing the restoration of Sufism to Islamic orthodoxy, but subtly recasting normative standards for proper religion in the modern Indonesian state. Earlier generations of Modernist Muslims and other scripturalists had settled for political compromises over definitions of religion (*agama*) under the constitution, whereby religions would be understood as scripturalist, 'rational', congregational and exclusive. In contrast, later generations, which have enjoyed the rapid economic development of Suharto's New Order and have been drawn into intensely globalized processes of twenty-first century modernization, are acting out different conceptions of religious modernity. Still making use of highly rationalized forms of organization for religious purposes (like formally constituted foundations, business firms and the like), many of Indonesia's religiously committed cosmopolitan Muslims have nonetheless rejected the dry scripturalism favoured by older Modernists in favour of some kind of experiential spirituality identified with Sufism.

Intellectual rationality, as well as institutional rationalization, however, still play a part in cosmopolitan Sufi religiosity. The skills of critical thinking learned through years of general education and applied to Islam in their short courses have whet the appetites of numerous adult-course students for choice, both in sources of religious commentary and forms of religious expression. Rational-critical skills acquired through the university-style programs also assist in the exercise of autonomy in the religious sphere, giving people confidence to go on, after completing the courses, to find for themselves the means to spiritual satisfaction in a still under-developed and partially restricted religious market. In exercising choice and creating their own ways to meet newly perceived spiritual needs, the new Sufis have inverted the negative valence attached to experiential religiosity in high modern constructions of religion. Also, by being prepared to make use of spiritual and psychological insights and techniques from other traditions and assimilate these to Islam's traditions of depth spirituality, the negative associations once attached to eclecticism in religion are now being partially erased.

There are strong resemblances here to patterns of religiosity in the non-Muslim world, and not simply, I would suggest, because so much religious product is now being imported (like so much else) from the West. Rather, the processes of modernization and globalization all over the world stimulate similar processes of systems differentiation and institutional rationalization, albeit contained within the frames of different historical legacies (cf. Eisenstadt, 2002). Moreover, the Christian and Islamic worlds, colonists and colonized, one-time first world and third world, globalized producers and consumers, all have been and continue to be linked in mutually shaping dialogues about what the processes of social change do imply and should mean for our religious lives. That post-Enlightenment Protestants, post-Vatican II Catholics and Modernist Muslim 'puritans' should all find their dearest conceptions of modern religion supplanted by a later generation of spiritual seekers, more aware of the limitations of science and eager to experience religion not simply through the intellect but through the whole person (cf. Lambert, 1999; Voye, 1999), should come as no surprise.

Acknowledgments

The research upon which this paper is based was funded by the Australian Research Council under its ARC Discovery program and by grants from Griffith University. This support, and the help of the many Indonesian colleagues and friends who offered their time and insights, are warmly appreciated, as are the helpful editorial comments of Martin van Bruinessen.

13

GOD BY ALL MEANS ... ECLECTIC FAITH AND SUFI RESURGENCE AMONG THE MOROCCAN BOURGEOISIE

Patrick Haenni and *Raphaël Voix*

> Life is a mystery to be lived; it is not a problem to be solved.
> Driss Benzouine[1]

With the suicide bombings of 16 May 2003 in Casablanca, Moroccans' belief that their country was an exception among violence-ridden Muslim societies died. In spite of the institution of the king as 'the Commander of the believers'[2] and the assumption that the religious field is controlled by the state, Moroccan society has been subjected to the same forces of Islamization that have already affected its neighbours. The Islamist movement has gained strength on the political scene, waves of revived piety have spread through society, semi-clandestine groups have gained control over marginalized suburbs and, although contested, the tide of *hijab* rises even among the urban bourgeoisie. This is a time of identity struggles, be it where modes of radical contestation or of peaceful predication are concerned.

Nonetheless, recently Moroccans have found other more discreet ways of embracing Islamization, ways where hybridity and cultural extraversion are accepted. Among these is the re-composition of religious belief in New Age terms.[3] Since the 1990s, this cultural move has become a popular mode of re-Islamization among the Muslim bourgeoisie. Whether in Jakarta, Tehran, Cairo or Casablanca, a new way of situating oneself vis-à-vis what is sacred is emerging wherein the interest of the individual has replaced espousal of great causes such as Pan-Arabism or Islamism.[4] This chapter aims to explore the specific logic of these dynamics within circles of the Moroccan bourgeoisie.[5]

The Formation of a New Age Movement in Morocco

Moroccans were introduced, indirectly, to the possibility of new kinds of relationship between body and spirit in the context of 1960s 'flower power'. From that time, imported psycho-spiritual movements began to develop among the expatriate community in Morocco. Courses in hatha-yoga, (a somato-psychic practice stemming from various Indian religious traditions) and gatherings for *zazen* meditation (a silent sitting practice stemming from a Japanese Buddhist tradition) were taught in private '*dojo*' (Japanese-style meditation or training halls). Martial arts centres also appeared during this period. Typically, trainers would come from Europe to give courses, weekend workshops and conferences. These movements would later open up the Moroccan bourgeoisie to the global spiritual marketplace (cf. Howell, 2005).

In the 1960s and 1970s, yoga and zen were purely imported products, but in the 1980s they began to take root among Moroccans. In 1989, Driss Benzouine, a former *beatnik* with a passion for mystical India and a follower of Osho,[6] became the president of the Moroccan Yoga Association. He brought about profound changes in two directions. He opened the Association to a wide range of therapeutic, esoteric and mystical practices (personal development, metamorphic massages, rebuilding and so forth) by bringing trainers on a regular basis from Europe to Morocco. Through these activities, the idea of the pluralism of esoteric mystical teachings spread among Moroccan practitioners. Benzouine also organized the first training of local teachers in Morocco, producing the first generation of locally trained Moroccan teachers. In 2005 there were approximately 15 people teaching yoga in public, in places like health spas, dance halls, lycées and universities.

The evolution of zen in Morocco is similar to that of yoga. In 1977, French doctor Claude Durix,[7] a prolific writer and disciple of Taisen Deshimaru, founded the Zen Association of Morocco to spread the teachings of his master.[8] In 1981, Deshimaru himself initiated the first six Moroccans in the course of a retreat that brought together more than 200 people in the suburbs of Marrakech.[9] When Durix died in the late 1980s, his young Moroccan disciple, Driss Badidi, became head of the Zen Association of Morocco. However, Driss Badidi subsequently broke off with the International Zen Association and spread his own teachings.[10] He had two explicit objectives: to distance himself from Buddhist traditions, and to identify convergences between zen and the mystical traditions of Islam. He recalls that about 50 Moroccans received spiritual direction from him.

In the course of the 1990s, his spiritual techniques became progressively more local in character. These techniques took root not only within expatriate circles but also among the Moroccan bourgeoisie which was then undergoing profound changes in political and religious orientation.

A Cosmopolitan Middle Class

Largely secularized, assimilated to French culture, and open onto the world through business networks and travel, the Moroccan bourgeoisie is becoming more and more outward-oriented. This orientation begins with education in French-style schools (the *lycée*), which is in many cases followed with higher studies at a foreign university. This has given rise to cosmopolitan networks of friends, not only during study in France but also upon return in Morocco, where these elites are now to be found mingling in French or other foreign expatriate circles. Correspondingly, their knowledge of Arabic remains underdeveloped and is often limited to the Moroccan dialect, which they use as the language of communication outside their Parisian networks. Consequently, their relationship with the sacred is often lived out in diglossia, as in the case of Miriam who recites the Qur'an 'in French in order to understand it and in Arabic in order to live it'.

Moreover, as is the case for all of Morocco, the transnational networks of the Diaspora constitute an essential bridge connecting these bourgeois circles with the world outside. But religion is often problematic for them. As a result of what is often a minimal or otherwise impoverished traditional religious education, they soon develop a relationship with the sacred that is distant or even outspokenly hostile. They are highly critical of the religiosity of their parents, which they consider as 'ritualistic', associated with the 'Islam of the jinn',[11] and unattractive because it is too 'mechanical' and, in a nutshell, 'too superstitious'.

By comparison with other Muslim communities in the Arab world, these Moroccan circles are particularly striking in that they present themselves in public as highly secularized, but they have been experiencing, for at least the past half decade or so, a real process of Islamization. They tend to avoid visible signs of their religious identity, frequently serve wine at meals, and may even profess atheism or refuse to identify themselves as Muslims. The Islamization may take, in a few cases, the form of a political conversion (from the nationalist left to Islamism), but it is more typically of a moral nature (as evident, e.g., in the increasing adoption of chic *hijab*, or attraction to the discourse of the popular Egyptian preacher Amr Khaled), or has a primarily spiritual inspiration (as seen, e.g., in the increased popularity of Sufi brotherhoods and various forms of individualistic Sufism).

Understanding the latter trend of re-Islamization of the Moroccan bourgeoisie requires appreciation of the unprecedented developments that preceded it in Morocco. Cosmopolitan Moroccans have been Islamized only feebly, and their imaginary has been built up at the crossroads of a double-stranded history. They have lived to the rhythm of the turpitudes of the Arab world (the defeat of 1967, Camp David, civil war, and then the Israeli invasion of Lebanon). They also have had to absorb the impact of great events in contemporary Western history: May 1968, the Vietnam War, and the sexual revolution. In the 1970s and 1980s, Moroccan university campuses were mostly dominated by the leftist currents, whether socialist, Marxist, or Trotskyist. Many members of the Moroccan bourgeoisie have passed through a period of commitment to the radical left and experienced a succession of cycles of hope and disillusionment similar to that of the European left. For some in Morocco, it was political Islam that took over and presented itself as the next hope on the horizon.[12] Within the Moroccan bourgeoisie, however, the loss of the ideals of the nationalist left has only rarely led to a conversion to the cause of political Islam. We submit the hypothesis that this is because disillusionment with politics took place in parallel with a recomposition of religiosity around the New Age orientations, which neutralized the attraction of political Islam while at the same time restoring a certain fascination with new forms of privatized Islam. In this new context 'the invention of the self' (cf. Kaufmann, 2003) was based on movements of re-traditionalization paradoxically propitious for modes of ultra-modern religious subjectivities.[13]

Varieties of New Age Experience in a Muslim Context

For many of those who gave up their flirtation with radical left politics, what became the new ideals to strive for were self-realization, internal equilibrium and spiritual peace. The individual was at the very heart of all these concerns. This was evident in the authors' research in Morocco between 2001 and 2003. Many of the people with whom we spoke had followed life paths rich with experimentation in several spiritual practices (yoga and zen), martial arts (aikido and karate) or psycho-spiritual techniques (meditation, personal development, etc). They had discovered these practices either in the West during their studies, or in Morocco through expatriate or local community networks. In their self-reports it is evident that each person had constructed an imaginary informed by borrowings from each of his or her domains of experience.

Hanae, a kinotherapist in Casablanca, provides an example. She recalled it was through a yoga course that she learned 'one does not have just a physical body, but different bodies surrounding each other'. She considers this perspective compatible with her Muslim beliefs. Others, while affirming that they are Muslims, nonetheless believe in reincarnation even though that belief does not conform with (mainstream) Muslim dogma.[14] Raja, for example, believes that in a previous life she was Indian, arguing that her first name also exists in Sanskrit where it means 'royalty'. Another common departure from Muslim orthodoxy is a very explicit monistic vision of the world, which proclaims the primacy of the individual and relativism. 'If you believe in the tremendous capacity of the human being to find oneself within oneself, and thereby finding one's Creator', declares Hanae, 'it is not important if a person is a Buddhist, a Christian, an atheist or a Jew'.[15] For Youssif, a 28 year old businessman, Islam is also but a means; the ultimate aim is God. 'If you are a Buddhist', he said, 'you are right; for those who are secular or atheists, that is their way. As for me, as a Muslim, I am also right'.[16]

For Youssif, the demarcation lines separating the sacred and the profane have become blurred. Something similar is happening with Miriam. She puts yoga, dancing and Islamic prayer on the same level:

> The well-being I feel during meditation I also manage to feel when I dance. That is the only moment when I truly feel the connection of body and spirit. I go into a trance, I feel myself to be in a superior world. This may be thanks to the Qur'an when I praise God, or to the use of my prayer beads when I do *dhikr*, reciting the names of God.

The building of modalities of belief in such groups resembles the reconstruction of ways of believing in the West analyzed by Babès (1996), Champion (1990) and Hervieu-Léger (2001). In them, a mental universe is structured around four axes: individualism, religious relativism, hybridity and loss of religious plausibility. Individualism is apparent in the strong affirmation of the centrality and autonomy of the individual leading to a monistic vision of the sacred, in defiance of any religious authority. Religious relativism is apparent in the conviction that different spiritual trajectories are equally true and equally effective – as a result of which, the engagement with them often remains exploratory and unfinished. Hybridity shows itself in the non-polemic and eclectic mobilization of multiple referents. The loss of religious plausibility may be due to either the very ignorance of the religious tradition, or to the reflexive objectification of the tradition.

Re-appropriation of the Sacred through Sufism

The aforementioned styles of Moroccan bourgeois religiosity reconstitute the sacred outside the confines of local culture, by avoiding conventionally institutionalized forms of religion. Instead, beliefs close to those of New Age are developed and acculturation is the order of the day. However, as a result of Arab nationalism and Islamism, other Muslims are obsessed with the boundaries of their faith and draw the line wherever mystical or esoteric notions are raised. The dilution of the religious by these New Age followers clashes with the desire of followers of the Salafi trend to impose their own views everywhere. In answer to westernized middle-class Muslim cultural extraversion, all groups engaged in forms of re-Islamization evince a fixation on identity. This conflict, we argue, is what generates the strong impulse that is now evident to reformulate foreign spiritual influences by indexing them to Islam and by searching for local Islamic equivalents to attractive non-Islamic religious practices. This is the context in which the Moroccan bourgeoisie has embraced Sufism along with eclecticism.

For the past few years, Sufism has been attracting followers of the New Age within the Moroccan bourgeoisie, and particularly those who previously were not inclined to submit themselves to a religious tradition. Yet such an evolution, lived and presented in terms of identity reconciliation, does not constitute a return to their 'roots' for these people, for three reasons. First, looking at the dynamics of conversion, we see that the Moroccan bourgeoisie no longer have any 'roots'. Their families are secular, they are educated in French institutions, and they have had minimal religious education. For such people, interest in Sufism must be the result of an attraction to a *modern* discourse about Sufism, not the remnant of traditional practices. Second, we shall see that conversion to Sufism, at least for some of the new followers, does not modify the modalities of believing that they held before. Finally, the Moroccan bourgeoisie is re-structuring itself around two tendencies, one close to contemporary individualism and relativism and claiming the right to multiple spiritual commitments, and the other affirming the absolute superiority of Sufism compared to other possible paths. This polarization is also one of the features of religious modernity.

To Liberate Oneself from the Islam of the Jinn: the Moroccan bourgeoisie and the Budshishiyya

The Budshishiyya, a new branch of the Qadiriyya brotherhood, was founded in 1942 by Abu Madyan ibn Munawwar al-Budshish among the Berber tribe of Beni Snassen.[17] The new interest in Sufism has been a boon to this branch, which began as a rural and localized brotherhood in the province of Oujda, and from the 1960s has been expanding from this rural base. At the beginning confined to the western part of Morocco, it spread all over the kingdom and gained large numbers of adherents. At present, observers estimate the number of followers at several tens of thousands (Anonymous, 2001). In the process of spreading, the brotherhood left behind its rural nature and its early rural following, consolidating instead around members of the urban bourgeoisie, especially liberal professionals and students. According to the hagiographers, this phenomenon of expansion was linked to the reforms in the order that took their shape in the course of the 1960s. Initially a *tabarrukiyya* brotherhood, i.e. one focused on the acquisition of blessing and confined to a religious elite whose activities revolved around prayer and meditation, the Budshishiyya evolved into an actively proselytizing *tarbawiyya* brotherhood, i.e. a mass movement concentrating on the moral education of its recruits (Tozy, 1990). The recruitment policy of the brotherhood was transformed: whereas initially individuals had to present solid proof of their zeal to qualify for initiation, later the order began to proselytize actively among wider groups considered as potential disciples from the outset.

In the 1960s the brotherhood also began connecting with the French-speaking elite. The first instance was when the well-known socialist intellectual, `Abd al-Salam al-Wali, visited the mother *zawiya* of the brotherhood in Madagh and engaged in debates with Sidi Abu l-`Abbas, the father of the present leader of the brotherhood, Sidi Hamza. `Abd al-Salam apparently intended to counter the growing influence of Sidi Abu l-`Abbas, but he failed in this objective and instead came himself under the influence of the shaykh. Along with a number of his political associates, `Abd al-Salam joined the ranks of the Budshishiyya. The reorientation of the order bore fruit, and in the 1970s the Budshishiyya began attracting students of secondary schools and the humanities faculties on a massive scale (Tozy, 1990). One person who played a key role in this recruitment was the shaykh Yassine, who is now better known as the spiritual authority of the Islamist movement Al-`Adl wa-l-Ihsan, but who was then a teacher and a member of the brotherhood.[18]

Intellectuals of the brotherhood, such as Zakia Zouanet, Taha Abdel-Rehim and Ahmed Tawfiq (the former director of the National Library of Casablanca and presently the Minister of Religious Affairs) favoured the penetration of the French-speaking, westernized elites. An especially important role in this urban middle-class 'aggiornamento' of the brotherhood was played by Faouzi Skali, who is perhaps the most prominent intellectual convert. Faouzi Skali is a Moroccan lecturer trained in anthropology in Paris, who came to the Budshishiyya through reading the French 'Traditionalist' author and Sufi, René Guénon.[19] He soon elaborated a reformulation of the Sufi heritage in the modern language of contemporary spiritualities, emphasizing the importance of inner experience, humanism and dialogue (as against obedience and discipline). Faouzi Skali is also the founder and director of the Fez festival of the Sacred Music of the World. In 2001, he was designated by the United Nations as one among the 12 world personalities who had contributed to the dialogue of civilizations. Today, continuing along that same path, and working together with Lama Denis, a French Buddhist, and with Khaled Bentounes, the head of the `Alawiyya Sufi brotherhood, he is taking part in the project of restoring the 'house of wisdom' (*bayt al-hikma*) of Baghdad, which in the eighth century was the centre of exchange between Greek and Islamic civilization and is now to become an inter-religious centre devoted to culture and education in tolerance (Tincq, 2004).

From the middle of the 1980s, Skali became quite well known in France through a number of popular books on Sufism published at large-circulation publishing houses, and he brought many French people into the brotherhood (Voix, 2004). A decade later, part of cosmopolitan Morocco followed in the tracks of these French converts and turned to Sufism by a very similar process. Using the model of propagation of modern spiritual movements in the West, which he knew well, Faouzi Skali organized 'Sufi weekends' in Morocco on the pattern with which he had experimented in France (Voix, 2004). Here he presented a new vision of Sufism and a taste of the Sufi experience without commitment, in a form attractive and reassuring to the Moroccan bourgeoisie. Intellectuals thus drawn into these modern Sufi circles around Skali provide the brotherhood with a presence in the modern media landscape, publishing such journals as al-Ishara (the Sign), a glossy magazine with articles on Sufism and other forms of spirituality, and developing websites such as www.sufism.org, www.tariqa.org, and www.isthme.org. In

Europe, the magazine *Soufisme d'Orient et d'Occident* is also linked to Faouzi Skali and the Budshishiyya.

Among the factors contributing to the detachment of the Budshishiyya from its rural roots and its gentrification, attention should also be given to the key role played by the shaykh of the brotherhood, Sidi Hamza, in this process. After the death of his father in 1971, he began preaching a more orthodox mysticism, down-playing the profoundly ecstatic Sufism of his father's provincial culture of the Moroccan hinterland. Sidi Hamza's brand of Sufism placed greater stress on respect for the shari`a and gradually adopted a critical attitude towards *dhikr* ceremonies accompanied by music and self-flagellation. He is also responsible for 'de-localizing' the Sufism of his father's order: the *mawlid* of Madagh celebrates the birth of the Prophet and not that of a locally important saint; visits to tombs of saints are not encouraged, and the shaykh no longer functions as a political patron at the local level. Moreover, Sidi Hamza encourages recruitment of followers from the ranks of the elite, even though he himself does not come from an elite background. He also supports recruitment in the universities and often appoints deputy spiritual directors (*muqaddam*) from among university professors.[20] And he has given his blessing to the summer Sufi 'universities' organized by the brotherhood in Oujda near the mother *zawiya* of Madagh. More than 2000 participants attended the summer 'university' in 2003. Such activities have contributed to the intellectualization of the brotherhood.

Finally, the expansion of the Budshishiyya in Moroccan bourgeois circles was facilitated by its surprising adaptability and its easy accommodation with quasi-corporatist patterns of organization. Existing socio-professional allegiances have played a key role in the organization of Budshishiyya prayer groups. Thus, in Casablanca, the Budshishiyya has groups organized around a '*zawiya* of medical doctors' and a '*zawiya* of university professors'. In this way, the Sufi resurgence has taken on the social morphology of the wider urban society and confirms its hierarchies. Class-based habits also reproduce themselves in the spiritual setting. French is spoken in such Sufi circles; two out of the nine Budshishiyya *zawiya* of the city of Casablanca are French speaking.[21] All in all, according to the estimates of Ahmed Qustas, during the annual *mawlid*s of Madagh, close to half the brotherhood now come from educated Moroccan circles (Sedgwick, 2004a).

At least in the first stage of conversion to Sufism via Budshishiyya, what seduced the Moroccan bourgeoisie was the discourse of Skali rather than the image of the master to whom he owed allegiance. The trajectory covered by Driss Benzouine perfectly illustrates this dynamic. As mentioned above, in 1990 he met Sidi Hamza, the then master of the Budshishiyya brotherhood, in the mother *zawiya* in the north of Morocco. He returned both bothered and frustrated from what he considered to have been too expeditious a meeting. At that time, he felt no attraction whatsoever for the man who, a few years later, would become his master. However, in 1994 he attended a lecture of

Faouzi Skali that much impressed him and of which he said, 'It was enlightening; enlightening because he spoke a language one could understand … No religiosity, a pure spirituality. Rather than speaking of God, the talk was of the Being, he spoke of a progression towards knowledge of oneself and that moved me greatly'. Driss Benzouine took initiation into the brotherhood immediately thereafter. Clearly it was not the figure of the old shaykh that attracted him to Sufism but the modern discourse of Faouzi Skali, whose interpretations of Sufism made sense to him.

Another person from this educated middle-class environment who followed a similar trajectory is Khadija. She had lost her 'intimate connection with God' since the end of her childhood. While studying in France, she discovered yoga and became 'fascinated with India'. She became engrossed in Ayurveda and practiced Transcendental Meditation. After her return to Morocco, she discovered Skali's book *The Sufi Path* (Skali, 1985) and through him became involved in the Budshishiyya.

As a general observation, it appears that the new presence of a 'modern' and 'universal' Sufi discourse that was not embodied in traditional Sufi personalities but in culturally contemporary intermediaries allowed many members of the Moroccan bourgeoisie to 'reconcile themselves' with Islam. Thus Rachid Ben Rochd relates how his interest in Sufism was first awakened through contacts with his zen teacher, a French doctor living in Morocco. As he tells it:

> At that time, I approached Islam from a Western point of view. I considered it a violent and austere religion. He [the zen teacher] corrected my stereotypes. When I said to him that Islam was the religion of the *jihad*, he spoke to me of the *jihad al-nafs* [the struggle against one's desires and for inner growth]. When I spoke to him of violence and austerity, he said to me that Islam was also spirituality and goodness.

As for his formal allegiance to a Sufi order, it was a French convert who inducted him into the Darqawiyya. This represented a break with the tradition of his family – his father had been a disciple of the Tijaniyya.

Those young middle-class Moroccans turning to Sufism who, like Ben Rochd, belong to a family with prior Sufi connections, stay only rarely within the same Sufi networks as their parents. Rather, the appeal of Sufism increases along with modern socializing (in cultural centres and yoga classes, at public lectures, and at work) and global connections. A case we heard about during our field study is of the young Moroccan woman who came to the Budshishiyya in Chicago through the agency of a female Brazilian convert, who herself had been converted and induced into the brotherhood in Brazil by a Frenchman. In accordance with the dictates of cosmopolitanism, it has often been foreigners, converts to Islam or teachers of different oriental spiritual disciplines, who have shown the way to these new followers of

Budshishiyya. For Tahir Wazani, one of the active members of Budshishiyya in Casablanca, his move toward Sufism began through a meeting with a French Orientalist in the library of the French Cultural Centre. The Orientalist spoke to him of the beauty of the writings of the great Sufi Master, Ibn `Arabi.

The Budshishiyya has been able to establish itself among groups who recognized themselves in this imaginary of spirituality and the well-being associated with it, and it has succeeded in recapturing some of these groups' members. This accounts for the presence of several Sufi personalities around the association GERME (*Groupe d'Études et de Recherches sur le Mieux-Être* [Group for Study and Research into Better-being]), which proclaims an interest in spiritual growth and 'harmonious development of the human being'. The most recent congress of this association ended with a roundtable on the theme of 'Better-being in the Twenty-first Century', devoted mainly to various forms of alternative medicine. At that conference, Faouzi Skali spoke on the theme of 'Sufism as a path for personal accomplishment'.

In the same spirit, the wife of Tahir Wazani, herself a recent convert to Budshishiyya, launched the magazine *Bien-être et Santé* (Well-being and Health), devoted to the well-being of body and spirit. Her husband fills a section of the magazine titled 'Well-being and Spirituality', which is devoted to a presentation of Sufism from a therapeutic perspective.

Eclecticism, Relativism and Sufism: Crossroads of mystical traditions

Thus modified, Sufism manages to progressively re-inscribe 'the floating religious' orientation of aficionados of Oriental spiritualities into an Islamic religious tradition. Yet even though the centrality of the Islamic reference is re-affirmed, the new 'Sufism' continues to broadly accommodate contemporary notions of individualism, eclecticism and relativism. A kind of New Age pole opens up within the Sufism of the Moroccan middle classes, in which mystical sensitivities and modern individualism mingle.

Many question all forms of religious authority. Karima, a high-ranking professional working in a bank, considers herself to be 'anti-rules': 'I do not like to have anything imposed upon me', she says. Miriam, a young graphics expert working for an American firm, considers that:

> The essential thing is humane behaviour. All the rest, things that are forbidden, are between God and us. One is not to judge people for what they do or do not do ... I prefer someone who gets drunk yet whose behaviour is extraordinarily humane, [someone with] a kind heart and lots of love; [I prefer that] to someone who spends time flaunting religious practices but whose heart is black.

As for Najiyya, her questioning of religious authority is expressed in terms of individualism:

> My father was well versed in religion. As an adolescent, I had virulent discussions with him and I revolted against religion. Psychologically, I could not accept the status of women in Islam. In my mind I wondered why God sends us prophets and why we would not be able to find that light within ourselves.

The traditional relationship between master and disciple is questioned first. Thus Najiyya, even though a member of the Budshishiyya, never felt the need to go and see her shaykh, Sidi Hamza: 'I do not give much importance to the master, nor do I often think of him', she said. 'On the other hand, I think much of the Prophet because I touched him with my own hands in a vision, and I felt his infinite love. It's a concrete and not an abstract knowledge and I now feel much more connected to the Prophet'. Others find the traditional tutelary relationship 'exasperating', or they whisper their doubts as to whether Sidi Hamza is indeed a true master. Such confidences reveal much about the paradox of traditional, strongly hierarchical movements transmogrifying into movements based on contemporary individualism in response to a need for spirituality compatible with egalitarian ideals. New converts are frequently reluctant to sacrifice their autonomy on the altar of a newly found faith by entering into a master–disciple relationship, which they consider to be fundamentally unequal.

As a result of the more detached relationships with the shaykh and a more casual, modern attitude towards religious allegiance, many of these bourgeois Sufi disciples participate in several *tariqa* simultaneously. Thus, Ben Rochd, who considers himself to be 'beyond the paths and the gates', does not seek a form of belonging in the brotherhood environment but rather 'an atmosphere': 'Sufism is within me', he says. 'That is where I found my heart'. It is a heart anchored in both the Darqawiyya and the Budshishiyya, and also in the Tijaniyya. And Driss Benzouine, already a *muqaddam* of the Budshishiyya brotherhood, did not hesitate to travel to Cyprus to be initiated by Shaykh Nazim, the master of a transnational branch of the Naqshbandiyya order. He considered this order to be closer to his yoga sensitivities.

The new Moroccan Sufism is characterized by membership of multiple brotherhoods and the generalization of Sufism without allegiance. In such Sufism, *dhikr* is practiced individually and no longer in a single brotherhood. Even though this might displease the Sufi purists, as a form of 'believing without belonging' (Grace Davie), it affirms itself to be Muslim. Thus, little by little, Sufism asserts itself outside the framework of brotherhoods, or tends to partially dissociate itself from them. At the extreme end, it openly separates itself from the religious, as in the case of a young teacher close to the Ghaziyya brotherhood who considers that 'Sufism is not a matter of religion. It is not even a belief. When you believe, it is a form of attachment. If you do not manage to detach yourself, you will never achieve liberation'.

In today's Morocco, the practices that stem from Muslim mystical traditions are not spared ongoing transformations; they tend to attach themselves to the repertories of people's contemporary predilections for syncretistic combinations, which vary from one individual to the other. Najiyya now practices her *dhikr* in a semi-lotus position that she learned from yoga, her back straight, her eyes half closed and prayer beads in her hand. Latifa uses yoga as a preparatory exercise for the *dhikr*. Khadija couples the *dhikr* to the recitation of Hindu mantras taken from Transcendental Meditation. This is more than a simple pairing of practices or postures; syncretism is present in the profound lived experience of those practices – for example in the *hal*, those states of ecstasy that belong to Sufism. The same is true of the uncontrolled appearance of ecstatic *hal* during yoga sessions where *enstasis* rather than ecstasy is sought. Syncretism is evident as well in meditation courses now held in the desert. These are expressions of de-localized New Age spirituality, where people exclaim 'Allah' during a dynamic Osho style meditation and rework their cultural differences.

It is finally at the level of language that syncretisms are played out. Concepts born of the New Age gradually impose themselves as new ways of reading traditional Sufi concepts. The *sirr*, the spiritual 'secret', is described in terms of 'energy', of 'spiritual flows'. Allah becomes 'Being'. Religiosity is reinterpreted in terms of 'a way forward towards knowledge of oneself'. Najiyya considers that Satan becomes 'the total ill-being' in contradistinction to angels who are considered to be 'total well-being'. This background of syncretistic correspondences then allows Driss Badidi to find in zen, 'a means of rendering his Arab–Muslim identity more profound'. A new commitment thus constitutes itself within a 'de-localized' mystical Sufism, wherein religion is seen to reconstitute itself outside the local religious culture by borrowing its categories from an imported lexical field,[22] while at the same time presenting itself as a return to origins. This is the stance to be found in all the works of Rachid Ben Rochd (1997, 1999, 2000).

It is on the fertile soil of these cross-references of mystic traditions and allusions to multiple references that relativism develops. Najiyya considers that 'yoga and Sufism are one and the same thing'. For her, 'they completely identify with one another'. For Hanae, 'meditation or *dhikr* are always a means for one to re-centre on oneself'. Yet the relativism that approves of cultural hybridities and eclectic mixtures on the basis of the proclaimed equivalence of references is but one of the possible responses where the New Age meets the Sufi tradition. It is by no means the only reaction. Faced with syncretistic tendencies, the temptation of dissociation is strong. Postulating the intrinsic incompatibility of references, some of the new recruits to Sufism abandon hybridity in favour of a more exclusive commitment to Islam. Admiration for the words of the intellectuals of the brotherhood gives way to a cult of Sidi Hamza; the approach to Islam becomes more orthodox; religiosity becomes structured around the moral norms and interdictions of the *shari`a*. Some women practitioners drawn into these circles end up wearing the veil.

In Addition to Doubt ... the Loss of Plausibility and the Illusion of a Return to the Roots

Although it may be true that dissociation and return to orthodoxy constitutes a re-traditionalization, it takes place in a context marked by the loss of plausibility. The whole process of re-investing what is religious testifies to this. In it we see voluntarism, personal choice, turning away from the heritage of the parents, the modernity of intermediaries and the quest for new discourses (such as the academic discourse of Faouzi Skali, the humanist discourse of Driss Benzouine, or the universalist discourses to which all the leaders of the bourgeois spiritual renewal of Casablanca subscribe).

An example is provided by *Le yoga maghrébin*, a booklet by Ben Rochd devoted to proving that 'Maghribi traditions' contain the basic principles of yoga. Ben Rochd may critique 'the breaking off with tradition' provoked by modernism, and consider that 'it is in the traditions that we can find our sources of creation of energy and wisdom' – as the subtitle of the published volume claims (Ben Rochd, 1997). Yet his attempt to advocate 'a return to the soil in order to find the roots and the sources of energy that are intimately linked to it' (Ben Rochd, 1997: 19) is expressed in modern phraseology and, in addition, in French. The 'traditional culture' towards which the author wishes to return will, he hopes, 're-construct and develop the human person by awakening his awareness of the body and of his latent potentialities' (Ben Rochd, 1997: 3). He situates himself at the very heart of that 'ideology of intimacy' that belongs to a religious modernity based on 'an ideology of personal development, intellectual awareness and self realization' (Étienne, 2002: 54). When one goes back to 'the country of our sources', one always heads for a return to mostly re-invented traditions (as the '*yoga maghrébin*', for instance). Obviously, the rites remain specific; but commitment to Sufism is mostly lived according to universal spiritual models. This helps account for the similarities that people discover between the different roads towards personal realization. These roads, or paths, are related more to a common way of living today than to the content of the traditions on which they draw. Thus, universalism arises from the loss of cultural plausibility. One lives Sufism, just like the other forms of spirituality, in terms of personal development, combating stress, emotional experience, and setting one's heart at peace, i.e. through a discourse of modern individualism.

The Re-centring of Islam and the New Pluralism

The Sufi renewal among the Moroccan bourgeoisie cannot be summed up as a process of Islamization of a New Age movement that had originally emerged outside the sphere of religion and that mechanically leaves its imprint and style on Sufism. Not only did several more 'orthodox' conversions take place without prior passage through the New Age, but the converts coming from zen or from yoga also sometimes added to their New Age concepts a mystical and more traditional imaginary – going back to devotion to the master, respect for the traditions of a brotherhood, and practice of the order's specific form of *dhikr*.

Within the groups that we have studied in Morocco, the logics of everyday life, including competition, develop. The leaders of the New Age movement, in order to spare their followers impossible dilemmas and choices, stress a clear distinction between religion and spirituality wherein spirituality is reconstructed outside the frame of religion and people's culture of origin. Driss Badidi urges his followers 'to empty zen from its Buddhist shell' and keep from it only a posture and a style of breathing. He refuses to place statues of Buddha in his *dojo* (temple). He also refuses all kinds of iconography with Japanese references. Where the rites are concerned, he has replaced the *keza*, the initiation ceremony for new members that has too markedly Buddhist traits, with a simple ceremony of handing out a diploma. As for apparel, he has replaced the kimono with a simple shirt and training suit, symbolizing both the zen ethic of frugality and the will to redefine his teachings outside the frame of its 'Buddhist shell'.

But such assertions of the applicability of spiritual techniques across cultural boundaries do not prevent the establishment of a sort of Sufi dogmatism within the Budshishiyya. Various types of arguments are advanced to affirm the exclusiveness of Sufism – culturalist arguments, like 'you have to choose your path as close as possible to your culture', purist arguments, like 'Sufism cannot abide being mixed with other references',[23] or essentialist arguments, like 'Sufism, intrinsically superior, is an exclusive commitment or rather the logical final step of other spiritual roads'[24] These arguments are effective, for many in Morocco have come to believe that Asian spiritualities and Sufism are incompatible and that the latter is to be preferred to the former. The number of conversions increases, sometimes taking a collective form as with the '*zawiya* of medical doctors', which is composed almost entirely of former yogis who moved to Sufism thanks to the Budshishiyya.

Among such belated Sufi exclusivists, some continue to think of their old commitments in terms of a journey of spiritual progress but do not consider it acceptable to accumulate all that they found on the way. Khadija is one such case. After having practiced yoga very regularly for ten years, she has given it up for good. She attributed the appearance of unexplained physical pains to the incompatibility of the two spiritual practices of yoga and Sufism and gave up the former, substituting it with aqua-gymnastics. Raja resolved the dilemma of possible incompatibilities by alternating from one set of practices to the other. This former high-ranking bank official and senior yoga instructor was unable to accept giving up yoga after her conversion to Sufism, and established a form of 'pendulum spirituality', alternating between certain periods devoted to Sufism and others devoted to yoga.

Others, however, refuse to validate any spiritual paths outside the frame of Islam. Thus, for instance, Dr Rahim, who is in charge of the '*zawiya* of medical doctors'. Although he practiced yoga for several years and had been an avid reader of the hagiographies of Hindu mystics, he completely renounced on yoga, concluding, in a rather peremptory manner, that 'it is not by contracting one's sphincter that one becomes more at peace'.

If the centrality of Islam is once again confirmed by certain of the Moroccan bourgeoisie, paradoxically, zen and yoga, through the discourses, disqualifications and rivalries to which they are subjected, are recognized as being a valued part of a new religious pluralism. This pluralism runs against the identity politics in which Moroccan Islam has become embroiled. Thus, within the Moroccan bourgeoisie, the undeniable 'revenge of God', as Gilles Kepel has called it, has been achieved at the cost of restructuring the religious and at the cost of its realignment with the new religious reality that has established itself in Europe in the 1970s and 1980s: the opposition of groups with a fundamentalist tendency to other groups in connivance with contemporary relativism and individualism (Champion, 1993).

The Tensions of Modernity: Individual and dogma

As against those who search for the modernization of Islam in theological reform, we hope to have shown in this chapter that this modernization is in full swing – only, one has to look for it elsewhere. It is in the new modalities of Muslim faith, rather than in the reflections of those who speak in the name of the Muslims. In Morocco, spiritual renewal began initially outside the sphere of Islam. It was later re-appropriated by a refurbished Sufism that had detached itself from its rural roots and was universalistic. It became possible to live out Sufism in a New Age mode, heterodox and syncretistic. As a reaction to this, a more orthodox pole constituted itself, which enjoined the return to the religious dogma and demanded exclusive allegiances. The present polarization in syncretistic and purist tendencies that can be observed among the Moroccan middle class drawn into the Budshishiyya is hardly a new phenomenon in religious movements and appears to be part and parcel of religious modernity.

However, there is an important difference with the situation in Western Europe, where in the 1970s a new esoteric-mystical religiosity emerged, which broke off completely with the existing religious institutions. Françoise Champion, who studied this phenomenon, has remarked that what was really unprecedented in this situation was the fact that the de-institutionalization did not bring a restoration of the institutions in its wake (Champion, 1990). We believe that we have shown the situation in Morocco is in this respect different from the experience in 1970s Western Europe and that the new esoteric–mystical religiosity has been re-institutionalized through Sufism. Religious modernity thus may give rise to a dynamic of re-localization, re-institutionalization and the resurrection of religious dogma. Can we qualify this as a regression? Perhaps, but even so it is a modern process in that it takes place in a context that is structured by contemporary individualism.

Acknowledgement
Patrick Haenni and Raphaël Voix thank the French Research Institute (Centre d'études et de documentation économique juridique et sociale, CEDEJ) in Cairo for a grant to have their chapter translated from the original French.

14

THE DEVELOPMENT OF A MODERN WESTERN SUFISM

Celia A. Genn

Introduction

The recent enthusiasm for Jalaluddin Rumi's poetry in North America and Europe has brought Sufism to the attention of many Westerners in a liberal and liberating way that contrasts sharply with post-9/11 stereotypes of the Islamic tradition from which it derives. That Sufism should stimulate receptivity to Islam is not a new phenomenon. Sufism's encounter with the modern West over the last century continues a process in which it has historically been one of the main carriers of Islam into new cultures. Since Sufi masters teach that one may experience God directly, and not just through the Qur'an and sunna, their movements generate familiar tensions among Muslims who are concerned that orthodoxy not be eroded by heterodox innovations (*bid`a*). The encounter of Sufism with the West also creates new tensions as this ancient tradition grapples with twentieth and twenty-first century processes of modernization in religious and other organizations as well as changes in patterns of personal religiosity.

This chapter is about one of the earliest and most prominent Sufi movements in the West, the International Sufi Movement, which has recruited primarily Western participants. The Indian Sufi Master, Hazrat Inayat Khan (1882-1927), established this Sufi order in North America and Europe between 1910 and 1926. It was brought to Australia soon after, and over the twentieth century became established on virtually every continent. By teaching in English and not requiring prior conversion to Islam, Inayat Khan was the first to make Sufism widely accessible to Westerners. For over 50 years this was virtually the only Sufi order in the West and the only group readily available to Westerners.[1]

From the 1960s, the Sufi landscape in the West became more variegated and extensive, both in migrant communities and among Westerners. Changes to the Immigration and Nationality Act in the United States in 1965 allowed for a new wave of Muslim immigrants and spiritual teachers of Eastern religious traditions, including Sufism. Similarly, in Australia, most Sufi groups had their start with the rapid growth in Muslim immigrants after changes to Australian immigration policy in the late 1960s (Saeed, 2003: 1-12).

Sufism has never been a homogeneous tradition. In the contemporary West, the multitude of orders and the diversity of both ethnic composition and approaches mirror the diversity of Sufism across its many homelands in Asia and the Middle East. The many expressions of Sufism in the West also show how the conditions of modernity affect processes of indigenization. In migrant and non-migrant communities in the West, Sufism is taught through both traditional Muslim orders such as the Bektashiyya and Ni`matullahis (Webb, 1995: 251; Hermansen, 1998: 158) and non-traditional institutions. The latter include groups blending traditional and universalistic elements such as the Naqshbandi Haqqani order (Hermansen, 1998: 157) and the Bawa Muhaiyaddeen Fellowship (Webb, 1994) and groups with a universalist focus such as Inayat Khan's Sufi Movement (the Inayati order).[2] The term 'universalist' is used here in the sense of 'available' or 'belonging' to all people, not just those of a particular ethnic or religious background.

The diversity of organizational forms that Sufism is taking in the West has been analyzed in a growing popular and academic literature. Rawlinson attempts to construct a model for comparative religion focussing on experiential aspects and categorizing the Sufi and other 'Eastern' religious groups in the West as 'hot' or 'cool' and 'structured' or 'unstructured' (1997: 20-4, 97-110). In her studies of Sufi and other groups in Muslim North America, Hermansen uses a garden metaphor to build a typology in which the various combinations of traditional Sufi practice and Islamic identification shaped by the American context are called 'hybrid' or 'perennial' (1998, 2000). Foregrounding changes in the West, Werbner provides an ethnographically rich analysis of the range of Sufi groups and practices among immigrant communities in Great Britain and their links to South Asian centres (1996, 1998; and Chapter 11 of this volume), while Frishkopf notes consequences for the Burhaniyya order's social organization and presentation in its expansion from Egypt to Europe and North America (2001). All of these studies make it clear that Sufism in the West includes both strictly *shari`a*-oriented and more latitudinarian groups. A variety of perennialist, Muslim puritan, and eclectic approaches can be found. 'New Age' influences can also be found in some groups such as the Dances for Universal Peace (Sufi Dancing).[3]

Viewing Western Sufi groups as New Religious Movements (NRMs) can aid understanding of how Sufi traditions change in response to modernity and the need to indigenize in the Western environment. Recent literature on NRMs has called attention to several factors shaping the development of NRMs of non-Western origin in the contemporary West. These factors include the history of the particular imported tradition (King, 1989; Finney, 1991; Baumann, 2001), the social dynamics of home and host environments (Howell and Nelson, 1997, 2000; Howell, 1998), and the intention behind the cultural translation (Genn, 2004). As NRMs in the West, most Asian-origin religious traditions are engaged in processes of adaptation, not only from more 'traditional' social and religious contexts to those of 'modernity', but also from 'Eastern' to 'Western' contexts (Genn, 2004: 272-3). They also differ from other religious movements in the West in that generally they are spiritually, culturally and structurally unfamiliar to most Westerners.

The distinctive social dynamics of Hindu and Buddhist traditions in modern Western countries have been analyzed in this way and offer suggestive comparisons for the study of Sufism in the West. For example, a study of a Hindu-derived NRM in the West found that differences in the processes of organization-environment interaction in the Indian and Western contexts contributed to both cultural and social structural innovations in the West (Howell and Nelson, 1997). Studies of Buddhist traditions in the West show that Western participants tend to focus on particular aspects of the tradition, and that they are making changes with regard to matters including women's roles and democratic principles, concerns that are taking on relevance incipiently in Buddhist migrant circles (Fields, 1992; Prebish and Tanaka, 1998; Baumann, 2001). The non-migrant participants in these Asian-origin groups, like participants in Western Sufi groups (including the Inayati order), do not reflect the general population but are drawn predominately from well educated, middle and upper-middle class members of Western society (Barker, 1994: 128; Hermansen, 1998: 156; Genn, 2004: 176). This chapter treats Inayat Khan's Sufi movement as an NRM to assist in identifying important factors in its development, as well as to reflect on the social and cultural processes distinctive of the Asian imported religious traditions more broadly in the modern social context and on the adaptation experiences common to other Sufi groups in the West.

In this chapter I show that the distinctive, universalist form of Sufism articulated by the Inayati Sufi movement needs to be explained in terms of all three factors identified in studies of the adaptation of Asian-derived NRMs to the West. Thus, I show the importance of the movement's historical background, specifically the Indian heritage of its founder Hazrat Inayat Khan, as well as the founder's intention – to formulate a new vision of Sufism in the modern social environment of the West. I argue that for Inayat Khan's Sufi movement, its particular Indian cultural roots are especially important. This is because Islam and Sufism developed somewhat differently in India, Hazrat Inayat Khan's home country, than in other parts of the Islamic world.

In India, the Sufi tradition is pervasive in Islamic discourse and institutions (Metcalf and Metcalf, 2002: 8) and the Chishtiyya Sufi order to which Inayat Khan belonged reflects an historically pluralistic religious environment that allowed religious traditions to evolve with less distinct boundaries than are commonly drawn between Islam and other religious traditions elsewhere. Two key characteristics of the Chishti order are not often found in orders outside India and facilitated transition to the West. These are its emphasis on music (*sama'*) for spiritual training and attainment, and its willingness to accept students (*mureed*s)[4] from non-Muslim backgrounds without first demanding conversion to Islam (Harris et al., 1992: 124-5; Waseem in De Tassy, 1997: 174). Inayat Khan's own pluralistic religious background and his contact with the intellectual and social world of the Western powers in late nineteenth-century colonial India each contributed to his creative spiritual mission and to his success in bringing a universalized Sufism to the West. They help explain the evolution of his intention in creating a distinctive variant of Sufism, and the loose constraints on the form of Sufism that developed under his and his successors' guidance.

Among the social dynamics important to the development of culturally novel transplanted NRMs has been the adoption of modern forms of formal organization. The new interest in 'transnational' religions (e.g. Rudolph and Piscatori, 1997; Ebaugh and Chafetz, 2002) is suggestive of this, but as yet this factor has been given insufficient attention.[5] In this chapter, I show how the new formal and transnational organizational form adopted by the Inayati order helps explain the history of the ruptures that have occurred within the group. As an NRM in the West, the order has to not only resolve cultural tensions but to do so within a new organizational context. While traditional pre-modern Sufi orders were often transnational, this was only in the sense that informal links between masters and their initiates stretched across state boundaries. These links did not impose tight constraints on practice and in any case, with pre-modern communications technologies there were no means of monitoring local practices closely. The Inayati order, however, adopted a variety of elements from Western culture, including a formal organization and the new communications technologies that appeared over the twentieth century, to coordinate its worldwide activities and groups. Adopting this formal, transnational organizational pattern, unprecedented in Indian Sufi orders, has both potentiated and constrained the group's development.

Explaining the shape and development of the Inayati order in these ways brings a number of key processes of adaptation into focus. One is that of reworking the beliefs, practices and informal institutions of a long established tradition in novel ways. In this case, Inayat Khan specifically adapted traditional Indian Sufism to the new social and cultural environment and to his inclusive and mystical vision for religion in the 'modern' world. He employed a mix of pragmatism (such as introducing a formal organization and decreasing the number of spiritual exercises given to students) and idealism (including making Sufism available to all, whether Muslim or non-Muslim). He nonetheless retained those concepts of spiritual hierarchy and authority that he saw as intrinsic to the Sufi path, despite their unpopularity in the West.

In this chapter I look first at the role of the cultural heritage and intentions of Inayat Khan in the development and adaptation of the order in the West. I then outline the development of the organizational structure of the Sufi Movement in Europe and North America and the tensions evident in that evolution. I then turn to the Australian experience and consider the role of the cultural heritage, the founder's specific vision, the formal organization, and modern communications in the three main phases of the evolution of Inayati Sufism there. Sources of data, where not otherwise indicated, are from fieldwork I conducted with the International Sufi Movement between 1996 and 2005.

Cultural Heritage and Intention in a Transnational NRM

Vitally important to the development of Inayat Khan's Sufi Movement in the West was the nature of the particular Sufi cultural heritage that Inayat Khan sought to transplant. As was common in the late nineteenth century, Inayat Khan was initiated into the four major Indian Sufi orders,[6] but was trained by his *murshid*, Khwaja Mohammed Abu Hashim Madani, primarily within the Nizami branch of the Chishti order. This Indian Sufi order was characteristically inclusive and tolerant of religious pluralism, and included music (*sama'*) along with prayer and *zikar* (*dhikr* or the remembrance of God), as a key spiritual practice. Like other orders, it also upheld the central role of the spiritual teacher (*pir* or *murshid*), the disciple's relationship of trust and obedience with his or her teacher, and the sense of *pir-bhai* or the brotherhood/community of disciples of a particular teacher.

The Chishtiyya order was founded in India by Hazrat Khwaja Mu'inuddin Chishti who left his home in what is now Afghanistan for India in the twelfth century CE. Entering this pluralistic environment, Khwaja Mu'inuddin emphasized a message of universal love and peace. He chose the way of 'no compulsion in religion' (Qur'an 2: 256) drawing to Islam many Indians who were inspired by him. Along with others, Mu'inuddin Chishti was instrumental in creating in India a rich composite culture, blending Islamic and indigenous cultures, and reflected in art, music, religion and philosophy. Seven centuries later, in 1910, his spiritual descendant, Sufi Inayat Khan, left his home in India to bring Sufism to the West.

While Inayat Khan was a Muslim, the object of his mission to the West was not formal conversion to Islam. He took instead a non-proselytizing approach, which he described as providing 'personal guidance on the path, in the problems of both outer life and inner life' without requiring belief in 'any special creed or dogma' (1963: 270-1). Formal conversion to Islam, observance of ritual obligations and traditional dress, and so forth, were neither required nor forbidden by Inayat Khan, though *Islam*, in the sense of surrender to the Divine, was central in his teachings.[7] By redefining the relationship between Sufism and the exoteric tradition and practice of Islam, Inayat Khan's Sufi Movement drew on its Chishti heritage to resolve the tension between the universal, experiential and theological dimensions of Sufism and the ritual and legal particularisms of Islam. This represents a particular type of adaptation, as not all Western Sufi groups have done this.

The practice of complete gender equality was another unusual aspect of Inayat Khan's Sufi Movement. While women's situation in India and Islam is equivocal, the gender equality of this Sufi movement was a significant change from the general lack of encouragement for women mystics in the East (Rizvi, 1978: 403) and was also well in advance of such equality in the West. As early as in 1914, Inayat Khan wrote, 'I can see as clear as daylight that the time has come when women will lead humanity on to a higher evolution' (cited in Van Voorst van Beest and Guillaume-Schamhart, 1979: 243). From the beginning of his work in the West, he actively promoted women within the order.

Key aspects of Inayat Khan's Sufi message such as the 'unity of religious ideals' were conveyed through creating new rituals within the order, such as the Universal Worship service. In this service, respect for the unity and diversity of the world's religions is shown by lighting candles for each major tradition and reading from the scripture of each. Nevertheless, Inayat Khan held that spiritual development and full realization of the meaning of the unity of religious ideals also required the inner purification and transformation of individuals. For this he retained traditional institutions such as the *murshid–mureed* relationship and many of the traditional Chishti spiritual practices.

Inayat Khan made ongoing efforts to get to know the West, and as his knowledge and mission evolved, he continued to adapt his presentation. For example, while his early lectures contain much Islamic terminology, he soon employed examples and metaphors from science, Christianity and everyday Western life to convey his message. To address people's desire to live meaningfully despite growing disenchantment with religious authorities (Inayat Khan, 1979: 243), he distinguished mysticism from any form of religious dogma, explaining that, 'People mostly think that the spiritual message must be something concrete and definite in the way of doctrines and principles; but that … does not belong to the divine nature, which is unlimited and is life itself' (1963: 16). At times Inayat Khan described Sufism simply as 'the religion of the heart, the religion in which one thing is most important, and that is to seek God in the heart of mankind' (1973: 38). This approach was, he believed, part of a new spiritual awakening in the world (Inayat Khan, 1967: 153).

These early developments made Sufi training, tradition, philosophy and practices available to everybody, not just Muslims. They presented Sufism in a way that could readily be practised within a modern and increasingly secular society. Inayat Khan's lack of dogma and use of music were appealing in the

West, although the organizational and spiritual hierarchy and *murshid–mureed* relationship were understood less well and received a mixed response. Inayat Khan did not replicate traditional Indian Sufism but drew on strands within the Chishtiyya order in this first stage of developing a new and Western form of Sufism. For Inayat Khan, the changes were not a compromise with the West but rather an integral part of his vision for religion in the modern world (Genn, 2004).

Institutionalizing a Sufi Order in a Formal Organization
At first, as Inayat Khan travelled and taught in North America, Russia, Europe and the United Kingdom, he simply initiated interested people and gave them instruction and practices. As numbers grew, however, he realized that the traditional way of working could not succeed in the West (Inayat Khan in Van Voorst van Beest and Guillaume-Schamhart, 1979: 235) and that administration and development of his order required an organization. Thus, in 1923 he incorporated the International Sufi Movement in Geneva in the form that continues today. Use of a formal, incorporated organization for his work introduced an organizational pattern unprecedented in Indian Sufi orders. It was, for Inayat Khan, a practical rather than an ideological innovation, with significant consequences for the development of the order.

The administrative structure of the organization he established consists of an International Executive Committee and International and National Councils for five subsidiary Activities, each of which is represented on the Executive Committee. The central Activity is the Esoteric School or Sufi Order within which initiation, the *murshid–mureed* relationship and spiritual training take place. The Sister and Brotherhood, Spiritual Healing, and Spiritual Symbology Activities respectively reflect, though they also expand, restructure and formalize the ethos of service, healing capacities and vocations, and use of symbolism traditionally found within the Chishtiyya order. The Universal Worship Activity was developed to allow followers of all religions to come together, and is a significant innovation and departure from traditional Sufism. The organization as a whole, and each of the Activities within it, is structured hierarchically with overall authority in the Representative General who is also the Pir-o-Murshid. No real distinction is made between spiritual and organizational hierarchy, with places on the various councils dependent upon a *mureed's* level of initiation or recognition within a particular Activity.

For a spiritual tradition that has been carried previously by traditional, informal organization and informal networks, incorporation as a formal organization has a range of implications. For Westerners, a formal organization carries expectations of values and procedures common to other modern voluntary organizations, such as everyone being eligible for office and member initiative. Such expectations, however, clash with the values of classical Sufi (and other) tutelary institutions. This clash is not just with a non-

Western and pre-modern ethos of religious respect but also with the distinctive relationship between a student and a master in an esoteric, mystical tradition. Like some other Eastern traditions that have become NRMs in the West, the Inayati Sufi order retains the central master-disciple relationship, which traditionally has been at the heart of the teaching, learning and organization of a Sufi order (Valiuddin, 1980: 47). In the modern West, this personal relationship of spiritual guidance and allegiance is an unfamiliar religious structure that cuts across the usual expectations for participation in a voluntary organization. Embedding the concepts of spiritual hierarchy and guidance within a formal organization also exposes cultural tensions between the traditional Muslim understanding that there should be no fundamental divide between worldly and spiritual life and modern Western notions that these should be separate.

Other observers of the Inayat Khan movement have remarked on these tensions. Jironet identified a lack of understanding of 'the principles of a spiritual hierarchy in the Western society at large and among his co-workers' (Jironet, 1998: 78) as a major cause of the difficulties that Hazrat Inayat Khan encountered in the organization of the Sufi Movement. Similarly, an early observer of the Sufi Movement reported that some of Inayat Khan's followers had ambitions of controlling the organization or at least of 'a steady if honorary Sufi career ... with spectacular authority at every level' (Mahmood Khan, 2001: 125). Inayat Khan accommodated his leading followers with considerable latitude to direct the Activities, but resisted all attempts to separate organizational from spiritual authority or to control his mode of work.

A formal organization also imposes certain constraints on a group including a strain towards coherence and consistency. In a transnational organization such as the Sufi Movement, the Articles of Incorporation create an internationally coherent and consistent structure that enables the group, at least in theory, to maintain high levels of control over policy and practices across the organization. Such an arrangement then becomes a major 'defining feature of local constituencies', imposing a 'tendency towards unity and universality in both doctrine and structure' (Della Cava, 2001: 537-8). This tendency has increased over the twentieth century as modern communications technologies and modern forms of travel continue to amplify the capacity for coordination, control and coherence. As has occurred within the Inayati order, local adaptations, practice or policy differences that might be ignored or unnoticed in an informal context, come to attention and into tension with the central authority and directives, and contribute to splintering.

Another feature of religious organizations in modern secular societies is that, as voluntary associations, they 'cannot assume the loyal adherence of members' (Warner, 1994: 63), as have those traditional Sufi orders in which membership has been largely a family matter and ongoing adherence has been reinforced by community pressures. Rather, modern religious voluntary organizations must actively recruit and retain members in competitive religious markets. This poses particular challenges for the governance of voluntary associations constructed on the modified templates of pre-modern religious institutions. In particular, hierarchical structures, such as that found in the Inayati Sufi Movement, are frequently criticized as inappropriate to the modern world and a liability to the organization. However, democratic practices such as majority rule may themselves destabilize voluntary organizations and contribute to their fragility (Diani, 1992: 14, 18).

In NRMs such as the Sufi Movement there are therefore often ongoing issues as to effective and appropriate authority structures, and how to balance the need for members and willing workers with quality control and the integrity of the tradition. Inayat Khan and subsequent leaders have restricted who may represent the organization. Still the 'newness' of local Sufi Movement groups and the need for leaders, particularly in new areas, has at times led to dedicated but less than fully qualified *mureed*s in these roles. Another recruitment challenge for the Inayati order has been that many people attracted to its ideas and innovative Sufi message have been reluctant to join any organization (Van Voorst van Beest and Guillaume-Schamhart, 1979), and this is still so.

Differences between Inayat Khan's Sufi ethos and Western expectations, and the problems of formal transnational voluntary organization in the West, were challenges during his lifetime, but Inayat Khan was still able to hold the organization together. However, after his unexpected death in 1927 at the age of 44 on a return trip to India, the social dynamics engendered by these differences in ethos, values and operation led to a number of ruptures.

The formation of sub-lineages is not unusual within a Sufi order (Ernst, 1997: 136). In the Inayati case, however, tensions have been exacerbated because the order is nested in the formal organizational structure and any division has complex organizational implications. In 1929, the original International Sufi Movement split into a European branch led by Shaikh-ul-Mashaikh Maheboob Khan who was Inayat Khan's brother and companion in the West, and an American branch led by Rabia Martin, the woman who was Inayat Khan's first disciple in the West and whom he appointed as *Murshida*. Following this early split, the International Sufi Movement (the European branch) has continued under a succession of leaders with Inayat Khan's younger son, Pir-o-Murshid Hidayat Inayat-Khan, as the current Representative General. Two additional offshoots, Sufi Way (in Great Britain) and Sufi Contact (in the Netherlands) were formed around 1980. As in the earliest rupture, these were created by *mureed*s who, for different reasons, were unhappy with certain decisions at Headquarters, and saw their primary loyalty to a particular guide within the order rather than to the organization as a whole.

The first American branch collapsed in the late 1940s and I explore the reasons for that collapse and its major implications for the Australian Sufi Movement later in this chapter. In the late 1950s, a clash between 'Eastern' and 'Sufi' values of obedience and spiritual readiness, and 'Western' initiative and expectations, led Inayat Khan's elder son, Pir Vilayat (d. 2004), to break with the International Sufi Movement. Collaborating with Samuel Lewis (Murshid Sam), the creator of the Dances of Universal Peace, Pir Vilayat started what is now called the Sufi Order International in the United States. His son, Pir Zia, is the current leader. In 1977, when Pir Vilayat attempted to impose certain policies on all groups and *mureed*s in his Sufi Order, *mureed*s initiated by Samuel Lewis broke away to form a new organization, the Sufi Ruhaniat International. Pir Shabda Kahn is the current leader. The three major branches – the Movement, the Order and the Ruhaniat – are now all separate, but very similar, transnational organizations. From 1997, the loosely structured Federation of the Sufi Message has operated in the contrary direction, bringing the branches together to share practices, music and prayer. This Federation was initiated by Pir-o-Murshid Hidayat Inayat-Khan and is 'very close to being a "non-organization" since it has no official status, no leader, no budget and works by consensus' (Pasnak, 2003).

Unlike in many religious groups, ruptures within the Inayati order have not occurred over the 'correct' interpretation of doctrines or teachings. Most splits have occurred from the clash in values between the organizational structure and the ethos out of which it operates. This is despite the fact that rightful spiritual authority, loyalty, obedience, and the role of the 'teacher' are variously conceived. There has been some shift towards authority justified by tradition or rules since Inayat Khan's death. Nevertheless, a succession of new charismatic leaders in each of the branches has weakened the institutionalization of the founder's charisma and the rationalization that might otherwise have been expected (Birnbaum, 1969: 15). In most of the ruptures, the *murshid–mureed* relationship of mystical attraction and spiritual authority has been privileged over organizational demands or policies, resulting in new (albeit almost identical) branch organizations or new, less formal and somewhat maverick sub-groups. The groups are aware of the difficulties. As a participant in the United States commented wryly, 'Hearing the voice of God doesn't really work in an organization and the only solution is to get rid of the mystics so that you can run things properly' (Graham, 1993).

As this account of the organizational development shows, the combination in this Sufi order of a modern formal transnational voluntary organization with a charismatic monarchical model of spiritual authority creates a dualism of principle that has never been entirely resolved. While personalities and other issues have played a part, the social dynamics inherent in the pull between these organizational forms largely account for the history of ruptures.

Formal Organization and Modern Communications in the Australian Evolution of Inayat Khan's Sufi Movement

Various factors shaped the form in which Inayati Sufism first arrived in Australia. These include the origins of Inayat Khan's Sufi Movement in the Indian Chishti Sufi tradition, early adaptations made by Inayat Khan in accord with his mystical vision for religion in the modern world, and pragmatic decisions like adopting a formal organization. These factors, along with the early rupture between the European and American branches after Inayat Khan's death, have also influenced the ongoing development of the International Sufi Movement in Australia. The Australian case therefore demonstrates further the paradoxical role that a formal transnational organization can play in the adaptation of an Asian-derived NRM to the West. The Australian story also shows how the 'newness' of an NRM in the West poses particular challenges as well as opportunities for a tradition, and how the emerging communications technologies and other social and religious trends of the twentieth and twenty-first centuries provide ongoing stimulus for change. I explore these processes by considering the three main phases through which the Inayati Sufi order has now passed in Australia.

Phase 1: The Early Australian Encounter with Sufism (1927-50)

Inayati Sufism began in Australia when Baron von Frankenberg immigrated in 1927, the same year that the founder died in India. Although Von Frankenberg's father was a German aristocrat and his mother was born in Australia, he grew up in the United States and Germany. He had become a *mureed* in 1925 and spent six months with Pir-o-Murshid Inayat Khan, his Sufi Master, at the annual Sufi Summer Schools near Paris. In Australia, Von Frankenberg, or Shaikh Momin as he was known to his *mureed*s, made Sufi literature available and offered initiation and spiritual guidance to his mostly middle-class, well-educated and artistic groups of *mureed*s. Von Frankenberg was associated with the early American branch of the order and was appointed as its Australian Representative in the mid-1930s. The American leader, Murshida Rabia Martin, toured Australia and New Zealand in 1939, giving public lectures on Sufism and meeting with groups of *mureed*s. For a time all went well, and Von Frankenberg's active and enthusiastic Sufi Societies in Melbourne and Sydney provided an alternative spiritual path to many in a predominantly Christian society from the 1930s to the late 1940s.

However, Von Frankenberg's groups did not survive. When Rabia Martin (leader of the American branch) died in 1947, her designated successor, Ivy Duce, felt unqualified for the role. Duce soon took the unprecedented step of handing over the Inayati order to a spiritual teacher from a different tradition. This teacher, Meher Baba, convinced Duce that he was 'the Avatar of the Age' and that Inayat Khan wanted his order to become part of Meher Baba's organization. In Australia, as in America, the order split. While some of the *mureed*s in each country followed Duce in this new direction, more disagreed but lacked a leader, and many drifted away. Von Frankenberg appeared unable to take a clear stand, and with his death soon after in 1950, the first phase of the Sufi Movement in Australia effectively ended.

This early history in Australia demonstrates many of the same difficulties found elsewhere after the early and unexpected death of Inayat Khan. As is characteristic of NRMs, the first generation members were enthusiastic but inexperienced (Barker and Mayer, 1995). Many who stepped into positions of responsibility, like Von Frankenberg, had not had a long period of training with Inayat Khan. In Australia, given the communications and technology of the times, he was geographically isolated. The acrimonious split that followed Inayat Khan's death had also cut off this group from the depth of experience available in Europe through the brothers and companions of Inayat Khan, as was true of the early American group. A further obstacle for Von Frankenberg and the early Australian group was government restrictions on persons of German nationality or name during World War II. These restrictions meant that Von Frankenberg had to suspend Sufi meetings at his home, and since many *mureed*s were able to contact him only by letter during these years, this weakened the group.

The challenge posed by Duce and Meher Baba involved not just acceptance or otherwise of Meher Baba's claims, but also both organizational and esoteric issues of authority and allegiance and the practice of the *murshid–mureed* relationship. As elsewhere, *mureed*s had different understandings of who or what constituted the 'master'. Was their allegiance to the founder, Inayat Khan, to Duce as the current head of the branch with which they were associated, to their individual initiator, Von Frankenberg, or to someone or something else?

Some of those who followed Meher Baba did so because they were impressed by his claim to have a higher spiritual status than Inayat Khan. To these people, a God guru seemed better than a modest Sufi saint. This demonstrated another process affecting the development of NRMs of non-Western origin: Westerners internalizing imagined or aggrandized 'Eastern' values without fully understanding the nuances of the different traditions that carry them. These *mureed*s were unaware of the limit of claims made by teachers within different religious traditions, such that in some Hindu traditions it is a relatively common and accepted practice to claim enlightenment or even Avatarship, whereas in Sufism such claims are usually regarded as egotism, heresy and insolence. The problem for NRMs is not simply that of adapting an 'Eastern' tradition to the 'West', but also of managing the hypercorrect behaviour of Western participants.

In addition, the dilemma exposed ambiguity in understanding the universal or 'unity of religious ideals' perspective taught by Inayat Khan. In the spirit of the Islamic teaching that prophets have been sent to all nations, Inayat Khan included in pre-Mohammedan prophetship what he called 'the Hindu line and that of Beni Israel' (1963: 147-8) He taught that each Divine Messenger, in essence, presented the same Truth with outer differences due to differences in audience, time and place. Inayat Khan encouraged learning about different religions but did not see value in debating the relative status of prophets or the 'truth' claims of different religions. As he understood it, 'God', 'Truth' or 'Reality' was to be found in the inner life, in the human heart, not in the outer form of a religion.

Inayat Khan's perspective has similarities with the 'perennialism' of neo-traditionalists like Nasr (e.g. Nasr, 1972) though he did not, like Nasr, believe it necessary to combine inner spiritual work with a particular outer law or ritual. In this respect, his universalism is closer to Huxley's 'perennial philosophy' (1945). On the other hand, unlike more 'New Age' perennialists, Inayat Khan warned against an eclectic combining of spiritual practices or teachers, likening this to trying to travel in two boats at the same time. Universality, for Inayat Khan, meant the 'unity of religious ideals' and the brotherhood and sisterhood of all humanity, each a central tenet in his Sufi Movement. Experientially, however, universality was the result, not the starting point, and the inner work of purification and refinement was thought to be best achieved by an aspirant following a particular spiritual training in depth.

The collapse of the first phase in Australia demonstrates the early group's failure to resolve the complicated pulls between a universal spiritual perspective and following a particular spiritual path, as well as the clash between organizational and spiritual claims to authority and obedience. Von Frankenberg was both a Sufi *shaykh* with a circle of *mureed*s, and the representative of a formal transnational Sufi organization that was effectively being taken over, albeit with the agreement of the new American leader, by another organization with a very different agenda. NRM literature indicates that a process of 'recoupment' or 're-orientation' might have been expected within the Australian group at this time (Baumann, 1994: 44-5). This process involves critically examining ambiguities that have arisen and affirming both the identity of one's tradition and its borders with competing traditions. That this process did not occur, due to the confusions of loyalties and conflicting pulls in the transnational organization, was a major factor in the failure of this phase of Sufism in Australia to survive.

Phase 2: Founding the Sufi Movement in Australia (1950-90)

The second phase under Sharif Jansen was more successful. Jansen was Dutch, grew up in Indonesia, and migrated to Australia in 1951. He was a *mureed* of Inayat Khan's brother, Musharaff Khan, and in 1958 was appointed as the National Representative for Australia, affiliated this time with the European branch. His early Sufi groups included new people as well as some from the groups of Von Frankenberg. Interest in Sufism expanded greatly from the early 1970s, with many who were involved in the various counter-cultural movements of the time seeking his guidance. Jansen met with individuals and held group evening classes in his home in Sydney. The classes involved prayers, study of Inayat Khan's teaching papers, *zikar*, and on special occasions, the Universal Worship Service and the Healing Service. He also established and guided Sufi groups in New Zealand and other Australian cities.

In training his *mureed*s, Jansen adhered closely to Inayat Khan's teachings and insisted on the establishment of disciplined, ethical lifestyles as a prerequisite to more advanced training. Jansen had received a deep and traditional 'inner' Sufi training from Musharaff Khan and sought to pass on this form of training (a largely silent communion between a *mureed* and teacher, and unfolding within the *mureed* assisted from the Unseen) to his *mureed*s. He was a strong leader who required *mureed*s to regularly attend the Sufi classes and he discouraged any combining of these with the other spiritual paths and teachings available at the time.

Before the death in 1967 of Pir-o-Murshid Musharaff Khan, who was Jansen's teacher and the fourth Representative General of the International Sufi Movement, Jansen had a harmonious relationship with the international organization and regular correspondence with Musharaff Khan. However, Jansen had been unable to travel to Europe and attend the Sufi Summer Schools, and in those days before international communication technologies such as email, he was often isolated from ongoing developments. On several occasions, the practical and structured information taught in the Summer Schools did not find its way to him until years later. Insofar as the focus of the International Headquarters was at the time on the Sufi work in Europe and the United States, Jansen and the Australian group were somewhat neglected.

In 1975, Sharif Jansen and his wife attended the annual Summer School in the Netherlands but found the new leader, Fazal Inayat-Khan, to be very different in style from his predecessors. Fazal had attracted a large number of 'alternative' people, introduced practices from the human potential movement alongside Sufi activities, and allowed what Jansen saw as disrespectful behaviour in the Sufi Temple complex at Katwijk. When a meeting failed to resolve differences, Jansen withdrew the Australian groups from the International Sufi Movement organization. Back in Australia, he continued to hold Sufi classes and sought to protect his growing number of *mureed*s from the 'going astray' (Genn, 2004: 269-70) he perceived overseas. He was supported with letters and teaching papers from some of the older leaders in England and South Africa, although others, and the organization as a whole, regarded him as a maverick.

In sum, geographical isolation, a sole (immigrant) leader with a circle of *mureed*s, and conflict with and within the transnational organization shaped the first two phases of Inayati Sufism in Australia. Neither Von Frankenberg nor Jansen established an organization in Australia; rather, they just attracted around themselves groups of *mureed*s and interested people. Both early leaders were, however, deeply affected by events within their transnational Sufi organizations, and as happened overseas, ambiguities in the understanding and practice of the *murshid–mureed* relationship in the West and within a formal organization contributed to these. In the case of Jansen, his understanding of the *murshid–mureed* relationship led him to resist in Australia the changes taking place elsewhere in the transnational organization.[8] He continued to follow what he believed were the instructions of his *Murshid*, even when this meant leaving the organization. Jansen's personal charisma, his sole leadership in Australia and the loyalty of his *mureed*s served largely to postpone further major changes in this form of Sufism in Australia until after his death in 1990.

Phase 3: The Contemporary Western Sufi Community and Its Evolving Organization (1990s Onwards)

From around the start of the 1990s, modern communication technologies, greater ease of travel and increasing involvement with the transnational organization have effected a massive shift in the Australian Sufi Movement scene. An event that took place around 1990, shortly before Sharif Jansen's death, shows some of the issues that are now shaping the third contemporary phase of the group and some of the tensions that had actually already been building before that event.

While their *Murshid* was in hospital, the Sydney *mureed*s continued to gather regularly for study, *zikar*, music and other practices. On one such occasion, a long-time *mureed* and musician wanted to share her inspiration of putting to music a prayer, given by Inayat Khan, with a new first line that did not attribute gender to the Divine. She had replaced the words 'Beloved Lord, Almighty God', with 'O Thou the Healing Spirit of All'. The group had begun to sing when a male *mureed* interrupted and said that Inayat Khan had asked that his words not be changed. Doing so, the *mureed* said, was disrespectful to Inayat Khan and to Sharif Jansen, and as a *mureed* he felt obliged to stop it. The atmosphere that had been built up over several hours of chanting and practices shattered. A heavy silence followed and then discussion. Some harmony was restored in the group by the efforts of its members to recognize each other's sincerity, but the issues were not fully resolved and remain an ongoing source of tension in the group.

The issues raised by the incident related to gendered language; the practice of the *murshid–mureed* relationship; hierarchical verses self authority in spiritual guidance, rituals and practices; hierarchy versus democratic principles in organizational matters and styles of Australian decision-making and autonomy. After Jansen's death, tensions over these issues were great enough to rupture the group and two separate groups emerged. These are the Sufi Movement in Australia (SMIA), which is more traditional in the sense of closely following Sufism as taught by Inayat Khan, and Heartcentre, an innovative and autonomous community. During the 1990s and early 2000s, the Sufi Order International and the Sufi Ruhaniat International have also developed a presence in Australia and the Dances of Universal Peace (DUP), popularly known as Sufi Dancing has become more organized. DUP is not a Sufi order but functions as an ecumenical activity and frequently as a point of first contact for people who later join the order.

The main Inayati group in Australia, the SMIA (Sufi Movement in Australia) is now a formal Australian organization and affiliate of the International Sufi Movement. While there is some consultation, appointments within the Australian organization are mostly made overseas by the Pir-o-Murshid, who also authorizes leaders to hold Sufi classes and to initiate and guide *mureed*s. This Australian group increasingly functions along lines set by the transnational organization as can be seen from its constitution, the frequency of visits by overseas leaders to Australia, travel of Australian *mureed*s to international events, and the SMIA's use of communication technologies like email and the World Wide Web to keep up with developments in the international organization.

Most Australian participants are willing to grant authority to Pir-o-Murshid Hidayat Inayat-Khan and senior international representatives of the order like Murshid Nawab Pasnak. Even so, Australian culture tends to be informal, and within themselves Australian groups tend to de-emphasize hierarchy and resist local assertions of authority. Affordable air travel along with the emerging transnational email and cyber Sufi community have gone a long way to overcome both the large geographic distances across Australia and the previous isolation of Australian groups from the transnational organization. However, they have also inspired concerns about the structure of the organization and the lack of local autonomy, as well as confusion about the distinction between organizational and spiritual decisions. There is an ongoing and unresolved tension within the SMIA between concerns with the social and political implications of the hierarchical organizational structure, and the Sufi perception of an order, 'not as a social institution but as a mystical transmission that makes possible the entry of the individual into spiritual life' (Ernst, 1997: 122). These concerns have not occasioned any further splits in the Australian group, but they have caused some *mureed*s to withdraw from active involvement in the organization.

A significant and related ongoing issue for the groups is the different understandings and practice of the *murshid–mureed* relationship. While Inayat Khan made a number of adaptations to traditional Sufism, he saw this relationship as intrinsic to the Sufi path and training, and emphasized steadfastness within it. Spiritual hierarchy is inherent in the relationship, although interviews with teachers and students in the Inayati order indicate that its practice by the order, both now and in Inayat Khan's time, is arguably non-authoritarian, and Sufi Movement teachers do not claim infallibility. Spiritual hierarchy and authority within the order are balanced by a concept of 'spiritual liberty', or the individual's right to freedom of thought.

Nonetheless, changes in patterns of personal religiosity in the modern world are reflected in the emergence of a variety of alternatives as well as a more flexible practice of the *murshid–mureed* relationship. The New Age emphasis on 'self-authority' (Heelas, 1996; Roof, 1999) and today's spiritual 'marketplace' (Iannaccone, 1991) offer modern seekers new and diverse approaches to spiritual life. In addition, concerns about democracy and individualism, and the 'guru' scandals of the 1980s and 1990s involving sexual and other abuse within a number of Asian-origin religious groups in the West (see Rodarmor, 1983; Simpkinson, 1996),[9] have led to assertions that the master-disciple system of spiritual training is redundant or counterproductive (Wren-Lewis, 1994; Harvey, 1995). While there have been no scandals within the Inayati Sufi Movement, participants have been influenced by these broader changes and concerns. Some *mureed*s reject any form of hierarchy and say they get what they need spiritually from group activities, books and a network of friends within the group. Others have a guide but see that person as just a friend. Some say they receive direct guidance from Inayat Khan or God, so do not need a human teacher. Others decide for themselves what spiritual practices are best. Some, in a style reminiscent of a pre-*tariqa* Sufism,[10] seek guidance from a range of teachers within the Inayati order and, as is possible today, from other spiritual traditions as well.

It is not surprising that Westerners are grappling with the meaning of concepts like loyalty, commitment, trust and surrender and what these concepts offer in the twenty-first century. More striking is the support that traditional forms of the *murshid–mureed* relationship still command in this Western Sufi order and the strength of the bond between many *mureed*s and their guides. These *mureed*s believe they receive something extremely valuable and the model of the wise spiritual teacher and loving guide retains great appeal, as does the spiritual community built around it. In that the relationship offers a contrast to the emphasis in modern society on individualism and external achievement, and to the fragmentation and transitoriness of many relationships, this may also be partly a response to contemporary social conditions.

Putting the experience of the Inayati movement in Australia in broader perspective, it is clear that similar tensions are evident in other Asian-derived religious transplants. The changes in the Western cultural context over the course of twentieth century, particularly of increasing gender equity and less authoritarian and less formal relationships generally, have challenged many spiritual traditions, not just the Inayati order. Western culture itself varies, and national and local differences in perception and concerns make issues such as the use of gender-inclusive language in prayer and readings potentially divisive for a transnational organization. Recent research into the transnational religion of immigrants in the United States identifies the issue of internal differences within congregations as a consistent dilemma. Ebaugh and Chafetz (2000), for example, found that accommodating cultural and ethnic differences hurts the unity of a migrant religious organization, but failure to respond invites schism. While the Inayati group has not dealt with tension between global and local cultures by encouraging a mono-cultural uniformity, as some non-Western-origin NRMs have done, it still faces ongoing challenges in balancing integrity and recognition of the tradition with accommodation to Australian culture and concerns. The issue of gendered language was one factor in the split between the SMIA and Heartcentre groups, and it continues to be a concern for some within the SMIA.

Modern communication technologies and increasingly active engagement in the formal transnational International Sufi Movement organization are changing the practice of Inayati Sufism in Australia and elsewhere, as they are transforming those of other transnational Sufi orders. The processes are somewhat parallel to those that are transforming 'Muslim' identities from essentially local, cultural identities to more homogenized globalized religious identities (Gibb, 1998). However, many of the 'transplanted' Sufi networks in immigrant communities in North America, Western Europe and Australia are still largely extensions of networks in the home countries, embedded in parochial settings where Muslim, national, ethnic and local identities blend together (Lapidus, 2001: 37). For these groups the focus tends to be on the relationships created and maintained between source (homeland) and destination (new abode) and key tensions relate to the role of religion within immigrant communities in the West (Ebaugh and Chafetz, 2000). This is a form of transnational religion, though many instances might also be regarded as trans-state particularisms (Waldinger and Fitzgerald, 2004: 1182-3).

By contrast, the mostly Western adherents of Eastern-origin NRMs may be creating a new variant of transnational religion beyond traditional ethnic, cultural and religious boundaries. While many of these groups are using formal organizations to coordinate their work and to create coherent and consistent transnational networks, their emphasis is generally on the interior spiritual dimension of religion and individual experience, and often, in addition, on a concern for humanity as a whole. 'Reworked' traditions such as the Inayati order are practising across borders a Sufism that differs from both traditional informal Sufi networks and the transnational Sufism practised by contemporary immigrants.

The Inayati movement is to a degree culturally and geographically anchored by Headquarters in the Netherlands and the United States and by the sacred site of the *Dargah* (holy shrine or tomb) complex of Inayat Khan in India. Yet the practice of this Sufism does not require belonging to or embracing a particular culture or religion. The group's participants are also becoming more diverse. While the Inayati order is still predominantly 'Western', growing interest in the order in Asia and South America make it an increasingly multi-site phenomenon in which global and transnational aspects are interwoven with local specificity (cf. Kearney, 1995). At the Australian Sufi Summer School in 2004, the majority of participants were 'Westerners'

(Australians of European background), but there were also people of Turkish and Iranian Muslim background. A few of the 'Western' participants had formally converted to Islam, though in most cases before becoming involved with the Inayati order. Another recent Inayati Sufi gathering in Australia drew Muslim participants from Malaysia, and retreats at the *Dargah* of Hazrat Inayat Khan in New Delhi from 2003 to 2005 have been attended by Indian nationals, South American and Chinese *mureed*s, as well as Westerners from Australia, New Zealand, North America and Europe.

While the challenge of resolving cultural tensions within a new, formal transnational organization has contributed to ruptures within the Inayati movement, this organizational structure is paradoxically also allowing wider allegiances to form. Even for those whose participation remains local, membership of a transnational spiritual organization, with more or less common perspectives and practices across space, creates a sense of global belonging or family. In the Inayati movement this often extends beyond the *pir-bhai* or community of a traditional Sufi order to a sense of kinship with other religious organizations and individuals who combine a specific spiritual commitment with a universalist or inclusive outlook. As a social process, it mirrors that in modern social movements such as environmentalism, in which the movement exceeds the boundaries of any single group or organization (Diani, 1992). As Beyer (1994) argues, religions have generally responded to the expansion of a global system of communication in one of two ways: by defending their particularism or by attempting to develop a liberal religious ethic. Within this polarization, transnational spiritual groups may find common cause, and a place of belonging, with others beyond the traditional boundaries of religion.

Conclusion

This chapter has examined the Inayati order – its cultural history in Indian Chishti Sufism, the vision of its founder, and the challenges and opportunities presented by the Western social and cultural environment into which it has been projected. It shows how the interplay between these factors accounts for this Sufi movement's distinctively broad, universal interpretation of Sufism freed from a strictly Muslim religious identity, and its ready adoption of modern social forms. These innovations in the modern West, which have parallels in other Asian-derived religious imports, have contributed to the group's appeal. They have also, because the innovations have been combined with a number of traditional features retained by the order, generated tensions in the movement.

My analysis here of the Inayati movement as an NRM that has adopted the distinctive twentieth century tools of formal organization and used advances in communication that enable increasingly close interaction and coordination within a formal voluntary organization, sheds light on the kinds of tensions that have arisen in this and other Asian-derived but Western-adapted religious organizations. The various ruptures within the Inayati group occurred largely due to frictions between the formal organizational structure and the hierarchical concept of spiritual authority. On the other hand, the transnational organizational structure adopted by the Inayati order and other Asian-origin NRMs in the West is allowing the emergence across borders of a new kind of religion that emphasizes interior spirituality, personal experience and an inclusive vision transcending traditional ethnic, religious and organizational boundaries.

While long established religious traditions in the West are also grappling with the transition from 'traditional' social and religious contexts to those of 'modernity', Asian-origin NRMs are additionally and simultaneously undergoing processes of cultural translation from East to West. Many, like the Inayati order, have attracted Westerners. As I have shown in this chapter, a new membership, in addition to a new social and cultural environment and new modern forms of organization and communications, creates particular challenges and opportunities for the practice and development of a religious movement. The founder of the Inayati order made major changes, both visionary and pragmatic, in the West, but also, in accord with his understanding of spiritual efficacy and integrity, retained significant strands of the Indian Sufi heritage. The understanding and practice of previously unfamiliar spiritual concepts, as well as the distinction between the cultural and the spiritual dimensions of a transplanted religious tradition can be hazy or contested, with consequent issues for cultural translation, adaptation and legitimation.

Treating the Inayati order as an NRM in this chapter has shown that its problems of cross-cultural translation and the structural strains experienced by the organization in its new environments are not unique to that order. Identifying those problematic organizational dynamics has also helped to explain the distinctive pattern of continuity and innovation in this modern Western Sufi movement. This analysis both extends our understanding of adaptation processes in NRMs of non-Western origin to Western environments and demonstrates a strategy for the comparative analysis of Sufi movements in the West.

Inayat Khan's Sufi Movement does not adhere to some elements of 'orthodoxy' usually followed in Muslim-majority countries. Nonetheless, the group still defines itself as a Sufi order and it has several structural features, such as a *silsila* (chain of transmission), the central teacher-disciple (*murshid–mureed*) relationship, and spiritual practices such as *zikar* that are generally distinctive of Sufi orders. While the movement is innovative, it is not alone among Sufi groups in this regard, and it is not only the substantially non-migrant Sufi groups that have responded creatively to a Western and modern global context. Nor is this Sufi movement alone among modern Sufi communities in introducing changes to teachings and practices. Immigrant Sufi groups in the West are also changing in response to the modern environment (Werbner, 1996; Frishkopf, 2001), and Sufi groups in Muslim-majority countries are adopting experimental and innovative forms of Sufi practice and organization (Howell, 2001).

Although the universalist Sufism of the Inayati movement is in many ways a new impulse within Sufism and a 'Western' and 'modern' variant, like most NRMs it is not entirely new. Inayati Sufism's appreciation of and tolerance for the followers of all faiths and its valuing of spiritual freedom and experience bring forward characteristics of a centuries-old Sufi and Islamic tradition into the modern world and resonate with the conditions of modernity. The Inayati order retains in the West the appreciation of poetry, music and movement found in the Chishti order and it continues to provide a disciplined path of spiritual training. Even so, the development of the tradition in the West, including in Australia, has provided latitude for change that the movement may not have had in its home country, and, as is the case with other Asian-origin traditions, Westerners often practise Sufism in different ways and with different emphases.

Acknowledgement

I thank Julia Howell for her valuable suggestions and comments in preparing this chapter.

CONCLUDING REFLECTIONS

15

CONTEMPORARY SUFISM AND CURRENT SOCIAL THEORY

John O. Voll

'It's so hard to be a saint in the city', sang popular American singer, Bruce Springsteen, about the temptations of city living.[1] Springsteen's song echoes the vow of a nineteenth century Sudanese ascetic Sufi, Muhammad Ahmad, who later proclaimed his mission as Mahdi, the hoped-for messianic figure who would bring justice to the world. As a young man, Muhammad Ahmad was accosted by a city prostitute and vowed never to enter a city again until he could transform society.[2] Sufi saints and their devotional paths (*tariqa*s) with their popular followings have frequently been identified with rural, village, and tribal societies, in contrast to the religious mode of the literate scholars of the cities.[3] The popular Sufi brotherhoods and the saintly figures at their centres have been viewed as basically part of the folk religion of the illiterate believers in the 'Little Tradition' of rural village societies.[4] From this perspective, it is indeed 'hard to be a saint in the city'.

Sufi *tariqa*s have, however, long been an important part of urban life in the Muslim world. Allen Roberts and Mary Nooter Roberts (2003: 21) quoted Springsteen's song at the beginning of their book, *A Saint in the City*, which presents the vitality of *tariqa* life in the urban context in Senegal. The Mourides, the *tariqa* whose urban devotional life is the subject of the Roberts' book, provide an important contemporary example of the dynamic urban presence of Sufi brotherhoods in the contemporary world. The order now has centres in major cities around the world and the followers are well integrated into urban society, with the vitality of the Mouride community in New York City a good illustration (Sachs, 2003: 1, 17).[5]

Old Theories and New Circumstances

The continuing strength of Sufi brotherhoods in the contexts of contemporary societies surprises many people. As discussed in the

Introduction to this volume, much of the sociological literature on Muslim societies has identified the *tariqa*s with the illiterate and rural parts of society. In this perspective the *tariqa*s represent the disappearing 'traditional' elements of the contemporary social order. This image of *tariqa*s continues to influence scholarship and more general public opinion, in the West and in the Muslim world. In such a conceptual framework, the current success and growing visibility of *tariqa*s among professional educated people in the 'modern' sector of society and in modern and modernizing societies in general is neither expected nor predicted.

This situation requires that we re-evaluate some basic analytical assumptions underlying the study of Sufism, since it seems clear that the *tariqa*s of the twenty-first century are not simply residual elements of society and culture from pre-modern times. Instead, the brotherhoods appear to be remarkably effective modern and post-modern forms of societal organization and religious experience. The experience of the Khalwatiyya in Egypt, as Rachida Chih examines in this volume, illustrates the effectiveness of the institution of the *tariqa* in the context of modernity and highlights the need to reconceptualize the nature of Sufism in modern societies.

The surprise caused by the continuing effectiveness of Sufi orders is, in some ways, part of a broader surprise involving the continuing influence and strength of 'religion' itself in contemporary societies. Since the days of the eighteenth century Enlightenment, scholars in the West argued that 'religion' would be replaced by 'science' and have decreasing significance in human life. In the middle of the twentieth century, 'secularization theory' became a central part of the theories of modernization. The separation of religion from politics and the broader processes of the secularization of society came to be seen as an inherent part of modernization. In this framework, as Swatos and Christiano (1999: 213) noted of Shiner's (1967) conceptual study, 'Secularization theory's claims mean the "decline of religion", that is, religion's "previously accepted symbols, doctrines, and institutions lose their prestige and influence. The culmination of secularization would be a religionless society"'.

At the beginning of the twenty-first century it has become clear that such theoretical frameworks for understanding the nature of contemporary societies require significant modification, if not abandonment. By the end of the 1970s, important sociologists of religion were already engaged in a reassessment. Reflecting on a 1970 symposium, Long and Hadden (1979) sensed great change. They noted that while much of the literature assessed in the 1970 symposium pointed to the declining importance of religion in secularizing societies, a decade later attention had shifted to the 'unexpected return of religion to social prominence' (Long and Hadden, 1979: 280). By the end of the twentieth century, prominent sociologist of religion, Rodney Stark, would proclaim:

> Let us declare an end to the social scientific faith in the theory of secularization, recognizing that it was the product of wishful thinking ... After nearly three centuries of utterly failed prophesies and misrepresentations of both present and past, it seems time to carry the secularization doctrine to the graveyard of failed theories, and there to whisper '*requiescat in pace*' [rest in peace]. (Stark, 1999: 269-70)

Recognition of the continuing vitality and importance of 'religion' in the contemporary world is an important part of contemporary scholarship. Theories of modernization are being revised significantly in broad recognition of what Berger (1999) has called 'the desecularization of the world'. While Johnston and Sampson's 1994 volume identified religion as 'the missing dimension of statecraft', Hatzopoulos and Petito (2003: 1-4) have argued that the 'worldwide resurgence of religion' requires a transformation of the modern discipline of International Relations. The study of 'religious movements' has become an important part of a number of disciplines whose scholars examine the 'resurgence of religion'. As Sharma (1994: 366) noted, the study of cults and new religious movements (NRM) that emerged out of the tumult of the 1960s has important methodological implications in the study of religion. Similarly, Smith (1996: 2) observed that although religion's important contribution to social movements was hitherto 'conspicuously under-explored – arguably virtually ignored – in the academic literature on social movements', a number of scholars are 'correcting a curious neglect, or bringing religion back in'.

In the worlds of mass media and scholarship, much attention has been given to the global 'resurgence of religion', with special attention given to developments within the Muslim world. However, most of this attention and research has been given to militant and politically activist movements. The so-called 'fundamentalists' are viewed as central to the resurgence. When scholars speak of the explanatory failure of 'secularization theory', many discuss only Muslim 'fundamentalists', as did, for example, Stark (1999: 267-8) and Berger (1999: 7-8). There is little recognition that while membership in the militant groups may be in the thousands, there are many millions of Muslims who are not fundamentalists, who are active participants in Sufi *tariqa*s around the world.

The dynamism and vitality of Sufi brotherhoods continues to receive little attention and to surprise the many who have expected otherwise. Scholars whose work is still influenced in some way by secularist expectations continue to view the orders as residues of 'traditional' popular folk religion. Another manifestation of a secularist analytical orientation is emphasis on religion as a personal matter, identified with the 'inner' spiritual life. In a futurist volume looking toward the year 2000, Stendahl (1969: 223-4) noted how such an approach emphasizes the mystic dimensions of religious life and tends to view 'institutional religion' negatively. Even then he had observed the weakness of this approach, noting, 'It is unrealistic to believe that "institutional religion" will fade away, while its non-institutional forms continue or even increase. There will, of course, be substantial changes in the structures of these institutions, but that does not make them less institutional' (Stendahl, 1969: 225).

In these contexts, it becomes necessary to identify new analytical and theoretical frameworks for understanding the continuing significance of *tariqa*s in the modern and contemporary world. Even though some of these frameworks have been used effectively in analysing the general phenomenon of 'religious resurgence' in the late twentieth century, recognition of the continuing importance of religion needs to be extended more explicitly to understanding the nature and significance of Sufi brotherhoods in the contemporary world.

In this Conclusion to the volume, I examine three new approaches to understanding *tariqa*s and their place in the contemporary world. These approaches have been exemplified in various ways in this volume, but need to be flagged as significant alternatives to older approaches that are limited by their linkages to the secularization hypothesis or to outmoded models of Muslim society. The first of the new approaches involves focusing on the relationship between the organizations of 'traditional' popular folk religion and those of contemporary popular religion. The second focuses on the relationships between globalization and the development of *tariqa* structures, and the third views *tariqa*s within the framework of conceptualizations of religion in the 'postmodern' world.

Folk Islam and Pop Culture

Within the broader context of a global religious resurgence, the *tariqa* form of organization continues to be important as a structural format for 'popular' religious life in the Muslim world, whether urban or rural. The wide variety of 'popular' religious practices among South Asians in Great Britain, as analysed by Pnina Werbner in this volume, highlights the continuing vitality of these forms of communal and individual faith. The contrasts between 'modern' and 'traditional' that many of the widely accepted concepts posit about modernity clearly do not apply. Since the older analytical frameworks do not 'explain' this situation, it is useful to see if current theoretical frameworks can help.

Many empirical studies show the continuing vitality of *tariqa*s and their importance in contemporary societies. However less effort has been directed to developing a theoretical framework to replace the older ones based on secularization/modernization theory or the Orientalist understanding of 'popular Islam'. One possible replacement framework is social movement theory, which was developed to study other types of movements and in other contexts.[6] In general terms, one might view the whole effort to maintain an authentic sense of Islamic faith and identity in the dramatically new contexts of modernity as a 'social movement'. Within this context, social movement organizations can take many different forms. McAdam, McCarthy and Zald (1996: 3) observed how some scholars of social movement theory examine different types of organizational formats as the '*mobilizing structures* through which groups seek to organize' and examine '*those collective vehicles, informal as well as formal, through which people mobilize and engage in collective action*' (italics in original). In the following discussion, I consider some concrete evidence of the continuing dynamism of *tariqa*s and present possible explanations using aspects of social movement theory.

Many recent studies have made it clear that the sharp contrasts that older descriptions of Sufi organizations make between rural–urban, intellectual–illiterate and spiritual–institutional need to be modified. Many ulama, especially in pre-modern Muslim societies, were major figures in *tariqa*s and the brotherhoods were a vital part of urban as well as rural society. There were elite orders and ones that primarily reflected the religious life of the masses. However, the contrast between elite culture and mass culture in general cannot be ignored. One element of this contrast was the tension between urban scholarly puritanism and the many practices of popular Islam associated with the *tariqa*s and Sufi saint-groups that the puritanism resisted and opposed.

Throughout Islamic history, reformers have clashed with some aspects of Sufism and some of the chapters in this volume confirm that these tensions continue. We see contemporary forms in Michael Laffan's analysis of the debates about Sufism in the recent Indonesian periodicals, *Salafy* and *Sufi*, and in Matthijs van den Bos' examination of the interactions between Sufi groups and the state in the Islamic Republic of Iran. A different dynamic is involved when the reformers themselves are Sufis. Itzchak Weismann notes the long tradition of activist reformism that might be called 'Sufi fundamentalism', which he observes is often identified with the Naqshbandiyya in South Asia and, as he explores in detail in twentieth century Syria. These studies provide important evidence that Sufism continues to be an interactive alternative to both modernism and Islamism, even as the nature of popular religious practice and mass culture is changing in the varied contexts of modernity.

One significant dynamic of societal evolution in the modern era has been a transformation of the nature of 'mass culture' and its relationship to elite culture. Already in 1930, an influential 'diagnosis' of modern times by Spanish philosopher José Ortega y Gasset (1932: 11) spoke of 'the revolt of the masses' and 'the accession of the masses to complete social power'. At the beginning of the twenty-first century, Fareed Zakaria (2003: 13-15) speaks about the global democratization of culture and politics and 'the shift of power downward'. Even relatively poor societies have experienced a rising level of general awareness of the world beyond the particular locality and higher levels of education and literacy. Ronald Inglehart's important study concludes, 'As ordinary people obtain greater resources, going from being illiterate peasants to become relatively secure, well-educated people, the balance between elites and masses shifts in favour of the masses' (Inglehart, 1997: 340). While this study dealt primarily with advanced industrial societies, it has more general applicability in the context of contemporary globalization and development, given the increasing difficulty of separating developments in 'less industrialized' and in dominant, 'highly industrialized' societies.

Mass culture – the culture of 'ordinary people' – has not remained static in the past century. Rapidly changing technologies have transformed the abilities of the 'common person' to communicate and participate in the activities of society beyond the immediate locality. In this transformation, what may be thought of as 'traditional' popular culture in fact has been disappearing, as transforming lifestyles inherently transform the explicit content of 'popular religion'. One might capture the change conceptually from looking at the changing nature of the life of 'ordinary people', with the suggestion that 'traditional popular culture' has changed into 'pop culture'. Here people who are not scholars in religion or from the 'religious establishments' play an increasingly visible and important role in defining the religious dimensions of societal life.

Since *tariqa*s were an important part of the structures of popular Islam, their place in society has changed as popular culture itself has changed. One manifestation of this change is that some *tariqa*s have made the transition, with Sufism a dimension of 'pop culture' in many different societal contexts. This transition has been associated in some cases with organizational innovation, and in other cases with old-style structures becoming involved in activities of the new pop culture.

Different types of *tariqa*s have found ways to become effective organizations in contemporary societies. Building on established traditions and existing associational networks, *tariqa*s have often emerged as more effective 'modern associations' than organizations structured in a more explicitly modern manner. This process involves interaction with changing political systems as state and society are transformed in the modern era. The interaction between *tariqa*s and the state in the later Ottoman Empire and in the modern Turkish Republic provides an important case study of the continuities and changes involved. Brian Silverstein presents in this volume a comprehensive analysis of these processes, noting how Sufi organizations survive in the contexts of legal secularism. The Naqshbandi experience is, as Silverstein notes, an important element in this situation.

The Naqshbandi order is one of the major *tariqa*s in the Muslim world and has organizational roots that go back to the fourteenth century in Central Asia. In the modern era it provided the organizational base for movements of reform and activist resistance to European imperial expansion as well as being a major element in popular piety in many areas. In the new Turkish Republic created by Mustafa Kemal Ataturk in the 1920s, the order was banned as a part of the secularization programs of Kemalism. However, this did not mean an end to the order in Turkey. As Hakan Yavuz (1999: 129) observed,

What the reformist Turkish state perceived as out-of-date institutions became a 'womb' for fostering flexible and adaptive informal institutions and discourses. These networks have been the main intellectual and philosophical sources of the contemporary Islamic movements in Turkey ... In response to repression, most of these orders [the Naqshbandi networks] gradually transformed from strictly religious associations into educational and cultural informal associations with religious underpinnings.

The Naqshbandi order has also been remarkably successful in other parts of the Muslim world, in terms of visibility and influence as well as in developing new modes of operation in the rapidly changing conditions of the contemporary world. In Syria, the Kaftariyya branch of the brotherhood has long played a prominent role in religious affairs. Its leader, Shaykh Ahmad Kaftaru (d. 2004) was appointed Mufti of Damascus in 1951 and became Grand Mufti of Syria in 1964. He was at the centre of an international network of scholars and former students. His organization operates schools (including doctoral-level study in Islamic law) and a *da'wah* (missionary) organization, conducts publishing activities, and maintains an effective presence on the Internet.[7] In Central Asia, many Soviet officials viewed the Naqshbandiyya as the most potentially effective opposition to Soviet rule, and after the break-up of the Soviet Union, the newly independent regimes worked with the Naqshbandiyya as an effective counter to the possible influence of radical 'fundamentalist' movements (Goble, 2000). In Indonesia, the Naqshbandiyya has been an active part of the Islamic resurgence and some of its branches have been especially successful in appealing to 'well-educated urbanites' (Howell, 2001: 717).

In each of these regions, the Naqshbandiyya responded organizationally in ways that were different from each other, but effective. The Naqshbandi example shows the strength and durability of the Sufi modes of popular religion in the contexts of rapidly changing modern and contemporary societies. The transition from being a major part of 'traditional' popular Islamic culture to playing a significant role in mass culture in Muslim societies reflects the continuing strength of the *tariqa* traditions in the contemporary world. In general, Julia Howell's conclusion about Indonesian Sufism applies in many parts of the world:

Sufism, once strongly associated with the 'traditional' rural sector of Indonesian society, clearly has not died out ... [and] in the period of Indonesia's most rapid economic development under the New Order government, Sufism has inspired new enthusiasm, even in the sectors of Indonesian society most intensely engaged in modernization and globalization: the urban middle and upper classes. This interest is expressed through the participation of urbanites in the long-established, rural-based Sufi orders, the *tarekat*, but also through novel institutional forms in the towns and cities. (Howell, 2001: 722)

These developments show that the *tariqa* organizational format continues to be significant and it is important to seek explanation. Why are the *tariqa*-style organization and the Sufi traditions a major mode of expression of the new popular religion of ordinary people? And why are *tariqa*s still important as vehicles for social movements affirming Islamic identity in the context of modernity? The answers from within the older theoretical frameworks are that there are still many people who are attracted to old style religion and that the significance of *tariqa*s is simply a sign of limited modernization. Yet, the evidence shows that much of the contemporary strength of the *tariqa* traditions comes from their support by people in the most 'modern' sectors of society. Some helpful alternative answers are suggested by contemporary social movement theory, particularly as it relates to social movement organization.

The organizational structures of social movements do not simply appear in a vacuum. They arise within already existing patterns of interaction among individuals and groups. As McCarthy (1996: 147) notes,

> In any concrete social setting, a range of mobilizing structural elements are more or less available to activists as they attempt to create new movements or nurture and direct ongoing ones. More embedded social processes spawn and alter many concrete social patterns that constitute the range of mobilizing structural forms which are available to activists at any point in time, but they can invent new ones as well as radically alter and creatively combine available ones as they try to achieve their collective purposes.

In Muslim societies, the *tariqa* structure is part of the available range of alternatives and appears to be widely used as the organizational format for ordinary people expressing the new popular Islam as it interacts with social, economic and political dimensions of life. McCarthy's discussion of the choice of structures provides a possible explanation for this continued vitality of adapted *tariqa* forms in contemporary modern societies:

> The structures of everyday life may ultimately be changed by collective action, but in the short run they are relatively fixed, and serve as the relational underpinning for most collective action. The portions of mobilizing structural repertoires where the most creating effort occurs is in putting those structures to new or newly recombined uses and in building new mobilizing structures out of them. Collective actors, probably most often, adopt mobilizing structural forms that are known to them from direct experience. Saul Alinsky's oft noted advice to organizers to avoid tactics 'outside the experience of your people'

suggests a logic internal to groups for such routine adoption of familiar forms. (MCarthy, 1996: 147-8)

The 'familiar forms' of the *tariqa*s as a part of the 'structures of everyday life' make them a natural format for activity, which suggests that the various contemporary forms of the Naqshbandiyya are striking examples of how this process works. The older theories of Sufi organization would find, for example, the experience of Shaykh Kaftaru in Syria paradoxical and surprising, while McCarthy's discussion of mobilizing structures provides a way of understanding Naqshbandi successes as a natural development within the context of the social movement of new Islamic affirmation.

*Tariqa*s and Globalization

In the descriptions presented in long-established scholarship, *tariqa*s are frequently the core of distinctive local Muslim cultures and societies. From Southeast Asia to West Africa, the brotherhoods are viewed as the important, flexible institutions of the Islamic 'frontier'. By being open to including distinctive local customs in what would be defined as Islam, the Sufi teachers allowed for a gradual Islamization of societies. Distinctively 'local' modes of Muslim identity developed through the incorporation of local practices into the framework of 'Islamic practices'. In this way it becomes possible to define, for example, a contrast between 'Islam in Africa' and 'African Islam'. Introducing a wide-ranging volume of essays on this topic, Rosander (1997: 1) distinguished clearly:

When speaking about 'African Islam' we refer to the 'contextualized' or '*localized*' forms which are found particularly in Sufi contexts. African Islam has frequently been depicted as culturally as well as religiously flexible and accommodating. The expression 'Islam in Africa', we use to designate Islamist tendencies, which could also be called reformist/activist tendencies. Their aims are to 'purify' African Islam from *local* or indigenous African ideas and practices as well as from Western influences [emphasis added].

'Local' Islam with its distinctive practices is the target of modernizing reformers and Islamist puritans alike. A contrast is made between 'local' and 'global' Islam, with the Sufi brotherhoods seen as playing a critical role in creating and maintaining the local. In general, local and parochial identities and interests were defined in modernization theory as being destined to disappear in the broader identities of 'nation' or even more cosmopolitan structures of 'mass society'.

It is, of course, undeniable that distinctive local Muslim identities exist and that Sufi teachers and associations have played an important role in shaping those identities. Scholars speak of 'African Islam', 'Malaysian Islam', and many other similarly distinctive Muslim local cultural identities. The distinction between this 'local Islam' with its recognizable continuities with pre-Islamic customs and culture and 'global Islam' can be made forcefully.

In an earlier work (Voll, 1994), I explained how global Islam has been described as a distinctive world-system. Richard Eaton (1990: 43) characterized it as:

> a world system linking men and women through informal networks of scholars and saints, built upon shared understandings of how to see the world and structure one's relationship to it. Above all, it was a world system constructed around a book, the Qur'an, and of humanity's attempt to respond to its message, by fulfilling both its external project of building a righteous social order and its internal project for drawing humans nearer to their maker.

This broad sense of a universal message and a global community identity was spread by itinerant scholars and religious teachers and was (and is) the 'global Islam' that is contrasted to 'local Islam'.

Donald Wright's study of the interaction of global and local elements in Niumi, a 'very small place in [West] Africa', provides important insights into this global–local interaction. Wright notes that this global Islam was brought to West Africa by travelling shaykhs and scholars and that West African Muslims came to see themselves as:

> part of a vast community, an *intellectual* world system stretching across the desert they knew and into lands they could barely imagine, held together by scholars and saints and mystics and jurists and common folk all praying toward the same central shrine and living by the same law, parts of which they memorized in the same language. For this world system, economic unity was a factor, but not the major one. Perhaps it was spiritual unity as much as anything that tied together peoples of the Muslim realm across the Afro-Eurasian landmass. (Wright, 1997: 19-20)

A similar sense of the coming of global Islam and transforming local identities is presented in Richard Eaton's analysis of the Islamization of Bengal. He identifies 'three analytically distinct aspects to the process, each referring to a different relationship between Islamic and Indian superhuman agencies' (Eaton, 1993: 269). His description of the three parts of the process helps to define the more general global–local relations in the processes of conversion in many parts of the Muslim world:

> By *inclusion* is meant the process by which Islamic superhuman agencies became accepted by local Bengali cosmologies alongside local divinities already embedded therein. By *identification* is meant the process by which Islamic superhuman agencies ceased merely to coexist alongside Bengali

agencies, but actually merged with them ... And finally, by *displacement* is meant the process by which the names of Islamic superhuman agencies replaced those of other divinities in local cosmologies. (Eaton, 1993: 269)

In both Niumi and Bengal, there is a valid distinction between the local base and the global Islamic world system that comes to the locality. However, as both Eaton and Wright make clear in discussing the long-term processes of change involved in Islamization, very rapidly 'Islam' becomes an important part of what might be considered 'local'. This situation is common throughout the Muslim world. Muslim reforming teachers and modern scholars might view the product of 'inclusion' and 'identification' in terms similar to those used by 'the Maghribi elite and French scholars' to describe some of the popular Sufi orders in North Africa: 'They are said to be "corrupted by the base imagination of *le peuple*, by survivals from the ancient religions of the circum-Mediterranean culture area, and by pagan influences from sub-Saharan Africa"' (Rosander, 1997: 4, quoting Crapanzano, 1973: 1). However, relatively rapidly, whatever puritanical elite scholars might think, the self-identification of the adherents of this popular Islamic faith was that they were 'Muslim'. This identification needs to be considered legitimate in that it is no longer the purely 'local' base of the starting point. It has been shaped indelibly by global Islam and cannot be understood without reference in some way to that global dimension. This creates something of a paradox since in some ways, the global *is* the local, at least in part.

A symmetrically similar possible paradox is created by the contemporary conditions of globalization. Muslims are part of the major global migrations that have taken place in the modern era. In the past, common patterns of immigrant behaviour involved assimilation of migrants into the cultures of the host societies. However, these patterns are being changed. Frequently, migration does not mean absorption of the migrants into a controlling homogeneous culture. Instead, global movements of people create increasingly culturally heterogeneous societies resulting from globalization. In this, the migrant groups are not simply maintaining old homeland identities in new places, but over time create distinctive identities that are an important part of the very processes of globalization themselves. Just as 'the global' increasingly appears as a part of the local, 'local' particularities are a necessary part of the emerging global.

Sufi orders help to illustrate this heterogeneous global condition. The global extension of the Mouride brotherhood provides a good example. Mouridism continues to be a special and particular identity but its communal life in places like New York is a part of patterns of globalization and helps to define the processes of the continuing globalization of New York City.

The old conceptualization of the *tariqa*s as the core of local particularist tradition as it interacts with a 'global' universalist Islam does not provide much assistance in examining the current global–local, universal–particular dimensions of *tariqa* life. Scholars like Eaton have already moved beyond the old-fashioned dichotomy distinguishing the popular folk Islam of the illiterate and rural peoples and the 'pure' Islam of the urban scholars in analysis of pre-modern societies. However, in the contemporary world, analysts sometimes continue the old particular–universal contrast within the context of current modes of globalization. Many see a sharp polarity between particularist 'jihad' modes and a 'McWorld', with 'jihad' representing the belligerent particularism emphasizing distinctive 'local' identities and McWorld representing those globalizing forces 'pressing nations into one homogeneous global theme park, one McWorld tied together by communications, information, entertainment, and commerce' (Barber, 1996: 4).

In the context of globalization, religion is viewed as an important support for particularist jihad. In more formal terms, Peter Beyer (1994: 108) speaks of the 'historical affinity of religion to socio-cultural particularisms', and religion as 'an important resource' for activist movements of particularism. Such religious movements 'often display the conservative option with its typical stress on the relativizing forces of globalization as prime manifestations of evil in the world' (Beyer, 1994: 108). In an analysis of Islamic developments in Western Europe, Olivier Roy examines the nature of globalization experiences on Muslims in Europe. He distinguishes between 'diasporic' Islam in which Muslim immigrants maintain a sense of identity with their countries of origin and 'universal' Islam which 'is defined in essence by European Muslims' identification with a universal *umma*, or community of the faithful' (Roy, 2003: 63). In this line of analysis, 'universal' Islam is in fact exclusivist and particularist in its vision and is the source of recruits for the jihad mode in the contemporary world. The contrast remains between the militant particularist and a more homogenizing mode of integration into European society as a kind of 'Muslim church' (Roy, 2003: 63).

Sufi movements and associations in the contemporary world frequently do not fit comfortably in this new analytical dichotomy, any more than they fit into the old rural–urban, local–global polarities of analysts. Global and local, the particular and the universal, are combined in important ways and are complementary rather than contradictory elements. Many of the chapters in this volume provide important examples of the complementary interaction of global and local. Pnina Werbner's affirmation of the need to understand the combination of 'localism' and 'transnationalism' as critical to understanding Sufism as a global movement provides an important frame. Leonardo Villalón notes the impact of the experience of Senegalese Murids who have been part of the global diaspora in adapting the Murid Sufi model. The new modes of 'Sufi spirituality' among middle- and upper-class cosmopolitan Muslims in Indonesia, as Julia Howell discusses, are clearly part of a synthesis of global and local that transcends the jihad/McWorld categories. Similarly, the 'living saints' in Indonesia described by Martin van Bruinessen combine cosmopolitan 'global' perspectives with distinctive 'local' identities. A similar synthesis of global and local can be seen in the development of the activities of the Tablighi Jama'at, as Yoginder Sikand describes. This double dimension of global and local is explicit in the processes Werbner describes, by which British-based Sufi groups construct national and international networks that connect towns and cities in Britain and Pakistan.

In considering these and many other movements and contexts, the need for a conceptual framework that recognizes the interconnections between 'global' and 'local' becomes clear. Such a framework could provide interesting and useful ways of examining the nature of contemporary *tariqa*s and their relationships to global and local developments. Contributions from scholars like Roland Robertson are changing theoretical understandings of the processes of globalization and modernization in more general terms that provide ways of analysing the continuing development of *tariqa*s in the contemporary world.

These new frameworks do not define 'globalization' as a single, linear phenomenon. Instead they recognize many different globalizations taking place simultaneously such that one might even speak, as does Hoffmann (2002), of a 'clash of globalizations'. In this context, 'McWorld' is increasingly heterogeneous, and one of the distinguishing characteristics of contemporary globality is its diversity based on the shaping of what is thought to be global by what is local. As Eisenstadt (2000) argues, rather than a uniform, homogeneous and global modernity emerging by the end of the twentieth century, 'multiple modernities' have emerged. Robertson (1995) uses the term 'glocalization' for the interacting syntheses of 'global' and 'local'.

The concept of 'glocalization' opens the way for setting analyses of contemporary Sufism in a framework that goes beyond the old polarities conceptualizing the *tariqa*s as manifestations of 'the local' in tension with cosmopolitan 'pure' Islam of the global. It relates, for example, to the context in Senegal where, as Leo Villalón notes in this volume, the Sufi orders have engaged in debates and discussions with representatives of new forms of 'reformist' and 'arabizing' Islam. Here debates about what it means to be 'Muslim', 'African' and 'Modern' have blurred these distinctions and produced new and hybrid forms of religious modernity, rooted deeply in Sufism but borrowing from other elements of the Islamic tradition. One can also see glocalization as an important part of the distinctively Indonesian modes of Islamic resurgence and cosmopolitan Sufism that Howell analyses in her chapter. Similarly, the 'living saints' who van Bruinessen notes and the 'saints' of Neo-liberal Mali who Benjamin Soares discusses are operating in 'glocal' contexts.

The global–local framework has been used most frequently in studies of politically activist and protest groups, yet *tariqa*s reflect many of the same experiences. Saskia Sassen's descriptions of such activist groups resonates with the current characteristics of at least some dimensions of Muslim spirituality as expressed in *tariqa*s, as this example indicates:

> The fact that the network is global does not mean that everything has to happen at the global level. This is not the cosmopolitan route to the global. This is about the global as the multiplication of the local ... The individuals and groups involved do not have to become cosmopolitan in the process; they may well remain domestic or local in their orientation, engaged with their households and local community struggles. And yet, they may experience themselves as participants in emergent forms of globality, or, more concretely, in specific global social circuits. (Sassen, 2002-03: 19)

*Tariqa*s and Sufism have long been vehicles for bringing together the particular and the universal into an effective synthesis of religious experiences. Conceptualizations that emphasize the 'local' nature of *tariqa*s and set that in tension with the 'global' provide an inadequate framework for analysis of *tariqa*s in the contemporary world and historically. The concept of 'glocalization' developed by Robertson and others provides a way of going beyond the limits of the old theories of popular local religion and Sufism, and so enable more accurate analysis in an increasingly globalized human community.

Contemporary Sufism and Postmaterialism

Contemporary Sufism and *tariqa*s are frequently viewed within the conceptual framework of the continuities and contrasts of 'pre-modern' and 'modern' modes of religious institutions and experiences. The late twentieth century 'resurgence of Islam' is regularly described as a response by Muslims to 'modernity'. Discussions of the pluralism of the modern world with its 'multiple modernities' also tend to remain within the framework of this pre-modern ('traditional')–modern polarity.

There is, however, significant recognition that what has come to be considered 'modernity' represents a phase in human history with distinctive characteristics. Although the term 'modern' continues to retain elements of the definition casting 'modern' as whatever was current, as opposed to the past, 'modernity' and 'modernization' assume content that involves specific characteristics. As King (1995: 110) noted, the referent for this meaning is 'the Enlightenment project in Europe, with its emphasis on rationality, order, the state, control and the belief in progress'. As early as the 1960s, some observers and scholars argued that the era of that particular package of elements that comprised 'modernity' was passing. Peter Drucker (1965: xi-xiii) claimed:

> At some unmarked point during the past twenty years we imperceptibly moved out of the Modern Age and into a new, as yet nameless, era. Our

view of the world changed ... There is a new spiritual center to human existence .... [There has been a] philosophical shift from the Cartesian universe of mechanical cause to the new universe of pattern, purpose and process.

Twenty-five years later in his study of the 'hidden agenda' of modernity, Stephen Toulmin (1990: 20) noted, 'It is unrealistic as things stand to imagine a future that preserves the hallmarks of Modernity: the intellectual autonomy of distinct sciences, a confident reliance on self-justifying technologies, and separate independent nation-states with unqualified sovereignty'. This new phase is regularly identified by terminology that emphasizes what it is not, that is, by using the prefix 'post-'. The most common identification speaks of the contemporary phase as 'post-modern'. In this framework, the term 'post-modern' is not concerned, at least directly, with the issues of literary and analytical criticism that have created much controversy. Rather, it identifies simply the current historical phase which has moved away from the particular package of characteristics that have come to be identified with 'modernity'.

The role of religion in this post-modern era is significantly different from the role set for it within 'modernity'. Major religious institutions and perspectives are changing as the post-modern contexts within which they exist also change. It is useful to ask about the place of *tariqa*s in the post-modern context. Scholars developing social movement theory suggest frameworks for this consideration, although these theorists have not themselves addressed the question of 'post-modern *tariqa*s'. However, the 'new Sufis' who Benjamin Soares discusses in this volume provide possibly significant examples of the distinctive styles of Sufism emerging by the early twenty-first century. These 'new Sufis' reflect the dynamics of societies that may have continuities with the past but are clearly different from the formats that developed in modern colonial societies and the political systems that developed in many parts of the Muslim world following achievement of independence. The post-colonial New Sufis of Mali illustrate new modes of entrepreneurial religious marketing and concepts of religious synthesis that are distinctive to the current era. Similarly, the new approaches of the Budshishiyya in Morocco, which Raphaël Voix and Patrick Haenni analyze in this volume, show the new modes of conceptual synthesis and popular organization that are an important part of Muslim life in the Maghrib.

Scholars suggest that the nature of major social movements has changed significantly in the past 50 years, and the changes help to define the nature of what can be thought of as 'post modern' movements. The new social movements that began to emerge in the 1960s involved issues different from those that mobilized people in earlier industrial modern society. The older issues that defined the nature of social movements involved conflict over distribution of material goods. Jurgen Habermas (1981: 33) asserted that in the new social movements the question 'is not one of compensations that the welfare state can provide. Rather, the question is how to defend or reinstate endangered lifestyles, or how to put reformed lifestyles into practice. In short, the new conflicts are not sparked by *problems of distribution*, but concern the *grammar of forms of life*. Articulation of this 'grammar' is fundamentally a religious project and the transition from 'modern' to 'post-modern' issues is an important dimension in the 'religious resurgence' of the late twentieth century.

One important dimension of this transition in the nature of social movements is a changing sense of values, especially the rise of 'postmaterialism'. Ronald Inglehart (1990: 45) articulated the perspective of various observers that 'postmaterialist values underlie many of the new social movements'. This contrasts with important aspects of value priorities in modern industrial societies. Thus he noted:

> Postmaterialists emphasize fundamentally different value priorities from those that have dominated industrial society for many decades ... In the takeoff phase of industrial revolution, economic growth was the central problem. The postmaterialists who have become increasingly numerous in recent decades place less emphasis on economic growth and more emphasis on the non-economic quality of life ... It is not that the postmaterialists reject the fruits of prosperity – but simply that their value priorities are less strongly dominated by the imperatives that were central to early industrial society. (Inglehart, 1990: 45)

In this context of 'postmodernization' that is seen as replacing modernization, Inglehart (1990: 324) pointed to the development of a new paradigm, claiming that, 'A new worldview is gradually replacing the paradigm that has dominated industrializing societies since the Industrial Revolution. It reflects a shift in what people want out of life. It is transforming basic norms governing politics, work, religion, family, and sexual behaviour'.

Although religious dimensions of the emergence of the postmodern are very significant, old-style modes of religious operation are not necessarily being restored. The most visible movements of religious resurgence at the end of the twentieth century were 'fundamentalist' and relatively radical in their rejection of the old-style religious establishments and institutions. Inglehart (1990: 328) observed in the findings of a major international survey that confidence in the old institutions of 'organized religion' may be declining but 'spiritual concerns are not vanishing: on the contrary, we find a consistent cross-national tendency for people to spend *more* time thinking about the meaning and purpose of life'. Although much of the research on postmodernism/postmaterialism has examined long industrialized societies, the concerns identified are fully global. As Robertson and Chirico (1985: 239) observed:

> The globalization process itself raises religious and quasi-religious questions ... Religion is centred in the process of globalization by virtue of both the religious or quasi-religious matters raised as a result of universalistic tendencies involving mankind and relations between societies *and* by the particularizing responses to the universalistic tendencies.

Using this analysis of the emergence of postmaterialism as the lens for examining the nature of some *tariqa*s in the contemporary world, rather than the old 'traditional–modern' analytical framework, we find that at least some *tariqa*s are better understood as manifestations of postmodernism and postmaterialism. Possibly the most visible postmaterialism style of Sufism is the New Age Sufism that began to draw a significant following in the United States and Western Europe in the 1960s. These movements have some important roots in the International Sufi Movement, as Celia Genn discusses in this volume, although there are many distinctive trends within this Western Sufism. For many urban middle-class professionals as well as those seeking alternative lifestyles, a major part of the appeal of Western Sufism is the provision of resources for spiritualist escape from materialist society.[8]

The analytical framework developed by Inglehart and others places new movements in the historical context of the postmodern and postmaterialist era. Using this framework in the study of contemporary *tariqa*s would not necessarily change particular analytical descriptions of those groups. However, it offers the possibility of providing a broader global context for comparison. Postmodern *tariqa*s are distinctive but they also can be seen as part of broader global patterns of adaptation to conditions in which the agenda of modernity is no longer as dominant as it was in the earlier era of modernization. The postmaterialist hypothesis offers a way of moving beyond the old framework that identified *tariqa*s as part of the 'pre-modern' that was interacting with modernity.

Conclusion

Many of the old analytical frameworks used to understand Sufi orders and the roles they played in society are still very influential and have some utility. However, long established stereotypes of the orders as being basically the vehicles for expressing rural superstitious piety are not useful for trying to understand *tariqa*s and their place in the modern and contemporary worlds. It may be 'hard to be a saint in the city', but saints and brotherhoods thrive in contemporary urban society.

The continuing vitality of Sufism and *tariqa*s contradicts the older Orientalist stereotypes and traditional anthropological descriptions. This dynamism also represents a contradiction of the important axiom of old-style modernization theory that saw secularization as an inherent part of the processes of modernization. Broadly recognizing the failure of secularization theory enables recognition of a *modern* resurgence of religion that is more than simply a residual pre-modern resistance to modernization.

It is important for scholars dealing with the place of Sufism and *tariqa*s in the modern and contemporary world to be self-conscious in analyzing the theoretical frameworks and assumptions that underlie contemporary research. Some new theoretical approaches in the social sciences and humanities can provide assistance. The three general areas of study outlined above provide examples of how such theory can assist the study of *tariqa*s.

To summarize, first, there is a broad transition within Sufi movements from being the core of old-fashioned popular Islam to being important vehicles for the expression of new styles of popular or mass Islam in the context of modern and modernizing societies. Why the *tariqa* format continues is an important question and some aspects of social movement theory provide useful suggestions for the answer. From this theoretical perspective, it is not surprising that the *tariqa*-style organization would be an effective framework for new modes of religious expression since it is an important part of the institutional repertoire of Muslim societies and could be expected to be more effective than an unfamiliar mode of organization.

Second, the relationship between 'global' and 'local' is important in defining and shaping the nature and dynamism of *tariqa*s. Sometimes the global and the local are in tension but often they are complementary. Robertson's suggestion that processes of *glocalization* are of great significance in the contemporary world provides a useful framework for exploring the continuing dynamism of *tariqa* structures.

A third area where new theoretical perspectives can be helpful comes with recognition that some important aspects of contemporary society and religious life are postmodern in nature and postmaterialist in defining value priorities. Such a framework helps scholars of contemporary Sufism go beyond the old dichotomy of 'modern' and 'traditional', recognizing that some modes of Sufism are neither 'traditional' nor 'modern'.

New studies employing these three theoretical frameworks will not necessarily refute conclusions reached in earlier studies of modern and contemporary *tariqa*s. However, the new frameworks can provide the impetus and the conceptual tools for better understanding *tariqa*s within contemporary global patterns of societal and religious development.

Acknowledgement

I express my gratitude for insights from the conference in Bogor, Indonesia, in 2003 – through conference discussions, paper abstracts and what are now chapters in this volume. In this Conclusion, I note specific chapters, although it will be clear to readers that the full written piece is informed by the work of all conference participants, to whom I am grateful.

NOTES

Chapter One

1 We use the term 'Islamist' to denote those Islamic movements that have an explicit political agenda for the transformation of society and/or state based on the implementation of some version of Islamic law, and 'neo-fundamentalist' for those movements that strive to purge religious beliefs and practices of all that is not based on the Qur'an or the example of the Prophet. These categories are not mutually exclusive. Many neo-fundamentalist movements call themselves 'Salafi', a term that indicates that they emulate the example of the 'pious predecessors' (*al-salaf al-salih*), the first two or three generations of followers of the Prophet.

Chapter Two

1 In France, scholars affiliated with the École des Hautes Études en Sciences Sociales have, from the 1980s, published a series of edited volumes on the history and present situation of the *tariqa* in the modern world: Popovic and Veinstein (1986, 1996); Gaborieau, Popovic and Zarcone (1990).
2 This approach was developed in my book-length study of Egyptian *tariqa*, Chih (2000a).
3 In an insightful study of the 'prophetic model' of the spiritual master, Denis Gril (2002) has analyzed the references in the Qur'an and *hadith* on which Sufis base their conception of the spiritual master. This article echoes an earlier statement by Michel Chodkiewicz (1996).
4 Among contemporary Egyptian Sufis, the term *khidma* refers to the place (a tent, an apartment, or even just the corridor of a house) where the members of a *tariqa* or the adherents of a saint perform their *dhikr* and serve tea and food during a *mawlid*.
5 Gilsenan (1973); De Jong (1983) and Luizard (1991) largely follow the analysis of De Jong.
6 Besides the studies of Gilsenan and De Jong mentioned above, there are three relevant studies by Pierre-Jean Luizard (1990, 1991, 1992).
7 For a typology of models of sainthood in medieval Morocco, see the conclusions of the subtle study by Cornell (1998).

Chapter Three

1 Smith (1957: 162).
2 Quoted in M. Kara (1985: 988).

3   In the later Empire, the major orders in the central Ottoman lands of Anatolia and the Balkans were (besides the heterodox Malamiyya and Bektashiyye) Khalwatiyya, Qadiriyya, Mevleviyye, Naqshbandiyya and Rufa`iyya.
4   For an overview of the official and unofficial statuses of Sufi orders in contemporary Turkey, as well as a review of the literature on the topic, see Raudvere (2002).
5   On debates in Islamist scholarship in contemporary Turkey, see Silverstein (2005).
6   This is not to deny that old genealogies are frequently claimed for practices that are in fact of recent vintage (often in the context of modern nationalisms), and Asad readily admits this. See the essays in Hobsbawm and Ranger (1983). However, this does not mean that a definition of traditions as inventions is adequate.
7   By 'politics of continuity' I do not mean to impute cynical intentions, nor, to be sure, is this a reference to 'inventions'. The term refers to that dimension of power in all traditions, which Arendt (1968) defined specifically as 'authority'.
8   On the career of modern techniques of governance in Turkey, see the recent ethnography of the Turkish state by Navaro-Yashin (2002).
9   Gümüşhanevi (d. 1311/1893) is a luminary in the *cemaat*'s *silsila* and was a major Islamic scholarly personality of the Ottoman nineteenth century. See Gündüz (1984).
10 The state of the art in Turkish historiography has converged on this point, and has come to emphasize the continuities from particularly the Second Constitutional period starting in 1908 into the early Republic; see Zürcher (1994). This perspective has been elided meticulously by the vast majority of works on Islamist historiography in Turkey, according to which much of Republican history is indeed a story of alienation (Silverstein, 2005). See the revisionist work by I. Kara (2001).
11 Schimmel (1975: 366) defines sohbet as 'intimate conversation between master and disciple conducted on a very high spiritual level'.
12 Several good histories of the Khalidi sub-order are available; see especially the essays in Gaborieau et al. (1990); Algar (1990) and Hourani (1981). On Naqshbandis in Republican Turkey see also Mardin (1991).
13 Coşan was born in 1938 in Çanakkale and raised in Istanbul in an observant family of Naqshbandis. He graduated from the Faculty of Arabic and Persian Literature at Istanbul University, moving to Ankara University's Faculty of Theology in 1960, where he completed his doctorate in 1965, became docent in 1973, professor in 1982, and retired in 1987. He married Kotku's daughter, and succeeded him upon Kotku's passing in 1980. Coşan's two daughters studied in Turkey, while his son studied business in the United States. See Çakır (1990) and Yavuz (1999). Some community members have reportedly transferred their allegiance to Esad's son, Nureddin.
14 Until very recently the *hadith*s were read from Ahmed Ziyaüddin Gümüşhanevi's concordance, *Ramuz el-Ehadith*, compiled from the six authoritative collections and published in 1858. The *Ramuz* became a kind of handbook for the Gümüşhanevi branches of the Naqshbandi order in Anatolia and the Balkans, and is known to have been the basis of *sohbet* lessons in the main Gümüşhanevi Naqshbandi lodge in Istanbul up until the closure of the lodges in 1925. However as of summer 2006 and reportedly at the suggestion of Nureddin, some of the *cemaat* has taken the significant step of abandoning *Ramuz* in favour of the six '*sahih*' collections that 'all Muslims agree upon' (as I was told), admitting that a very few of the hadith in the *Ramuz* were disputed as 'weak'.
15 The *dhikr* was commonly 100 *Istighfar*, 100 *Kelime-i Tevhid*, 100 *Lafza-ı Celal* ('Allah'), 100 *Salavat-ı Şerife* and '*Allahumme sally wa Allahumme Barik*' followed by 100 *Sura al-Ikhlas*, and sometimes 100 *Sura al-Inshira*. See Algar's (1976) discussion of Naqshbandi *dhikr* and its relative 'sobriety' in comparison with its function in other orders (e.g. its role in their inducement of certain types of 'ecstatic' states). Also see his description of Naqshbandi *dhikr*s in Bosnia in the early 1970s in Algar (1971).

16 Religious minorities like Armenian and Greek Christian and Jewish communities are also referred to as *cemaat*s.
17 The sense of *terbiye* as synonymous with (and a translation of) the French and English 'education' was an innovation of the nineteenth century (Mitchell, 1991: 87-9). In the later decades of the nineteenth century, Redhouse (1996 [1890]) recorded several senses in the Turkish-speaking parts of the Empire, in order: rearing, nursing, training or educating, hence culture, good manners, good breeding; a correcting, chastising, admonition; regulating or improving by the use of chemical or other agents, including seasoning for food; bringing up or training; correcting or punishing. Sufis use '*terbiye*' in the older sense of 'breeding' and 'cultivating' through correction (as in tying a growing plant to influence its formation). The term is now synonymous with education and training in the Arab world, but in Turkey it is falling out of use with regard to education, and tends to be increasingly associated with parents' upbringing of children.
18 The *silsila* of this order's shaykhs is given in Appendix B to Özal (1999).
19 For a discussion of debates about ethical, epistemological and political issues surrounding contemporary relationships to past precedent among Muslim scholars in Turkey, see Silverstein (2005).
20 See Abu-Manneh (1990). Mevlana Khalid was not from Baghdad, and did not even spend much time there. He was a Kurd from Shahrazur, eventually settling in Damascus, where, as of the author's visits in 1997 and 1999, his tomb continued to attract visitors and an attached lodge (*tekke*) hosts *dhikr*.
21 On the various shadings of love in Sufi practice, see Schimmel (1975).
22 The notion of presence here contrasts with that which Derrida (1973) identified as characteristic of Western metaphysics, whereby meaning and knowledge have been idealized as the presence of a pure origin to an identical meaning.
23 On women's experiences of Sufism in a different order in contemporary Turkey, see Raudvere (2002).
24 Cf. Bourdieu (1990: 54), who wrote, '(T)he structures characterizing a determinate class of conditions of existence produce the structures of the *habitus*, which in their turn are the basis of the perception and appreciation of all subsequent experiences'.
25 On the social, political, economic and architectural aspects of the *tekke* and *zaviye* in the later Empire, see the essays in Lifchez (1992).
26 In 1882 and 1890, there were 260 and 305 *tekke*s respectively in Istanbul, of which 52 and 65 were Naqshbandi (Karpat, 2001: 107). Kreiser (1992: 49) estimated that between 60 and 85 per cent of these were continuously occupied.
27 On debates about the status of the orders and of Islamic institutions and personnel associated with them, during what ended up being the closing years of the Empire through the War of Independence and into the Republic, see Jäschke (1972) and İ. Kara (1997, vol. 2).
28 M. Kara (1980: 322-9).
29 For the text of Law 677, see M. Kara (2002: 151).
30 I heard this expression on numerous occasions.
31 The recent work of Mustafa Kara and his students has been important in this regard, as has the work of İsmail Kara. See, for example, M. Kara (2001) and the essays in İ. Kara (1998).
32 For a summary of these views and source materials see M. Kara (2002).
33 Accounts of Republican era *sohbet*s prior to those of Mehmed Zahid Kotku are few. In addition to the references cited here, see Gürdoğan (1996: 34-6) and M. Kara (2002: 262).
34 Interestingly, Schimmel (1975: 366) writes of a Naqshbandi-affiliated journal called *Sohbet Dergisi*, published in Istanbul in 1952-53.
35 Karpat (2000: xvi) estimates that between 40 and 50 per cent of the population of today's Turkey is of Balkan, Caucasian or Crimean ancestry. With intermarriage of the

302   SUFISM AND THE 'MODERN' IN ISLAM

     immigrants with local Kurds less common than marriage with other groups, it is likely that a very high percentage of Turks of non-Kurdish origin have ancestry in these regions.
36 Arms and financing for Kosovar Albanians were certainly being organized quietly by Albanian diaspora around the world, including in Istanbul (where I met an Albanian–American allegedly doing just that). But the Turkish authorities had committed themselves to coordinating their responses through NATO, and such material support was done discretely in Turkey. Emotional ties to Kosovo and the rest of the Balkans run high in Turkey, however, and the Turkish authorities flew in several thousand Kosovar Albanian families to temporarily shelter them in camps set up by the military near Kırklareli, in Thrace.
37 It is also through foundations that religious minorities such as Armenian and Greek Christians and Jews are to provide for the administration of their communities' facilities, such as houses of worship, schools, lands and archives. Again, the importance of regulations on foundations can hardly be overstated, and indeed the liberalization of such regulations is a part of the reforms being undertaken by authorities in line with EU accession protocols.
38 On foundations and associations in the corporate life of Naqshbandis in Turkey see Yavuz (2003: 133-50); on observant, non-Sufi communities in Turkey see White (2002: 178-211).
39 An interesting account of this period and how it was experienced by sympathizers of the orders is given in Zarcone (1993).
40 See the extremely important collection of writings by prominent Islamist intellectuals from this period in the two volumes of I. Kara (1997).
41 See the description of the experiences of this period by Turks of various persuasions in Navaro-Yashin (2002).
42 In January 2001, retired general and former secretary of the Joint Chiefs of Staff, Erol Özkasnak, referred to *28 Şubat* as a 'post-modern coup'. *Radikal*, 15 January 2001. See also useful discussion of the period in Raudvere (2002).

Chapter Four

1 The best overviews of available information on the Khaksar are given in Gramlich's three-volume study of the Shi'i orders (1965, 1976, 1981) and in Chahardahi (1361/1982-3).
2 A Sufi rebellion in Qum in February 2006 seems to mark the advent of a new era in relations between Sufis, clerics and the state. In a move unprecedented in the Islamic Republic and even under the Pahlavi dynasty, hundreds of Sufis from all over Iran, of diverse ethnic background, rushed to help besieged fellow dervishes of the Sultan`alishahi order resisting expropriation of the order's religious centre in Qum by state authorities. The protests met violence – deaths and hundreds of wounded, and the deliberate destruction of properties including the contested religious centre and the local sheikh's house in Qum. Information on the troubles in Qum and elsewhere in Iran can be found on the order's website http://www.icchome.org/main/hosseinieh.aspx (accessed 17 February 2006). Since Mahmud Ahmadinejad replaced Khatami as president in June 2005, Iranian Sufis have had to bear an intensified onslaught on Sufi mysticism, the order reports. This came to the fore ideologically through anti-Sufi articles in leading newspapers such as *Kayhan* and *Jumhuri-yi Islami* and strong anti-Sufi statements made publicly by clerics such as Grand Ayatullah Husayn Nuri-Hamadani, and materially through assaults by vigilantes and state officials on the order's religious centres in several cities.
3 This perspective is particularly evident in Zarrinkoob (1970) and Zarrinkub (1369/1990). This author is highly respected in Sufi circles in Iran.
4 The magazines involved included *Vahid* and *Mehr*.

5 An example of such criticism is the anonymous tract, *Pasukhi bi intibah-nama-yi hay'at-i mushawara-yi anjuman-i ukhuwwat*, (1333/1954), which targets the innovative Sufism of leaders of the Brotherhood Society.
6 These relations with Khomeini are documented in Parishanzada (1377/1998: 67-7) and Madani (1376/1997: 162-3).
7 This common spiritual ancestry is explained in Tanha'i (1379/2000: 232, 324) and in further correspondence with the author, 8 March 2004.
8 Correspondence Office of *ayatullah al-`uzma* Makarim-Shirazi, 22 September 1997.
9 Correspondence Office of *ayatullah al-`uzma* Musavi-Ardabili, 23 August 1997.
10 Examples of this genre are Madani (1376/1997) and Salih`alishah (1375/1996).
11 For the Safi'alishahi order, see Chahardahi (1361/1982-3: 182).
12 Cf. last paragraph of Ashghal-e husayniyya-yi darawish-i Gunabadi dar Qum tawassut-i idara-yi ittila`at-i Qum, through the 'juz'iyyat' link on http://www.icchome.org/main/hosseinieh.aspx.
13 For just one explicit example of this praise of Rumi's Sufism, see Surush (1378/1999); on Soroush's critique of institutionalized Sufism, see Matin-Asgari (1997: 103).
14 Interview with a Sultan'alishahi shaykh, 16 August 2001.
15 Although it probably had nothing to do with its Sufism, the last major publicity surrounding the Safi`alishahi order concerned an *anti*-regime event. Ansar-i Hizbullah militants violently disturbed the mourning ceremony that was held on the property of Safi`alishah's grave in Tehran in November 2002 in remembrance of the political murders of Daryush Furuhar and his wife. See Ahmadi (1381/2002).
16 The tension or conflict between the religious and the political that is the second element of Roy's definition of post-Islamism is less apparent in the case of the Sufi orders, but it is clearly present in developments in the relations between Shi`i religiosity in society (notably the 'new religious thought') and the state doctrine of *wilayat-i faqih*.
17 Interview with author, 26 August 2001.
18 The Freedom Movement was created by a group of intellectuals, among whom was Mehdi Bazargan, the Islamic Republic's first prime minister. Its members were influential in the government immediately after the revolution but were subsequently sidelined by hardliners. Khomeini banned the movement shortly before his death, but it retains a presence in Iran as an intellectual force.
19 I wish to thank Husayn Abu'l-Hasan Tanha'i for providing me with copies of his work and answering my queries.
20 Earlier Sultan`alishahi formulations are discussed in van den Bos (2002b: 198-201). A later article, van den Bos (2002c), discusses other Sufi conceptions of *walayat*.
21 Letter from Tanha'i to the author, 8 March 2004.
22 While Durkheim's initial formulation of the social has by now become obsolete, it did define an exclusive social object and as a result provided historical legitimacy for sociology as a science. It may still be invoked to that end. Durkheim's *fait social* refers to a *sui generis* class of facts, which are both coercive and external to the individual (Lukes, 1982: 52; Tabataba'i 1379 [1374]). The *fait social* concerns 'ways of acting, thinking and feeling, exterior to the individual, which are invested with a coercive power, and which impose themselves upon him' ('*des manières d'agir, de penser et de sentir, extérieures à l'individu, et qui sont douées d'un pouvoir de coercition qui s'imposent à lui*' (Durkheim, 1977: 5).

Chapter Five

1 See, e.g., Brenner (1993) on Mali; Coulon (1988) on Senegal; Loimeier (1997) on Nigeria; Hiskett (1984) on West Africa; and Triaud and Robinson (2000) on the Tijaniyya; cf. Launay (1992) on Côte d'Ivoire.
2 See, for example, Babou (2002); Diouf (2000); Perry (1997); and Riccio (2004).

3   Each of the major leaders of the Sufi orders has representatives and deputies based in Bamako. Some of the sons and grandsons of prominent heads of Sufi orders/leaders are also based in the Malian capital.
4   For a broader discussion of Islam in contemporary Mali, see Soares (2005, 2006).
5   On Muhammad Taqiyyu Allah (b. 1878), the son of Muhammed Abd Allah (d. 1905), see Marty (1921: 301ff). Numerous references to him appear in the colonial archives from the 1920s when colonial authorities first identified him as a prominent Muslim religious leader. Although informants have told me Muhammad Taqiyyu Allah died during the colonial period, I have been unable to determine the year of his death.
6   See, for example, Pazo (2000).
7   ww.cheicksoufibilal.com
8   Although Iranians have a presence in Mali, Bilal has no relation with the Bilal Muslim Mission, the Iranian organization, which seeks to attract Africans to the Shia.
9   See the list of his six publications in the bibliography.
10 Cheikh Ahmad Tall has even provided a preface to Bilal's latest publication (as of, 2005) in which he praises Bilal as a 'saint of the twenty-first century'. See Bilal (n.d. 6).
11 For a list of some of these texts from the region, see Hunwick (2003).
12 Zahan's (1960) study of these societies indicates that they were all present in Adama's village and the surrounding areas when Zahan conducted his research in the 1950s, shortly before Adama was born.
13 On Sékou Salah Siby's colonial-era career, see Soares (2004a).
14 For coverage of Daouda Yattara in the print media, see, for example, Sangho (2002); Traoré (2002); and Guindo (2003).
15 As recent research on Pentecostals in Africa has shown [e.g., Hackett (2003); Meyer (1998); and van Dijk (1998)], this association with 'traditional' African religion would be completely anathema to most African Pentecostals.

Chapter Six

1   For an interesting and perceptive description of one of these local conflicts involving one of the most outspokenly anti-Islamic *abangan* movements see Geertz (1959). The case described there suggests a number of reasons of why social change has worked in favour of orthodox Islam and against syncretistic beliefs and practices.
2   In his book on the early New Order, Australian journalist Hamish McDonald gave a fascinating account of Suharto's efforts to strengthen his political power through his dealings with the spirit world (McDonald, 1980). The extremely pragmatic nature of his political mysticism became especially clear when Suharto's legitimacy was challenged by another mystic, Sawito, who claimed that Suharto had lost the *wahyu*, the supernatural endorsement of his rule from the spirit world.
3   For a more detailed overview of Sufi orders in Indonesia than can be given here, see van Bruinessen (1994a).
4   Elaborate classifications are a common element in Indonesian Shattari manuscripts and recur in the cosmologies of various *abangan* mystical movements. Even the Naqshbandiyya, arguably the most *shari`a*-oriented of the orders, gave rise to a number of syncretistic local sects devoted to magic and the martial arts. See van Bruinessen (1992: 208-11, 216-8).
5   Three such teachers on the Muslim side of the spectrum, who were active in the 1880s, were studied by Drewes (1925), and the same milieu is the subject of a more recent study by Kumar (1985). Major studies of more contemporary syncretistic mystical teachers and their following are Howell (1976) and Suwandi (2000).
6   The oldest extant pesantren, at Tegalsari in East Java, was established in the late eighteenth century. Pesantren appear to have remained few and far between until the late nineteenth century, when their numbers began rapidly increasing (van Bruinessen, 1994c).

7   On *kanuragan*, see de Grave (2001), a study of martial arts traditions in Java though not specifically of pesantren-based *kanuragan*, which is mentioned briefly on pp. 154-6.
8   Chapter IV of Korver's (1982) study of the SI gives examples of the millenarian fervour in various parts of the country.
9   Details on the organization and expansion of the Sarekat Islam are in Korver (1982, Chapter VII) and an analysis of the social composition of the leaders and membership are in Chapter VIII.
10 Conflicts in local branches and between the central committee and local committees are described in Kartodirdjo et al. (1975). On the emergence of the Sarekat Abang in Jambi, South Sumatra, see Muttalib (1981).
11 Permai, the political wing of the *kebatinan* movement Perjalanan, was especially influential among plantation workers in West and East Java. It is the *abangan* movement that is one of the protagonists in Geertz (1959). The national organizer, Rustama Kartawinata, was the son of the charismatic founder of the movement.
12 Another local order that repeatedly received media attention during the New Order period and was treated with even more suspicion was the Mufarridiyya, which originated in North Sumatra. It was said to harbour former 'communists', but the accusations concerned primarily the fact that its founder claimed to have received instructions for the ritual devotions directly from two angels, with whom he and advanced followers were in constant communication. See Effendi (1990b).
13 On the Naqshbandiyya in West Sumatra, see van Bruinessen (1992, Chapters VIII and X). On Perti, see Latief (1988).
14 The name of the association was changed several times but the initials remained the same; 'Partai' changed into 'Persatuan', 'Union', and the other P came to stand for various terms meaning 'follower' or 'defender'. For Haji Jalaluddin's activities, see van Bruinessen (2006); for the subsequent history of the PPTI, see Effendi (1990a).
15 The internal conflicts in PPTI are the subject of a perceptive study by Effendi (1990a).
16 Abdurrahman Wahid, a grandson of Hasjim Asj'ari, was the NU's chairman from 1984 to 1999 and then for a year and a half was Indonesia's ineffectual fourth president. When a coalition of forces was preparing to bring him down, NU-affiliated martial arts groups led by *kanuragan* experts prepared to intimidate the opposition and keep Wahid in power by controlling the streets (van Bruinessen, 2002: 34; de Grave, 2001: 155-6).
17 The by-laws of the Jam'iyyah gave only a vague definition of what is meant by *mu`tabar*: belonging to the *ahl al-sunna wa-l-jama`a* and following one of the four orthodox schools of Islamic law. In conversations, the following criteria were usually mentioned: an unbroken chain of transmission from the Prophet, obedience to the *shari`a*, and rejection of Monistic mysticism (*wahdat al-wujud*).
18 Rejected by NU circles, the founder of the Siddiqiyya, Kiai Mukhtar Mu'thi, was one of the first to affiliate himself with Golkar, resulting in some government patronage and a further increase in *abangan* followers in search of protection.
19 One of the founders, Idham Chalid, told me he accepted to become the chairman of this association in the early New Order, when he already was overburdened with other official functions, at the request of 'those in power' (*yang berkuasa*), who wished to 'secure' (*mengamankan*) the potentially contentious Sufi orders with their mass following (interviews in Jakarta 22 and 30 January 1990).
20 There was, as is not unusual, a conflict over the succession. Musta'in clashed with his father's chief *khalifa*, Usman al-Ishaqi, who claimed, probably rightly, that he had been nominated as the legitimate successor. Many branches of the order, however, chose Musta'in as their supreme shaykh, and Musta'in succeeded in establishing dozens of new local branches. Usman al-Ishaqi and after him his son Asrori continued to lord over an equally extensive network of local branches.
21 Formally this was the Fifth congress of the Jam'iyyah, but the first one on which written documentation exists, an 87-page booklet containing speeches, the by-laws of

     the Jam'iyyah as adopted by the congress, and a summary of the discussions on religious questions (Thoriqot Mu'tabaroh, 1977). Kiai Musta'in was the chairmen of the organizing committee and delivered one of the opening speeches; the congress elected him as the Jam'iyyah chairman.

22 A younger and less influential *tarekat* teacher, who in his youth had studied in the pesantren at Rejoso and whom I interviewed in Madura in 1988, told me that towards the 1982 elections he had consulted Kiai Musta'in on whether he too should join Golkar. Musta'in had advised against it, telling him 'I joined Golkar in order to colour it; but you are not strong enough and it will colour you'.

23 As well as my own observations and interviews, this section is indebted to Lombard (1985: 154-7) and Dhofier (1999) (originally a PhD thesis submitted to ANU in 1980). The political struggles within NU and the strategy to destroy Musta'in's influence are described in greater detail in van Bruinessen (1994b: 169-80). Later developments are analysed in Sujuthi (2001).

24 The debates and conflicts surrounding these decisions are the subject of van Bruinessen (1994b).

25 Rare quantitative data on the spread of the Qadiriyya wa-Naqshbandiyya to urban audiences (in two districts) are provided in Howell at al. (1998); see also Howell (2001). Perceptive observations on the trend towards orthodoxy in Suryalaya and its close relations with the governments are made in an early, little-known but excellent article by Soebardi (1978). A good overview of the expansion of the order from Suryalaya is given by Mulyati (2004).

26 For a fascinating study of an *abangan* cult around a *wali*, in whose teachings one finds no recognisable Islamic elements, see Suwandi (2000). Many *abangan* and *kebatinan* teachers have claimed a special connection with the *wali sanga* discussed below. See, for example, Howell (1976).

27 Geertz (1986) chose Sunan Kalijaga to exemplify what he called the classical Javanese style of Islam.

28 There are several later *wali* whose legendary biographies echo Siti Jenar's (see Feener, 1998), and several more recent mystics have emulated sayings and actions attributed to Siti Jenar.

29 I visited this graveyard not long after Gus Mik's death and found to my surprise that Kiai Achmad Siddiq (who had lived hundreds of kilometres further east) was also buried there, along with a third person, who appeared to be a *hafiz*. Only a few dozen pilgrims were visiting the grave at this time.

30 Personal communication. In 1992-93 the armed forces fought a fierce struggle with Suharto over the composition of the cabinet for the next five-year period. The military succeeded in imposing General Try Sutrisno as the vice-president but the previously most powerful general, Bennie Moerdani, was not returned to the cabinet, which for the first time had a clear 'green' (Islamic) colour. Gus Mik's services had been enlisted by Try Sutrisno or his close supporters. One explanation that close tances gave for Gus Mik's death placed its cause in struggles in the spirit world.

31 These observations are based on numerous conversations that I had over the years with Abdurrahman Wahid, his brother Hasyim Wahid and other NU personalities, and several meetings with Mbah Lim. Unfortunately I never met Gus Mik in person. The supernatural intervened in re than before during Abdurrahman Wahid's presidency; see van Bruinessen (2002).

32 Mustafa Bisri wrote a foreword to the biography of the orthodox *wali*, Kiai Hamid of Pasuruan (Ahmad, 2001), in which he contrasted this real *wali* with the numerous so-called *wali* (*wali tiban*, 'ready-made saints'), of whom so much had been heard in the past years.

33 I have written more extensively on Kadirun Yahya in van Bruinessen (1992, Ch. XI) and van Bruinessen (2006).

Chapter Seven

1. For a general overview of the brotherhood, see Algar (1990).
2. For a considered evaluation of Sirhindi's political role, see Friedmann (1971).
3. For biography of Kuftaru, see especially Habash (1996) and Böttcher (1998: 149-54).
4. On Kuftaru's father, see Habash (1989).
5. See Kuftaru's interview in Naddaf (1997: 62-108, 150-92).
6. On both Abu al-Nasr Khalaf and Muhammad al-Hamid, see Weismann (2005).
7. For fuller discussion see Mayer (1983); Lobmeyer (1995) and Hinnebusch (1996).
8. The other two books in the series are *al-Mustakhlas fi tazkiyat al-anfus* (Cairo, 1984), which is modelled on Ghazali's magnum opus *Ihya `ulum al-din* (The Revival of Religious Sciences), and *Mudhakkirat fi manazil al-siddiqiyin wa-l-rabbaniyin* (Notes from the Houses of the Saintly Ones) (Cairo, 1986), which is based on Ibn `Ata'illah's *Kitab al-hikam* (The Book of Maxims).
9. On `Abd al-Fattah Abu Ghudda, see Weismann (forthcoming) and Al Rashid (1999). Al Rashid's work conceals Abu Ghudda's Sufi and Muslim Brothers affiliations.
10. On `Isa al-Bayanuni's Naqshbandi affiliation, see al-Bayanuni (1344/1925: 2-3).
11. On the Muslim World League organization, see Schulze (1990).
12. http://www.aboghodda.com. Accessed 20 July 2002.
13. For a full list and a short description of each book, see Al Rashid (1999: 178-215). See also the analysis of his publishing activity and oral transmission in the context of the articulation of authority by the `ulama under the impact of modern print technology, in Zaman (2002: 55-6). In this respect, the biographer's systematic overlooking of Abu-Ghudda's Sufi background, although understandable in view of his move to Saudi Arabia, is all the more striking.
14. See al-Muhasibi (1964: 7). This is the first of eight printings, two of them new expanded editions.
15. For the early phase of Nadwat al-`Ulama, see Metcalf (1982: 335-47); Hashmi (1989: 117-46); and particularly Malik (1994).
16. On Shibli Nu`mani, see Troll (1993) and Azami (1994).
17. On Ahmad Shahid, see Ahmad (1964).
18. On Adam Banuri, see Rizvi (1983).
19. Nadwi explains in the introduction that he was inspired to write this exposition of Sirhindi's life and work in the late 1970s, in an attempt to demonstrate to the contemporary radical Islamist movements that a revivalist strategy should aim at guiding the government rather than overthrowing it.
20. On this movement, see Masud (2000) and the excellent study by Sikand (2002).
21. About this journey, see his travelogue, al-Nadwi (1975).
22. Those who have made this claim include Sivan (1985: 23); Roy (1994: 35); and Moussalli (1999: 21-2).
23. For his encounters with Sayyid Qutb, who however had not yet developed his radical ideas, see al-Nadwi (1975: 95-7, 125-6, 188-90).
24. In Hama, Nadwi visited the Ibn Rushd school where Hamid was the teacher of religion.
25. For the discussion that follows I used al-Nadwi (1986), which is the fourth edition of this book. The work was first published in 1966. It is interesting to note that in the Urdu version of the book, which appeared in 1979, the title includes the Sufi term: *Tazkiya wa ihsan ya tasawwuf wa suluk*. Hartung (2003: 106-12) and my personal communication with Hartung.

Chapter Eight

1. For a detailed study of the Tablighi Jama`at, see Sikand (2002).
2. For biographical details, see Nadwi (1983) and Anwar ul-Haq (1972).

3 A *chilla* consists of 40 days. The practice of spending *chilla*s in spiritual retreat and meditation is clearly of Sufi provenance.
4 For detailed discussion of the *chhe batein*, see Bulandshahri (n.d.) and Nizami (1993).
5 I have discussed this process in detail in Sikand (2002).
6 For further discussion, see Sikand (1999).
7 For details, see Hardy (1980).

Chapter Nine

1 The Jakarta Charter was a draft constitution of 1945 that had a provision stipulating the application of the *shari`a* for the future-nation's Muslims. For more on the charter and the debates surrounding it, see Boland (1982: 29ff).
2 Information on the Ihya'us Sunnah is derived from information provided by Noorhaidi Hasan and is gratefully acknowledged. See Hasan (2006).
3 The overwhelming majority of Indonesian traditionalists are adherents of the Shafi`i *madhhab*.
4 Likewise, a dictionary is the first text used to explain the possibility of 'debate' in Islam, with Thalib using various Arabic words for debate to commence his discussion. See Thalib (1997).
5 For a brief treatment of Hamzah Fansuri as background to the rise of '*shari`a*-oriented' reformism and its impact on Southeast Asia in the seventeenth century, see Azra (2004).
6 Since the 1980s, Mizan has developed a reputation for publishing works on Islam that take in an extremely broad and stimulating perspective, including discussions of philosophy and Iran. The review of Abdul Hadi's book appears in Junaidi (1996).
7 The teaching of the *wujudiyya*, that is, the adherents of the doctrine of *wahdat al-wujud* (lit. 'unity of being'), developed out of later understandings of the thought of Ibn al-`Arabi (1165-1240). This doctrine allows for the theoretical possibility of the mystic attaining unity with the Divine essence of God. For a discussion of the polemic surrounding Ibn al-`Arabi's thought in the later Islamic tradition, see Knysh (1999).
8 In Sufi parlance, *majdhub* also designates a state experienced by a passive mystic as opposed to an active 'strider' (*salik*) on the mystic path. More recently it has been a key term used to attack Sufi practices in general, where, according to *Encyclopaedia of Islam*, it is 'a frequently used extenuating and exculpating designation of eccentric ecstatics, love-maddened persons, holy fools, and despisers of the law'. See the entry 'Madjdhûb' by Gramlich (1991).
9 Al-Fatani's family had long played a role in the Jawi tradition in Mainland Southeast Asia, and Ahmad bin Muhammad Zayn was no exception. As of 1884, he was appointed in charge of the newly established Government Press in Mecca.
10 Muhammad bin Ali al-Shawkani (1760-1834) is one of the major instigators of reformism in the late eighteenth century who affirmed the principle of independent rational investigation of the sources of Islam by the process of *ijtihad*. While a fellow traveller in some respects, given his Zaydi Shi`a heritage and distaste for the Wahhabiyya, it is curious to find him cited. On al-Shawkani and his ideas, see Haykel (2003).
11 According to classical conceptions of Sufism, religion (*din*) is enacted at three gradated levels: Islam is effectuated in adherence to the *shari`a*, *iman* is formed through practice of the rituals of an order (*tariqa*), and *ihsan* comes of knowledge of 'reality' (*haqiqa*).
12 This act, known as *istighatha*, is often carried out in NU circles, and was initiated as a mass activity by Abdurrahman Wahid.
13 This description is derived from two interviews in Jakarta, one at the then Danau Batur office on 31 July 2002 and another in Kuningan on 21 February 2003. An earlier version of this part of the chapter was presented at the workshop on 'Modern

Adaptations of Sufi-based Popular Islam' held at the Centre for Modern Oriental Studies, Berlin, 4-5 April 2003 (publication forthcoming).

14 In fact, Luqman himself regards his teacher, Kiai Abdul Jalil Mustaqim of the Pesantren Pesulukan Thariqat Agung, at Tulung Agung, East Java, as the *murshid* of his order. This seems to imply that Luqman is most likely the Jakarta representative of Mustaqim.
15 Here references were given to www.sufinet.com and www.sufinet.org.com. Neither site is now active, although once the journal was revived in mid-2003, it had a new associated domain: www.sufinews.com.
16 Such plans were announced at the July 2003 workshop organized by NU members in Cairo and the Egyptian Philosophical Society (Laffan, 2003).
17 For preliminary notes on this phenomenon, see Hasan and Mufid (2002: 23).
18 Most commonly cited are his article on the Naqshbandiyya in Indonesia (van Bruinessen, 1990b), and an article on books in Arabic script used in the *pesantren* milieu (van Bruinessen, 1990a).
19 I visited this well-appointed house on Jalan Brawijaya with Ahmad Syafii Mufid on 1 August 2002.
20 Said Aqil Siradj, Personal communication, Cairo, August 2003.

Chapter Ten

1 See, for example, Samuel Huntington's (1984) list of variables that correlate with the likelihood of democracy. He notes that Islam is a religion 'not hospitable to democracy'. The list is dated, and Huntington's predictions proved patently wrong in the post-Cold War setting, but the discussion of these variables continues to dominate much of the political science literature on democracy.
2 'Marabout' is a French term, from Arabic *murabit*, but widely used. Other terms are used in local languages, including *sëriñ* (often spelled 'serigne') in Wolof and *ceerno* in Pulaar (Wolof is the Senegalese lingua franca, and Pulaar the next most widely used African language, alongside French as the official language). *Serigne* and *Shaykh* are both often used as titles of respect.
3 The Arabized term for this order is used very rarely; in English the name is at times spelled 'Murid'.
4 For more on the history and spread of the Tijaniyya, see Triaud and Robinson (2000); the most extensive study of the founding of the Mourides is the excellent dissertation by Cheikh Anta Babou (2002a)
5 Shaykh Mortada Mbacké, another son of Amadou Bamba and younger brother – and thus presumed heir – to the current caliph, died in August 2004.
6 The Wolof term *daaira* is derived from the Arabic *da'ira*, meaning 'circle', and so called because the role of host for meetings of these groups circulates among group members. The term is also frequently spelled 'dahira' and used in the Wolofized Arabic names of such groups, such as the Dahiratoul Moustarchidina wal Moustarchidaty, which I discuss below. It should not be confused with *daara* (from Arabic *daar*, house), which in Senegal refers either to Qur'anic schools or to Mouride agricultural settlements in the service of a marabout.
7 Wade insisted on this explanation in an interview with this author carried out on 21 April 2001, at the presidential palace in Dakar.
8 Personal communication. Cheikh Guèye is the author of a superb book examining the origins and meaning of the city of Touba within the Mouride order (Guèye, 2002).
9 I am indebted to my colleague Abdoulaye Kane for his keen insights into this dynamic. For more on this émigré community and its modernizing influences, see A. Kane (2001, 2002).
10 For an excellent discussion and analysis of this phenomenon and the varying motivations for veiling among young women, see Augis (2002).

11 For a discussion of the role of family succession tensions in the rise of one such movement, see Villalón (2000).
12 The historian, civil society activist, and former Minister of Culture, Professor Penda Mbow, in a talk to an academic audience in Dakar in June 2003.
13 On this see, for example, Kane, 2001, 2002; Beck, 2003; Bava, 2002, Ebin, 1990, 1993; and Carter, 1997.
14 A full accounting of the status of Touba, beyond the scope of this chapter, would necessitate an examination of its particular status within independent Senegal, as a *de facto* free trade zone and autonomous city that is beyond the reach of the Senegalese state. For analyses of Touba, see Ross (1995), and especially the superb and voluminous work by Guèye (2002).
15 Following Shaykh Mourtada's death on 7 August 2004, his son Serigne Mame Mor Mbacké has undertaken various trips abroad to visit Mouride *daairas*. He would thus seem to be continuing the important role played by his father in maintaining the ties between the family and the émigré communities.
16 Similar and comparable events are held elsewhere in the world, and celebrated in Senegal. In 2003, for example, an article in the daily *Le Quotidien* (5 June 2003) reported on the fourth annual visit by Shaykh Mourtada to the Mouride community in Italy, on the occasion of the Islamic Cultural Week dedicated to Cheikh Amadou Bamba, and jointly organized by all of the Mouride *daairas* in Italy.
17 Allen Roberts, personal communication. It merits noting here as well that, with the involvement of the author, the exhibit was also shown at the University of Florida's Harn Museum of Art in early 2005.
18 The 'Baye Lahatte' refers to the oversized robes worn by followers of the Hizbut Tarquiyyah and various successor movements, and named after the third caliph of the order, Abdou (or 'Baye', father) Lahatte Mbacké. The *maxtume* is a leather pouch or box worn on a cord around the neck by many Mourides, containing pages of Amadou Bamba's poetry known as *khassaides* (from the Arabic *qasa'id*, or odes), and frequently sung at Mouride rituals and ceremonies.

Chapter Eleven

1 For a full discussion of this issue, see P. Werbner (2001, 2003: 129-33).
2 See, for example, the contributions by Ballard, Shaw and others in Ballard (1994).
3 On this variability, see Basu and Werbner (1998).
4 Eaton (1978), who argues for this view, cites Trimingham (1971). In fact, however, Trimingham recognizes that *ta'ifa* were the major vehicle for the spread of Sufi orders and were not a separate phase.
5 According to Richard Werbner (1977: XVIII), such correspondence theories draw on simplistic Durkheimian or Marxist approaches. He also cites Robertson Smith's theory of sacrifice among the Semites as an example.
6 Regional cult analysis was first formulated by contributors to an edited volume, *Regional Cults* (R. Werbner, 1977). It drew on central place analysis and responded to Victor Turner's theorization of pilgrimage and pilgrimage centres (Turner, 1974).
7 On South Asia see, for example, Gilmartin (1984, 1988); Eaton (1978, 1984, 1993); Mann (1989); Liebeskind (1998); and Bayly (1989). On North Africa see Eickelman (1976, 1977) and Evans-Pritchard (1949).
8 Baji Saeeda died about a year after I completed my study in 2000.

Chapter Twelve

1 This is not to comment on the actual character of the *tarekat*, which were in any case diverse and varied from circle to circle. Moreover, exponents of a number of Sufi

orders joined in criticism of other orders they considered deviant (Van Bruinessen, 1994, 1999).

2   Evidence of the Sufi heritage is evident, for example in Subud, Sapta Dharma, Sumarah, and Sadhar Mapan.

3   For examples of reports in the Indonesian popular press see *Amanah* 36 (1987, cover and pp. 6-10), *Ulumul Qur'an* I (1): 92-7 (1989); and *Gatra* 46 (6): http://www.gatra.com/VI/46/LKH2-46.ht (2000).

4   Indonesia's first constitution, drafted before independence and promulgated a day after independence in August 1945, was abrogated by the Federal Constitution of 1949 and Provisional Constitution of 1950. It was restored in July 1959 and stands today with a number of subsequent revisions.

5   'Orthodox' Sufi orders in this context refers to the *mu'tabarah* Sufi orders.

6   President Sukarno nonetheless cultivated the popular perception that he had acquired the mystical power objects that were the traditional marks of Javanese kingship.

7   Several Buddhist groups taught meditation in the 1950s after Theravada-trained monks joined in the reformation of Indonesian Buddhism. But lay Buddhist practice was structured around regular congregational worship services and official representations of Buddhism published by the Department of Religion foregrounded reformed Buddhism's congregational features.

8   After the collapse of Suharto's New Order, the Department of Education and Culture was restructured, separating out the administration of 'culture'. The 'faiths' (*golongan kepercayaan*) are now lodged within the Department of Culture and Tourism. To some ears, 'culture and tourism' has a less serious ring than 'education and culture', and thus signals a further marginalization of *kebatinan*.

9   The revelations upon which Pangestu teachings are based were given out by Raden (Prince) Soenarto Mertowardojo (Hardjoprakoso and Sumodiharjo, 1987).

10 Author's interview with Paramadina's former Manager of Islamic Studies, Budhy Munawar-Rachman, in Jakarta in March 2004.

11 The Indonesian cognate, *spirituil* and the related *spiritualitas*, have gained considerable currency in recent years as English language competence has become widespread along with the idea of a generic depth dimension common to many different religions. These English cognates have substantially displaced the previously current term *kebatinan*, which in its literal meaning and most general sense means 'inwardness' (as in the inner spiritual life), as opposed to its narrower usage as a way of referring to an indigenous mystical tradition, as indicated earlier. Nurcholish Madjid and his some of his younger associates like Komaruddin Hidayat have done much to promote this usage through their writings, but Nurcholish, in particular, took great care to distinguish the spiritual basis of Islamic life from the New Age and 'cults' (Kull, 2005: 149ff).

12 When established in 1998, the university was called 'Universitas ParamadinaMulya'. The name has since been abbreviated.

13 Note that ICNIS was discontinued in the late 1990s and IIMaN ceased to offer regular courses around 2005.

14 Nurcholish Madjid, the principal founding figure in Paramadina, generally looked with disfavour on the New Age, particularly on what he called 'cults'. He had the same objection to them as to the *tarekat* and to fundamentalist movements in which people surrender responsibility for their understandings of, and relationship to, God and accept what Majdid saw as unacceptably limiting, exclusivist, hierarchical religious structures (Kull, 2005). Nonetheless, Paramadina programming featuring guest speakers from Hindu-style yoga groups like the Brahma Kumaris and the Anand Ashram were welcomed occasionally in the spirit of promoting inter-faith understanding. This was consistent with the positive value placed on religious pluralism by Nurcholish and other Paramadina intellectuals.

15 Here, a personalised litany recommended to individuals for specific purposes by a spiritual advisor.

Chapter Thirteen

1 Driss Benzouine is one of the three key figures in Sufi renewal in Morocco who we discuss in this chapter. Before moving into Sufism, he was a follower of Osho (previously known as Baghwan Shree Rajneesh; see Note 7), who had adopted this motto. The fact that this motto finds its origin with the nineteenth century Danish philosopher Søren Kierkegaard (1813-1955) illustrates well the syncretism developing in Sufism in Morocco that we discuss in this chapter.
2 The king is set as a model for the Muslim community as well as a supreme religious authority vested with divine legitimacy as the Commander of the Believers (*amir al-mu'minin*). On this aspect of royal legitimacy see Tozy (1990) and Leveau (1985).
3 New Age is understood here as those new modes of belief in which eclecticism dominates and the well-being of the individual is set as the objective of a personal quest that constitutes itself at the crossroads of spirituality and psychological therapies.
4 For studies of the processes in these three cities, see Howell (2000), Khosrokhavar and Roy (1999) and Haenni (2004).
5 The chapter is based on field study that the authors conducted in Rabat and Casablanca over three weeks in June 2000. We spoke with more than 20 people – members of *Sufi* brotherhoods and practitioners of yoga and/or zen meditation. Exercising discretion, with the exception of public figures, we mention here only the given names of these people who were kind enough to agree to our request for interviews. The conversations, sometimes repeated and semi-directed, were centred on the spiritual itineraries and the practices and rituals in the circles of the initiates. Our work in this chapter has also greatly benefited from data that Raphael Voix collected during a previous field study he conducted between December 2001 and June 2002. Key figures in this Sufi renewal (Driss Badidi, Rachid ben Rochd, Driss Benzouine and Faouzi Skali) received us warmly in their circles, explaining, often patiently, their practices and the universe of meanings within which they are carried out. May they find here an expression of our gratitude for their time and patience.
6 Osho (1931-90), previously known as Baghwan Shree Rajneesh, is a controversial Indian guru who attracted large followings to his communes in Pune (India) and in Rajneeshpuram (Oregon). He is famous for the mixture of therapies and meditations he developed, and for the libertine behaviour he advocated among his followers. For an introduction to the movement, see Palmer and Sharma (1993).
7 Durix is a trained doctor and prolific writer. In the course of 30 years, he has written more than ten books concerning zen, Muslim tradition, Japanese calligraphy and the like (e.g., Durix, 1980, 2002).
8 The Japanese monk, Taisen Deshimaru (1940-82) was a disciple of Kodo Sawaki and propagated Japanese Soto zen in Europe. In 1967 he settled in Paris, and in 1970 created the International Zen Association to spread his teachings.
9 This concerned the first level of initiation, called 'bodhisattva'. It corresponds to what the Christian tradition calls the 'novitiate': the first and non-final vows. This is followed by a second level known as *Zinho* that marks the proper passage into inner-worldly monastic life. The latter degree of initiation also confers the right to initiate new followers. It should be noted that, contrary to some claims, according to the International Zen Association, no Moroccan has so far received this initiation.
10 The International Zen Association (IZA) was set up in 1970 by Taisen Deshimaru to help enable him to spread the practice and the teaching of Japanese Soto zen. The IZA brought together more than 200 centres (*dojos*) mainly in Europe. It owns the domain of Gendronière near Blois, which became a zen temple and where the followers come together every year. The IZA is a member of the Buddhist Union of France. In

Morocco, as elsewhere, to be ordained within the IZA commits the follower to a life of service and asceticism, yet it does not imply a vow of chastity. It does imply the follower will undertake a certain number of rites of passage including the change of the follower's first name to something like 'Peaceful Harmony', 'Silence Monk', 'White Cloud' or 'Muse'.

11 The word *jinn* means 'spirit', often in the sense of a malign force. The expression 'Islam of the *jinn*' refers to a traditional Islam that is mainly rural and superstitious.

12 This shift from a Marxist perspective to Islamism is discussed extensively in Burgat (1995).

13 For a complete overview, see the October 2002 issue of *Politique Africaine*, devoted to 'Les sujets de Dieu'.

14 Usually this concerns a belief in reincarnation as it developed in Western esotericism and not in the type of metempsychosis as described in Hinduism or Buddhism. The former considers only the possibility of reincarnation in human form, whereas the latter extends the possibility to encompass all living forms.

15 Hanae alludes here to a well-known phrase (allegedly a *hadith*) attributed to Ibn `Arabi, '*man `arafa nafsahu fa-qadd `arafa rabbahu*', 'who knows himself, he verily knows his Lord' (editors' note).

16 Interestingly, the pluralism of beliefs to which these informants subscribe explicitly allows space to two categories of faith that are absent from the classical Muslim precepts regarding tolerance, i.e., the Asian religions (Buddhism and Hinduism) and atheism. The classical precepts are generally limited to 'the people of the book', i.e., Christians and Jews.

17 On the Budshishiyya as described by one of his members, see Ben Driss (2002); on the history of the order and its role in Moroccan society, see Tozy (1990) and Sedgwick (2004).

18 It was Shaykh Yassine's position as a teacher that first opened the doors of the world of modern education to the Budshishiyya. He later was to leave the brotherhood, apparently in connection with a rivalry over the succession to Abu l-`Abbas, from which Sidi Hamza emerged victorious (Mohamed Tozy, oral communication). The Budshishiyya's strategy of active recruitment among the professional classes is a legacy of Shaykh Yassine's activities.

19 See Sedgwick (2004a). On Guénon's Traditionalism and the influence he exerted on the conversion of western intellectuals to Sufism, see the book by that author on the Traditionalist movement (Sedgwick, 2004b).

20 In the Budshishiyya, the *muqaddam* are representatives of the shaykh who leads local branches. They are responsible for the local *zawiya*, and they are authorized to perform initiations.

21 The people we studied belonged mainly to those two *zawiyas*.

22 Here we are reasoning by analogy with the ideas of Wilhelm Halbfass concerning neo-Hinduism (Halbfass, 1988). He shows how the nationalist discourse reconstituted Hinduism on the basis of the mental categories of the British education given to Indian elites of the end of the nineteenth century.

23 A metaphor frequently used in the Budshishiyya to caution against combining different paths is that one cannot take two medicines at the same time without risking the side effects of their interaction. But individualism also has its defenders. A nurse who we interviewed responded to this cautioning with the common-sense comment that, barring counter-indications, combining several medicines is not a problem.

24 Thus, alluding to the ethic of the void proper to zen, a French convert, Faroul, remarked to Ben Rochd that if zen corresponds to crossing of the desert, Sufism is the oasis that one must find in the desert. Along the same lines, Ben Rochd considers Sufism the highest stage of 'Maghribi yoga'.

Chapter Fourteen

1. A Western branch of the Shadhili order was begun around 1907, but it was very small and effectively secret. See Rawlinson (1997: 21-3).
2. When it began in 1910, Inayat Khan's Sufi Movement was effectively the only order in the West and did not need to be distinguished from others. It now has a number of branches and, following the traditional practice in naming orders, I refer to these collectively as the Inayati order.
3. Colloquially known as Sufi Dancing, this was begun in the 1960s by Samuel Lewis, an American disciple of Hazrat Inayat Khan. It has become a formal and worldwide organization (Wilson, 1998: 195-6).
4. I maintain the Anglo–Indian spelling of 'mureed' rather than the more usual transliteration as 'murid', in accordance with usage in the Inayati Sufi movement.
5. Levitt (2004) considers different types of organization but only within migrant communities.
6. These are the Chishti, Qadiri, Naqshbandi and Suhrawardi orders.
7. The current (2006) leader of the Sufi Order International, Pir Zia Inayat-Khan, represents this attitude as 'generic' Islam as opposed to formal or 'brand name' Islam.
8. Many of the changes introduced by Fazal Inayat-Khan were temporary and he stepped down from the leadership in 1982.
9. While Simpkinson (1996) documents incidents within Western Buddhist groups, she also recognizes that no religious tradition is immune from the issue of sexual or other abuse by spiritual leaders.
10. Before the *tariqa*s or orders were established (around the twelfth century), students of Sufism were not bound to a single shaikh and often travelled to take spiritual direction from a number of masters. The *tariqa*s, each centred around one spiritual master, formalized and institutionalized the practice of Sufism and the *murshid–mureed* relationship.

Chapter Fifteen

1. Bruce Springsteen Compact Disk, 'Greetings from Asbury Park, N.J.', Columbia Records/CBS Inc., 1973, track 9.
2. 'Summary Translation of the Mahadi's Book', in Khartoum University Library, Sudan Collection, 1677/48CM, typescript, 25 August 1936.
3. See, for example, the analysis in Gellner (1968).
4. The terminology comes from the 'Great Tradition'/'Little Tradition' distinction that Robert Redfield made in such works as The Little Community and Peasant Society and Culture (1960).
5. The effective adaptations of this brotherhood are discussed more fully in Leonardo Villalón's chapter in this volume.
6. The author expresses his gratitude to Michael O. Voll for his helpful suggestions and analyses of the literature concerning social movement theory.
7. Itzchak Weismann provides an important analysis of the background of the Kaftariyya in this volume. See also Stenberg (1999).
8. In addition to Genn's chapter, see the studies of 'New Age Sufism' in the West by Hermansen et al. (1997).

NOTES ON CONTRIBUTORS

Rachida Chih is Associate Research Fellow at the Centre National de la Recherche Scientifique (CNRS) and a Member of the Centre d'études turques, ottomanes, balkaniques et centrasiatiques (Cetobac) in Paris. She holds a PhD in Arabic and Islamic Studies from the University of Provence, in Aix en Provence. She is the author of *Le soufisme au quotidien. Confréries d'Egypte au XXe siècle* (Sufism and everyday life. Sufi orders in twentieth century Egypt), Paris: Sindbad, 2000, and edited, with Denis Gril, a collection of articles on reading hagiographies, *Le saint et son milieu* (Cairo: IFAO, 2000); with Catherine Mayeur-Jaouen, *Le soufisme à l'époque ottomane* (Cairo: IFAO, 2010); and with Catherine Mayeur-Jaouen and Rüdiger Seesemann, *Sufism, Literary Production and Printing in the 19th Century* (Würzburg: Ergon Verlag, forthcoming). She can be contacted at rachidachih@yahoo.co.uk.

Celia Genn is an Honorary Research Fellow in the School of History, Philosophy, Religion and Classics at the University of Queensland in Brisbane, Australia. She is a sociologist with a research focus on Sufism and Asian-origin religious movements in South Asian and Western societies. She received the Dean's Commendation for her PhD thesis, *Exploration and Analysis of the Origins, Nature, and Development of the Sufi Movement in Australia* (2004). Celia has recently lectured in religious studies at the University of Queensland and University of New England (Armidale, Australia), and in Asian studies at Griffith University (Brisbane, Australia). Her publications include 'The Chishtiyya Diaspora: An Expanding Circle?' in *Indian Diaspora: Retrospect and Prospect*, edited by Brij Maharaj, K. Laxmi Narayan and Dave Sangha (New Delhi: Sage Publications, 2006). She can be contacted at cgenn@bigpond.com.

Patrick Haenni is a researcher in the French Centre of Economic, Juristic and Social Studies and Documentations (CEDEJ) in Egypt. A political scientist, he is interested in the Islamization process and religious entrepreneurs, particularly in Egypt. His current research explores relations between new forms of religiosity, globalization and reform of the post-colonial state in the Middle East. His most recent works (in French, German and English) concern possibilities for ideological break-up beyond Islamism, state building and political empowerment in a former Islamic stronghold in Cairo, post-Salafist Islam, rediscovery of a worldwide liberalism in contemporary Islams, and the diversity of the rhetoric of democracy in different Islamic contexts. His recent books are *L'ordre des caïds. Conjurer la dissidence urbaine au Caire*. Paris: Karthala, 2005; and *L'islam de marché, l'autre révolution conservatrice*. Paris: Le Seuil, 2005. Patrick can be contacted at patrickhaenni@bluewin.ch.

Julia Day Howell is Professor of the Sociology of Religion at the Centre for the Religion and Society and the Centre for the Study of Contemporary Muslim Societies at the University of Western Sydney. She did her postgraduate studies in Anthropology at the London School of Economics and at Stanford University. Her earlier work dealt with Indic religious traditions in Indonesia and New Religious Movements of Asian origin in the West. Her recent work on Islam among Indonesia's cosmopolitan urbanities, focusing especially on Sufi expressions of Islam, contributes to the comparative sociology of Islam in contemporary societies. It also addresses issues of Islam and religious pluralism in democratic states, and examines new forms of piety in modern, media saturated social settings. In addition, she has also done collaborative work with psychologists in Indonesia and Australia on religious experiences and is presently contributing to the sociology of religious emotion with her work on Sufi ritual performance. She has published widely in Indonesian as well as English. Her publications include articles in leading area studies journals, such as the *Journal of Asian Studies* and *Modern Asian Studies*, and those dealing with her primary disciplinary specialties like *Sociology of Religion*, *Journal for the Scientific Study of Religion*, *Social Compass*, and the *Journal of Contemporary Religion*. She can be contacted at j.howell@uws.edu.au.

Michael Laffan is Professor of History at Princeton University. His first book, *Islamic Nationhood and Colonial Indonesia* (RoutledgeCurzon, 2003), considers Islam's place in framing imaginings of Indonesia in the late colonial period, while his more recent foray, *The Makings of Indonesian Islam* (Princeton University Press, 2011), explores the ways in which Indonesians and Dutch scholar-officials made sense of the place of *tariqa* mysticism in society and history. He is now working on a project concerning the life and times of an Arab exile to Cape Town. He can be contacted at mlaffan@princeton.edu.

Yoginder Sikand is an independent writer based in New Delhi. He followed his PhD at the University of London with post-doctoral study at the International Institute for the Study of Islam in the Modern World in Leiden. He edits a monthly webmagazine, Qalandar (www.islaminterfaith.org), which deals essentially with issues concerning Islam, Muslims and inter-community relations in South Asia. Yoginder has written several journal articles and for the popular press. His books include: *Bastions of the Believers: Madrasas and Islamic Education in India*. New Delhi: Penguin India, 2005; *Muslims in India Since 1947: Islamic Perspectives on Inter-Faith Relations*. London: RoutledgeCurzon, 2004; *Struggling to be Heard: South Asian Muslim Voices*. New Delhi: Global Media Publications, 2004; *Sacred Spaces: Exploring Traditions of Shared Faith in India*. New Delhi: Penguin India, 2003; and *The Origins and Development of the Tablighi Jamaat (1920–2000): A Cross-Country Comparative Study*. New Delhi: Orient Longman, 2002. Yoginder can be contacted at ysikand@yahoo.com.

Brian Silverstein is Associate Professor of Anthropology at the University of Arizona. He has published on Islam and modernity in Turkey, Turkish Islamist intellectuals, Sufism in the late Ottoman Empire and Republic of Turkey, and more recently on institutional reform in Turkey. His book, *Islam and Modernity in Turkey* (Palgrave, 2011), based on two years of fieldwork in Istanbul and regional cities, examines Islamic disciplines of ethical self-formation in Turkey and their articulation with mass media and norms of liberal citizenship. He can be contacted at bsilver@email.arizona.edu.

Benjamin Soares, an anthropologist, is a senior researcher at the African Studies Centre in Leiden, The Netherlands. He has taught at Northwestern University, the University of Chicago, and the University of Sussex and held fellowships at the University of Chicago and the École des Hautes Études en Sciences Sociales in Paris. His publications include *Islam and the Prayer Economy* (University of Michigan Press & Edinburgh University Press, 2005); the edited collections *Islam and Muslim Politics in Africa* (Palgrave, 2007) and *Islam, État et société en Afrique* (Karthala, 2008), both with René Otayek; *Muslim-Christian Encounters in Africa* (Brill, 2006); and *Islam, Politics, Anthropology* (Wiley-Blackwell, 2010), with Filippo Osella. He can be contacted at BSoares@ascleiden.nl.

Martin van Bruinessen is Emeritus Professor of Comparative Studies of Modern Muslim Societies at Utrecht University in the Netherlands. He is an anthropologist with a strong interest in history and politics, and with fieldwork experience in Kurdistan, Afghanistan and Indonesia. His publications include *Agha, Shaikh and State: The Social and Political Structures of Kurdistan* (Zed Books, 1992); and *Mullas, Sufis and Heretics: The Role of Religion in Kurdish Society* (Istanbul: Isis Press, 2000); the edited volumes *The Madrasa in Asia* (with Farish A. Noor and Yoginder Sikand, Amsterdam University Press, 2008); *Producing Islamic Knowledge: Transmission and Dissemination in Western Europe* (with Stefano Allievi, Routledge, 2011); and numerous articles. His present research concerns religious authority and knowledge in Southeast Asia as mediated by transnational Islamic movements. He can be contacted at m.vanbruinessen@uu.nl.

Matthijs van den Bos is a Lecturer in International Studies at Birkbeck, University of London. His research and teaching have focused on transnational networks, international migration, (European) Shiism, Sufism, political anthropology/sociology, democratization, classification theory, and new media. His dissertation, 'Mystic Regimes,' investigates the long-term socio-political development of two Shiite (Ne'matollahi) Sufi orders in Iran. His publications include *Mystic Regimes. Sufism and the State in Iran, From the Late Qajar Era to the Islamic Republic* (Brill, 2002); 'Dhahabiyya' (forthcoming in *Encyclopaedia of Islam*, 3rd ed.); 'European Shiism? Counterpoints from Shiites' organization in Europe', *Ethnicities* 12 (2012); 'Notes on Sufism and Freemasonry in Iran, 1900–97', *Journal of the History of Sufism* 4 (2003–04); 'Transnational Orientalism: Henry Corbin in Iran', *Anthropos* 100(2005); and 'Hyperlinked Dutch–Iranian Cyberspace', *International Sociology*, 21(2006). He can be contacted at altresid-info@yahoo.com.

Leonardo A. Villalón is Director of the Centre for African Studies and Associate Professor of Political Science at the University of Florida. His research has focused on issues of Islam and politics and on democratization in Senegal, Mali and Niger. He has written numerous articles and book chapters on politics and religion in West Africa. He is the author of *Islamic Society and State Power in Senegal*. New York: Cambridge University Press, 1995; and co-editor of *The African State at a Critical Juncture: Between Disintegration and Reconfiguration*. Boulder, CO., London: Lynne Rienner, 1998; and *The Fate of Africa's Democratic Experiments: Elites and Institutions*. Bloomington, IN: Indiana University Press, 2005. He taught for two years as a Fulbright senior scholar at the Université Cheikh Anta Diop in Dakar, Senegal. He has also taught at the Université Gaston Berger in St. Louis, Senegal, and has lectured and directed seminars and workshops at various institutions across West Africa. Leonardo can be contacted at villalon@africa.ufl.edu.

Raphaël Voix is a PhD student at the Anthropology and Comparative Sociology Research Centre of the Paris X University, France. His research deals with contemporary religious movements in India and their transnational links, specializing in the hatha-yogic traditions of West Bengal. He has also examined a new form of adhesion to Sufi orders through research on French converts to the Moroccan Tariqa Budshishiyya. Raphaël Voix can be contacted at rvoix@jerevox.com.

John O. Voll is Professor of History and Associate Director of the Prince Alwaleed Bin Talal Centre for Muslim-Christian Understanding at Georgetown University. He is a past president of the Middle East Studies Association of North America. Among his publications are *Islam: Continuity and Change in the Modern World*. Syracuse, NY: Syracuse University Press, 1994; and with John L. Esposito, *Makers of Contemporary Islam*. New York: Oxford University Press, 2001. John can be contacted at vollj@georgetown.edu.

Itzchak Weismann is Professor of Islamic studies and Head of the Jewish-Arab Center at the University of Haifa. His research interests focus on modern Islam, particularly fundamentalist and radical Islamic movements and Sufism. He is the author of *Taste of Modernity: Sufism, Salafiyya, and Arabism in Late Ottoman Damascus* (Brill, 2001), *The Naqshbandiyya: Orthodoxy and Activism in a Worldwide Sufi Tradition* (Routledge, 2007), and co-editor of *Ottoman Reform and Islamic Regeneration* (I.B.Tauris, 2005), and *Islamic Myths and Memories: Mediators of Globalization*, forthcoming. He also published numerous articles on Islam in modern Syria, the Arab East at large and India. As head of the Jewish-Arab Center, Prof. Weismann works to promote good relations between Jews and Arabs in Israel. He can be contacted at Weismann@research.haifa.ac.il.

Pnina Werbner is Professor Emerita of Social Anthropology at Keele. She is the author of *The Migration Process: Capital, Gifts and Offerings among British Pakistanis* (Berg, 1990 and 2002); *Imagined Diasporas among Manchester Muslims* (James Currey, and School of American Research, 2002); and *Pilgrims of Love: The Anthropology of a Global Sufi Cult* (Hurst, and Indiana University Press, 2003), and the editor of *Anthropology and the New Cosmopolitanism: Rooted, Feminist and Vernacular Perspective* (Berg Publishers, 2008). Recent co-edited collections include, with Tariq Modood, *Debating Cultural Hybridity* (Zed Books, 1997); with Tariq Modood, *The Politics of Multiculturalism in the New Europe* (Zed Books, 1997); with Helene Basu, *Embodying Charisma: Modernity, Locality and the Performance of Emotion in Sufi Cults* (Routledge, 1998); with Nira Yuval-Davis, *Women, Citizenship and Difference* (Zed Books, 1999); and a special issue of the journal *Diaspora* on The Materiality of Diaspora, 9(1) 2000. Her fieldwork includes research in Britain, Pakistan, and Botswana. She can be contacted at P.Werbner@keele.ac.uk.

A NOTE ON TRANSLITERATION

The chapters in this volume use sources and terms from a range of Islamic languages, including Arabic, Persian, Turkish, Indonesian, Javanese, Urdu and Wolof. The editors have not attempted to devise a unified transliteration for all of these languages. For the first three we used the style of *International Journal of Middle East Affairs*, and for the other languages the locally most common transliteration. For certain widely known concepts, like *shari`a* or *tasawwuf*, we have used the transcription from the Arabic throughout, but other concepts may appear in different forms in different chapters. Especially where terms appear to have acquired new shades of meaning in their current cultural context, we have maintained the form the term has in the language at hand in the chapter. Thus we have *hizmet* in the chapter on Turkey and its Arabic form, *khidma*, in the chapter on Egypt. Where such an originally Arabic term appears in a form that some readers may not recognize immediately, we have also supplied the Arabic form of the term at its first appearance. The glossary at the end of the volume lists all terms that may need some explanation in the various forms in which these terms appear in this volume.

REFERENCES

Chapter One

Ansari, Sarah F.D. 1996. The Islamic World in the Era of Western Domination, 1800 to the Present. In *The Cambridge Illustrated History of the Islamic World*, edited by Francis Robinson, pp. 90-121. Cambridge: Cambridge University Press.

Arberry, A.J. 1950. *Sufism*. London: Allen and Unwin.

Atay, Tayfun, 1996. *Bati'da bir Naksi cemaati: Seyh Nâzım Kıbrısî örneği*. Istanbul: Iletisim Yayinlari.

Azra, Azyumardi. 2004. *The Origins of Islamic Reformism in Southeast Asia: Networks of Malay–Indonesian and Middle Eastern 'Ulama' in the Seventeenth and Eighteenth Centuries*. Crows Nest, NSW: Allen and Unwin.

Baldick, Julian. 1989. *Mystical Islam: An Introduction to Sufism*. London: I.B. Tauris.

Bourguignon, Erika. ed. 1973. *Religion, Altered States of Consciousness and Social Change*. Columbus: Ohio University Press.

Berger, Peter L. 1967. *The Sacred Canopy: Elements of a Sociological Theory of Religion*. New York: Doubleday.

Bruinessen, Martin van. 1992. *Agha, Shaikh and State: The Social and Political Structures of Kurdistan*. London: Zed Books.

Campbell, Colin. 1978. The Secret Religion of the Educated Classes, *Sociological Analysis*, 39(2): 146-56.

Casanova, Jose. 1994. *Public Religions in the Modern World*. Chicago: The University of Chicago Press.

Copans, Jean. 2000. Mourides des champs, mourides des villes, mourides du téléphone portable et de l'internet. Les renouvellements de l'économie politique d'une confrérie, *Afrique contemporaine*, 194: 24-33.

Cruise O'Brien, Donal B. 1971. *The Mourides of Senegal: The Political and Economic Organization of an Islamic Brotherhood*. Oxford: Clarendon Press.

—— 1988. Charisma Comes to Town: Mouride Urbanization 1945-1986. *Charisma and Brotherhood in African Islam*, edited by Donal B. Cruise O'Brien and Christian Coulon, pp. 135-55. Oxford: Clarendon Press.

Damrel, David W. 2006. Aspects of the Naqshbandi–Haqqani Order in North America. In *Sufism in the West*, edited by John Hinnels and Jamal Malik, pp. 115-26. London: Routledge.

De Jong, Frederick. 1974. Review of Gilsenan 1973, *Journal of Semitic Studies*, 19(2): 322-28.

De Jong, Frederick and Radtke, Bernd. eds. 1999. *Mysticism Contested: Thirteen Centuries of Controversies and Polemics*. Leiden: Brill.

Chapter One (cont.)

Evans-Pritchard, E.E. 1949. *The Sanusi of Cyrenaica*. London: Oxford University Press.

Geertz, Clifford. 1960. *The Religion of Java*. Glencoe, Ill.: The Free Press.

——— 1968. *Islam Observed*. Chicago: University of Chicago Press.

Gellner, Ernest. 1969. *The Saints of the Atlas*. Chicago: University of Chicago Press.

——— 1981. *Muslim Society*. Cambridge: Cambridge University Press.

——— 1992. *Postmodernism, Reason and Religion*. London and New York: Routledge.

Gilsenan, Michael. 1967. Some Factors in the Decline of Sufi Orders in Modern Egypt, *The Muslim World*, 57: 11-18.

——— 1973. *Saint and Sufi in Modern Egypt: An Essay in the Sociology of Religion*. Oxford: Oxford University Press.

——— 1985. Trajectories of Contemporary Sufism. In *Islamic Dilemmas: Reformers, Nationalists and Industrialization*, edited by Ernest Gellner, pp. 187-98. Amsterdam: Mouton.

Heelas, Paul and Woodhead, Linda. 2005. *The Spiritual Revolution: Why Religion is Giving Way to Spirituality*. Oxford, UK: Blackwell.

Hermansen, Marcia. 1998. In the Garden of American Sufi Movements: Hybrids and Perennials. In *New Trends and Developments in the World of Islam*, edited by Peter B. Clarke, pp. 155-77. London: Luzac Oriental.

——— 2000. Hybrid Identity Formations in Muslim America: The Case of American Sufi Movements, *The Muslim World*, 90: 158-97.

Hoffman, Valerie J. 1995. *Sufism, Mystics, and Saints in Modern Egypt*. Columbia, S.C.: University of South Carolina Press.

——— 1999. Annihilation in the Messenger of God: The Development of a Sufi Practice, *International Journal of Middle East Studies*, 31: 351-69.

Howell, Julia Day. 2001. Sufism and the Indonesian Islamic Revival, *Journal of Asian Studies*, 60(3): 701-29.

Howell, Julia Day; Subandi; and Nelson, Peter L. 1998. Indonesian Sufism: Sign of Resurgence. In *New Trends and Developments in the World of Islam*, edited by Peter B. Clarke, pp. 277-98. London: Luzac Oriental.

Huntington, Samuel P. 1997. *The Clash of Civilizations and the Remaking of the World Order*. London: Simon and Schuster.

Johansen, Julian. 1996. *Sufism and Islamic Reform in Egypt: The Battle for Islamic Tradition*. Oxford: Clarendon Press.

King, Ursula. 1997. Spirituality. In *A New Handbook of Living Religions*, edited by John R. Hinnells, pp. 667-81. London: Penguin.

Kurzman, Charles. 1998. *Liberal Islam: A Sourcebook*. Oxford: Oxford University Press.

Lewis, Bernard. 2002. *What Went Wrong? The Clash between Islam and Modernity in the Middle East*. London: Weidenfeld and Nicolson.

Lewis, I.M. 1971. *Ecstatic Religion: An Anthropological Study of Spirit Possession and Shamanism*. Harmondsworth: Penguin.

Malik, Iftikhar H. 2004. *Islam and Modernity: Muslims in Europe and the United States*. London: Pluto Press.

Malik, Jamal and Hinnells, John. eds. 2006. *Sufism in the West*. London: Routledge.

Mardin, Serif. 1993. The Naqshibendi Order of Turkey. In *Fundamentalisms and the State: Remaking Polities, Economies, and Militance*, edited by Martin E. Marty and R. Scott Appleby, pp. 204-32. Chicago: The University of Chicago Press.

Martin, David. 1978. *A General Theory of Secularization*. Oxford: Blackwell.

——— 2002. *Pentecostalism: The World Their Parish*. Oxford: Blackwell.

Munson, Henry, Jr. 1993. *Religion and Power in Morocco*. New Haven: Yale University Press.

Nasr, Seyyed Hossein. ed. 1987. *Islamic Spirituality I: Foundations*. New York: Crossroad.

——— ed. 1991. *Islamic Spirituality II: Manifestations*. New York: Crossroad.

Chapter One (cont.)

Nielsen, Jorgen S.; Draper, Mustafa and Yemelianova, Galina. 2006. Transnational Sufism: The Haqqaniyya. In *Sufism in the West*, edited by Jamal Malik and John Hinnells, pp. 103-14. London: Routledge.

O'Fahey, R.S. 1990. *Enigmatic Saint: Ahmad ibn Idris and the Idrisi Tradition.* Evanston, Ill: Northwestern University Press.

O'Fahey, R.S. and Radtke, Bernd. 1993. Neo-Sufism Reconsidered, *Der Islam*, 70: 52-87.

Otto, Rudolf. 1970. *The Idea of the Holy*, 2nd edn, trans. by John W. Harvey. London: Oxford University Press.

Özal, Korkut. 1999. Twenty Years with Mehmed Zahid Kotku: A Personal Story. In *Naqshbandis in Western and Central Asia*, edited by Elisabeth Özdalga, pp. 159-85. Istanbul: Swedish Research Institute.

Özdalga, Elisabeth. ed. 1999. *Naqshbandis in Western and Central Asia.* Istanbul: Swedish Research Institute.

Radtke, Bernd. 1996. Ijtihad and Neo-Sufism, *Asiatische Studien*, 48: 909-21.

────── 1996. Sufism in the 18th Century: An Attempt at a Provisional Appraisal, *Die Welt des Islams*, 36: 326-64.

Robertson, Roland. 1995. Glocalization: Time–Space and Homogeneity–Heterogeneity. In *Global Modernities*, edited by Mike Featherstone, Scott Lash and Roland Robertson, pp. 25-44. London: Sage Publications.

Safi, Omid. ed. 2003. *Progressive Muslims: On Justice, Gender and Pluralism.* Oxford: Oneworld.

Sirriyeh, Elizabeth. 1999. *Sufis and Anti-Sufis: The Defense, Rethinking and Rejection of Sufism in the Modern World.* Richmond: Curzon.

Swatos, William H. Jr. 1983. Enchantment and Disenchantment in Modernity: The Significance of 'Religion' as a Sociological Category, *Sociological Analysis*, 44(4): 321-38.

Swatos, William H. Jr. and Christiano, Kevin J. 1999. Introduction – Secularization Theory: The Course of a Concept, *Sociology of Religion*, 60(3): 209-28.

Triaud, Jean-Louis and Robinson, David. eds. 2000. *La Tijâniyya: une confrérie musulmane à la conquête de l'Afrique.* Paris: Karthala.

Trimingham, J. Spencer. 1971. *The Sufi Orders in Islam.* Oxford: Clarendon Press.

Troeltsch, Ernst. 1931. *The Social Teachings of the Christian Churches*, vol. 2. New York. McMillan.

Umar, Muhammad Sani. 1993. Changing Islamic Identity in Nigeria from the 1960s to the 1980s: From Sufism to Anti-Sufism. In *Muslim Identity and Social Change in Sub-Saharan Africa*, edited by Louis Brenner, pp. 154-78. London: Hurst and Company.

Villalón, Leonardo A. 1995. *Islamic Society and State Power in Senegal: Disciples and Citizens in Fatick.* Cambridge: Cambridge University Press.

Voll, John O. 1972. Mahdis, Walis and New Men in the Sudan. In *Scholars, Saints and Sufis*, edited by Nikki Keddie, pp. 367-84. Berkeley: University of California Press.

────── 1980. Hadith Scholars and Tariqahs: An Ulama Group in the 18th Century Haramayn and Their Impact in the Islamic World, *Journal of Asian and African Studies*, 15: 264-73.

────── 1995. Sufi Orders. In *The Oxford Encyclopedia of the Modern Islamic World*, vol. 4, edited by John L. Esposito, pp. 109-17. New York, etc.: Oxford University Press.

Weismann, Itzchak. 2000. *Taste of Modernity: Sufism, Salafiyya, and Arabism in Late Ottoman Damascus.* Leiden: Brill.

Werbner, Pnina. 2003. *Pilgrims of Love: The Anthropology of a Global Sufi Cult.* Bloomington: Indiana University Press.

Westerlund, David and Rosander, Eva Evers. eds. 1997. *African Islam and Islam in Africa: Encounters between Sufis and Islamists.* London: Hurst.

Yavuz, M. Hakan. 1999. The Matrix of Modern Turkish Islamic Movements: The Naqshbandi Order. In *Naqshbandis in Western and Central Asia*, edited by Elisabeth Özdalga, pp. 129-46. Istanbul: Swedish Research Institute in Istanbul.

Chapter One (cont.)

Yavuz, M. Hakan and Esposito, John L. eds. 2003. *Turkish Islam and the Secular State: The Gülen Movement*. New York: Syracuse University Press.

Zarcone, Thierry. 1992. Les Naksibendi et la république turque: de la persécution au repositionnement théologique, politique et social (1925-1991), *Turcica*, 24: 133-51.

Chapter Two

Arberry, A.J. 1950. *Sufism*. London: George Allen & Unwin.

Brown, Peter. 1982. *Society and the Holy in Late Antiquity*. London: Faber and Faber.

Chih, Rachida. 1998. Cheminements et situation actuelle d'un ordre mystique réformateur: la Khalwatiyya en Égypte (fin XVe siècle à nos jours), *Studia Islamica*, 88: 181-201.

—— 2000a. *Le soufisme au quotidien: confréries d'Egypte au XXe siècle*. Paris: Sindbad (Actes Sud).

—— 2000b. Les débuts d'une tarîqa. Formation et essor de la Khalwatiyya égyptienne au XVIIIe siècle d'après l'hagiographie de son fondateur, M.b. Sâlim al-Hifnî (m. 1181/1767). In *Le saint et son milieu, ou comment lire les sources hagiographiques*, edited by Rachida Chih and Denis Gril, pp. 137-49. Le Caire: Institut Français d'Archéologie Orientale.

Chodkiewicz, Michel. 1986. *Le sceau des saints. Prophétie et sainteté dans la doctrine d'Ibn Arabi*. Paris: Gallimard.

—— 1996. Le modèle prophétique de la sainteté en islam, *Lettre d'information de l'Afemam*, 10: 505-18.

Cornell, Vincent J. 1998. *Realm of the Saint: Power and Authority in Moroccan Sufism*. Austin: University of Texas Press.

De Jong, Frederick. 1978. *Turuq and Turuq-linked Institutions in Nineteenth Century Egypt: A Historical Study in Organizational Dimensions of Islamic Mysticism*. Leiden: Brill.

—— 1983. Aspects of the Political Involvement of the Sufi Orders in Twentieth Century Egypt (1907/1970): An Exploratory Stocktaking. In *Islam, Radicalism and Nationalism in Egypt and the Sudan*, edited by Gabriel R. Warburg and Uri M. Kupferschmidt, pp. 183-212. New York: Praeger.

Delanoue, Gilbert. 1982. *Moralistes et politiques musulmans dans l'Égypte du XIXe siècle (1798-1882)*, 2 vols. Le Caire: IFAO.

Elboudrari, Hassan. 1985. Quand les saints font la ville: lecture anthropologique de la pratique sociale d'un saint marocain du XVIIe siècle, *Annales ESC*, 40(3): 489-508.

Gaborieau, Marc; Popovic, Alexandre and Zarcone, Thierry. eds. 1990. *Naqshbandis: cheminements et situation actuelle d'un ordre mystique musulman*. Istanbul–Paris: Editions Isis.

Gaborieau, Marc and Zeghal, Malika. eds. 2004. *Autorités religieuses en islam*, special issue of *Archives des Sciences Sociales des Religions*, 49(125).

Geertz, Clifford. 1968. *Islam Observed: Religious Development in Morocco and Indonesia*. New Haven: Yale University Press.

Gellner, Ernest. 1969. *The Saints of the Atlas*. Chicago: University of Chicago Press.

—— 1981. *Muslim Society*. Cambridge: Cambridge University Press.

Gilsenan, Michael. 1967. Some Factors in the Decline of Sufi Orders in Modern Egypt, *The Muslim World*, 57: 11-18.

—— 1973. *Saint and Sufi in Modern Egypt. An Essay in the Sociology of Religion*. Oxford: Clarendon Press.

Goldziher, Ignaz. 1880. Le culte des saints chez les musulmans, *Revue de l'histoire des religions*, 2: 227-351.

Gril, Denis. ed. 1986. *La Risâla de Safî al-Dîn abî'l-Mansûr ibn Zâfir*. Le Caire: Institut Français d'Archéologie Orientale.

Gril, Denis. 1996. La voie. In *Les voies d'Allah: les ordres mystiques dans le monde musulman des origines à aujourd'hui*, edited by Alexandre Popovic and Gilles Veinstein, pp. 87-103. Paris: Fayard.

Chapter Two (cont.)

Gril, Denis. 2002. Le modèle prophétique du maître spirituel en islam. In *Maestro e discepolo. Temi e problemi della direzione spirituale tra VI secolo a.c. e VII secolo d.c.*, edited by Giovanni Filoramo, pp. 345-60. Piacenza: Centro di alti studi in scienze religiose di Piacenza.

Luizard, Pierre-Jean. 1990. Le soufisme égyptien contemporain, *Égypte-Monde arabe*, 2: 35-94.

——— 1991. Le role des confréries soufies dans le système politique égyptien, *Maghreb-Machrek*, 131: 26-53.

——— 1992. Le soufisme réformiste: l'exemple de trois confréries. In *Modernisation et nouvelles formes de mobilisation sociale*, Dossiers du Cedej, pp. 91-107, Cairo: CEDEJ.

Popovic, Alexandre and Veinstein, Gilles. eds. 1986. *Les ordres mystiques dans l'islam: cheminements et situation actuelle*. Paris: Ecole des Hautes Etudes en Sciences Sociales.

——— 1996. *Les voies d'Allah: les ordres mystiques dans le monde musulman des origines à aujourd'hui*. Paris: Fayard.

Tâhir, A.R. and Mahmûd, A.R. 1961. *Al-`Ârif al-Dûmî*. Cairo (printed privately).

Touati, Houari. 1989. Approche sémiologique d'un document hagiographique algérien, *Annales ESC*, 44/5: 1205-28.

Trimingham, J. Spencer. 1971. *The Sufi Orders in Islam*. Oxford: Clarendon Press.

Zeghal, Malika. 1996. *Gardiens de l'islam: les ulamas d'al-Azhar dans l'Égypte contemporaine*. Paris: Presses des Sciences politiques.

Chapter Three

Abu-Manneh, Butrus. 1990. Khalwa and Rabita in the Khalidi Suborder. In *Naqshbandis: cheminements et situation actuelle d'un ordre mystique musulman*, edited by Marc Gaborieau, Alexandre Popovic and Thierry Zarcone, pp. 283-302. Istanbul: Isis.

Algar, Hamid. 1971. Some Notes on the Naqshbandi Tarikat in Bosnia, *Die Welt des Islams*, 13: 168-203.

——— 1976. Silent and Vocal Dhikr in the Naqshbandi Order. In *Akten des VII. Kongresses für Arabistik und Islamwissenschaft*, edited by Albert Dietrich, pp. 39-46. Göttingen: Vandenhoek and Ruprecht.

——— 1990. A Brief History of the Naqshbandi Order. In *Naqshbandis: cheminements et situation actuelle d'un ordre mystique musulman*, edited by Marc Gaborieau, Alexandre Popovic and Thierry Zarcone, pp. 3-44. Istanbul: Isis.

——— 1992. Devotional Practices of the Khalidi Naqshbandis of Ottoman Turkey. In *The Dervish Lodge: Architecture, Art, and Sufism in Ottoman Turkey*, edited by R. Lifchez, pp. 209-27. Berkeley: The University of California Press.

Arendt, Hannah 1968. *Between Past and Future*. New York: Viking.

Asad, Talal. 1986. *The Idea of an Anthropology of Islam*, Occasional Paper. Washington DC: Center for Contemporary Arab Studies, Georgetown University.

——— 1993. *Genealogies of Religion: Disciplines and Reasons of Power in Christianity and Islam*. Baltimore: Johns Hopkins University Press.

Bourdieu. Pierre. 1990. *The Logic of Practice*, trans. by R. Nice. Stanford: Stanford University Press.

Crapanzano, Vincent. 1973. *The Hamadsha: A Study in Moroccan Ethnopsychiatry*. Berkeley: University of California Press.

Çakır, Ruşen. 1990. *Ayet ve slogan: Türkiye'de İslami oluşumlar*. Istanbul: Metis Yayınları.

Derrida, Jacques. 1973. *Speech and Phenomena, and Other Essays on Husserl's Theory of Signs*, trans. by David Allison. Evanston: Northwestern University Press.

Ersöz, Ahmet. 1992. *Abdülaziz Bekkine Hazretleri*. Izmir: Nil Yayınları.

Foucault, Michel. 1979. *Discipline and Punish: The Birth of the Prison*, trans. by Alan Sheridan. New York: Vintage.

——— 1980. *The History of Sexuality*, vol. 1, trans by Robert Hurley. New York: Vintage.

Chapter Three (cont.)

Foucault, Michel. 1991. Governmentality. In *The Foucault Effect: Studies in Governmentality: With Two Lectures by and an Interview with Michel Foucault*, edited by Graham Burchell, Colin Gordon and Peter Miller, pp. 87-104. London: Harvester Wheatsheaf.

Gaborieau, Marc; Popovic, Alexandre and Zarcone, Thierry. eds. 1990. *Naqshbandis: cheminements et situation actuelle d'un ordre mystique musulman*. Istanbul-Paris: Editions Isis.

Gilsenan, Michael. 1973. *Saint and Sufi in Modern Egypt. An Essay in the Sociology of Religion*. Oxford: Clarendon Press.

Gündüz, İrfan. 1984. *Gümüşhânevî Ahmed Ziyâüddîn (KS). Hayatı-eserleri-tarîkat anlayışı ve Hâlidiyye tarîkatı*. Ankara: Seha Neşriyat.

Gürdoğan, Ersin Nazif. 1996. *Görünmeyen üniversite*, Istanbul: İz Yayıncılık.

Hobsbawm, Eric and Ranger, Terence. eds. 1983. *The Invention of Tradition*. Cambridge: Cambridge University Press.

Hourani, Albert. 1981. Sufism and Modern Islam: Shaikh Khalid and the Naqshbandi Order. In *The Emergence of the Modern Middle East*, edited by Albert Hourani, pp. 75-89. Berkeley: University of California Press.

Jäschke, Gotthard. 1972. *Yeni Türkiye'de İslamlık*. Ankara: Bilgi.

Kafadar, Cemal. 1992. The New Visibility of Sufism in Turkish Studies and Cultural Life. In *The Dervish Lodge: Architecture, Art, and Sufism in Ottoman Turkey*, edited by R. Lifchez, pp. 307-22. Berkeley: The University of California Press.

Kara, İsmail. ed. 1997. *Türkiye'de İslâmcılık düşüncesi, cilt 1, 2*. Istanbul: Kitabevi.

Kara, İsmail. 1991. Sonuç yerine: Tekkeler kapandı mı?, *Dergâh*, 16: 14-15; 20.

—— 1998. *Şeyhefendinin rüyasındaki Türkiye*. Istanbul: Kitabevi.

—— 2001 (1994). *İslâmcıların siyasi görüşleri*. Istanbul: Dergâh.

—— 2004. Bir kâseden bin neşve peydâ, *Dergâh*, 173: 16-19.

Kara, Mustafa. 1980. *Din, hayat, sanat açısından tekkeler ve zaviyeler*. Istanbul: Dergâh.

—— 1985. Tanzimat'ta Cumhuriyet'e tasavvuf ve tarikatlar. In *Tanzimat'tan Cumhuriyet'e Türkiye Ansiklopedisi*, edited by Murat Belge, pp. 978-94. Istanbul: İletişim.

—— 2001. Bir Şeyh efendi'nin Meşrutiyet ve Cumhuriyet'e bakışı, *Dergâh*, 134: 14-18.

—— 2002. *Metinlerle günümüz tasavvuf hareketleri*. Istanbul: Dergâh.

Karpat, Kemal H. ed. 2000. *Ottoman Past and Today's Turkey*. Leiden: Brill.

Karpat, Kemal H. 2001. *The Politicization of Islam: Reconstructing Identity, State, Faith and Community in the Late Ottoman State*. Oxford: Oxford University Press.

Keyder, Çağlar. 1987. *State and Class in Turkey: A Study in Capitalist Development*. London: Verso.

Kreiser, Klaus. 1992. The Dervish Living. In *The Dervish Lodge: Architecture, Art, and Sufism in Ottoman Turkey*, edited by Raymond Lifchez, pp. 49-56. Berkeley: The University of California Press.

Lifchez, Raymond. ed. 1992. *The Dervish Lodge: Architecture, Art, and Sufism in Ottoman Turkey*. Berkeley: The University of California Press.

MacIntyre, Alasdair. 1984. *After Virtue*, 2nd edn. Notre Dame: Notre Dame University Press.

Mardin, Şerif. 1991. The Nakşibendi Order in Turkish History. In *Islam in Modern Turkey: Religion, Politics and Literature in a Secular State*, edited by Richard Tapper, pp. 121-42. London: I.B. Tauris.

Meeker, Michael E. 2002. *A Nation of Empire: The Ottoman Legacy of Turkish Modernity*. Berkeley: University of California Press.

Meier, Fritz. 1994. *Zwei Abhandlungen über die Naqšbandiyya. I. Die Herzensbindung an den Meister. II. Kraftakt und Faustrecht des Heiligen, Beiruter Texte und Studien, Bd.58*. Stuttgart: Steiner.

Mitchell, Timothy. 1991. *Colonizing Egypt*, 2nd edn. Berkeley: University of California Press.

Navaro-Yashin, Yael. 2002. *Faces of the State: Secularism and Public Life in Turkey*. Princeton: Princeton University Press.

Chapter Three (cont.)

Necatioğlu, Halil. 1990. İslam alimlerinin tartışılmaz değeri ve üstünlüğü, *İslam*, January.
Ong, Aihwa. 1995. The State Versus Islam: Malay Families, Women's Bodies, and the Body Politic in Malaysia. In *Bewitching Women, Pious Men: Gender and Body Politics in Southeast Asia*, edited by Aihwa Ong and Michael Peletz, pp. 159-94. Berkeley: University of California Press.
Özal, Korkut. 1999. Twenty Years with Mehmed Zahid Kotku: A Personal Story. In *Naqshbandis in Western and Central Asia*, edited by Elisabeth Özdalga, pp. 159-85. Istanbul: Swedish Research Institute in Istanbul.
Radikal, 15 January 2001
Raudvere, Catharina. 2002. *The Book and the Roses: Sufi Women, Visibility, and Zikir in Contemporary Istanbul*. Istanbul: Swedish Research Institute.
Redhouse, Sir James. 1996 (1890). *A Turkish and English Lexicon*, new edn. Beirut: Librairie du Liban.
Schimmel, Annemarie. 1975. *Mystical Dimensions of Islam*. Chapel Hill: The University of North Carolina Press.
Silverstein, Brian. 2003. Islam and Modernity in Turkey: Power, Tradition and Historicity in the European Provinces of the Muslim World, *Anthropological Quarterly*, 76: 497-517.
⸻ 2005. Islamist Critique in Modern Turkey: Hermeneutics, Tradition, Genealogy, *Comparative Studies in Society and History*, 47: 134-60.
⸻ (2009). "Sufism and Governmentality in the Late Ottoman Empire," *Comparative Studies of South Asia, Africa and the Middle East*, 29(2): 171-185.
Sitembölükbaşi, Şaban. 1995. *Türkiye'de İslâm'in yeniden inkişafi*. Ankara: Türkiye Diyanet Vakfi.
Smith, Wilfred Cantwell. 1957. *Islam in Modern History*. Princeton: Princeton University Press.
Trimingham, J. Spencer. 1998. *The Sufi Orders in Islam*. Oxford: Clarendon Press.
White, Jenny B. 2002. *Islamist Mobilization in Turkey: A Study in Vernacular Politics*. London: University of Washington Press.
Yavuz, Hakan. 1999. The Matrix of Modern Turkish Islamic Movements: The Naqshbandi Order. In *Naqshbandis in Western and Central Asia*, edited by Elisabeth Özdalga, pp. 129–46. Istanbul: Swedish Research Institute in Istanbul.
⸻ 2003. *Islamic Political Identity in Turkey*. New York: Oxford University Press.
Zarcone, Thierry. 1993. *Mystiques, philosphes et franc-maçons en islam*. Paris: Jean Maisonneuve Editeur.
Zürcher, Erik J. 1994. *Turkey: A Modern History*, revised edn. London: I.B. Tauris.

Chapter Four

Afarinish. 2003. Ra'is-i kumisiyun-i asl-i 90: guzarish-niha'i dar-bara-yi shikayat-i khanaqahha-yi Ni`matullahi bi tasvib rasid, *Afarinesh*. http://www.afarineshdaily.com/newspapers/news13811108/politic4.asp?name=politic. Accessed 28 January 2003.
Ahmadi, Kiyan. 1381/2002 Sada-yi zalzala mi-ayad, Parvana!, *Naw-andish*, November-December/Azar, 30(4): 8-9.
Al-i Ahmad, Jalal. 1372/1993 [1344/1962]. *Gharbzadagi*. Tehran: Intisharat-i Firdaws.
Algar, Hamid. 1993. Dhahabiya. In *Encyclopaedia Iranica*, vi, pp. 578-81. Costa Mesa, Cal.: Mazda.
Alinejad, Mahmoud. 1999. Imagination, Meaning and Revolution. The Sources of the Revolutionary Power of Islam in Iran. PhD dissertation, University of Amsterdam.
Anonymous. 1333/1954. *Pasukhi bi intibah-nama-yi hay'at-i mushawara-yi anjuman-i ukhuwwat*. Tehran: n.p.
Azimi, Fakhreddin. 1998. Entezam. In *Encyclopaedia Iranica*, viii, pp. 461-63. Costa Mesa, Cal.: Mazda.

Chapter Four (cont.)

Baldick, Julian. 1993. *Imaginary Muslims. The Uwaysi Sufis of Central Asia.* New York: New York University Press.

Bianchi, Gabriella. 2000. Shocked Darvish Sheik Back in Wild Kurdestan. http://www.iranreporter.com/story.asp?id=28. Accessed 20 March 2006.

Boroujerdi, Mehrzad. 1996. *Iranian Intellectuals and the West: The Tormented Triumph of Nativism.* Syracuse, NY: Syracuse University Press.

Chahardahi, Nur al-din Mudarrisi. 1352/1973. Silsila-yi Ni`matullahi-Munis`alishahi, *Vahid*, 11(5): 526-31.

──── 1361/1982-3. *Sayri dar tasawwuf.* Tehran: Intisharat-i Ishraqi.

Dabashi, Hamid. 1993. *Theology of Discontent: The Ideological Foundation of the Islamic Revolution in Iran.* New York: New York University Press.

Durkheim, Emile. 1977 [1895]. *Les règles de la méthode sociologique.* Paris: Presses Universitaires de France.

Esfandiari, Golnaz. 2006. *Iran: Qom Authorities Crack Down On Sufis, Radio Free Europe/Radio Liberty.* http://www.rferl.org/featuresarticle/2006/02/2ecd7fd6-2aa1-489a-b2ac-4e64bbd71d50.html. Accessed 17 February 2006.

Fanon, Frantz. 1968 [1959]. *Sociologie d'une révolution (l'an V de la révolution algérienne).* Paris: Maspéro.

Fischer, Michael M.J. 1980. *Iran: From Religious Dispute to Revolution.* Cambridge, Mass.: Harvard University Press.

Ghaffari, Emir Nosrateddine. 1964. *Les soufis de l'Iran. Apologie d'une civilisation.* Tehran: Tchap-Rangine.

Ghahari, Keivandokht. 2001. *Nationalismus und Modernismus in Iran in der Periode zwischen dem Zerfall der Qajaren-Dynastie und der Machtfestigung Reza Schahs.* Berlin: Klaus Schwarz Verlag.

Gramlich, Richard. 1965. *Die schiitischen Derwischorden Persiens 1: Die Affiliationen.* Wiesbaden: Deutsche Morgenländische Gesellschaft; Kommissionsverlag Franz Steiner.

──── 1976. *Die schiitischen Derwischorden Persiens 2: Glaube und Lehre,* Wiesbaden: Deutsche Morgenländische Gesellschaft; Kommissionsverlag Franz Steiner.

──── 1981. *Die schiitischen Derwischorden Persiens 3: Brauchtum und Riten,* Wiesbaden: Deutsche Morgenländische Gesellschaft; Kommissionsverlag Franz Steiner.

Hasuri, `Ali. 1375/1997. `Irfan wa naqsh-i tarikhi-yi an, *Jami`a-yi salam*, 6(29): 6-9.

Homayouni, Massoud. 1991. *Memoirs of a Sufi Master in Iran.* London: The Mawlana Centre.

Humayuni, Mas`ud. 1371/1992. *Tarikh-i silsilaha-yi tariqa-yi Ni`matullahiyya dar Iran,* London: Bunyad-i `irfan-i Mawlana.

Iran House. 2002. Iran Bars World Sufism Conference, *Middle East Times*, 19 August. http://www.iranhouseindia.com/year03/rep-sufism.htm. Accessed 20 March 2006.

Iran House. 2003. National Seminar on 'Erfan wa Tasaww[o]f-e Islami', 7 and 8 December, http://www.iranhouseindia.com/year03/rep-sufism.htm. Accessed 20 March 2006.

Kadivar, Muhsin. 1378/1999 [1377/1998]. *Hukumat-i wila'i* (Andisha-yi Siyasi dar Islam, 2). Tehran: Nashr-i nay.

──── 1380/2001 [1376/1998] *Nazariyyaha-yi dawlat dar fiqh-i shi`a* (Andisha-yi Siyasi dar Islam, 1). Tehran: Nashr-i nay.

Kasrawi, Ahmad. 1342/1963. *Sufigari.* Tehran: Matbu`at-i Furughi.

Khosrokhavar, Farhad and Roy, Olivier. 1999. *Iran: Comment sortir d'une révolution religieuse.* Paris: Éditions du Seuil.

Lewisohn, Leonard. 1998. An Introduction to the History of Modern Persian Sufism, Part I, The Ni`matullahi Order: Persecution, Revival and Schism, *Bulletin of the School of Oriental and African Studies*, 61(3): 437-64.

──── 1999. An Introduction to the History of Modern Persian Sufism, Part II, A Sociocultural Profile of Sufism, from the Dhahabi Revival to the Present Day, *Bulletin of the School of Oriental and African Studies*, 62(1): 36-59.

Chapter Four (cont.)

Lukes, Steven. ed. 1982. *The Rules of Sociological Method by Emile Durkheim, with an Introduction by Steven Lukes*. New York: Free Press.

Madani, Muhammad. 1376/1997. *Dar khanaqah-i Baydukht chi mi-guzarad?* Tehran: n.p.

Matin-Asgari, Afshin. 1997. `Abdolkarim Sorush and the Secularization of Islamic Thought in Iran, *Iranian studies*, 30(1-2): 95-115.

Miller, W. 1923. Shi`ah Mysticism (The Sufis of Gunabad), *The Moslem World*, 13: 343-63.

Mujtahid-Shabistari, Muhammad. 1379/2000. *Naqdi bar qira'at-i rasmi az din*. Tehran: Intisharat-i tarh-i naw.

Nasr, Seyyed Hossein. 1979. Introduction. In *A Shi`ite Anthology*, edited by M.H. Tabataba'i, pp. 5-13. Qum: Ansariyan Publications.

―――― 1991. Sufism and Spirituality in Persia. In *Islamic Spirituality: Manifestations*, edited by S.H. Nasr, pp. 206-22. London: SCM Press Ltd.

Nurbakhsh, Javad. 1980. *Masters of the Path: A History of the Masters of the Nimatullahi Sufi Order*. New York: Khaniqahi-Nimatullahi Publications.

Parishanzada, Abu'l-Hasan. 1377/1998. *Gushayish-i raz (pasukh bi kitab-i 'Raz-gusha'-yi Kaywan Qazwini*. Tehran: Intisharat-i Haqiqat.

Rahnema, Ali. 2000. *An Islamic Utopian: A Political Biography of Ali Shari`ati*. London: I.B. Tauris.

Ridgeon, Lloyd. 2006. *Castigator of Sufism: Ahmad Kasravi and the Iranian Mystical Tradition*. London: Routledge.

Roy, Olivier. 2001. Qu'est-ce que le postislamisme?, *Esprit*, (8): 52-3.

Salih`alishah [Sayyid Taqi Wahidi]. 1375/1996. *Az ku-yi sufiyan ta huzur-i `arifan*. Tehran: n.p.

Sauerwein, Uwe. 2002. Per Trance zur göttlichen Wahrheit. Gesänge fur die Seele im Haus der Kulturen der Welt: Sufi-Meister aus dem Iran eröffneten Festival 'Sacred Music', *Berliner Morgenpost*, 8 December, http://morgenpost.berlin1.de/print.php/archiv2002/021208/feuilleton/story568292.html. Accessed 20 March 2006.

Shayegan, Daryush. 1992. *Cultural Schizophrenia: Islamic Societies Confronting the West*. Syracuse, N.Y.: Syracuse University Press.

Surush, `Abd al-karim. 1378/1999. Mawlawi wa tasawwuf-i `ishqi, *Iran*, 26 Mehr/18 October, p. 10.

Tabanda, Dr. Hajj Nur `Ali [Majdhub`alishah]. 1378/1999-2000. *Majmu`i-yi maqalat-i fiqhi wa ijtima`i*. Tehran: Intisharat-i Haqiqat.

Tabanda, Hajj Sultanhusayn [Riza`alishah]. 1354/1975. *Nazar-i madhhabi bi i`lamiyya-yi huquq-i bashar. Nigarish-i Sultanhusayn Tabanda Gunabadi*. Tehran: Chapkhana-yi Payruz.

Tabataba'i, Jawad. 1379/2000 [1374/1995]. *Ibn-i Khaldun wa `ulum-i ijtima`i*. Tehran: Intisharat-i tarh-e naw.

Tanha'i, H.A. 1378/1999. *Tarikh-i andisha wa nazariyyat-i jami`a-shinasi az ibtida ta kunun. Jild-i 2:Jami`a-shinasi-yi tarikhi-yi islam*. Tehran: Nashr-i Ruzigar.

―――― 1379/2000. *Jami`a-shinasi-yi nazari-yi islam. Mutala`a-yi guzida'i az nazariyyat-i jami`a-shinakhti wa insan-shinakhti-yi mutafikkirin, falasifa wa sufiyan-i musalman*. Mashhad: Nashr-i sukhan-gostar.

Van den Bos, Matthijs. 2002a. A Modern Iranian Shiite Friend of God – Nur`alishah II (1867–1918), *Persica*, XVIII: 1-15.

―――― 2002b. *Mystic Regimes: Sufism and the State in Iran, from the Late Qajar Era to the Islamic Republic*. Leiden: Brill.

―――― 2002c. Sufi Authority in Khatami's Iran. Some Fieldwork Notes, *Oriente Moderno*, XXI(LXXXII): 351-78.

Zarrinkoob, Abdol-Hosein [Zarrinkub]. 1970. Persian Sufism in its Historical Perspective, *Iranian Studies*, 3(3): 139-220.

Zarrinkub, `Abd al-husayn. 1369/1990. *Dunbala-yi just-u-ju dar tasawwuf-i Iran*. Tehran: Amir Kabir.

Chapter Five

Abun-Nasr, Jamil M. 1965. *The Tijaniyya: A Sufi Order in the Modern World*. London: Oxford University Press.

Anonymous. 2000. Cheick Soufi Bilal et la Quadria, *Kabako*, 224, 10 March, p. 2.

Anonymous. 2002. Le saint Cheikh Salah avait prédit, *Le Réflet*, 248, 21 August, p. 2.

Anonymous. 2003. Religion: La Tijania démystifiée par Cheick Soufi Bilal, *Kabako*, 312, 7 June, p. 25.

Babou, Cheikh Anta. 2002. Brotherhood Solidarity, Education, and Migration: The Role of the Dahiras among Murid Muslim Community in New York, *African Affairs*, 101: 151-70.

Bilal, Cheick Soufi. n.d. 1. *La Qadria*. n.p.

Bilal, Cheick Soufi. n.d. 2. *Sourate ikhlaç en [sic] dix prières superérogatoires*. n.p.

Bilal, Cheick Soufi. n.d. 3. *La Tijania voie spirituelle de Cheick Ahamad Tijane*. n.p.

Bilal, Cheick Soufi. n.d. 4. *La célébration du Maouloud*. n.p.

Bilal, Cheick Soufi. n.d. 5. *La lumière du Ramadan*. n.p.

Bilal, Cheick Soufi. n.d. 6. *Nouroul anwar (origines des creatures)*. n.p.

Bouaré, O. 2003. Réconciliation entre les villages. Cheick Soufi Bilal joue à la Colombe, *Kabako*, 328, 11 December, p. 6.

Brenner, Louis. 1993. Constructing Muslim Identities in Mali. In *Muslim Identity and Social Change in Sub-Saharan Africa*, edited by L. Brenner, pp. 59-78. Bloomington: Indiana University Press.

Cardaire, Marcel. 1954. *L'islam et le terroir africain*. Koulouba: Institut français d'Afrique noire.

Coulon, Christian. 1988. *Les musulmans et le pouvoir en Afrique noire*, 2nd edn. Paris: Karthala.

Cruise O'Brien, Donal B. 1971. *The Mourides of Senegal*. Oxford: Clarendon Press.

——— 1975. *Saints and Politicians*. Cambridge: Cambridge University Press.

Dijk, Rijk. van. 1998. Pentecostalism, Cultural Memory and the State: Contested Representations of Time in Postcolonial Malawi. In *Memory and the Postcolony*, edited by Richard Werbner, pp. 155-81. London and New York: Zed Books.

Diouf, Mamadou. 2000. The Senegalese Murid Trade Diaspora and the Making of a Vernacular Cosmopolitanism, *Public Culture*, 12 (3): 679-702.

Guindo, A.L. 2003. Daouda Yattara, Sitanè: Le courage d'une croyance, la force d'une conviction, *Liberté*, 161, 7 January, p. 2.

Hackett, Rosalind I.J. 1986. African New Religious Movements, *African Studies Review*, 29(3): 141-6.

——— 2003. Discourses of Demonization in Africa and Beyond, *Diogenes*, 50(3): 61-75.

Hiskett, Mervyn. 1984. *The Development of Islam in West Africa*. London: Longman.

Hunwick, John O. 2003. *Arabic Literature of Africa, Vol. IV: The Writings of Western Sudanic Africa*. Leiden: Brill.

Jules-Rosette, Bennetta, ed. 1979. *The New Religions of Africa*. Trenton: Ablex Publishing.

Launay, Robert. 1992. *Beyond the Stream: Islam and Society in a West Africa Town*. Berkeley: University of California Press.

Loimeier, Roman. 1997. *Islamic Reform and Political Change in Northern Nigeria*. Evanston: Northwestern University Press.

Mann, Gregory. 2003. Fetishizing Religion: Allah Koura and French 'Islamic Policy' in Late Colonial French Soudan (Mali), *Journal of African History*, 44: 263-82.

Marty, Paul. 1921. *Études sur l'islam et les tribus du Soudan: Les tribus maures du Sahel et du Hodh*, vol. 3. Paris: Ernest Leroux.

Meyer, Birgit. 1998. 'Make a Complete Break with the Past': Memory and Postcolonial Modernity in Ghanaian Pentecostal Discourse. In *Memory and the Postcolony*, edited by Richard Werbner, pp. 182-208. London and New York: Zed Books.

Pazo. 2000. Djicoroni Para. Cheick Soufi Bilal sauve les situations désespérées à coups de chapelet, *Kabako*, 232, 30 June, p. 4.

Chapter Five (cont.)

Perry, Donna L. 1997. Rural Ideologies and Urban Imaginings: Wolof Immigrants in New York City, *Africa Today*, 44(2): 229-60.

Riccio, Bruno. 2004. Transnational Mouridism and the Afro-Muslim Critique of Italy, *Journal of Ethnic and Migration Studies*, 30(5): 929-44.

Royer, Patrick. 1999. Le Massa et l'eau de Moussa: Cultes régionaux, 'traditions' locales et sorcellerie en Afrique de l'Ouest, *Cahiers d'études africaines*, 39(2): 337-66.

Savishinsky, Neil J. 1994. Rastafari in the Promised Land: The Spread of a Jamaican Socioreligious Movement among the Youth of West Africa, *African Studies Review*, 37(3): 19-50.

Seesemann, Rüdiger. 2002. 'Ein Dialog der Taubstummen': französische vs. britische Wahrnehmungen des Islam im spätkolonialen Westafrika, *Africa Spectrum*, 37(2): 109-39.

Sangho, Ben Sidy Kalil. 2002. Daouda Yattara dit Sitanè: Rencontre avec un serviteur de Satan, *Nouvel Horizon*, 1853, 19 February, pp. 5-6, 8.

Soares, Benjamin F. 1999. Muslim Proselytization as Purification: Religious Pluralism and Conflict in Contemporary Mali. In *Proselytization and Communal Self-Determination in Africa*, edited by Abdullahi A. An-Na'im, pp. 228-45. Maryknoll, NY: Orbis Books.

——— 2004a. Islam and Public Piety in Mali. In *Public Islam and the Common Good*, edited by Armando Salvatore and Dale F. Eickelman, pp. 205-26. Leiden: Brill.

——— 2004b. Muslim Saints in the Age of Neoliberalism. In *Producing African Futures: Ritual and Reproduction in a Neoliberal Age*, edited by Brad Weiss, pp. 79-105. Leiden: Brill.

——— 2005. *Islam and the Prayer Economy: History and Authority in a Malian Town*. Edinburgh and Ann Arbor: Edinburgh University Press and the University of Michigan Press.

——— 2006. Islam in Mali in the Neoliberal Era, *African Affairs*, 105(418): 77-95.

Tall, Cheikh Ahmad. 1995. *Niche des secrets: Recueil d'arcanes mystiques dans la tradition soufie (islamique)*, 2nd edn. Dakar: n.p.

Traoré, M.S. 2002. Sciences occultes: Le Satan de Kanadiguila se fache, *L'Observateur*, 701, 21 February, p. 6.

Triaud, Jean-Louis and David Robinson. eds. 2000. *La Tijâniyya: une confrérie musulmane à la conquête de l'Afrique*. Paris: Karthala.

Villalón, Leonardo A. 1995. *Islamic Society and State Power in Senegal: Disciples and Citizens in Fatick*. Cambridge: Cambridge University Press.

Zahan, Dominique. 1960. *Sociétés d'initiation Bambara: Le N'domo, le Korè*. Paris and the Hague: Mouton.

Chapter Six

Abdurrahman, Moeslim. 1978. Sufisme di Kediri. In *Sufisme di Indonesia* [special issue of journal *Dialog*], 23-40.

——— 1990. Die Tijaniyya in Indonesien: orthodox oder häretisch?. In *Islamische mystische Bruderschaften im heutigen Indonesien*, edited by Werner Kraus, pp. 131-44. Hamburg: Institut fur Asienkunde.

Ahmad, Hamid. 2001. *Percik-percik keteladanan Kiai Hamid Pasuruan*. Pasuruan: Lembaga Informasi dan Studi Islam (L'Islam) Yayasan Ma'had as-Salafiyah.

Bruinessen, Martin van. 1990. The Origins and Development of the Naqshbandi Order in Indonesia, *Der Islam*, 67: 150-79.

——— 1992. *Tarekat Naqsyabandiyah di Indonesia. Survei historis, geografis, dan sosiologis.* Bandung: Mizan.

——— 1994a. The Origins and Development of Sufi Orders (Tarekat) in Southeast Asia, *Studia Islamika - Indonesian Journal for Islamic Studies*, 1(1): 1-23.

——— 1994b. *NU: tradisi, relasi-relasi kuasa, pencarian wacana baru*. Yogyakarta: LKiS.

Chapter Six (cont.)

Bruinessen, Martin van. 1994c. Pesantren and Kitab Kuning: Continuity and Change in a Tradition of Religious Learning. In *Texts from the Islands: Oral and Written Traditions of Indonesia and the Malay World*, edited by Wolfgang Marschall, pp. 121-46. Berne: The University of Berne Institute of Ethnology.

―――― 1999. Controversies and Polemics Involving the Sufi Orders in Twentieth-century Indonesia. In *Islamic Mysticism Contested: Thirteen Centuries of Controversies and Polemics*, edited by Frederick de Jong and Bernd Radtke, pp. 705-28. Leiden: Brill.

―――― 2002. Back to Situbondo? Nahdlatul Ulama Attitudes towards Abdurrahman Wahid's Presidency and His Fall. In *Indonesia: In Search of Transition*, edited by Henk Schulte Nordholt and Irwan Abdullah, pp. 15-46. Yogyakarta: Pustaka Pelajar.

―――― 2006. After the Days of Abû Qubays: Indonesian Transformations of the Naqshbandiyya Khâlidiyya, *Journal of the History of Sufism*, 5.

Dhofier, Zamakhsyari. 1999. *The Pesantren Tradition: The Role of the Kyai in the Maintenance of Traditional Islam in Java*. Arizona: Arizona State University, Program for Southeast Asian Studies.

Drewes, G.W.J. 1925. *Drie Javaansche Goeroe's. Hun leven, onderricht en messiasprediking*. Leiden: A. Vros [diss. Leiden].

Effendi, Djohan. 1990a. PPTI: eine konfliktreiche Tarekat-Organisation. In *Islamische mystische Bruderschaften im heutigen Indonesien*, edited by Werner Kraus, pp. 91-100. Hamburg: Institut fur Asienkunde.

―――― 1990b. Über nichtortodoxe und synkretistische Bruderschaften im gegenwartigen Indonesien. In *Islamische mystische Bruderschaften im heutigen Indonesien*, edited by Werner Kraus, pp. 101-30. Hamburg: Institut für Asienkunde.

Feener, R. Michael. 1998. A Re-examination of the Place of al-Hallaj in the Development of Southeast Asian Islam, *Bijdragen tot de Taal-, Land- en Volkenkunde*, 154: 571-92.

Geertz, Clifford. 1959. Ritual and Social Change: A Javanese Example, *American Anthropologist*, 61: 991-1012.

―――― 1960. *The Religion of Java*. New York: The Free Press.

―――― 1968. *Islam Observed: Religious Development in Morocco and Indonesia*. New Haven: Yale University Press.

Grave, Jean-Marc de. 2001. *Initiation rituelle et arts martiaux: Trois écoles de kanuragan javanais*. Paris: L'Harmattan.

Hassan, Kamal. 1980. *Muslim Intellectual Response to New Order Modernization in Indonesia*. Kuala Lumpur: Dewan Bahasa.

Howell, Julia Day. 1976. *Vehicles for the Kalki Avatar: The Experiments of a Javanese Guru in Rationalizing Ecstatic Religion*. PhD dissertation. Stanford University.

―――― 2001. Sufism and the Indonesian Islamic Revival, *The Journal of Asian Studies*, 60: 701-29.

Howell, Julia Day, Subandi, and Nelson, Peter L. 1998. Indonesian Sufism: Signs of Resurgence. In *New Trends and Developments in the World of Islam*, edited by Peter B. Clarke, pp. 277-97. London: Luzac Oriental.

Jay, Robert. 1957. *Santri and Abangan: Religious Schism in Rural Central Java*. Cambridge, Mass.: Harvard University Press.

Kartodirdjo, Sartono, Soeroto, Soeri and Hatmosuprobo, Suhardjo. eds. 1975. *Sarekat Islam local*. Jakarta: Arsip Nasional Republik Indonesia.

Korver, A.P.E. 1982. *Sarekat Islam 1912-1916. Opkomst, bloei en structuur van Indonesie's eerste massabeweging*. Amsterdam: Historisch Seminarium van de Universiteit van Amsterdam.

Kumar, Ann. 1985. *The Diary of a Javanese Muslim: Religion, Politics and the Pesantren 1883-1886*, Canberra: Australian National University, Faculty of Asian Studies.

Latief, Sanusi. 1988. *Gerakan kaum tua di Minangkabau*. PhD dissertation. IAIN, Jakarta.

Lombard, Denys. 1985. Les tarékat en Insulinde. In *Les ordres mystiques en Islam*, edited by Alexandre Popovic and Gilles Veinstein, pp. 139-63. Paris: E.H.E.S.S.

McDonald, Hamish. 1980. *Suharto's Indonesia*, Blackburn, Victoria: Fontana Books.

Chapter Six (cont.)

Millie, Julian Patrick. 2006. *Splashed by the Saint: Ritual Reading and Islamic Sanctity in West Java.* PhD thesis. Universiteit Leiden, Leiden.

Mulyati, Sri. 2004. Tarekat Qadiriyyah wa Naqsyabandiyyah: tarekat temuan tokoh Indonesia asli. In *Tarekat tarekat muktabarah di Indonesia*, edited by Sri Mulyati, pp. 253-90. Jakarta: Prenada Media.

Muttalib, Jang A. 1981. Social Movements in Jambi during the Early 20th Century, *Prisma: The Indonesian Indicator*, 22: 17-28.

Reeve, David. 1985. *Golkar of Indonesia: An Alternative to the Party System.* Singapore: Oxford University Press.

Soebardi, Soebakin. 1978. The Pesantren Tarikat of Surialaya in West Java. In *Spectrum: Essays Presented to S.T. Alisjahbana*, edited by S. Udin, pp. 215-36. Jakarta: Dian Rakyat.

Stange, Paul. 1980. *The Sumarah Movement in Javanese Mysticism.* PhD thesis. University of Wisconsin, Madison.

Sujuthi, Mahmud. 2001. *Politik tarekat Qadiriyah wa Naqsyabandiyah Jombang: studi tentang hubungan agama, negara dan masyarakat.* Yogyakarta: Galang Press.

Suwandi, Raharjo. 2000. *A Quest for Justice: The Millenary Aspirations of a Contemporary Javanese Wali.* Leiden: KITLV Press.

Thoriqot Mu'tabaroh. 1977. *Dokumentasi & keputusan Konggres ke V Jam'iyyah Ahli Thoriqot Mu'tabaroh di Madiun, tgl 2 s/d 5 Agustus 1975M.* Semarang: Pucuk Pimpinan Thoriqot Mu'tabaroh.

Chapter Seven

Abu Ghudda, `Abd al-Fattah. 1992. *Safahat min sabr al-`ulama `ala shada'id al-`ilm wa-l-tahsil*, 3rd edn. Aleppo: Maktab al-matba`at al-islamiyya.

Abu-Manneh, Butrus. 2001. *Studies on Islam and the Ottoman Empire in the 19th Century. 1826-1876.* Istanbul: Isis Press.

Ahmad, Aziz. 1964. *Studies in Islamic Culture in the Indian Environment.* Oxford: Oxford University Press.

Ahmad, Aziz. 1967. *Islamic Modernism in India and Pakistan, 1857-1964.* London: Oxford University Press.

Alam, Muzaffar. 1986. *The Crisis of Empire in Mughal North India, 1707-1748.* Oxford: Oxford University Press.

Algar, Hamid. 1990. A Brief History of the Naqshbandi Order. In *Naqshbandis: cheminements et situation actuelle d'un ordre mystique musulman*, edited by Marc Gaborieau, Alexandre Popovic and Thierry Zarcone, pp. 3-44. Istanbul and Paris: Isis Press.

Al Rashid, Muhammad ibn `Abdallah. 1999. *Imdad al-fattah bi-asanid wa-muruyyat al-Shaykh `Abd al-Fattah.* Riyad: Maktabat al-Imam al-Shafi`i.

Azami, Neyaz Ahmad. 1994. Shibli on Muslim Education and Politics, *Islam and the Modern Age*, 25: 190-205.

al-Bani, Muhammad Bashir. n.d. *al-Murshid al-mujaddid.* Damascus.

Barbir, Karl K. 1990. All in the Family: The Muradis of Damascus. In *IIIrd Congress on the Social and Economic History of Turkey, Princeton University, 24-26 August 1983*, edited by Heath W. Lowry and Ralph S. Hattox, pp. 327-35. Istanbul, Washington and Paris: Isis Press.

Batatu, Hanna. 1982. Syria's Muslim Brethren, *Merip Reports*, 110: 14.

al-Bayanuni, `Isa. 1344/1925. *al-Arab fi adab mukhtasar kitab abwab al-rahiq fi adab al-tariq.* Aleppo: al-Matba`a al-`ilmiyya.

Bayly, C.A. 1988. *Indian Society and the Making of British India.* Cambridge: Cambridge University Press.

Böttcher, Annabelle. 1998. *Syrische Religionspolitik unter Asad.* Freiburg: Arnold-Bergsträsser-Institut.

Chapter Seven (cont.)

Bredi, Daniella. 1999. Sadat in South Asia: The Case of Abu'l-Hasan `Ali Nadwi, *Oriente Moderno*, 18: 375-92.

De Jong, Frederick. 1990. The Naqshbandiyya in Egypt and Syria: Aspects of Its History and Observations Concerning its Present-day Condition. In *Naqshbandis: cheminements et situation actuelle d'un ordre mystique musulman*, edited by Marc Gaborieau, Alexandre Popovic and Thierry Zarcone, pp. 589-601. Istanbul and Paris: Isis Press.

Friedmann, Yohanan. 1971. *Shaykh Ahmad Sirhindi: An Outline of His Thought and a Study of His Image in the Eyes of Posterity*. Montreal: McGill–Queen's University Press.

Geoffroy, Eric. 1997. Sufism, réformisme et pouvoir en Syrie contemporaine, *Égypte/Monde Arabe*, 29: 11-18.

Habash, Muhammad. 1989. *al-Shaykh Amin Kuftaru fi dhikra khamsin `am `ala wafatihi*. Damascus: Dar al-ma`rifa.

Habash, Muhammad. 1996. *al-Shaykh Ahmad Kuftaru wa-minhajuhu fi al-tajdid wa-l-islah*. Damascus: Dar al-nur.

al-Hafiz, Muhammad Muti` and Nizar Abaza. 1986. *Ta'rikh `ulama Dimashq fi al-qarn al-rabi` `ashar al-hijri*, vol. 2. Damascus: Dar al-fikr.

Hansen, Thomas Blom. 1999. *The Saffron Wave: Democracy and Hindu Nationalism in Modern India*. Princeton: Princeton University Press.

Hardy, Peter. 1972. *The Muslims of British India*. Cambridge, Cambridge University Press.

Hartung, Jan-Peter. 2003. *Viele Wege und ein Ziel: Leben und Wirken von Sayyid Abu l-Hasan `Ali al-Hasani Nadwi 1914-1999*. Wurzburg: Ergon.

Hashmi, Syed Mansoor Ali Akhtar. 1989. *Muslim Response to Western Education: A Study of Four Pioneer Institutions*. New Delhi: Commonwealth Publishers.

Hawwa, Sa`id. n.d. *Jund Allah: Thaqafa wa-akhlaq*. Beirut: Dar al-kutub al-`ilmiyya.

Hawwa, Sa`id. 1981. *Tarbiyatuna al-ruhiyya*, 2nd edn. Amman: Maktabat al-risala al-haditha.

Hawwa, Sa`id. 1984. *Ihya al-rabbaniyya*. Cairo: Dar al-Salam.

Hawwa, Sa`id. 1986. *Mudhakkirat fi manazil al-siddiqiyin wa-l-rabbaniyin*. Cairo: Dar al-salam.

Hawwa, Sa`id. 1987. *Hadhihi tajribati ... wa-hadhihi shahadati*. Cairo: Maktabat Wahba.

al-Hindi, Abu al-Hayat Muhammad `Abd al-Hayy al-Lakhnawi. 1988. *Sibahat al-fikr fi al-jahr bi-l-dhikr*. Aleppo: Maktab al-matbu`at al-`ilmiyya.

al-Hindi, `Abd al-Hayy al-Lakhnawi. 1963. *al-Raf` wa-l-takmil fi al-jarh wa-l-ta`dil*, edited by `Abd al-Fattah Abu Ghudda. Aleppo: Maktab al-matbu`at al-`ilmiyya.

Hinnebusch, Raymond A. 1990. *Authoritarian Power and State Formation in Ba'thist Syria: Army, Party, and Peasant*. Boulder, Col.: Westview Press.

Hinnebusch, Raymond A. 1996. State and Islamism in Syria. In *Islamic Fundamentalism*, edited by Abdel Salam Sidahmed and Anoushiravan Ehteshami, pp. 199-214. Boulder, Col.: Westview Press.

Hodgson, Marshal G.S. 1974. *The Venture of Islam: Conscience and History in a World Civilization*, vol. 3. Chicago: University of Chicago Press.

Kepel, Gilles. 1985. *The Prophet and Pharaoh: Muslim Extremism in Egypt*. London: al-Saqi.

Lelyveld, David. 1978. *Alighar's First Generation: Muslim Solidarity in British India*. Princeton: Princeton University Press.

Levtzion, Nehemia and Voll, John O. eds. 1978. *Eighteenth Century Renewal and Reform Movements in Islam*, Syracuse: Syracuse University Press.

Lobmeyer, Hans Gunter. 1995. *Opposition und Wiederstand in Syrien*. Hamburg: Deutsches Orient-Institut.

Malik, Jamal. 1994. The Making of a Council: The Nadwat al-`Ulama, *Islamic Culture*, 68: 11-40.

Masud, Muhammad Khalid. ed. 2000. *Travellers in Faith: Studies of the Tablighi Jama`at as a Transnational Islamic Movement for Faith Renewal*. Leiden: Brill.

Mayer, Thomas. 1983. The Islamic Opposition in Syria, 1961-1982, *Orient*, 4: 589-609.

Metcalf, Barbara D. 1982. *Islamic Revival in British India: Deoband 1860-1900*. Princeton: Princeton University Press.

Chapter Seven (cont.)

Mitchell, Richard. 1969. *The Society of the Muslim Brothers*. London: Oxford University Press.

Moussalli, Ahmad S. 1999. *Moderate and Radical Islamic Fundamentalism: The Quest for Modernity, Legitimacy, and the Islamic State*. Gainesville, Fl.: University Press of Florida.

al-Muhasibi, Al-Harith. 1964. *Risalat al-mustarshidin*, edited by `Abd al-Fattah Abu Ghudda. Aleppo: Al-Harith al-Muhasibi.

Mukarram, Ahmed. 1992. Some Aspects of Contemporary Islamic Thought: Guidance and Governance in the Work of Mawlana Abul Hasan Ali Nadwi and Mawlana Abul Aala Mawdudi. PhD dissertation. University of Oxford, Oxford.

Naddaf, Imad `Abd al-Latif. 1997. *Al-Shaykh Ahmad Kuftaru yatahaddath*. Beirut: Dar al-rashid.

Nadwi, Maulana Abul Hasan Ali. 1994. *Saviours of Islamic Spirit, Volume 3: Shaikh Ahmad Mujaddid Alf Thani*, ed. and trans. by Mohiuddin Ahmad, 2nd edn. Lucknow: Academy of Islamic Press and Publications.

al-Nadwi, Abu al-Hasan al-Hasani. 1380/1961. Faragh yajibu an yumla, *Hadarat al-Islam*, 1(9): 25-33.

al-Nadwi, Abu al-Hasan `Ali al-Hasani. 1384/1964. Bayni wa-bayna faqid al-Islam al-Ustadh al-Duktur al-Siba'i, *Hadarat al-Islam*, 5(6): 8-15.

al-Nadwi, Abu al-Hasan `Ali al-Hasani. 1394/1974. *Min nahr Kabul ila nahr al-Yarmuk*. Ankara: Dar al-Hilal.

al-Nadwi, Abu al-Hasan `Ali al-Hasan. 1975. *Mudhakkirat sa'ih fi al-sharq al-`arabi*, 2nd edn. Beirut: Muassasat al-Risala.

al-Nadwi, Abu al-Hasan `Ali al-Hasani. 1980. *Ridda ... la Abu Bakr laha*. Lucknow: al-Majma` al-Islami al-Hindi.

al-Nadwi, Abu al-Hasan `Ali al-Hasani. 1986. *Rabbaniyya la rahbaniyya*, 4th edn. Beirut: Mu'assasat al-risala.

al-Nadwi, Muhammad Akram. 1998. *Nafahat al-Hind wa-l-Yaman bi-asanid al-Shaykh Abi al-Hasan*. Riyad: Maktabat al-Imam al-Shafi`i.

Nasr, Seyyed Vali Reza. 1994. *The Vanguard of the Islamic Revolution: The Jama`at -i Islami of Pakistan*. Berkeley and Los Angeles: University of California Press.

Nizami, Khaliq Ahmad. 1989. *Akbar and Religion*. Delhi: DK Publishers.

Rizvi, Athar Abbas. 1983. *A History of Sufism in India*, vol. 2. New Delhi: Munshiram Manoharlal.

Robinson, Francis. 2001. *The `Ulama of Farangi Mahall and Islamic Culture in South Asia*. New Delhi: Permanent Black.

Roy, Olivier. 1994. *The Failure of Political Islam*, trans. by Carol Volk. London and New York: I.B. Tauris.

Saeedullah. 1973. *The Life and Works of Muhammad Siddiq Hasan Khan, Nawab of Bophal, 1248-1307*. Lahore: Sh. Muhammad Ashraf.

Schulze, Reinhard. 1990. *Islamischer Internationalismus im 20. Jahrhundert: Untersuchungen zur Geschichte der Islamischen Weltliga*. Leiden: Brill.

al-Shaykhani, Muhammad. 1990. *al-Tarbiya al-ruhiyya bayn al-Sufiyin wa-l-Salafiyin*. Damascus: Dar Qutayba.

Sikand, Yoginder. 2002. *The Origins and Development of the Tablighi Jama`at 1920-2000: A Cross-country Comparative Study*. New Delhi: Orient Longman.

Sirriyeh, Elizabeth. 1999. *Sufis and Anti-Sufis: The Defence, Rethinking and Rejection of Sufism in the Modern World*. Richmond, Surrey: Curzon Press.

Sivan, Emmanuel. 1985. *Radical Islam: Medieval Theology and Modern Politics*. New Haven and London: Yale University Press.

Stenberg, Leif. 1999. Naqshbandiyya in Damascus: Strategies to Establish and Strengthen the Order in a Changing Society. In *Naqshbandis in Western and Central Asia*, edited by Elizabeth Özdalga, pp. 101-16. Istanbul: Swedish Research Institute in Istanbul.

Troll, Christian W. 1993. Muhammad Shibli Nu'mani (1857-1914) and the Reform of Muslim Religious Education, *Islam and the Modern Age*, 24: 1-19.

Chapter Seven (cont.)

Veer, Peter van der. 1994. *Religious Nationalism: Hindus and Muslims in India*. Berkeley, Cal.: University of California Press.
Weismann, Itzchak. 1993. Sa'id Hawwa: The Making of a Radical Muslim Thinker in Modern Syria, *Middle Eastern Studies*, 29: 601-23.
Weismann, Itzchak. 1997. Sa'id Hawwa and Islamic Revivalism in Ba'thist Syria, *Studia Islamica*, 85: 143-9.
Weismann, Itzchak. 2001. *Taste of Modernity: Sufism, Salafiyya, and Arabism in Late Ottoman Damascus*. Leiden: Brill.
Weismann, Itzchak. 2003a. The Forgotten Shaykh: `Isa al-Kurdi and the Transformation of the Naqshbandi–Khalidi Order in Twentieth Century Syria, *Die Welt des Islams*, 43: 273-93.
Weismann, Itzchak. 2003b. The Naqshbandiyya–Khalidiyya and the Salafi Challenge in Iraq, *Journal of the History of Sufism*, 4: 229-40.
Weismann, Itzchak. 2005. The Politics of Popular Islam: Sufis, Salafis, and Muslim Brothers in Twentieth-century Hamah, *International Journal of Middle East Studies*, 37: 39-58.
Weismann, Itzchak. forthcoming. The Hidden Hand: The Naqshbandi–Khalidi Brotherhood and Orthodox–Fundamentalist Cooperation in Aleppo, *Journal of the History of Sufism*.
Zaman, Muhammad Qasim. 2002. *The Ulama in Contemporary Islam: Custodians of Change*. Princeton: Princeton University Press.

Chapter Eight

Anwar ul-Haq, M. 1972. *The Faith Movement of Mawlana Muhammad Ilyas*. London: George Allen & Unwin.
Bakhsh, Rahim. 1995. *Tablighi Jama`at ke Tarikhi Halat, Malfuzat-o Makatibat-i Bani-i Tabligh, Muhsin-i Mewat, Muballigh-i Islam al-Haj Shah Hazrat Maulana Muhammad Ilyas*. Roodpa: Muhammad Hasan.
Bulandshahri, Ashiq Ilahi. n.d. *Aqsi Chhe Batein*. Delhi: Jaseem Book Depot.
Faruqi, Zia ur-Rahman. 1992. `*Ulama-i Deoband: Kaun Hain, Kya Hain*. Deoband: Dar ul-Kitab.
Hardy, Peter. 1980. *Partners in Freedom – and True Muslims: The Political Thought of Some Muslim Scholars in British India*. Westport: Greenwood Press.
Ilyas, Muhammad. 1989. A Call to Muslims. In *The Teachings of Tabligh*. New Delhi: Idara-i Isha'at-i Diniyat.
Metcalf, Barbara Daly. 2002. *Islamic Revival in British India: Deoband, 1860-1900*. New Delhi: Oxford University Press.
Metcalf, Barbara Daly. 2003. Travelers' Tales in the Tablighi Jama'at, *Annals of the American Academy of Political and Social Science*, 588: 136-48.
Nadwi, Sayyed Abul Hasan Ali. 1983. *Life and Mission of Maulana Muhammad Ilyas*, trans. by Mohammad Asif Kidwai. Lucknow: Academy of Islamic Research and Publications, Nadwat ul-'Ulama.
Nizami, Muhammad Khalid. ed. 1993. Paigham-i Falah. Dhanbad: Dini Ta'limi Board.
Numani, Manzur. ed. 1991. *Malfuzat-i Hazrat Maulana Muhammad Ilyas*. New Delhi: Idara-i Isha'at-i Diniyat.
Pemberton, Kelley. 2002. Islamic and Islamicizing Discourses: Ritual Performance, Didactic Texts, and the Reformist Challenge in the South Asian Sufi Milieu, *Annual of Urdu Studies*, 17.
Powlett, P.W. 1878. *Gazetteer of Ulwar*. London: Trubner.
Sikand, Yoginder. 1999. Women and the Tablighi Jama'at, *Islam and Christian–Muslim Relations*, 10: 41-52.
―――― 2002. *The Origins and Development of the Tablighi-Jama`at (1920-2000): A Cross-country Comparative Study*. Hyderabad: Orient Longman.

Chapter Nine

al-Albani, Nasir al-Din. 1995. Mengapa harus kita pakai nama Salafi?, *Salafy*, 1, Sha`ban 1416: 8-10.

Anonymous. 1996. Mengenal para Imam Ahlussunnah, Ashabul Hadits, *Salafy*, 4, Dhu 'l-Qa`da 1416: 10-15.

Anonymous. 1999. Imam at-Turtusi: Membongkar kedustaan kitab *Ihya' Ulumuddin*, *Salafy*, 32, 1420:39.

Azra, Azyumardi. 2004. *The Origins of Islamic Reformism in Southeast Asia: Networks of Malay–Indonesian and Middle Eastern `Ulama in the Seventeenth and Eighteenth Centuries*. Leiden: KITLV Press.

Boland, B.J. 1982. *The Struggle of Islam in Modern Indonesia*, revised edition. The Hague: Nijhoff.

Bruinessen, Martin van. 1990a. Kitab Kuning: Books in Arabic Script Used in the Pesantren Milieu, *Bijdragen tot de Taal-, Land- en Volkenkunde*, 146: 226-69.

——— 1990b. The Origins and Development of the Naqshbandi Order in Indonesia, *Der Islam*, 67: 150-79.

——— 2002. Genealogies of Islamic Radicalism in Post-Suharto Indonesia, *South East Asia Research*, 10(2): 117-54.

Fairuz, Abu. 1998. Baiat: Siasat agar orang terikat, *Salafy*, 25, 1418: 52-3.

al-Fatani, Ahmad bin Muhammad Zayn bin Mustafa. 1957. *al-Fatawa al-Fataniyya*. Siam: al-Matba`a al-Fataniyya.

Gramlich, R. 1991. Madjdhûb. In *The Encyclopaedia of Islam*, 2nd edn, 5, p. 1029. Leiden: Brill.

Hadi, Abdul. 1995. *Hamzah Fansuri: Risalah tasawuf dan puisi-puisinya*. Bandung: Mizan.

Hakiem, Luqman. 2000a. Milenium Sufi, *Sufi*, 1(1), April/Muharram 1421: 1-3.

Hakiem, Luqman. 2000b. Mentas dari oase kegersangan, *Sufi*, 1(1), April/Muharram 1421:5.

Hakiem, Luqman. 2000c. [Interview with Sahal Mahfudz] *Sufi*, 1(1), April/Muharram 1421: 6-10.

Hakiem, Luqman. 2000d. [Interview with Abdul Hadi] *Sufi*, 1(1), April/Muharram 1421: 11-13.

Hakiem, Luqman. 2000e. [Interview with Rifai Hasan] *Sufi*, 1(1), April/Muharram 1421: 14-17.

Hakiem, Luqman. 2001. Ghurur: Tipudaya perjalanan Sufi, *Sufi*, 13, June: 8-9.

Hamdani, Ahmad. 1997a. Mungkinkah kita melihat Allah?, *Salafy*, 15, Dhu 'l-qa`da 1417: 30-8.

Hamdani, Ahmad. 1997b. Tawasul, *Salafy*, 21, 1418: 42-52.

al-Haqqani, Nazim Adil. 2001. Banyak lilin tapi tak bercahaya, *Sufi*, 13, June: 50-51.

Hasan, Noorhaidi and Mufid, Ahmad Syafii. 2002. When Executives Chant Dhikr, *ILAS Newsletter*, 28, August: 23.

Hasan, Noorhaidi. 2005. Between Transnational Interest and Domestic Politics: Understanding Middle Eastern *Fatwas* on Jihad in the Moluccas, *Islamic Law & Society*, 12(1): 73-92.

Hasan, Noorhaidi. 2006. *Laskar Jihad: Islam, Militancy and the Quest for Identity in Post-New Order Indonesia*, Ithaca, NY: Cornell Southeast Asia Program.

Haykel, Bernard. 2003. *Revival and Reform in Islam: The Legacy of Muhammad al-Shawkani*. Cambridge: Cambridge University Press.

al-Hilali, Salim. 1997. Imam Nawawi: Seorang imam dari Nawa, *Salafy*, 20, 1418: 63-64.

Ichwan, Moch. Nur. 2001. Differing Responses to an Ahmadi Translation and Exegesis: The Holy Qur'ân in Egypt and Indonesia, *Archipel*, 62: 143-61.

De Jong, Frederick and Radtke, Bernd. eds. 1999. *Islamic Mysticism Contested: Thirteen Centuries of Controversies and Polemics*. Leiden, Boston and Köln: Brill.

Junaidi. 1996. Review of Abdul Hadi, *Hamzah Fansuri: Risalah Tasawuf dan Puisi-puisiny*, *Salafy*, 5, Dhu 'l-hijja 1416: 67-69.

Chapter Nine (cont.)

al-Kaf, Salim Abdullah. 1996. Studi kritis terhadap Studi kritis: Bantahan terhadap buku Studi kritis faham Wahabi, karya Ja`far Subhani, *Salafy*, 10 and 11, Jumadil Awal and Rajab 1417: 33-37, 18-29.

Knysh, Alexander D. 1999. *Ibn `Arabi in the Later Islamic Tradition: The Making of a Polemical Image in Medieval Islam*, Albany: SUNY Press.

Kraus, Werner. 1999. Sufis und ihre Widersacher in Kelantan/Malaysia: Die Polemik gegen die Ahmadiyya zu beginn des 20. Jahrhunderts. In *Islamic Mysticism Contested: Thirteen Centuries of Controversies and Polemics*, edited by Frederick De Jong and Bernd Radtke, pp. 728-756. Leiden: Brill.

Laffan, Michael. 2003. When Kiais Came to Cairo, *Archipel*, 66: 5-12.

Al-Medani, Muhammad Ali Ishmah. 1997. Hadits tentang Wali Allah, *Salafy*, 18, Safar 1418: 40-45.

Mufid, Husnu. 2002. Melihat orang terbang sambil towaf, *Posmo*, 4(174): 10.

Mu`thi, Abdul. 1998. Jebakan-jebakan Iblis, *Salafy*, 24, 1418: 10-17.

Nur, Mukhtar M. and Al-Makasari, Abu Abdillah. 1997. Tabaruk, *Salafy*, 22, 1418: 34-39.

al-Salafi, Abd al-Mu`ti. 1995. al-Adzkar, *Salafy*, 1, Sha`ban 1416: 74.

as-Sewed, Muhammad. 1995. Awal mula terjadinya kesyirikan di jazirah Arab, *Salafy*, 1, Sha`ban 1416: 31-8.

Siradj, Said Aqiel. 2000. Rekonstruksi Sufisme, *Sufi*, 1(1), April/Muharram 1421: 18-20.

Sirriyeh, Elizabeth. 1999. *Sufis and Anti-Sufis. The Defence, Rethinking and Rejection of Sufism in the Modern World*. London: Curzon.

Skovgaard-Petersen, Jakob. 1997. *Defining Islam for the Egyptian State: Muftis and Fatwas of the Dar al-Ifta*. Brill: Leiden.

Thalib, Ja`far Umar and as-Sewed, Umar. 1995. Sambutan redaksi, *Salafy*, 1, Sha`ban 1416:1

Thalib, Ja`far Umar. 1995a. Waspada terhadap Islam sempalan, *Salafy*, 1, Sha`ban 1416: 11-13.

Thalib, Ja`far Umar. 1995b. Sejarah dan pahaman Ahlus Sunnah wal Jama`ah, *Salafy*, 1, Sha`ban 1416: 14-17.

Thalib, Ja`far Umar. 1995c. Da`wah Salafi di persimpagan jalan, *Salafy*, 1, Sha`ban 1416: 39-42.

Thalib, Ja`far Umar. 1997. Hukum berdebat dalam Islam, *Salafy*, 13, Sha`ban 1417: 3-8.

Thalib, Ja`far Umar. 1998. Para pemikir yang diulamakan, *Salafy*, 26, 1419: 10-19.

Chapter Ten

Augis, Erin. 2002. *Dakar's Sunnite Women: The Politics of Person*. PhD dissertation. University of Chicago, USA.

Babou, Cheikh Anta. 2002a. *Amadu Bamba and the Founding of the Muridiyya: The History of a Muslim Brotherhood in Senegal (1853-1913)*. PhD dissertation. Michigan State University.

———— 2002b. Brotherhood Solidarity, Education, and Migration: The Role of the Dahiras among the Murid Muslim Community in New York, *African Affairs*, 101: 151-70.

Bathily, Abdoulaye; Diouf, Mamadou and Mbodj, Mohamed. 1995. The Senegalese Student Movement from its Inception to 1989. In *African Studies in Social Movements and Democracy*, edited by Mahmood Mamdani and Ernest Wamba-dia-Wamba. Dakar: CODESRIA.

Bava, Sophie. 2002. Entre Touba et Marseille: Le mouride migrant et la société locale. In *La Société sénégalaise entre le local et le global*, edited by Momar-Coumba Diop, pp. 579-94. Paris: Karthala.

Beck, Linda. 2003. Who are the *Sénégalais d'Amérique*? Unpublished manuscript.

Behrman, Lucy. 1970. *Muslim Brotherhoods and Politics in Senegal*. Cambridge, MA: Harvard University Press.

Chapter Ten (cont.)

Carter, Donald M. 1997. *States of Grace: Senegalese in Italy and the New European Immigration*. Minneapolis: University of Minnesota Press.

Copans, Jean. 1980. *Les Marabouts de l'arachide: La confrérie mouride et les paysans du Sénégal*. Paris: Sycomore.

Coulon, Christian. 1981. *Le Marabout et le prince: Islam et pouvoir au Sénégal*. Paris: A. Pedone.

Cruise O'Brien, Donal B. 1983. Sufi Politics in Senegal. In *Islam in the Political Process*, edited by James P. Piscatori, pp. 122-37. Cambridge: Cambridge University Press.

Cruise O'Brien, Donal B. 1988. Charisma Comes to Town: Mouride Urbanization 1945-1986. In *Charisma and Brotherhood in African Islam*, edited by Donal Cruise O'Brien and Christian Coulon, pp. 135-55. Oxford: Clarendon Press.

Da Costa, Peter. 1994. Senegal: Shades of Algeria?, *Africa Report*. May-June: 58-61.

Diouf, Mamadou. 2000. The Senegalese Murid Trade Diaspora and the Making of a Vernacular Cosmopolitanism, *Public Culture*, 12(3): 679-702.

Ebin, Victoria. 1990. Commerçants et missionaries: une confrérie sénégalaise à New York, *Hommes et Migrations*, 1132, May: 25-31.

——— 1993. Les Commerçants Mourides à Marseille et à New York. In *Grands Commerçants d'Afrique de l'Ouest*, edited by E. Grégoire and P. Labazée, pp. 101-23. Paris: Karthala.

——— 1996. Making Room Versus Creating Space: The Construction of Spatial Categories by Itinerant Mouride Traders. In *Making Muslim Space in North America and Europe*, edited by B. Metcalf, pp. 92-109. Berkeley: University of California Press.

Frasques. 2002. Un Jour de Bamba à New York. Dakar (undated special edition of popular magazine).

Gomez-Perez, Muriel. 1991. Associations Islamiques à Dakar, *Islam et Sociétés au Sud du Sahara*, 5: 5-19.

Guèye, Cheikh. 2002. *Touba: La capitale des mourides*. Paris: Karthala.

Huntington, Samuel. 1984. Will More Countries Become Democratic?, *Political Science Quarterly*, 99(2): 193-218.

Kane, Abdoulaye. 2001. *Les caméléons de la finance populaire au Sénégal et dans la Diaspora: Dynamiques des Tontines et de caisses villageoises entre Thilogne, Dakar et la France*. PhD dissertation. Amsterdam School for Social Science Research, University of Amsterdam.

——— 2002. Senegal's Village Diaspora and the People Left Behind. In *The Transnational Family: New European Frontiers and Global Networks*, edited by Deborah Bryceson and Ulla Vuorela, pp. 245-63. Oxford/New York: Berg Publishers.

Kane, Ousmane. 1997. Muslim Missionaries and African States. In *Transnational Religion and Fading States*, edited by Susanne Hoeber Rudolph and James Piscatori, pp. 47-62. Boulder, CO: Westview Press.

Kane, Ousmane and Villalón, Leonardo A. 1995. Entre Confrérisme, Réformisme et Islamisme: Les Mustarchidin du Sénégal. Analyse et Traduction Commentée de Discours Electoral de Moustapha Sy et Réponse de Abdou Aziz Sy Junior, *Islam et Sociétés au Sud du Sahara*, 9: 119-201.

Loimeier, Roman. 1996. The Secular State and Islam in Senegal. In *Questioning the Secular State: The Worldwide Resurgence of Religion and Politics*, edited by David Westerlund, pp. 183-97. New York: St. Martin's Press.

Mbow, Penda. 2003. Civisme, Laïcité, République. Unpublished manuscript.

McLaughlin, Fiona. 2000. 'In the Name of God I Will Sing Again, Mawdo Malik the Good': Popular Music and the Senegalese Sufi Tariqas. *Journal of Religion in Africa*, 30(2): 191-207.

——— 1997. Islam and Popular Music in Senegal: The Emergence of a 'New Tradition', *Africa*, 67(4): 560-81.

MICA (Mouride Islamic Community in America). 2002. *Education: A Key Function in Muridism. A Message from Shaykh Mourtada Mbacke ibn Khadimou Rassoul*, July. New York.

Chapter Ten (cont.)

Piga, Adriana. 2003. Un Survol sur la dialectique entre soufisme et anti-soufisme au Sénégal contemporain. In *Islam et Villes en Afrique au sud du Sahara*, edited by Adriana Piga, pp. 305-21. Paris: Karthala.

Riccio, Bruno. 2003. L'urbanisation mouride et les migrations transnationales sénégalaises. In *Islam et Villes en Afrique au sud du Sahara*, edited by Adriana Piga, pp. 359-75. Paris: Karthala.

Roberts, Allan F. and Roberts, Mary Nooter (with Armenian, Gassia and Gueye, Ousmane). 2003. *A Saint in the City: Sufi Arts of Urban Senegal*. Los Angeles: UCLA Fowler Museum of Cultural History.

Robinson, David. 2000. *Paths of Accommodation: Muslim Societies and French Colonial Authorities in Senegal and Mauritania, 1880-1920*. Athens, Ohio: Ohio University Press.

Rosander, Eva Evers and Westerlund, David. eds. 1997. *African Islam and Islam in Africa: Encounters between Sufis and Islamists*. Athens, Ohio: Ohio University Press.

Ross, Eric. 1995. Touba: A Spiritual Metropolis in the Modern World, *Canadian Journal of African Studies*, 29(2): 222-59.

Sambe, Bakary. 2003. Nouveau visage du militantisme islamique sénégalais depuis les années 80: l'opposition confréries/associations est-elle encore pertinente?'. Paper presented at the International Conference on Political Islam South of the Sahara, Université Paris VII, September.

Sene, Ibra. 2003. Islam as a Site of Agency, Mediation, and Resistance: Hizbut Tarqiyya (Senegal), 1975-2002. Paper presented at the Annual Meeting of the African Studies Association, Washington, DC, 30 October - 1 November.

Triaud, Jean-Louis. 2000. Islam in Africa under French Colonial Rule. In *The History of Islam in Africa*, edited by Nehemia Levtzion and Randall L. Pouwels, pp. 169-87. Athens, Ohio: Ohio University Press.

Triaud, Jean-Louis and Robinson, David. eds. 2000. *La Tijaniyya: une confrérie musulmane à la conquête de l'Afrique*. Paris: Karthala.

Villalón, Leonardo A. 1994. Sufi Rituals as Rallies: Religious Ceremonies in the Politics of Senegalese State–Society Relations, *Comparative Politics*, 26(4): 415-37.

—— 1995. *Islamic Society and State Power in Senegal: Disciples and Citizens in Fatick*. Cambridge: Cambridge University Press.

—— 1999. Generational Changes, Political Stagnation, and the Evolving Dynamics of Religion and Politics in Senegal, *Africa Today*, 46(3/4): 129-47.

—— 2000. The Moustarchidine of Senegal: The Family Politics of a Contemporary Tijan Movement. In *La Tijaniyya: une confrérie musulmane à la conquête de l'Afrique*, edited by Jean-Louis Triaud and David Robinson, pp. 469-97. Paris: Karthala.

Villalón, Leonardo, and Kane, Ousmane. 1998. Senegal: The Crisis of Democracy and the Emergence of an Islamic Opposition. In *The African State at a Critical Juncture: Between Disintegration and Reconfiguration*, edited by Leonardo A. Villalón and Phillip A. Huxtable, pp. 143-66. Boulder: Lynne Rienner.

Chapter Eleven

Al-Abidi, Akhtar Moeed Shah. 2002. *Divine Prophecy Divine*. London: Janus Publishing Company.

Ballard, Roger. ed. 1994. *Desh Pardesh: The South Asian Presence in Britain*. London: Hurst.

Bayly, Susan. 1989. *Saints, Goddesses and Kings: Muslims and Christians in South Indian Society, 1700-1900*. Cambridge: Cambridge University Press.

Buehler, Arthur F. 1998. *Sufi Heirs of the Prophet: The Indian Naqshbaniyya and the Rise of the Mediating Sufi Shaykh*. Columbia, NC: University of North Carolina Press.

Eade, John and Sallnow, Michael J. 1991. Introduction. In *Contesting the Sacred: The Anthropology of Christian Pilgrimage*, edited by John Eade and Michael J. Sallnow, pp. 1-29. London: Routledge.

Chapter Eleven (cont.)

Eaton, Richard W. 1978. *Sufis of Bijapur, 1300-1700*. Princeton NJ: Princeton University Press.
—— 1983. *The Rise of Islam and the Bengal Frontier, 1204-1760*. Berkeley: University of California Press.
—— 1984. The Political and Religious Authority of the Shrine of Baba Farid. In *Moral Conduct and Authority: The Place of Adab in South Asian Islam*, edited by Barbara Daly Metcalf, pp. 333-56. Berkeley: University of California Press.
Eickelman, Dale F. 1976. *Moroccan Islam*. Austin: University of Texas Press.
—— 1977. Ideological Change and Regional Cults: Maraboutism and Ties of 'Closeness' in Western Morocco. In *Regional Cults*, edited by Richard P. Werbner, pp. 3-28, ASA Monographs No. 16, London and New York: Academic Press.
Evans-Pritchard, E.E. 1949. *The Sanusi of Cyrenaica*. Oxford: Clarendon Press.
Fahd, Tofic. 1999a. Djafr. In *Encyclopaedia of Islam*. Leiden: Brill.
—— 1999b. Huruf. In *Encyclopaedia of Islam*. Leiden: Brill.
Geertz, Clifford. 1968. *Islam Observed*. New Haven: Yale University Press.
Gilmartin, David. 1984. Shrines, Succession, and Sources of Moral Authority. In *Moral Conduct and Authority: The Place of Adab in South Asian Islam*, edited by Barbara Daly Metcalf, pp. 221-40. Berkeley: University of California Press.
—— 1988. *Empire and Islam*. Berkeley: University of California Press.
Gilsenan, Michael. 1973. *Saint and Sufi in Modern Egypt*. Oxford: Clarendon Press.
Hetherington, Kevin. 1994. The Contemporary Significance of Schmalenbach's Concept of the Bund, *The Sociological Review*, 42, 1: 1-25.
Lewis, Philip. 1984. Pirs, Shrines and Pakistani Islam, *Al-Mushir*, XXVI: 1-22.
Liebeskind, Claudia. 1998. *Piety on its Knees: Three Sufi Traditions in South Asia in Modern Times*. Delhi: Oxford University Press.
Malik, Jamal. ed. 2004. *Muslims in Europe: From the Margins to the Centre*. Munster: LIT Verlag.
Mann, Elizabeth A. 1989. Religion, Money and Status: Competition for Resources at the Shrine of Shah Jamal, Aligarh. In *Muslim Shrines in India: Their Character, History and Significance*, edited by Christian W. Troll, pp. 145-71. Delhi: Oxford University Press.
Schimmel, Annemarie. 1975. *Mystical Dimensions of Islam*. Chapel Hill: North Carolina University Press.
Schmalenbach, H. 1977. Communion – A Sociological Category. In *Herman Schmalenbach: On Society and Experience*, trans and ed. by G. Luschen and G. Stone, pp. 64-125. Chicago: University of Chicago Press.
Trimingham, J.S. 1971. *The Sufi Orders in Islam*. London: Oxford University at the Clarendon Press.
Turner, Victor. 1974. *Dramas, Fields, and Metaphors*. Cornell: Cornell University Press.
Werbner, Pnina. 1995. Powerful Knowledge in a Global Sufi Cult: Reflections on the Poetics of Travelling Theories. In *The Pursuit of Certainty: Religious and Cultural Formulations*. ASA Dicennial Conference Series on 'The Uses of Knowledge: Global and Local Relations', edited by Wendy James, pp. 134-60. London: Routledge.
—— 1996a. The Making of Muslim Dissent: Hybridized Discourses, Lay Preachers and Radical Rhetoric among British Pakistanis, *American Ethnologist*, 23(1): 102-22.
—— 1996b. Stamping the Earth with the Name of Allah: Zikr and the Sacralising of Space among British Muslims, *Cultural Anthropology*, 11(3): 309-38 [also in *Making Muslim Space in North America and Europe*, edited by Barbara Daly Metcalf, pp. 167-85. Berkeley: University of California Press].
—— 2001. Murids of the Saints: Migration, Diaspora and Redemptive Sociality in Sufi Regional and Global Cults, *International Journal of Punjab Studies*, 8(1): 35-55 [also in *Muslim Traditions and Modern Techniques of Power*, Yearbook of the Sociology of Islam 3, edited by Armando Salvatore, pp. 265-91. Hamburg: LIT Verlag].

——— 2002. *Imagined Diasporas among Manchester Muslims*. Oxford and Sante Fe: James Currey and School of American Research (SAR).
——— 2003. *Pilgrims of Love: The Anthropology of a Global Sufi Cult*. London and Bloomington: Hurst Publishers and Indiana University Press.
Werbner, Richard P. ed. 1977. *Regional Cults*, ASA Monograph 16. London and New York: Academic Press.

Chapter Twelve

Anshari, E.S. 1979. *The Jakarta Charter 1945: The Struggle for an Islamic Constitution in Indonesia*. Kuala Lumpur: Muslim Youth Movement of Malaysia.
Arberry, A.J. 1950. *Sufism*. London: Allen & Unwin.
Aveling, Harry, ed. and trans. 2001. *Secrets Need Words: Indonesian Poetry, 1966-1998*. Southeast Asia Series, No. 105. Athens: Ohio University Center for International Studies.
Azra, Azyumardi. 2004. *The Origins of Islamic Reformism in Southeast Asia: Networks of Malay-Indonesian and Middle Eastern 'Ulama in the Seventeenth and Eighteenth Centuries*. Crows Nest, NSW: Allen & Unwin.
Barton, Greg. 1991. The International Context of the Emergence of Islamic Neo-Modernism in Indonesia. In *Islam in the Indonesian Social Context*, edited by M. Ricklefs, pp. 69-82. Clayton, VIC: Monash University CSEAS.
——— 1995. Neo-Modernism: A Vital Synthesis of Traditionalist and Modernist Islamic Thought in Indonesia, *Studia Islamika*, 2(3): 1-75 (Jakarta).
Boland, B.J. 1971. *The Struggle of Islam in Modern Indonesia*. The Hague: Martinus Nijhoff.
Bruinessen, Martin van. 1994. The Origins and Development of Sufi Orders (*Tarekat*) in Southeast Asia, *Studia Islamika*, 1(1): 1-23.
Bruinessen, Martin van. 1999. Controversies and Polemics Involving the Sufi Orders in Twentieth-Century Indonesia. In *Islamic Mysticism Contested: Thirteen Centuries of Controversies and Polemics*, edited by F. de Jong and B. Radtke, pp. 705-28. Leiden: Brill.
Damanik, Ali Said. 2002. *Fenomena Partai Keadilan: transformasi 20 tahun gerakan Tarbiyah di Indonesia*. Bandung: Teraju.
Dick, H. 1985. The Rise of a Middle Class and the Changing Concept of Equity in Indonesia. *Indonesia*, 39: 71-92.
Eickelman, D.F. 1992. Mass Higher Education and the Religious Imagination in Contemporary Arab Societies, *American Ethnologist*, 19(4): 1-13.
Eickelman, D.F. and Anderson, J.W. 1999. Redefining Muslim Publics. In *New Media in the Muslim World: The Emerging Public Sphere*, edited by D.F. Eickelman and J.W. Anderson. Indianapolis: Indiana University Press.
Eisenstadt, S.N. ed. 2002. *Multiple Modernities*. London: Transaction Publishers.
Fathimah, S. 1999. *Modernism and the Contextualization of Islamic Doctrines: The Reform of Indonesian Islam Proposed by Nurcholish Madjid*. MA thesis. McGill University, Montreal.
Geertz, Clifford. 1960a. The Javanese Kijai: The Changing Role of a Cultural Broker. *Comparative Studies in Society and History*, 2(2): 228-56.
——— 1960b. *The Religion of Java*. NY: Free Press.
——— 1968. *Islam Observed*. Chicago: University of Chicago Press.
Gellner, Ernest. 1981. *Muslim Society*. Cambridge: Cambridge University Press.
——— 1992. *Postmodernism, Reason and Religion*. London and New York: Routledge.
Hamka. [1939] 1990. *Tasauf Moderen*. Jakarta: Pustaka Panjimas.
Hardjoprakoso, R.T. and R. Trihardono Sumodiharjo. eds. 1978. *True Light (Sasangka Jati): A Collection of the Teachings of the World Teacher (Guru Sejati, Suksma Sejati) Delivered via His Disciple R. Sunarto Mertowardojo*, 2nd revised ed., trans. by R. Marsaid Susila Sastradiharja. Jakarta: [Pangestu].
Hefner, R. 1997. Print Islam: Mass Media and Ideological Rivalries among Indonesian Muslims. *Indonesia*, October, 64: 77-104.

Chapter Twelve (cont.)

Hefner, R. 2000. *Civil Islam, Muslims and Democratization in Indonesia*. Princeton: Princeton University Press.

────── 2003. Civic Pluralism Denied? The New Media and *Jihadi* Violence in Indonesia. In *New Media in the Muslim World: The Emerging Public Sphere*, 2nd ed., edited by D.F. Eickelman and Jon W. Anderson: Bloomington: Indiana University Press.

Hodgson, M.G.S. 1974. *The Venture of Islam*. Chicago: Chicago University Press.

Howell, Julia Day. 1978. Modernizing Religious Reform and the Far Eastern Religions in Twentieth Century Indonesia. In *Spectrum: Essays Presented to Professor Sutan Takdir Alisjahbana*, edited by Sam Udin, pp. 260-76. Jakarta: Dian Rakyat.

────── 1982. Indonesia: Searching for Consensus. In *Religions and Societies: Asia and the Middle East*, edited by Carlo Caldarola, pp. 497-548. The Hague: Mouton.

────── 2001. Sufism and the Indonesian Islamic Revival. *Journal of Asian Studies*, 60(3): 701-29.

Howell, Julia Day; Subandi; and Nelson, Peter L. 2001. New Faces of Indonesian Sufism: A Demographic Profile of Tarekat Qodiriyyah–Naqsyabandiyyah, Pesantren Suryalaya, in the 1990s. *Review of Indonesian and Malaysian Affairs*, 35(2): 33-60.

Hugo, Graeme. 1997. Changing Patterns and Processes of Population Mobility. In *Indonesia Assessment: Population and Human Resources*, edited by Gavin Jones and Terence Hull, pp. 68-100. Canberra and Singapore: Research School for Pacific and Asian Studies, ANU, and Institute of Southeast Asian Studies (Singapore).

Jabali, Fuad and Makruf, Jamhari. 2002. *IAIN dan Modernisasi Islam di Indonesia*. Ciputat: Logos Wacana Ilmu.

Kraince, Richard G. 2000. The Role of Islamic Student Groups in the Reformasi Struggle: KAMMI (Kesatuan Aksi Mahasiswa Muslim Indonesia), *Studia Islamika*, 7(1): 1-50.

Kull, Ann. 2005. *Piety and Politics: Nurcholish Madjid and His Interpretation of Islam in Modern Indonesia*. Lund: Lund Studies in History of Religions, vol. 21.

Lambert, Yves. 1999. Religion in Modernity as a New Axial Age: Secularization or New Religious Forms. *Sociology of Religion*, 60(3): 303-34.

Mulder, Niels. 1998. *Mysticism in Java, Ideology in Indonesia*. Amsterdam: The Pepin Press.

Noer, Deliar. 1973. *The Modernist Muslim Movement in Indonesia, 1900-1942*. Singapore: Oxford University Press.

Oey-Gardiner, Mayling. 1997. Educational Developments, Achievements and Challenges. In *Indonesia Assessment: Population and Human Resources*, edited by Gavin Jones and Terence Hull, pp. 135-66. Canberra and Singapore: Research School for Pacific and Asian Studies, ANU, and Institute of Southeast Asian Studies (Singapore).

Rasjidi, H.M. 1967. *Islam dan Kebatinan*. Jakarta: Jajasan Islam Studi Club Indonesia.

Riddell, P. 2001. *Islam and the Malay–Indonesian World: Transmission and Responses*. London: Hurst.

Robison, Richard. 1996. The Middle Class and the Bourgeoisie in Indonesia. In *The New Rich in Asia: Mobile Phones, McDonald's and Middle-Class Revolution*, edited by Richard Robison and David S.G. Goodman, pp. 79-104. London: Routledge.

Roy, Olivier. 2004. *Globalised Islam: The Search for a New Ummah*. London: Hurst & Co.

Sekretariat PHDP [Parisada Hindu Darma Pusat]. 1970. *Pokok Pokok Sejarah Perkembangan Parisda Hindu Dharma*. Denpasar.

Sila, Muhammad Adlin. 2000. *Tasawuf Perkotaan: Kasus Pusat Kajian Tasawuf (PKT) Tazkiyah Sejati Jakarta*. Jakarta: Badan Penelitian dan Pengembangan Agama.

Soedjatmoko. 1965. Cultural Motivations to Progress: The 'Exterior' and 'Interior' Views. In *Religion and Progress in Modern Asia*, edited by Robert N. Bellah, pp. 1-14. New York: Free Press.

Stange, Paul. 1986. Legitimate Mysticism in Java, *Review of Indonesian and Malaysian Affairs*, 20(2): 76-117.

Steenbrink, Karel. 1972. Het Indonesisch Godsdienstministerie en de Godsdiensten. *Wereld en Zending*, 1: 174-99.

Chapter Twelve (cont.)

Subagya, Rahmat. 1976. *Kepercayaan, Kebatinan, Kerohanian, Kejiwaan dan Agama.* Yogyakarta: Yayasan Kanisius.

Suryadinata, Leo. 1998. State and Minority Religion in Contemporary Indonesia: Recent Government Policy towards Confucianism, Tridharma and Buddhism. In *Nation-State, Identity and Religion in Southeast Asia*, edited by Tsuneo Ayabe, pp. 5-23. Singapore: Singapore Society of Asian Studies.

Syafi'i, Ahmad. 1996. Gerakan Tarekat Desekitar Muria. In *Tradisi di Tengah Akselerasi Modernisasi*, edited by Badan Penelitian dan Pengembangan Agama, Departmen Agama, RI, pp. 19-34. Jakarta: Badan Penelitian dan Pengembangan Agama, Departmen Agama RI.

Tanter, R. and Young, K. 1990. *The Politics of Middle Class Indonesia.* Clayton, Vic.: Monash CSEAS.

Thoyibi, M. 1996. *Kaum Terpelajar dalam Tarekat Naqsyabandiyah di Yogyakarta dan Surakarta.* Research Report. Surakarta: Universitas Muhammadiyah Surakarta.

Voye, Liane. 1999. Secularization in a Context of Advanced Modernity. *Sociology of Religion*, 60(3): 275-88.

Woodward, Mark R. 1989. *Islam in Java: Normative Piety and Mysticism in the Sultanate of Yogyakarta.* Tuscon: University of Arizona Press.

Chapter Thirteen

Anonymous. 2001. Le soufisme en tant que prolongement de l'initiation spirituelle: Célébration du Mawlid Annabaoui par la Tarika Kadiriya Boutchichia à la Zaouia de Madagh. In *Le Matin du Sahara et du Maghrib*. http://www.tariqa.org/rp/mawlild_Madagh.php. Accessed 8 June 2001.

Babès, Leïla. ed. 1996. *Les nouvelles manières de croire: judaisme, christianisme, islam, nouvelles religiosités.* Paris: Editions de l'Atelier.

Ben Driss, Karim. 2002. *Sidi Hamza al-Qâdiri Boudchich: le renouveau du soufisme au Maroc.* Paris: Albouraq.

Ben Rochd, Rachid. 1997. *Au pays de nos sources. Dans la tradition se trouvent nos sources de création d'énergie et de sagesse.* Casablanca: Déchra [originally published as: *Le yoga maghrébin*].

——— 1999. *Ben Rochd, témoin de notre époque: la baraka au service de l'entreprise.* Casablanca: Déchra.

——— 2000. *Islam entre islamisme et anti-islamisme.* Casablanca: Déchra.

Burgat, François. 2002. *L'islamisme en face*, Paris: La Découverte [English translation: 2003. *Face to Face with Political Islam.* London: I.B. Tauris].

Champion, Françoise. 1990. *De l'émotion en religion: renouveaux et traditions.* Paris: Centurion.

——— 1993. Religieux flottant, éclectisme et syncrétismes. In *Le fait religieux*, edited by Jean Delumeau, pp. 741-72. Paris: Fayard.

Davie, Grace. 1994. *Religion in Britain Since 1945: Believing Without Belonging.* Oxford: Blackwell.

Durix, Claude. 1980. *Zen, ni lotus, ni robots.* Paris: Editions du Cerf.

——— 2002. *Le Maroc et le Saint Abd as Salam, le serviteur de la paix.* Paris: Editions du Cerf.

Étienne, Bruno. 2002. Fondements du politique en Méditerranée, *La pensée de midi*, 7: 51-64

Haenni, Patrick. 2003. Grâce a Dieu, ils n'ont pas perdu le nord! L'islamisation ajustée au temps mondial, *Boèce, Revue Romande de Sciences Humaines*, 7: 67-80.

Halbfass, Wilhelm. 1988. *India and Europe.* Albany, NY: SUNY Press.

Hervieu-Léger, Danièle. 2001. *La religion en miettes ou la question des sects.* Paris: Calmann-Levy.

Howell, Julia Day. 2000. Indonesia's Urban Sufis: Challenging Stereotypes of Islamic Revival, *ISIM. International Institute for the Study of Islam in the Modern World Newsletter*, 6:17.

Chapter Thirteen (cont.)

Howell, Julia Day. 2005. Muslims, the New Age and Marginal Religions in Indonesia: Changing Meanings of Religious Pluralism, *Social Compass*, 52(4): 473-93.

Kaufmann, Jean-Claude. 2003. *L'invention de soi*. Paris: Armand Colin.

Khosrokhavar, Farhad and Roy, Olivier. 1999. *Iran: comment sortir d'une révolution religieuse*. Paris: Seuil.

Leveau, Rémy. 1985. *Le fellah marocain, défenseur du trône*, 2me édn, revue et augmentée. Paris: Presses de la Fondation Nationale des Sciences Politiques.

Palmer, Susan and Sharma, Arvind. 1993. *The Rajneesh Papers: Studies in a New Religious Movement*. Delhi: Motilal Banarsidas Publishers.

Politique Africaine. 2002. Les sujets de Dieu, 87, October.

Sedgwick, Mark J.R. 2004a. In Search of the Counterreformation: Anti-Sufi Stereotypes and the Budshishiyya's Response. In *An Islamic Reformation?*, edited by Michaelle Browers and Charles Kurzman, pp. 124-45. Lanham, MD: Lexington Books.

——— 2004b. *Against the Modern World: Traditionalism and the Secret Intellectual History of the Twentieth Century*. New York: Oxford University Press.

Skali, Faouzi. 1985. *La voie soufie*. Paris: Albin Michel.

Tincq, Henri. 2004. Soufis et bouddhistes veulent restaurer la Maison de la Sagesse, *Le Monde*, 2 January.

Tozy, Mohamed. 1990. Le prince, le clerc et l'Etat: la restructuration du champ religieux au Maroc. In *Intellectuels et militants de l'islam contemporain*, edited by Gilles Kepel and Yann Richard, pp. 71-101. Paris: Seuil.

——— 1999. *Monarchie et islam politique au Maroc*. Paris: Presses de Sciences Po.

Voix, Raphaël. 2004. Implantation d'une confrérie marocaine en France: mécanismes, méthodes et acteurs, *Ateliers*, 28: 221-48.

Chapter Fourteen

Barker, Eileen. 1994. New Religious Movements in Europe. In *Religion in Europe: Contemporary Perspectives*, edited by Sean Gill, Gavin D'Costa, and Ursula King, pp. 120-40. Kampen, The Netherlands: Kok Pharos Publishing House.

Barker, Eileen and Mayer, Jean-Francois. 1995. Introduction, *Social Compass*, 42: 147-63.

Baumann, Martin. 1994. The Transplantation of Buddhism to Germany: Processive Modes and Strategies of Adaptation, *Method and Theory in the Study of Religion*, 6: 35-61.

——— 2001. Global Buddhism: Developmental Periods, Regional Histories, and a New Analytical Perspective, *Journal of Global Buddhism*, 2: 1-43.

Beyer, Peter. 1994. *Religion and Globalization*. London: Sage Publications.

Birnbaum, N. 1969. *Sociology and Religion*, Englewood Cliffs, NJ: Prentice-Hall.

Della Cava, Ralph. 2001. Transnational Religions: The Roman Catholic Church in Brazil and the Orthodox Church in Russia, *Sociology of Religion*, 62: 535-50.

Diani, Mario. 1992. The Concept of Social Movement, *The Sociological Review*, 92: 1-25.

Ebaugh, Helen Rose and Chafetz, Janet Saltzman. 2000. *Religion and the New Immigrants: Continuities and Adaptations in Immigrant Congregations*. Walnut Creek, CA: AltaMira Press.

——— eds. 2002. *Religion across Borders: Transnational Immigrant Networks*. Walnut Creek, CA: AltaMira Press.

Ernst, Carl W. 1997. *Sufism: An Essential Introduction to the Philosophy and Practice of the Mystical Tradition of Islam*. Boston: Shambhala.

Fields, Rick. 1992. *How the Swans Came to the Lake: A Narrative History of Buddhism in America*. Boston: Shambhala.

Finney, Henry C. 1991. American Zen's Japan Connection, *Sociological Analysis*, 52: 379-96.

Frishkopf, Michael. 2001. Changing Modalities in the Globalization of Islamic Saint Veneration and Mysticism: Sidi Ibrahim al-Dasuqi, Shaykh Muhammad 'Uthman al-Burhani, and Their Sufi Orders (Part 2), *Religious Studies and Theology*, 20: 37-67.

Chapter Fourteen (cont.)

Genn, Celia A. 2004. *Exploration and Analysis of the Origins, Nature and Development of the Sufi Movement in Australia*. PhD dissertation. University of Queensland, Australia.

Gibb, Camilla. 1998. Religious Identification in Transnational Contexts: Being and Becoming Muslim in Ethiopia and Canada, *Diaspora*, 7: 247-67.

Graham, Donald A. 'Sharif'. 1993. What is Unique about the Message?, www.wisdomschild.com/About_Sufism/unique.html. Accessed 9 September 2004.

Harris, Ian; Mews, Stuart; Morris, Paul and Shepherd, John. eds. 1992. *Contemporary Religions: A World Guide*. London: Longman.

Harvey, Andrew. 1995. *The Return of the Mother*. Berkeley: Frog Ltd.

Heelas, Paul. 1996. *The New Age Movement: The Celebration of the Self and the Sacralization of Modernity*. Oxford: Blackwell Publishers.

Hermansen, Marcia. 1998. In the Garden of American Sufi Movements: Hybrids and Perennials. In *New Trends and Developments in the World of Islam*, edited by Peter B. Clarke, pp. 155-77. London: Luzac Oriental.

—— 2000. Hybrid Identity Formations in Muslim America: The Case of American Sufi Movements, *The Muslim World*, 90: 158-97.

Howell, Julia Day. 1998. Gender Role Experimentation in New Religious Movements: The Case of the Brahma Kumaris, *Journal for the Scientific Study of Religion*, 37: 453-61.

Howell, Julia Day. 2001. Sufism and the Indonesian Islamic Revival, *Journal of Asian Studies*, 60: 701-29.

Howell, Julia Day and Nelson, Peter L. 1997. The Brahma-Kumaris in the Western World, Part I: Structural Adaptation and 'Success' in Transplantation of an Asian New Religious Movement, *Research in the Social Scientific Study of Religion*, 8: 1-34.

—— 2000. The Brahma-Kumaris in the Western World, Part II: Demographic Change and Secularisation in an Asian New Religious Movement, *Research in the Social Scientific Study of Religion*, 11: 225-39.

Huxley, Aldous. 1945. *The Perennial Philosophy*. New York: Harper & Brothers.

Iannaccone, L.R. 1991. The Consequences of Religious Market Structure: Adam Smith and the Economics of Religion, *Rationality and Society*, 3: 156-77.

Jironet, Karin. 1998. *The Image of Spiritual Liberty in the Sufi Movement Following Hazrat Inayat Khan*, PhD dissertation. University of Amsterdam.

Johnson, Paul Edward. 1990. Unraveling in Democratically Governed Groups, *Rationality and Society*, 2: 4-34.

Kearney, M. 1995. The Local and the Global: The Anthropology of Globalization and Transnationalism, *Annual Review of Anthropology*, 24: 547-65.

Khan, Inayat. 1963. *The Unity of Religious Ideals, Volume IX of XIII Volumes*. London: Barrie and Jenkins.

—— 1967. *The Vision of God and Man, Volume XII of XIII Volumes*. London: Barrie and Jenkins.

—— 1973. *The Smiling Forehead: Selected Writings of Hazrat Inayat Khan*. San Francisco: The Rainbridge.

—— 1979. *The Path of Initiation, Volume X of XIII Volumes*. Katwijk: Servire.

Khan, Mahmood. 2001. Hazrat Inayat Khan: A Biographical Perspective. In *A Pearl in Wine: Essays on the Life, Music and Sufism of Hazrat Inayat Khan*, edited by Zia Inayat-Khan, pp. 65-126. New Lebanon: Omega Publications.

King, Ursula. 1989. Some Reflections on Sociological Approaches to the Study of Modern Hinduism, *Numen*, 36: 72-97.

Lapidus, Ira M. 2001. Between Universalism and Particularism: The Historical Bases of Muslim Communal, National, and Global Identities, *Global Networks: A Journal of Transnational Affairs*, 1: 37-55.

Levitt, Peggy. 2004. Redefining the Boundaries of Belonging: The Institutional Character of Transnational Religious Life, *Sociology of Religion*, 65: 1-18.

Chapter Fourteen (cont.)

Metcalf, Barbara Daly and Metcalf, Thomas R. 2002. *A Concise History of India*. Cambridge: Cambridge University Press.

Nasr, Seyyed Hossein. 1972. *Sufi Essays*. Albany: State University of New York Press.

Pasnak, Nawab. 2003. Laughter and Love and Kansas City, *Spirit Matters: The Newsletter of the Sufi Movement in Australia*, 6:6.

Prebish, Charles S. and Tanaka, Kenneth K. 1998. *The Faces of Buddhism in America*. Berkeley: University of California Press.

Rawlinson, Andrew. 1997. *The Book of Enlightened Masters: Western Teachers in Eastern Traditions*. Chicago: Open Court.

Rizvi, Saiyid Athar Abbas. 1978. *A History of Sufism in India: Early Sufism and its History in India to 1600AD*. New Delhi: Munshiram Manoharlal Publishers.

Rodarmor, W. 1983. The Secret Life of Swami Muktananda, *Co-Evolution Quarterly*, Winter: 104-11.

Roof, Wade Clark. 1999. *Spiritual Marketplace: Baby Boomers and the Remaking of American Religion*. Princeton: Princeton University Press.

Rothstein, Mikael. 1996. Patterns of Diffusion and Religious Globalization: An Empirical Survey of New Religious Movements, *Temenos*, 3: 195-220.

Rudolph, S.H. and Piscatori, J. eds. 1997. *Transnational Religion and Fading States*. Boulder CO: Westview Press.

Saeed, Abdullah. 2003. *Islam in Australia*. Sydney: Allen & Unwin.

Simpkinson, Anne A. 1996. Soul Betrayal, *Common Boundary*, 14: 24-37.

Tully, Mark. 1998. Transnational Religion: Fading States. Edited by Susanne Hoeber Rudolph and James Piscatori, Boulder, CO, Oxford: Westview, 1997 - Book Review, *International Affairs*, 74: 654-56.

Valiuddin, Mir. 1980. *Contemplative Disciplines in Sufism*. London: East–West Publications.

Voorst van Beest, Munira van and Guillaume-Schamhart, Elise. eds. 1979. *Biography of Pir-o-Murshid Inayat Khan*. London: East–West Publications.

Waldinger, Roger and Fitzgerald, David. 2004. Transnationalism in Question, *The American Journal of Sociology*, 109: 1177-95.

Warner, R. Stephen. 1994. The Place of the Congregation in the American Religious Configuration. In *American Congregations*, edited by J.P. Wind and J.W. Lewis, pp. 54-99. Chicago, IL: University of Chicago Press.

Waseem, M. ed. and trans. 1997. Appendix. In *Muslim Festivals in India and Other Essays*, edited by Garcin De Tassy, pp. 171-86. Oxford: Oxford University Press.

Webb, Gisela. 1994. Tradition and Innovation in Contemporary American Islamic Spirituality: The Bawa Muhaiyaddeen Fellowship. In *Muslim Communities in North America*, edited by Yvonne Yazbeck Haddad and Jane Idleman Smith, pp. 75-132. Albany: State University of New York Press.

—— 1995. Sufism in America. In *America's Alternative Religions*, edited by Timothy Miller, pp. 249-58. Albury, New York: State University of New York Press.

Weber, Max. 1957. *The Theory of Social and Economic Organization*. New York: Free Press.

Werbner, Pnina. 1996. Stamping the Earth with the Name of Allah: Zikr and the Sacralizing of Space among British Muslims. In *Making Muslim Space in North America and Europe*, edited by Barbara Daly Metcalf, pp. 167-85. Berkeley and Los Angeles: University of California Press.

—— 1998. Langar: Pilgrimage, Sacred Exchange and Perpetual Sacrifice in a Sufi Saint's Lodge. In *Embodying Charisma: Modernity, Locality and the Performance of Emotion in Sufi Cults*, edited by Pnina Werbner and Helene Basu, pp. 95-116. London: Routledge.

Wilson, Peter. 1998. The Strange Fate of Sufism in the New Age. In *New Trends and Developments in the World of Islam*, edited by Peter B. Clarke, pp. 179-210. London: Luzac Oriental.

Wren-Lewis, John. 1994. Death Knell of the Guru System? Perfectionism Versus Enlightenment, *Journal of Humanistic Psychology*, 34: 46-61.

Chapter Fifteen

Barber, Benjamin R. 1996. *Jihad vs. McWorld*. New York: Ballantine Books.

Berger, Peter L. ed. 1999. *The Desecularization of the World: Resurgent Religion and World Politics*. Washington: Ethics and Public Policy Center.

Beyer, Peter. 1994. *Religion and Globalization*. London: Sage Publications.

Crapanzano, Vincent. 1973. *The Hamadsha: A Study of Moroccan Ethnopsychiatry*. Berkeley: University of California Press.

Drucker, Peter F. 1965. *Landmarks of Tomorrow: A Report on the New 'Post-Modern' World*. New York: Harper and Row.

Eaton, Richard M. 1990. *Islamic History as Global History*. Washington: American Historical Association.

Eaton, Richard M. 1993. *The Rise of Islam and the Bengal Frontier, 1204-1760*. Berkeley: University of California Press.

Eisenstadt, S.N. 2000. The Reconstruction of Religious Arenas in the Framework of 'Multiple Modernities', *Millennium: Journal of International Studies*, 29(3): 591-611.

Gellner, Ernest. 1968. A Pendulum Swing Theory of Islam, *Annales Marocaines de Sociologie*, 1: 5-14. Reprinted in *Sociology of Religion*, edited by Roland Robertson, pp. 127-38. Baltimore: Penguin, 1969.

Goble, Paul. 2000. Fighting Fundamentalism with Sufism, *Central Asia Monitor*, 5, cover story.

Habermas, Jurgen. 1981. New Social Movements, *Telos*, 49: 33-37.

Hatzopoulos, Pavlos and Petito, Fabio. 2003. The Return from Exile: An Introduction. In *Religion in International Relations: The Return From Exile*, edited by Fabio Petito and Pavlos Hatzopoulos, pp. 1-20. New York: Palgrave Macmillan.

Hermansen, Marcia. 1997. In the Garden of American Sufi Movements: Hybrids and Perennials. In *New Trends and Developments in the World of Islam*, edited by Peter Clarke, pp. 155-78. London: Luzac Oriental Press.

Hoffmann, Stanley. 2002. The Clash of Globalizations, *Foreign Affairs* (July/August), 81(4): 104-15.

Howell, Julia Day. 2001. Sufism and the Indonesian Islamic Revival, *The Journal of Asian Studies*, 60(3): 701-29.

Inglehart, Ronald. 1990. Values, Ideology, and Cognitive Mobilization in New Social Movements. In *Challenging the Political Order: New Social and Political Movements in Western Democracies*, edited by Russell J. Dalton and Manfred Kuechler, pp. 43-66. Cambridge: Polity Press.

Inglehart, Ronald. 2003. *Modernization and Postmodernization: Cultural, Economic, and Political Change in 43 Societies*. Princeton: Princeton University Press.

Jervis, James, 1997. The Sufi Order in the West and Pir Vilāyat 'Ināyat Khān: Space-Age Spirituality in Contemporary Euro-America. In *New Trends and Developments in the World of Islam*, edited by Peter Clarke, pp. 211-60. London: Luzac Oriental Press.

Johnston, Douglas and Sampson, Cynthia. eds. 1994. *Religion, the Missing Dimension of Statecraft*. New York: Oxford University Press.

King, Anthony D. 1995. The Times and Spaces of Modernity (or Who Needs Postmodernism). In *Global Modernities*, edited by Mike Featherstone, Scott Lash and Roland Robertson, pp. 108-23. London: Sage Publications.

Long, Theodore E. and Hadden, Jeffrey K. 1979. Sects, Cults and Religious Movements, *Sociological Analysis*, 40(4): 280-82.

McAdam, Doug; McCarthy, John D. and Zald, Mayer N. 1996. Introduction: Opportunities, Mobilizing Structures, and Framing Processes: Toward a Synthetic, Comparative Perspective on Social Movements. In *Comparative Perspectives on Social Movements: Political Opportunities, Mobilizing Structures, and Cultural Framings*, edited by Doug McAdam, John D. McCarthy and Mayer N. Zald, pp. 1-20. Cambridge: Cambridge University Press.

Chapter Fifteen (cont.)

McCarthy, John D. 1996. Constraints and Opportunities in Adopting, Adapting, and Inventing. In *Comparative Perspectives on Social Movements: Political Opportunities, Mobilizing Structures, and Cultural Framings*, edited by Doug McAdam, John D. McCarthy and Mayer N. Zald, pp. 141-51. Cambridge: Cambridge University Press.

Ortega y Gasset, José. 1932. *The Revolt of the Masses* (anonymous translator). New York: W.W. Norton & Co. Inc.

Redfield, Robert. 1960. *The Little Community and Peasant Society and Culture*. Chicago: University of Chicago Press.

Roberts, Allen F. and Roberts, Mary Nooter. 2003. *A Saint in the City: Sufi Arts of Urban Senegal*. Los Angeles: UCLA Fowler Museum of Cultural History.

Robertson, Roland. 1995. Glocalization: Time–Space and Homogeneity–Heterogeneity. In *Global Modernities*, edited by Mike Featherstone, Scott Lash and Roland Robertson, pp. 25-44. London: Sage Publications.

Robertson, Roland and Chirico, JoAnn. 1985. Humanity, Globalization, and Worldwide Religious Resurgence: A Theoretical Exploration, *Sociological Analysis*, 46: 239.

Rosander, Eva Evers. 1997. Introduction: The Islamization of 'Tradition' and 'Modernity'. In *African Islam and Islam in Africa: Encounters between Sufis and Islamists*, edited by David Westerlund and Eva Evers Rosander, pp. 1-27. Athens, Ohio: Ohio University Press.

Roy, Olivier. 2003. EuroIslam: The Jihad Within?, *The National Interest* (Spring), 71: 63-73.

Sachs, Susan. 2003. In Harlem's Fabric, Bright Threads of Senegal. *New York Times*, 28 July 2003, pp. 1, 17.

Sassen, Saskia. 2002-03. Globalization or Denationalization, *Items & Issues* (Social Science Research Council), 4(1): 15-19.

Shiner, L. 1967. The Concept of Secularization in Empirical Research, *Journal for the Scientific Study of Religion*, 6: 207-20.

Sharma, Arvind. 1994. The Methodological Implications of the New Religious Movements. In *Religions sans Frontieres? Present and Future Trends of Migration, Culture and Communication*, edited by Robert Cipriani, pp. 357-66. Rome: Presidenza del Consiglio dei Ministri, Dipartimento per l'Informazione e l'Editoria.

Smith, Christian. 1996. Correcting a Curious Neglect, or Bringing Religion Back In. In *Disruptive Religion: The Force of Faith in Social-Movement Activism*, edited by Christian Smith, pp. 1-46. New York: Routledge.

Somers, Jeffrey. 1997. Whirling and the West: The Mevlevi Dervishes in the West. In *New Trends and Developments in the World of Islam*, edited by Peter Clarke, pp. 261-76. London: Luzac Oriental Press.

Stark, Rodney. 1999. Secularization, R.I.P., *Sociology of Religion*, 60(3): 249-73.

Stenberg, Leif. 1999. Naqshbandiyya in Damascus: Strategies to Establish and Strengthen the Order in a Changing Society. In *Naqshbandis in Western and Central Asia: Change and Continuity*, edited by Elizabeth Özdalga, pp. 101-16. Istanbul: Swedish Research Institute in Istanbul.

Stendahl, Krister. 1969. Religion, Mysticism, and the Institutional Church. In *Toward the Year 2000: Work in Progress*, edited by Daniel Bell, pp. 222-27. Boston: Beacon Press.

Summary Translation of the Mahadi's Book. In Khartoum University Library, Sudan Collection, 1677/48CM, typescript, 25 August 1936.

Swatos Jr, William H. and Christiano, Kevin J. 1999. Introduction – Secularization Theory: The Course of a Concept, *Sociology of Religion*, 60(3): 209-28.

Toulmin, Stephen. 1990. *Cosmopolis: The Hidden Agenda of Modernity*. New York: Free Press.

Trimingham, J.S. 1968. *Islam in the Sudan* (Reprint of 1949 edition). London: Cass.

Voll, John Obert. 1994. Islam as a Special World-System, *Journal of World History*, 5(2): 213-26.

Wilson, Peter. 1997. The Strange Fate of Sufism in the New Age. In *New Trends and Developments in the World of Islam*, edited by Peter Clarke, pp. 179-209. London: Luzac Oriental Press.

Chapter Fifteen (cont.)

Wright, Donald R. 1997. *The World and a Very Small Place in Africa.* Armonk: M.E. Sharpe.

Yavuz, Hakan. 1999. The Matrix of Modern Turkish Islamic Movements: The Naqshbandi Sufi Order. In *Naqshbandis in Western and Central Asia: Change and Continuity,* edited by Elizabeth Özdalga, pp. 129-46. Istanbul: Swedish Research Institute in Istanbul.

Zakaria, Fareed. 2003. *The Future of Freedom: Illiberal Democracy at Home and Abroad.* New York: W.W. Norton.

GLOSSARY

[abbreviations: A – Arabic; P – Persian; T – Turkish; I – Indonesian; J – Javanese; U – Urdu; W – Wolof]

abangan (J): adherents of vernacular versions of Islam incorporating numerous local (Javanese) beliefs and practices that are frowned upon by more strictly practising Muslims or *santri*

adab (A): moral etiquette

`*ada* (A), *adat* (I): indigenous custom, customary practices

agama (I): religion

`*ahd* (A): pact

ahl al-sunna wa-l-jama`a (A): 'people of the path of the Prophet and the community': the orthodox mainstream of Islam

akhlaq (A), *ahlak* (T): moral behaviour

`*alam al-arwah* (A), `*alam-i arwah* (P): the world of the souls, one of a hierarchy of planes of existence beyond the phenomenal world

`*alim*, pl. `*ulama* (A): religious scholar

`*aqida* (A): doctrine, belief

asma (A): [God's] names (plural of *ism*)

awliya (A): saints (plural of *wali*)

awqaf (A): pious foundations (plural of *waqf*)

baraka (A), *barkat* (P/U): divine grace

bay`a* (A), *bay`at (P/U): oath of allegiance

bid`a* (A), *bid`at (P): 'innovation', a practice or belief for which there is no precedent in the Qur'an or the practice of the Prophet

cemaat (T), *jama`a* (A): congregation, faith community

daaira (W): local congregation of followers of a Sufi order, a cellular pattern of organization that emerged in Senegal (from Arabic *da'ira*, 'circle')

dam (P/U): a spell, usually consisting of a Qur'anic verse (literally, 'breath')

dargah (P), *dergâh* (T): Sufi lodge; Sufi shrine (especially in South Asia)

darwish (P): the term used in Iran for the 'low' variety of Sufi: the intoxicated, begging vagrant

da`wa (A), *da'wah / dakwah* (I): the call to Islam: predication

dergâh (T): Sufi lodge

dhikr (A), *dzikir* (I), *zikar* (U), *zikir* (T): 'remembrance [of God]', recitation of God's names or other short formulas as a spiritual discipline

du`a (A): supplicatory prayer

evrad (T), *awrad* (A): plural of *vird* (T), *wird* (A), litanies

faqir (A/P): ascetic, world renouncer (literally, 'poor')

fatwa (A): an authoritative opinion on a matter of religious importance, given in answer to a question

fayz (P) emanation, the divine grace exuding from a saint

fiqh (A): Islamic jurisprudence, legal thought

gàmmu (W): annual pilgrimage of the Tijaniyya in Senegal

golongan kebatinan (I): a mystical group

golongan kepercayaan (I): lit. a 'faith' group; since the 1970s, the official term for mystical groups in Indonesia

gyarvi sharif (U): commemoration of the miraculous life and deeds of Shaykh `Abd al-Qadir Jilani (South Asia)

hadith (A): account of a deed or saying of the Prophet

hafiz (A): 'memorizer': a person who knows the Qur'an by heart

hajj (A): the annual pilgrimage to Mecca

hal (A): state of 'higher' consciousness

haqq (A): truth, higher reality, God

hikma (A), *hikmat* (P): metaphysical lore, the various 'sciences' that entered Muslim civilization from the Hellenistic tradition, including Hermeticism and Greek medicine

hızmet (T), *khidma* (A): service (to the community)

hululiyya (A): the belief that God can manifest Himself or be incarnate in human beings; also, the sects holding this belief

husayniyya (P): convention hall for commemorations of Husayn's martyrdom; some Shi`i Sufi orders also use this name for their convention halls

`*id* (A), *eid* (P): festival (term used for the feast of sacrifice, the feast at the end of the fasting month, and the celebration of the Prophet's birthday)

ifta (A): the issuance of *fatwa*s, opinions on matters of religious importance

ihsan (A): spiritual perfection

ijaza (A): authorization

ijma` (A): consensus of the scholars, one of the sources of Islamic law

ijtihad (A): independent judgment (exercised where no unambiguous scriptural basis is available)

ikhtilaf (A/P): difference of opinion, especially concerning the fine points on which the various schools of *fiqh* differ; *ikhtilafi* matters are those non-essential details on which different views legitimately coexist. Used in contrast to *ittifaq*, consensus of the ulama.

`*irfan* (P): gnosis, mysticism – the term used in Iran for the metaphysical thought of the great Persian Sufi poets

irshad (A/P): spiritual guidance

ittifaq (A): consensus (of the `*ulama*); *ittifaqi* matters are those on which the various schools of *fiqh* are in complete agreement (cf. *ikhtilaf*)

ittihadiyya (A): the belief that human beings can achieve union with God; also, sects holding that belief

jadhba (A): rapture, mystical ecstasy

jafr (A): the science of numerology

jama`a (A): congregation, faith community

kanuragan (J): magic, especially the types used in martial arts (invulnerability techniques and the acquisition of extraordinary powers)

karamat (A): supernatural powers, miraculous acts performed by a saint

kasektèn (J): spiritual power

kebatinan (J): esotericism, Javanese syncretistic mysticism

khalifa (A): representative, deputy

khanqah, khanaqah (P): Sufi lodge

khatm-i Khwajagan (P): invocation of the memory or spirit of the saints of the Naqshbandi *silsila*

Khwajagan (P): the Central Asian Sufi saints among whom the Naqshbandi order first took shape

khidma (A): service (to the community). Also (in Egypt): the place – tent, apartment, corridor of a house – where the members of a *tariqa* or the adherents of a saint perform their *dhikr* and serve tea and food during a *mawlid*

kiai (J): charismatic teacher of religion in a *pesantren*, a traditional religious school

langar (U): festive meal, cooked by volunteers and distributed freely at Sufi shrines in South Asia

madhhab (A), *mazhab* (P), *mezhep* (T): school of *fiqh*, Islamic jurisprudence

madrasa (A/P), *medrese* (T): traditional centre of religious education

màggal (W): annual pilgrimage of the Mouride brotherhood

majdhub (A): ecstatic mystic

masjid (A): mosque

maulvi (U): low-ranking religious functionary

mawlid (A): commemoration of the Prophet's birthday; also (especially in Egypt) saint's day celebration

mazar (A/P): saint's shrine

meşihat (T): the (Ottoman) office of the Shaykh al-Islam

milad al-nabi (A): birth of the Prophet

mufti (A), *müftü* (T): scholar who issues *fatwa*s, authoritative opinions, on matters of religious importance

muhibb (A): devotee, follower of a shaykh who is not bound to him by a pact or oath

muqaddam (A): spiritual director; in most orders using this term, the *muqaddam* is a local representative of the supreme shaykh

muqallid (A): person who follows the rulings of the founder and leading scholars of a school of Islamic law (*madhhab*) rather than exercising independent judgment

muraqaba (A): contemplation, meditation

murid (A): disciple, follower of a shaykh bound to him by a pact or oath

murshid (A): spiritual teacher, guide

mustarshid (A): person in search of spiritual guidance

namaz (P/T): the Muslim prayer (Arabic: *salat*)

pengajian (I): Islamic religious instruction classes

pesantren (J/I): the Javanese version of the *madrasa*, a school, normally with dormitory facilities and adjoining the home of a qualified scholar (*ulama* or *kiai*), that provides children a traditional Islamic education

pir (P): Sufi teacher

pir-bhai (South Asia): the brotherhood / community of disciples of a particular teacher (*pir*)

Pir-o-Murshid: title of the supreme teacher in the Inayati Sufi movement

postnishin (P), *postnişin* (T): head of a Sufi lodge; more especially the chief successor of the founder of an order

qalandar (P): the archetypical begging, vagrant, drug-using dervish (cf. *darwish*)

qutb (A/P): 'pole', the supreme spiritual authority of a Sufi order

rabbaniyya (A): godliness

rabita (A): a method of establishing a spiritual connection with the teacher through visualization of the latter's image [binding the heart to the master]

rahbaniyya (A): monasticism (conceived as a non-Muslim institution)

rawda (A): Sufi lodge in urban Egypt (lit. 'garden')

ridda (A): apostasy

sabr (A/P/T): patience

saha (A): Sufi lodge in Upper Egypt, residence of the shaykh, where he receives his followers (lit. 'court')

sajjada (A/P): prayer mat

sajjada-nishin (P): the current successor to the founder of a Sufi order or a saint buried in a shrine; hence also: the keeper of a Sufi shrine *al-salaf al-salih* (A): 'the Pious Forebears', i.e. the first generations of Islam

salafiyya (A): movement to purge Islam of all foreign accretions and return to the practice of the first generations of Islam

salat (A), *sholat* (I/J): the Muslim prayer, performed five times a day

salawat (A): formulaic invocation of divine blessing on the Prophet and his family

sama` (A): listening to music as a spiritual practice

sama'an (J): [listening to] the recital of the Qur'an

santri (I/J): student in a *pesantren*, a traditional religious school. Also: a conscientiously practicing Muslim

sawab (P/U), *sevap* (T), from *thawab* (A): religious merit, reward

sayyid, pl. *sada* (A): descendant of the Prophet

shari`a (A), *şeriat* (T): the rules of proper Islamic behaviour, 'Islamic law'

shaykh (A), *şeyh* (T), *syekh* (I): religious authority, esp. the head of a Sufi order

shirk (A): associating anything with God, attributing divine power to other entities besides God

sifat (A): [God's] attributes

silsila: spiritual genealogy of master–disciple links, leading back to the founder of an order and ultimately to the Prophet

sohbet (T), *suhba* (A): companionship, conversation; more specifically, keeping the company of the shaykh and one's fellow disciples

sunna (A), *sunnat* (P), *sunnah* (I): the path of the Prophet: the Prophet's exemplary words and deeds

tabarruk (A): seeking blessing

tabligh (A): predication, propagation

ta'ifa (A): social group, sect, denomination, association (lit. 'part, portion'); also: Sufi order

taqarrub (A): drawing close to God

taqlid (A): following the rulings of the founder and leading scholars of a school of Islamic law (*madhhab*) rather than exercising independent judgment (*ijtihad*)

taqwa (A): piety, fear of God

tarawih (A): supererogatory prayers performed in the month of Ramadan, after the evening prayer

tarbiya (A), *terbiye* (T): Islamic moral education, disciplining

tariqa, pl. *turuq* (A), *tarikat* (T), *tarixa* (W): Sufi order

tasawwuf (A), *tasavvuf* (T): Sufism, Islamic mysticism

tawassul (A): prayer for intercession by a saint

tawakkul (A): absolute trust in God

tawba (A): repentance

tazkiya (A): purification; in Sufism, ethical and other spiritual practices for cleansing the soul of distractions from God

tazkiyat al-nafs (A): purifying the soul of base emotions in order to be more receptive to an awareness of God's love (an expression that appears in the Qur'an)

tekke (T): Sufi lodge

`ulama (A): the scholars of Islam

umma (A): the community of believers

`umra (A), *umrah / umroh* (I): an abbreviated form of pilgrimage to Mecca omitting part of the full hajj ritual course and usually done outside the hajj season

`urs (A/P/U): death anniversary of a saint or shaykh (South Asia)

vakıf (T), *waqf* (A): pious foundation

vird (T), *wird* (A): litany

wahdat al-wujud (A): the metaphysical Sufi doctrine of Unity of Being, introduced by Ibn `Arabi, according to which the phenomenal world has emanated from the Divine Self and is not essentially different and separate from Him.

walaya (A), *walayat* (P): sainthood, friendship with / closeness to God.

wali (A): friend of God, saint

wali sanga (J): the nine saints considered as the primary actors of the Islamization of Java

waqf (A): pious foundation

wara` (A): piety

wazifa (A): litany consisting of prayers and other formulas, recited repetitively.

wilaya (A), *wilayat* (P): authority, guardianship

wilayat-i faqih (P): 'guardianship of the jurist', Khomeini's concept of rule by the clergy

wird, pl. *awrad* (A), *wirid* (I), *vird* (T): litany, formula

wujudiyya (A): see *wahdat al-wujud*

zawiya (A/P), *zaviye* (T): Sufi lodge

zikar (U), *zikir* (T): the recitation of God's name or other short formulas as a spiritual discipline (from Ar. *dhikr*, literally 'remembering')

ziyara (A): visitation of saints' graves, pilgrimage

zuhd (A): ascetic withdrawal, renunciation

INDEX

Aah Gym (Abdullah Gymnastiar) 229
Abah Anom 105-6, 111, 112, 235
abangan 92-4, 98, 104, 109, 111, 304, 306
`Abduh, Muhammad 149
Abdul Hadi W.M. 154, 165, 167, 218
Abdullah, Sufi 213-5, 216
Abdurrahman Wahid 101, 104, 106, 110, 111, 163, 171, 305, 306
Abidi, Shaykh (Shahji) 202-7, 212-3, 214
Abu Ghudda, `Abd al-Fattah 117, 121-2, 124, 125, 126, 127-8, 307
Abu'l-`Abbas, Sidi 246
Adalet ve Kalkınma Partisi (AKP) 57-9
Adama Yalcouyé (Sufi Adama) 86-91
Ahl-i Hadith 115, 117, 133
Ahmad Shahid, Sayyid – see Barelwi, Sayyid Ahmad
Ahmadiyya movement 161
Ahmadiyya (Sufi order) 25, 155
`Alawiyya (Sufi order) 247

al-Albani, Nasir al-Din 152, 153, 155, 156
America 184-8, 265-6
Aqil Siradj – see Said Aqil Siradj
Arberry, A.J. 8, 218
Arya Samaj 132, 137, 143
Asad, Talal 40, 43
Australia 257, 267-77
al-Azhar 22, 23, 24, 31, 33, 34, 35, 37-8, 121
Azimiyya 200-2, 207, 215

Badidi, Driss 242, 252
al-Bakri, Mustafa Kamal 23
Bamba (Mbacké), Amadou 174, 181, 183, 187
al-Banna, Hasan 121, 124, 127, 161
Banuri, Adam 123
Barelvi movement 198
Barelwi, Sayyid Ahmad (Shahid) 123, 127
Bawa Muhaiyaddeen Fellowship 258
bay`a, bay`at 27, 29, 30, 160-1, 211
Bekkine, Abdülaziz 47-8
Bektashiyya 258, 300

Ben Rochd, Rachid 249, 251, 252, 253
Bentounes, Khaled 247
Benzouine, Driss 241, 242, 248-9, 251, 253, 312
Bilal, Cheick Soufi 81-6, 88, 91
Bin Baz, `Abd al-`Aziz 152
Britain 195-216, 265
Buddhism 223-5, 242, 244, 247, 259, 311
al-Budshish, Abu Madyan b. Munawwar 246
Budshishiyya 246-55, 312
Buehler, Arthur 197-8
al-Bukhori, Jefry 229
bureaucratization 63, 96-7, 98, 99-100, 103, 112, 263-6
Burhamiyya 9, 25, 258

cemaat 48, 49, 50, 53-4, 301
charisma 29, 31, 95, 266, 271
Chishti, Hazrat Khwaja Mu`inuddin 261
Chishtiyya 196, 259-63
Cissé, Hassan 85
colonialism 10, 116, 127, 179, 183, 188
Confucianism 223-5
Coşan, Esad 42, 48-9, 50, 56-7, 300

daaira 175-6, 179, 181, 182, 185, 186, 187, 188, 190, 309
Dadash, Hajji 63
al-Dardir, Ahmad 23-4
Darqawiyya 249, 251
Daouda Yattara 89, 90
De Jong, Fred 9, 22, 24
Deoband movement 129, 130-2, 139, 145-7, 198, 208, 210
Deshimaru, Taisen 242, 312
Dhahabiyya 61, 65, 68
dhikr 26, 32, 35, 42, 49, 119, 134, 153, 158, 198-9, 201-2, 203, 204, 208, 209, 211-2, 213-4, 218, 220, 234, 238, 248, 252, 254, 261, 271, 300
Dhu'l-Riyasatayn Ni`matullahiyya 61, 62, 67, 68, 70
Diouf, Abdou 176, 177, 181
Dogon 86-9
Duce, Ivy 267-8
al-Dumi, `Abd al-Jawad 24-5, 26, 27, 34-5
Durix, Claude 243, 312
Durkheim, Émile 75, 303

ecstatic Sufism 155, 308
Egypt 21-38
Erbakan, Necmettin 55
Erdoğan, Recep Tayyip 55, 57

Farooqui, Shaykh 208-12
al-Fatani, Ahmad b. Muhammad Zayn 155
Fazal Inayat-Khan 270, 314
folk religion 178, 225, 283, 284
Foucault, Michel 59
Frankenberg, Baron von 267-9, 270
Freemasonry 97-8

Gangohi, Maulana Rashid Ahmad 131
Geertz, Clifford 8, 92-3, 197, 218
Gellner, Ernest 8, 17, 218
Ghazali, Abu Hamid 94, 107, 168, 307
al-Ghazali, Muhammad 124
Gilsenan, Michael 9, 37, 53
globalization 289-94, 296-7
Golkar 99-100, 102, 103, 104, 105
Gus Mik (Hamim Djazuli) 106, 108-9, 110, 306
Gümüşhanevi, Ahmed Ziyaüddin 48, 55, 57, 300
gyarvi sharif 213, 214

al-Hallaj, Husayn b. Mansur 107, 157
Hamallah 84
Hamid of Pasuruan 107-8
Hamka 16, 218-9, 230
Hamza, Sidi 246, 248, 251, 252
al-Haqqani, Muhammad Nazim al-`Adil (al-Qubrusi) 169-70, 251
Haqqaniyya – see Naqshbandiyya Haqqaniyya
Hawwa, Sa`id 117, 119, 120, 124, 126-8
Hidayat Inayat-Khan 266, 272
al-Hifni, Muhammad b. Salim 23
Hinduism 132, 133, 137-8, 143, 147, 223-5, 252, 259, 268
Hizb ut-Tahrir 198
Hizbut Tarqiyyah 181-2, 310
Hoffman, Valerie 9
hululiyya 157

Ibn `Arabi, Muhyi al-Din 94, 250, 308
Ibn `Ata'illah 107, 307
Ibn Qudama al-Maqdisi 159-60, 169
Ibn Taymiyya 127, 154
Idham Chalid 103, 104, 305
ijtihad 117, 139, 308
Ilham, M. Arifin 229
Ilyas, Maulana Muhammad 129-48 *passim*
Inayat Khan, Hazrat 16, 17, 257-77 *passim*
India 115-7, 122-8, 129-48, 259-63, 274, 275
Indonesia 92-112, 149-71, 217-40
Inglehart, Ronald 285-6, 296
Iran 61-75
Iranshahr, Husayn Kazimzada 64
Iskender Pasha community 55, 56, 58, 59
Islamization 290-1

ittihadiyya 157

jafr 205-7
Jalaluddin, Haji 99-100, 112
Jama`at-i Islami 115, 124, 198
Jamaatou Ibadou Rahmane 180, 182
Jam'iyyah Ahlith Thoriqah Mu'tabaroh 101-3, 161, 166, 169, 305-6
Jansen, Sharif 269-71
al-Jaza'iri, `Abd al-Qadir 127
jihad 10, 123, 127, 131, 151, 161, 170, 183, 292
al-Jilani, `Abd al-Qadir 105, 127, 163, 168
al-Jili, Abd al-Karim 94
al-Junayd 167

kabbalism 204
al-Kabbani, Muhammad Hisham 169
Kadirun Yahya 111, 306
Kadivar, Muhsin 70, 74
Kalijaga, Sunan 107
kanuragan 95, 101, 105, 107, 305
Kasrawi, Ahmad 66
al-Kawthari, Muhammad Zahid 121, 126
kebatinan movements 97-8, 101, 104, 106, 218, 221, 222-3, 225-7, 229, 239, 305, 311
Khaksar 61, 302
Khalaf, Abu al-Nasr 119, 120, 121
Khalid, Mevlana 44, 301
Khalwatiyya 12-3, 21-38, 282, 300
khanqah 209
Khatami, Muhammad 68-9, 71
khatm-i Khwajagan 42
khidma 32, 299
Khomeini, Ayatollah Ruhollah 64-5, 73, 303
al-Khuli, al-Bahi 124

Kotku, Mehmed Zahid 48, 54-5, 57, 300, 301
Kubrawiyya 65
Kuftaru (Kaftaru), Ahmad 117, 118-9, 120, 124-5, 127-8, 287, 289
al-Kurdi, `Isa 118, 119

al-Lakhnawi, `Abd al-Hayy 126
langar 201, 212
Layène 174
Lewis, Samuel (Murshid Sam) 266, 272, 314
Luqman Hakiem 162-70 *passim*

McCarthy, John D. 288-9
madad 27, 29
Madani, Khwaja Mohammad Abu Hashim 261
Madjid, Nurcholish 163, 169, 230, 233, 311
Madni, Maulana Hussain Ahmad 145
madrasa 129, 141-2, 145
mahdist movements 174, 281
Maktab Tariqat Uwaysi Shahmaqsudi 61, 68
Malamiyya 300
Mali 76-91
Mansur Yusuf 229
marabout 13, 79, 173-5, 179, 180, 184, 309
Martin, Rabia (Murshida) 265, 267
Masyumi 93
Mawdudi, Abu'l-A`la 117, 124
mawlid (`id milad al-nabi*) 32, 35, 198, 213, 215, 248
Mbah Lim (Muslim Rifa'i Imampura) 106, 109-10, 306
media, audio-visual 80, 81, 82, 85, 86, 89, 229, 231
Meher Baba 267-8
messianism 95, 96, 174, 281
Mevleviyye 47, 300

Minangkabau 99
modernization theory 5, 17-8, 197, 218, 282
Mongiri, Muhammad `Ali 123, 127
Morocco 241-56
Mourides, Muridiyya 11-2, 13, 77, 82, 174-91 *passim*, 281, 291
al-Muhajiroun 198
Muhammad Ahmad (Mahdi) 281
Muhammadiyah (Indonesia) 149, 217
muhibb, muhabba 27, 28, 44
Mujtahid-Shabistari, Muhammad 70, 74
muraqaba hall, meeting 201, 207
Musharaff Khan 269-70
music 260, 261, 262, 271, 277
Muslich of Mranggen 103
Muslim Baye Fall 82-3, 88
Muslim Brothers (al-Ikhwan al-Muslimun) 115, 117, 119, 124, 125, 127, 161
Musta'in Romly 101-3, 104, 112, 305-6

Nadwat al-`Ulama 117, 122-4
Nadwi, Abu al-Hasan `Ali 118, 123-8
Nahdlatul Ulama (NU) 93, 99, 100-4, 106, 110-11, 163, 164
Naqshbandiyya 10, 12, 13, 16, 17, 39-60, 99-100, 104, 111, 118, 119, 120, 124-5, 196, 213, 285, 286-9, 300, 301, 304
Naqshbandiyya, Gümüşhanevi branch 44, 300
Naqshbandiyya Haqqaniyya 12, 169-70, 237, 251, 258
Naqshbandiyya Khalidiyya 39-60, 99-100, 104, 111, 118, 119, 120, 121, 300
Naqshbandiyya Mujaddidiyya 117, 118, 123, 127, 196, 208-10

Nasr, Seyyed Hossein 269
Nazim al-Qubrusi – see al-Haqqani, Muhammad Nazim
neo-Sufism 10-1, 64
Netherlands 265, 270, 274
networks, scholarly 95-6
New Age 6, 15, 16, 231, 237, 238-9, 242, 244-5, 250-6, 258, 269, 273, 311
New Religious Movements 6, 88, 224, 258-61, 264-5, 268, 269, 274, 275-7, 283
New York 184, 186
Niasse, Abdoulaye 174
Niasse, Ibrahima 85, 175, 185
Ni`matullahiyya 61-75, 258
Ni`matullahiyya, Dhu'l-Riyasatayn branch 61, 62, 67, 68, 70
Ni`matullahiyya, Safi`alishahi branch 61, 63, 66, 67-8
Ni`matullahiyya, Sultan`alishahi branch 61, 63, 64, 66, 67, 70, 71-4
Nurbakhsh, Jawad 62
Nurcu movement 12, 43

Pakistani migrants 195-216 *passim*
Pan-Africanism 82
Paramadina 230-3, 237, 311
perennialism 268
Perti (Persatuan Tarbiyah Islamiyah) 99
pesantren 93, 95, 100, 162-3, 168, 228, 304
pilgrimage 176, 179, 181, 200; see also *ziyara*
post-modernity 295-7
PPTI (Partai Politik Tarekat Islam) 99-100, 103, 105, 305

Qadiriyya 69, 77, 78, 79, 80, 83, 84, 85, 87, 174, 196, 213, 246
Qadiriyya wa-Naqshbandiyya 100-4, 105-6, 111, 235, 306

Qutb, Sayyid 117, 161

rabbaniyya 119-121, 123, 127, 128
rabita 54, 119
rahbaniyya ('monasticism') 127, 143
Rakhmat, Jalaluddin 169, 233, 235, 236
Rastafarianism 82-3, 88
Ratu Adil 95, 96
rawda 35-7
Refah Partisi 51, 55, 56, 57
Reformism, Muslim 7, 129-34, 149, 161-2, 180-1, 184, 217
regional cult 199-200
Rida, Rashid 149
Rifa'i Hasan 167
Robertson, Ronald 18
Rufa`iyya 300
Rumi, Jalal al-Din 70, 127, 257, 303

Saeeda, Baji 200-2
Safi`alishahiyya 61, 63, 66, 67-8
saha 29-32
Sahal Mahfudz 164-7
Said Aqil Siradj 165, 167-8, 171
Salafism 14-5, 24, 115, 117, 120, 122, 150, 151-9, 180, 182, 299
sama` 260, 261, 262
Sanusiyya 10, 127
santri 92-4, 98, 109, 110, 111, 228
Sarekat Abang 97, 305
Sarekat Islam 96-7, 305
secularization thesis 5, 282-3, 287-8
Sékou Salah Siby 87
Senegal 77, 83, 85, 172-91
Senghor, Léopold Sédar 176
Shadhiliyya 9, 37, 150
Shahji (Shaykh Abidi) 202-7, 212
shari`a-centred Sufism 9, 10-1, 92, 107-8, 111, 115-28, 130, 131, 134, 145, 153, 159, 258
Shari`ati, `Ali 71, 72-3

Sharqawi, Ahmad 24, 27
Shattariyya 94, 101, 104, 235
Shawkani, Muhammad b. `Ali 156, 308
Shaykh Said rebellion (Turkey) 46
Shibli Nu`mani 123
al-Siba'i, Mustafa 125
Siddiqiyya 98, 101, 104, 305
silsila 26, 42, 98
Sirhindi, Ahmad 44, 117, 123, 307
Siti Jenar, Shaykh 107, 108, 306
Skali, Faouzi 247-9, 253
social movement theory 283, 284, 288
sohbet – see *suhba*
Soroush, Abdolkarim 69, 70
Stark, Rodney 282-3
Sufi Dancing 258, 266, 272, 314
Sufi Movement, International 257-77
Sufi Movement in Australia 271-5
Sufi Order International 266, 272
Sufi Ruhaniat International 266, 272
Sufi shrines 134-5, 137, 139-40, 155, 209, 213, 274, 275
Suharto 92, 94, 102, 106, 109, 110, 111, 151, 219, 225, 229, 304, 306, 311
suhba 27, 28, 36, 42-5, 48, 50, 51, 54, 300, 301
Suhrawardiyya 196
Sukarno 223, 225, 311
Sultan`alishahiyya 61, 63, 64, 66, 67, 70, 71-4
syncreticism 86-90, 92-3, 97-8, 111, 133, 136-7, 139, 141, 218, 223, 255
Sy, Abdoul Aziz 178
Sy, El Hadj Malik 174, 180, 183
Sy, Moustapha 180-1
Syria 117-22

Taal, El Hadj Umar 179, 183

Tabanda, Hajj Sultanhusayn 63
Tabanda, Nur`alishah 71
Tablighi Jama`at 16, 124, 126, 127, 129-48, 198
Taliban 208, 210
Tall, Ahmad 83, 86, 304
Tanha'i, Husayn Abu'l-Hasan 72-5
Taqiyyu Allah, Muhammad 81, 84, 87, 304
tarbiya 43, 118, 246, 301
tawassul 26, 27, 153, 158; see also *khatm-i Khwajagan*
al-Tayyib al-Hasani, Ahmad 24, 25-6, 27, 30
al-Tayyib, Ahmad (mufti) 31, 33, 150
al-Tayyib, Muhammad Muhammad Ahmad 29-34
Tazkiyah Sejati 230, 231, 232, 233, 235
tazkiyat al-nafs 119, 120, 121, 125
tekke 45-8, 301
Thalib, Ja`far Umar 152, 170
Thanwi, Ashraf Ali 131, 145
Theosophy 64, 97-8, 224
Tijaniyya 13, 77, 78, 79, 83, 84-5, 101, 104, 174-91 *passim*, 235, 249, 251
Timbuktu 81
Tönnies, Ferdinand 18
Touba 174, 177, 181-2, 185, 186, 188, 310
transnationalism 11-2, 15, 68,
Traoré, Moussa 80, 89-90
Turkey 39-60

`*urs* 198, 201, 213, 215

vakıf 45, 49, 51-3
Vilayat, Pir 266

Wade, Abdoulaye 177-8
al-Wadi`i, Muqbil b. Hadi 152
Wahhabism 133, 150, 162, 308

wahdat al-wujud 157-8; see also *wujudiyya*
Wahidiyya 98, 101, 104
wali, walaya 25, 28-9, 30-1, 32, 33-4, 73-5, 106-11, 156
wali sanga 106-7, 162
wazifa 204, 214
wilayat-i faqih 73, 74
Weber, Max 17-8, 29, 37, 144, 221
Wolof 174
wujudiyya 107, 133, 154, 308

Yassine 247, 312
Yavuz, Hakan 286-7
Yoga 237, 242, 244, 251, 252, 253, 254

Zainuddin MZ 229
zawiya 174, 175, 176, 185, 187-8, 246, 248, 254
Zen 242, 244, 254, 312
Zia Inayat-Khan, Pir 266, 314
zikir – see *dhikr*
Zindapir 203, 213, 214, 216
ziyara 93, 155; see also pilgrimage and Sufi shrines

www.ingramcontent.com/pod-product-compliance
Ingram Content Group UK Ltd.
Pitfield, Milton Keynes, MK11 3LW, UK
UKHW050053230326
469204UK00012B/343